ABINGDON
BIBLE HANDBOOK

DATE DUE

ABINGDON
BIBLE
HANDBOOK

EDWARD P. BLAIR

ABINGDON PRESS
Nashville — New York

ABINGDON BIBLE HANDBOOK

Copyright © 1975 by Abingdon Press

All rights reserved

Library of Congress Cataloging in Publication Data

BLAIR, EDWARD PAYSON, 1910- Abingdon Bible handbook.
Bibliography: p. Includes index.
1. Bible—Introductions. I. Title.
BS475.2.B5   220'.02'02   75-6774
ISBN 0-687-00169-2

Scripture quotations unless otherwise noted are from the Revised Standard Version of the Bible, copyrighted 1946, 1952, and 1971 by the Division of Christian Education, National Council of Churches, and are used by permission.

Scripture quotations noted NEB are from the New English Bible, copyright © the Delegates of the Oxford University Press and the Syndics of the Cambridge University Press, 1961, 1970.

Quotations noted TLB are from *The Living Bible,* copyright © 1971 Tyndale House Publishers, Wheaton, Illinois. Used by permission.

Quotations noted TEV are from Today's English Version of the New Testament. Copyright © American Bible Society 1966.

Quotations noted JB are from The Jerusalem Bible, copyright © 1966 by Darton, Longman & Todd, Ltd. and Doubleday & Company, Inc. Used by permission of the publisher.

Scripture quotations noted NIV are from the New International Version.

Chapters 14 and 16 are from *The Book of Deuteronomy and the Book of Joshua* by Edward P. Blair. Volume 5 of *The Layman's Bible Commentary.* © 1964 by M. E. Bratcher. Used by permission of John Knox Press.

Charts on pages 460 and 462 originally appeared in Edward Blair's book *Leader's Guide to the Study of the Sermon on the Mount.* Copyright © 1968 by Abingdon Press.

MANUFACTURED BY THE PARTHENON PRESS AT NASHVILLE, TENNESSEE, UNITED STATES OF AMERICA

To the many people everywhere
who are eager to have
authentic knowledge
about the matters
of which they
are partly
informed
    (see Luke 1:4 NEB)

FOREWORD

The translation and distribution of the Bible in our time far surpass the circulation of books and study aids that help us understand it and benefit from its rich treasures.

The question put to the Ethiopian eunuch by Philip, "Do you understand what you are reading?" and the despairing reply of the eunuch, "How can I understand . . . unless someone explains it to me?" (Acts 8:30-31 TEV) reflect the condition of millions of people today who take the Bible in their hands.

It is true that much in the Bible is crystal clear and needs no explanation. The Bible societies of the world have files bulging with testimonies from people of many races, cultures, and walks of life who have found help from reading the Scriptures unaided. But it also is true that tragic misconceptions about the Bible have confused and poisoned the faith and life of multitudes. It evidently is not enough for us to read the Bible; we must know how to interpret what we read.

I have written this *Handbook* for you who find the Bible difficult or impossible to penetrate by yourself. It is my belief that if you will pay a reasonable price in time and effort and will work prayerfully and persistently with good biblical tools, you can come to a mature understanding of the Bible and its meaning for your life. Especially is this so if you will join or form a group dedicated to serious Bible study, where procedures, questions, insights, and applications to contemporary life can be shared and evaluated.

The use of this *Handbook* is no substitute for direct reading of the Bible. The *Handbook* is intended to serve as a companion on your journey of firsthand exploration. I agree with Walter Russell Bowie, who once said that the best guide in the study of the Bible is the guide who "does not try to say too much. He tells the inquirer what lies ahead of him if he wants to look, and how he can get to the vantage point at which the wonders of the Bible will most fully make him open his own eyes" (in Walter D. Ferguson, *Journey Through the Bible* [1947], p. ix).

Part I ("The Bible Today") presents information you should have when you take the Bible in your hands: the meaning of the word "Bible"; the

7

contents of the Bible as used by Jews, Protestants, and Roman Catholics, and why the contents differ among these groups; the makeup and major characteristics of the Bible; ancient and modern translations and the best versions for use by contemporary English readers; basic principles for interpreting the Bible correctly; and practical suggestions for reading it.

Part II ("The Bible in History") sets the books of the Bible in the times in which they were first written and read. Basic to correct interpretation is knowledge of the circumstances and needs of the original readers, the purpose or purposes of the authors, the process by which the books came into being, their structure and central emphases, the transmission of their texts by the communities that preserved them, and the like. The books bear the marks of the ancient cultures out of which they came. You must understand these marks before you can grasp the contents of these books and relate them to your life.

Part III ("The Bible and Faith and Life") deals with some of the basic teachings of the Bible and shows how the beliefs behind these teachings form a structure of faith and a pattern of life. It discusses biblical perspectives on God, Satan, man, miracles, the way of salvation, the church, the Christian's situation in the world, and the future. A final section treats the question of the Bible's inspiration and authority for contemporary readers. You will find clues to the solution of some present-day problems of faith and life in this section.

This *Handbook* does not attempt a book-by-book and chapter-by-chapter commentary on the Bible. Commentaries in handbooks are usually so superficial as to be almost valueless. Instead, I have offered in Part II introductions to all the books of the Bible (including the Apocrypha). These are meant to set the course for your firsthand reading of the individual books and supply you with important background material and the scholarly judgments you need to understand them. I recommend that, in addition to this *Handbook,* you secure a good one-volume commentary on the Bible for consultation (see p. 481).

In fairness to you I should state my point of view at the outset.

I hold that the Bible is more than a relic of antiquity which one is free to consider or ignore as his fancy directs; that it is more than a repository of information about man's past and a source of delightful human interest stories and salty wisdom; that it is more than great literature which educated people of our time should be acquainted with, like the works of Shakespeare; that it is more than a record of man's search for God and the good life.

I believe that the Bible is the story of God's search for man; of God's redemptive deeds in the life of the people of Israel and of "the one-man Israel," Jesus Christ; of the saving activity of God's Spirit in the world through the church; of God's establishment through Jesus and his disciples of the outpost of the new order called in the New Testament "the kingdom of God."

I believe that Jesus Christ fulfills the world's hope for peace, justice, prosperity, and stability, and that unswerving faith in him as Lord and Savior and unconditional obedience to him will bring personal and social salvation, here and hereafter.

I believe that the Bible presents the Word of God in the words of men so that I and all people may understand and obey. I shall not have dealt seriously with this message until I have understood it as far as possible with my mind, responded to it with my will and my emotions, sought to communicate it to others, and endeavored to live out its implications in my everyday life.

I believe that I must open my mind to all truth, from whatever source it may come. I must follow no opinions about the Bible simply because they are old and long honored. If the Holy Spirit is to lead me into all truth (John 16:13), I must be willing to change my views when solid evidence points in new directions. I must live and work in the confidence that nothing that is really true can undermine my Christian knowledge and experience, for God is the God of truth and truth builds up and frees (Eph. 4:15; John 8:32). I must, however, "test everything [and] hold fast what is good" (I Thess. 5:21), knowing that God's Spirit will illumine and guide me.

This *Handbook* attempts, therefore, to combine sound scholarship and Christian devotion. It tries to be fair to the evidence. I have often presented more than one point of view. I have listed good Roman Catholic books, as well as conservative and liberal Protestant works, under the caption "For Further Reading." God's Spirit is at work today in remarkable ways in all communions where Bible study is taken seriously.

It is impossible to express my debt to others who directly or indirectly have influenced the contents of this *Handbook*. In the realm of learning, Jesus' statement to the disciples, as reported in the Gospel of John, indicates where credit usually should go: "Others have done the hard work, and you have reaped the benefits of their labor" (4:38 NIV). Only rarely have I quoted other scholars directly, but my debt to them is great, as my fellow workers in the biblical field will know quite well.

Words of thanks are due my wife, Vivian, for her patient and skillful assistance throughout the project; and Harry Thomas Frank and John C. Trever for their many fine photographs.

It remains only to wish for all of you into whose hands this *Handbook* comes an exhilarating and insightful journey through the Bible.

Edward P. Blair

CONTENTS

B. The Apocrypha

CONTENTS

Part III. THE BIBLE AND FAITH AND LIFE

PART I
THE BIBLE TODAY

1. The Bible's Name and Contents

"The Bible" means literally "the books." The term rests ultimately on the Greek word *biblos* (papyrus) and comes to us by way of the Greek *biblion* (book), the Greek and Latin *biblia* (books), and the Old French word *bible*.

Jews of the time of Jesus used such terms as "the books," "the holy books," and "the book of the law" in referring to their sacred texts (Dan. 9:2; I Macc. 3:48; 12:9).

New Testament writers referred to these texts as "the scriptures" (Matt. 21:42), "the holy scriptures" (Rom. 1:2), "the law" (John 12:34), "the law of Moses and . . . the prophets" (Acts 28:23), and "the law of Moses and the prophets and the psalms" (Luke 24:44). "Scripture" is simply the Latin rendering of the Greek word for "writing."

From about A.D. 400 "the books," without qualifying adjectives and meaning "*the* Books," became the standard term of reference for the whole body of sacred writings.

The exact contents of the Bible and the arrangement of its books have varied considerably in different places and periods of Jewish and Christian history.

1. The Hebrew Bible

Since the second century A.D. the Hebrew Bible has consisted of the thirty-nine books included in Protestant editions of the Old Testament but grouped in such a way as to number twenty-four and in a different order. I and II Samuel, I and II Kings, I and II Chronicles, Ezra and Nehemiah, and the Twelve (Minor) Prophets were each regarded as one book.

The books often used their opening words as titles, such as "In the beginning" for our Genesis and "And these are the names" for our Exodus.

Present-day Jews use the names customary among Christians but keep the traditional Jewish arrangement, as follows:

    I. *The Law* (Torah): Genesis, Exodus, Leviticus, Numbers, Deuteronomy

   II. *The Prophets*

        The Former Prophets: Joshua, Judges, Samuel, Kings

        The Latter Prophets: Isaiah, Jeremiah, Ezekiel, the Twelve (Ho-

sea, Joel, Amos, Obadiah, Jonah, Micah, Nahum, Habakkuk,
Zephaniah, Haggai, Zechariah, Malachi)

III. *The Writings:* Psalms, Proverbs, Job, *Song of Songs, *Ruth, *Lamentations, *Ecclesiastes, *Esther, Daniel, Ezra-Nehemiah, Chronicles (the books with an asterisk were called "Festival Scrolls")

2. The Greek Bible (the Septuagint or LXX)

This was the Bible used by Greek-speaking Jews of the Greco-Roman
world and by early Gentile Christians. It arose largely from a translation of
the Hebrew Bible made during the third to first centuries B.C.

Besides the twenty-four books contained in the Hebrew Bible, seventeen
other books or portions of books were included. Fourteen of these seventeen, plus II Esdras, now comprise the Apocrypha of Protestant Bibles.
Roman Catholics accept twelve of these books or portions as of equal inspiration and authority with the books of the Hebrew Bible. (See below, on
the Roman Catholic Old Testament.)

The order of books in the Greek Bible differs somewhat in different
ancient manuscripts. The list offered here is from A. Rahlfs, *Septuaginta*
(with minor changes):

I. *Books of Law and History*

Genesis	Kingdoms I-IV (our	of Ezra and our
Exodus	I-II Samuel	Ezra-Nehemiah)
Leviticus	and I-II Kings)	Esther (with addi-
Numbers	Paralipomena I-II	tions now in our
Deuteronomy	(our I-II Chroni-	Apocrypha)
Joshua	cles)	Judith
Judges	Esdras I-II (an	Tobit
Ruth	apocryphal book	Maccabees I-IV

II. *Poetic and Prophetic Books*

Psalms	Job	Hosea
Odes (including the	Wisdom of Solo-	Amos
Prayer of Ma-	mon	Micah
nasseh)	Wisdom of Jesus	Joel
Proverbs	the Son of	Obadiah
Ecclesiastes	Sirach	Jonah
Song of Songs	Psalms of Solomon	Nahum

Habakkuk
Zephaniah
Haggai
Zechariah
Malachi
Isaiah
Jeremiah

Baruch
Lamentations
Letter of Jeremiah
Ezekiel
Daniel (with addi-
    tions, including
    The Prayer of

Azariah and the
Song of the Three
Young Men,
Susanna, and Bel
and the Dragon)

3. The Latin Bible

This Bible came into existence between the second and fifth centuries A.D. through the work of many Christian translators, notably Jerome (died 420). Jerome's predecessors had translated the Old Testament from the Greek Bible, whereas Jerome rendered it from the Hebrew Bible.

In general contents and arrangement, the Latin Bible followed the Greek Bible. The identity and number of the books included in Latin manuscripts varied somewhat before the Council of Trent (A.D. 1546). As fixed by the council, the list excluded I Esdras (the apocryphal Esdras) and the Prayer of Manasseh, which, with a second apocryphal book of Esdras, were placed in an appendix. III and IV Maccabees apparently were never included in Latin Bibles.

Since the Council of Trent the Latin Bible has contained the following books:

Old Testament

Genesis
Exodus
Leviticus
Numbers
Deuteronomy
Joshua
Judges
Ruth
I-IV Kingdoms
    (our books of Samuel
    and Kings)
I-II Paralipomena
    (our books of Chronicles)
I-II Esdras (our Ezra and
    Nehemiah)

Tobit
Judith
Esther
Job
Psalms
Proverbs
Ecclesiastes
Song of Songs
Wisdom of Solomon
Ecclesiasticus (The Wisdom
    of Jesus the Son of
    Sirach)
Isaiah
Jeremiah
Lamentations

Baruch	Habakkuk
Ezekiel	Zephaniah
Daniel	Haggai
Hosea	Zechariah
Joel	Malachi
Amos	I-II Maccabees
Obadiah	Appendix: The Prayer of
Jonah	Manasseh and two apocryphal
Micah	books of Esdras
Nahum	

New Testament

The twenty-seven books in the order customary in Protestant Bibles

4. Contemporary English Bibles

a. Roman Catholic

The New American Bible (1970)—the most important contemporary Roman Catholic Bible—contains the exact list of books as noted above, except that it introduces I and II Maccabees between Esther and Job and uses the names I and II Samuel, I and II Kings, I and II Chronicles, Ezra, and Nehemiah instead of the older terminology. The books in the appendix of the Latin Bible are not included.

b. Jewish

These follow the content and order of the Hebrew Bible. They employ the names for the individual books traditional among Christians. The books of the New Testament, of course, are not included.

c. Protestant

The Old Testament in Protestant Bibles contains only the books present in the Hebrew Bible. The additional books of the Greek and the Latin Bibles are either omitted altogether or printed in a separate section under the caption "the Apocrypha." The books of the Apocrypha, long omitted from Protestant Bibles, are now being re-introduced, as in some editions of the RSV and the NEB. (On the history of the Apocrypha, see chap. 48.)

Protestant and Roman Catholic Bibles always have agreed on the content and arrangement of the New Testament.

2. Major Characteristics of the Bible

1. The Bible Is One Book and Many Books

So accustomed are we to the printed Bible published in one bound volume that we are apt to forget that its different books were written by many different persons in many periods of ancient history and that the books at first circulated independently. Only gradually were they gathered together into smaller and then greater collections, until a collection of collections was formed. Certain of the writers were separated by more than a thousand years.

But the Bible is also one book. It arose out of the religious experience of one people (Israel) with their God (Yahweh). The Bible explains the origin of this people, the character of their history, the nature of their institutions, the purpose of their existence, and their ultimate destiny as the people of God. The Christian church regarded itself as the true Israel of God (Gal. 6:16; I Pet. 2:9-10) and the events of its founding as the fulfillment of the purpose of God as expressed in the holy writings (Luke 24:25-27, 44-46; Acts 2:16 ff.; Rom. 1:1-2).

Thus the church came to see Jewish scriptures and Christian writings as complementary—as together bearing witness to the mighty deeds of God in the forming of a people of his own out of the stock of Israel and, through the true Israel, out of the nations of the world. The Bible is therefore *one* book with a pervading theme: God's activity in the redemption of the world through a chosen, renewed, and obedient people.

2. The Bible Is a Collection of Approved Books

Both Israels—the old and the new—produced a large literature. Much of it is not now contained in our Bible, even in those Bibles that include the Apocrypha.

In the Old Testament we find mention of books now lost: "the Book of the Wars of the Lord" (Num. 21:14); "the Book of Jashar" (Josh. 10:13); "the Book of the Acts of Solomon" (I Kings 11:41); "the Book of the Chronicles of the Kings of Israel" (I Kings 14:19); "the Book of the Chronicles of the Kings of Judah" (I Kings 14:29); and others.

Many books not mentioned in our Bible (including the Apocrypha) circulated in Judaism before, during, and after the rise of Christianity. Among them were commentaries on and paraphrases of Old Testament books; collections of Old Testament passages and of hymns; books about worship, about the end of the age, and about the beliefs and practices of religious groups (see pp. 396-403).

Christianity produced much literature not included in the New Testament as finally agreed upon by A.D. 400, such as: many Gospels and related works; many writings about the Apostles; and several books that professed to unveil the future (apocalypses).

The books that appear in our Bible are thus only a part of the large literature of the Judeo-Christian religion. Our biblical books came to the fore and maintained their prestige not only because of their assumed connection with persons believed to have been God-inspired but because of their value for worship, instruction, and guidance of life in the communities for which they were written. For the most part, they became "approved" books in their communities long before they were included by official action in a closed collection (see chap. 3).

3. The Bible, as Known in the Christian Church, Is a Two-Stage Book

The stages are: promise (the Old Testament, or more accurately, the Old Covenant) and fulfillment (the New Testament or New Covenant).

Traditionally in English and Latin Bibles the Christian church has referred to the books it inherited from Judaism as "the Old Testament" (Latin, *testamentum*).

Actually, the Hebrews spoke of a *berit* or covenant which God had made with the fathers, particularly with Moses at Mt. Sinai. By this word they meant a promise, an agreement, or an arrangement involving two parties, in which at least one party was bound by an oath. The Greek Bible translated the Hebrew word *berit* (covenant) by the word *diatheke* (meaning usually "covenant" but sometimes "will" or "testament"—that is, a declaration of intention concerning the disposal of an estate upon the maker's death).

It is not a "will" that is intended in the terms Old Testament and New Testament, but an arrangement or agreement between contracting parties involving promises and sealed with oaths. Therefore, "Old Covenant" and "New Covenant" are to be preferred in modern translations.

The Bible represents the Old Covenant as proposed by God, accepted by Israel, and sealed in solemn ceremony at Mt. Sinai. God promised to bless Israel with his presence and to protect and guide it to a place of preeminence among the peoples of the world—*if* Israel would be exclusively loyal to him, become like him in character, express this God-likeness in individual and national life, witness to the nations concerning his saving activity in Israel's history, and invite the nations to join in the benefits and responsibilities of the covenant relationship.

But Israel was faithless to the terms of the covenant, as the great prophets unceasingly pointed out. The nation worshiped other gods, trusted for security in military alliances made with idolatrous foreign powers, aped the false way of life of the peoples around, and finally experienced national disaster as the consequence of infidelity to its covenant God. Instead of becoming a light to the nations, it withdrew into something like a ghetto existence. God's name, rather than being honored among the nations, was blasphemed because of Israel's shameless conduct (Isa. 52:5; Rom. 2:24). The prophets Isaiah, Jeremiah, Ezekiel, and others looked forward to the day when Israel would be fully obedient to the terms of the covenant, when its national life would be renewed inwardly and outwardly and its world mission faithfully carried out. But within the pages of the Old Testament all this remains unfulfilled promise.

The New Testament resounds with the note of fulfillment. It says that the righteous leader promised as the fulfiller of Israel's God-appointed destiny appeared with the birth, ministry, and death-resurrection of Jesus of Nazareth. It declares that he inaugurated a new and fully effective covenant between God and Israel. It claims that, as participants in the new covenant, his followers are made loyal to God, are inwardly cleansed, are indwelt by God's Spirit, are living in loving relationships with their brothers as children in a common family, and are faithfully carrying out their work of witnessing to the nations. The New Testament regards the church as the outpost of the kingdom of God and holds that the church enjoys in foretaste the life of the final kingdom.

4. The Bible Is Both an Ancient and a Very Modern Book

It contains old tribal traditions reaching back into the second millennium B.C. One of the sources behind the Pentateuch ("J"—see pp. 84-86) seems to have been composed as early as the tenth or ninth century B.C. "The Court History of David" (II Sam. 9–20 and I Kings 1, 2), unquestionably the finest piece of historical narrative in the Old Testament, was written probably in the age of King Solomon—centuries before the rise of historical writing among the Greeks.

The books of the Old Testament were created to meet the needs of the ancient communities in which they first appeared. A proper interpretation of them requires that we see them primarily as written for the circumstances of the authors' own time.

The prophets of the Old Testament were declarers of the divine will for the men of their own age. They were not primarily predictors of the future for *our* benefit.

Paul's letters were practical directives for the church of his day. He did not write, as one scholar has put it, "with the thought that posterity [was] looking over his shoulder." Another writer has remarked that if Paul had possessed a magic carpet, he would not have written his letters at all.

Even a book like the Revelation to John—so loudly claimed in some circles today as having been incomprehensible until now by any but ourselves, who live in the time of the final fulfillment of prophecy—was actually "tailored" for the church in Asia Minor at the end of the first century A.D. Its first readers certainly understood it far better than we can.

Furthermore, these ancient books, addressed to ancient people and situations long gone, were transmitted through the centuries by copyists who reproduced them by hand. The original manuscripts on animal skins and papyrus soon perished. The thousands of copies showed variations due to inaccurate copying. Scholars have been at work for some two hundred years comparing the many manuscripts and recovering as far as possible the original text of the biblical books (see chap. 92).

The Bible is an heirloom of great antiquity, bequeathed to us by countless persons who produced it and passed it along to us.

Yet, when all this has been said, the Bible remains a strangely modern book, often strikingly relevant to our contemporary life. This is so in part because the human situation in every age remains fundamentally the same. We are born, grow up in families, marry, beget children, and work for a living in a natural order often hostile to our best efforts. We struggle against human enemies and cringe before the leering face of death. In every age men are tempted to worship the creature rather than the Creator and to seek self-gratification rather than the well-being of all people. Though the cultural setting of man's life varies from age to age, his basic situation remains the same.

Thus Abraham, who desperately wanted what life had denied him (a son), who sought by devious means to obtain an heir, and who at length learned to trust in God in the face of human impossibility, holds up a mirror in which we see our own frustrations, lack of faith, and need of divine help. Thus Job, whose life was reduced to ashes in overpowering disasters and who found God at the end of his questioning, comforts us in our tribulations. Thus Jesus and Paul, who left father and mother, brothers and sisters, and houses and lands in obedience to the divine call and the claims of the kingdom of God, draw us after them.

The early church and Christians through the centuries have found that, under the Holy Spirit as teacher (John 14:26; 16:13-15), the sacred writings are "profitable for teaching, for reproof, for correction, and for training in righteousness, that the man of God may be complete, equipped for every good work" (II Tim. 3:16).

5. The Bible Is a Book of Rich Variety

It contains many types of literature: songs and other poetic material, historical narratives, laws, liturgies, prophetic utterances, wise sayings, short stories, Gospels, letters, sermons, apocalypses.

There is reading matter for every mood. One can skip through lush meadows to the music of the birds, drink from sparkling fountains, and loll under the cedars of Lebanon (Ps. 104). One can ride the waves in a ship of Solomon's fleet in search of the gold of Ophir (I Kings 9). One can dawdle in the pleasure gardens of kings, sipping wine from golden goblets and watching maidens from the royal harem entertain the banqueters (Esther 1–2).

"The glory of Lebanon" (Isa. 35:2)—a gorge near the famous cedars of Lebanon

One can enter into the awful silence of the temple, cry out for mercy before a majestic and holy God, and depart with sins forgiven and a mission to perform (Isa. 6). One can vent his anger over the rank injustices in life, lament the day of his birth, and perhaps battle his way to faith (Job and Jeremiah) or turn to bitter pessimism (Ecclesiastes). One can spend his life in unselfish service and know the agony of vicarious suffering and death (Isa. 53 and the Gospels). One can peer into the future with prophets and seers, tremble before the great white throne, and shout "hallelujah" with the redeemed or wail with the damned (Daniel and Revelation).

The Bible is a book that plumbs the depths of human experience on all its sides.

6. The Bible Is a Picture Book

Its pictures are, of course, word pictures. But so graphic are they that we see the scenes almost as if we were looking at photographs.

Isaiah's description of the daughters of Zion walking with outstretched necks, glancing wantonly as they mince along with tinkling feet (Isa. 3:16) is almost as effective as a motion picture of the scene would be. Jeremiah's word picture of the drought in Judah (Jer. 14:2-6) is so realistic that our lips seem almost cracked like the parched earth and we fairly pant with the wild asses on the barren heights.

The picture language of the Bible is technically called metaphorical language. A metaphor offers a comparison between two objects or realms of experience. When we speak of the head of a table, a leg of a chair, the foot of a bed, the face of a cliff, an arm of a sea, the hands of a watch, we characterize one object in terms of another.

In the Bible almost every page glistens with metaphors. Judah is "a lion's whelp," Israel "a wild vine" and "a wild ass . . . in her heat sniffing the wind." Jesus is said to be "the Lamb of God" or "our pascal lamb." He is represented as "the bridegroom," and the church as his "bride." Christians are "the light of the world."

Skillful use of metaphor is characteristic of great literature.

7. The Bible Is an Inspired and an Inspiring Storybook

The Hebrews were a storytelling people, in some respects like their Arabic-speaking kin, who spun the delightful tales of the Arabian Nights.

Some of the world's best stories are to be found in the Bible. Many literary experts regard the Joseph narrative, for example, as a supreme example of the storyteller's art.

"The Lord is my shepherd" (Ps. 23:1)—perhaps the best-loved of biblical metaphors. Here a shepherd leads his flock at modern Jericho.

The real power of the Bible lies in its central story—the story of redemption. The theme of this story is what God has done through the life of Israel to save all mankind from sin and folly and to bring people of every race and condition into a kingdom of love and brotherhood.

The story describes how God called the Hebrews to be his means of revelation, how he made himself known to them when he delivered them from the land of Egypt, how he disclosed his will for their life in the giving of the Law at Mount Sinai, how he led them into the Promised Land, how he spoke urgent words to them through the prophets and disciplined them at the hands of foreign nations. It tells how at length he sent his Son to them; how, through the Son's life, death, and resurrection, the power of evil was broken and a new Spirit-filled community brought into being. It affirms that through Jesus Christ salvation has been made available to all people. It declares that the power of this community will increase, that the kingdoms of this world will become the kingdom of our Lord and of his Christ, and that finally God's purpose for men will be fully realized: he and his children will dwell together in intimate fellowship forever.

Because of the wonderful story told in the Bible and confirmed in human experience, Christians have always regarded the Bible as an inspired book. It came out of the life of an inspired people, a people granted unusual intimacy with God and special understanding of his will. The Bible is the record written by these people about God's encounter with them. When we read it we find what God is like, what men are like, what God has done and is doing for them and with them, and what he wants us to be and do. In the Bible we have a message from God and about God. We thus say that the Bible is the Word of God.

We do not, of course, mean that every word contained in the Bible was placed there by God. We must remember that God works in the world through people who are responsive, usable, and human. God's own Son became truly human that God might speak to us in a language we mortals could understand. To grasp this message one must view the Bible as a whole, not in piecemeal fashion, as though there were something magical about the individual words.

The Bible tells us what we need to know in order to be saved. It does not satisfy our curiosity about important questions in the fields of science, philosophy, history, psychology, and the like. Its function is to bring us to Christ, to bring us to maturity in him, and to send us out into the world to witness by our life and good deeds to his saving power. It gives us a great hope—that "earth may be fair and all her children one"—and it assures us that "eye hath not seen, nor ear heard, neither have entered into the heart of man, the things which God hath prepared for them that love him" (I Cor. 2:9 KJV).

(For further discussion of the inspiration and authority of the Bible see chap. 103.)

For Further Reading

Kelly, Balmer H., ed. *The Layman's Bible Commentary,* Vol. I, 1959.
Mellor, Enid B., ed. *The Making of the Old Testament,* 1972.
Robert, A., and Feuillet, A. *Interpreting the Scriptures,* 1969.

3. Holy Scriptures and Sacred Canon

"Holy Scriptures" means "writings that have been set apart." The synagogue and the church considered them different from secular literature because they believed them to have been inspired by God.

"Sacred canon" represents a further stage at which a list of such holy writings was drawn up as a closed collection, not to be added to, subtracted from, or altered in any way.

"Canon," from an ancient Semitic word meaning "reed," came to mean an authoritative standard by which other things are measured. As applied to the Bible, the word means that in this particular collection of writings—as against other writings—the Divine purpose and will for men are to be found.

1. The Formation of the Old Testament Canon

We have seen in the lists in chapter 1 that the Old Testament canon varies in Jewish, Greek, Roman Catholic, and Protestant Bibles. Over and above the contents of the Jewish Bible there are some fifteen books or portions of books that were accepted as in some sense authoritative by Greek-reading Jews of around the time of Jesus.

Protestants have sometimes included these as an appendix to the Old Testament, under the label "Apocrypha," or excluded them altogether. Roman Catholics accept twelve of these as "deuterocanonical" (see p. 196) and include them in various places in the text of the Old Testament.

It is important to remember that the Hebrew Bible consists of three sections: the Law or the Torah (the Pentateuch), the Prophets, and the Writings.

a. Stages in the Formation of the Old Testament Canon

(1) The Recognition of the Authority of Deuteronomy

Upon discovery of this book (or part of it) in the temple in 622 B.C., King Josiah recognized its authority as the word of Moses and of God and based a sweeping reform on its laws (II Kings 22:3–23:25).

(2) The Exaltation of "the Law" (the Torah, the Pentateuch)

The written sources used in the compilation of the Pentateuch are apparently considerably older than the Pentateuch itself (see chap. 9). These sources and the laws and teachings contained in them clearly were regarded as authoritative for the life of Israel long before they became embodied in our Pentateuch.

The Pentateuch in its present form seems to have been completed in the fifth century B.C. and accepted as God's word for the nation by Ezra and his contemporaries in the fifth or early fourth century (Neh. 8:1–10:39).

Conservative scholars, however, hold that the Pentateuch was completed much earlier, perhaps by the time of Samuel in the eleventh century B.C., and was considered binding on Israel from that time.

(3) The Assembling of "the Prophets"

This collection embraces the Former or Earlier Prophets (Joshua to Kings) and the Latter or Later Prophets (Isaiah, Jeremiah, Ezekiel, and the Twelve, that is, "the Minor Prophets").

All these books presumably enjoyed a growing authority from the time of their compilation.

They became a closed collection by around 200 B.C., to judge from evidence in the apocryphal book the Wisdom of Jesus the Son of Sirach of the second century B.C.

(4) The Selection of "the Writings"

In Jewish circles at the time of Jesus much literature not in the Law and the Prophets also was read, including the eleven books now in "the Writings," those books and portions now in the Apocrypha of Protestant Bibles, and sectarian works like the Dead Sea Scrolls.

No attempt was made to draw up a list of approved books from this miscellaneous literature until late in the first or in the second century A.D. Then rabbis at Jamnia, where there was a rabbinical school, and rabbis elsewhere set out to determine which books in this category should be accepted as canonical. By the third century the eleven books now in the third section of the Hebrew Bible were firmly established among Jews and the rest excluded.

b. The Christian Church and the Old Testament Canon

The wide use of the Greek Bible in the early church and its translation into Latin led to the perpetuation of the books and portions Protestants now assign to the Apocrypha. Though individuals and sections of the early church, on the basis of knowledge of the more limited Jewish canon, questioned or forbade use of the additional books and portions, these latter were included by the councils of Hippo (393) and Carthage (397) and eventually declared canonical by the Council of Trent (1546).

Martin Luther denied the authority of the additional books and portions and relegated them to an appendix to the Old Testament with this superscription: "Apocrypha, these are books which are not held equal to the sacred Scriptures, and yet are useful and good for reading."

Since Luther's time they have both been included and omitted from the Protestant Bible. Since the Council of Trent declared twelve of them canonical, they have had a secure place in the Roman Catholic Bible.

c. Standards by Which Jews Judged Their Books

We have no certain knowledge here. Several suggestions have been made:
Was a book written by an inspired prophet or by someone connected with him?

Did its teaching conform to the Law of God as traditionally understood?

Was it suitable for reading and instruction in the public worship of temple and synagogue? Did it celebrate authentically the mighty acts of God in Israel's behalf, and did it remind Israel of its God-appointed responsibilities within the covenant relationship?

d. Factors Leading to the Final Canonization of the Jewish Scriptures

Several historical factors made an approved collection of books necessary for Jews:

The collapse of the Jewish revolutionary movements against the authority of Rome (A.D. 66–73 and 132–135) and the need felt by Jewish leaders to ban the inflammatory apocalyptic literature which had supported these movements (see pp. 342-43).

The rise of Christianity with a literature which was regarded by Jewish leaders as "heretical."

The Septuagint (Greek Old Testament) had fallen into disfavor with Jews because of its popularity in the Christian church.

2. The Formation of the New Testament Canon

Since Christianity arose before the third section of the Old Testament canon (the Writings) was fixed in the first and second centuries A.D., Christian literature was free to circulate and gain acceptance by Jews as well as Gentiles. Christians believed that the Holy Spirit had been given to the church and that prophecy had returned to Israel (Acts 21:9; I Cor. 12:28; Rev. 22:6, 9). All New Testament writings lay claim to authority, either implicitly or explicitly.

a. Stages in the Formation of the New Testament Canon

(1) The Collection of the Letters of Paul

Paul's letters were recognized by many of their first readers as divinely inspired. This is evident from the fact that those letters were preserved and that the churches addressed continued for the most part in the directions Paul pointed out.

Who first brought together Paul's letters into a collection is not known. One supposition holds that the author of Ephesians—a disciple of Paul, possibly the one-time runaway slave Onesimus—collected his master's letters about A.D. 90 and wrote Ephesians under his master's name as an introduction to the collection. This hypothesis cannot be verified.

Near the end of the first century Clement of Rome referred to I Corinthians as "written with true inspiration." He appealed to the authority of Paul along with that of the Old Testament.

Early in the second century Ignatius wrote to the church at Ephesus that Paul "in every letter makes mention of you in Christ Jesus"—thus indicating Ignatius' knowledge of a collection of Paul's letters.

The author of II Peter (first half of second century) knew the collected letters of Paul and referred to them as on a level with "the other scriptures" (3:16), that is, probably the Old Testament and possibly some Christian writings which had gained wide acceptance in the church.

The heretic Marcion published his own edition of Paul's letters about A.D. 140. This shows that the collected letters of Paul were well known in the church of Marcion's day.

(2) The Emergence of Four Gospels

The church regarded both the words of the historical Jesus and those of the resurrected Christ as inspired and authoritative. (For examples of words of the resurrected Christ, see Matt. 28:18-20; Acts 1:6-8.)

The author of Luke-Acts tells us that many accounts of Christian beginnings existed when he wrote. These were based on the reports handed down by the original eyewitnesses (Luke 1:1-2). Only four accounts were included in the church's canon. Why were these four preserved?

The answer may be that each of the four became recognized as authoritative in a different important early center of the church. If this is so, these four Gospels were first circulated locally before they were circulated throughout the church.

The four Gospels were slow in gaining general acceptance. By and large the early church preferred oral reports about Jesus and the apostles. Papias (second quarter of the second century) said that "things out of books were less useful to me than what could be learned from a living and abiding voice"—meaning, as the context shows, from some living person who had had contact with disciples of the original apostles.

Though early church writers (such as Clement of Rome, Ignatius) some-

Photo by H. T. Frank

The Bible in Anglo-Saxon; precursor of the various English texts. The Anglo-Saxon is written between the lines of the Latin text.

times cited material like that in our Gospels, the first clear reference to any of our four Gospels appears in the writings of Papias. He mentions Mark's Gospel and refers to a collection of "oracles" (sayings of Jesus) in "the Hebrew language" (that is, in Aramaic) by Matthew. This collection of sayings of Jesus is probably not our Gospel of Matthew but rather perhaps a source used extensively by Matthew, possibly "Q" (see p. 214).

Justin Martyr (died about 165) referred to our Gospels as "memoirs" of the apostles and of those who followed the apostles. He believed the deeds and words of Jesus were authoritatively reported in them. He indicated that on Sundays in its liturgy the church of his time read from these apostolic memoirs as well as from the Old Testament prophets. Here it is no longer the oral tradition about Jesus but the written records of him that are the center of attention and authority.

A harmony of the Gospels, known as the Diatessaron, prepared by the Syrian Tatian (around 170), appears to have used only our four Gospels. This indicates that these four Gospels had come to a place of preeminence by that time. In about 180 Irenaeus offered an elaborate argument for the validity of *four* Gospels: since there are four winds and four directions, so there must of necessity be four Gospels.

Many other Gospels appeared in the church during the second and following centuries, but they did not gain universal acceptance. They consist of:

(a) Gospels of Our Canonical Type

Their authors took traditional material about Jesus, like that in our four Gospels, and used it to advance untraditional or "heretical" theology. (Papyrus Oxyrhynchus 840, Papyrus Edgerton 2, the Gospel of Peter, and the Gospel of the Egyptians are of this sort.)

(b) Gospels of a Gnostic Type

These present Jesus as the revealer of secret knowledge, given to the disciples in dialogues and visions. These Gospels also stemmed from groups the church regarded as heretical. (Representative of this type are: the Gospel of Thomas, the Apocryphon of John, the Sophia Jesu Christi [The Wisdom of Jesus Christ], and the Dialogue of the Redeemer.)

(c) Gospels Which Supplement and Embellish the Canonical
        Gospels

He.e the desire was to satisfy curiosity by filling in gaps in the church's knowledge of Jesus. This was done from pious fancy and from legends from foreign sources. (Belonging to this type are: the Protevangelium of James, the Infancy Story of Thomas, and the Gospel of Nicodemus [Acts of Pilate and Christ's Descent into Hell].)

It is evident that our four Gospels made their way to the fore early, that by about 140–200 they had established themselves widely in church favor and use, and that they maintained their favored position until the New Testament canon was closed (see below).

(3) The Selection of the Rest of the New Testament

In the period around 140–200 most of the remaining books of the New Testament rose to a place of wide acceptance and authority.

Irenaeus, Tertullian, and Clement of Alexandria (all around the end of the second century) agreed on the authority of the following: the four Gospels, thirteen epistles of Paul, the Acts of the Apostles, I Peter, I John, and the Revelation to John. An agreement on Hebrews, James, II Peter, II and III John, and Jude had not yet been reached, and the authority of the Revelation to John was still contested in some quarters (particularly in the Eastern part of the church).

Some books of high quality were popular at this time but were not finally accepted into the New Testament canon: I Clement, the Shepherd of Hermas, the Epistle of Barnabas, the Didache, and the Apocalypse of Peter, for example.

(4) The Fixing of the New Testament Canon

Marcion seems to have made the first closed collection of Christian writings. He was a Gnostic (see pp. 304-7) who rejected the Old Testament and everything "Jewish" and put in place of the Old Testament "the Gospel" (an abridged edition of the Gospel of Luke) and "the Apostle" (ten edited letters of Paul). How much influence this "heretic" had in causing the church finally to draw up an approved list of books is not known.

It was not until Eusebius, around 325, that a careful attempt was made to distinguish approved from unapproved books. With him, therefore, canonization may be said to have begun. He made note of acknowledged, disputed, and rejected books. Among the disputed he named James, II Peter, Jude, II and III John, and the Revelation to John.

In his Easter letter of A.D. 367 Athanasius of Alexandria listed as canonical the books now contained in our New Testament.

Church councils at Rome (382), at Hippo (393), at Carthage (397), and again at Carthage (419) fixed the list at those now present in our New Testament.

In some parts of the church, controversy over the inclusion of the Revelation to John and some of the General Epistles continued until the beginning of the sixth century.

b. Standards by Which Christian Books Were Judged

In general, three standards operated through the centuries in the church's selection of its authoritative—and, finally, canonical—literature:

The extent of the acceptance and use in the church of a particular writing

The fidelity of its contents to the church's traditional teaching

The defensibility of its claim to apostolic origin (either written or authorized by an apostle)

For Further Reading
Barclay, W. *The Making of the Bible,* 1961.
Brown, R. E., Fitzmyer, J. A., and Murphy, R. E., eds. *The Jerome Biblical Commentary,* 1968, pp. 515-34.
Filson, F. V. *Which Books Belong in the Bible?* 1957.
Laymon, C. M., ed. *The Interpreter's One-Volume Commentary on the Bible,* 1971, pp. 1209-24.

4. The Translation and Distribution of the Bible

A translation of the Bible into a language different from those in which it was originally written (Hebrew, Aramaic, and Greek) is called a "version."

1. Ancient Versions

The Septuagint ("Seventy" or LXX): the Greek translation of the Old Testament, begun in Egypt around 250 B.C. and completed over a couple of centuries; allegedly made by seventy (or seventy-two) men

The Aramaic Targums: oral paraphrases of the Old Testament, used in Jewish synagogues for the benefit of hearers accustomed to Aramaic rather than Hebrew; eventually reduced to writing (some of them possibly as early as the latter part of the second century B.C.)

The Latin versions: the Old Latin translations and the Vulgate ("Common"), the latter made by Jerome (about A.D. 400) and probably by other translators after him

The Syriac versions: the Old Syriac, the Peshitta ("Simple"), and others, from the second to the seventh centuries

The Coptic versions from Egypt: the Sahidic, the Bohairic, etc., from the third and later centuries

The Gothic version: made by Bishop Ulfilas, the apostle to the Goths in the fourth century

The Armenian version (fifth century)

The Georgian version (fifth to eleventh centuries)

The Ethiopic version (fifth century?)

Arabic versions (of uncertain dates)

2. Medieval and Modern Versions

The spread of Christianity brought with it the translation of the Bible into the major languages of the world: Dutch, English, French, German, modern Greek, Hungarian, Italian, Portuguese, Danish, Icelandic, Swedish, Spanish, Slavic (Bulgarian, Polish, Russian), etc.

By the time of the invention of printing (mid-fifteenth century) the Bible had been put, in whole or in part, into thirty-three languages: twenty-two European, seven Asiatic, four African.

A spurt forward came in the nineteenth century, the century of missionary expansion, when the Bible was translated into some five hundred additional languages and dialects.

Today the Bible is unquestionably the world's most widely read book.

In whole or in part it has been translated into more than fifteen hundred languages. It has been estimated that more than 90 percent of the world's inhabitants have the entire Bible in their own language and more than 97 percent have at least one book of the Bible. The Gospel according to Mark, the most widely translated of the Bible's books, has been put into some eight hundred languages.

There remain more than a thousand minor languages into which the Bible is yet to be translated. The work of translation and revision of existing translations is being carried on in some 130 countries by several thousand skilled and dedicated people. Each year translators begin work in about a score of new languages.

By the end of the twentieth century the Bible societies of the world probably will distribute annually about one billion copies of Bibles, New Testaments, Gospels, and Scripture portions—approximately one piece for every seven persons expected to be living in the world by then.

The American Bible Society

Distributing scripture to farmers in Japan

Eugene A. Nida, the Executive Secretary for Translations of the American Bible Society, has written, "Despite the claim that the Bible is no longer intelligible to modern man, there are more people reading and studying the Scriptures, whether individually or in small groups, than at any time in the history of Christianity" (*Religion Across Cultures* [1968], p. 59).

For Further Reading

> Nida, Eugene A. *God's Word in Man's Language,* 1952.
> The files of the *American Bible Society Record.*

5. English Versions in Use Today

(For a description of biblical manuscripts and textual research, see chapter 92.)

THE KING JAMES VERSION (THE AUTHORIZED VERSION)
THE MODERN KING JAMES VERSION OF THE HOLY BIBLE

The King James Version, prepared by forty-seven scholars appointed by James I, was begun in 1604 and published in 1611. The translators were instructed to revise the Bishops' Bible, the version then officially in use, but to alter it "as little as the truth of the original will permit."

Much of the wording of the King James Version reflects the language of earlier English Bibles (the Geneva Bible, the Great Bible, Matthew's Bible, Coverdale's Bible, and Tyndale's translation of the New Testament and part of the Old). Approximately 80 percent of the words of the New Testament in the King James Version derive ultimately from Tyndale's work.

There were several editions of the King James Version, the last in 1638. In 1701 Archbishop Ussher's chronology was introduced into the margins.

The simplicity, dignity, power, and aptness of expression of this version have made it a classic in the English-speaking world. However, some of its English words are now archaic; for example, "chapmen" for "traders" (II Chron. 9:14); "ear" for "plow" (I Sam. 8:12); "leasing" for "lies" (Ps. 5:6); "neesings" for "sneezings" (Job 41:18); "holden" for "kept from" (Luke 24:16); "let" for "prevented" (Rom. 1:13). Also, there were inaccuracies in many places in the Hebrew and Greek texts from which the King James Version was made, as we know from the thousands of biblical

Photo by H. T. Frank

The title page of the original King James Bible (1611)

manuscripts found since 1611 (see chap. 92). Advances in knowledge of biblical languages, customs, history, and theological concepts have made other translations necessary.

In 1962 a version of the King James Bible edited by Jay P. Green appeared. It substitutes modern words and expressions for archaic ones but leaves the basic text unchanged (even where the best ancient manuscripts now known show a passage to be missing, as in Mark 16:9-21; John 5:4; 7:53–8:11). It starts from the assumption that "the people do not want a new Bible; they just want the old one in a form they can read and understand."

THE REVISED VERSION
THE AMERICAN STANDARD VERSION
THE NEW AMERICAN STANDARD BIBLE

In 1870 British scholars began a revision of the King James Version to bring it abreast of the vast increase of biblical knowledge since 1611. Revision committees were formed in England and in the United States for the work, the American committees serving as advisers to the British. The revision was called the Revised Version.

At the beginning the committees hoped that the revision could be adopted on both sides of the Atlantic. However, strong differences of judgment developed between the English and American groups. This led to the publication of the American preferences in appendixes to the British edition of the New Testament (1881) and of the Old Testament (1885) and finally to an American edition of both Testaments in 1901, under the name the American Standard Version. A British revision of the Apocrypha appeared in 1896, but no such revision was made by the Americans.

The Revised Version and the American Standard Version mark a great advance over the King James Version in accuracy of the text of the Bible (that is, in determining the original text of the Bible, free from copyists' errors). But in English style both revisions are inferior. Beauty and force are sacrificed to word-for-word literalness in translation. Such literalness makes the revisions superior for study purposes but of less value for public worship and private devotion. The revisers improved on the King James Version by printing much of the Bible's poetry in poetic form and by arranging the text in paragraphs. Marginal notes suggest variant readings.

By mid-twentieth century in America many one-man translations—like Moffatt's, Knox's, Phillips'—and the Revised Standard Version had begun to replace the American Standard Version. To keep this version alive the

Lockman Foundation issued it in a revised form as the New American Standard Bible (New Testament, 1963; both Testaments, 1971).

Some changes in the wording and content of the biblical text were adopted on the basis of present knowledge of ancient manuscripts. Marginal notes were altered and expanded, and English style was improved. Unfortunately, paragraphing was abandoned and a verse-by-verse-printing (as in the King James Version) resumed.

THE REVISED STANDARD VERSION

From 1930 to 1957 committees of American scholars, under authorization of many major American churches which worked together in the International Council of Religious Education and in the National Council of Churches of the U.S.A., carried out a revision of the American Standard Version and made in addition a translation of the Apocrypha.

The revisers were asked to prepare a version "which embodies the best results of modern scholarship as to the meaning of the Scriptures, and expresses this meaning in English diction which is designed for use in public and private worship and preserves those qualities which have given to the King James Version a supreme place in English literature."

The New Testament appeared in 1946, the Old Testament in 1952, and the Apocrypha in 1957. A standing revision committee has improved the translation in various places in editions published since those dates.

The Revised Standard Version has been widely used by Protestants and Roman Catholics, and, to some extent, by Jews.

Roman Catholics in England issued in 1966 a special Catholic edition, which included the deuterocanonical books in the order in which they appear in the Latin Vulgate (pp. 19-20). In 1973 the Revised Standard Version Common Bible (The Holy Bible—An Ecumenical Edition) was published for use by Protestant, Roman Catholic, and Orthodox readers. In this edition the apocryphal or deuterocanonical books stand between the Testaments.

The reception accorded the Revised Standard Version has been mixed. Many persons in both America and England have hailed it as a reliable, up-to-date, modern English translation which preserves the dignity of the King James Version but speaks to the man in the pew in a language he can understand. Others have villified both the version and the translators on the ground that "modernist" tendencies controlled the translation—a charge difficult, if not impossible, to prove. Some scholars have felt that the translators were too captive to traditional language and should have shown more originality and creativity in their renderings. It is possible that the greatest weakness of the version is its attempt to be both classical and contemporary in its style.

In spite of its faults, it will stand as one of the great translations of this generation.

THE NEW TESTAMENT IN MODERN SPEECH
by Richard F. Weymouth

An English headmaster and classical scholar translated into modern English an edition of the Greek New Testament he himself had produced. It was published in 1903, after his death, with the editorial help of E. Hampden-Cook, a Congregational minister. In 1927 James A. Robertson revised the translation.

The strength of the translation lies in its close attention to the exact force of the Greek tenses. Weymouth's "modern speech" attempts to preserve "a tinge of antiquity" so that there should be a "dignity of style that befits the sacred themes." Weymouth wanted his translation to serve as "a succinct and compressed running commentary (not doctrinal) to be used side by side with its elder compeers" (the King James Version and the English Revised Version). He did not intend the churches to use it for public reading.

THE BIBLE: A NEW TRANSLATION
by James Moffatt

Moffatt, a brilliant Scot, began his career as a translator of the Bible with The Historical New Testament (1901). This work arranged the books of the New Testament in the order of their supposed dates and literary growth.

In 1913 a second work appeared, The New Testament: A New Translation, and in 1924 an Old Testament translation—The Old Testament: A New Translation. Both Testaments were brought together in 1928 in a New Translation of the Bible. A final, revised form of this came out in 1935.

Of the many one-man translations of the Bible, Moffatt's has been among the widest in use. He swept aside "Bible English" and put the original languages in strong contemporary speech.

Criticism of Moffatt's work has been directed at the Scottish idioms in his English and at the extent to which he injected into his translation particular theories about the biblical text. He rearranged the order of certain chapters and verses (for example, the position of John 14) and even changed the Hebrew or Greek text (for example, I Sam. 14:11; I Pet. 3: 19). Furthermore, he attempted to indicate the various sources behind the Pentateuch by varying the style of type in different passages.

His use of "the Eternal" for the personal name of God was not altogether a happy choice. His translation of the Old Testament is generally regarded as of less value than that of the New.

Moffatt put his genius for translation at the service of the committee that prepared the Revised Standard Version. He served as Executive Secretary of this committee from 1937 until his death in 1944.

THE NEW TESTAMENT, AN AMERICAN TRANSLATION
by Edgar J. Goodspeed
THE OLD TESTAMENT, AN AMERICAN TRANSLATION
by T. J. Meek, Leroy Waterman, A. R. Gordon, and J. M. P. Smith

Goodspeed's translation of the New Testament into the language of everyday life appeared in 1923. A somewhat similar translation of the Old Testament by four scholars paralleled it in 1927. The two were joined in 1931 to form The Bible, an American Translation. In 1939 The Complete Bible, an American Translation was published. It contained a revision of the Old Testament translation (by T. J. Meek), Goodspeed's translation of the Apocrypha, and his New Testament.

Freshness and imagination marked the translation in both Testaments. Since four men worked on different parts of the Old Testament, there is some variety in the style there. In the Old Testament section one does not find the degree of passion shown by Goodspeed to translate in the plain language of the street and the marketplace. Simplicity and directness are, however, the rule everywhere. The translation aims at being American "in the sense that the writings of Lincoln, Roosevelt, and Wilson are American," says J. M. P. Smith.

THE BIBLE IN BASIC ENGLISH

Using only about 1,000 different English words, a committee in England, under the leadership of S. H. Hooke of the University of London, produced The New Testament in Basic English in 1941 and the entire Bible in 1949. Obviously, the use of so limited an English vocabulary required the translators to exercise great ingenuity in the rendering of difficult passages. The result is a translation of amazing simplicity. This version has been especially popular with those who were learning to speak and write the English language.

THE CONFRATERNITY VERSION

The standard English Roman Catholic Bible between the sixteenth and twentieth centuries was the Douay-Rheims-Challoner Version, begun by Gregory Martin in 1582 and much revised, especially by Challoner between 1749 and 1763. It is a translation of the Latin Vulgate.

The Confraternity Version of the New Testament (1941), made by American scholars appointed by the Episcopal Committee of the Confraternity of Christian Doctrine, is a revision of the Douay-Rheims-Challoner New Testament. The revisers followed the Latin Vulgate but constantly consulted the Greek text and noted differences in the footnotes. They modernized the English style and wording.

The Episcopal Committee began a revision of the Douay-Rheims-Challoner Old Testament but abandoned it after Pope Pius XII in 1943 permitted and encouraged official translations of the Bible from the original languages.

HOLY BIBLE
translated by Ronald A. Knox

This is one of the best-known Roman Catholic English versions of the twentieth century.

It is a translation of the Latin Vulgate in the light of the Hebrew and Greek originals. The New Testament, undertaken at the request of the Hierarchy of England and Wales in 1939, appeared in 1944. The Old Testament, requested by the Cardinal Archbishop of Westminster, was published in two volumes (1948 and 1950). The one-volume edition of the Holy Bible came out in 1955.

Monsignor Knox was a master of English style. His translation is fresh, sometimes witty, and generally skillful. Footnotes explain differences between the text of the Latin Vulgate and the Hebrew and Greek originals and clarify obscure terms and customs for the reader. The notes occasionally reflect characteristic positions of Roman Catholic theology.

Since Knox's version is a translation of a translation, with only secondary attention to the Hebrew and Greek originals, it cannot be relied on completely for precise knowledge of the meaning of the original texts. However, it makes delightful reading.

THE AUTHENTIC NEW TESTAMENT
by Hugh J. Schonfield

The translator, a British Jew who has written extensively on the New Testament, believes he is the first Jew to translate the New Testament into English (1955). He holds that because of his Jewish background and learning he can translate the New Testament better than a Gentile can. He has drawn heavily on Jewish sources in his translating and commenting (in extensive footnotes).

Schonfield attempts to reveal the New Testament exactly as it was written, to cut away convention and tradition in the way it is translated, and to give the reader "a New Testament authentic in accent and atmosphere."

A lengthy introduction to first-century Christianity, to the Palestinian background of the New Testament, and to the New Testament texts themselves prepares the way for the translation. Maps, plans, and illustrations increase the usefulness of the work.

Traditional chapter and verse divisions are abandoned. The New Testament text is divided into sections under numbers and captions as the translator sees fit. Many captions are strikingly appropriate. Rearrangement in the order of passages within individual books and conjectural changes in the wording are sometimes made.

The translation is often vivid and forceful. Fresh words are selected for old ones (for example, "envoys" for "apostles"; "the News" for "the gospel").

The reader who is accustomed to the more traditional translations of the New Testament will often be startled by what he finds here, but it will stimulate him to ask questions about the New Testament that he would not otherwise have considered.

THE FOUR GOSPELS
by E. V. Rieu
THE ACTS OF THE APOSTLES
by C. H. Rieu

E. V. Rieu, a distinguished classical scholar, translator of Homer, and general editor of the Penguin Classics, turned his skill to the translation of the Gospels (1952). His son, C. H. Rieu, followed in 1957 with a translation of the Acts of the Apostles. (Both the Gospels and the Acts are in the Penguin series.)

The father undertook the translation of the Gospels largely for the benefit of people who, like himself, were outside the direct influence of the church. The son, a lay reader in the church, remarked when he heard of his father's project, "It will be very interesting to see what Father makes of the Gospels. It'll be still more interesting to see what the Gospels make of Father." At the end of the task, the father confessed, "It changed me. My work changed me. And I came to the conclusion . . . that these works (the Gospels) bear the seal of the Son of Man and God. And they are the Magna Charta of the human spirit."

E. V. Rieu approached the Gospels without theological assumptions, as if they had been newly discovered manuscripts like the Dead Sea Scrolls. He believed that that translation is best which comes nearest to affecting modern readers in the way the original readers were affected.

He placed Mark first, for it was first written. He printed in footnotes the quotations of the Old Testament contained in the text of the Gospels—an indefensible procedure, especially in the Gospel of Matthew, where the quotations are part of the fabric of Matthew's style. He made chapter, but not verse, divisions.

C. H. Rieu tried to put the Greek of the Acts into the sort of English the author would have used if he had written in English today. He largely avoided the language of piety, on the one hand, and colloquial or slang expressions, on the other. Headings, italics for Old Testament quotations, and varieties of type make the translation easy to read.

THE HOLY BIBLE FROM ANCIENT EASTERN MANUSCRIPTS
by George M. Lamsa

This is a translation into English (1957) of the Syriac version of the Bible, known as the Peshitta ("Simple"). The Peshitta was a translation into Syriac of the Hebrew Old Testament and the Greek New Testament. It came out of the Syriac church of Edessa (Upper Mesopotamia), probably in the second century A.D. or a little later.

Lamsa, a native of Kurdistan, whose mother tongue is akin to the old Syriac (Aramaic) language, has made extravagant claims for the originality and accuracy of the Peshitta. He holds that it more accurately represents the true biblical text, that it preserves the Hebrew-Aramaic idioms and world view that lay behind the Greek and Latin translations of the Bible, and that in it we hear the authentic words of the first apostles.

Lamsa's scholarship is of dubious quality. In the introduction to his translation he advocates impossible positions, such as that the Gospels are earlier than Paul's epistles and that both are translations from Aramaic originals.

The Peshitta has value for scholarly investigators of the text of the Bible; but it does not preserve simple access to the Bible's original text, as Lamsa claims.

THE NEW TESTAMENT—A NEW TRANSLATION IN PLAIN ENGLISH
by Charles Kingsley Williams

The translator was a British educator and missionary, who meant his translation for people whose native language was not English.

He used the Greek text that was the basis for the Revised Version of 1881 and limited his English vocabulary to about 2,000 words (thus "plain English").

Special features of the translation are: short sentences, using only common words; the avoidance of quotation marks in direct speech; the printing of a much larger proportion of the translation in poetic form than usual (for example, most of the text of the Revelation to John); fresh words instead of traditional ones ("hypocrites" becomes "double-dealers"); footnotes, offering alternative translations and explanations of various sorts; and a glossary.

As a whole, the work is fresh, smooth, and often insightful, as when "reconciled" is rendered "brought into friendship with God."

The translation first appeared in 1952 in England, and an American edition came out in 1963.

THE HOLY BIBLE. THE BERKELEY VERSION
by Gerritt Verkuyl and others

Verkuyl, for many years a member of the Board of Christian Education of the Presbyterian Church U.S.A., brought out his translation of the New Testament in 1945 and thereafter supervised work on the Old Testament by twenty scholars (mostly conservatives). The whole Bible appeared in 1959.

"I aimed," he has said, "at a translation less interpretive than Moffatt's, more cultured in language than Goodspeed's, more American than Weymouth's, and freer from the King James Version than the Revised Standard."

The translation offers brief footnotes to the biblical text, and dates—

unfortunately often of questionable accuracy—in the margins to indicate the period referred to in the biblical material. Conservative positions usually predominate in the dating of the books as to their supposed time of writing. Weights, measures, and money are given in modern American terms.

In general, the translation of the Old Testament is better than that of the New. The whole is a conservative counterpart to the Revised Standard Version.

In 1970 a revision of the New Testament by unnamed scholars appeared under the title The Modern Language New Testament—The New Berkeley Version.

THE AMPLIFIED BIBLE

This translation stems basically from the work of Frances E. Siewert, who devoted a lifetime of research to it. It was issued under the auspices of the Lockman Foundation. It appeared first in three sections (New Testament, 1958; Job to Malachi, 1962; Genesis to Esther, 1964) and as a whole Bible in 1965.

Its purpose is "to reveal, together with the single-word English equivalent to each key Hebrew [and Greek] word, any other clarifying shades of meaning that may have been concealed by the traditional word-for-word method of translation." Multiple English words and phrases are inserted in brackets in the text to suggest the range of meanings in key biblical words and phrases.

This loading of the text with synonyms results in a very wordy translation. I Cor. 10:13, for example, is translated in the Revised Standard Version with 44 words but here with 139 words. Precise translation results from the selection of the proper meaning of a word to express the thought the biblical writer intended. It does not help to list meanings the biblical writer did not have in mind.

Dubious interpretations are often inserted in the brackets. For example, Gen. 1:26 is rendered, "God said, Let us (Father, Son, and Holy Spirit) make mankind in Our image," whereas the "us" may refer to God and his heavenly court (Ps. 82:1; 89:5-7) or it may be a plural of majesty, such as ancient kings used in self-glorification. In I Cor. 7:38 the insertion of the words "the father" and "his daughter, virgin" limits the interpretation to one possibility out of three—hardly a fair procedure from the standpoint of the unwary.

This translation and amplification should be used with caution.

THE NEW JEWISH VERSION

Since 1955 a committee of distinguished Jewish scholars from the three major branches of Judaism in America, under the auspices of the Jewish Publication Society, has been working to produce a new translation of the Jewish Bible according to the traditional text.

To date, the following biblical portions have been completed: the Torah (the Pentateuch), 1962; the Megilloth (Song of Songs, Ruth, Lamentations, Koheleth [Ecclesiastes], Esther) and the book of Jonah, 1971; the Psalms and Isaiah, 1973; Jeremiah, 1974.

Prior to this, American Judaism relied on a Jewish revision of the Revised Version of 1885, published in 1917. The New Jewish Version is a completely new translation.

This version rejects the mechanical word-for-word approach to translation taken by the Septuagint and the King James Version, replaces coordinate Hebrew sentences connected by "and" with appropriate independent and subordinate clauses, takes account in footnotes of the variations in wording of ancient manuscripts, and maintains a conservative attitude toward changes of the traditional text.

The translators, who are fully abreast of the latest linguistic researches and archaeological discoveries, have given us a reliable translation in simple, contemporary English. The high quality of the first installments promises large success for the whole project.

THE NEW TESTAMENT IN MODERN ENGLISH
FOUR PROPHETS: AMOS, HOSEA, FIRST ISAIAH, MICAH
both by J. B. Phillips

Starting in 1947 with Letters to Young Churches, J. B. Phillips of England has published highly successful additional translations of the Scriptures as follows: The Gospels in Modern English, 1952; The Young Church in Action, 1955 (a translation of the book of the Acts); The Book of Revelation, 1957; The New Testament in Modern English, 1958 (his translation of the entire New Testament); and Four Prophets: Amos, Hosea, First Isaiah, Micah, 1963.

Three principles have controlled his work: the translation must not sound like a translation; the translator must not obtrude his own personality; he must do his best to create in the reader an effect equivalent to that produced in the original readers by the author. Phillips has met these tests to a high degree.

With the exception of the New Testament in Modern English, each book introduces the text of the various biblical writings with information about such matters as the author, the date, and the theme. The volume on the Acts includes as an appendix an imaginative expansion by Phillips of four sermons reported in condensed form in the Acts.

Phillips' translation is often quite free, approaching paraphrase. It is not a word-for-word but a meaning-for-meaning translation.

The widespread use of his translation testifies to the high degree of his success in communicating the vitality of the biblical writings to the average person.

THE NEW WORLD TRANSLATION OF THE HOLY SCRIPTURES

The Jehovah's Witnesses published this translation in 1960. By 1971 it had reached a total of over ten million copies in five languages.

It aims to be "as literal as possible to the point of understandableness." Paraphrase, therefore, seldom appears.

Good recent Hebrew and Greek texts have been used as the basis of the translation.

A great point is made of the faithful rendering in this version of the divine name as "Jehovah" (Yahweh). The translators restored this name where they believed ancient editors or copyists inserted "Lord" or "God" in its place (for example, Gen. 18:3). The Foreword decries the concealment of the divine name Jehovah or Yahweh by the term "the Lord" in modern translations.

The translation is often awkward and sadly deficient on the side of English style. It is also marred by attempts to justify the doctrines of Jehovah's Witnesses through the translation and notes on the text. This is particularly visible in the reduction of the New Testament's view of the deity of Christ (for example, "the Word was a God"—John 1:1).

THE NEW ENGLISH BIBLE

The proposal for this new translation arose in 1946 in the Church of Scotland. Soon the Church of England, the major free churches of England (Methodist, Baptist, Congregationalist, Presbyterian, the Society of Friends), the churches of Wales and Ireland, and the Bible societies of England and Scotland gave their support to the project.

The directors, appointed by the Joint Committee on the New Translation of the Bible, were C. H. Dodd, G. R. Driver, and W. D. McHardy. Four panels of translators, representative of the best scholarship of the British Isles, were named by the Joint Committee. They dealt respectively with the Old Testament, the New Testament, the Apocrypha, and with English style.

The New Testament appeared in 1961, and the Old Testament and the Apocrypha, together with a revised edition of the New Testament, in 1970.

The Hebrew and Aramaic text of the Old Testament translated in this version is the traditional text in the best present-day edition. However, the translators made many changes, based on the Dead Sea Scrolls, the ancient versions, variations in Hebrew manuscripts, and conjecture. Footnotes indicate alternative translations, the literal meaning of the Hebrew, the meaning of proper names, corrections of the text, changes in order of material, and the like.

The New Testament rests on no one Greek text. The translators carefully considered variant readings of ancient manuscripts and versions, selected the wording which appeared to be the most original, and recorded serious alternative possibilities in the footnotes.

General introductions to the Old Testament, the Apocrypha, and the New Testament are offered, so that the reader may understand the procedures and issues involved in translating each portion. The text is printed in paragraphs under sectional headings.

The New English Bible is a genuinely new translation, not a revision of an existing one. It employs colloquial, dignified, forceful, direct English idiom and avoids archaic expressions and modern slang. Some Briticisms, however, do appear. Word-for-word translating is rare.

This version is intended for both public and private reading. It has the advantage of team scholarship by England's and Scotland's finest biblical scholars and of official authorization by the major non-Roman churches of the British Isles.

GOOD NEWS FOR MODERN MAN
(TODAY'S ENGLISH VERSION)

This important version of the New Testament began with the appearance in 1964 of a translation of the Gospel of Mark entitled The Right Time. It was made by Robert G. Bratcher, a biblical scholar and translation expert of the American Bible Society. Assisted by an advisory committee of American and British scholars, Bratcher published his translation of the whole New Testament, Good News for Modern Man (Today's English Version), in 1966.

The Old Testament in this version is scheduled to appear in 1976.

Today's English Version is a sparkling, new translation in the language of today. It avoids traditional biblical vocabulary and style. Its phenomenal sale (some 41 million copies by 1973) attests to the translator's success in achieving readability and authenticity.

Dubious passages (such as John 5:3b-4, 7:53–8:11; Mark 16:9-20; Acts 8:37) are placed in brackets. There are no footnotes offering alternative readings. The Greek text employed is that edited by Aland, Black, Metzger, and Wikgren for the United Bible Societies (1966). There are some departures from it, however.

Line drawings by Annie Vallotton illustrate the text. Sectional captions and effective paragraphing help the reader. A glossary of terms, places, and persons mentioned in the New Testament and an index of important subjects, persons, places, and events contribute to the usefulness of the translation.

THE JERUSALEM BIBLE

This valuable English translation (1966)—with introductory essays, extensive footnotes, tables, and maps—is in the best tradition of liberal Roman Catholic scholarship. Its editor was Alexander Jones of Christ's College, Liverpool. He was assisted by twenty-seven principal collaborators. Behind it lies a French work of 1948–54, done by a large company of scholars under the leadership of the famous Dominican Roland DeVaux of Jerusalem, which appeared in a one-volume edition in 1956.

The English biblical text, while following the French translation, reflects the constant use of the Hebrew and Greek texts of the Bible by the editor and his collaborators. The Latin Vulgate, though referred to frequently in the footnotes, has dropped far into the background.

The books translated include those called "deuterocanonical" by Roman Catholics ("apocryphal" by Protestants).

The scholarship is for the most part admirable. As in every translation, the theology of the translators has left its mark in some places (for example, at Matt. 1:25; 18:18; 19:9). The position on historical-critical problems is often quite conservative. Included in the translated text are some passages not found in the best ancient manuscripts (for example, Mark 16:9-20; John 5:3b-4; 7:53–8:11), though footnotes indicate that there is textual evidence against the passages.

THE NEW AMERICAN BIBLE

This Roman Catholic translation of the Bible from the original languages was more than a quarter-century in the making. It appeared in 1970 as the fruit of the labor of some fifty scholars, four of them Protestants. The sponsor was the Episcopal Committee of the Confraternity of Christian Doctrine.

The inspiration for the new version came from a papal encyclical of 1943 which authorized translation from the original languages and approved "cooperation with separated brethren" in the work. A new era in Roman Catholic biblical translation thus began.

The makers of this version declare that they have aimed at a translation, not a paraphrase, in order to retain something of the original flavor and the eccentricities of the various biblical writings.

Introductions to biblical books, extensive footnotes, captions in the text, an essay on biblical geography, and a glossary of biblical terms guide the reader effectively. The spelling of proper names conforms to that found in the King James Version and in most English Bibles since—a considerable departure from traditional Roman Catholic practice.

The books of the Apocrypha (called deuterocanonical books by Roman Catholics) are printed in their traditional places through the Old Testament.

The translation as a whole is skillful and in the mainstream of recent ecumenical biblical scholarship. Only rarely are distinctive Roman Catholic doctrines evident in the introductions or footnotes. Protestants, as well as Roman Catholics, can use this version with great profit.

THE LIVING BIBLE PARAPHRASED

All accurate translation is to a large extent paraphrase, a restatement of an author's thought in different words. What is more than translation in paraphrase is properly "commentary." There is indeed a sizable slice of commentary in this paraphrased Bible, which reflects, as the Preface states, "a rigid evangelical position."

The paraphrase was made by Kenneth N. Taylor and, according to the Preface, was scrutinized by Greek and Hebrew scholars and critics of English style. The text paraphrased is the American Standard Version of 1901 (with some revisions).

Literary form received little attention in the arrangement of the text. The poetic parts of the Bible are mostly printed as prose.

Footnotes to the text are provided. They offer alternative translations, meanings believed implied, literal renderings, and interpretative comments. Unfortunately, the "implied" sometimes suggests what is not implied by the text (see, for example, the notes on John 13:20; Rom. 3:21; Heb. 5:7; 9:18).

Sometimes the interpretative comments inject conclusions on historical matters which are highly debatable, if not erroneous. For example, it is not true that "all commentators believe him [the disciple sitting next to Jesus at the table] to be John, the writer of this book" (footnote on John 13:23). Conclusions on historical matters are sometimes wrongly written into the text. An illustration is the use of the first person in Ps. 132, whereby David is unjustifiably made the author.

Inaccuracies and inadequacies of translation appear. For example, "the tree of Conscience" (Gen. 2:9, 17) introduces a Greek concept into a Hebrew phrase; getting to heaven does not properly render Paul's meaning in the words "salvation" and "righteousness" (Rom. 1:16, 17; 3:21; 4:4, 5); the difficult statement of Jesus in Mark 13:30 is avoided, not translated or paraphrased; a particular and possibly incorrect theory of the atonement is introduced in Rom. 3:25 and I John 2:2.

On the other hand, the economy and felicity of expression often delight the reader: "I would only be making noise" (I Cor. 13:1); "nothing you do for the Lord is ever wasted" (I Cor. 15:58). There is a helpful tendency to make the general and abstract simple and concrete (I Cor. 13:7, 12).

Your major question concerning this paraphrase probably will be, How can I know what is Bible and what is commentary? The answer must be that without a good translation (or several good translations) at your elbow for constant comparison you cannot.

You will find the paraphrase helpful if you will use it for rapid reading and not for detailed investigation of the historical and theological meaning of individual passages and if you will check it in key places against standard translations.

THE NEW TESTAMENT—A NEW TRANSLATION
by William Barclay

Perhaps the finest contemporary interpreter of the New Testament for the average person is William Barclay of the University of Glasgow. His many articles, commentaries, word studies, and monographs, his years of teaching, and his unusual success in writing at a popular level, have superbly equipped him for translating the New Testament for today's readers.

The translation appears in two volumes: The Gospels and the Acts of the Apostles (1968); and The Letters and the Revelation (1969). Its aim is to make the New Testament understandable by the average person without the use of commentaries.

The translation is accurate, clear, and often sparkling. Barclay does not hesitate to paraphrase when a translation would fall short of conveying the biblical author's intention. In a section in Vol. 2 titled "Notes on Passages," he justifies expanding twenty-two passages in order to bring out their meaning for contemporary readers. Fortunately, his fine scholarship gives him the right to paraphrase where needed to convey proper meaning.

The reader finds many helps: a section on problems and principles in translating the New Testament; brief introductions to all the New Testament books and to groups of books; definitions of and comments on many important New Testament words, alphabetically arranged; notes on certain difficult passages; and occasionally introductory notes and footnotes to the translation.

THE NEW INTERNATIONAL VERSION

The New Testament in this version appeared in 1973. The Old Testament is scheduled for 1976.

With the New York Bible Society as sponsor, over one hundred conservative, evangelical Protestant scholars from many denominations and English-speaking countries have undertaken the translation.

This version will meet the needs of churches that have been dissatisfied, on the one hand, with the alleged "liberal" tendencies of the Revised Standard Version, Today's English Version, the New English Bible, and many of the one-man translations, and on the other, with the paraphrases and amplifications popular in conservative circles today (such as, The Living Bible Paraphrased, The Amplified Bible).

The translation is new, not a revision of any earlier version. It takes account of the best contemporary textual knowledge. Where there is a serious doubt about the way a passage should be translated, an alternate rendering is offered in a footnote. A few explanatory words, where needed, are inserted in brackets in the text. Footnotes are kept to a bare minimum.

English style received attention, and a flowing, dignified, and yet common vocabulary resulted.

Captions divide the text into logical units, and paragraph divisions assist the reader in comprehension. Commonly recognized poetic parts of the New Testament are printed in poetic form.

As would be expected in a conservative translation, old terms are kept where new, more meaningful ones might convey more to the contemporary mind. So we find "forgive us our debts," "sanctify," "saints," "righteousness," "justified," "predestined," "holiness." Some renditions are questionable: "understood" (John 1:5); "sacrifice of atonement" and "atoning sacrifice" (Rom. 3:25; I John 2:2). Some are infelicitous (for example, "one and only" in John 3:16), and some are not fully abreast of present knowledge (as, "our daily bread" [Matt. 6:11], where a footnote should at least suggest the translation "our bread for tomorrow").

Many splendid renditions appear: "keeps on sinning" (I John 3:6, compare vs. 9); "faith expressing itself through love" (Gal. 5:6); "let us keep in step with the Spirit" (Gal. 5:25); "faith is being sure of what we hope for" (Heb. 11:1); "in all things God works for the good of those who love him" (Rom. 8:28).

The merits of the translation far outweigh its limitations. It is likely to become the standard version for conservative, evangelical churches.

For Further Reading

Bruce, F. F. *The English Bible,* 1961.
MacGregor, Geddes. *A Literary History of the Bible,* 1968.
May, Herbert G. *Our English Bible in the Making,* rev. ed. 1965.

6. The Interpretation of the Bible

The Protestant Reformation put the Bible in the hands of the common man, asked him to read and digest it, to apply its teachings to his personal and social life, and to weigh all church pronouncements in the light of its teachings.

The Roman Catholic Church long challenged the Protestant emphasis on scriptural, rather than ecclesiastical, authority and the responsibility of every man to interpret and apply the Bible for himself. The Catholic position was that the church, under its apostles and their successors, was invested with final authority by Christ; that the church, from whose life the Bible sprang, is properly the Bible's custodian and interpreter; and that individual lay interpreters are seldom learned and skillful enough to interpret it without serious error.

Since Pope Pius XII's encyclical *Divino Afflante Spiritu* of 1943 and the famous church council known as Vatican II, a revolution has occurred in Roman Catholic attitudes toward the Bible. Vatican II declared: "It is necessary that the faithful have full access to Sacred Scripture." This far-seeing and progressive council saw that, with respect to non-Catholics, "Sacred Scripture makes an excellent tool in the powerful hand of God for the attainment of that unity which the Savior offers to all men." It is a fact that common biblical interest and study have done much to unite Protestants and Catholics.

There is growing agreement today among Catholic and Protestant scholars on the nature of the Scriptures and how readers should relate to them. We now see that the Bible is not an "it"—a *thing* to be analyzed, dissected, rearranged according to our view of historical development, set in its cultural framework, and thus "mastered" by us. The Bible is more a "thou" than an "it." Behind the written words stand persons. Written words are the thoughts, feelings, and desires of persons, indicated by the hand through symbols instead of by the tongue. Words, whether oral or written, are persons in projection or extension.

In the Bible we are addressed by persons. We are to listen carefully, ponder the message until the meaning is clear, and respond to it in some appropriate way. We are to carry on a conversation or dialogue with the persons behind the words; we are not to treat the Bible as if it were a laboratory specimen.

The dialogue with the Bible thus involves two major steps: (1) we are to examine the text carefully so we understand exactly what its authors intended to say; (2) we are to let the text examine us so that its message may have its intended effect.

Both steps can be taken by individuals working independently, or they can be taken with others. Martin Luther found transformation through his own dialogue with Paul in the letter to the Romans. The synagogue at Beroea undertook group study of the Scriptures to see if Paul's message concerning the Savior Jesus was valid, with striking results for many (Acts 17:11-12).

Actually, for the fullest dialogue with the Bible both individual and group involvement are necessary. The Bible has a very personal word and a social word. By sharing in a group what has been communicated to individuals alone, everyone will grasp more adequately the full message and respond in a way that embraces both individual and group life. Furthermore, a group approach to the Scriptures will correct subjective, eccentric interpretations and applications.

Here are some guidelines within these two major steps:

1. Careful Examination of the Text

a. Interpret Biblical Materials in the Light of the Circumstances in Which They Were Originally Written and Read.

Biblical writers directed their message to people of their own day. Their readers had particular needs and problems due to the events and circumstances of their place and time. The message was delivered in language and forms of thought the readers could understand.

We must, therefore, project ourselves as best we can into the first readers' situation. We must investigate the social, economic, political, and religious conditions and the customs and the major events of their time. We must find out all we can about the author and his reasons for addressing *those* people at *that* particular moment.

b. Interpret Biblical Passages in the Light of Their Basic Literary Type.

All present-day writings fall into forms or types, according to their purpose and function. The business letter has its characteristic formal marks, as do the love letter and the letter home from a family member. If entertainment is the goal, there are the jingle, the short story, the skit, the novel. If the purpose is serious instruction, there are the essay, the drama, the textbook. If motivation to action is intended, there are the sermon, the religious tract, the political pamphlet.

Ancient writings also had specific relation to life situations, forms adapted to functions. In fact, ancient writers were probably more bound by conventional forms than are modern authors.

Ancient customs required poetic pieces for many occasions in life: wedding songs, work songs, funeral dirges, victory songs, songs for worship, prophetic oracles (declarations) in times of national crisis, laments for occasions of national mourning, and the like.

Prose compositions filled their appointed functions in personal and national life: speeches, sermons, prayers, contracts, personal and official letters, legal codes, genealogies, official annals, historical narratives, autobiographies, sagas (traditional stories about ancestors and national heroes), fables, riddles, visions of the future (apocalypses), gospels, and letters to churches.

Every type of literature has characteristics of its own, including a customary vocabulary and style, a certain formal structure, and a particular kind of thought content.

Poetry must not be interpreted as if it were prose. Poetry makes large

THE INTERPRETATION OF THE BIBLE   59

use of figurative language and thus suggests more than it actually says. Hebrew poetry has a distinctive characteristic called "parallelism," which puts ideas together in various ways (see p. 131). Alphabetic poems are poems in which each line begins with a different letter of the Hebrew alphabet in sequence.

The prose compositions present wide variations which must be taken into account in order to understand them. Sagas require treatment different from chronicles or annals. Gospels are not biographies or works of history but rather testimonials to faith in Jesus as Savior and Lord. Letters to specific churches are quite unlike essays addressed to a general public.

The approach to the Bible from the standpoint of its literary forms or types is absolutely basic to the correct understanding of it.

c. Interpret Words and Passages in the Light of Their Historical and Literary Context.

It is common knowledge that many words have changed their meaning over a considerable period of time. For example, when the King James Version was issued, "prevent" meant "to go before"; today it means "to hinder."

It is important, therefore, to investigate the basic meaning or meanings of an important biblical word in the time when it was used in the biblical passage under consideration. These possible meanings should then be tested to see which fits the passage best.

Derivation of words (etymology) can be misleading. The English word "nice" comes from the Latin *nescius,* meaning "ignorant." This is not what "nice" means today! The meaning of a word is determined by its context, not by what root it may have come from.

There are two kinds of context: the immediate and the remote. Words constitute links in a chain. Each chain consists of an idea. Ideas put together form paragraphs, sections, and whole books. The immediate context is the sentence in which the word belongs, the sentences immediately before and after, and the paragraph as a whole in which the word is imbedded.

The remote context consists of the larger associations of the word or passage. There are degrees of remoteness, of course. The section, the book as a whole, other books written by the same author, and the other literature of the same period belong to the remote context.

Our task in a particular passage is to discover the direction in which the author's thought is moving and to see which of several possible meanings of a difficult word or phrase best contributes to the progress of thought.

d. Respect the Individuality of the Various Biblical Writers.

If the Bible consists of a library of books written by many different authors over a period of nearly a thousand years, we should expect considerable diversity in point of view among the writings. The personality and experience of each writer are stamped on his creation.

We must not import Paul's theology into Matthew's account of Jesus' ministry, or Luke's theology into John's Gospel. If we do, we shall distort the distinctive witness of each writer and reduce the rich, many-sided testimony concerning Jesus to one uninspired and uninspiring version.

We can see the damage to sound biblical interpretation caused by failure to respect the individuality of the various writers in one commentator's exposition of Gen. 1:16. He declares that "the greater light" (the sun) and "the lesser light" (the moon) stand for "Christ and His people" on the ground that in Mal. 4:2 "the sun of righteousness . . . with healing in its wings" refers to Jesus Christ and in Rev. 12:1 the moon represents Israel and the church. To import Jesus Christ and the church into the creation story in this manner violates all sound principles of interpretation.

We do the authors no honor if we force them all into one pattern. It is when we see clearly how different they are that we shall appreciate how similar they are.

e. Take Biblical Materials, First of All, in Their Literal Sense.

The literal sense is the meaning intended by the author or authors in a particular piece of writing. The literal sense differs from meanings the material may have taken on in the minds of others, contemporary or later in time. These other, more-than-literal meanings are sometimes called "spiritual," "allegorical," "typological," or "symbolic."

The literal sense allows for the use of metaphorical devices (similies, metaphors, parables, allegories, symbols) as legitimate ways of conveying meaning. The literal sense rules out only meanings foreign to the author's original intent.

In the history of the church, secondary, alien meanings often overshadowed the literal or historical sense. Particular interpreters of the biblical text put what it meant to them ahead of what it meant when it was first written. It has been the merit of modern historical study to cut through these alien interpretations to the original meanings.

f. Look at Specific Passages in the Light of the Whole Bible and the History of the Christian Church.

It is quite right to hold that biblical materials can mean more to us than they did or could to their original authors.

If God was working out a purpose in the total history of Israel and the Christian church, it is not strange that early participants in that history could not understand the full meaning of their words and deeds and that it should be given to later persons to grasp that meaning in the light of subsequent events.

New Testament writers saw many Old Testament statements and events as pointing beyond themselves to a fulfillment realized in Jesus Christ and the Christian church.

Isaiah 53, when read today in the light of the career of Jesus of Nazareth, takes on a meaning in harmony with, but not fully identical with, its meaning when written, some five centuries before the coming of Jesus. Likewise, Jeremiah's prophecy concerning the new covenant (31:31-34) was fulfilled by God (Heb. 8) in a way Jeremiah did not and could not conceive of.

In short, we may not exhaust the full meaning of a passage simply by determining by historical methods what was originally meant by the man who wrote it. However, we distort rather than interpret Scripture if the full meaning we see in a passage is not to some extent in harmony with the literal sense.

2. Examination of the Reader by the Text

A generation ago many biblical interpreters scrutinized the Bible "objectively," in a somewhat detached scientific manner. They assumed that different interpreters, using the same tools of interpretation, would arrive at the same results—provided they kept their personal points of view out of their work.

Today we see that a strict objectivity is impossible. We are the product of unique personal experiences and of a particular family, national, and cultural background. We cannot divest ourselves of our presuppositions and our social conditioning any more than we can shed our skin or change the color of our eyes. We can only seek to understand and allow for our background.

In regard to answering the ultimate questions of life, we are no better off than ancient people; certainly we are in no position to sit in judgment on them. In fact, what they were and what they wrote down scrutinize us quite as much as we scrutinize them.

If this is true, then statements about our attitude as we seek to understand the biblical text are in order.

> a. We Should Come to the Bible with an Alert, Open Mind, and Be Ready to Accept and Obey Whatever Message the Spirit of God May Impart.

Some people come to the Bible for arguments with which to uphold their opinions and prejudices rather than to discover the will of God for their lives and find strength to obey it.

Others come for an aesthetic experience. They want to sample the Bible's stories and savor its ancient wisdom. They too have no interest in God's word and its relation to their lives. They sometimes claim that no religious orientation or special piety is needed for interpreting the Bible; all one needs are the proper tools of literary interpretation.

Such persons can perhaps enter part way into biblical truth, but its deeper dimensions elude them. What would a person who has never made the venture of faith in Jesus Christ make out of Galatians 2:20: "I have been crucified with Christ; it is no longer I who live, but Christ who lives in me; and the life I now live in the flesh I live by faith in the Son of God, who loved me and gave himself for me"? It is doubtful that those with only a literary interest in the Bible can understand the radiant sense of salvation that fills the New Testament.

The reader of the Bible needs eyes alert to literary discipline, but he also needs "eyes of faith" and the willingness to act on the truth he discovers there.

A spirit of quiet expectancy and receptivity is essential in one's encounter with the writers of the Bible. One scholar has said, "The attitude of Bible-reading is rather that of a lover waiting at the trysting-place than that of a general storming a citadel" (Alan Richardson, *Preface to Bible-Study,* 1944, p. 17).

> b. In Sustained, Prayerful Exposure to the Bible, Both in Individual and Group Study, We Shall See Ourselves, Our World, and God in the Mirror of the Bible.

The amazing popularity of the Bible in our world today attests to its power to affect contemporary readers. But how can people trained in modern science and with a modern world view derive any benefit from documents nineteen hundred or more years old? As someone has put it, the issue is, "What can a bunch of camel drivers say to us who live in the jet age?"

The relevance of ancient documents was a problem faced by Hellenistic, Jewish, and Christian writers of the time of Paul and the early church and, indeed, by thinkers in every age since. What was the meaning of the old Greek myths and the writings of Homer for philosophically minded people centuries later? How were the ancient laws of Moses and the institutions of Israel, described in the books of the fathers, to be related to the thought and practices of Jews living under cultural conditions vastly different from the time of Moses? Christians of every age have had to decide what the Scriptures should mean for them. The problem will remain as long as the Scriptures and human life continue.

There is no neat formula for deciding what in ancient documents is relevant for modern readers and precisely how. We can venture only a few suggestions here.

Present-day Christian existentialists have said that what binds us to ancient men is our common humanity. In every age men have fundamentally the same problems, needs, and aspirations. Hunger, sickness, human and natural enemies, and death beset us. The great human ventures are alike: love and marriage, the conception and birth of children, the struggle for economic and political security, the quest for life's meaning, and the like.

Not only are the needs of men much the same, but the resources available to them are similar. Men may seek to control the hostile forces of nature through the practice of magic and to overcome human enemies through military power. One may seek by individual or collective wits (including traditional "wisdom") to work out a secure position in an insecure world. Or one may accept one's lot as inevitable, the will of God or the gods, and attempt to make the best of one's circumstances. Or again one may believe that human effort may be undergirded by divine strength and seek through prayer and action to determine the divine will and to ally oneself with it.

Human existence—in its limitations and possibilities—thus offers us common ground with the men of all ages.

The Bible, the Old Testament as well as the New, is supremely the place where God reveals man and his predicament to man himself; that is why we can hold up the Old Testament . . . as a mirror in which we can see our own reflected image. In the Old Testament, we might say, God shows us as in a mirror what we are; and in the New Testament he reveals to us the image of what we shall become, shining in the face of Jesus Christ. (Alan Richardson, *The Bible in the Age of Science,* 1961, p. 121.)

The Bible characterizes human existence in pictorial, symbolic, dramatic language.

It represents good and evil, God and the devil, angels and demons as locked in military combat, with men enticed and pressured to ally themselves with one side or the other. It says that the struggle will be resolved

Courtesy of the Oriental Institute, The University of Chicago

Winged bull with human face, once flanking the main entrance to the throne room of Sargon II at Khorsabad (8th century B.C.)

in a military-type victory, the field of battle bestrewed with the corpses of the slain (for example, Rev. 19:11-21).

When God is represented as a heavenly king, who sits on a throne with a rainbow around it (Rev. 4:1-6), or when he is said, as in Ps. 80:1, to be "enthroned upon the cherubim"—that is, upon winged lions or bulls such as decorated the thrones of ancient kings—it is obvious that language and concepts ordinarily applied to human kings are used metaphorically of God.

We must recognize the dramatic, symbolic, pictorial language and search for the concepts underlying it. We must distinguish between *what* is said and *how* it is said. Ancient picture language, while admittedly difficult for modern men, is not impossible to penetrate, if the modern reader is alert to its nature and function.

By looking in the biblical mirror, doors to a kind of existence beyond our imagination may open to us and our world.

For Further Reading

> Brown, R. E.; Fitzmyer, J. A.; and Murphy, R. E., eds. *The Jerome Biblical Commentary,* 1968, Vol. II, pp. 605-23.
> Keck, L. E. *Taking the Bible Seriously,* 1962.
> Mickelsen, A. Berkeley. *Interpreting the Bible,* 1963.
> Richardson, Alan. *A Preface to Bible Study,* 1944.
> _____. *The Bible in the Age of Science,* 1961.
> Smart, James D. *The Interpretation of Scripture,* 1961.
> Swaim, J. Carter. *Right and Wrong Ways to Use the Bible,* 1953.

7. Specific Approaches to the Bible

Most Bible-reading is "catch-as-catch can" reading—a few verses before retiring at night, a paragraph between cups of coffee at the breakfast table, a sample or two to make us feel right before we go to church on Sunday morning. We somehow expect the Bible to yield up its treasures in two minutes flat.

While there may be some value in such casual reading, there are dangers also. We may lift passages out of context and misinterpret and misapply them.

One Bible student properly reminds us that in Bible reading we need not snapshots but time exposures. We should read when our faculties are most alert, when we have time to ponder the deeper meanings for ourselves, our family, our business, our community, and our world.

All in-depth reading of the Bible—like all proper scientific study—proceeds through four basic steps: exact observation of data; interpretation of data; verification of results; and the application of results to life. This is a "see-for-yourself" procedure.

Too many people's knowledge of the Bible is secondhand. They are content to read about it in a reference book or a commentary. Some have a basic fear that they will get lost in the Bible's dry lists, archaic vocabulary, and curious symbols. They never experience the thrill of firsthand discovery, develop mature powers of judgment in biblical matters, and come through to a rich personal understanding of the significance of biblical perspectives for their own lives.

We should read the Bible with the kind of excited curiosity a scientist has when he is on the track of a new discovery. We should read it the way a young man in the first stages of love pores over a letter from his beloved—not once, hurriedly; but repeatedly, with attention to every detail and the exact meaning of every word.

Such reading requires planning and preparation: regular periods set aside for uninterrupted individual and group study; a proper physical environment; and adequate working tools.

Working equipment should include the following books:

> a modern translation by a competent scholar or group of scholars
> > (a second translation for sake of comparison is advisable)
> a concordance to that translation (if one has been published)
> a good one-volume commentary on the Bible
> a theological wordbook or a Bible dictionary
> an atlas to the lands of the Bible

If you can secure only one work besides a modern translation, it should be a one-volume commentary. (For suggestions, see p. 481.)

Adequate understanding of the Bible comes only by reading it in logical units. Such units may be whole books, sections, or paragraphs. If the material is poetry, the poem or the stanza may constitute the unit. Chapters may or may not be logical units.

As we shall see below, you can identify units smaller than a whole book. Help is given in modern translations, which divide the text into sections and paragraphs, often headed by titles. Or blank space in the text may indicate a logical division.

The books of the Bible divide roughly into those that are unified, or substantially so, and those that are clearly not unified.

I. *Unified or Substantially Unified Books*

Old Testament

Genesis, Exodus, Numbers, Deuteronomy, Joshua, Judges, Ruth, I and II Samuel, I and II Kings, I and II Chronicles, Esther, Daniel, Joel, Obadiah, Jonah, Zephaniah, Haggai, Malachi

Apocrypha

I Esdras, Tobit, Judith, the Letter of Jeremiah, Susanna, Bel and the Dragon, the Prayer of Manasseh, I and II Maccabees

New Testament

Matthew, Mark, Luke-Acts, John, Romans, I Corinthians, Galatians, Ephesians, Philippians, Colossians, I and II Thessalonians, I and II Timothy, Titus, Philemon, Hebrews, I and II Peter, I, II, and III John, Jude, Revelation

II. *Nonunified Books*

Old Testament

Leviticus, Ezra, Nehemiah, Job, Psalms, Proverbs, Ecclesiastes, Song of Solomon, Isaiah, Jeremiah, Lamentations, Ezekiel, Hosea, Amos, Micah, Nahum, Habakkuk, Zechariah

Apocrypha

II Esdras, Additions to the Book of Esther, The Wisdom of Solomon, Ecclesiasticus (The Wisdom of Jesus the Son of Sirach), Baruch, The Prayer of Azariah and the Song of the Three Young Men

New Testament

II Corinthians, James

Some of the books are like great snowballs which, as they rolled down through the centuries following their first appearance in written form, gathered up material of the same or different type. They are collections of pieces rather than logically coherent compositions.

Whether a book had one or several authors is not the decisive considera-tion in determining how it should be read. It is quite possible for several writers to contribute to a book in such a way that the final result holds to-gether fairly logically.

1. Reading the Unified and Substantially Unified Books

The procedure I am about to suggest is purposely detailed. It is unlikely that you will have the time and patience individually to follow out all the steps. Make a selection of what you wish to do. If you work in a group, you may parcel out the steps and offer reports to the group on the results.

a. Survey the Whole Book.

Individual books of the Bible have no table of contents or preface by which we can get an idea of the whole. We can accomplish this only by rapid reading or scanning.

You should read books through *at one sitting,* if at all possible. Only thus can you gain a total impression. One writer has said that more than half of the sixty-six books printed in the traditional Protestant Bible can be read through in an average of about twenty minutes. The larger ones can be read selectively and scanned.

In this first survey of the whole book you should look for answers to the following questions:

(1) What type of literature is this?

As noted in the previous chapter, literature must be interpreted in the light of its basic character.

(2) What occasioned the writing of the book?

Is the author's name given, and are there any indications concerning his whereabouts and circumstances?

Are there any references to datable historical events that may offer a clue to the time of writing?

Are there references to the condition and circumstances of the original readers and therefore to the author's reason for writing?

(3) What are the writer's characteristic words, phrases, concepts, and moods?

What words and phrases are most repeated and most central to his thought?

Was he joyful, angry, reflective, argumentative, hopeful when he wrote?

(4) What gives the book its unity?

Is the unifying factor a subject, a person, a group of persons, a problem, an event of the past, present, or future?

Attempt to state the unity in a sentence or a short paragraph.

(5) What is the structure of the book?

Has the writer anywhere stated his plan or outline?

What are the major blocks of material, and where are the turning points or shifts in subject matter? Note the blank spaces (as in the RSV) or the captions in the text (as in the NEB), which modern editors placed there as an aid to understanding the book's contents.

Make a brief outline of the book.

(6) What impact has the reading of this book made on you?

What do you like and dislike about it? What is puzzling? What message of value has come through to you?

(7) How do your results from firsthand reading compare with the conclusions of others who have studied the book?

Turn now to the discussion of this book in Part II of this *Handbook* or to a standard introduction to the Old or New Testament or to the introductory portion of a good commentary on the book or to an article on it in a Bible dictionary.

Correct and supplement your conclusions.

b. Examine the Parts of the Book.

After you have determined the general layout of a book from your initial survey, you should consider the individual parts which make up the whole.

Be selective in using the steps presented here for examining the parts. Not all parts are worthy of the same depth of scrutiny. The richer and more closely packed a book is, the more detailed the examination should be. Some books should be studied by major divisions only; others should be studied by the sections that comprise the major divisions; and still others deserve a careful analysis of paragraphs and sentences.

Books are like people. Some intrigue and some fatigue. The initial survey should indicate how much time and effort you want to spend on each.

In examining a part of a book consider the following questions:

(1) What type of material is contained here?

The type may vary in the different parts. It is always important to be aware of the character of the material, as we noted in chap. 6.

(2) What important variations in the wording do the footnotes offer on

the basis of ancient manuscripts and versions? How do the alternate words affect the meaning of the passage?

(3) Is the part composed of smaller units?

A major division will usually break down into sections and paragraphs.

The logical parts are not necessarily identical with the traditional chapter divisions. These divisions were made in the thirteenth century and frequently do not break the material at logical points. (In the RSV the translators frequently overrode the chapter divisions: for example, at Gen. 27:46–28:5; Exod. 5:22–6:1; I Sam. 3:19–4:1; Mark 8:34–9:1; I Cor. 10:31–11:1).

Many contemporary English translations assist the reader by printing the text in paragraphs and by indicating the larger divisions through the use of captions (headings). Rather than relying entirely on the printed captions, you should construct your own. This will help you summarize the material and see the relationship of the parts.

Give special attention to connecting words, such as *and, but, because, for, since, so, therefore, hence, however, nevertheless, finally*. These words help you dissect the thought of a passage at the joints.

You must develop X-ray eyes so you can see the skeleton of a book. When you have discovered it, you should put it down in the form of a chart or outline.

(4) What use, if any, is made of figures of speech (similies, metaphors, symbols)? What idea is each figure attempting to convey?

(5) What are the key words around which the thought of the section or paragraph revolves?

To discover the key words of a short unit of biblical material, you should strike out every word that can be eliminated without sacrificing the basic meaning, as we do when we compose a telegram. Examine the remaining important words in the light of the flow of the thought of the passage. It is often possible to determine the meaning of unfamiliar words simply by the drift of thought around them.

It is helpful also to locate through the use of a concordance other usages of important words in the biblical book under consideration. Read them in their contexts. And finally, consult a lexicon, a Bible dictionary, or a commentary on the meaning of the words in question.

(6) What in the passage is still unclear?

Unfamiliar customs, institutions, events, persons, and world views may still remain puzzling to you after the above steps have been taken. Here you should consult a good commentary. A reader of the Bible only cheats himself by sliding over things he does not understand.

(7) What was the writer's purpose in this part or section?

To answer this question the situation of the first readers must be brought into focus again. What did the writer want to tell them and why? What would they have missed if the part under consideration had been left out?

(8) What does the passage mean in your own words?

As a clinching act, write out the thought of the passage in your own words. If the passage is short, paraphrase it; if long, summarize it.

(9) What is the significance of this passage for you and your contemporaries?

See the section "Examination of the Reader by the Text" (chap. 6).

c. Review the Whole Book.

A well-known literary scholar has written: "In the case of the higher literary forms the whole is a different thing from the sum of the parts. It is quite possible to have considered every detail of a literary work and yet to be far from understanding the work as a whole" (R. G. Moulton, *The Bible at a Single View* [1919], p. 103).

The investigation by major divisions, sections, and paragraphs will lead you to more mature conclusions about the whole book than the initial survey produced. Therefore, a final survey is in order.

(1) Investigate the special themes that run like threads through the book.

Locate every passage dealing with one theme. It is best to find these passages by rereading the book. A concordance can help if you look up the principal words used in presenting the theme.

Group the passages according to what they contain and consider them together. Consult commentaries for help on difficult passages.

Draw up conclusions from studying the theme and compare them with the results of others as contained in Part II of this *Handbook,* in introductions to the Old and the New Testaments, and in special volumes on the biblical book under consideration.

(2) Restate the theme or message of the book and show how the major parts contribute to its presentation.

You can do this by a logical outline or a chart of the book's contents. How detailed you make it will be determined by the extent of your interest in those contents.

(3) Relate the message of the entire book to the situation of its first readers. How did it speak to their needs?

(4) Summarize the meaning of the book for your own life and its possible significance for our times.

As pointed out before, the Bible evaluates us quite as much as we evaluate it. Here we must pray for understanding, that we neither fall into credulous acceptance of everything we read in the Bible or proudly and self-righteously reject what does not meet our preconceptions.

Perhaps three questions will help here.

How does my life look from the standpoint of this book—my personal beliefs, my emotions, my attitudes toward myself and toward others, my actions, my goals?

How would contemporary life be affected if the message here were universally accepted and acted on?

How does the teaching of this book check out with truth from other sources—from science, psychology, sociology, philosophy?

2. Reading the Nonunified Books

As explained above, nonunified books are collections of literary pieces, loosely—and often illogically—arranged.

These books fall into several classes: many of the books of the prophets; the books of poetry; the books of wisdom; additions to canonical books; an apocalypse; a letter of Paul's.

How shall we treat books that are themselves little libraries of material?

It is obvious that we must rearrange or group the pieces in some orderly way if we are to understand their contents. The rearrangement may follow chronological (historical) or logical lines. If the biblical material has to do with the words and deeds of persons, we must reconstruct the life situations of these persons with some accuracy. Hence, attention to chronological sequence is important. If the material has no biographical base, a logical grouping may yield maximum understanding.

We can touch on only the major classes of the nonunified books here.

a. The Books of the Prophets

The books of the prophets deal with the words, and often the deeds, of these prophets. The life situation of each prophet is thus the key to understanding what he said and did.

In reading the nonunified prophetic books, take the following steps:

(1) If the book is short, read it through rapidly for a general idea of its contents. If it is long, sample it by scanning and reading selectively. Of

particular importance are references to the times in which the prophet lived and the situation of the people to whom he spoke.

(2) Read in a good secondary source a discussion of the prophet's times: in a Bible dictionary (under the name of the prophet), in an introduction to the Old Testament, in a history of Israel, in a commentary, or in Part II of this *Handbook*. Fix in mind the main events and situations of his period.

(3) Insofar as possible, with the help of the secondary source chosen, relate the various portions of the prophetic book to their proper historical background.

(4) Project yourself into each situation in which the prophet spoke. Imagine the circumstances—the place, the people addressed, the bystanders, the dress, the manner, and the temper of the speaker. Analyze his words on that occasion.

(5) Try to catch the recurrent themes in the prophet's message. What is his view of God, of man and his deeds, of the proper God-man and man-man relationship? What does he have to say about the future and why?

(6) Summarize the contribution of the prophet to the life of his people and his influence on later generations. What would Israel have lacked if he had not been born and called to his prophetic ministry?

(7) Compare your conclusions on the above points with positions in standard reference books.

(8) What of importance for us and our day is present in the words and deeds of this ancient prophet?

b. The Books of Poetry and the Books of Wisdom

In reading the books of poetry and the books of wisdom we are dealing with poetic pieces. As noted in Part II (chap. 24), Hebrew poetry falls into several major types, which must be related to the life situations out of which they arose (see also p. 58).

Before reading books of this kind, it is best to consult brief introductions, such as in Part II of this *Handbook,* in a Bible dictionary, or in a standard introduction to the Old Testament. They will indicate the basic nature and structure of each book so that it may be read piece by piece in some logical and understandable way.

For example, it is best to read the Psalms by types (see chap. 26), and a book like Job requires some knowledge of its dramatic structure for intelligent reading. Do not try to go it alone on complicated collections of material such as the poetic and wisdom books contain.

c. Prose Books

In reading nonunified prose material you need to be aware of the loose arrangement of the book, so that you will not try to discover a unity which is not there. Here too the help of other reference books will point the way to intelligent reading.

Finally, keep firmly in mind that the focus of attention should always be the biblical material itself, never some secondary discussion of it.

For Further Reading

> Adler, Mortimer J. *How to Read a Book,* 1940.
> Blair, Edward P. *The Bible and You,* 1953.
> Kelly, Balmer H., ed. *The Layman's Bible Commentary,* Vol. I, 1959, pp. 143-71.
> Love, Julian Price. *How to Read the Bible,* rev. ed., 1959.

8. Programs of Reading the Bible

We come now to the question concerning the order in which we should read the books of the Bible.

People read the Bible from many different points of view. Literary men read it because of its superb literary qualities. Historians pore over its pages for information about ancient cultures, personages, and events. Scientists test its assertions concerning the origins of the earth and man. Philosophers and religious educators trace in it the development of moral standards.

The Bible itself, so far as it speaks of its purpose, leads us to believe that we should read it from quite different motives. According to John 5:39-40 Jesus said to the Jews, "You search the scriptures, because you think that in them you have eternal life; and it is they that bear witness to me; yet you refuse to come to me that you may have life." From this passage we learn that the Scriptures point to Jesus Christ, the source of eternal life, and that they lead people to him. In II Tim. 3:14-17 we read that the Scriptures lead to salvation through faith in Christ, train the believer in righteousness, and equip persons for Christian service. The Bible nowhere suggests that we should view it as a book of history, philosophy, morality, science, or as a masterpiece of literature.

In recent decades biblical scholars have been seeing more clearly what the basic nature and purpose of the Bible is. Amid all its diversity of subject matter and points of view an underlying unity can be discovered. This unity consists in the story of what God has done, is doing, and will do for the redemption of men. The center of his activity is Jesus Christ and the church. Jesus is the long-promised deliverer of Israel, and the church is the faithful remnant through which God will save both Israel and the nations. All God's deeds lead to Jesus Christ, and all subsequent events are shaped by the fact that he came.

If Jesus Christ is the point of brightest illumination concerning the purpose and activity of God, it is clear that we should see all the rest of the Bible in relation to him. This means that we should start with those materials which most fully present him to view, the four Gospels. Then we should trace the impact Jesus had on his first followers, as portrayed in the Acts of the Apostles, in the letters of Paul to specific churches, and in the general letters of the early church. We then read on to Jesus' final triumph over the powers of evil, to his inauguration of the heavenly kingdom of God, and to the glories of the church's life in that kingdom, as pictured in the book of Revelation.

Now we should search to discover how God set the stage for the coming of Jesus: how mankind came to be in need of redemption; how God found redemptive agents and sought to educate them for their role in the world; how unresponsive people thwarted him and how he yet persisted; and how he ultimately raised up a deliverer and a remnant people who fulfilled his purpose for the world.

The books of the Apocrypha also celebrate the deeds of God in the life of the nation and of its righteous individuals. In those writings we see God as a mighty protector in national and personal crises, as the giver of spiritual and material blessings, as the revealer of truth to his chosen servants, and as the guarantor of his people's future when they fully obey his law. The longing of the nation for full redemption shines through this literature.

You will now have a choice between two reading programs which follow this line of approach: a longer and a shorter program. The first covers the entire contents of the Bible, including the Apocrypha. The second includes the major books and portions of books—enough to offer an adequate view of the sweep of the biblical materials.

The order of the books follows no one principle. I have tried to join theological, chronological, and historical-critical considerations with a commonsense approach, in the attempt to find a sequence that will lead to maximum understanding when supplemented by the help on the individual books offered in Part II of this *Handbook*.

The Longer Program

The New Testament

1. Mark
2. Matthew
3. John
4-5. Luke-Acts
6. I Thessalonians
7. II Thessalonians
8. I Corinthians
9. II Corinthians
    (chief attention
    to chaps. 1–9)
10. Galatians
11. Romans
12. Philemon
13. Colossians
14. Philippians
15. Ephesians
16. II Timothy
17. Titus
18. I Timothy
19. I Peter
20. Hebrews
21. James
22. I John
23. II John
24. III John
25. Jude
26. II Peter
27. Revelation (chaps. 1–5 and 19:6–22: 21; sample 6:1–19:5)

The Old Testament

28. Genesis
29. Exodus (chief attention to chaps. 1–24)
30. Leviticus (scan and sample)
31. Numbers (chief attention to 10:11–21:35)
32. Deuteronomy (chief attention to chaps. 1–11 and 27–34)
33. Joshua (chief attention to chaps. 1–12 and 22–24)
34. Judges (chief attention to chaps. 1–16)
35-36. I-II Samuel
37-38. I-II Kings (scan and sample)
39-40. I-II Chronicles (scan and sample)
41-42. Ezra-Nehemiah (chief attention to Nehemiah)
43. Amos
44. Hosea
45. Micah
46. Isaiah (chaps. 1–39; chief attention to chaps. 1–12)
47. Zephaniah
48. Jeremiah (chief attention to chaps. 1–25 and 30–33)
49. Nahum
50. Habakkuk
51. Ezekiel (chief attention to chaps. 1–24 and 33–39)
52. Obadiah
53. Lamentations
54. Isaiah (chaps. 40–66)
55. Haggai
56. Zechariah (chief attention to chaps. 1–8)
57. Malachi
58. Joel
59. Ruth
60. Jonah
61. Psalms (read some representatives of each major type)

62. Job (less attention to chaps. 32–37)
63. Proverbs (chief attention to chaps. 1–9)
64. Song of Solomon
65. Ecclesiastes
66. Esther
67. Daniel

The Apocrypha

68. I Esdras (special attention to 3:1–5:6)
69. The Prayer of Manasseh
70. The Letter of Jeremiah
71. Baruch
72. Additions to the Book of Esther (scan and sample)
73. Tobit
74. Ecclesiasticus (The Wisdom of Jesus the Son of Sirach) (sample either Book I [chaps. 1–23] or Book II [chaps. 24–50])
75. I Maccabees (special attention to 1:1–9:22)
76. II Maccabees
77. Judith
78. The Prayer of Azariah and the Song of the Three Young Men
79. Susanna
80. Bel and the Dragon
81. The Wisdom of Solomon (chief attention to chaps. 1–9)
82. II Esdras (chief attention to chaps. 3–14)

The Shorter Program

The New Testament

1. Mark
2. John
3. Luke-Acts
4. I Thessalonians
5. I Corinthians
6. Romans
7. Philemon
8. Philippians
9. Ephesians
10. II Timothy
11. I Peter
12. I John
13. Revelation (chaps. 1–5 and 19:6–22: 21; sample 6:1– 19:5)

The Old Testament

14. Genesis
15. Exodus (chaps. 1–24)
16. Numbers (10:11–21:35)
17. Deuteronomy (chaps. 1–11)
18. Joshua (chaps. 1–12 and 22–24)
19. Judges (sample)
20. I-II Samuel (sample)
21. I-II Kings (sample)
22. Nehemiah
23. Amos
24. Isaiah (chaps. 1–12)
25. Jeremiah (chaps. 1–25, 30– 33)

25

26. Isaiah (chaps. 40–55)
27. Ruth
28. Jonah
29. Psalms (some examples of the major types)

30. Job (chaps. 1–14 and 38–42)
31. Proverbs (chaps. 1–9)
32. Daniel (chaps. 1–6; sample chaps. 7–12)

The Apocrypha

33. Tobit
34. Ecclesiasticus (The Wisdom of Jesus the Son of Sirach) (sample chaps. 1–23)
35. I Maccabees (1:1–9:22) or II Maccabees

36. Judith
37. The Wisdom of Solomon (chaps. 1–9)
38. II Esdras (chaps. 3–14)

Additional Note

In addition to reading the Bible by books, you may wish to follow themes that run through the Bible or considerable parts of it and also to approach it by way of its principal characters.

Both methods are valid, if used by skillful interpreters. In following a theme, if you simply join passage to passage, without regard to the specific context of each, you will distort meanings and arrive at erroneous conclusions.

The meaning of words and the content of ideas changed through the centuries. What is said in Genesis does not necessarily agree with what is said in Isaiah or in Romans.

You should undertake the tracing of themes only after you have a careful grounding in the literature of the Bible in its historical setting. This method is thus for advanced students of the Bible.

The same remarks apply to the study of the Bible by its principle characters. By considering verses, chapters, and portions of books without regard to the literary and historical contexts, an inexperienced reader can understand neither the characteristics of nor the reasons for particular portraits in the various passages. It is best for such a reader to view biblical characters in the context of the entire biblical books in which they appear.

PART II
THE BIBLE IN HISTORY

9. The Pentateuch

1. Name

The term "Pentateuch" (Greek for "five scrolls") apparently arose during the first century A.D. among Alexandrian Jews as a name for the first five books of the Old Testament. The early church fathers Tertullian and Origen used the term in the second and third centuries.

Hebrew-speaking Jews normally called the five books "The Law" (Torah), "The Law of Moses," "The Book of the Law of Moses," or "The Book of Moses."

2. Contents

The Pentateuch seeks to explain how Israel became the chosen and covenanted people of God and what this relationship to God involved for the life and destiny of Israel and all mankind.

Genesis tells how God chose the covenant family from among the peoples of the earth; Exodus, how he redeemed this chosen family—greatly enlarged—from bondage in Egypt and how he entered into a covenant with it at Mt. Sinai; Leviticus, how he consecrated the new nation for service and educated it in worship; Numbers, how he purged and disciplined it according to the provisions of the covenant during its wandering in the wilderness; and Deuteronomy, how Moses exhorted it to perpetual fidelity to God and to the terms of the covenant it had accepted.

The concept of the covenant must be clearly grasped if the Pentateuch is to be understood. Ancient kings (*e.g.,* Hittite) entered into written covenants with vassal states. These agreements had several elements: a preamble, naming the author of the covenant, with his titles, attributes, and genealogy; a historical statement concerning the benevolent acts performed by the king in behalf of the vassal state; a list of the obligations imposed on and accepted by the vassal; a statement requiring the deposit of the covenant document in the temple and its periodic public reading; a list of deities who stood as witnesses to the covenant; blessings and curses which would ensue if the covenant was kept or broken. Most of these elements appear in the Pentateuch (see especially Exod. 20:1-17; Deut. 5:6-21; 31:9-13, 26; and chaps. 27–28), showing that Israel thought of its relationship to God in the same general fashion as these covenants.

Photo by H. T. Frank
A Canaanite incense stand from Megiddo
(Late Bronze Age)

In the Pentateuch the covenant is represented as arising out of God's gracious choice of Israel. That choice is an expression of his desire to enter into communion with a people of his own and to bless them with his presence and gifts.

In order to experience the blessings, Israel would have to fulfill faithfully conditions determined by God's character and purposes.

Such is the general perspective from which the Pentateuch was put together.

3. Authorship and Sources

The Pentateuch nowhere clearly claims that Moses was the author of the whole of it. Passages that refer to Moses' writing down "all the words of the Lord," "this law," and the like (see Exod. 17:14; 24:4; 34:27; Num. 33:1-2; Deut. 31:9, 22) refer only to certain parts which seem to be included in the whole.

Though Philo and Josephus—Jewish writers of the first century A.D.—explicitly attribute to Moses the account of his own death (Deut. 34:5-12), the Talmud (c. A.D. 500) regards this story as having been written by Joshua. It is obvious that certain statements in the Pentateuch imply a time of writing later than Moses (e.g., Gen. 12:6; 13:7; 36:31; Deut. 34:6).

The best conservative Old Testament scholars of today allow for later additions to and revisions of the Pentateuch and argue only that it is substantially and essentially Mosaic. (See Additional Note, pp. 89-90.)

Most liberal scholars agree that Moses stands behind the Pentateuch as its originating cause, but they hold that what parts of it he may actually have written, if any, can no longer be determined. They believe that for many centuries after his death traditions about him and about the patriarchs were passed on in Israel, both in oral and written form, until they were finally gathered together in the fifth century B.C. into the Pentateuch as we now have it.

These scholars have assembled much evidence from the Pentateuch that it was put together in several stages over a period of some 700 years. The stages, as identified by them, are:

a. Oral Recital in Both Poetry and Prose of Israel's Early Traditions

Israel's traditions about the past were told orally in many different ways before they were collected in written documents. Some of these units are now identifiable in the Pentateuch, much as individual stones are to be seen in a mosaic.

For example, there are songs (Gen. 4:23-24; Exod. 15:1-18; Num. 21:14-15, 17-18, 27-30; etc.); symbolic stories (with mythical features) about the origin of the world, mankind, and nature (Gen. 1–3); sagas, i.e., popular lore about family and national heroes (Gen. 12–50 and much of Exodus and Numbers); sermonic and liturgical materials (Deuteronomy); and legal matter (e.g., Exod. 20:22–23:33).

It appears that materials of these and other types were recited by skilled storytellers at family and tribal gatherings and by priests at the places of worship on the occasion of sacred festivals.

b. Earliest Basic Oral or Written Narrative

At an early time, possibly as early as the eleventh or tenth century B.C., some creative person or persons put together the stories of God's dealings with the fathers, which had taken shape in oral form, along the general lines now in the Pentateuch. We may perhaps see the pattern which shaped the miscellaneous pieces in the confessions of faith (the "credos") recited at the sacred festivals (Deut. 26:5-10; Josh. 24).

This hypothetical oral or written composition has been called by some scholars "G" (for "Groundwork") or "T" (for "Tradition"). Its existence seems necessary to explain the common features of the various documents which followed it.

c. Written Sources of the Pentateuch

More than 200 years of careful study of the Pentateuch have led most scholars to the conclusion that several written sources were woven together (with many deletions, additions, and alterations) to form our Pentateuch. The sources have been given the symbols N (also designated L, S, or J^1), J, E, D, P.

Ancient writers did not use quotation marks when they assembled materials. They simply wove together their written and oral sources, making additions, deletions, and alterations as they saw fit. The sources lying behind their work are evident to the careful observer.

(1) The N (L, S, J^1) Source

N stands for "Nomadic," L for "Lay" (*i.e.,* unaffected by priestly points of view), S for "South" or "Seir," and J^1 for the first Judean document using "Yahweh" as the characteristic name for the deity. The same document is meant by all the above symbols, each favored by a different scholar or group of scholars according to different understandings of its dominant feature.

This source shows hostility toward settled civilization, glorifies the desert and the God of the desert mountain, and holds that man at his best lives as a nomad.

Some representative passages assigned to it are:
Gen. 4:17-24; 6:1-4; 9:21-27; 11:1-9; most of 12:1-9; most of chaps. 18–19; 25:1-6, 21-26, 29-34; chap. 38
Exod. 3:21-22; 4:1-9, 19-26; 12:21-27; 15:20-27; 24:1-2, 9-11; 32:17-18, 25-29
Num. 11:1-3; 21:1-3; 32:39-42

(2) The J Source

The symbol comes from German scholars who spelled "Yahweh" as "Jahweh," thus J. This document uses the name "Yahweh" from the beginning of its narrative (Gen. 4:26), as well as after God's appearance to Moses (Exod. 3:15; 6:3). (On the name "Yahweh," see p. 425.) The symbol is appropriate also because the writing may have come from Judah (probably from the royal court in Jerusalem). It is a Judean version of the source G (see b., above).

Beginning with the creation of the world and man (Gen. 2:4b ff.), this source stresses man's rebellion against God, God's judgment in the flood, God's call of the obedient Abraham and his family, the bondage in and exodus from Egypt, the revelation at Sinai and the giving of the Law,

The Wilderness of Judea, at Nebi Musa

the wandering in the wilderness, the appointment of Joshua, and the death of Moses. Whether the story included an account of the conquest under Joshua and the settlement and organization of Israel in the land is not clear.

In this document the writer affirms God's intent to redeem fallen man through a chosen family. He shows how God's purpose won out over seemingly unsurmountable obstacles.

In contrast to N, which glorifies nomadic life, J prefers agricultural life and Yahweh-worship as it developed in the new land. The benefits and possibilities of the Davidic monarchy are stressed. The author is both nationalistic (emphasizing the promised land as Yahweh's special gift to Israel) and universalistic (presenting Israel as God's means of blessing the world).

The style of J is clear, simple, and powerful. The story has epic proportions and qualities.

Scholars have usually placed the author between the time of David and Solomon (tenth century) and Amaziah (beginning of the eighth).

Some representative passages are:
Gen. 2:4b–3:24; 4:1-16, 25-26; 6:5-8; 7:1–8:22; 9:18-20, 28-29; 10:8-19, 24-30; 11:28-30; 15:7-12; 16:4-14; 21:1-7; 22:20-24; 27:1-45; 28:13-16
Exod. 2:1-14; 5:1–6:1; 7:14–10:29; 19:2-25; 23:20-33
Num. 10:29-36; 11:4-35; chap. 16; 20:14-21
Deut. 31:14, 16, 23; 34:1-6

(3) The E Source

E stands for "Elohistic." The source has been given this name and symbol because its author, called "the Elohist," prior to Exodus 3:14-15 refers to God as "Elohim" (a Hebrew word for "God" or "deity"), not as "Yahweh."

Like J, this source is a version of G. It probably was composed in the Northern Kingdom about the time of Jeroboam II, the middle of the eighth century B.C.

E seems to have begun its story of God's dealings with Israel at our present Gen. 15:1, with the Abraham narrative. It runs parallel to J through the Pentateuch and is much like J, but its content is somewhat different and it has its own point of view.

J glorifies Abraham, but E exalts Jacob and Joseph. It gives prominence to the northern sanctuaries of Bethel and Shechem. It exalts Moses as a great prophet. The author shows considerable interest in prophecy, even calling Abraham a prophet (Gen. 20:7). Like the great ethical prophets, he emphasizes the conditional nature of God's promises to Israel: if Israel obeys the terms of the covenant it will become a kingdom of priests and a holy nation (Exod. 19:5-6). God's judgment on Israel for failure to obey and serve his redemptive purposes will be severe. We hear here the notes sounded by Amos and Hosea.

Some representative passages are:
Gen. chap. 15; chap. 20; 21:8-34; 22:1-19; chap. 24; 27:1-45; 28:10-12, 17-18, 20-22; most of chaps. 39–50

Exod. 3:1-15; 5:1–6:1; much of chaps. 7–10; chaps. 20–23 and 32
Num. 11:4-35; chap. 12; chaps. 13–14; 22:2–24:25
Deut. 31:14-17, 23; chap. 33; 34:1

(4) The Union of N, J, and E

Whether N and J were joined before E was written or whether N was added after the union of J and E has not been determined.

J and E seem to have been woven together by an editor in Jerusalem (or Judah) after the fall of Samaria in 721 B.C., possibly in the time of Hezekiah (early seventh century B.C.). The editor's aim was to create a complete history of the people of God to promote the fidelity of both northern and southern Israel to the God of the fathers.

(5) The D Source

D (from "Deuteronomy") stands for a layer of material in the Pentateuch and in the books of Joshua through II Kings which has definite stylistic and theological characteristics. The chief example of this layer is the book of Deuteronomy (except for most of chaps. 31–34). Only touches of D appear in Genesis to Numbers.

The origin of this material is uncertain. It may have arisen out of a code of royal law developed in northern Israel (perhaps in the eighth century B.C.) as a revision and expansion of earlier traditional law. This code may have been brought to Jerusalem after the fall of the Northern Kingdom (721 B.C.) and put into a sermonic form much like our present book of Deuteronomy. Or the sermonic setting of the laws may be much older than that and have come from the practice of preaching the ancestral law at a great covenant renewal ceremony held periodically at the city of Shechem in the Northern Kingdom. Deuteronomy thus would contain a portion of the liturgy of ancient Israel, preserved perhaps by Levites of the north, one of whom put the traditional sermons into much their present form around 700 B.C.

However the book of Deuteronomy first arose, it seems clear that a shorter form of it greatly affected the reformation carried out by King Josiah in 622 B.C. Scholars generally agree that the book of the Law found in the temple by Hilkiah (II Kings 22) was essentially our book of Deuteronomy. So powerful an impression did this book make on Josiah when it was read to him that he immediately set in operation its prescriptions for the life of the nation.

The book found in the temple probably contained what is now Deuteronomy 4:44–26:19 and chap. 28, in substantially its present form.

Later expansion added 1:1–4:43, chap. 27, and chaps. 29–34. The same men who expanded the temple book also edited or composed the material now to be found in Joshua to II Kings. It is likely that NJE and Deuteronomy were joined by these writers during the Exile in Babylon (c. 550 B.C.).

The central notes of Deuteronomy are "remember," "obey," "behold": all Israelites should remember God's gracious attitudes and deeds; they should obey his commandments in unswerving loyalty and fidelity; they are to behold what he has in store for them, if they remain faithful to him. He will set them high above all the nations that he has made (26:19), or he will make them "a horror to all the kingdoms of the earth" (28:25). Throughout the Deuteronomic material it is shown that God exalts those who obey him absolutely and abases those who do not.

(6) The P Source

P is the symbol applied to the "Priestly Document," the latest material in the Pentateuch. It is most interested in ritual institutions, priestly regulations, and statistical data (genealogies, tribal lists, census tabulations, chronological notations). P now forms the framework in which the Pentateuch is set.

The P material in the Pentateuch runs from the creation story (Gen. 1:1–2:4a) through the death of Moses (Deut. 34:7–9). The revelation at Sinai, for which all else is regarded as preparation, is the consuming interest of P; for there God gave to Moses the rules for Israel's worship. The book of Leviticus, with its elaborate ritual regulations, is entirely P material.

Careful study has shown that P gathers together many traditions, lists, and records of varying dates and character. It is thus a literary collection, rather than a unity. It seems to have been put together in Babylonia in the sixth or fifth century B.C.

P wishes to fix in Israel's life after the Exile a detailed pattern of worship and to show that this worship has divine authority since it came from God through Moses at Mt. Sinai. The magnificent God, whose glory could be seen only by Moses, has established ways of access to himself: the tabernacle, the holy priesthood, the sacrifices and other ritual acts. Israel, as God's holy people, must center its life in worship, if its destiny, as appointed by God, is to be achieved.

Some representative passages are:
Gen. 1:1–2:4a; chap. 5; 9:1-17; much of chap. 10; 11:10-27; chap. 17; chap. 23; 25:7-20; 27:46–28:9

Exod. 6:2–7:13; 12:1-20, 40-51; 25:1–31:17; 34:29-35; chaps. 35–40
The whole of Leviticus
Num. 1:1–10:28; chap. 15; chaps. 17–19; most of 25:6–36:13
Deut. 34:7-9

d. The Completed Pentateuch

The P material was added to NJED probably in Babylonia in the fifth century B.C., shortly before the time of Ezra. Ezra brought a book of the Law from Babylon, read it in the hearing of all Israel, and based a sweeping reformation on it (Neh. 8:1–10:39). This book seems to have been the completed Pentateuch (rather than the P document), since some of Ezra's reforms appear to rest on Pentateuchal passages not in P. From the time of Ezra on (c. 400 B.C.), the Pentateuch had unique authority as the Law of God for the life of Israel.

The majority of scholars today believe that the Pentateuch is the product of many minds from many centuries and a veritable treasure chest of Israel's historical memories. They also believe that the documents from which the Pentateuch was formed, though written much later than the events they describe, contain much authentic information about the origins of Israel (see p. 385).

It is clear that Moses stands behind the Pentateuch and the institutions, laws, religious concepts, and ceremonies described there. He was the central actor under God in the liberation of Israel from Egypt and in the organization of Israel's life on its many sides. Although not all the laws, institutions, concepts, and ceremonies ascribed to Moses in the Pentateuch stemmed from him—some are later developments and adaptations in his spirit, made necessary by Israel's changing situation—this fact does not reduce his stature but rather enhances it.

If Moses was not the "author" of the Pentateuch, in the modern understanding of that term, he was its fountainhead. And the book of which he is the veritable center and heart is thus not inappropriately called "the Book of Moses" (Mark 12:26).

Additional Note

A few contemporary scholars challenge the view of the origin of the Pentateuch given above. They reject the alleged sources NJEDP as spurious and the standards by which they have been identified in the Pentateuch as based on inadequate and inaccurate knowledge of ancient literary methods and on wrong philosophical and theological presuppositions.

They hold that Moses did in fact write the Pentateuch in substantially its present form during the years of wilderness wandering. He used traditions about the patriarchs known to him and other Israelites and gave his own eyewitness account of the events of the Exodus and the wilderness sojourn.

They explain the obviously later-than-Moses elements in the Pentateuch (later words, grammar and spelling, forms of place names, and references to later institutions) as due to the activity of scribes after Moses who revised the Mosaic document to make it understandable to people of their time.

They view the duplicate stories, pointed out by the majority of scholars as evidence of the combination of different documents (such as the two stories of creation in Gen. 1:1–2:4a and 2:4b-25 and the double story of the danger to Sarah from foreign rulers in Gen. 12:9-20 and 20:1-18), as illustrating the love of repetition on the part of individual ancient writers, not as evidence of different sources.

They deny that poetic pieces in the Pentateuch are older than prose narratives and that there was any long period of oral transmission, such as the documentary hypothesis requires. Even the editing by scribes was substantially complete by the death of Samuel (late eleventh century), they say.

The prevailing view today, however, is the documentary hypothesis described above.

10. Genesis

1. Title

The word "Genesis" means "beginning." This title comes from the Greek translation of the Old Testament (the Septuagint). The Hebrews, like other peoples of the ancient East, titled literary works after their opening word or words. For example, Genesis was called originally "In the beginning," and Leviticus "And he called." The Septuagint and the Vulgate tended to name books after their contents, not their opening words, and from these titles the English names are derived.

2. Contents

The subject of Genesis is: Why and how God chose Israel to be his redemptive people. The *why* is explained in chaps. 1–11 and the *how* in chaps. 12–50.

Courtesy of the Oriental Institute, The University of Chicago
A reconstruction (after E. Unger) of the tower of Babel (Babylon)

a. Gen. 1–11: The Corrupted Creation

Chaps. 1–11 show mankind's need of redemption.

Genesis opens with two accounts of creation (P's in 1:1–2:4a and J's in 2:4b-25). The first account, in magnificent, formal cadences and in balanced, seven-part structure, celebrates the creation of the heavens and the earth and all things therein. It shows that the created order resulted from the purposive act of one transcendent God. All that God created was good. He made man, the highest of his creatures, in his moral image and appointed him to have dominion over the created order. He intended man to worship his Creator and live in perpetual fellowship with him.

The second creation story deals, in much simpler language and style, not so much with the origin of the universe as with the beginnings of life on the earth. In this story God creates man before vegetation, animal life, and woman. He shapes man out of earth, animates him by his breath, and places him in a beautiful Garden "to till it and keep it." To supply man a companion, God creates animals, which prove inadequate, and then woman.

Instead of recognizing their creaturely dependence and rendering obedience to God, Adam (meaning "earthling") and Eve (interpreted in 3:20 as "the mother of all living") attempt to break out of their status as human beings. They wish to possess the powers that belong to God alone: unlimited knowledge and immortality. Their rebellion against God and their alienation from him end quite other than they had planned: in God's curse and their expulsion from the Garden.

The story of Cain's murder of Abel shows how the break between man and God becomes also a breach in human relationships. Sin is now a fact of human existence. It crouches as a demon at the door of the evildoer (4:7). It must be mastered. Blood feuds between agriculturalists (Cain) and herdsmen (Abel), with their rival forms of worship, mar the earth. Men begin to build cities and forge a civilization without God (4:17-22). Revenge, violence, and death become awful realities of human experience (4:23-24). Even heavenly beings—so an ancient myth said—formed unions with the daughters of men, and giants came into being (6:1-4).

So wicked did men as a whole become that God was sorry he had made them (6:5-6). His judgment on them came in the form of a great flood which all but destroyed mankind from the earth. Even after the flood evil men in their arrogant desire to make a name for themselves, to ensure their security and self-sufficiency, built a great city and a great tower. God met their arrogance by confusing their languages and by scattering them over the face of the earth. Thus he decisively broke up the challenge to his sovereignty. The story shows that the tragic divisions in the human family are not the will of God but the result of man's pride, arrogance, self-trust, and self-worship.

While Genesis records the judgment of God on rebellious men, it also depicts his unfailing mercy toward them. He seeks to deliver them from the condition into which their folly has brought them. Though man's struggle with evil will be long and acute (3:15), we learn that God will make a way of escape. A remnant—a righteous line obedient to him—will become his saving instrument in the world.

Adam's son Seth is shown as the father of the faithful. In his days (or those of his son Enosh) "men began to call on the name of the Lord [Hebrew, *Yahweh*]" (4:26). (Other traditions [E and P] connect the beginning of Yahweh worship with Moses—Exod. 3:13 ff.; 6:2-3). The righteous line of Seth at length produced Enoch and Noah who "walked with God" (Gen. 5:22, 24; 6:9); that is, they lived in intimate moral fellowship with him. Noah became God's instrument in the preservation of mankind from the judgment of the flood and a participant with him in a special covenant relationship (9:1-17). From him came Shem, who was especially blessed above his brothers (9:26-27); and from Shem descended the line leading to Abraham, the father of the redemptive people Israel.

b. Gen. 12–50: The Redemptive Family

The stories of the Patriarchs (Abraham, Isaac, Jacob, Joseph) occupy most of the book of Genesis. Technically most of these stories should be called sagas (material dealing with the exploits of tribal heroes and their clans, transmitted in oral form from generation to generation).

Several groups of material may be identified in chaps. 12–50: (1) the Abraham saga (12:1–25:18); (2) the Jacob (and Isaac) saga (25:19–36:43); (3) the Joseph story (chaps. 37–50).

(1) The Abraham Saga (12:1–25:18)

This material deals with God's call of Abraham, his journeys to and in the land of Canaan, his descent into Egypt, his relations with his nephew Lot, his experiences in securing a true son and heir, his dispute with Abimelech, his test of faith in the ordeal concerning Isaac, his purchase of a family burial cave, his obtaining a wife for Isaac, and the death of Abraham.

Several emphases appear in this material.

First, there is God's call and his constant guidance of Abraham. Abraham's departure for a new land is spiritually motivated: God thrusts him out from his kindred and his father's house into a new existence. The life in a new land is designed to lead to a great destiny—the forming of a new nation which will be a blessing to the whole earth.

Some scholars see in Abraham's response to God's call the beginnings of the rejection of polytheism (the worship of many gods) and the planting of the seed of monotheism (the worship of one God), a crucial turning point in the life of mankind. It appears that for Abraham no other God had existence or meaning. He entered into a covenant with the God who called him (chap. 17) and rendered this God exclusive attention and obedience.

Second, Abraham's wholehearted response to this God is stressed. He departed from Haran "as the Lord had told him" (12:4). He built in the new land a string of altars where he had heard the voice of God and worshiped (12:7, 8; 13:4, 18). He believed God's promise that he would have a son (15:6). His absolute obedience to God in relation to the covenant of circumcision (chap. 17) and the offering up of Isaac (chap. 22) stand out.

Third, his humane and righteous attitudes are frequently highlighted. He allowed Lot first choice of land (chap. 13) and then rescued him from the consequences of that choice by defeating four foreign kings at great personal cost (chap. 14). He interceded for righteous Lot and his family in the wicked city of Sodom (chap. 18). He was unselfish in his refusal to receive spoils of war from the king of Sodom (14:21-24).

Fourth, God's purpose to redeem all mankind is repeatedly emphasized (12:2-3; 17:3-7; 18:18; 22:17-18; 26:3-5; 28:14). To reverse the effects of

Adam's fall is apparently what God intends. God will work out this purpose in spite of delays, lack of faith on the part of his chosen instruments (18:11-15; chap. 16), and interference by foreign rulers (12:9-20; chap. 20).

(2) The Jacob (and Isaac) Saga (25:19–36:43)

Isaac is not a main character in Genesis. The amount of material dealing with him is small (chiefly chap. 26), and when he does appear he is a pale reflection of Abraham or background for the schemes and triumphs of Jacob. He is a connecting link in the chain of descent of the righteous line, the official bearer of the covenant and its promises (26:24), but he is basically only stage setting for the more significant Jacob and his sons.

The Jacob saga revolves around two poles: Jacob's deceit, treachery, self-centeredness, and general perversity, on the one hand; and the divine grace operating in an undeserving life, on the other.

The first is illustrated in such stories as those about the unscrupulous way he obtained the birthright from Esau (25:29-34), the theft of Isaac's blessing (chap. 27), the sharp-witted fleecing of Laban (30:25-43), and the insincere promise to Esau at the time of reconciliation (33:12-17).

The second is seen in the dream at Bethel (28:10-22), where the divine assurance and promise come to a fearful, fleeing youth, and in the crisis at Peniel, where Jacob prevailed in his struggle with the divine visitor (32:24-32). The latter experience seems to say that Jacob, after an encounter with God and with himself as he really was, emerged a changed man, ready for the tasks to be assigned him in the redemptive purpose of God. The change of his name from Jacob (explained as meaning "he takes by the heel" or "he supplants") to Israel (interpreted as "he who strives with God" or "God strives") is symbolic of a new self, a new status before God, and a divine destiny.

Jacob in Genesis is clearly a symbol for the nation Israel. Both were unsuited for the role God had cast for them, but God made them useful through his transforming and empowering grace.

(3) The Joseph Story (Chaps. 37–50)

The story of Joseph is widely regarded as one of the literary masterpieces of the world. Unlike the Abraham-Isaac-Jacob material, which consists of individual episodes drawn together into a loose narrative, the Joseph story is tightly written and moves carefully, and almost without interruption, to its climax and resolution. The closely knit character of the story argues against a background in oral tradition. It was probably put together from JE and P by a skillful writer.

Its purpose is to join the varied traditions concerning Abraham, Isaac, and Jacob with those about Moses, the Exodus, and the conquest of Canaan. It shows how Israel got to Egypt and how God prepared the way for the work of Moses and the birth of the nation.

The story moves through well-marked stages: how Joseph became a slave in Egypt (chap. 37); his rise to power (39:1–41:57); the coming of his brothers to Egypt (42:1–45:28); Jacob in Egypt, his burial in Canaan, and the death of Joseph (46:1–50:26). The only major digression is found in chap. 38 (the story of Judah and Tamar).

The central message of the Joseph story is that God cares for his chosen people. He turns foul deeds against them into a source of ultimate blessing. The story shows that people are free to do what they choose, but they cannot control the consequences of their choices. These are in the hands of God. This teaching comes to focus in 50:20, where the magnanimous Joseph says to his brothers, "As for you, you meant evil against me; but God meant it for good, to bring it about that many people should be kept alive, as they are today."

3. Sources and Historical Value

For a discussion of the literary sources of Genesis, see the comments on the Pentateuch (chap. 9, section 3). Here we need consider only the cultural sources and attempt an estimate of the historical value of the book.

Except for the Joseph story, archaeological discoveries show that much of the content of Genesis reflects traditions, customs, and conceptions derived from Mesopotamia. This agrees with the clear claim in the book that Mesopotamia was the ancestral home of the patriarchs. Abraham and Lot must have brought with them at least some of their cultural heritage.

Furthermore, Canaan was heavily influenced by Mesopotamian culture long before their arrival and long after.

Both stories of creation in Genesis show the marks of Mesopotamian thought, literary forms, and language. The Babylonian creation epic *Enuma Elish* ("When above"), discovered among the ruins of the library of King Asshurbanapal (*c.* 668–627 B.C.) in Nineveh, offers an account of creation both strikingly similar to and different from P's in Gen. 1:1–2:4a. The order of the events of creation is the same, and many details are alike. However, the differences, growing out of the belief in many gods in the one case and in one all-powerful God in the other, are equally striking. (See also p. 386.)

The story of the Fall contains similarities to the Gilgamesh Epic and the Myth of Adapa. The list of long-lived, pre-flood patriarchs in Gen. 5 seems to rest on a Mesopotamian tradition of similar kings. The flood story strikingly parallels that in the Gilgamesh Epic (see pp. 387-88). The Tower of Babel narrative (11:1-9) unmistakably reflects knowledge of Mesopotamian ziggurats (pyramidal temples).

The Abraham-Isaac-Jacob stories contain many references to Mesopotamian customs and beliefs.

For example, at Haran in upper Mesopotamia a husband could adopt his wife as a sister, regardless of actual blood ties, and thereby secure for her special standing and protection in society. This undoubtedly explains why Abraham and Isaac represented Sarah and Rebekah as their sisters (12:9-20;

Photo by H. T. Frank

Bedouin tents. Some scholars think the patriarchs of Israel had a life-style similar to the Bedouins.

20:1-18; 26:6-11)—an attempt to show that they were especially important before the law and to their husbands and thus legally untouchable.

The adoption of a slave as a son and heir, with the stipulation that the subsequent birth of an actual son would require the adopted son to give way as principal heir to the real son, was standard practice in upper Mesopotamia and explains the Eliezer-Isaac situation (Gen. 15:2 ff.).

The theft of Laban's household gods by Rachel was her way of securing title to Laban's estate for herself and Jacob, as we know from tablets discovered from this region (see p. 385).

Genesis consists of stories of various types from hoary antiquity, many of them from Mesopotamia (especially those in Gen. 1–11), some from Egypt (the Joseph narrative), and the rest from traditions about the patriarchs handed down in Canaan. All were assimilated into the theological perspective of Israel by deeply religious Hebrew writers and made instruments of the revelation of God's redemptive purpose. The stories must be looked on not as histories in a narrow sense, but as vehicles for the communication of profound religious truth.

The historical content of Gen. 12–50 is somewhat larger than that of Gen. 1–11. The customs reflected in the patriarchal stories agree in general with the cultural situation as we know it from archaeology. This gives us confidence that much reliable information about the patriarchs and their respective tribal groups has been handed down in the traditions.

11. Exodus

1. Title

In Hebrew the title consists of the opening words, "And these are the names." In the Septuagint "Exodos" means "a going out," with reference, of course, to the going out from Egypt in the time of Moses.

2. Contents and Theology

Genesis tells why and how God chose, led, and preserved (in Egypt) the redemptive family. Exodus records how this family became a free nation under God—how he redeemed it from bondage, sealed it in a covenant relationship with himself, and prepared it, through the construction of the tabernacle, for his perpetual presence.

The book may be outlined as follows:

I. The redemption from Egyptian bondage (chaps. 1–18)
II. The sealing of the covenant between God and Israel at Mt. Sinai (chaps. 19–24)
III. Israel's preparation for God's abiding presence (chaps. 25–40)

The dominant personality of Exodus, as in Genesis, is God (El Shaddai, Yahweh). In these books Abraham, Isaac, Jacob, Joseph, and Moses are the human instruments through whom he works.

The theological heart of Exodus is God's revelation of himself. It is God's purpose that all shall "know" who he is, what he is doing or has done, and what he will do for his people.

First of all, God knows his people's suffering in Egypt (3:7) and he knows Moses' name (33:12, 17). To *know*, according to these passages, means to care about and to seek to help the one known.

Then Moses is to know God's name, nature, and purposes (3:13-17; 6:2-8)—that "Yahweh" cares about Israel and about Moses himself (33:17).

Israel is to know what Moses knows, not only by Moses' words (6:6-8) but also by God's mighty acts in its behalf (16:6-12; 29:46). The children in succeeding generations are to know what God has done for Israel (10:2).

Pharaoh and the Egyptians are to know who the true God is (7:5, 17; 14:4), that there is no god like him in all the earth (8:10; 9:14), and that all the earth is his (9:29).

Photo by H. T. Frank

Mudbricks drying in the sun. Such bricks were used for houses in Egypt (see Exod. 5:7-8) and parts of Palestine.

The whole book deals in one way or another with God's self-revelation, not only of his identity, nature, sovereignty, and purposes, but of his will for Israel's life.

The latter is spelled out in the terms of the covenant sealed at Mt. Sinai: in the unqualified stipulations of the Ten Commandments, covering relations with God and with one's fellows (20:3-17); in the provisions of civil law (21:1–23:9); in laws governing worship (20:22-26; 23:10-19); and the like.

The lengthy sections concerning the making of the tabernacle (chaps. 25–31; 35–40) suggest: (1) God's loftiness (transcendence), his holiness (his separation from all that is common and unclean), and his desire to be present with his people (his immanence); and (2) the conditions on which sinful people can approach him. These sections thus play their part in the self-revelation of God, as presented in the book of Exodus.

3. Historical Background

Precisely when the family of Jacob descended into Egypt cannot be determined. Many scholars think the career of Joseph fits best into Egyptian history in the time of the Hyksos (meaning "rulers of foreign countries"). They were invaders of mixed ethnic origin who ruled Egypt around 1650 to 1542 B.C. These foreign kings (among whom there appear to have been Semitic elements) might well

Photo by H. T. Frank

Akhenaten (c. 1364-1347 B.C.), worshiper of Aten (the Solar Disk) as the only god of Egypt, with his wife and children

have looked with favor on a brilliant foreign youth and have promoted him to a position of responsibility in the government. Egyptian records indicate that it was customary to admit Bedouins and Asiatics in time of famine.

Whether all the Israelite tribes or only part of them went down into Egypt—and thus whether all participated in the Exodus—is not clear. Various pieces of evidence, such as the cordial relations of the invading Israelites under Joshua with the inhabitants of Shechem (Josh. 24), indicate that groups related to Israel had remained in Canaan. It is unlikely that the seventy persons who are said to have descended into Egypt (Gen. 46:27; Exod. 1:5) comprised all the Israelites born during a period of some 200 years' settlement in Canaan prior to the descent into Egypt.

The date of the Exodus is likewise uncertain. The preferred view today is that it occurred about 1280 B.C. under Ramesses II (c. 1290–1224 B.C.). This pharaoh and his predecessor, Sethos I (c. 1305–1290), were oppressors of Israel (Exod. 1:8-11) who forced the Israelites to work at fortifying Pithom and Ramesses (the latter city called at various times Zoan, Avaris, or Tanis) in the delta. Archaeology has dated the conquest of Canaan under Joshua in the latter part of the thirteenth century, thus allowing about a generation for the wandering in the wilderness. The memorial stone of the Egyptian king Marniptah, set up about 1220 B.C., indicates that Israel was established in parts of Canaan by that date.

4. Meaning of the Exodus

The miracle of the deliverance from Egypt made an indelible impression on the memory of Israel. In later centuries poets, prophets, wise men, and priests celebrated it as a mighty demonstration of the mercy of God expressed toward his people.

The Exodus was to Jews and the Old Testament what the life, death, and resurrection of Jesus were for the first Christians and the New Testament—a merciful act by which unworthy, helpless people were delivered from bondage into glorious liberty as the people of God.

Old Testament writers saw the giving of the Law at Sinai as God's gracious instruction of his children concerning what he expected of those whom he had redeemed.

(For a discussion of authorship, sources, and dates, see chap. 9.)

12. Leviticus

1. Title

The Hebrew title is "And he called." Our title is derived from the Septuagint and the Latin Vulgate and suggests that this book pertains to the work of the Levitical priests who guided the worship of the people of God.

2. Contents and Sources

Leviticus, in contrast to Genesis and Exodus, contains very little narrative (only chaps. 8–9; 10:1-7, 16-20; 24: 10-14, 23). It consists almost wholly of regulations for governing the relationship between Israel and God.

God is "holy" (*i.e.*, high above all that is profane and unclean). This book tells how a secular and unclean people can relate themselves to a God of indescribable glory and absolute purity—how they can meet the divine command, "You shall be holy; for I the Lord your God am holy" (11: 44-45; 19:2; 20:26; 21:8).

The book falls into several parts:

I. Laws concerning sacrifices (chaps. 1–7)
II. The ceremony of consecration of the priesthood (chaps. 8–9)
III. Laws concerning ritual purity (clean and unclean) (chaps. 11–15)
IV. The Day of Atonement ceremony (chap. 16)
V. The Law of Holiness (chaps. 17–26)
VI. Laws concerning vows and tithes (chap. 27)

Leviticus belongs to the P layer of the Pentateuch (see pp. 88-89). Its priestly editor incorporated into P an older independent source now called the Holiness Code (chaps. 17–26).

Many of the laws of this code and of the rest of Leviticus are ancient, some probably taken from Canaanite practice and transformed in their new setting. This great body of religious law and ritual served as a guide for priestly service in the postexilic temple.

3. The Significance of Leviticus

Leviticus expresses the ancient Jews' conviction that God—the only God— is supremely pure, that people are unclean sinners, whose ways are an abomination to God. However, God wants to make them like himself so he and they can dwell together in fellowship (Lev. 26:11-12).

The way of reconciliation and cleansing set forth in Leviticus is shaped by the understandings and forms of worship current in the ancient world. Animal sacrifice apparently was universal—a gift to the deity expressing gratitude and penitence, with a view to establishing communion between God and worshipers. Israel looked on it as a means of showing and promoting true fellowship with God and one's fellows. It thus served a valid function at that stage of man's experience.

New Testament writers saw the sacrificial system as pointing beyond itself to the perfect atoning sacrifice, Jesus Christ, who "gave himself up for us, a fragrant offering and sacrifice to God" (Eph. 5:2), to bring about perfect reconciliation with God (Heb. 9–10), and to lead us into complete and enduring fellowship with him (I Pet. 2:21-25; 3:18).

13. Numbers

1. Title

The Hebrew title "In the Wilderness" is a more adequate designation than the Septuagint and Latin Vulgate title "Numbers." The numbering of the tribes (chaps. 1–4, 26) is only a small portion of the book, and it is only one aspect of Israel's many-sided life "in the wilderness."

2. Contents and Sources

In general, the book describes miscellaneous experiences of Israel from the final days of sojourning at Mt. Sinai until the encampment on the plains of Moab before entering the Promised Land. The material is loosely organized, laws and narratives being combined in a not altogether logical way.

J, E, and P are the sources from which the contents are derived, approximately three-fourths having come from P. (See chap. 9.)

The geographical setting suggests the outline of the book:

    I.   Organization of Israel at Sinai for wilderness life and travel (1:1–10:10)

    II.   God's disciplining of Israel in the wilderness of Paran (10:11–21:35)

    III.   Experiences in the plains of Moab (22:1–36:13)

According to the book's own chronology (which comes from the P source), only twenty days are covered in Part I (see 1:1 and 10:11). Part II involves about thirty-eight years

Photo by H. T. Frank
Fertility goddess, 10th century B.C., from Taanach

(10:11; 33:38, the latter passage dating Aaron's death as recorded in 20:23-29). Part III spans about six months (33:38; Deut. 1:3). The P tradition that Israel spent forty years in the wilderness (Exod. 16:35; Num. 14:33-34; 32:13) has shaped the whole book. (For a historical evaluation of this, see below.)

Perhaps the dominant note of Numbers is God's patient discipline of faithless, rebellious, impetuous, licentious Israel, that he might prepare an unworthy but chosen nation to inherit the Promised Land.

3. Historical and Religious Significance

We must sift carefully the traditions in Numbers about Israel's life in the wilderness in any fair estimate of their historical value.

It is hardly believable that Israel in the wilderness should have been able to count 603,550 fighting men (1:46). This number would make the total company of Israelites about two million, an impossible multitude in view of the shortage of water and food in this desolate area.

Many scholars believe that the census lists of chaps. 1 and 26 originally related to a later period (the times of the Judges or of David) and are out of place chronologically here. It has been suggested also that the Hebrew word now translated "thousand" (e.g., in 1:21) may mean a unit or subsection of a tribe. Thus the tribe of Reuben (1:21) would have had 46 subsections totaling 500 persons, rather than 46,500. Clearly the numbers as they now stand are impossible for the wilderness period.

Since ancient peoples often reckoned a generation by the round number forty years (as did the Phoenicians and the Carthaginians), we apparently have a traditional number here signifying a generation. Actually a generation (from father's birth to son's birth) was about twenty to twenty-five years. The chronology of Numbers is thus traditional and not strictly historical.

It is altogether probable that Israel, after the escape from Egypt, wandered from oasis to oasis in the wilderness south of Canaan for about a generation, unable to penetrate the well-fortified land (chaps. 13-14). Their principal base was Kadesh-Barnea, an important oasis about fifty miles south of Beersheba. Finally they skirted the edges of settled, fortified areas (Edom and Moab) and attacked the land of Canaan from the east.

The legal sections of Numbers (e.g., chaps. 5-6; 8:1-9:14; chaps. 28-29) obviously have been inserted into the narrative setting with little regard for suitability of context. The purpose seems to be to connect the various laws with the Mosaic period to give them Mosaic authority.

The stories in Numbers offer a vivid picture of the frustrations, petulance, rivalry, rebellion against authority, rashness, licentiousness, and occasional heroism and nobility that characterized Israel's life in the wilderness. The stories emphasize the importance of wholehearted trust in God and unflinching obedience to his will, and portray his unending patience in the disciplining of his stubborn children.

14. Deuteronomy

1. Title and Importance

Our name "Deuteronomy" came from the Septuagint by way of the Latin Vulgate.

The Septuagint mistranslated the Hebrew phrase "a copy of this law" in Deut. 17:18 by rendering it "second (or repeated) law" (*deuteronomion*).

This word apparently became the name of the book because it indicates a prominent aspect of the material: a repetition by Moses of the deeds of Yahweh and the content of his Law for the benefit of the generation about to enter the Promised Land.

Deuteronomy is one of the four Old Testament books most quoted in the New Testament (the others are Isaiah, Psalms, and Genesis). Jesus used its words in resisting the tempter in the wilderness (Matt. 4:4, 7, 10). Like the Jewish teachers of his time, he summarized the primary demand of God by quoting Deut. 6:5: "You shall love the Lord your God with all your heart, and with all your soul, and with all your might" (Matt. 22:37; Mark 12:30; Luke 10:27-28).

It seems that Deuteronomy was the first book of the Bible to be regarded as canonical, that is, as containing an authoritative standard for the life of the covenant people (see p. 29).

2. Contents

Deuteronomy is not a book of law in a narrow sense. It is a book of sermons about the gracious deeds of God in Israel's behalf and *how* Israel

Photo by H. T. Frank

Large altar for burnt offerings at Canaanite Megiddo

should respond to these deeds and *why*.

The theme of the preaching is: In view of God's love for his people, his gracious deliverance of them from the bondage of Egypt, and his gift of the covenant at Horeb (Sinai), they should respond by loving him, remaining staunchly loyal to him, and wholeheartedly obeying his will as expressed in the terms of the covenant. If they obey his laws, God will bless them with rich life in the new land; if they do not, they will be blighted with a horrible curse and perish in that land.

The central notes of Deuteronomy are "remember," "obey," "behold": *remember* God's gracious attitudes and deeds; *obey* his words in unswerving loyalty and fidelity; *behold* what he has in store for his people!

The book falls into the following parts:

I. First address of Moses: what God has done (1:1–4:43)
The mighty acts of God, which call for exclusive loyalty to him, are recited.

II. Second address of Moses: what God requires (4:44–28:68)
The meaning and obligation of the covenant relationship, its specific terms, and the enforcement by God of those terms are set forth.

III. Third address of Moses: what God proposes (29:1–30:20)
A renewal of the covenant by the new generation is contemplated.

IV. Narrative about the change in leadership from Moses to Joshua (31:1–34:12)

3. Circumstances of Writing

Most scholars believe that Deuteronomy, in whole or in part, was the book found in the temple by Hilkiah the priest, in the time of King Josiah.

This book became the basis of a sweeping religious reformation (II Kings 22–23). The reforms instituted by Josiah—the rooting out of polytheism; the reestablishment of exclusive worship of the ancestral God of Israel and the centralization of his worship in one sanctuary at Jerusalem; the abolition of child sacrifice, sacred prostitution, and the practice of divination and magic—are in line with the teaching of Deuteronomy. The threats and promises of the book (chaps. 27–28) seem to have had an electric effect on this king (II Kings 22:11-13; 23:1-3).

We do not know how long the book had been in existence before its discovery in the temple. (See the remarks on the D source in the article on the Pentateuch, pp. 87-88). Much of its material seems old. Some of it may contain reminiscences of actual words of Moses, preserved by Levitical preachers of the còvenant in northern Israel.

4. Theological Emphases

a. Yahweh is the Lord of the nations and of history. He has assigned all people their lands and their forms of worship (2:5, 9; 4:19; 32:8).

b. Out of his love he chose Israel

as his special possession (7:6-8). He gave Israel a goodly land, a law to govern its life, a form of worship, and the promise of a magnificent future (28:1-14).

c. Israel must give exclusive loyalty to Yahweh (4:1-40). It must eliminate idolatrous peoples and the worship of other gods from its land by "holy war" (7:1-5), centralize its worship at the one sanctuary in Jerusalem (12:2-28), and faithfully perform the ceremonies prescribed by God (14:22–16:17).

d. God's love should be reciprocated with love, and this love should bring about obedience to his righteous will in all areas of personal and national life.

Members of the covenant community must be loving and faithful both to God and to one another. Lost property is to be restored speedily to its owner (22:1-4). Money is to be lent to a neighbor without interest charges (23:19-20). The cloak of a poor man, offered as security, must be returned before nightfall (24:12-13). A widow's garment is not to be taken as security (24:17). Generosity toward the poor will dictate leaving some of the harvest for them to gather (24:19-21). Fellow Israelites are not to be forced into slavery or sold (24:7).

The withholding of wages from servants is strictly forbidden (24:14-15). Honest weights and measures must be used in all transactions (25:13-15). The God of love and mercy requires love and mercy of those who live in fellowship with him.

5. Abiding Significance

On the historical side, we may say that Deuteronomy is to the teaching of Moses what the Gospel of John is to the teaching of Jesus. Authentic notes of each teacher are undoubtedly preserved in each writing, but both bodies of teaching have been transposed into a different key and made to apply to new situations. Moses stands behind Deuteronomy, even as Jesus stands behind the Fourth Gospel.

Deuteronomy stands at the center of Judeo-Christian theology. The heart of the gospel in both Testaments is that we should love and serve God because he first loved and redeemed us. Deuteronomy presents God's deeds as the basis of his requirements, a point made strongly by both Jesus and Paul. And that true ethical behavior springs out of a loving, dedicated heart is a profound and important insight.

15. The Historical Books

The historical books of the Old Testament are Joshua, Judges, Ruth, I-II Samuel, I-II Kings, I-II Chronicles, Ezra-Nehemiah, Esther.

The word "historical" may be misleading here. These books do not contain history in the modern sense of that term. Although they possess materials of great value to the historian, they are shaped so strongly by theological interests that often they are more like preaching than straightforward historical narrative.

That this is so is suggested by the fact that in the Hebrew Bible the books of Joshua through Kings are called "The Former (or Early) Prophets," while Isaiah, Jeremiah, Ezekiel and the Twelve (Minor) Prophets are called "The Latter (or Later) Prophets." This terminology recognizes the truth that the books of Joshua through Kings record Israel's obedience or disobedience to the word of God as spoken through his special agents; and the books point out the blessed or dire consequences in personal and national life of that obedience or disobedience.

While these books are related to the writings of the Latter (or Later) Prophets on the one hand, they are related to the Pentateuch on the other. In content they continue the story of God's redemptive activity in the life of Israel.

Deuteronomy ends with the appointment of Joshua as a successor to Moses and with the story of the latter's death. The book of Joshua picks up the story there and records the conquest and division of the land and the farewell addresses and death of Joshua.

The books following record God's activity in the period of the Judges of Israel, in the formation of the monarchy under Saul, David, and Solomon and in its disruption after Solomon's death; and they trace the progressive degradation of the two kingdoms (Northern and Southern) until the destruction of each at the hands of Israel's enemies.

I-II Chronicles and Ezra-Nehemiah point out strongly the wisdom of personal and national obedience to God and the folly of disobedience.

So close is the book of Joshua to the content, style, and assumed sources of the Pentateuch that many scholars prefer to include it with the five books before it and speak of the "Hexateuch" (six scrolls or books). J, E, D, P appear to underlie the book of Joshua, P terminating with this book. Other scholars have argued that J, E, and D run through II Kings and that the books Joshua through II Kings have a common literary history with the books of the Pentateuch.

Yet other scholars prefer to split Deuteronomy off from Genesis to Numbers and to speak only of a "Tetrateuch" (four scrolls or books). They argue that Deuteronomy is the first book of a long Deuteronomistic history of Israel extending through II Kings. They deny the existence of the main Pentateuchal sources J and E in Joshua to Kings and argue that a writer or writers with the Deuteronomic point of view put the narrative in these books together out of many fragments. They hold that Deuteronomy was separated from Joshua to Kings when Moses' authorship of the opening books of the Bible became a fixed dogma in Judaism.

Thus whether Deuteronomy belonged originally with the books before it or after it is a debated point.

16. Joshua

1. Title

The English title is from the Septuagint and the Latin Vulgate, which named books by their contents rather than their opening words.

The name Joshua (Hebrew, *Yehoshua* or *Yeshua*) means "Yahweh is salvation." The Greek form of the name is *Iesous* (English, Jesus). There are two great Joshuas in Judeo-Christian literature, the second being Joshua of Nazareth.

2. Contents and Theology

The book falls into three major parts:

I. The conquest of Canaan (1: 1–12:24)
II. The division of the land (13: 1–21:45)
III. Final acts and instructions of Joshua (22:1–24:33)

The book of Joshua is both a climax and a new beginning. It records the fulfillment of the promise made to Abraham concerning the gift of the land of Canaan (Gen. 12, 15) and the beginning of a long life for the people of Israel in that land. The exodus from Egypt and the covenant in the wilderness have meaning in Israel's history only because a homeland was won in which a redeemed people

Photo by H. T. Frank

Neolithic tower at Jericho from about 6800 B.C.

could work out their destiny under God.

The point of view throughout is identical with that in Deuteronomy.

God is regarded as a holy and jealous God, who tolerates no worship of other gods by his people. He is the Lord of history, who works out the pattern of events in such a way as to fulfill his own purposes. (Note the sovereign "I" in 24:2-13.) He has called Israel into being and guided its destiny at every stage. He has given his people a homeland. This land has been won not by Israel's bow or sword but by the terror or panic sent by the Lord on the land's inhabitants (24:12). Although much territory remains to be taken, the whole land is included in God's promise, and it will be possessed if Israel will be loyal and obedient to God.

In view of the gracious purpose and deeds of the Lord, Israel should love and serve him faithfully (23:11; 24:14-15). This means abhorrence of other gods, no intermarriage with foreign peoples (23:12-13), and complete destruction of forbidden possessions (chap. 7). The only path to national security and prosperity is exclusive loyalty to God with the whole heart and soul (22:5).

3. Author, Sources, and Date

Most interpreters believe that the book of Joshua was put together from a variety of sources—some of them of early date—by a compiler who lived not earlier than the late seventh century B.C. and probably in the sixth.

This writer may have been the author of the book of Deuteronomy in its present form. The stylistic and theological characteristics of Deuteronomy and Joshua are strikingly similar. It is possible that Joshua is the second part of a great Deuteronomic history of Israel reaching from Moses to the fall of Jerusalem. It seems that some portions of Joshua were added after the great history was completed (possibly Josh. 13–21 and 24).

We cannot say precisely what sources were used in compiling the book of Joshua.

It is debatable whether the old JE narrative furnished any of the material of chaps. 1–12. The JE narrative must have contained an account of the fulfillment of the promise made to Abraham (Gen. 12, 15) in the gift of the land. Hence, some interpreters hold that this fulfillment in altered form appears in the narrative of Josh. 1–12.

The material contained in Josh. 13–21 seems to have come from lists of tribal borders and towns, of cities of refuge, and of Levitical cities, dating probably from the eleventh to the seventh centuries. Some who deny that JE materials underlie the story of the conquest of the land in Joshua find the source of this material in sanctuary and tribal traditions freely reworked by the Deuteronomic author.

A few scholars, who reject the documentary hypothesis concerning the formation of the Pentateuch (see Additional Note, p. 89), have either ascribed the bulk of the book to Joshua himself (with minor later additions) or assigned its writing to an unknown person of the time of Samuel (middle of the eleventh century), with the suggestion that Samuel may have contributed in some way to its composition.

No certainty on authorship, sources, or date is possible. Whatever the sources and whoever the author, the narrative he put together about the conquest and its aftermath offers informative and absorbing reading.

4. Historical Significance

Opinions differ sharply on the historical value of the book of Joshua. Scholars have long noted that the massive, sweeping, and almost uniformly successful character of Joshua's campaigns, as presented in this book, differs from the painful, piecemeal, tribe-by-tribe efforts at conquest described in the first chapter of Judges. It has been customary to accept the Judges account and discredit that in Joshua as consisting of fanciful hero tales told through the romanticizing haze of the years, and of popular stories which arose in explanation of various customs and landmarks. Sim-

Photo by H. T. Frank

Israelite road leading into the city of Dan; from the time of Jeroboam I (922-901 B.C.)

ilarly, little of value for understanding the settlement of the tribes in the conquered land has been seen in the lists offered in Josh. 13–21, so late and confused have these materials seemed to be.

As a result of archaeological research, however, some interpreters have come to see more grounds for confidence in the historical value of the Joshua materials. Excavation has established conclusively that several important cities of western Palestine (Bethel, Lachish, Debir, Hazor) were destroyed in the latter half of the thirteenth century B.C., the probable period of the Israelite invasion. Heavy layers of ash, topped by primitive Israelite structures quite different from Canaanite workmanship, offer mute evidence of the ferocity of the Israelite attack and the completeness of the devastation. These cities are located in the center, the south, and the north of the land, the locale of Joshua's sweeping attacks.

It may be that the record in Joshua is schematic and gives too much credit to Joshua, that some cities claimed as destroyed by him could not have been thus taken (Jericho, Ai—see pp. 382-83), and that in reality most of the land was yet to be conquered territory by territory. But the probability of smashing campaigns by Joshua in the center, in the south, and in the north cannot be denied. Some sections of Joshua seem aware of the gradual subjugation of the land (13:2-6; 15:13-19, 63; 23:7-13).

It seems that the evidence of both Joshua and Judges is needed for a full picture of the conquest.

17. Judges

1. Title

"Judges" was the title given to the book in the Hebrew Old Testament as well as in the Septuagint and the Latin Vulgate.

The title came from the text of the book (*e.g.*, 2:16-18), where the term seems to mean not legal experts who rendered decisions in a court of law, but heroes who, by divine call and empowerment, delivered Israel from the oppression of surrounding enemies. However, these heroes evidently had judicial functions during the period of their leadership (4:5). They were virtual dictators in all matters pertaining to the life of their followers.

Some scholars hold that two types of leaders are combined in the book: tribal military heroes and city or district rulers. According to this hypothesis, the great Judges (Othniel, Ehud, Deborah, Gideon, Jephthah, and Samson) were military heroes, and the minor ones (Shamgar, Tola, Jair, Ibzan, Elon, Abdon) were city or district rulers. Both types may be included under the Hebrew word "judges" because God's Spirit was be-lieved to guide both the warriors and the magistrates of Israel.

2. General Contents and Theology

The book contains three major parts:
I.   An introductory summary of the conquest of the land (1:1–2:5)
II. The narratives concerning the judges (2:6–16:31)
III. An appendix concerning the founding of the sanctuary at Dan and the war against the Benjaminites (chaps. 17–21)

Part I offers an account of the conquest of Canaan roughly parallel to that in the book of Joshua, though with a sharply different emphasis. Here the conquest proceeds by tribes, there by a united attack on the whole land.

The material in Part I lays a good foundation for the rest of the book, since it explains the source of many of Israel's troubles in this period: the presence of Canaanite inhabitants in many of the chief cities and the influence of their religion (Baalism) on the life of Israel.

Part II contains the courageous and often bloody exploits of the "judges." Twelve—six major and six minor (Abimelech, a thirteenth, seems a supplemental figure in the story of Gideon)—are placed before the reader, the minor ones with little more than brief mention.

The stories about the six major judges illustrate a theology of history

Photo by H. T. Frank

Remains of the 16th-century B.C. east gate at Shechem

characteristic of the book of Deuteronomy, especially of chap. 28. This is that exclusive loyalty to God and faithful obedience to *all* his laws bring national prosperity and security, but disobedience results in complete disaster.

This point of view is illustrated from the experience of Israel in the time of the judges. The experience runs in a repeated cycle: the people of Israel are faithful to Yahweh during the days of the God-sent leader; after his death, they turn away and worship the baals; an enemy conquers and oppresses them; they repent and cry to Yahweh for deliverance; God shows mercy and sends a deliverer; they are faithful to Yahweh during the lifetime of the deliverer; then, again, they worship the baals; again, an enemy overcomes them; etc.

Part III is only loosely connected with the preceding material. It apparently seeks to illustrate the statement: "In those days there was no king in Israel; every man did what was right in his own eyes" (17:6; 21:25; *cf.* 18:1; 19:1). The writer, by showing the relative anarchy of the period of the judges because Israel had no central authority, prepares for the narrative yet to come about the rise of the monarchy. The two stories offered here (chaps. 17–21) exalt the importance of the Levites and may well have come from pre-monarchical Levitical traditions.

3. Sources and Historical Value

Basic to the book are old hero stories which were told in the individual tribes at various local centers and sanctuaries. The Song of Deborah (chap. 5) may have been composed and sung soon after the event described in it (twelfth century B.C.). Various short pieces seem to be of early date (Jotham's fable, 9:7-15; Samson's riddles, 14:14, 18; 15:16, for example).

These and other old materials were put together in some hero narrative (possibly as part of JE) between the tenth and the seventh centuries B.C. A version of this narrative was issued in the late seventh or sixth century by a Deuteronomic editor (or editors) who cast the whole in the cyclic theology of history described above. A final edition, including some additions and changes, seems to have been made in the postexilic period, perhaps in the fifth century B.C.

Conservative scholars give a different view of the book's origin. They hold that its true sources have no relationship to the hypothetical Pentateuchal sources (JEDP, etc.) but are oral and written traditions about tribal and national heroes preserved at various early sanctuaries. Some unknown writer (possibly Samuel or a disciple) put them together in the early years of the reign of David (*c.* 1000 B.C.).

The book offers a graphic picture of Israelite life in the first years of the settlement in Canaan. The tribes, loosely federated, maintained a precarious hold on part of the land, while they attempted to beat off attacks of local Canaanite groups and parry the thrusts of enemies from neighboring countries. Wars among Israelite tribes (chaps. 19–21) weakened their resources and their resistance to common enemies. Without a central government, Israel of necessity had to rely on voluntary cooperation of the tribes, tribes too often interested in their own local affairs to help their brethren at a distance. Baal religion which, along with an agricultural way of life, Israelites picked up from the Canaanites, weakened loyalty to Yahweh, the God of the desert of Sinai, and contributed to the disunity of the tribes. The book of Judges accurately mirrors all these conditions.

That the judges did not rule over all Israel in succession, as the book claims, but rather to some degree at the same time in the various tribes is evident from the fact that altogether 410 years are assigned to the period of the judges in the chronological notations of the book. I Kings 6:1 puts only 480 years between the Exodus and the building of the temple under Solomon. It seems certain that many of the judges were tribal, rather than national, figures, whose careers overlapped and who together occupied a period of not more than about 200 years.

4. Religious Significance

The basic conviction expressed in the book is like that in Deuteronomy and Joshua: God requires of his covenant people loyalty to himself and complete rejection of false religion. His blessings depend on unswerving obedience. To follow any other god is to forfeit personal and national destiny. For a wandering people to return to him is the highest wisdom, the way to forgiveness, success, peace.

This is the teaching of the prophets written boldly in this book. Christianity largely transferred the rewards and the punishments to the spiritual realm, but it did not abandon the concept of recompense for loyalty and disloyalty to the true God.

18. Ruth

1. Basic Nature and Contents

The book of Ruth, named after one of its three principal characters, appears in the Septuagint and the Latin Vulgate after the book of Judges because of the opening words: "In the days when the judges ruled . . ." (Ruth 1:1).

In the Hebrew Bible Ruth falls among the Writings—that is, after the Former (Early) and Latter (Later) Prophets. It originally had no connection with the book of Judges, the statement in the Talmud that "Samuel wrote his own book and Judges and Ruth" to the contrary notwithstanding.

In form it is an entertaining and instructive short story, based on an old narrative or possibly a poem long told in Israel. The writer of the story in its present form has shaped it into what Goethe called "the liveliest little epic and idyllic whole that tradition has given us."

The story of the loyalty of Ruth, the widowed Moabitess, to her mother-in-law, Naomi; of the journey of both to Bethlehem (Naomi's ancestral home); of Ruth's marriage to Boaz; and of the birth to them of Obed, the grandfather of David, is so well known as to need no outlining in detail here.

2. Purpose and Date

Several purposes of the book have been suggested:

a. To revive or reinforce the obligation of a male relative to take a dead man's sonless widow as a wife in order to raise up an heir for the deceased;

b. To protest against the policy of exclusion of foreigners carried out by Ezra and Nehemiah (Neh. 13:1-3, 23-27; cf. Ezra 10) by showing that God blessed the union of a Jew and a Moabitess with the gift of Obed, the grandfather of David;

c. To show how God guides and helps those who are faithful to their obligations to him and who are merciful toward one another, even to foreigners.

The language of the book, the nature of its religious teaching, and its position in the Hebrew Bible among the Writings (the third division of the Old Testament Canon) suggest to most scholars that it was written in its present form in the fifth or fourth century B.C. A minority position is that the book was composed much earlier: during the reign of David (c. 1000–961 B.C.) or slightly later.

We do not know the identity of the author. It is evident that he was a man of culture, deep piety, and largeness of heart.

19. I-II Samuel

1. Title

I and II Samuel were originally one book and were so presented in Hebrew manuscripts before the fifteenth century A.D.

The separation into two books dates to the Septuagint, which, moreover, put Samuel and Kings under the title "Kingdoms" and numbered them from one to four. Greek, unlike Hebrew, is written with vowels as well as consonants and requires about one and three quarters more space than Hebrew. Therefore, two rolls became necessary for the translation of each Hebrew book. The division into four books passed into the Latin Vulgate and into English editions.

The Hebrew Bible called the original book "Samuel" either because Samuel was regarded in Jewish tradition (based on I Chron. 29:29-30) as its author or because he was a main character in the book.

The name is not altogether appropriate. Samuel could not have written it, since his death is reported in I Sam. 25:1 and all the events of I Sam. 25–31 and II Samuel occurred thereafter. Furthermore, Saul and

David surely had equal right to be considered in the naming, since they figure so largely in the narrative.

Jewish burials on the Mount of Olives. The tower is the traditional tomb of Absalom.

2. Contents and Theology

In general, I-II Samuel covers the story of the founding of the Israelite monarchy by Samuel and the careers of its first two kings, Saul and David.

The narrative falls into the following major parts:

I. The Samuel stories (I Sam. 1–7)
II. Samuel and Saul (I Sam. 8–15)
III. Saul and David (I Sam. 16–31)
IV. David (II Sam. 1–20)
V. Appendixes (II Sam. 21–24)

In its present form I-II Samuel elaborates the theme that obedience to God by personal righteousness in attitudes and deeds is the basic requirement for leadership of God's chosen people. It draws a contrast between disobedient, evil leaders, and God-fearing, good leaders.

God rejected the priest Eli and his sons because they violated the standards of priestly conduct. They were weak, licentious, and greedy (I Sam. 2:12-17, 22-25, 27-36). Samuel, on the other hand, was "a man of God," fully obedient to God's voice (I Sam. 3). The people declared that he was righteous all his days (I Sam. 12:1-5).

Saul was a promising young man upon whom the Spirit of God came in mighty power (I Sam. 11:6). He did not realize his promise because he did not obey the word of Yahweh (I Sam. 13:13-14; chap. 15; 28:17-18). He finally confessed that God had rejected him because of his unrighteous attitudes and deeds (I Sam. 24:17-20).

David, by contrast, also was chosen by God for leadership and filled with his Spirit (I Sam. 16:1-13). He showed himself zealous for God's cause (I Sam. 17:36), continually "strengthened himself in the Lord his God" (I Sam. 30:6), and lived in humility among his fellows (I Sam. 18:18, 23). He showed consideration and respect for his personal enemy Saul (I Sam. 24:6; 26:9; II Sam. 1), manifested zeal for the worship of God by bringing the ark to Jerusalem and planning the building of a temple (II Sam. 6–7), and achieved victory in all his foreign conquests by the power of the Lord (II Sam. 8:6). He "administered justice and equity to all his people" (II Sam. 8:15). He was "a man after his [God's] own heart" (I Sam. 13:14).

And yet even David was judged by God when he sinned by coveting his neighbor's wife and arranging that neighbor's death (II Sam. 11). Even his repentance (II Sam. 12:13) could not avert the tragic consequences that sin brought in its wake. David's house was shaken to its very foundations (II Sam. 11–20).

The whole narrative in I-II Samuel makes abundantly clear that God has a standard by which he judges rulers. When they violate his will and refuse to cooperate with his purposes, he removes them from leadership or severely punishes them.

3. Sources, Authorship, and Date

Many students of the book have claimed that written sources lie behind it.

They point to duplicate accounts of the same events and to contradictory perspectives in them. In regard to the establishment of the monarchy, one account (I Sam. 9:1–10:16; 11:1-11, 15) represents the monarchy as God's intention and his gracious gift to save his people from their enemies (9:16). Another (I Sam. 8; 10:17-27; chap. 12) holds that its establishment was due to the people's wish and was an act of rebellion against God. Twice God rejects Saul (I Sam. 13:8–14; 15:10-31); twice David is introduced to Saul (I Sam. 16–17); twice David flees to the King of Gath (I Sam. 21:10-15; chap. 27); twice he has mercy on Saul (I Sam. 24 and 26); etc. It seems that different sources had different versions of these events.

Much of I-II Samuel is loosely written, with episodes hooked together. II Sam. 9–20 and I Kings 1–2, however, contain a tightly constructed narrative, obviously done by an accomplished writer. An eyewitness of the events described seems to have written this narrative in the age of Solomon (tenth century B.C.). Ahimaaz, the son of the high priest Zadok, or Abiathar, the high priest under David, may have been its author.

Underlying the remainder of I-II Samuel may be some of the same sources imbedded in the Pentateuch (N or L, J, E). Another possibility is that many miscellaneous fragments were put together from diverse sources. It appears that Deuteronomic editors (seventh to sixth century B.C.) also worked on the book (though their marks are less evident than in Joshua and Judges). Postexilic additions are visible in II Sam. 21–24 and in a few other places in the narrative.

Against this view of the origin of I-II Samuel stand several conservative scholars who deny that there are any duplicate and contradictory narratives which can form the basis for source analysis. They grant the prior existence of the "Throne Succession" source (II Sam. 9–20), certain stories concerning the Ark (I Sam. 4:1–7:2), and pieces of tradition about Saul and David. They put the compilation, by an unknown author, at about 920–900 B.C.

4. Historical and Religious Value

Scholars agree that the most valuable section of I-II Samuel for the historian is II Sam. 9–20 (and its conclusion in I Kings 1–2). This narrative has been called "the Court History of David" or "the History of the Throne Succession." Its realistic, true-to-life presentation of people and events, its factual and psychological accuracy, and its artful structure make it the

THE
UNITED KINGDOM
(c. 1000 - 922 B.C.)

0   25   50   75

SCALE OF MILES

HITTITES

TIPHSAH

PHOENICIA

The Great Sea

DAMASCUS

TYRE

S Y R I A

I S R A E L

MEGIDDO

R. Jordan

GIBEAH   GILGAL

RAMAH   JERICHO

JERUSALEM

BETHLEHEM

PHILISTIA

GAZA

AMMON

BEER - SHEBA

Dead Sea

MOAB

E D O M

A R A B A H

EZION -
GEBER

finest specimen of historical writing in the Old Testament. Neighboring civilization produced nothing like this until the time of the Greek historians centuries later.

The Samuel and Saul stories are less complete, seem less consistent with one another, and less historically accurate than those about David. They are sagas rather than eyewitness narratives. But they convey to us a substantially accurate picture of the times when the monarchy was formed in the face of Philistine pressure on Israel.

The lively stories of I-II Samuel drive home powerfully the view that priests and kings are subject to divine law and that the will of God is absolute righteousness in attitudes and deeds.

20. I-II Kings

1. Title

The Hebrew Bible's "Samuel" and "Kings" were divided by the translators of the Septuagint into four books called "Kingdoms" and designated individually by the first four letters of the Greek alphabet. The Vulgate continued the division into four books and called them at first "Kingdoms" but later "Kings." English Bibles use the fourfold division but keep the Hebrew designations "Samuel" and "Kings."

2. Contents, Literary Method, and Point of View

The history of the kings of the united and the divided kingdoms presented in I-II Kings runs from Solomon (c. 961–922 B.C.) to Jehoiachin's release from prison in Babylonia (c. 561 B.C.), a period of some 400 years.

Three major divisions of the work appear:

  I.   The accession and the reign of Solomon (I Kings 1–11)

 II.   The kings of the divided monarchy (I Kings 12–II Kings 17)

III.   The kings of the surviving Southern Kingdom (II Kings 18–25)

I-II Kings opens with events which follow those in II Samuel 20. (We noted above that II Sam. 9–20 and I Kings 1–2 comprise a "Court History of David," II Sam. 21–24 forming appendixes.)

The record of the reigns of the various kings is set in a more or less stereotyped pattern, consisting of an introduction, some important facts about each reign, and a conclusion.

The introduction includes: (1) the year of the king's accession, dated by reference to the year of reign of the king in the opposite kingdom (Israel or Judah); (2) his age at his accession (for kings of Judah only); (3) the length of his reign; (4) his capital city; (5) his mother's name (for kings of Judah only); (6) a judgment concerning his loyalty to Yahweh, as de-

Photo by H. T. Frank

Samaria: a fine example of Phoenician masonry from the 9th century B.C. This wall enclosed the royal Israelite quarters.

termined by his attitude toward religious cults other than that of the temple of Yahweh at Jerusalem.

The facts offered vary from the briefest notices to rather full accounts of the king's reign.

The conclusion contains: (1) a reference to a source where additional information about the king can be found; (2) a mention of his death and place of burial; (3) the name and relationship of his successor.

The kings of Israel (the Northern Kingdom) are almost without exception condemned for infidelity to Yahweh in that they followed in the "way of Jeroboam" who made Israel sin by setting up shrines at Bethel and Dan (I Kings 12:28 ff.). Even Jehu, who

launched a great attack on the worship of Baal in Israel but did not eliminate the worship at Bethel and Dan, is censured (II Kings 10:28-31).

As for the kings of Judah, only Hezekiah and Josiah are unconditionally approved; some (Asa, Jehoshaphat, Jehoash, Amaziah, Uzziah, and Jotham) receive limited approval; and the rest are condemned for doing wrong in the eyes of Yahweh. David is regarded as the ideal king. His successors are measured by comparison with him.

Emphasis in the book falls on persons and events of religious importance. Much attention is given to the work of Elijah and Elisha, because they championed the cause of Yahweh in the struggle with Baal worship. Kings considered unimportant religiously, however great they were politically and commercially, are passed over quickly. Omri, the founder of the city of Samaria, the conquerer of Moab, and certainly one of the greatest figures in the history of the Northern Kingdom is given only six verses (I Kings 16:23-28). The religious reformers Hezekiah (II Kings 18–20) and Josiah (II Kings 22:1–23:30) are treated in great detail. Solomon's building of the temple and its dedication are given top attention (I Kings 6–8). While there is political, economic, and sociological information in the book, it is everywhere evident that the major concern is religious. The authors wanted to show how loyal the leaders were to the covenant made with Yahweh at Sinai—to the worship of *one* God at *one* sanctuary and to his will as expressed in the Law.

3. Sources and Editorial Work

The chief sources used seem to be: (1) the Court History of David (I Kings 1–2); (2) the Book of the Acts of Solomon (I Kings 11:41); (3) records of the Jerusalem temple (perhaps drawn on for the account of the temple's description and furnishings—I Kings 6–7); (4) the Book of the Chronicles of the Kings of Israel and the Book of the Chronicles of the Kings of Judah (I Kings 14:19, 29, and many other references), apparently annals or official chronicles or records based on them; (5) a collection of Elijah and Elisha stories; (6) an Isaiah source (II Kings 18:13–20:19); and (7) an Ahab source (I Kings 20; 22:1-38). The two books of "Chronicles" above are not our I-II Chronicles but much earlier and very different works.

Some scholars think that the writers of I-II Kings used N (L), J, and E— the sources lying behind the Penta-

Photo from Southeastern Films

The Howland-Garber model reconstruction of Solomon's Temple

Courtesy of the Oriental Institute, The University of Chicago
Bronze statuette of a Canaanite god (El or Baal), covered with gold leaf, from Megiddo, about 13th century B.C.

teuch (or Hexateuch)—but this is unlikely.

A writer, or writers, who held to the theology expressed in the book of Deuteronomy seems to have put these many sources together. He believed, as we saw above, in the importance of absolute loyalty to one God (Yahweh), who was to be worshiped in one temple (at Jerusalem). He bitterly opposed worship at Bethel and Dan and at local shrines. He believed also that those who are loyal to Yahweh prosper, while the unfaithful are punished (see I Kings 2:2-4). He designed his record of the kings of Israel and Judah to demonstrate this.

Two Deuteronomic writers may have worked on the book, the first in the latter part of the seventh century and the second about the middle of the sixth, or one editor may have compiled the book around 550 B.C.

4. Historical and Religious Value

The historical value lies primarily in the basic information, derived from reliable contemporary sources, with which the record is so lavishly furnished.

Without the record contained in I-II Kings the outside sources (Assyrian monuments and annals, Egyptian records, the Moabite Stone, and the like) would have much less meaning for Bible students.

The zeal for pure worship, for hearing and obeying the word of God as spoken through faithful prophets, and for learning the lessons of history as a guide to the present and future mark these writers as faithful members of the people of God.

21. I-II Chronicles

1. Title and Position in the Old Testament

I and II Chronicles, like I and II Kings, were originally one book. It became two when translated into Greek, because of the greater space required when vowelless Hebrew is translated into voweled Greek.

Its Hebrew name was "The Words (or Matters) of the Days," that is, the events of the times. In the Septuagint it is called "The Things Omitted" (*i.e.,* omitted from the books of Samuel and Kings). Jerome, the translator of the Vulgate, suggested that the work be called "a chronicle of the whole divine history." It is from this that the English title "Chronicles" comes.

It is clear from the language, style, method of writing, interests, and general point of view that I-II Chronicles and Ezra-Nehemiah were composed as one continuous work by the same author. The proclamation of Cyrus in II Chron. 36:22-23, presented in fuller form in Ezra 1:1-3, ties the two portions of the work together.

In the Hebrew Bible, Ezra-Nehemiah precedes, rather than follows, I-II Chronicles, in defiance of the sequence of events the books record. Apparently Ezra-Nehemiah became part of the canon earlier than I-II Chronicles, because Ezra-Nehemiah contains information available in no other work, whereas I-II Chronicles largely duplicates (with additions and alterations) material already present in other canonical books. When admitted to canonical status, I-II Chronicles was simply added on as the last work of the total collection, without regard to its proper chronological and logical place.

For Jesus, the Hebrew Scriptures consisted of Genesis to Chronicles.

2. Contents, Purpose, and Theology

I-II Chronicles divides into the following sections:

I. Genealogical l i s t s—f r o m Adam to Saul (I Chron. 1–9)
II. The reign of David—especially his provision for Israel's worship (I Chron. 10–29)
III. The reign of Solomon—especially his building of the temple (II Chron. 1–9)
IV. The reigns of the kings of Judah—from Rehoboam to the edict of Cyrus (II Chron. 10–36)

Though I-II Chronicles appears to offer a history of the Jews from Adam to the Babylonian exile, the author's real concern is not with history as such but with exalting Jewish worship, Jewish institutions, and Jewish national life in a time when the struggling Jewish community of the postexilic period was overshadowed by great foreign powers (Persia, Greece) and faced with a rival temple and worship in Samaria (see p. 405).

The author wishes to demonstrate the supremacy of the Jews and their religion over all rival peoples and cults. He accomplishes this by showing how God, dwelling in his temple in Jerusalem and worshiped by a holy people, fulfilled his purpose, long ago announced to the forefathers of the Jews, of establishing his imperishable kingdom on earth. Though the Judean kingdom may appear insignificant in the eyes of the "great" peoples of the world, it is a kingdom with a noble past and a glowing future. For the only true God dwells in Jerusalem, and he is worshiped there in proper forms and ceremonies by accredited priests and a holy people. Let no one despise the Jews, but let them consider the authenticity, the antiquity, and the authority of their religion, and let them recognize the great destiny of this people under the only true God!

It is also clear in these books that God rewarded those kings who worshiped him exclusively and obeyed his laws and that he punished those who did not. The author explains that the exception to this divine principle of retribution—the unusually long reign of the wicked Manasseh—was due to his repentance and conversion while he was a captive in Babylon and his subsequent restoration by God to his throne in Jerusalem (II Chron. 33:11-13). II Kings 21:1-18 knows nothing of Manasseh's captivity, repentance, and restoration.

3. Sources, Date, and Authorship

The sources of I-II Chronicles are, first of all, the books of Genesis to Joshua (for the genealogies of I Chron. 1–9) and the books of Samuel and Kings (for much of the remaining material). The Chronicler uses these canonical sources with considerable freedom, selecting, omitting, modifying, and adding to create the impression he wishes to give.

For example, he omits almost all material from the book of Kings having to do with the Northern Kingdom, so that he may show how the Judean kings carried out God's purpose in the founding and continuance of the Jerusalem temple worship. He passes over the abundant material in Samuel and Kings about the personal life and deeds of Saul and David, since this material has no bearing on the life and worship of the sacred community in Jerusalem. He modifies when necessary, as in his story of Manasseh's repentance and restoration and in the attributing of David's census to Satan instead of to Yahweh (I Chron. 21:1; II Sam. 24:1). He adds much material about the ceremony of transporting the ark to Jerusalem (II Sam. 6:12-23; I Chron. 15–16) and about David's preparations for building the temple in Jerusalem and establishing its ritual (I Chron. 22–29). He skillfully shifts the credit for planning and building the temple from Solomon (I Kings 5–7) to David. He is anxious to connect David prominently with the Jerusalem temple worship.

The Chronicler refers to several uncertain sources: "The Book of the Kings of Israel and Judah" (II Chron. 27:7; 35:27); "The Chronicles of the Kings of Israel" (II Chron. 33:18); "The Commentary on the Book of the

Photo by H. T. Frank

The Black Obelisk of Shalmaneser III, showing King Jehu of Israel prostrating himself before the Assyrian king and bringing tribute

Kings" (II Chron. 24:27); the chronicles, prophecies, visions, and stories of various prophets (I Chron. 29:29; II Chron. 9:29; 20:34; 26:22; 32:32; 33:19). Those titles which contain reference to "kings" may all refer to a lengthy commentary on the kings of Israel and Judah (II Chron. 24:27) no longer in existence. The prophetic writings mentioned, in part at least, may also have belonged to the same commentary (II Chron. 20:34; 32: 32). This commentary may, in fact, have been a commentary on our books of Samuel and Kings.

The main sources seem thus to be our books of Samuel and Kings and a commentary based on this material.

Since the Chronicler's record in I-II Chronicles and Ezra-Nehemiah runs down through the career of Ezra, who came to Jerusalem in 458, 428,

Photo by H. T. Frank
The horned altar at Megiddo, from the time of Solomon

or 398 B.C. (see p. 127), and since the genealogies run to a somewhat later time still, the author may have lived in the late fifth, fourth, or even the third century B.C. His strong interest in the temple—its origin, its personnel (priests, Levites, musicians, custodians, etc.), its liturgy, and its authority and significance for the Jews and the world—makes it likely that he was a religious functionary there, perhaps a Levite and a singer.

4. Historical and Religious Significance

The Chronicler's use of his sources, so far as this can be checked, and the emphases of his writing show that he was a religious teacher rather than a historian. In rewriting the history of his people from Adam to Ezra (from David to Ezra in detail) he sought to demonstrate the divine origin, great antiquity, and permanent validity of the Jews' religious institutions and practices—so that all the world would know that God, the only God, was with them, protecting them, and helping them toward a divine destiny.

He wrote *interpreted* history, *apologetic* history, more so than any other Old Testament writer. Every piece of his work must be sifted critically if one's objective is the recovery of historical *facts*. Sometimes he offers supplementary material of historical value. The work is, of course, of great significance for a knowledge of the times in which he lived.

The writer's belief that true worship of God and absolute loyalty to him are the indispensable bases of national existence as the people of God is in line with the best emphases of the Old Testament. Some of the sermons and prayers of the book give expression to noble faith, and have influenced life and worship through the centuries. (See, *e.g.,* I Chron. 29: 10-19, esp. vs. 14.)

22. Ezra-Nehemiah

1. Relation to I-II Chronicles, Place in Canon, and Name

The Hebrew Ezra-Nehemiah constituted one book. Like the books of Samuel, Kings, and Chronicles it was divided into two in the Septuagint.

Ezra-Nehemiah is the second volume of the Chronicler's theological interpretation of the history of the Jews. I-II Chronicles is the first.

The Hebrew Bible has Chronicles last in the Old Testament canon, im-

Photo by H. T. Frank

The 6th century B.C. Tomb of Cyrus the Great, Pasargadae, Iran (ancient Persia) mediately preceded by Ezra-Nehemiah. This order is probably due to the prior acceptance of Ezra-Nehemiah into the canon. The Septuagint, the Latin Vulgate, and our English Bibles preserve the true order.

After the separation of Ezra-Nehemiah from I-II Chronicles and its division into two books, the two were variously designated. In the Septuagint our Ezra and Nehemiah are books two and three (designated by the second and third letters of the Greek alphabet) of the books called "Esdras." The first is now in the Apocrypha (see p. 197). In the Vulgate Ezra and Nehemiah are numbers one and two of four books called "Esdras" (see pp. 19-20). In Hebrew texts since the fifteenth century the names "Ezra" and "Nehemiah" have been used, as in English Bibles.

2. Contents and Order of Material

Ezra-Nehemiah covers a relatively brief period: from the Edict of Cyrus (538 B.C.), providing for the return of the Jews to their land and the rebuilding of their temple in Jerusalem (Ezra 1:2-4; 6:3-5), through the work of Ezra and Nehemiah (sometime between 458 and 398 B.C.; see below), around one hundred years.

The Chronicler tells us nothing directly about the life of the Jews in exile in Babylon. The center of his interest is the worship of God in the temple at Jerusalem and the holy community there. Ezra-Nehemiah shows how this worship and communal life, interrupted by God's punishment of his people through foreign captivity, was restored by God's providence through the work of Sheshbazzar, Zerubbabel, Ezra, and Nehemiah. All these men are portrayed as zealous for the worship and service of God. Their efforts centered in two endeavors: the rebuilding of the temple and the holy city; and the bringing of the life of the Jews into complete conformity with the Law of God as given through Moses.

We may divide Ezra-Nehemiah into two unequal parts: (1) events leading to the rebuilding of the temple in Jerusalem (Ezra 1-6); (2) the work of Ezra and Nehemiah in restoring the holy community in Judah (Ezra 7-Neh. 13).

The order of materials in Ezra-Nehemiah is considerably confused. Two illustrations must suffice.

Those who returned from exile, listed in Ezra, chap. 2, presumably accompanied Sheshbazzar, prince of Judah, on the first return from Babylon, shortly after the edict of Cyrus (538 B.C.). Ezra 2:2 and Neh. 7:7 (at which point the entire list is reproduced again), however, associate this group with "Zerubbabel, Jeshua, Nehemiah." Zerubbabel appears to have been Sheshbazzar's nephew and successor as governor of Judah, who led a second return at some time between 538 and 522 B.C. Jeshua was the high priest associated with him (Ezra 5:2; Hag. 1:1). Nehemiah does not come to Judah until 445 B.C. The list in Ezra 2 telescopes periods and persons; the nearly 50,000 persons embraced by it (2:64-65) thus seem to include the total number of several returns. Or it may be that the whole list is a census list of the time of Nehemiah.

Events in the time of Artaxerxes (465–424 B.C.), discussed in Ezra 4: 7-23, are placed before the time of Darius (522–486 B.C.), as we clearly see in Ezra 4:23-24.

For proper understanding we must rearrange the text about as follows: Ezra 1:1–4:6; 4:24–6:22; 4:7-23; Neh. 1:1–7:5; chaps. 11–13; 9:38–10:39; Ezra 7–10; Neh. 8:1–9:37. (Neh. 7:6–73 duplicates Ezra 2:1-70.)

3. Sources

The sources of Ezra-Nehemiah are more identifiable than those of I-II Chronicles. They appear to have been about as follows:

a. Ezra memoirs (in the first person)—Ezra 7:27–9:5 (or possibly 7:11–9:15);

b. Nehemiah memoirs (in the first person)—Neh. 1:1–7:5; 11:1-2; 12:27 13:31;

c. Aramaic sources—Ezra 4:8–6: 18; 7:12-26, consisting of official documents and narrative material;

d. Lists—Ezra 2; Neh. 7:6-73a; Ezra 8:1-14.

4. Historical and Religious Value

We have seen that Ezra-Nehemiah is somewhat disorganized in contents. When the text is carefully rearranged, the contents are of the highest value, since they offer us our major source of knowledge of the period of restoration in Judah after the Exile in Babylonia.

Problems remain, however. How is the work of Sheshbazzar and of Zerubbabel related? When did Ezra come to Jerusalem, and how did his work relate to that of Nehemiah? The following reconstruction of the history of the period has gained favor with many scholars:

a. a return under the edict of Cyrus (about 538 B.C.), led by Sheshbazzar, who made some ineffective attempts to begin rebuilding the temple;

b. another return under Cyrus or Cambyses (sometime between 538 and 522 B.C.), led by Zerubbabel and Jeshua, who, under the stimulus of the prophets Haggai and Zechariah, succeeded in rebuilding the temple and reinstituting its worship;

c. two visits of Nehemiah and his companions in the time of Artaxerxes I (465–424 B.C.), resulting in the building of the walls of Jerusalem and in certain social and religious reforms;

d. the coming of Ezra, the scribe, in 458 or 428 B.C., in the time of Artaxerxes I (465–424 B.C.), or in 398 B.C., in the time of Artaxerxes II (404–358 B.C.), to exalt the Law of Moses over the life of the people in Judah.

Most readers regard the memoirs of Nehemiah as the most valuable part of the book. These memoirs recount the story of a great, unselfish man, beset by staggering problems, who by constant prayer, incessant work, and indomitable will power built the walls of Jerusalem and revived the national life of the Jews.

23. Esther

1. Title and Place in the Old Testament

The book takes its title from its heroine's non-Jewish name, Esther (perhaps from a Persian word meaning "star" or from the name of the Akkadian goddess Ishtar). Her Hebrew name is given in 2:7 as Hadassah (meaning "myrtle").

In the Hebrew Old Testament the book falls in the third division (the Writings), but in the Septuagint it stands after the historical and before the prophetic books, as in the English Bible today.

The Septuagint text of Esther contains many passages not in the Hebrew text. We now call these passages the Additions to Esther. They seek to deepen the religious content of the originally quite secular book (see below) and to bolster its reliability. Jerome gathered these additions together at the end of the Hebrew book, as chaps. 11–16. Luther placed them among the Apocrypha, where they stand today in Protestant Bibles (see p. 196).

Jews of the first and second centuries A.D. questioned the right of this book to a place in the Canon, probably because of its secular character. Luther heartily disliked the book. He regarded it as too Judaistic and full of "heathen perverseness."

2. Contents and Literary Form

The story centers in a deliverance of the Jewish people brought about by a Jewish maiden who became the queen of the Persian king Ahasuerus (Xerxes I [486–465 B.C.]; less probably, Artaxerxes II [404–358 B.C.]). In cooperation with her cousin, Mordecai, she cleverly turned an intended extermination of Jews all over the Persian world into the liquidation of the perpetrators of the plot. In joy over the deliverance, the Jews inaugurated an annual festival called Purim.

It is evident that the story reflects some historical information about Persian palaces, manners, and customs in the time of the great Persian kings. However, various details make it difficult to regard it as historical in a narrow sense. Xerxes' queen, according to Herodotus, was Amestris, not Vashti or Esther. Mordecai, carried off from Jerusalem in 597 B.C. (2:6), can hardly have become grand vizier of Persia in the twelfth year of Xerxes

Courtesy of the Oriental Institute, The University of Chicago

Black limestone bull head from the portico of the throne hall, palace of Artaxerxes I, 5th century B.C. Persepolis, Persia (Iran)

(3:7; 8:2). At that time he would have been more than 124 years old! The extermination by the Jews, by permission of the Persian king, of more than 75,000 of his non-Jewish subjects (9:1-16) and a gallows 83 feet high (5:14) are strange, to say the least.

There have been attempts to explain these historical difficulties. Esther may have supplanted Amestris, even though Herodotus does not record this. The person carried into captivity in 597 may have been Kish, the great-grandfather of Mordecai. Exaggerated numbers are frequent in the Old Testament and do not argue against the basic historical truth of the events.

If the story is not fully historical, it is a historical romance based on some actual (but otherwise unknown) deliverance of the Jewish people in Persia. It wishes to show that the Jews are altogether invincible (4:14; 6:13)—that evil planned against them returns on the head of the planners.

A further aim is to explain the origin of the Feast of Purim as it had come to be observed in the time of the writer and to urge its faithful observance.

3. Point of View, Author, and Date of Writing

The book as a whole has a somewhat secular point of view when compared with Jewish literature in general. God, prayer, and corporate worship are nowhere mentioned. Yet the writer appears to believe in an overruling providence (4:14) and in fasting (4:16; 9:31). He is conscious of the uniqueness of Jewish law and the separateness of the Jewish people (3:8). His spirit as a whole may be said to be nationalistic rather than truly religious.

The writer's date is unknown. He has been placed late in the Persian period (550–331 B.C.) or in the Greek period (331–63 B.C.). The secular viewpoint would fit well the religious situation about 200–175 B.C., before the revival of religious zeal under the Maccabees, though an earlier date (c. 350 B.C.) by a Jew living in Persia is not impossible.

The Feast of Purim is not mentioned again until II Macc. (15:36-37), about 50 B.C. Esther is the only book of the Old Testament not represented in the manuscript finds at Qumran (see p. 400).

24. The Poetic and Wisdom Literature

Poetic compositions originated very early (third millennium B.C.) among the people of the ancient Near East, particularly in Mesopotamia. The Canaanites, by about the middle of the second millenium B.C., had an extensive written literature, much of which was in poetic form.

Archaeologists have recovered myths, epics, legends, religious rituals, hymns, prayers, laments, oracles and prophecies, proverbs and precepts, work songs, and love poems as illustrative of the poetry of the ancient Near East.

The Hebrews, like their neighbors, made extensive use of poetic form. Approximately one third of the Old Testament is in poetry. In ancient cultures poetry was regarded as vigorous and virile, appropriate for national victory celebrations, national festivals, and important declarations on national policy by the prophets. It also gave expression to deep inner feelings and personal experiences.

Hebrew poetry may be classified roughly into lyric poetry (hymns, laments, prayers, songs of thanksgiving, battle songs, victory songs, harvest songs, love songs, etc.), oracular poetry (pronouncements of Yahweh through priest and prophet), and didactic poetry (proverbs, riddles, fables, dialogues, wisdom psalms).

The Wisdom literature (Proverbs, Job, Ecclesiastes, some of the Psalms, the Wisdom of Jesus the Son of Sirach, and the Wisdom of Solomon) belongs to the didactic (instructional) poetry of Israel. This poetry was created and passed along by sages who, since ancient times in the Near East, sought to instruct young men how to live effective lives and how to have successful careers through observing fundamentally right principles of conduct. Right conduct consisted of those actions which caused a person to fit well into the existing order of the universe, to achieve some mastery of life, and to surmount successfully its problems.

Wisdom of this sort was widespread outside, as well as within, Israel, as I Kings 4:30-31 shows. The sages were usually attached to the court and conducted "schools" for young men seeking government service. Considerable amounts of Mesopotamian and Egyptian wisdom have come to light. Prov. 22:17–23:11 so closely parallels the Instruction of Amenemope from Egypt that it seems to be an imitation of that work (see p. 139).

Solomon was a sage of wide repute (I Kings 4:29-34). He apparently had great knowledge and understanding of the world of nature (vs. 33). In the book of Proverbs, reflections on people and human relationships are ascribed to him also (Prov. 10:1; 25:1). It is probable that there gathered around him at his court many sages who created, gathered, and classified knowledge of both nature and humankind. In Jeremiah's time "the wise" were a recognized class along with priests and prophets (Jer. 18:18).

In the postexilic period the originally rather secular, universal wisdom came under the influence of Jewish religion and nationalism. Yahweh became the source of all wisdom and the Jews its privileged custodians. The highest form of wisdom—indeed, all wisdom—was found in the Law of Moses, and the "fear of Yahweh" became "the beginning of wisdom." Priestly scribes (men learned in the Law, in the Prophets, and in the Wisdom tradition) became the teachers of the nation.

Hebrew poetry has recognizable features. One is "parallelism," which has to do with the way lines are put together. The second line of a couplet may repeat in different words the thought of the first line (*e.g.,* Ps. 51:3; 103:10); or the second line may offer a contrast to the first line (*e.g.,* Ps. 1:6; Prov. 3:5); or the second line may complete the thought begun in the first (*e.g.,* Ps. 2:6; Isa. 40:1); or one line may employ a simile or a metaphor to illustrate the thought present in the other (*e.g.,* Ps. 42:1; 103:11); or the successive lines may mount up by repetition and extension (*e.g.,* Ps. 3:1-2; 29:1-2); or four lines may be arranged so that the first is parallel to the fourth and the second to the third (*e.g.,* Ps. 51:1).

Stanzas or strophes may be formed out of groups of lines. Sometimes alphabetic poems appear, in which each line begins with a different letter of the Hebrew alphabet in sequence.

Hebrew poetry also has rhythm. A common pattern is a three-beat first line, followed by a two-beat second line (the dirge meter, as in the book of Lamentations). Couplets with three stresses in each line (as often in Isa. 40–55 and Proverbs) are frequent. Other patterns appear: two-beat lines and four-beat lines. Often the metric patterns are mixed in one poem. Metrical fluidity, rather than exactness, is characteristic of Hebrew and other Near Eastern poetry.

Rhyme, except where accidental, is not a feature of Hebrew poetry.

25. Job

The book of Job is one of the recognized literary masterpieces of the Bible. Its haunting question about the meaning of human suffering and its suggestions concerning how a sufferer should conduct himself when misfortune descends mercilessly upon him are superbly treated.

The book takes its place alongside the great ancient Sumerian and Akkadian theodicies (works dealing with the problem of divine justice) and Greek tragedies and stands in an honored place in the line of similar literature reaching all the way to Dostoevski, Thomas Hardy, Eugene O'Neill, and Archibald MacLeish.

1. Contents and Structure

The book divides naturally into three parts:

    I.   The Prologue (chaps. 1–2)
   II.   The Discourses (3:1–42:6)
  III.   The Epilogue (42:7-17)

The Prologue portrays Job as a God-fearing, righteous, and prosperous man, whom God allowed Satan to test to see whether his piety was motivated by selfish interests. The testing included the loss of all his possessions, his children, and his health, and misunderstanding by his wife. The Prologue pictures Job as enduring the test—as holding fast to faith in God as the giver of both good and evil (2:9) and as not blaming God for the treatment he had received. It ends with an account of the visit of three friends.

The Discourses fall into three divisions:

a. Dialogue in three cycles of speeches:
    (1) Speeches by Job (chap. 3), Eliphaz (chaps. 4–5), Job (chaps. 6–7), Bildad (chap. 8), Job (chaps. 9–10), Zophar (chap. 11), Job (chaps. 12–14)
    (2) Speeches by Eliphaz (chap. 15), Job (chaps. 16–17), Bildad (chap. 18), Job (chap. 19), Zophar (chap. 20), Job (chap. 21)
    (3) Speeches by Eliphaz (chap. 22), Job (chaps. 23–24), Bildad (chap. 25), Job (chaps. 26–31)
b. The Speeches of Elihu (chaps. 32–37)
c. The Discourses of God (chaps. 38–41) and Job's response (42: 1-6)

The Epilogue deals with God's rebuke of Job's friends, with provisions for their deliverance from punishment, and with the full restoration of Job to health, family, prosperity, and a long life.

2. Literary Forms

The Prologue and Epilogue are in prose (for the most part), and the Discourses are in poetry.

The prose parts seem to preserve an ancient, popular folktale, probably pre-Israelite, similar to other old Near-Eastern stories (chiefly Egyptian and Mesopotamian) dealing with the problem of bitter suffering in relation to divine justice. Whether the folktale came to the author of the Discourses in written or oral form is not known.

The poetic Discourses center in a dispute between Job and his friends over the cause and the cure of suffering. Here the style and thought reach a lofty level, in fact, as exalted and effective as any writing in the Old Testament. The writers of these poems (see below) are clearly educated men, acquainted with the traditions of Israel and of surrounding peoples and with the myths and science of their day.

The poems show points of contact with several literary forms—laments, lawsuits, epics, tragic dramas, dialogue-debates—but actually they fall into no one classification. It is generally agreed that they are unique in the literature of the ancient Near East.

3. Authorship, Place of Writing, and Date

It seems that several persons contributed to the book as it now lies before us.

The Prologue-Epilogue, as noted above, may have existed before the poetic parts were written and possibly may represent an Israelite writer's adaptation of an ancient Canaanite or Edomite epic poem.

More than one person may have written the Discourses.

The principal poet probably contributed at least chaps. 3-31 (except for some alterations in chaps. 24-27 and the whole of chap. 28). The poem on Wisdom in chap. 28, though a masterpiece of writing, does not fit its context and may come from another hand.

The Speeches of Elihu (chaps. 32-37) may be insertions by a later writer, to judge from their somewhat different syle, repetitious theology, and argumentative tone. Elihu is not mentioned along with Job's friends in the Epilogue.

The Discourses of God (chaps. 38-41) and Job's brief responses (40:3-5; 42:1-6) may or may not have come from the writer of chaps. 3-31. Job's demand that the Almighty answer him (31:35) requires some word from God. Strangely, two speeches of God are offered (38:1-40:2 and 40:6 ff.) and two responses of Job (40:3-5; 42:1-6). Whether both of the speeches and responses are original, or only one of each, or none, remains a question. But the double responses of both God and Job have considerable effectiveness, whether resulting from the work of one author or more.

Though materials of foreign origin may appear in the book, in its present form it was almost certainly composed in Palestine. Some of the vocabulary appears to be relatively late, and the maturity of the theology argues for a late, rather than an early, period in Israel's history. The fifth or fourth century B.C. (with some additions and alterations in the third century) seems an appropriate time.

A few scholars today argue that the book is the work of one author, who may have lived at any time between the age of Solomon and the end of the fifth century B.C. They explain the presence of poetical material in a prose framework as in harmony with the ancient Mesopotamian practice of enclosing the main part of a literary work in language of contrasting style. They are unimpressed by the alleged differences in theology and style in the various parts of the book.

4. Teaching and Purpose

The central question with which the book deals is: What should the righteous man expect to receive from the hand of God? Should he expect only good fortune or should he also expect bad fortune?

The Prologue-Epilogue affirms clearly that both come to the righteous from God. Job first had great prosperity, but then everything was swept away from him except his life. At last prosperity returned to him. God had brought it *all* on him. Foolish, undiscerning people expect only good to come to the righteous from the hand of God, but the wise know that evil also comes to them from him (2:10) as a test of their loyalty to him. Job passed the test and was approved by God.

The Dialogue in the three speech-cycles exhibits the wrong views of Job's friends. They hold that the righteous man should expect only good fortune from God. If bad fortune comes, it is clear evidence that he is not really righteous. He should confess his secret sins, repent, and be restored to God's favor. Job bitterly repudiates such a view. He insists that his suffering is not due to unconfessed sin in his life, and he cries out for a fair hearing before God. He expects ultimate vindication by God.

The speeches of Elihu add little to the discussion of the problem. They reaffirm the view that God sends suffering to turn the wicked from their sins.

The Discourses of God and Job's final response indicate that the righteous man should humbly and silently trust in God's goodness and justice in bad fortune as well as good, believing that even bitter suffering issues from God's mysterious but purposeful activity. Whatever his condition, the righteous man can rest in the knowledge that God is, that he stands in right relationship with God, and that he can look forward in his suffering to eventual liberation by God.

The book of Job clearly is a protest against the long-standing view that in this life righteousness always results in prosperity, and wickedness in misfortune. This viewpoint is present, for example, in I-II Kings, I-II Chronicles, and some of the Psalms.

The idea that both good and evil come to the righteous from the hand of God for some ultimate purpose, which the righteous may not understand, laid the foundation for the New Testament interpretation of the cross and the suffering of Christians.

26. The Psalms

Jesus and the early Christians loved the Psalms. So also did the covenanters at Qumran, to judge from the many manuscripts of the Psalms found in the caves there. (On the Dead Sea Scrolls, see pp. 399-403).

Through the centuries since, Christians and Jews alike, in their agonies and in their victories, have found spiritual strength and the language of praise in the words of the Psalms.

Martin Luther called the Psalter "a Bible in miniature" and affirmed that in it "all things which are set forth more at length in the rest of the Scriptures are collected into a beautiful manual of wonderful and attractive brevity."

1. Title and General Contents

"Psalms" comes from the title of the book in the Septuagint (psalmoi) and means "songs." Ancient Jews called the book *"tehillim"*—hymns. "Psalter," meaning "stringed instrument," derives from the title *psalterion* found in some manuscripts of the book in the Septuagint.

The Psalter now contains 150 psalms, arranged in five books: I, 1–41; II, 42–72; III, 73–89; IV, 90–106; V, 107–150, each concluding with a doxology. The Septuagint has an additional psalm at the end, number 151, and divides and numbers some of the psalms differently. The division into five books was probably made in imitation of the Pentateuch.

The Psalter is a great collection of smaller collections of psalms without logical arrangement. Some psalms appear twice (14 = 53; 40:13-17 = 70; 57:7-11 + 60:5-12 = 108). The comment "The prayers of David, the son of Jesse, are ended" in 72:20 is contradicted by later notes (see the titles of Psalms 86, 101, 103). Psalms of "the Sons of Korah" (42–49; 84–85; 87–88) and of "Asaph" (50, 73–83) point to different origins, as does the variation in the divine name (chiefly "Yahweh" in Books I, IV, V, and "Elohim" in Books II, III).

2. The Superscriptions and Notations

These contain a variety of items, such as: musical directions ("with

Courtesy of the Oriental Institute, The University of Chicago
Terra cotta plaque of a musician (Ischali, Iraq)

stringed instruments"); names of tunes ("according to the Hind of the Dawn"); indications of authorship and circumstances of composition ("A Psalm of David, when he fled from Absalom his son"); designations of earlier collections ("Asaph," "Korah" —see above); names of types of compositions ("Mizmor" or "Shir," a song; "Maskil," a didactic poem; "Tehillah," a hymn or song of praise; "Tepillah," a prayer; "Mikhtam" and "Shiggayon" are of uncertain meaning). "Selah" may mean "musical interlude."

3. Types and Use

The prevailing view now is that the psalms were composed largely for use in worship—in the public and private ceremonies of the temple—and that they may be classified according to their basic nature and function in worship. The principal types are:

a. *Hymns*—songs of praise to Yahweh for his greatness as revealed in the creation of the world.

They celebrate Yahweh as King of the universe and praise his city, Zion, with its sanctuary.

The hymns were chanted by temple singers, congregation, and individuals, often accompanied by musical instruments, at the great annual festivals, at processions, sacrifices, and private ceremonies in the temple.

Representatives of this class are: 8; 15; 19:1-6; 24; 29; 46; 47; 48; 93; 96–99; 122.

b. *Laments* (or Entreaties)—by individuals and by the nation, invoking God's help in time of personal and national disaster and expressing hope of God's deliverance.

Individuals came to the temple for healing when sick and for justice when accused by enemies. There they poured out their complaints before God. The nation in times of calamity cried out, "Why?" and "How long?" and implored God's merciful deliverance.

Representatives of this class are: 3; 4; 6; 10; 22; 26; 36; 39; 51; 80; 90; 102; 137.

c. *Songs of Thanksgiving*—offered by individuals and the nation in the temple, after receiving some benefit from the hands of God.

Belonging to this group are: 30; 32; 40:1-11; 63; 65; 67; 107; 111; 116; 136.

Some scholars list other types— Royal Psalms (2; 18; 20; 45; 72; 110; 144), Wisdom Psalms (1; 37; 49; 73; 112; 128), Liturgies (15; 24; 50; 85; 118), Pilgrim Psalms (84; 122), and still others.

4. Authorship and Date

Seventy-three of the psalms are ascribed to David and some to other individuals (Moses, Solomon, Ethan the Ezrahite, Heman the Ezrahite, Asaph, and the sons of Korah). Thus the Psalter does not claim that David is the author of all the psalms, as many persons believe today. Some psalms clearly reflect the destruction of Jerusalem and the experience of Israel in exile in Babylonia (sixth century B.C.), for example, 74, 126, 137.

Some psalms appear to be adaptations of earlier texts: 19:1-6 may

Photo by H. T. Frank

Wadi Qelt, between Jerusalem and Jericho, with the monastery of St. George, a "valley of the shadow of death" (Ps. 23)

represent a rewriting of an ancient Canaanite hymn to the sun; Ps. 29 may have come from a reworking of a Canaanite hymn to the storm god Baal; and Ps. 104 seems to borrow from a Canaanite version of the Egyptian sun hymn of Amenhotep IV. Canaanite terms and ideas influenced quite deeply the worship materials of Israel.

The writing of the Psalms reached from about the tenth century B.C. (the time of David) to the early postexilic period (fifth through fourth centuries B.C.). David, who had poetic gifts and musical talent (I Sam. 16:16-18; II Sam. 1:17-27; 6:5), took the first step toward a hymnody for Israel's worship. Many persons over a half dozen centuries or more added their creations to the collection. The men of Qumran, who gave us the Dead Sea Scrolls, were experts in the composition of psalms.

5. Religious Teachings and Significance

The Psalms are songs of praise to the creator, sustainer, and redeemer God and prayers that he will deliver, protect, and sustain his people.

They glorify the place where he reveals himself (Jerusalem, the city of the great king, and the holy temple) and exalt the instrument of his revelation (the Law).

They emphasize the importance of living by the standards of the Law and point out the blessed consequences of obedience and the dire results of disobedience. Righteous kings, people, and individuals, worshiping God aright in his city and his temple, will declare his praise among the nations.

The Psalms celebrate God's wonderful works in the past and invoke similar mercies for the future. "Great is the Lord, and greatly to be praised" (96:4). "Hallelujah!"

Jesus nourished his life on the Psalms (Matt. 26:30; Mark 15:34; Luke 23:46), and Paul urged the Christians at Colossae to "sing psalms and hymns and spiritual songs with thankfulness in your hearts to God" (Col. 3:16). Both Judaism and Christianity have been singing religions.

27. The Proverbs

In addition to the priests and the prophets of Israel, there existed a class of wise men to whom we owe the material of the book of Proverbs.

These sages, probably attached to the court, assembled the wisdom of their time, both Israelite and foreign, for the benefit of court workers, including trainees. The aim of these teachers was to produce wise and good men who would know how to live well and work effectively.

Though some parts of the book have a pronounced religious cast, much of the teaching is grounded in human experience rather than in divine revelation. Formal, institutional religion and even Israel's unique historical experiences play little part in the book.

The practical moral philosophy has had a strong appeal through the centuries to religious and secular people alike.

1. Name, Superscriptions, and Collections

"The Proverbs" comes from the title that heads the book in the Hebrew text: "The proverbs of Solomon, son of David, king of Israel" (1:1).

The Hebrew word behind "proverbs" *(mashal)* means basically "a comparison" or "a likeness" and properly designates a statement which shows the real nature of something by a comparison with something else. It can also mean a standard of behavior and an utterance of hidden truth. The statement so designated can vary in form from a single line to a complex, lengthy poem. The meaning of the word is thus broader than the English word "proverb."

Several superscriptions in the book assign the various parts to different authors or collectors: Solomon (1:1, 10:1; 25:1); the Wise (22:17; 24:23); Agur (30:1); Lemuel (31:1). In 25:1 we are told that some of the proverbs of Solomon were transmitted by "men of Hezekiah," probably professional scribes at Hezekiah's court.

Several collections of proverbs are contained in our present book, as follows:

a. chaps. 1–9 (ascribed to Solomon)

b. 10:1–22:16 (ascribed to Solomon)

c. 22:17–24:22 (ascribed to the Wise)

d. 24:23–34 (also ascribed to the Wise)

e. chaps. 25–29 (ascribed to Solomon; transmitted by Hezekiah's scribes)

f. chap. 30 (ascribed to Agur of Massa)

g. chap. 31 (ascribed to Lemuel, king of Massa)

2. Authorship and Date

The superscriptions do not claim that all the proverbs of the book came from Solomon. Like the Psalms, Proverbs is a great collection of collections, probably put in its present form after the Exile. However, a few scholars argue that the whole content of the book is preexilic.

I Kings 4:29-34 asserts that Solomon uttered 3,000 proverbs concerning nature (trees, hyssop, beasts, birds, reptiles, fish). However, those ascribed to him in the book of Proverbs concern people and human relationships. Both types, of course, may have come from him, I Kings and the book of Proverbs each reflecting a different type.

Solomon was clearly a patron of learning. At his court and under subsequent kings (*e.g.,* Hezekiah, Prov. 25:1) wisdom materials from many sources were accumulated. After the Exile most of these materials, whatever their actual origin, were ascribed to Solomon, under whose patronage this type of learning and literature received emphasis in Israel.

Agur and Lemuel of Massa (30:1, 31:1) are unknown persons. They apparently belonged to an Ishmaelite tribe of north Arabia (Gen. 25:14). Sages similar to Solomon lived in many countries of the Middle East (I Kings 4:30-31). Extensive bodies of Wisdom material have been recovered from Egypt and Mesopotamia, one piece from Egypt ("The Instruction of Amenemope") being closely parallel to Prov. 22:17–23:11. The Edomites were especially renowned for their wise men (Jer. 49:7). All these men were the "scholars" of antiquity.

The earliest materials of the book of Proverbs appear in chaps. 10–29. These have the greatest claim to Solomonic origin. Chaps. 30–31, forming an appendix to the book, are of uncertain date (likely postexilic). Chaps. 1–9 contain some of the later ma-

Photo by John C. Trever

The Step Pyramid of King Zoser of Egypt, built about 2600 B.C.

terials, whether late preexilic or post-exilic is disputed.

The book in its present form seems to date to about the fifth or fourth century B.C.

3. Nature and Value of the Teaching in the Proverbs

Since the book of Proverbs consists of a collection of collections from several periods of Israel's history, the teaching of the book will hardly be of one kind. There is, furthermore, no systematic arrangement of the proverbs in the book; hence, conclusions concerning the teaching as a whole are difficult.

In general, formal emphases of Israel's religion are less evident in chaps. 10–31 than in chaps. 1–9.

Belief in God as creator and ruler of the world undergirds chaps. 10–31, but it is held that people must achieve their goals largely through their own efforts. The wise person will shun every attitude and practice that works against his best interests (laziness, drunkenness, licentiousness, bad company, etc.) and devote his intelligence and honest efforts to his highest goals. Wisdom here is practical common sense, which will enable people to lead a prosperous and happy life. The Lord takes account of what one does and rewards or punishes accordingly.

Chaps. 1–9 are more explicitly "religious." All wisdom comes from God. Wisdom, which was active at the creation, has come to earth and persistently seeks admission to the minds of men. They are free to accept or reject God's gift. If they accept, they will know how to live well in this world; if they reject, they will feel the full consequences of their folly. The wise (the righteous) are always rewarded; fools (the unrighteous) are invariably punished—in *this* life!

The theology of Israel's sages appears to be both too self-centered and too limited in scope. While beneficial results usually or often follow righteous living, it is not invariably so, as the book of Job and the experience of righteous martyrs show.

28. Ecclesiastes

This is the strangest book in the Bible. Many readers have regarded it as an illegitimate child among the sons of inspiration, so radically different from traditional biblical teachings are the views expressed in it.

Some Jews of the late first century A.D. disputed its right to a place in their sacred scriptures. The book was apparently little valued by early Christians, for it is not cited in the New Testament. Christian interpreters through the centuries have strained to find justification for its place in the Bible. Today, however, discerning readers agree that it makes its own unique contribution to the literature concerning man's quest for meaningful faith.

1. Title

"Ecclesiastes" comes from the Septuagint, where it is a translation of the Hebrew *Qoheleth,* the title given to the author in 1:1: "The words of Qoheleth, the son of David, king in Jerusalem."

Qoheleth means "speaker or teacher of the assembly." "Schoolmaster" or "teacher" is nearer the true meaning than "preacher" (KJV, RSV). What the author's real name was is unknown.

2. Arrangement of Material

The book consists of a loosely organized series of reflections on God, the world, and the meaning of life.

They are spoken in the first person (1:12-18; 2:1 ff.), in the second person (5:1-8; 11:1-6), and in the third person (1:2-11; 3:1-8; 7:1-8; 10:1-3). They state what "I" have seen, known, and done; what you—"young man"— should know, be, and do; and what is generally true.

No clear outline of the contents is possible. The sages paid little attention to logical arrangement of materials. The only general statement we can make is that the author set forth his basic philosophy in the first part of the book and the ethic deriving from it in the second. "All is vanity," established at the beginning, becomes the basis for "Rejoice, O young man, in your youth" at the end. Some sections (*e.g.,* 10:1-20) would fit in as well almost anywhere in the book as in their present position.

3. Philosophical and Religious Outlook

The book contains a curious mixture of doubt and faith—of rationalism, skepticism, pessimism, and fatalism, on the one hand, and traditional or orthodox confessions, on the other. How to relate these two strands of thought is a difficult problem.

Some thirty times this or that or "all" is said to be "vanity" or "vain" (*i.e.,* a vapor, a breath, something unsubstantial or fleeting). Meaningless change and endless repetition are the law of life, with no permanent gain, result, or new achievement. "There is nothing new under the sun" (1:9). Since all is meaningless flux—in nature and in human life—all man's strivings are worthless. Wisdom, wealth, women, and even righteousness bring sorrow and disappointment. The fate of the righteous and the wicked is the same: death—a fate which comes to humans and animals alike (3:19-21). Wise and righteous men fare no better in life than do fools and the unrighteous (2:14-16; 7:15-16; 8:14; 9:2-3, 11).

There is deep skepticism about the possibility of knowing and understanding God. God is impenetrable mystery, whose purposes and work no one, not even the wise man, can fathom (8:16-17). This mysterious God has consigned all men to one fate: "one fate comes to all" (9:3); "time and chance happen to them all" (9:11). Every man should "accept his lot" in life (5:19). There is no knowledge available concerning "what is good for man while he lives the few days of his vain life" (6:12). And there is no blessed future life (3:19-21; 9:10). It would be better not to have been born at all (4:3; 6:3).

Over against this dreary pessimism and cynicism, one finds optimistic, orthodox statements. Wisdom and the wise are sometimes praised and valued (2:13-14; 7:19; 8:1; 9:17-18). God's judgment of the righteous and the wicked is affirmed (3:17; 11:9; 12:14), together with the promise that "it will be well with those who fear God, . . . but it will not be well with the wicked" (8:12-13). The fear of God is commanded (5:7; 7:18; 8:13; 12:13). The enjoyment of life and work is repeatedly affirmed as man's duty and privilege, as gifts from the hand of God (2:24; 3:12, 22; 5:18-19; 8:15).

Some interpreters of the book have suggested that an orthodox editor or editors attempted to soften the pessimism of the book by adding orthodox statements. Many scholars, however, believe that the two points of view are not wholly irreconcilable in one mind.

It is clear that the author believed in God, but in a different kind of God from that revealed in the Law and the Prophets. For him God was unrevealed mystery, who decreed unalterably what the world should be like ("crooked" rather than "straight" —7:13). Man cannot alter the nature of his existence in this world. He simply accepts it and finds what enjoyment he can from living in it. He cannot be sure that a righteous life will yield any better results than an evil one. Death will end everything for everyone. Resignation to what is, is the advice offered to youth in this book. Such resignation will bring a certain pleasure in living. The fear of God is reverence and acceptance of the unalterable.

4. The Author and Date

The "teacher" was a wise man who devoted himself to "weighing and studying and arranging proverbs with great care" (12:9).

He probably lived in Jerusalem in the fourth or third century B.C., although it is not impossible that his home was Alexandria or Phoenicia.

He seems to have been acquainted with Egyptian, Mesopotamian, and Greek thought, which differs from orthodox Hebrew beliefs. Like the author of the book of Job, he challenged traditional beliefs—particularly the doctrine of retribution in this life.

Several facts show that the book was not written by Solomon but was attributed to him by a postexilic Hebrew sage: the late Hebrew language of the book, the inappropriateness of several statements for the lips of Solomon (1:16; 4:13; 10:16-17), the generally pessimistic and fatalistic character of its thought, and its position in the latest section of the Hebrew Canon (see pp. 18, 30).

5. Significance

The book gives expression to the ancient and modern struggle to find faith and meaning in a world that often seems meaningless and full of contradictions. It joins its voice to the book of Job in questioning simple answers to the difficult problems of human existence. It acts, as one writer has put it, "as a counterweight to smug assurance and unreflective belief" (R. B. Y. Scott, *Proverbs, Ecclesiastes* [*The Anchor Bible*], 1965, p. 207). As such, it meets the disillusioned of our time where they are and offers them a point of beginning for exploring other biblical books which reveal the purpose of God in our "mysterious" existence.

Additional Note

Conservative scholarship is divided on the question of the authorship and date of Ecclesiastes.

One position argues for direct authorship by King Solomon (tenth century B.C.). It explains the peculiarities of language in the book as due to Canaanite (Phoenician) influences on the mind of Solomon and as characteristic of the style of wisdom writers of that period. It defends the theology as possible for Solomon. It holds that the book's purpose is to present Solomon's final conclusion: that life has no meaning apart from God and his holy will.

The other position is that the book was written in the fifth century B.C. by a wise man, accustomed to the use of Aramaic as well as Hebrew, who undertook to represent the mind of Solomon on the meaning of human existence. This subject may well have occupied the attention of the historical Solomon toward the end of his life.

Advocates of this view point out that the book makes no direct claim to authorship by Solomon and that some passages seem to contradict such authorship.

They agree with the first position that the author intended to show that life is devoid of meaning without God and the wisdom that comes from him.

29. The Song of Solomon

1. Title

In the Hebrew text the title is "The Song of Songs, which pertains to Solomon" (1:1).

"The Song of Songs," after the pattern of such expressions as "the holy of holies" or "vanity of vanities," is a superlative and means "the finest song."

2. Authorship, Date, and Place of Origin

It is not certain that the title attributes the authorship to Solomon.

"Which pertains to Solomon" can mean "belonging to," "in honor of," "in the fashion of," "concerning," or "by" (in the sense of authorship).

The title evidently was placed at the head of the book by an ancient editor who wished to connect it in some way with Solomon, the reputed author of 1,005 songs (I Kings 4:32).

Solomon is mentioned several times in the songs (1:5; 3:7, 9, 11; 8:11-12) but not in such a way as to imply that he wrote them.

It is likely that a collection of songs

of various dates (some of them possibly quite old) was drawn together by an unknown editor of the postexilic period (fifth or fourth century B.C.). Certain words and constructions fit the postexilic period best.

The rural scenes, as well as some of the language, suggest to some interpreters the northern part of the country, rather than Judea, as the place of origin; but this is uncertain.

A few scholars still cling to Solomon's authorship. They deny that the language contains late (postexilic) forms and words, and they point out characteristics in the songs typical of Solomon (interest in flora and fauna, cavalry, and imported cosmetics). They claim also that the geographical situation reflected in the book argues for a tenth century date.

3. Form and Contents

In form, interpreters view the book in different ways: as a poem, as a drama, or as a collection of originally separate love songs.

One of the traditional pools of Solomon near Bethlehem (cf. Song of Sol. 4:15-16)

It is difficult to find any clear theme in the book, such as a unified poem possesses. And marks of dramatic structure, in which various actors play various parts (or one actor assumes several roles), are indistinct or nonexistent.

It is probably best to regard the book as a collection of originally disconnected songs, about twenty-five in number, which were joined together into a continuous text by a wise man of the postexilic period.

4. Interpretation

How to understand the Song of Songs has given rise to wide differences of opinion.

The poems obviously celebrate the glories of courtship and marriage, often describing in frankest terms the charms of the female beloved, the strength and beauty of her lover, and the pleasures of loving relationships. Even nature is included in the pleasure-loving sensuousness that characterizes this poetry. Nowhere is the name of God mentioned, and any attempt at religious instruction is veiled, if present at all.

What is the meaning of this poetry? Various positions are possible:

a. The poetry is allegorical or parabolic. The lover is really God or Christ, and the beloved is Israel or the church. Advocates of this view point out that both Testaments speak of the relation of God and Christ to Israel and the church and use the symbol of marriage. Many Jews and Christians, ancient and modern, have so viewed the book. Others have argued that the relation between God and the individual human soul is described here.

b. The poems had their origin in the worship of non-Israelite fertility deities. In those religions the lover was the dying and rising fertility god whose beloved was his sister or mother. Their relationships were celebrated in songs at agricultural festivals. Israel adapted these songs for use at its own agricultural festivals, and thus they passed in a modified form into Israel's liturgy.

c. The Song of Songs is a dramatic portrayal of the relationships between King Solomon and the (female) Shulammite (6:13), who has been identified by some as Abishag of I Kings 1:1-4, 15; 2:17-22. The poems celebrate their conjugal love. (A variation holds that Abishag rejected Solomon and remained faithful to her shepherd lover.)

d. The poems are oriental love poetry, some of them perhaps composed for and sung at wedding festivities. Poetry of this sort is common in the modern Near East. It hails the bridegroom and bride as "king" and "queen" and celebrates the physical attributes of the pair.

5. Value

The last view, the dominant one today, justifies the inclusion of the Song of Songs in the Bible by pointing out the Hebrews' simple delight in sexuality as a gift of the Creator.

Jewish scholars near the end of the first century A.D. debated the propriety of the book's inclusion in the Canon. Individual Christian scholars of modern times have questioned it also. However, many interpreters today praise its frank acceptance and celebration of the gentleness, the strength, and the delights of human love—as God's ordained purpose for mankind.

30. The Prophets

The high point of Old Testament religion is to be seen in the prophetic books.

The prophets, often scorned in their own day, came to be venerated in later centuries as men of clear vision, matchless faith and experience, and heroic courage.

Jesus and the primitive church drank deeply from the springs of prophetic teaching and experience, as the many references to the prophets in the Gospels and the Epistles show.

Even many secular men of our time regard the prophets as authentic human beings, unshackled by tradition and free from oppressive attitudes and practices—thus prototypes of the kind of humanity that must come into being.

1. Place in the Canon

The Hebrew Bible has two groups of prophetic books: the Earlier Prophets (Joshua, Judges, Samuel, Kings) and the Later Prophets (Isaiah, Jeremiah, Ezekiel, and the Twelve). As indicated earlier (chap. 15), theological interests so dominate Joshua to Kings that these books are often more like preaching than straightforward historical narrative. It is thus appropriate to call them "the Earlier (or Former) Prophets."

The Greek Bible, followed by the Latin and the English Bibles, puts the prophetic books after the poetic and Wisdom books (*i.e.,* after Job, Psalms, Proverbs, Ecclesiastes, Song of Solomon) and adds to the prophetic books Lamentations and Daniel (and some additional material not preserved in the Hebrew Bible). We thus get the sequence: the Pentateuch, the historical books, the poetic and Wisdom books, and the prophetic books.

2. Meaning of "Prophet" and the Prophet's Role and Message

The meaning of *nabi,* the Hebrew word for prophet, is uncertain. It may come from a root meaning "to call" and thus may designate "one who is called" or possibly "one who calls out", *i.e.,* a spokesman or announcer.

Prophets in some respects like Israel's existed in ancient Mesopotamian and Canaanite religion. Eighteenth-century B.C. tablets from Mari on the Euphrates mention male and female messengers of God, attached to a temple, who received messages through omens, dreams, and ecstatic experiences and delivered these messages as oracles. An Egyptian papyrus of the eleventh century B.C. relates the experiences of Wen-Amon in Phoenicia, where a young attendant of the prince of Byblos was seized with a prophetic ecstasy and delivered to that prince a divine oracle. The Old Testament frequently speaks of prophets of the Canaanite god Baal (I Kings 18:19-20; II Kings 10:19) and, indeed, of prophets in many surrounding lands (Jer. 27:9).

However, Israel's prophets were markedly different from those in neighboring countries, just as Israel's God was different from theirs. The prophets regarded Israel's God as the Lord of nature and history, who redeemed the Hebrews from Egypt, chose and sealed them as his people at Mt. Sinai, and revealed his righteous will to them in the Law given by Moses. He called the prophets to become like him in character and to speak for him to the nation. The prophets kept alive the memory of the redemptive events and Israel's obligations to their covenant God. They proclaimed God's will in the crises the nation faced and pointed out the consequences of obedience and disobedience. They were primarily proclaimers of the divine will, not predicters of the future, though they did foresee what kind of a future would emerge out of the present when their hearers obeyed or disobeyed God's will.

Some of Israel's prophets were attached to the sanctuaries of the land and some to the court. The former served alongside the priests, delivering to the people the word of God on this matter and that, and interceding with God for them. Court prophets advised the rulers, particularly in times of crisis. Both may be called professional prophets.

The professional prophets were strongly nationalistic. They held that Yahweh's people were invincible so long as they kept up the religious practices through which atonement for sins could be achieved. Israel's relation to Yahweh as the chosen people guaranteed victory over every enemy (Jer. 14:13-16).

Along with the professional prophets stood the great individual, non-professional prophets. They had no claim to the prophetic office other than God's call. Amos, for example, said, "I am no prophet, nor a prophet's son; but I am a herdsman, and a dresser of sycamore trees, and the Lord took me from following the flock, and the Lord said to me, 'Go, prophesy to my people Israel'" (Amos 7:14-15).

These God-appointed prophets did not assure Israel of an irrevocable claim on God. They saw God as righteous judge of both Israel and the nations, who would punish Israel for its sins by defeat at the hands of foreign powers, unless there was radical repentance and amendment of life. The continuance of religious ceremonies without personal and social righteousness was offensive to God, they said, and would lead to disaster. Religious practices, backed by personal and social righteousness, would lead to individual and national security and to all the blessings God had promised for the coming age.

These prophets did not oppose on principle the ceremonies carried on at the temple, even though their words appear radical (Amos 5:21-24; Isa. 1:11-15; Jer. 7:21-22). They held that such practices, *divorced from righteous living,* are of no avail before God.

Disasters at the hands of Assyria (721 B.C.) and of Babylon (598 B.C. and 587 B.C.) proved the professional prophets wrong. After the Exile in Babylonia they ceased to function as a class and were absorbed into the guilds of temple singers. The great nonprofessional prophets were increasingly venerated, and their words and deeds were remembered and collected.

3. Formation of the Prophetic Books

The prophets ordinarily delivered their message in oral form. In exceptional circumstances they put it in writing (Isa. 8:1-4; 30:8; Jer. 36; Ezek. 43:11). They also taught by their lives, as evidenced by Hosea's marriage (Hos. 1–3), Isaiah's nakedness (Isa. 20:2-3), Jeremiah's celibacy (Jer. 16), Ezekiel's strange actions (Ezek. 4:3; 12:6, 11; 24:24).

They used many forms of expression: the oracle (the pronouncement of a divine message, usually introduced by "Thus says Yahweh," in which the immediate future is shown to be favorable or unfavorable according to the course of action taken); the threat (an announcement of judgment because of sin); the promise (the offer of salvation as a consequence of repentance and amendment of life); exhortations; the report of a vision or a symbolic action; the use of standard rhetorical forms such as hymns, laments, dirges, love songs, proverbs, prose narratives, etc. Their preaching and teaching contained great variety of form and style.

The compilation of the prophetic books probably went through the following stages:

a. The writing down of some of the prophetic utterances by disciples, with or without the express command of the prophet, for the sake of extending the effectiveness of the message;

b. The gathering of written materials into small collections;

c. The joining of small collections into larger ones;

d. The assembling of larger collections into prophetic books, with additional matter supplied by the editor or editors.

Some prophetic books are fairly logically arranged; others are quite unsystematic. Some have relatively little editorial matter, but others have large blocks of it. (For details, see the comments on the individual books below.)

4. The "Major" and "Minor" Prophets

Popularly and traditionally, the prophets have been classified as "major" and "minor" on the basis of the size of the books that bear their names. The "major" prophets are thus Isaiah, Jeremiah, and Ezekiel; the "minor" are twelve in number (Hosea, Joel, Amos, Obadiah, Jonah, Micah, Nahum, Habakkuk, Zephaniah, Haggai, Zechariah, Malachi). No estimate of the relative importance of the prophets in the life of Israel or in the fulfillment of the purposes of God is intended by the distinction—a distinction made at least from the time of Augustine (354–430 A.D.).

31. Isaiah

Isaiah—so full of glowing promises concerning Israel's future—was one of the favorite books of the Jews of Jesus' time, to judge by the number of copies of it discovered at Qumran by the Dead Sea (see p. 401). Early Christians also loved this book, because they believed the promises in it were fulfilled in the coming of Jesus and the formation of the church.

1. Place in the Canon

In the Hebrew Bible Isaiah heads the section known as the Later Prophets. In the Septuagint the Twelve (Minor) Prophets come first. The Latin Vulgate and modern versions follow the Hebrew order.

Isaiah's first place in the Hebrew Bible is probably due to its size, and thus apparent importance, not strictly to chronological considerations. Amos and Hosea of the Twelve Prophets were written earlier than Isaiah.

2. Unity and Authorship

There are three major positions:

a. The whole book comes from Isaiah, the son of Amoz, who lived in Jerusalem in the eighth to seventh centuries B.C. Apart from a couple of Jewish scholars, one in the second

ASSYRIAN EMPIRE
EIGHTH CENTURY B.C.
Cities and States paying tribute
SCALE OF MILES
0   100   500

and the other in the twelfth century A.D., no one seems to have doubted the unity of the book until the eighteenth century. In our time, a few Old Testament scholars support the traditional view. (See Additional Note, below).

b. The book contains the prophecies of two men: chaps. 1–39, of Isaiah of Jerusalem; and chaps. 40–66, of an unknown prophet of the Babylonian exile (sixth century B.C.). The mention of Cyrus as liberator of the Jews (44:28; 45:1), the contemplated fall of Babylon (not Assyria) in 47:1 and 48:14, and the difference between the two sections in literary style and theological emphases have led many to assume a dual origin for the book.

c. The book contains the utterances of three prophets, at least: chaps. 1–39, largely from Isaiah of Jerusalem; chaps. 40–55, from a sixth century prophet of the Babylonian exile (so-called Second Isaiah); chaps. 56–66, from a third prophet (Third Isaiah), who lived in Palestine in the late sixth or early fifth century. Contributions from still other prophets may have been made to the material in chaps. 56–66.

It seems clear to most scholars that we must assume several authors for the book. Isa. 36–39 corresponds closely to II Kings 18:13–20:19 and appears to be taken from that historical work. Pieces in Isa. 1–35 (*e.g.,* chaps. 24–27) bear the marks of postexilic authorship. The book as we now have it appears to be a collection of collections of prophetic sayings reaching from Isaiah of Jerusalem (eighth century B.C.) to postexilic writers who assembled and edited the whole. We may think of the various contributors as standing in an "Isaiah tradition," as disciples in some sense of the original Isaiah.

3. Isaiah, Son of Amoz (Chaps. 1–39)

Isaiah was a Jerusalemite, probably from an aristocratic family and possibly educated as a priest or a scribe (wise man). He was married to a prophetess and had two sons (7:3; 8:1-4).

He was called to be a prophet "in the year that King Uzziah [Azariah] died" (6:1), about 742 B.C. He prophesied during the reigns of Jotham, Ahaz, and Hezekiah, when Judah was seeking desperately to adjust to the pressure of Assyrian power under the great kings Tiglath-Pileser III (745–727), Shalmaneser V (726–722), Sargon II (721–705), and Sennacherib (704–681). His latest prophecies, so far as we know, date to the year 701. Tradition says he died a martyr under King Manasseh (687–642).

His vision of God in the temple at the time of his call impressed him with the holiness of God and his own and his nation's sin. He learned also the possibility and reality of cleansing. He sought to turn his people away from trust in false gods and foreign alliances for national security to absolute trust in Yahweh; from greed on the part of the wealthy to concern for the poor and oppressed; from lavish ritual, relied on as a guarantee of Yahweh's favor and protection, to righteous living and good deeds.

He kept on preaching fearlessly even though he was convinced that the nation would not repent but would experience God's judgments at the hand of Assyria. He believed that God would preserve a remnant and through it, under a righteous king of the line of David, Israel's destiny would be realized.

We may outline the materials in chaps. 1–39 as follows:

a. Prophecies (chaps. 1–35)
  (1) Concerning Judah and Jerusalem (chaps. 1–12)
  (2) Concerning foreign nations (chaps. 13–23)
  (3) Concerning God's final universal judgments and the salvation of Israel (chaps. 24–27)
  (4) Concerning the Assyrian crisis of the time of King Hezekiah (chaps. 28–33)
  (5) Concerning the fall of Edom and the restoration of Israel (chaps. 34–35)
b. Historical appendix (chaps. 36–39)
  Concerning the Assyrian threat to Jerusalem and that city's miraculous deliverance in the time of King Hezekiah; and concerning the sickness and recovery of Hezekiah and the coming of messengers from Babylonia.

4. The "Isaiah" of the Exile (Second Isaiah) (Chaps. 40–55)

The name of this prophet is unknown (hence, "Second Isaiah" or "Deutero-Isaiah"). His ministry probably fell between the beginning of the Persian king Cyrus' victorious career (c. 550 B.C.) and his capture of Babylon (539 B.C.), which resulted in the liberation of the Jews from Babylonia in 538.

The contents of Isa. 40–55 are difficult to analyze. There seem to be about fifty poems in the section, grouped according to similarity of content. We may distinguish two general stages in the thought development:

a. The deliverance of Israel from Babylonian captivity, by the power of the only true God, Yahweh, is to come about through Cyrus (chaps. 40–48).
b. Israel, having suffered God's judgment and been punished by exile, and having been restored to and exalted in its homeland by Yahweh, will see in its sufferings and exaltation God's redemptive activity for itself and for the nations (chaps. 49–55).

Second Isaiah declared the nonexistence of the gods of Babylon and of the nations (44:9-20). He emphasized the omnipotence of the only God, Yahweh, and his beneficence toward Israel and all peoples (chap. 40; 55:5). He urged his fellow Jews to have absolute confidence in their God, who would lead them tenderly back to their homeland and establish them eternally as a purged, renewed, holy people under his sovereign, universal rule (49:8-23).

Second Isaiah spoke of a servant of Yahweh through whom redemption would come to all people (42:1-4; 52:13–53:12). Whether this servant is the nation of Israel as a whole (44:1-2, 21), or a righteous remnant within it (49:3-6), or a single righteous individual (a prophet? the Messiah?), or all three, has been much debated.

Whoever the servant is, the teaching is unmistakable here that unmerited suffering, gladly accepted by the righteous in the course of their work for God, moves the unrighteous who behold it to repentance and renewal of life (see II Macc. 7:37-38).

Jesus, "the one-man Israel," seems to have accepted this calling and work for himself (Mark 9:12; 10:45; 14:24; Luke 22:37), thereby drawing both Jews and Gentiles to the God of Israel and to membership in his family.

5. The "Isaiah" after the Exile (Third Isaiah) (Chaps. 56–66)

Chaps. 56–66 seem to reflect religious conditions in Judea after the return from Babylonian exile.

The temple appears to be standing and foreigners (proselytes) to be participating in the worship of Yahweh (56:1-8). Bad conditions exist: false worship under corrupt religious leaders (56:9–57:13), many wicked people (59:1-15), and insincere performance or nonobservance of religious duties (58:3-5, 13). The walls of the city are not yet rebuilt (58:12). These conditions suggest the period between the rebuilding of the temple in 520–515 B.C. and the reforms of Nehemiah and Ezra about the second half of the fifth century B.C.

This prophet emphasized strongly the importance of repentance, pure worship, and exact obedience to the Law, together with consideration for the poor, the oppressed, and even the foreigner. He clearly tried to keep his people from sinking to the level of corrupt peoples living in and around his land and to lift the worship of Yahweh by righteous Jews and sincere proselytes to its proper level. He made glowing promises for the future—on condition of Israel's obedience to God.

Some fourteen different pieces of material are included in these chapters, some of the pieces possibly from still other hands.

Additional Note

Staunch scholarly defenders of the unity of Isaiah are still vocal.

They point out the lack of agreement among those who dissect the book and assign its parts to various authors, editors, and historical situations, that is, to two or three Isaiahs and multiple editors, all but one of them unknown in name, place, and time.

They believe it strange that the identity of so great a prophet as the Second Isaiah is alleged to have been should have been altogether forgotten.

They hold that the historical situation reflected in the various parts of our present book is substantially identical. In all parts the Hebrews and the writer are assumed to be in Palestine. The idolatry opposed by the writer (44:9-20; 57:5, 7; 65:2-4) is almost everywhere plainly of the Canaanite variety, such as existed in Israel in the time of the eighth-century Isaiah (1:29; 2:8 ff.; 8:19). They claim that idolatry was not a real threat to Israel during the Exile or after, inasmuch as God's judgment in the destruction of Judah at the hands of Nebuchadnez-

Photo by H. T. Frank

A watchtower from which owner guarded ripening crops (Isa. 5:2)

zar had cured the nation of idolatrous ways.

They point out many agreements in language and style between the latter and former parts of the book and find close correspondence between the theology of the latter part and the theology of Micah, a contemporary of Isaiah. They argue that there is even a correspondence in the order of the materials in the two parts of the book.

They affirm that the eighth-century Isaiah was capable of predicting the Exile, and even the coming of Cyrus as future deliverer (44:28; 45:1); for prediction was an authentic function of Old Testament prophets (I Kings 13: 1 ff.; Mic. 5:2; Ezek. 26:2 ff.).

One such scholar holds that the book is an anthology of Isaiah's utterances, containing examples of his thought and style in the various periods of his life, which was put together as a manual of instruction in two parts (chaps. 1–33 and 34–66) by his disciples within a half-century of his death (*i.e., c.* 630 B.C.).

32. Jeremiah

The book of Jeremiah is particularly rich in information about the life, the personality, the times, and the message of the prophet who stands behind it. We know more about Jeremiah than about any other Old Testament prophet.

1. The Man and His Times

Jeremiah's ministry, like Isaiah's, extended over some four decades. He was born at Anathoth, a village of Benjamin, about two and one-half miles northeast of Jerusalem, apparently into a family of exiled priests (I Kings 2:26-27). The date of his birth is unknown, but it probably was about 650 B.C., during the closing years of the long reign of King Manasseh (687–642).

His call to the prophetic office occurred during the reign of Josiah (640–609), about the year 627 (Jer. 1:2). His ministry was carried out under kings Josiah, Jehoahaz (609), Jehoiakim (609–598), Jehoiachin (598/597), and Zedekiah (597–587). After the deportation of Judean captives to Babylon in 587 Jeremiah was taken forcibly into Egypt, where he continued to prophesy for an unknown length of time until his death there.

Jeremiah sought to supply direction for his nation at a time when it was striving to adjust to the pressure of foreign military powers. King Manasseh had found it impossible to resist Assyria. He had paid tribute and had recognized officially in Jerusalem the overlord's gods, with the inevitable contamination of Judah's religion and national life.

In the closing years of the reign of King Asshurbanapal of Assyria (668–627) Assyrian power over the west weakened, and King Josiah struck for freedom (c. 628). He launched sweeping reforms aimed at achieving full independence from Assyria politically and religiously. These reforms came to their climax in 622, after the discovery of the book of the Law (some form of our book of Deuteronomy) in the temple (II Kings 22). Jeremiah had a high estimate of Josiah and his work

Photo by H. T. Frank

Entrance to the palace of King Jehoiakim at Ramat Rahel, south of Jerusalem, an extravagance built by forced labor and severely criticized by Jeremiah (22:13-15)

(Jer. 22:15-16), though he soon came to see the superficiality and inadequacy of the reformation.

After Josiah's death, in 609, at the hands of the Egyptian king Neco II, Jeremiah found himself in bitter conflict with evil Jehoiakim, who had been made king by Neco against the wishes of the Judean people. They had crowned Jehoahaz three months before, only to have him deposed by Neco. Jehoiakim remained a vassal of Egypt until 605, when Nebuchadnezzar of Babylon defeated the Egyptians at Carchemish and took over control of the west.

Within a short time Jehoiakim transferred his allegiance to Nebuchadnezzar. However, relying on the help of Egypt, he rebelled against Nebuchadnezzar. This brought the Babylonian army into Judah in 598. The sudden death of Jehoiakim (perhaps by assassination) resulted in the crowning of the eighteen-year-old Jehoiachin, who, after a three-month reign (598/597), was carried to Babylonia by Nebuchadnezzar, together with high officials, prominent citizens, and much booty. The Babylonians put Mattaniah (Zedekiah) on the throne as a sworn vassal (597).

Zedekiah (597–587), a vacillating king, began plotting rebellion with other western kings (594/593). Encouraged by fanatical nationalists and some surrounding peoples, especially the Egyptians, by 589 he had broken his covenant with Nebuchadnezzar and launched on a course of open rebellion. The army of Nebuchadnezzar soon appeared and systematically destroyed the fortified cities of Judah.

After a long and terrible siege, Jerusalem was captured and destroyed (587). Zedekiah was blinded and carried in chains to Babylon. Other prominent persons and a sizable group of the population were deported. The kingdom of Judah came to its final end.

Jeremiah favored the policies of only Josiah. He found Jehoiakim greedy, disloyal to traditional Yahwism, paganizing, opportunistic, oppressive, unjust. He rebuked Zedekiah for repudiating his covenant with Nebuchadnezzar. He saw Nebuchadnezzar's rule over Judah as God's punishment for the people's sins, a punishment from which they should not seek to escape. He predicted destruction of the nation as the consequence of rebellion, the promises of false prophets to the contrary notwithstanding.

Jeremiah was considered a traitor by most of his countrymen and subjected to untold suffering and perhaps a martyr's death in Egypt.

2. The Book and Its Making

The book may be divided as follows:

I. Jeremiah's prophecies concerning Judah and Jerusalem (chaps. 1–25)

II. Biographical narratives about Jeremiah (chaps. 26–45)

III. Prophecies concerning foreign nations (chaps. 46–51)

IV. A historical appendix (chap. 52)

The process by which the book came to its present form is fairly evident. According to chap. 36, Jeremiah dictated two scrolls to Baruch, his scribe. Jehoiakim disdainfully burned the first one shortly after the battle of Carchemish (605). Jeremiah dictated the second not long afterward and somewhat expanded its contents over the first (36:28-32). It appears that this second scroll forms the basis for our present chaps. 1–25. These chapters seem also to include some later utterances of Jeremiah.

Chaps. 1–25 contain pronouncements of Jeremiah probably from the beginning of his ministry to the fall of Jerusalem in 587 and some autobiographical pieces (e.g., 1:4-19; 3:6-13; 11:18-23; 12:1-6; 13:1-14; 16:1-13).

Chaps. 26–45 are almost entirely in prose. It appears that Baruch wrote them about the experiences of Jeremiah. The order of events is not chronological. The "Book of Consolation" (chaps. 30–31) is an independent collection of expanded sayings of Jere-

miah introduced here by Baruch or a later editor in connection with the story of Jeremiah's act of faith in the nation's future (chap. 32).

The prophecies concerning foreign nations (chaps. 46–51) contain genuine sayings of Jeremiah but show signs of later expansion. Jeremiah considered himself "a prophet to the nations" (1:5).

The historical appendix (chap. 52) agrees quite closely with II Kings 24: 18–25:30 and probably came from that source. It means to suggest that Jeremiah's threats against Judah and Jerusalem were fulfilled.

Several editors had a hand in the composition of the book, and its text was not fixed for a long time. The Septuagint shows this, for its text of Jeremiah is about one-eighth shorter than the Hebrew text.

3. The Message of Jeremiah

Jeremiah's roots lie deep in the religion of Moses and of the prophets before him, particularly Hosea. Like Hosea he saw Israel as Yahweh's beloved bride who deserted her Divine Lover for false lovers. But the Divine Lover never gave up. He pursued the unfaithful one in unfailing compassion and sought to restore the broken relationship. Jeremiah pled long and intensely with his nation in the attempt to bring it to repentance.

Jeremiah saw that Yahweh was not satisfied with formal obedience to his laws. He believed that Josiah's reformation, which had centralized worship in the Jerusalem temple and cleansed it of foreign elements, had been un-

Photo by H. T. Frank

A cooking pot from the time of Jeremiah (7th-6th centuries B.C.)

successful in reaching the hearts of the worshipers and bringing mercy and justice in everyday relationships. He looked forward to the day when God's law would be written in the heart and would find expression in a new kind of human relationship (31:31-34).

Jeremiah opposed the pursuit of national security by alliance with foreign powers and recognition of their idolatrous religion. He resisted the many influential false prophets who claimed that Israel's covenant relation with Yahweh would guarantee her security, if the provisions of that covenant (such as pure temple worship) were maintained. He contended that only personal and national heart-loyalty and

Photo by H. T. Frank

A letter in Hebrew on a piece of pottery, written during the siege of Judah by Nebuchadnezzar (Jer. 34:7). This letter was one of many found at Lachish.

life-loyalty would avail. Without these, temple worship was irrelevant. God would allow even the destruction of the temple. Without these, Yahweh would abandon his people to the terrors of the covenant-judgments (Deut. 28).

Jeremiah saw no hope for his nation in the course it was taking. He regarded Nebuchadnezzar's punishment of Zedekiah's rebellion as an act of God to purge the nation and prepare it for a new and righteous future beyond the Exile. In that future a righteous king (23:5-6) would lead his people and the nations into perfect knowledge of God and obedience to God's will.

4. Jeremiah and Jesus

What we learn about Jeremiah reminds us strangely of Jesus, a similarity noted by some in New Testament times (Matt. 16:13-14).

Both grew up and served as God's messengers to the nation in a time of fanatical nationalistic rebellion against foreign powers (Assyria and Babylon for Jeremiah; Rome for Jesus). Both sought unsuccessfully to avoid catastrophe for their country by counseling repentance and absolute loyalty to God, who alone could assure Israel's future. Both challenged the hollow ceremonialism, divorced from practical morality, that characterized temple worship in their time and predicted the destruction of the temple. Both reacted against the legalism of book religion and advocated a religion of the heart. Both loved their people deeply, preached in virile, poetic language, often dramatically acted out the message, and wept over the people's hardness of heart. Both suffered deeply at the hands of those they loved; and it seems that both were martyred for their efforts. Jesus brought into being the new covenant envisioned by Jeremiah (Heb. 8:8-13). Both looked beyond the tragedy of national destruction to a New Age in which the purposes of God for Israel and the world would be fulfilled.

Photo by H. T. Frank

Tell ed-Duweir, site of the ancient city of Lachish

33. Lamentations

1. Name and Place in Canon

The Hebrew title comes from the opening word of chaps. 1, 2, and 4, which means "Ah, how!" Funeral dirges began with this word. The English title comes from the Latin Vulgate's *lamentationes*. In some ancient translations, "of Jeremiah" or "of Jeremiah the prophet" was added to the title, and the book was placed after the book of Jeremiah.

In the Hebrew Bible its position is in the third division of the canon (The Writings).

2. Literary Style and Type

The five poems of this book, corresponding to the five chapters, present a mixture of literary types: funeral dirges in which dead Jerusalem is mourned (1, 2, 4), individual laments (3 and some parts of the others), and community laments (5 and parts of others). Most of the poems are in the meter of the elegy or dirge.

The poems are carefully constructed and patterned in various ways after the order of the Hebrew alphabet.

For example, in poems 1 and 2 the first line of each three-line stanza (strophe) begins with a different letter of the Hebrew alphabet in sequence, while in poem 3 each letter of the alphabet is used to begin three successive lines before the next letter is introduced. Poem 5 has as many lines as there are letters in the Hebrew alphabet (22), though the letters are not in sequence.

This neat structuring of the material interferes somewhat with free, logical flowing of ideas. It may be that the alphabetic form was a memory device to help the leader and congregation through the laments (see below). It may also suggest completeness, as we would say, "from A to Z."

3. Contents

Poem 1 (chap. 1): Desolate, devastated Jerusalem weeps over her condition, confesses her sins, acclaims God's punishment as just, and prays for vengeance on her enemies.

Poem 2 (chap. 2): The destruction of Jerusalem is Yahweh's doing alone, in fulfillment of his word of judgment.

Poem 3 (chap. 3): The awful consequences of God's judgments lead to a consideration of his great mercy—for he is a God of both judgment and mercy.

Poem 4 (chap. 4): The horrors of the siege and the devastation of Jerusalem, brought on by the sins of prophets and priests, were unrelieved by the nation's ally (Egypt); gloating Edom will be punished.

Poem 5 (chap. 5): The miseries resulting from the capture of Jerusalem lead to a prayer for restoration by the eternal King Yahweh.

4. Date, Authorship, and Purpose

The poems reflect at close range the events and conditions of the fall of Jerusalem in 587 B.C. They were probably written by one or more eyewitnesses of those tragic events, perhaps for use at an annual ceremony of mourning for the ruined temple and city. Such lamentation began soon after the destruction (Jer. 41:5) and continued in the postexilic period (Zech. 7:3; 8:19). A date between 587 and 540 is likely.

The tradition that they were written by Jeremiah has iittle to support it. Jeremiah could hardly have said that the voice of prophecy had been silenced (Lam. 2:9), nor would he have praised vacillating King Zedekiah (4: 20). The artificial style of construction is unlike anything in Jeremiah's prophecies. The writer or writers are unknown.

There are, however, a few scholars today who argue for Jeremiah's authorship.

5. Value

In these poems we have moving penitential liturgy. It contemplates the stark consequences of human sin and misery, sees God's hand in them for ultimate good (3:37-39), and hopes fervently in the midst of tragedy for deliverance and a bright future by the mercy of God.

The book has long been chanted by Jews on the fast day recalling the fall of Jerusalem in 587 (the ninth of Ab [Jul.–Aug.]) and is used today by Christians during Holy Week in calling to mind the sufferings of Jesus.

34. Ezekiel

To most people today Ezekiel is a curious and puzzling prophet. His strange otherworldly visions, his "abnormal" personality, his obscure imagery, his monotonous and harsh language and style, his interest in correct religious forms and ceremonies, his high regard for meticulous fulfillment of the Law—all remove him from the areas of interest of most contemporary Western people.

To the courageous and imaginative, however, who are willing to enter sympathetically into Ezekiel's world and situation, the rewards are considerable. His emphasis on individual responsibility before God and on inner conversion (God's gift of a new heart and a new spirit) alone entitles him to an honored place among Israel's teachers and among the forerunners of Christianity.

temple in Jerusalem. He was carried as a captive to Babylonia along with King Jehoiachin and others in 597 B.C. He lived in a house of his own in the community of Telabib by the river Chebar (3:15; 8:1). There in 593 B.C. he received his call to become a prophet (1:2). His beloved wife died at Telabib at the time of the siege of Jerusalem by Nebuchadnezzar (588 B.C.). He used her death as a symbol of the inevitable destruction of beloved Jerusalem and the temple and his numb unexpressed grief as a symbol of the people's appropriate reaction to God's righteous judgment on that city (24:15-24). His ministry in Babylonia continued until around 571 B.C. (29:17). He often delivered the word of the Lord to elders of the exiles who came to his house (8:1; 14:1).

1. The Man

Information in the book does not allow certainty concerning the outline of his life and career. Scholars have made many conflicting constructions of it.

According to the most probable view, at the beginning of his career Ezekiel was a priest attached to the

2. The Book

The contents are, for the most part, well organized and may be outlined as follows:

    I.   Warnings and threats directed to Judah and Jerusalem (chaps. 1–24)

   II.   Warnings and threats directed to foreign nations (chaps. 25–32)

III. Promises concerning the future of Judah and Jerusalem (chaps. 33–48)

There is evidence that the book was added to and altered by Ezekiel's disciples and successors. The additions seem to fall in line with Ezekiel's own point of view. Duplicate passages (3: 17-19=33:7-9; 18:25-29=33:17-20; etc.) and chronological displacements (26:1; 29:1; etc.) offer proof of a complicated literary history. Ezekiel's authorship may be justly claimed for the bulk of the material, however. When the book reached its present form is not known. Responsible estimates range from the sixth to the fourth centuries B.C.

3. Ezekiel's Message

Ezekiel's prophecies before the fall of Jerusalem in 587 B.C. apparently were intended both for the exiles and the inhabitants of Judah and Jerusalem. He wished all to understand that Jerusalem was doomed on account of its sins, to prepare them for its fall by separating them from dependence on it, and to declare God's will concerning its future. After the fall he sought to bring about a renewal of the life of the exiles so that they could enter into that future as God's chastened and redeemed people.

Ezekiel also pronounced God's judgments on the nations which gloated over Jerusalem's destruction and lived in defiance of the will of God (chaps. 25–32).

His hope embraced many elements: the resurrection of the nation (the dry bones will come alive); the return to Zion; the uniting of Israel and Judah into one kingdom; the reign of God's servant, a descendant of David, over it; marvelous fertility of the land; the rebuilding and glorification of the temple and careful observance of its holy rites; and the worship of a holy God by a people indwelt by his Spirit. This renewed people will obey God's will from the heart. A new covenant will be established, which will stand forever. God and his people will live together in mutual possession ("You shall be my people, and I will be your God").

The dominant theological notes in Ezekiel's message are: the loftiness and absolute holiness of God; his activity and nearness in his Spirit; the sinfulness of man; the certainty of divine judgment on sinners; individual, as well as collective, responsibility before God; inner conversion and renewal of the repentant; the certainty of a glorious future for God's renewed people.

4. Forms of Thought and Literary Style

Ezekiel was a many-sided prophet, perhaps the most versatile in Israel's entire history. He was a priest, a prophet, a pastor ("watchman"), an apocalyptist, a theologian, a religious and political planner, a poet, an artist.

As priest he had a deep concern for ritual and personal purity, for correct corporate worship, and for exact obedience to the law of God. The holiness of God overshadowed all his life and thought.

As prophet he exposed Israel's and

the nations' sins and announced the coming judgment of God. He called his hearers to repentance and promised God's mercy on all who sincerely turned to him.

As pastor he was called to warn, protect, and comfort his people.

As apocalyptist he was caught up into visionary trances and described God's truth in dramatic symbols.

As theologian he interpreted the meaning of the catastrophe of Jerusalem's fall and the conditions of national restoration and renewal.

As religious and political planner he laid the foundation for the postexilic community, with its life centered in the new temple.

As poet and artist he was strikingly imaginative, his creations often bordering on the bizarre. He communicated through powerful allegories, metaphors, symbols, and symbolic actions. He spoke and wrote in both prose and poetry. His laments are particularly powerful (e.g., 19:2-14).

5. Influence

Ezekiel left his mark on the postexilic community. He contributed to its passion for separation from the unclean, its strong legalism, and its growing apocalypticism (see below). On most of the New Testament Ezekiel has left little impression, but the visions of the Revelation to John owe much to him, as does the figure of the good shepherd in the Gospel of John (Ezek. 34; John 10:1-30).

35. Daniel

The stories of the book of Daniel are beloved wherever the Bible is known. They are great stories, full of adventure, suspense, pageantry, and emotion.

Few, however, understand their purpose and meaning in the book to which they belong. This is because they are lifted out of their context. Actually, they bear the same relation to the book as illustrations to sermons. The author meant them to be seen in relation to great truths which the book as a whole expounds.

The stories comprise chaps. 1–6. Chaps. 7–12 report the visions of Daniel. Though perplexing in some ways, the stories are on the whole fairly easy to grasp. But to understand their purpose requires penetrating the mysteries of the visions. This is difficult for many people.

1. Literary Type

Daniel and the Revelation to John belong to a type of literature called "apocalyptic." This literature became fashionable among Jews between about 200 B.C. and A.D. 100. Christians adopted and developed it. (For its characteristics see chap. 91.)

The word "apocalypse" means "unveiling," "disclosure," "revelation." The claim is made in the apocalypses that God has revealed to a particular prophet his purpose to overthrow the enemies of his people and give freedom, prosperity, world sovereignty, and religious leadership to them. God's secret plan for accomplishing this result is revealed as well. The enemies are referred to only through symbols (the oppressor Antiochus IV is "a little horn"—Dan. 8:9).

The message of apocalypses is: Wait patiently and in faith for God's plan to be accomplished; do not worship the oppressor's gods or accept his pagan way of life; obey God's law as revealed to the fathers; do acts of righteousness; at the last you will be on the winning side; God's program for the future is being accomplished and is on schedule.

2. Contents

The subject matter of the book of Daniel falls into two parts:
I. The deeds of Daniel and his companions (chaps. 1–6)
II. The visions of Daniel (chaps. 7–12)

In Part I the author portrays Daniel as a true Jew, loyal to God under the pressures of life in a foreign land (Babylon). His God-given ability in the interpretation of dreams brings him to a high position at court.

In Part II there are four visions. They reveal to Daniel what will come to pass before the enemies of Israel are defeated and the kingdom of God, with Israel ruling the nations, comes. Here Daniel, the interpreter of the visions of others (chaps. 1–6), has trouble understanding his own, so confusing is their content and so remote

their fulfillment. The angel Gabriel helps him discern in part their meaning concerning God's plan for the consummation of history (8:15-19), but their full import still lies beyond his grasp (8:27).

Part II outlines the succession of four empires which will dominate the world until the coming of God's kingdom. They seem to be the Babylonian, Median, Persian, and Greek empires. The amount of detail offered about the last of these is impressive (chap. 11). The history of this empire (apparently presented here as unfulfilled prophecy) is traced to the time of Antiochus IV (175–163 B.C.), who defiled the temple in Jerusalem and whose paganizing activities brought on the Maccabean rebellion and the suffering and death of Jews loyal to God (11:21-39). Antiochus' death is predicted (11:45) and the kingdom of God is promised soon, after the resurrection of many of the

The Ishtar Gate (reconstructed) in the walls of Babylon at the time of King Nebuchadnezzar (6th century B.C.)

dead (12:2). Daniel is directed to seal up the prophecy until the time of its fulfillment draws near (12:4, 9).

For some unknown reason, parts of the book are in Hebrew (1:1–2:4a and chaps. 8–12), and a considerable portion is in Aramaic (2:4b–7:28).

3. Author and Date

Chaps. 8–12, written in the first person, seem clearly to attribute the writing of the book to Daniel. The author places him in Babylon during the reigns of Nebuchadnezzar, Belshazzar, Darius, and Cyrus. According to 1:1, Nebuchadnezzar took him from Jerusalem to Babylon in 606 (or 605) B.C.

Modern scholarship as a whole, in spite of some dissent (see Additional Note, below), questions the authorship of the book by a sixth-century person and concludes that it was written around 165 B.C. by an unknown author *about*, rather than *by*, an ancient Daniel. Some of the reasons for this conclusion are:

a. The writer's knowledge of the third and second centuries B.C. seems considerably fuller and more accurate than of the sixth century.

The stories about events in the sixth century (chaps. 1–6) may belong to a literary type known as *haggadah* (popular stories told to set forth religious or moral truths). Such stories were not meant as exact history, though they sometimes were based on historical facts.

A story of this kind may be that of the three young men who refused to worship Nebuchadnezzar's image and came out of the super-heated fiery furnace without even their hair singed (chap. 3). The historical fact is that Jews in Babylon and in Palestine repeatedly underwent pressure to conform to pagan religious practices and social customs. The teaching is that no real harm can come to those who refuse, because God is on their side. He will support them, refine them by their suffering and death, and ultimately give them life in the coming age (11:33-35; 12:1-3).

The narratives of chaps. 1–6, if haggadic, were written not by someone contemporary with the events described but by an author who looked back through the centuries with the eyes of a preacher and teacher. The stories he used may have had a long period of popular use and retelling. Scholars have pointed out various historical inaccuracies in them (such as the attributing to Nebuchadnezzar of a mental illness actually experienced by Nabonidus [chap. 4] and the wrong sequence of foreign kings given in 6:28 and 9:1).

Dan. 11:2-39, on the contrary, contains an astonishingly detailed and accurate chronicle of events during the Greek period down to the Seleucid king Antiochus IV (175–163 B.C.). The last events mentioned seem to be the profanation of the Jerusalem temple by this impious ruler and the rebellion it evoked (11:31-35), events of 167–164 B.C.

b. The Hebrew and Aramaic of the book are of late, rather than of sixth-century, type; and some Persian and Greek words point to a late date.

c. The book appears in the latest

section of the Hebrew canon (the Writings), not in the earlier division called the Prophets. It apparently was unknown to the writer of Ecclesiasticus (The Wisdom of Jesus the Son of Sirach), about 200–180 B.C.

d. The religious concepts (angelology, resurrection of the dead, etc.) and the literary form (apocalypse) fit better in the second than in the sixth century B.C.

e. The figure of Daniel in the book appears to be drawn in part against the backdrop of traditions about a very ancient Daniel (or Dan'el), referred to in Ezek. 14:14, 20, along with Noah and Job. This Dan'el appears as a just and merciful king in the Canaanite Ras Shamra tablets of the fourteenth century B.C. Daniel stories had long been told in the Middle East. Our author apparently gathered together some of these in the second century and added to them visions of his own.

In the light of the above data, the date of the writing of the book would be between 167 and 164 B.C.

4. Historical Situation and Message

Antiochus IV ("Epiphanes," *i.e.,* "the god manifest"), king of Syria-Palestine, aided by Greek-influenced Palestinian Jews, sought to unite his territories with the cohesive force of Greek religion and culture, including the worship of himself as the visible manifestation of Zeus. He built an altar to Zeus on the altar of burnt offering in the Jerusalem temple. He forbade the offering of sacrifices to Yahweh, the circumcision of children,

and the observance of the Sabbath and dietary laws; and he ordered all copies of the Jewish scriptures destroyed. He raided the temple treasury to get money for his administrative and military operations. (See the discussion of I and II Maccabees, chaps. 62–63.)

His policies brought on bitter opposition by Jews loyal to their ancestral religion, including the writer of the book of Daniel. This writer undertook in this crisis to encourage his fellow Jews to resist Antiochus' demands and to remain faithful to the laws of God. He showed how Daniel and his three friends were exposed to similar pressure during the Exile but refused to give in, and how God protected them and made them prosper. He predicted the speedy overthrow of Antiochus and the coming of the kingdom of God about three and one-half years after the defiling of the temple (7:25; 8:14; 12:7, 11, 12). In this kingdom the faithful would be rewarded for their loyalty.

The central truths of the book, both in the stories and in the visions, are the following:

a. There is one God in the universe, to whom all people owe allegiance. Though they are asked to bow down to false gods, the truly wise will stoutly refuse.

b. This God revealed his holy and righteous will in his laws. Loyalty to these laws will pay in the end.

c. Rulers govern by divine sufferance and are held responsible for the way they rule. When they flout God's laws, he removes them from their thrones.

d. This God is the Lord of history,

whose will for human society is being carried out, in spite of indications to the contrary. He makes even the deeds of dictators advance his holy purposes.

e. It is his plan to sweep evil and evildoers aside and to give his faithful servants a kingdom of righteousness.

f. This kingdom is God's gift, not man's achievement. The stone was cut out without hands (2:31-45). But the saints have their part to play. They are to be loyal in life, outspoken in witness, and heroic in active deed.

g. Suffering, patiently and loyally borne, can result in purification of life.

h. The righteous dead have not died in vain. They will participate in God's ultimate triumph over the forces of evil.

5. Contemporary Significance

As we have seen, the book of Daniel was written to give hope to Jews in a bitter crisis of the second century B.C. by holding out to them the promise of God's deliverance and the gift of his kingdom. The writer apparently believed this kingdom would come in about three and one-half years. In this prediction events proved him wrong, as events always do to those who set dates. Jesus refused to set dates for the coming of the kingdom (Mark 13:32; cf. Acts 1:7). He preferred to leave this matter in the Father's hands.

Those who make Daniel into a divinely revealed blueprint of events in *our* time and seek to determine from it where we stand on God's time clock ignore the original purpose of this book and make God's business their business. But to share the faith of the writer as stated in the central truths above is the highest wisdom.

Additional Note

Most conservative scholars argue that the book of Daniel is a literary unit and that it was written in its entirety in the sixth century B.C. by the Jewish statesman whose name it bears. One such scholar of our time, however, allows for the possibility of compilation by someone else, not later than the middle of the fifth century B.C.

All claim that chaps. 1–6 are fully accurate historically. They believe also that the predictions of the future contained in the visions are authentic, divinely inspired predictions, not history disguised as prophecy.

They interpret the four kingdoms of the book as the Babylonian, the Medo-Persian, the Greek, and the Roman (rather than the Babylonian, Median, Persian, and Greek), on the ground that Darius the Mede (5:31; 6:1 ff.) was thought of by the author not as an independent monarch but as the Median governor of Babylon under appointment of King Cyrus, the Persian.

Such a construction of the succession of kingdoms avoids the conclusion that the author's prediction concerning the nearness of the end of the age and the coming of the kingdom of God (three and one-half years from the defiling of the temple by Antiochus IV) failed to come to pass. This construction allows for the contention that we are still in the Roman period and that the prophecies concerning the end will yet be literally fulfilled.

By interpreting the fourth kingdom as Rome it is possible, by a certain way of reading Dan. 9:25-26, to find a reference to the coming of Jesus, his crucifixion, and the destruction of Jerusalem by the Romans. Those who take the fourth kingdom to be Greece identify the "anointed one, a prince" (vs. 25) with Cyrus, Zerubbabel, or the priest Joshua (Hag. 1:1) and the "anointed one" who is "cut off" (vs. 26) with the high priest Onias III, who was deposed about 175 B.C. and subsequently murdered.

Conservative interpreters see Antiochus IV of the third (Greek) empire as typifying the Antichrist, who is to come after the fourth (Roman) empire, and find the Antichrist's work sketched in 11:40-45.

It is evident that strong differences in the interpretation of the book of Daniel and in the understanding of its meaning for us today exist among scholars of different theological positions.

36. Hosea

In the Hebrew Bible Hosea stands first in the collection of shorter prophetic books known as "The Twelve." This collection is now generally called "The Minor Prophets" (see chap. 30).

The order of these Twelve is not strictly chronological. Amos, for example, was earlier than Hosea. But those who put the Hebrew Bible together apparently attempted a rough chronological grouping. Hosea, Joel, Amos, Obadiah, Jonah, and Micah were believed to belong to the period of the height of Assyrian power over Israel and Judah (second half of the eighth century B.C.). Nahum, Habakkuk, and Zephaniah were thought to belong to the period of the end of Assyrian power (the last third of the seventh century). Haggai, Zechariah, and Malachi were recognized as belonging to the Persian period (sixth through fifth centuries). It is possible that Hosea was put first in the first group because it is the longest book of that group.

1. Life and Times of Hosea

Hosea carried out his ministry in the Northern Kingdom during the closing days of the reign of Jeroboam II (786–746) and for some time after that king's death, possibly as late as 725. Though some of his words reflect knowledge of conditions in the Southern Kingdom (5:8–6:6), he directed his message toward the situation in the north.

He lived in a turbulent age. Jeroboam II expanded the borders of Israel and brought great prosperity to his kingdom, at least to the upper classes. The rich, however, oppressed the poor.

The poor, robbed and dispossessed, could get no justice in the courts. Religious decay had set in. Though king and people worshiped Yahweh in great shrines, pagan fertility rites glorifying Baal had a place in these shrines and also flourished independently (Hos. 1–3; 4:6-14). Professional prophets fell in with the spirit of the times and offered no rebuke in the name of Yahweh and the Mosaic tradition.

The death of Jeroboam brought the Northern Kingdom to a virtual state of anarchy. Five kings reigned in a period of ten years. Several of them died at the hands of illegitimate pretenders. Assyria, under the powerful Tiglath-Pileser III (745–727), took advantage of the anarchic situation, extended its authority over the Northern Kingdom, and exacted heavy tribute. Soon an anti-Assyrian coalition, involving usurper Pekah of the Northern Kingdom and King Rezin of Damascus, sought to force King Ahaz of Judah into the coalition. Tiglath-Pileser forthwith destroyed the coalition and brought the west to its knees.

A final attempt at rebellion against Assyria was made by King Hoshea (732–724) of the Northern Kingdom, who hoped in vain for help from Egypt. Tiglath-Pileser's successors, Shalmaneser V and Sargon II, after a two-year siege of the capital city of Samaria, brought an end to the Northern Kingdom and deported 27,290 of its citizens to upper Mesopotamia and Media (721 B.C.).

Hosea apparently died shortly before the fall of the Northern Kingdom.

Little is known of Hosea's personal life. We learn only that his father's name was Beeri (1:1) and that his relationship with his wife, Gomer, was to him a symbol of Yahweh's relationship with Israel. It is evident from the high quality of his prophetic utterances that he was an educated man.

2. The Book

The contents fall into two unequal divisions:
  I. Hosea's marital experience and its meaning (chaps. 1–3)
  II. Hosea's prophetic utterances (chaps. 4–14)

The second division contains threats against corrupt priests, idolatrous and immoral people, and the royal family, together with some promises of restoration after repentance, when God's judgments are over.

The content of chaps. 4–14 consists of small collections of material arranged according to catchwords (i.e., material drawn together by the presence of identical words in disconnected pieces) and according to similarity of subject matter.

A Judean editor probably compiled the book from separate pieces carried to Judah sometime after the fall of the Northern Kingdom (721). It received its final form in the exilic or early postexilic period.

Conservative scholars, however, argue that the book was substantially completed within the lifetime of the prophet himself.

3. Hosea's Marriage

The book seems to present the prophet's personal marital experience as a parable of God's relationship with Israel.

Unfortunately, the details of Hosea's domestic life, as alluded to in chaps. 1 and 3, are far from clear. Different reconstructions are possible.

a. Hosea married *one* woman, Gomer, who either was a prostitute (probably attached to a Baal temple) when he married her or became a prostitute after he married her. He had children by her to whom he gave symbolic names as a means of conveying his message about the coming judgment of the nation by God (1: 4-8). She later left his home, perhaps through divorce, became the property of another, and was finally bought back by Hosea and restored to his home.

b. Hosea married *two* women: the first was the bride of his youth, Gomer, who either was at that time, or later became, a prostitute. Hosea divorced her as a symbol of Yahweh's coming repudiation of Israel. He later bought an unnamed prostitute, married her, and took her into his home, as a symbol of God's coming mercy on unworthy Israel.

Some interpreters have taken chaps. 1 and 3 allegorically—not as reports of a real marriage but only as a literary device by which to convey the message of God's judgment and love. Others have held that a dream or a vision lies behind the stories.

It is best to understand the chapters realistically, as actual events of the prophet's life.

The real problem is whether Hosea's message of God's judgment and love arose from his personal tragic marital experience or whether his message was prior to and led to his marriage (or marriages) as a way of dramatizing that message for his hearers. The prophets often engaged in deeds that symbolized their teaching (Isa. 20; Jer. 19).

We may conclude this much, at least: that Hosea had an unfortunate marriage, whatever its exact nature; that he saw a parallel between it and God's relation with Israel; and that by his actions in the marital relationship he sought to declare both God's judgment and his mercy on the nation.

4. Hosea's Message

Hosea describes the connection between God and Israel as a marriage relation (1:2; 2:16) or as a father-son relationship (11:1). The bond between God and his people began with the exodus from Egypt (12:9; 13:4) and issued from God's love (11:1). God delighted in his people at first (9:10), but shortly they turned to other gods (11:2; 13:5-6). Their history was one of rebellion (9:9; 10:9).

Baal worship had perverted their national and personal life. They had come to believe that the Baals, not Yahweh, were responsible for the fertility of flocks and fields and must therefore be worshiped (2:5-8; 4:13). They engaged in sacred prostitution as practiced in the Baal cult (4:13-14).

The political and religious leaders were an affront to God. The priests and prophets were corrupt and blind (4:4-9). Political leaders grabbed for the throne through assassination (4:2), law and order collapsed (7:1), security was sought through foreign alliances instead of through trust in God (5:13; 7:11).

The nation was heading toward destruction at the hands of Assyria. Yahweh will turn the nation over to the disaster of exile and new bondage (8:13; 9:3).

But God's love will reach beyond punishment to a new beginning. Cast off, repentant Israel will be restored to its bountiful home (14:4-8) and to the protection and perpetual fellowship of its merciful God (2:14-23).

5. Influence

Hosea's influence on Jeremiah, Jesus, and the early church was profound.

Jeremiah also represented Yahweh as a spurned lover who persistently pursued his beloved with a view to restoring her to exclusive relationship (Jer. 2:1–4:4).

Jesus' compassion for the outcasts

Photo by H. T. Frank
Sacred pillar in the fortress temple of Baal-berith at Shechem, possibly the "great stone" referred to in Josh. 24:26

(the irreligious, the harlots, and the tax collectors) reflects the attitude of Hosea that God desires steadfast love and not sacrifices (Hos. 6:6; Matt. 9:13; 12:7).

The early church saw God's magnificent love manifested in the adoption of an unworthy people (the Gentiles) as his own (I Pet. 2:10; Hos. 2:23).

37. Joel

Joel (probably meaning, "Yahweh is God") is a short but powerful book. The man behind it apparently was a priest-prophet, about whom we are told nothing other than that he was "the son of Pethuel" (1:1). He was the bearer of "the word of Yahweh" (1:1) in a national crisis in his generation, a word that has echoes in the New Testament and meaning for our time.

1. The Occasion and Date of the Prophecy

Joel 1:2–2:27 describes in vivid symbolic language a horrible plague of locusts and a severe drought that have impoverished the land and reduced its inhabitants to despair and mourning. So severe is the famine that the offerings of food and drink for temple worship are no longer possible (1:9, 13).

It is the prophet's role to interpret for the sufferers the meaning of this tragic experience.

We cannot be certain when it took place. Plagues of locusts, droughts, and resulting famines have occurred regularly in Palestine. There is no nonbiblical or other biblical evidence

for a great disaster such as the book of Joel describes.

But some general indications are at hand. The language and religious ideas, especially concerning the future, belong to a late date, almost certainly postexilic. Joel seems to be acquainted with several prophetic writings—Isaiah, Jeremiah, Ezekiel, Obadiah, Zephaniah, Malachi—whose ideas and words he echoes. The political and religious situation in Jerusalem fits the postexilic period: no king, but elders and priests as leaders; religious life centering in the temple, especially in the daily offerings; the dispersal of the inhabitants of Judah and Jerusalem among the nations; and Jews having been sold as slaves to Greeks. The best date is perhaps 400–350 B.C.

A few scholars have argued for a preexilic date, in the time of Jeremiah (late seventh century) or even in the late ninth century, but on grounds generally regarded as inadequate.

Some have claimed that the book does not describe an actual plague and drought but predicts these for the future in connection with the coming day of the Lord (i.e., the day of judgment). However, the graphic, realistic description, plus the call for a day of repentance by the whole nation (1:14; 2:12-17), and the prophet's interpretation of the meaning of the catastrophe (the locusts are the Lord's army for the judgment of his people—2:11, 25) all convince the reader that a real event is being described.

2. Contents and Unity

The book falls into two parts:
I. The disaster (locusts and drought) and the national religious response (lamentation, repentance, prayer, hearing of God's promise) (1:2–2:27)
II. God's gift of his Spirit, his final judgment of the nations, and the triumph and glorification of Jerusalem (2:28–3:21)

In English Bibles Joel is divided into three chapters. The Hebrew Bible has four chapters, the third chapter beginning at our 2:28 and the fourth at our 3:1.

Some students of the book have argued that the two parts come from two authors. They see stylistic and thought differences between the parts, especially the apocalyptic character (see chap. 91) of the second part. However, the view is gaining ground that the whole book stems from the mind of one prophet, each of the parts and perhaps even sections of them having originated at different times in his life.

3. Message

Joel's horror that temple sacrifice has ceased, his high regard for the priests as "the ministers of the Lord" (1:9, 13; 2:17) and "ministers of the altar" (1:13), his veneration of the temple as "the house of the Lord" and place of "solemn assembly" (1:14), and his passion for Jerusalem, the holy city and dwelling-place of God (3:17-18) make it probable that he was a priest whom God's word turned into a prophet.

This word came to him at the time of a great locust plague and drought. Joel saw them as a judgment of God on his sinful people. The locusts are the army of the Lord, he said (2:11, 25). Deliverance can come only by true repentance (returning to the Lord and trusting in his gracious forgiveness and goodness—2:12-14), carried out in solemn national assembly in the temple.

It seems that Joel saw the locust plague as the beginning of the woes that were to introduce God's final age. By punishment Israel would return to God. God would pour out his Spirit on his renewed people (2:28-29), make them mighty warriors able to conquer the nations (3:9-12), and exalt Judah and Jerusalem to world leadership (3:16-21). The "day of the Lord" (1:15; 2:11, 31; 3:14), as the time of judgment and salvation, is the keynote of Joel's prophecy.

4. Significance

Joel was a man of his times and of all times.

His view that natural disasters are God's punishments for men's sins must be qualified. That they are opportunities for repentance and renewal cannot be denied.

His concept of the people of God as mighty warriors who "beat [their] plowshares into swords, and [their] pruning hooks into spears" (3:10)— a strange reversal of Isa. 2:4 and Mic. 4:3—and slay the nations round about reminds us of the Zealot movement during Jesus' time (see p. 409).

His vision of the New Age as the time of pouring out of God's Spirit on all flesh and of the worship of God by a renewed people in Jerusalem

had its impact on the New Testament. Peter quoted the passage about the Spirit on the day of Pentecost (Acts 2:16-21), and the idea of the New Jerusalem underlies the Revelation to John.

For Joel, salvation seems to be limited to Jews ("all flesh" for him is not "all nations" but all classes or groups of Jews), whereas in some Old Testament passages and in the New Testament salvation is open to all nations (see chaps. 40, 75).

38. Amos

One of the mightiest preachers of Israel was the shepherd-herdsman and caretaker of sycamore trees, Amos of Tekoa in the Southern Kingdom.

He was not a prophet or a prophet's son (7:14); that is, he was not a professional prophet attached to the court and temple at Jerusalem. He was a skilled, middle-class laborer, whom God called to be a prophet (7:15).

His prophetic ministry, so far as we know, was short and apparently limited to the Northern Kingdom. This was not his home country. He regarded Israel as one people and felt himself called to deliver God's message in the especially needy north.

1. The Historical Situation

The superscription of the book (1:1) dates Amos' prophetic activity to the reigns of Uzziah (Azariah) of

Judah (783–742) and Jeroboam (II) of Israel (786–746). The mention of the earthquake here does not help in precise dating, for it is undatable. The general prosperity of the times, as indicated in the book, points to a late period in these reigns, perhaps to 760–750.

Both kings defeated their enemies, expanded their borders, achieved internal stability, and engaged in extensive commerce. (On the times see pp. 167-68.) We learn from Amos that the upper class "built houses of hewn stone" and "planted pleasant vineyards" (5:11). They lolled on "beds of ivory" (6:4), feasted, drank wine, and anointed themselves with costly oils (6:4-6). Base women of Samaria debauched themselves and their husbands (4:1). Merchants could scarcely wait for the Sabbath and the days of the new moon to end, so eager were they to be on with their moneymaking (8:4-5). But in the midst of prosperity there was poverty. The wealthy grew richer by exploiting the poor through sharp lending practices (2: 8a), fines (2:8b), and bribing judges in court (2:6-7a; 5:7, 12; 6:12).

We learn that there was a royal sanctuary at Bethel, presided over by a priest named Amaziah, who considered it his duty to protect Jeroboam's interests (7:10-13). There were also sanctuaries at Gilgal (4:4; 5:5) and Dan (8:14). We do not know whether Amos visited these as well as Bethel.

The worship of Yahweh at the sanctuaries consisted of daily ceremonies in which various types of sacrifices and offerings were presented (4:4-5) and of occasional great festal gatherings. At the latter, "fatted beasts" were offered (5:22), and singing, eating, drinking, and even sexual intercourse were indulged in (5:23; 2:7-8). There was also out-and-out idolatry in the worship of Assyrian gods (5:26).

Around opulent, decadent Israel were corrupt neighbors who had little regard for basic human rights: Damascus, Gaza, Tyre, Edom, Ammon, Moab (1:3–2:3). And farther away were predatory Assyria and Egypt, waiting to plunder the palaces of Israel (3:9-11).

2. Contents and Growth of the Book

I. Title and theme (1:1-2)
II. The coming doom of surrounding nations and of Judah and Israel (1:3–2:16)
III. The sins of Israel and the coming destruction (3:1–6: 14)
IV. The prophet's visions and the messages derived from them (7:1–9:15).

In the fourth section a piece concerning Amos' encounter with Amaziah appears (7:10-17), apparently because of the mention of Jeroboam in 7:9.

It is likely that Amos himself wrote much of the present book, probably by dictation to a scribe. The first-person account of his message and visions (5:1; 7:1-9; 8:1 ff.; 9:1 ff.) supports this conclusion.

Others seem to have contributed some of the material. For example, 7:10-17 is in the third person and interrupts the first-person reporting. Some scholars have assigned the oracles against Tyre (1:9-10), Edom (1: 11-12), and Judah (2:4-5) to a period later than Amos, as well as some hymnic pieces (4:13; 5:8-9; 9:5-6) and the conclusion of the book (9:8-15 or 11-15). It is probable that Amos' written materials were edited and added to by later hands, possibly as late as the early postexilic period.

3. Amos' Career and Message

How long Amos preached is unknown. After his call (7:14-15) he went to the Northern Kingdom, perhaps to the capital city, Samaria (3:9; 4:1; 6:1), possibly to the sanctuary at Gilgal (4:4; 5:5), and certainly to the state sanctuary at Bethel (7:10-17). At the latter place, perhaps at the time of an important festival, his pronounce-

Plowing in present-day Samaria is still done with oxen (cf. Amos 6:12)

ment of doom on the Northern Kingdom and its king, Jeroboam, led to an accusation of treason by the high priest, Amaziah. This priest banished Amos, apparently by command of Jeroboam. Amos then seems to have returned to Tekoa. Whether he had a further prophetic ministry in Judah is unknown, but it is unlikely. His career as a prophet may have lasted only two or three months.

That short ministry left a lasting impression on the nation and on the centuries since, so potent were the words of Amos.

His message may be summarized as follows:

a. The God of Israel is the Lord of the whole earth. Though he stands in a special relationship to Israel (3:2), his interest and activity are directed also toward the Ethiopians, Philistines, and Syrians. He gave homelands to them as well as to Israel (9:7). He holds not only the people of Israel accountable for their actions but also their enemies, for his jurisdiction extends over all nations (1:3–2:3).

b. He is a God of righteousness. There is nothing fickle, cruel, or unethical about him. God and the good are closely identified (5:4, 14). He is forever against nations and individuals who do wrong. His chief complaint against the people of Israel is that "they do not know how to do right" (3:10).

c. God's requirements are moral.

Elaborate sacrificial rites at the sanctuaries do not bring his favor (5:21-24). What he wants of men is unfailing justice in their relationships with one another (5:24; 2:6-7; 4:1; 8:4-6). Sin is not a failure to worship in the right way; it is a failure to do what is right in daily living.

d. God supports those who do right and punishes those who do evil. Those who seek the good (God) will live (5:4, 6, 14). The unrighteous will be destroyed (1:3–2:16; 5:16; 6:4-14; etc.). God has no favorites, and he makes no exceptions. Israel has no special claim on him and will fare no better than other nations that have violated fundamental principles of morality. The "day of the Lord" (the day when God judges), instead of bringing victory and vindication to Israel, will result in destruction and humiliation (5:18-20).

4. Amos' Significance

Amos marks the beginning of a new era in the history of religion. No prophet before him saw so clearly the universal sovereignty of Israel's God and his unwavering requirement of right conduct by all men, especially those standing in closest relationship to him (3:2). Special privilege involves special responsibility, said Amos.

The call to repent and do the will of God or perish was reaffirmed by the prophets after him and formed the cornerstone of the preaching of Jesus (Luke 13:3-9; Mark 1:15).

The view that "God shows no partiality, but in every nation any one who fears him and does what is right is acceptable to him" (Acts 10:34-35) could hardly have arisen without the work of Amos.

39. Obadiah

This is the shortest book in the Old Testament.

Nothing is known of Obadiah, whose name means simply "Servant of Yahweh," a name borne by nearly a dozen other Old Testament persons.

From the character of his prophecies it appears that he lived at the time of the fall of Jerusalem, in 587 B.C. Some precise details (vss. 11-14) and the heat of his wrath against the country of Edom for their part in that event indicate that he was an eyewitness of the fall and composed his oracles soon after it.

Evidence for the time of his ministry is inconclusive. Scholars have suggested dates ranging from the ninth century to the fifth century or later.

Edom's basic sin was unbrotherliness in a time of misfortune. It failed to help Judah against its enemies, gloated over a brother nation's misfortune, looted at the time of the destruction, and captured and delivered to the enemy fugitives from the stricken country. Obadiah regarded this as strange and reprehensible conduct from blood relatives (Esau, the father of the Edomites, was Jacob's [Israel's] twin—Gen. 25:30; 36:1).

Obadiah called down the wrath of God on such perfidy. Edom, which inhabited the high, rugged mountains to the southeast, would be brought down and annihilated (vss. 3-4, 10). As the Edomites had done, so would it be done to them (vs. 15). The coming "day of the Lord" (vs. 15) would redress the injustice. Edom and other wicked nations would pass away, Israel would be saved (vss. 16-18), and Israel's God would be sovereign over all the earth (vs. 21).

Obadiah sounds like a nationalistic prophet of narrow and vengeful spirit. There is no forgiveness of enemies in what he said. He had, however, a lively sense of justice and called on God to correct injustice in the great day of judgment.

It is possible that verses 19-21, which contemplate a return of dispersed Israelites and their conquest of Edom and other territories, were added to Obadiah's prophecies at some later time.

40. Jonah

One of the best known, but least understood, stories of the Old Testament is that of Jonah and the great fish (commonly called a whale).

The sheer magnitude of the miracle described here unfortunately has drawn attention away from the book as a whole. The average man is left with a wonder tale which he may feel forced to reject as impossible or which he may try to swallow after the example of the fish's alleged treatment of Jonah!

What is needed is an approach to the Jonah narrative that will put the episode about the fish into proper perspective.

1. Name and Place in the Canon

Jonah means "dove." The dove seems to have been a traditional symbol for Israel (Ps. 74:19; Hos. 11:11).

This fact leads immediately to some questions. Did the author intend the man Jonah to symbolize the Jewish nation as a whole in its disobedience to God, in its prejudice against Gentile nations, and in its misunderstanding of God's purpose and methods? And did the Jews misunderstand when they should have known better because of their highly privileged position as God's spokesmen—his prophet-people?

Though occupying a place among the Twelve Prophets, the book differs from the other, eleven in that it is a narrative about a prophet rather than a record of his prophetic utterances together with some biographical material. It is nearer to the stories about prophets in I and II Kings than to the prophetic books proper.

It found a place among the Twelve Prophets because of the identification in 1:1 of its central character with "Jonah the son of Amittai," an obscure eighth-century prophet mentioned in II Kings 14:25.

2. Contents

The book falls naturally into two parts:

I. Jonah's flight from the Lord and from his prophetic mission (chaps. 1–2)

II. Jonah's reluctant obedience to God and his subsequent education by God (chaps. 3–4)

Jonah's "No" to God brings him speedily to disaster. He finds he cannot run away from God without dire consequences for himself and others. His "Yes" to God, however reluctant, brings him to new knowledge of God and his purpose for the world.

3. Historical and Literary Character

Controversy has long raged about whether or not the incidents described in the book actually happened. Did the author intend to write a sober piece of history about the eighth-century prophet mentioned in II Kings, concerning whom he had special information, or did he wish to create an allegory or a parable meant to convey religious truth without regard to historical fact?

Those who argue for the historicity of the story do so on several grounds:

a. A Jonah, the son of Amittai, actually existed during the period when the Assyrians ruled from the capital city of Nineveh (II Kings 14: 25). Further biographical information

about his ministry might well have been preserved.

b. Jesus accepted as fact the experience of Jonah in the belly of the fish and the conversion of the Ninevites (Matt. 12:40-41).

c. Other prophets (Elijah and Elisha) were concerned with foreign peoples, and the lives of these prophets were characterized by miraculous experiences.

d. Rejection of the historicity of the Jonah narrative rests on skepticism and unbelief in the power of the living God.

Those who believe that the author intended the narrative to be an allegory or a parable and that it belongs to the category of instructional, not biographical, literature argue as follows:

a. The problem in the narrative is not miracle in general but these particular "miracles": the storm as God's judgment on Jonah for his flight to Tarshish; the identification of Jonah as the culprit by the casting of lots; the miraculous cessation of the storm after Jonah is tossed into the sea; the fish's swallowing Jonah and, after seventy-two hours, depositing him safely on shore; the repentance of the King of Nineveh and all the inhabitants of that city; a plant growing tall enough in a night to offer shade to Jonah, and its withering in the same length of time. God is indeed the God of nature, they say, but this particular collection of wonders is strange, to say the least.

b. Nineveh is represented as so large that it required three days to cross it (3:3). Excavations there have shown the city to be about three miles long and somewhat less than one and one-half miles wide.

c. Jesus, if he was truly God become man, was limited in knowledge as all human beings are (Mark 13: 32). Omniscience is no more possible for one who is truly man than is omnipresence. He used the story of Jonah in his preaching, but this does not necessarily validate its historicity.

d. Israel's teachers were skilled in the use of stories, with or without historical foundation, to drive home religious truth. Such stories are Jotham's fable (Judges 9:7-15), Nathan's parable of the ewe lamb (II Sam. 12: 1-4), and Jesus' parables of the good Samaritan (Luke 10:30-37) and the rich man and Lazarus (Luke 16:19-31).

e. Jonah seems to be a symbol of Israel as a whole: in being called by God for a mission to all peoples; in disobediently fleeing from God's presence and from that mission; in reluctant obedience after chastening; in prejudice against foreign nations and unwillingness to believe in the magnificent graciousness of God toward all peoples.

4. Authorship, Date, and Literary Unity

Those who hold that the story is historically true believe it was written by the eighth-century prophet Jonah, mentioned in II Kings 14:25, probably soon after his return from Nineveh (about 750 B.C.).

Those who take the story as a parable regard it as having been composed by a postexilic writer (perhaps in the fifth or fourth century) out of traditional story material, some of which may have gathered about the figure of the eighth-century prophet Jonah. They hold that the identity of the writer is unknown and that the psalm in 2:2-9, a song of thanksgiving for rescue, is inappropriate to its context. Jonah should have been praying for deliverance from the fish! The psalm may have been added to the story after it was first written.

Those believing in a postexilic date also point to 3:3 as evidence that Nineveh no longer existed at the time of writing (it fell in 612 B.C.), that much of the language of the book fits the fifth and fourth centuries rather than the eighth, and that the story as a whole is directed to the postexilic situation.

5. Historical Situation, Message, and Significance

The main teaching of the book is that God loves the Assyrians, all people, and even the animals. His attitude is quite different from the Jewish desire for the destruction of foreign nations. God earnestly seeks their repentance and continued life. His love and mercy are not for Israel alone.

Together with this is the teaching that although God's chosen instruments often try to run from their assigned mission, they cannot ultimately escape him and their appointed work. "The hound of heaven" follows them, disciplines them, educates them, until they are fit instruments for his service. The fish story is a symbolic illustration of God's sustaining, disciplining activity.

This message fits best the postexilic time in Judah, when strong nationalistic, exclusivist emphases were dominant, particularly under Ezra and Nehemiah. Jewish men were forced to divorce foreign wives, Jewish worship was closed to participation by foreigners, and blood purity was highly regarded. (See p. 405.) Some large-

hearted writer, through a story about the past, sought to broaden the outlook of his narrow-minded contemporaries by portraying God as he actually is and Jews as they ought to be.

Jesus' compassionate attitude toward despised peoples probably owed much to Jonah. The book has been a pillar in the structure of the modern missionary movement.

41. Micah

1. Name, Place, and Date

Micah is an abbreviated form of Micaiah and means "Who is like Yah(weh)?"

A number of Old Testament persons bore this name. The best known today is the eighth-century prophet from Moresheth-gath (1:1, 14) in the low hill country, some twenty miles southwest of Jerusalem.

This Micah, like Amos, was a man of the country who was appalled at the sins of the big cities—in Micah's case, Samaria and Jerusalem. He was sympathetic to the needs of the poor, oppressed farmers and shepherds among whom he grew up. His home in the low hills above the Philistine plain, across which the armies of antiquity marched, helped him become an observer of international affairs.

Mic. 1:1 places the prophet's ministry during the reigns of Jotham (742–735), Ahaz (735–715), and Hezekiah (715–687). In Jeremiah's time the elders of the land remem-

bered vividly Micah's prophecy of the destruction of Jerusalem and the temple and dated it to the reign of Hezekiah (Jer. 26:18).

Some utterances of Micah are clearly prior to the fall of Samaria in 721 (1:2-9), and some may reflect the Assyrian campaigns in Judah of 711 and 701. Most of his sayings are undatable.

Micah was a younger contemporary of Isaiah and seems to have been influenced by the older prophet (compare Mic. 1:10-15 with Isa. 10:27*b*-32, and Mic. 2:1-3 with Isa. 5:8-10).

Presumably Micah preached mostly in Jerusalem.

2. Contents

The book contains threats and promises in alternating blocks of material.

    I.   The coming destruction of Israel and Judah because of their sins (chaps. 1–3)

Photo by H. T. Frank
The Canaanite high place at Gezer with its sacred pillars

II. The ultimate triumph of the reassembled and renewed people of God under a ruler born in Bethlehem (chaps. 4–5)

III. God's controversy with Israel because of its ingratitude, ceremonialism, and unbrotherly attitudes and acts (6:1–7:7)

IV. The eventual exaltation of Israel by its loving, forgiving God (7:8-20)

As the above outline shows, the disaster-deliverance motif is present twice in the book.

3. Authenticity of the Materials

Most students of the book agree that 1:2–3:12 contains authentic words of Micah. There is substantial support for 6:1–7:7 as his also. These sections contain threat of disaster, for the most part.

Some scholars have assigned all the prophecies of hope to disciples of Micah and later editors.

However, there is a growing tendency today to accept some, at least, of the prophecies of hope as authentic. Conservative scholars, of course, staunchly defend them.

Some sections appear to be later than the prophet's time: 2:12-13; 4:8-14; 7:7-20, for example. They reflect later circumstances: Zion's going to Babylon (4:10); and the rebuilding of the walls, apparently of Jerusalem (7:11).

The famous passage 4:1-4 is present in Isa. 2:2-4. Whether Isaiah or Micah or some unknown prophet composed it cannot be determined. The prophecy of the ruler to be born in Bethlehem (5:2-4) is also of uncertain origin. The value of these passages does not depend on the identity of their author.

4. Historical Circumstances and Message

For a description of Micah's times, see the discussion of the books of Isaiah and Hosea (chaps. 31, 36).

Micah was disturbed by the oppression of brother by brother: of the poor by the rich (2:1-2, 8-9), of subjects by their rulers (3:1-3), of citizens by unjust judges (3:11), of customers by merchants (6:10-12). "Each hunts his brother with a net" (7:2), says Micah, and "a man's enemies are the men of his own house" (7:6). Injustice and social disruption reached even into families.

He was disturbed also by corrupt religious leaders and empty ceremonialism. Both priests and prophets were greedy for gain. They often aided and abetted the rich against the poor, while assuring the nation of God's presence and protection (3:11). Micah repudiated the claim that God's protection and help are assured to Israel regardless of its obedience to the laws of God. Rather, the city of Jerusalem and the holy temple will be destroyed because of Israel's sins (3:12). Multitudinous offerings—and even child sacrifice—will not win the favor of God (6:6-7). What God really wants is the practice of justice in human dealings, gracious loyalty to one another in the bonds of the covenant relationship, and an obedient life in relation to God (6:8).

Whether Micah looked beyond God's judgment of the nation to a new day when the dispersed peoples would be reassembled in a renewed Zion under a ruler from Bethlehem is disputed. It is likely that he did, for elements of this hope can be found in the thought of Amos, Hosea, and Isaiah before him. At least, those who followed Micah cherished this hope, for in the present book judgment is tempered by mercy and disaster turns into deliverance under the hand of God.

5. Significance

Micah's powerful preaching of God's coming judgment left its mark on later generations, even providing support for Jeremiah's unpalatable prediction concerning the destruction of the temple (Jer. 26:16-19).

According to Matt. 10:35-36, Micah's words concerning family divisions (7:6) were quoted by Jesus.

The great declaration concerning God's true requirements (Mic. 6:8), which link ethical responsibility toward fellowmen with genuine piety before God, anticipated the summary of the Law by Jesus (Mark 12:29-31).

The early church saw in Mic. 5:2 a prophecy of the birth of Jesus (Matt. 2:6).

42. Nahum

The book of Nahum, like the book of Obadiah, is a collection of prophecies directed against a foreign nation. Like Obadiah's verbal assault on Edom for its hostility toward Judah, Nahum's clipped, pregnant words pour venom on Assyria and rejoice in the prospect of its obliteration. Both books exude nationalistic fervor and are weak in the religious insights characteristic of the great Hebrew prophets.

1. Nahum and His Times

The superscription (1:1) tells us that Nahum came from Elkosh, a place of unknown location.

From references in the book, his career may be dated at some time between the capture of Thebes in Egypt by the Assyrians in 663 B.C. (referred to in 3:8-10) and the fall of Nineveh in 612 (the destruction of Nineveh is clearly still future in the prophecies themselves).

With the death in 627 of Asshurbanapal, the last great Assyrian king, the Assyrian empire began to disintegrate. In 626 the Babylonians decisively defeated the Assyrians and gained their independence. From this time on, it would be apparent to perceptive observers that Assyria's days were numbered. Nahum's utterance thus probably derives from the period 626–612 B.C.

2. Contents and Authenticity

I.   The title (1:1)
II. An alphabetic hymn on the coming of Yahweh to judge his enemies (1:2-10)
III. Miscellaneous utterances containing threats toward Assyria and promises toward Judah (1:11-15)
IV. Ode on the fall of Nineveh (2:1–3:19)

The disconnected character of the contents up to 2:1 is obvious to any thoughtful reader. Many scholars believe that a later editor added the alphabetic hymn at the beginning and interspersed utterances of Nahum (1:11, 14) with comments and addditions of his own or adapted from traditional liturgy (1:12, 13, 15). He also may have added 2:2.

The heart of Nahum's work is clearly 2:1–3:19 (except perhaps for 2:2).

3. Literary and Religious Value

We have in this book a magnificent ode over the coming downfall of a cruel oppressor of Israel. It contains some of the finest poetry of the Old Testament.

Many students of the book have seen in it marks of temple liturgy—perhaps a liturgy for a thanksgiving celebration at the New Year festival following the destruction of Nineveh. The congregation may have recited the alphabetical hymn. Prophets attached to the temple may have taken a prominent role in this liturgy. If this view is correct, Nahum's utterances were put to use in the worship of Judah and thus preserved. It is possible that Nahum himself was attached to the temple as a cult prophet.

Nahum was overpowered by a sense of Yahweh's lordship of the nations and history. He saw Yahweh as a God who measures even the mighty Assyria, finds it wanting, and decrees its doom. He viewed Nineveh as "a bloody city, all full of lies and booty" (3:1), a great harlot who had betrayed the nations through deceitful and treacherous dealings (3:4-15). Those who used the sword would perish by the sword (2:11-12; 3:15) was Nahum's prediction.

There is no call to repentance and to amendment of life in the book—themes characteristic of Israel's great prophets. The passages seemingly later than Nahum strike tender notes that

supply a needed balance in the picture of God (1:7, 12, 15; 2:2).

Nahum was a great poet, if not a great religious thinker. In his attitude toward Assyria his views are a far cry from the large-heartedness of the author of the book of Jonah!

43. Habakkuk

Habakkuk was the first prophet to raise in sharp form the problem of the suffering of righteous Israel at the hands of unrighteous foreigners. The problem arose from Israel's belief that God rewards the righteous and punishes the unrighteous. Habakkuk has been called "the skeptic among the prophets."

While the book begins in doubt, it ends in faith, showing that the prophet in his personal struggle at last found grounds for believing in the justice and goodness of God.

1. The Title and the Name of the Prophet

The title (1:1) calls the contents of the book "the oracle of God which Habakkuk the prophet saw." The Hebrew word translated "oracle" is literally "burden" and came to be a technical term for a message from God given to a prophet for deliverance.

"Which Habakkuk . . . saw," rather than "heard," suggests that the message came in a vision (2:2).

Habakkuk is not a Hebrew name. It probably comes from an Akkadian

word meaning "a garden plant." We know nothing about him except what we find in this book.

2. Contents and Literary Form

The book contains mainly a dialogue between the prophet and God. In this respect Habakkuk was like his contemporary Jeremiah, who often gave himself to entreaties and arguments before God.

An outline of the contents follows:
I. Questions addressed to God about foreign oppressors (1:2–2:4)
First complaint of the prophet: injustice prevails (1:2-4).
First word from God: the Chaldeans are the agents of God's justice (1:5-11).
Second complaint of the prophet: God's agent is greedy and merciless (1:12-17).
Second word from God: Wait in patience and fidelity for God's vindication of the righteous (2:1-4).
II. Woes pronounced against the foreign oppressors (2:5-20)
III. A prayer expressing confi-

dence in God's deliverance (3:
1-19)

It is clear that chap. 3 was used in the worship of the temple, for it contains liturgical notations (*Shigionoth*— meaning unknown; *Selah*—perhaps a pause for a musical interlude; and the note to the choirmaster at the end). Scholars disagree on the question of Habakkuk's authorship of this psalm.

Whether chaps. 1 and 2 were used in temple worship has not been settled. Some experts regard the contents of the book as a whole as a prophetical liturgy. They believe that Habakkuk was a temple prophet who had a vision in the temple and who communicated this vision in liturgical form. Others think the material of these chapters is hardly suited for liturgical use.

Some scholars think Habakkuk simply imitated liturgical style without expecting actual use of the material in formal worship.

3. Date and Historical Situation

There is fairly wide agreement today that Habakkuk was a preexilic prophet, a contemporary of Jeremiah, though some scholars put him during the Babylonian Exile or in the postexilic period.

Crucial is the identification of the wicked one (or ones) in 1:4. Since the Chaldeans (1:6) seem to be deliverers from the oppressions of the wicked one (or ones), it is possible that the latter are the Assyrians or perhaps the wicked Judean king, Jehoiakim.

If the Assyrians are meant, the date of the prophecy would fall between 626 B.C. (the rise of the Chaldeans under Nabopolassar) and the reforms of Josiah in 622, which officially threw off Assyrian control. If Jehoiakim (and perhaps his evil associates) is meant, the prophecy would fall about the time when Nebuchadnezzar extended Babylonian authority over Judah, over Jehoiakim its king, and over the west as a whole (605 B.C.).

Faith must have been sorely tried at the close of the seventh century B.C. The righteous Josiah's reign (640– 609), which had seen the end of Assyrian rule and had reformed national life after the pattern set down in Deuteronomy (II Kings 22–23), was followed by a dark period under Jehoiakim, in which old idolatrous practices revived and injustice flourished (Jer. 22:13-17). Assyrian rule was exchanged for Babylonian; both were cruel and financially demanding.

Where was Israel's God in all this? Why did he allow his people to suffer bitterly at the hands of unrighteous tyrants, both within and outside the nation? Was he too weak to help, or too indifferent to care, or was he in some mysterious way ordering events according to his good purpose? If the latter, what was this purpose?

4. Message

Habakkuk said that his answer came out of a vision after much agony of soul (1:2-4, 13; 2:1).

The vision revealed to him was that God is not too weak or too indifferent to set the situation right. God was in fact using the Chaldeans as agents of his justice to punish the oppressors of his righteous people. But the Chaldeans themselves, violent, rapacious, tyrannical, would fall under the same judgment of God. They did not see themselves as agents of God, but they trusted arrogantly in their own god and their own strength (1:7-11). When their work of chastisement was done, the peoples they oppressed would rise up and plunder them (2: 7-8). National destruction, as the end of a course of bloody iniquity, is the result of the working of God's will (2:13). The whole world will see God's glory in the judgment of the evil Chaldeans (2:14).

What does the oppressed righteous man do in the meantime? He waits patiently for God's appointed time of vindication (2:3). The righteous will survive through their fidelity to God (2:4).

The oppressed righteous, then, may rejoice in Yahweh's mighty vindication, which is sure to come. Yahweh is reigning in his holy temple; let all the earth stand in awe of him (2:20). His mighty acts in Israel's past are a guarantee of his mighty and merciful

acts in the future (3:3-15). So in the midst of disaster the righteous person can say, "I will rejoice in the Lord, I will joy in the God of my salvation" (3:17-18).

5. Abiding Significance

Habakkuk was avidly studied by the community living by the Dead Sea in the time of Jesus (the community that gave us the Dead Sea Scrolls [see pp. 399-403]). One of those scrolls is a commentary on Habakkuk, which points out that Habakkuk was prophesying events of the commentator's own time.

Paul found in Habakkuk a pillar passage for his message of salvation by faith. For Paul, "faith" was trust in and obedience to Jesus, the Messiah, as the way to righteousness before God, whereas for Habakkuk it was trust in and fidelity to God as the deliverer of the already righteous.

Habakkuk's trust in God, who vindicates the righteous and defeats the purposes of evil men, offers a word of comfort to all who suffer injustice and the even greater agony of its seeming meaninglessness.

44. Zephaniah

The theme of Zephaniah's prophecies—the coming of the day of the Lord, the time of God's judgment of the nations and his salvation of a remnant in Israel—echoes in part the preaching of Amos and Isaiah.

Zephaniah (meaning "Yahweh protects"), according to the title of the book, was a descendant of Hezekiah, possibly King Hezekiah (715–687 B.C.). If the king was not meant, it seems there would have been little reason to carry the genealogy back four generations (1:1).

1. The Man and His Message

If Zephaniah was of royal blood, he was a relative of King Josiah (640–609 B.C.).

His prophecies, unlike Amos', show no particular concern for the socially depressed classes, but criticize the national life from the top: the court officials (1:8), the judges, the cult prophets, the priests (3:3-4), the idolatrous practices officially tolerated (1:4-6), the foreign customs and dress adopted by wealthy persons (1:8), the prosperous and religiously indifferent Jerusalemite householders (1:12-13), the proud boasters of the holy city (3:11).

He apparently belonged to the same devout religious circle that nourished Josiah in his youth and that repudiated, under the leadership of Josiah, the evil political and religious policies

Courtesy of the Oriental Institute, The University of Chicago

Two eunuchs leading a procession; relief from the Palace of Sargon II at Khorsabad (8th century B.C.)

of Manasseh (687–642) and Amon (642–640).

We can fairly well determine the date of Zephaniah's prophetic activity. He prophesied before Josiah's reformation began in 622 B.C. (II Kings 22–23), for he rebuked the practices Josiah eliminated (Zeph. 1:4-6). Zephaniah may have meant the Scythians when he referred to an enemy from the north as the coming destroyer of Jerusalem (1:10-13). According to the Greek historian Herodotus, the Scythians swept through Palestine around 625 B.C. Whether or not the Scythian invasion was in Zephaniah's mind, he fits nicely into the early years of the reign of Josiah, that is, about 630–625 B.C.

2. The Book

The book falls into the following parts:

    I.   The significance of the day of Yahweh for the world and for Judah (1:2–2:3)

    II.   Its significance for foreign nations (2:4-15)

    III.   Its significance for Jerusalem (3:1-8)

    IV.   Its significance for the righteous remnant (3:9-20)

Some sections of the book may come from writers later than Zephaniah, particularly parts of chaps. 2 and 3.

Conservative scholars hold to Zephaniah's authorship of the whole.

3. Theology and Influence

No prophet depicted more awesomely the terrors of God's coming "day of wrath" (*e.g.*, 1:15, 18) for the wicked in Judah and outside. On the other hand, he stressed God's magnificent mercy on the righteous remnant. The thought moves between doom on the entire world and its human and animal inhabitants, and the delights of salvation in a renewed world for those who escape the doom.

The righteous remnant is promised one language for the common worship of Yahweh (3:9). Thus the curse of Babel (Gen. 11:1-9) will be removed. The remnant will be humble, morally pure, and secure (3:12-13). Yahweh will reign over them in a community characterized by joy and singing (3: 14-18).

The doctrines of the day of Yahweh and of the righteous remnant to whom God would give his kingdom, taught by several of the great prophets, appear to have influenced the mind of Jesus.

No prophet said more potently than Zephaniah that God expects to deal decisively with evil men in this world and that the righteous are on the winning side.

45. Haggai

Haggai and Zechariah opened the third period in Hebrew prophecy. Before the Exile the prophets warned about the coming punishment of Israel and the nations. During the Exile they sought to comfort God's people and prepare them for a new future in their homeland. After the Exile they attempted to stimulate the rebuilding of the religious and political life of the restored community according to the Law of God.

The prophetic word was always shaped by the historical situation; it was therefore never static or stereotyped.

1. Name, Date, and Historical Situation

Haggai means "festal" or perhaps "born on the feast day." His ancestry is given neither in the book that bears his name nor in two references to him in Ezra (5:1; 6:14).

He may have seen the temple of Solomon before its destruction in 587 B.C. (Hag. 2:3). He may have served as a prophet to the Judean exiles in Babylonia and returned with Zerubbabel (Ezra 2:2). If so, he was an old man when he began the prophetic work reported in the book of Haggai. But there is no certainty here.

His prophecies fall within a four-month period (August to December) of the second year of Darius I (520 B.C.).

Some of the exiles had been back in Palestine since soon after Cyrus' edict of 538. Under the terms of this edict Sheshbazzar, a prince of Judah, and a small company of enthusiastic Jews had attempted to rebuild community life there (Ezra 1:5 ff.).

Whether Sheshbazzar began the

work of rebuilding the temple (Ezra 5:16) or whether this was first undertaken in 520 under Zerubbabel (Ezra 3:6-11; Zech. 4:9) is not clear. If Sheshbazzar made a beginning, the work did not proceed far.

Haggai, in 520, rebuked his hearers for preoccupation with building their own houses and neglect of a house for Yahweh (1:4, 9). Dismal economic conditions due to the devastated condition of the country, drought, the hostility of neighbors, and the like made sheer survival the central concern and prevented work on the temple.

Haggai's prophetic mission was to stimulate the beginning (or resumption) of temple reconstruction and to keep enthusiasm and activity alive until it was completed. He was assisted in this by Zechariah.

2. Contents and Compilation

The book consists of four dated utterances of Haggai:

I. Yahweh's command to the governor, the high priest, and the people to begin rebuilding the temple, and their response (1:1-15) (August–September, 520 B.C.)

II. Yahweh's word of encouragement to the builders concerning the future glory of the temple (2:1-9) (October, 520)

III. Yahweh's clarification about certain "unclean" matters affecting the life and future of the people (2:10-19) (December, 520)

IV. Yahweh's promise concerning Zerubbabel's coming role as messianic king (2:20-23) (December, 520)

Some scholars think the text is out of proper order in a few places. The most important suggested rearrangement is to place 2:15-19 after 1:15a and change "ninth" to "sixth" in 2:18.

The book obviously was put together by someone other than Haggai, who collected his utterances, prefaced them with introductions containing dates, and added a narrative portion (1:12-14). The editor may have lived quite close in time to Haggai.

3. Message and Abiding Value

Haggai's message was centered in the importance of the temple and its liturgy for the life of the community. He lamented the materialistic, self-centered attitude of the returned exiles, who put "paneled houses" above the house of God in their scale of values. He attributed the misfortunes that had befallen the people since their return to their neglect of the proper worship of God in a proper temple.

He said that if they would put God first by rebuilding the temple, their condition would change. In fact the glories of the Messianic Age would be theirs. God would judge the nations and bring their treasures into the temple, making it more splendid than the temple of Solomon (2:6-9). Zerubbabel, the governor (who was of Davidic descent), would be installed by God as messianic king to rule the nations (2:21-23).

When the people lost their enthusiasm because the new structure was not as splendid as the temple of Solomon, Haggai encouraged them with promises concerning its future glorification by God. When the deep and pervasive uncleanness of the people became apparent, and it seemed that this might frustrate their future under God, Haggai reaffirmed the certainty of that future. The past cannot defeat God's future, he said: "From this day on I will bless you" (2:19). Put God first, and things will come out beyond your fondest dreams, in spite of the failures of the past!

Haggai's criticisms of materialism and self-centeredness and his emphasis on God-centeredness are applicable to people of every age. However, his promise of material prosperity for those who put God first helped to raise questions about the undeserved suffering of the righteous, such as are dealt with in the book of Job. Israel by Haggai's time had not thought its way very deeply into this problem (see chaps. 25, 43).

46. Zechariah

1. Name, Identity, Date

Zechariah means "Yahweh has remembered."

Zech. 1:1 identifies the prophet as the son of Berechiah and grandson of Iddo. In Ezra 5:1 and 6:14 Zechariah is called "the son of Iddo." The explanation may be that "son" often means any descendant, or that some ancient editor inserted Berechiah into Zech. 1:1 because of the mistaken belief that this Zechariah was the same as the one mentioned in Isa. 8:2.

Neh. 12:16 makes Zechariah head of the priestly house of Iddo. In Neh. 12:4 we learn that Iddo came back from the Babylonian exile with Zerubbabel and Jeshua. From these facts it is clear that Zechariah belonged to a priestly family and that probably he had been in Babylonia.

Zechariah was a younger contemporary and associate of Haggai. Both directed their energies toward rebuilding the temple in 520-515 B.C. Zechariah's ministry began only about two months later than Haggai's (Zech. 1:1; Hag. 1:1). It continued longer than Haggai's four-month ministry, that is, to 518 B.C. (Zech. 7:1) and possibly to 515, when the temple was finished and dedicated. Zech. 3:8-9 probably was spoken on that occasion.

On the historical situation in which both men worked, see the discussion of Haggai (chap. 45).

2. Contents

The book falls into two distinct parts:

   I. The visions of Zechariah and additional prophecies about the future of the land (chaps. 1–8)

      a. Introduction: A call to repentance, referring to the

experience of the fathers (1:1-6)

b. The visions of the night regarding the coming of the New Age for the Jews (1:7–6:8)

c. The crowning of Joshua (and Zerubbabel) (6:9-15)

d. God's requirement for the time of restoration: not fasting but righteousness and love (chap. 7)

e. The future glory of Jerusalem and Judah (chap. 8)

II. Yahweh's judgment of the nations and the establishment of his universal kingdom (chaps. 9–14)

a. First prophecy: The coming humbling of the nations, the reassembling of the exiles, and Israel's need for a true shepherd (chaps. 9–11)

b. Second prophecy: The coming of the day of Yahweh when Jerusalem's enemies will be repulsed, its inhabitants will mourn over one who has been martyred, prophecy will cease, and Yahweh will appear in glorified Jerusalem to reign over and be worshiped by all the earth (chaps. 12–14)

3. The Literary Problem

All serious students of the book admit that the two parts identified above are quite different in character.

Chaps. 1–8 clearly reflect a definite historical occasion: the time of the rebuilding of the temple under Zerubbabel and Joshua (520–515). Chaps. 9–14 lack specific grounding in historical events and could be assigned, as far as historical references are concerned, to many points in the life of the nation from the eighth to the second centuries B.C.

The style, thought, and to some extent the language of the two parts differ. Chaps. 1–8 contain mostly visions with interpretations related to a specific occasion. They are in prose. Chaps. 9–14 contain many poetic pieces called oracles (9:1; 12:1), unrelated to any identifiable historical situation, and presenting in highly symbolic language the author's views concerning the day of the Lord and the final coming of the kingdom of God. So mysterious is some of this material (*e.g.*, 11:4-17) that scholars despair of discovering its meaning.

The most widely held view today assigns the materials of chaps. 1–8 to Zechariah, the prophet of 520 B.C., and attributes chaps. 9–14 to later

Photo by H. T. Frank
An oil lamp from the time of the Judges

minds, usually to a Second (chaps. 9–11) and to a Third (chaps. 12–14) Zechariah.

These later writers may have lived in the fourth and third centuries B.C. The reference to the triumph of the Jews over the sons of Greece (9:13) seems to point to the Greek period following Alexander the Great (after 331 B.C.), rather than to the Persian period of the prophet Zechariah.

Conservative scholarship once attributed chaps. 9–14 (or at least chap. 11) to Jeremiah because in Matt. 27:9 a passage now present in Zech. 11:12-13 is credited to Jeremiah. Today conservatives argue that Zechariah, the son of Berechiah, probably wrote both halves of the present book. Against the differences in style and theology of the two parts, they identify similarities. It is suggested that Zechariah may have written the second half late in his life (perhaps 480–470 B.C.).

4. Message and Significance

The Zechariah who worked with Haggai believed profoundly that the building of the new temple was God's first act in the drama of the end, and the end would involve the coming of the Messianic Age for God's people and the world.

Zechariah went so far as to have crowns made for Joshua and Zerubbabel. Though Zerubbabel's name no longer appears in the text of 6:9-14, the mention of "crowns," "the Branch" (which is appropriate to Zerubbabel as Messianic King—Hag. 2:20-23), "a priest by his throne" (Zech. 6:13), and "both" (6:13) show that Zerub-babel too, not just Joshua (6:11), was in the prophet's mind. For some reason the text has been altered by a later editor to exclude Zerubbabel. Possibly his reason was that Zerubbabel did not become the Messiah; the civil and religious life of the nation came under the leadership of the high priest alone. Thus the prophecy was brought into harmony with the course of history, and Joshua only is mentioned here.

Zechariah's concept of the New Age involved not only Jewish political supremacy over the nations but religious and moral leadership also. Idolatry, stealing, and perjury would be done away. Ceremonialism (fasting) would give way to justice, kindness, mercy for the oppressed, and good-heartedness (7:8-10; 8:16-17). God's presence among his people would arouse the desire of foreigners to share in his worship and experience the blessings of the New Age (8:20-23).

The person (or persons) responsible for chaps. 9–14 brings before us the certainty of the ultimate establishment of the kingdom of God over all peoples. The allusion to the mourning over "him whom they have pierced" (12:10) appears in the New Testament as a reference to Jesus (John 19:37; Rev. 1:7). The passage may echo Isa. 53. Whether the original reference was to Jesus or to another (unknown) prophet, Jesus fulfilled the prophecy in the way he fulfilled other Old Testament expectations: by incorporating in his life and death all that is valid in them, as he understood the will of God for himself and his people.

47. Malachi

1. Place in Canon

The last book of the Hebrew Bible is not Malachi but Chronicles. In the Latin Vulgate the last Old Testament books are I and II Maccabees, immediately preceded by Malachi.

When Luther removed all the books and portions of books not found in the Hebrew Bible to an appendix at the end of the Old Testament, Malachi fell in last place, where it remains in English Bibles to this day.

Malachi has a peculiar relationship to Zechariah. After Zech. 1–8 there are three segments of material which carry the same superscription: "An oracle, the Word of Yahweh" (Zech. 9:1; 12:1; Mal. 1:1). Since Malachi means "my messenger" and is probably not a proper name (see next section), it seems likely that three anonymous prophetic oracles were attached to Zech. 1–8. Later, perhaps to form a collection of *twelve* lesser prophets, Malachi was separated off to form the twelfth book. Then or later Malachi was regarded as a proper name.

2. Name, Date, Historical Circumstances

As noted above, Malachi means "my messenger." In 3:1 it is certainly not a proper name, though the editor who added the superscription in 1:1 may have so taken it. The Septuagint has in 1:1 "by the hand of his messenger," and later Jewish tradition sometimes ascribed the book to Ezra. It is hardly likely that Malachi was the prophet's name. What it was we do not know.

His approximate date is fairly easy to determine. A governor rules over Judah (1:8). The temple and its ritual are in full operation (1:6-14; 3:1, 10), but its services have become boring to both priests and worshipers (1:6-14; 3:8). The people are questioning the love of God for Israel and the justice of God, arguing that there is no profit in serving him (1:2-5; 2:17; 3:13-15). Divorce and marriage to heathen women are prevalent (2:11-16).

Such conditions suit the time just before Nehemiah and Ezra. The failure of Haggai's and Zechariah's glowing hopes for the future brought the struggling community to a state of despondency and cynicism. It was Nehemiah's and Ezra's task to restore the nation's faith, purity of life, and enthusiasm for the future. A date about 460 B.C. for Malachi seems correct.

3. Contents

Six basic sections are identifiable, in addition to a superscription and conclusion:

Superscription (1:1)

I. God's love for Israel (proved by his punishment of Edom) (1:2-5)

II. The priests' contempt for Yahweh (their polluted offerings in the temple and their false teaching), Gentile respect for him, and the coming judgment of the priests (1:6–2:9)

III. The lack of faithfulness of Jewish males to the ancestral covenant (divorce of wives and marriage with foreign women) (2:10-16)

IV. The people's disbelief in the justice of God (cynical complaints about the successes of evildoers and their participation in evil practices) and God's coming refining judgment (2:17–3:5)

V. Israel's departure from Yahweh's requirements (nonpayment of tithes and offerings) and the need for repentance (3:6-12)

VI. The arrogant unbelief of the ungodly (their claim that they get along in life quite as well as the godly) and Yahweh's eventual punishment of the wicked and reward of the righteous (3:13–4:3)

Conclusion to the Book of the Twelve Prophets: A command to obey the Law of Moses and to await the coming of Elijah, the restorer of Israel before the day of judgment (4:4-5)

The sections follow a basic pattern: first a declaration, then an objection, and finally a substantiation or proof. It is a kind of dialogue or debate form.

4. Message and Abiding Significance

Malachi addressed a people who believed God had let them down. The reestablishment of pure worship in a rebuilt temple had not brought the blessings predicted by Haggai and Zechariah. Instead, Judah was under the heel of a foreign government (Persia), crop failures and famine were frequent, the hostility of non-Jewish peoples in and around the nation was intense, and general hopelessness infected the national spirit. Of what use was the elaborate worship of God and personal fidelity to the Mosaic covenant? Those who ignored God and the Law seemed to succeed as well as those who piously attended to traditional duties.

Malachi championed the reverent worship of God when it was unpopular to do so. His argumentative style indicates that he was often locked in controversy with skeptics.

His main convictions may be summarized as follows:

a. God loves Israel in spite of all indications to the contrary. This love will be manifested at the coming day of Yahweh, if the people are faithful to God and to one another, as the Mosaic covenant directed.

b. Respect for God involves the giving of the best we have to him. Tossing him a few unwanted scraps will not do.

c. Earnest and reverent Gentile worship is more acceptable to God than insincere and indifferent Jewish worship ("my name is great among the nations"—1:11, 14).

d. Marriage is sacred and indissoluble. To cast off a faithful wife and to marry another (particularly a foreigner) is a violation of the covenant bond (3:5).

e. The coming kingdom is for the righteous. God intends to refine his people through an appointed messenger, so that the day of judgment will find them prepared for their future life in that kingdom.

Malachi was more legalistic and ritualistic than the great preexilic prophets. He was also oversimple in his stress on suffering as a direct consequence of sin, and prosperity as the fruit of righteousness (see the contrary view in Job). But his firm belief in God and in God's future for the righteous, when outward facts do not seem to justify it and when unbelievers are loudly cynical, entitles him to an honored place among the prophets and forerunners of Christianity.

The hope for the coming of Elijah and the return of the Lord to his temple reappears in the New Testament (Mark 6:15; 9:11-13; Matt. 11:10; and the primitive church's preoccupation with the temple, according to Acts 2:46; 3:1 ff.).

For Further Reading Concerning the Books of the Old Testament

Anderson, B. W. *Understanding the Old Testament,* 3rd ed., 1975.
Archer, Jr., G. L. *A Survey of Old Testament Introduction,* 1964.
Brown, R. E.; Fitzmyer, J. A.; and Murphy, R. E., eds. *The Jerome Biblical Commentary,* Vol. I, 1968.
Harrelson, Walter. *Interpreting the Old Testament,* 1964.
Harrison, R. K. *Introduction to the Old Testament,* 1969.
Jensen, Joseph. *God's Word to Israel,* 1968.
Wright, G. E., and Fuller, R. H. *The Book of the Acts of God,* 1957.
Young, E. J. *An Introduction to the Old Testament,* rev. ed., 1960.

48. The Apocryphal Books

The Apocrypha of the Old Testament, as presented in the Revised Standard Version and the New English Bible, consists of fifteen books or portions of books. None of these writings appears in the Hebrew Bible; but, with the exception of II Esdras, all are present in copies of the Septuagint (Greek Old Testament) and all, including II Esdras, appear in Latin manuscripts of the Bible.

The fifteen are:

I and II Esdras
Tobit
Judith
The Additions to the Book of Esther
The Wisdom of Solomon
Ecclesiasticus (the Wisdom of Jesus the Son of Sirach)

Baruch
The Letter of Jeremiah
The Prayer of Azariah and the Song of the Three Young Men
Susanna
Bel and the Dragon
The Prayer of Manasseh
I and II Maccabees

"Apocrypha" means "hidden things." As applied to writings it means "hidden" books, withdrawn from common use and suited only for the initiated, or books improper for use because they contain heretical teachings, or simply books outside the Hebrew canon.

Protestants use the term in the last sense and apply it to all fifteen books or portions. Roman Catholics use it in a somewhat different way. They speak of "protocanonical books" (those books recognized from the earliest times of the Christian church as authoritative), "deuterocanonical books" (those books and portions which came later to be recognized as authoritative in the church), and "apocryphal" (those books never recognized by the church as authoritative).

Of the fifteen that Protestants call "apocryphal," Roman Catholics apply the term only to three—the Prayer of Manasseh and I and II Esdras. The other twelve are regarded as deuterocanonical; they were declared "sacred" and "canonical" at the Council of Trent in 1546. The many other Jewish books not in the Hebrew Bible or the Latin Vulgate, which Protestants label "Pseudepigrapha" ("false books," because so many are attributed to persons who did not write them), are included by Roman Catholics, along with the three mentioned above, under the term "Apocrypha." Protestants have three categories: canonical, apocryphal, pseudepigraphic. Roman Catholics also have three: protocanonical, deuterocanonical, and apocryphal. But the books are distributed somewhat differently in the two systems.

The fifteen apocryphal books came under attack by the Protestants during the Reformation. Luther gathered them together as an appendix to the Old Testament under a caption which said that they "are not held to be equal to holy scripture and yet are profitable and good to read." The Reformed Church similarly segregated and appended them to the books of the Hebrew Bible.

As early as 1599 some English copies of the Bible omitted the apocryphal books altogether. The King James Version of 1611, however, contained them. The hostility of the Puritans toward the Apocrypha led increasingly to their omission from English Bibles. The important non–Roman Catholic English translations, commissioned by official religious organizations during the last 100 years, have included them: the English Revised Version (1895); the Revised Standard Version (1957); and the New English Bible (1970).

The apocryphal books are of uneven value. Some of them contain material of high religious and ethical significance. Others are fairly trivial. Their influence on literature, music, and art through the centuries has been profound. Some Roman Catholic doctrines (such as purgatory and masses for the dead) find in the Apocrypha their chief biblical support.

The Apocrypha and Pseudepigrapha (or the deuterocanonical and apocryphal books) help us understand Judaism at the time of Jesus. They also throw considerable light on the New Testament. Intelligent students of both Judaism and Christianity should know these books. And one will frequently find light by which to live breaking forth from them.

49. I Esdras

This book is called III Esdras in the Latin Vulgate, where, since the Council of Trent in 1546, it has appeared in an appendix after the New Testament. The books called Ezra and Nehemiah in Protestant Bibles are I and II Esdras in the Vulgate.

A Jewish author, probably toward the end of the second century B.C., excerpted and partially rewrote the end of II Chronicles, the book of Ezra, and part of Nehemiah. He supplemented his biblical sources with a charming, lengthy tale, probably of Persian origin. It tells about a contest among three pages or bodyguards of King Darius which, won by Zerubbabel, a Jew, resulted in Darius' helping to rebuild the Jerusalem temple.

The book covers Jewish history from King Josiah (640–609 B.C.) to the reforms of Ezra (458 or 428 or 398 B.C.). The writer's interest centers in the temple and its ceremonies. He has nothing of historical significance to contribute over and above his biblical sources.

Josephus used this book in the writing of his *Antiquities of the Jewish People* (c. A.D. 93).

50. II Esdras

This book appears in the Latin Vulgate as IV Esdras.

Like Daniel and the Revelation to John, it is an apocalypse (see pp. 342-43). It unveils the plan of God for the end of the world and the coming of the final age. The secrets of God are revealed to Ezra through seven visions which the angel Uriel interprets.

The main part of the book, the seven visions (chaps. 3–14), was written by a Jewish author about A.D. 100, that is, about 30 years after the destruction of Jerusalem by the Romans. Later, Christian writers added chaps. 1–2 and 15–16 (probably in the second and third centuries), with the double intent of showing that Chris-

Photo by H. T. Frank

Eagle and inscription of the XIIth Roman legion. Cut to pieces by Jewish rebels at Beth-horon in A.D. 66, this legion was later reconstituted and took part in the final assault on Jerusalem in A.D. 70.

tians, not Jews, are the heirs of the coming age and of pronouncing God's doom on the Roman empire.

Chaps. 3–14 represent Ezra as having experienced his seven visions in Babylon in the thirtieth year after the fall of Jerusalem (i.e., in 557 B.C.). (Ezra, of course, actually lived in the fifth century B.C.)

These chapters describe Ezra as greatly troubled over God's treatment of the Jews and his governing of the world in general. Why has he allowed people more unrighteous than the Jews to overrun and oppress them? Why has he made man's lot in the world so difficult, particularly the attainment of righteousness? Since sin has so deeply affected men's hearts and lives, and they are to be judged by the hard demands of the Law, perhaps it would be better if they had never been born. Why will so few be

saved? The author pours out all the hard questions that Israel's traditional faith and historical experiences (recently the fall of Jerusalem in A.D. 70) had aroused in thoughtful minds.

Ezra is told in his visions that the coming age, near at hand, will provide the solution to all present inequities and distresses. The righteous will be vindicated, the wicked punished. The Son of man (Messiah) will inaugurate that age. It will come when the predestined number of the righteous has been made up. Ezra must wait in faith. He cannot now expect to understand all the mysteries of God.

The book was widely read in the early Christian church, which preserved it. After the futile rebellion of Bar Kochba against Rome (A.D. 132–35), the Jews rejected it along with apocalyptic literature and theology in general.

51. Tobit

Tobit has long been one of the most popular of those books now called apocryphal or deuterocanonical. Luther wrote of it, "Is it history? Then it is a holy history. Is it fiction? Then it is a truly beautiful, wholesome and profitable fiction, the performance of a gifted poet."

It is not hard to prove that the book is fictitious. In 1:4 Tobit is described as a young man when the tribe of Naphtali (and the other northern tribes) split off from Jerusalem (922 B.C.); 1:2 says that he was deported to Nineveh by the Assyrians in the time of Shalmaneser (726–722 B.C.), and 14:15 that his son Tobias lived until after the destruction of Nineveh (612 B.C.). Sennacherib, rather than Sargon, is made the successor of Shalmaneser (1:15). Nebuchadnezzar and Ahasuerus (Xerxes), rather than Nabopolassar and Cyaxares, are made the conquerors of Nineveh (14:15). Inaccuracies are to be found also in the geography of the book.

The value of the story lies not in its historical contribution but in what it teaches about religious and domestic fidelity. The main characters are all models of piety and morality. They observe the Law faithfully and win out by God's help, given through the angel Raphael, over many serious troubles. Marriage and the home are glorified. Good deeds are exalted, and almsgiving is declared to atone for sins (4:6, 10; 12:9). The golden rule in negative form is to be found here (4:15). The characters are models of what true Jews ought to be. The story teaches that those who obey God faithfully experience his help in ways beyond their imagining.

The original language of the book was probably Aramaic. It could have been written in Palestine, Egypt, or Mesopotamia, most likely around 200 B.C. Some Hebrew and Aramaic fragments have been found at Qumran by the Dead Sea.

Several older folktales which circulated widely in the ancient world (the Grateful Dead, the Dangerous Bride, the Story of Ahikar) have been used in the narrative. The author combined and rewrote them from the standpoint of the devout Judaism of his time.

52. Judith

This superb example of the Jewish storyteller's art revolves around the exploits of a beautiful and daring woman who single-handedly delivered her nation from extermination at the hands of a powerful and arrogant enemy.

The story should be classified as

historical romance and not history because of the many inaccuracies it contains. Nebuchadnezzar, actually king of the Chaldeans in Babylon, is called king of the Assyrians, with his capital at Nineveh (1:1). The book's events are supposed to have occurred during his reign (605–562 B.C.), but we read that the crisis described took place when the Jews "had only recently returned from the captivity" (4:3), after the rebuilding of the temple (520–515 B.C.). The three-day march from Nineveh to southeastern Asia Minor (2:21)—a distance of some 300 miles—was, of course, impossible. It may be that the writer intentionally introduced inaccuracies to indicate subtly that the story was not to be taken literally.

"Judith" means "Jewess." The heroine of the story is devout and scrupulous in the observance of Jewish law. She implicitly trusts in the providence of God. She is prosperous, intelligent, and eminently desirable. She is the symbol of what the nation should be. Because she did not sin, God made her invincible. The author conceives of sin largely in legal and ceremonial terms. Lying to Nebuchadnezzar's general, Holofernes, and decapitating him was not sin, but eating his food would have been!

The story reflects the Maccabean struggle against the attempts of the Seleucid king Antiochus IV (Epiphanes) to destroy Judaism and to replace it with worship of himself as Zeus Olympus (167–164 B.C.). The clash between Nebuchadnezzar as God and the true God of the Jews is a prominent theme (3:8; 6:2, 4). Faithfulness to God and to his Law, even in peril of death, brings invincibility. Such is the teaching of the book.

Its date is probably about 150 B.C., its original language Hebrew, and the place of writing Palestine.

53. The Additions to the Book of Esther

The Greek and the Old Latin texts of the book of Esther include 107 verses not present in the Hebrew text. These verses belong to six sections which are distributed through the narrative. Jerome, when making the Latin Vulgate (c. A.D. 400), assembled them and placed them at the end of the book of Esther.

The printing of these sections together in the King James Version, as if they constituted 10:4–16:24 of the book of Esther, ignored their basic character as fragments and rendered them incomprehensible.

Present-day Roman Catholic Bibles print them in their proper place in the book of Esther, with a clear indication that they are additions to the Hebrew text.

The additions are of three types: prayers, which supply religious content to the book (see p. 129 about the secular character of the book of

Esther); texts of edicts only mentioned in the narrative, to increase the reader's sense of its trustworthiness; and details to strengthen the story.

The additions are early, perhaps from the late second century B.C. Some of them probably were introduced by a Jew named Lysimachus, who translated the Hebrew Esther into Greek.

There is general agreement that the additions have little or no historical value. Their purpose was to make the Esther narrative more palatable to pious Jews.

54. The Wisdom of Solomon

This book is probably the high-water mark of the Apocrypha.

Its lofty wrestling with the big problems of human existence, its artistic style, and its daring synthesis of Greek and Hebrew ideas endeared it to some of the best minds of the early church.

Some scholars believe that Paul knew the book and echoed its thought and language in various passages, particularly in Romans. But it may be that the background and training of the two writers was somewhat similar and that they drew from the same well of language and thought.

The book claims to have come from King Solomon (7:1-6; 9:7, 8, 12). This claim places it in the Wisdom tradition, behind which stood the figure of Solomon (see p. 130).

Many characteristics indicate that it came from a period centuries later than Solomon: the peculiar fusion of Hebrew and Greek thought; the technical Greek terms ("self-control," "prudence," "justice," and "courage" [8:7], which are the four cardinal virtues of Stoicism); the philosophical concepts (the preexistence and immortality of the soul); and the bombastic style of much of it.

The author probably lived in the first century B.C., where we do not know but probably in Alexandria.

Chaps. 1–5 show that, in spite of

The goddess Athena

appearances to the contrary, the suffering righteous (the Wise) will be rewarded by God with a blessed existence beyond death, while their wicked persecutors (the Fools) will vanish without a trace. The suffering of the righteous is the discipline a loving Father gives his sons.

Chaps. 6–9 contain praise of the attributes and works of Wisdom and show how Wisdom came to Solomon and will come to others.

Chaps. 10–19 deal with Wisdom's works in history, especially how Wisdom helped and saved Israel's forefathers. A discourse on the folly of idolatry (13:1–15:17) interrupts the historical account of Wisdom's activity.

A notable concept of the book is the associating of Wisdom, Logos (Word), and Holy Spirit as agents of God's activity in the world. In Paul (I Cor. 1:24; 12:8) and in the Gospel of John (1:1-18; 7:37-39; 20:22) a similar association occurs.

In the New Testament, suffering as a mark of sonship to the Father and as a learning experience is applied both to Jesus (Heb. 5:8-9) and to his followers (Rom. 8:14-25; Heb. 12:3-11).

55. Ecclesiasticus (the Wisdom of Jesus the Son of Sirach)

This is the longest book of the Apocrypha and one of the most important as well. It was known in the early Christian church as Ecclesiasticus, meaning probably "the church book" or "to be read in church."

Its contents consist of the teaching of a wise man and scribe (teacher of the Law) named Joshua ben Sira (in Hebrew), who had a school in Jerusalem (50:27; 51:23). Since he had traveled widely (34:11; 51:13), it is possible that he was in the diplomatic service.

This is the only book of the Apocrypha whose author's name is known. We are fortunate to learn from the prologue that the translator of the book (into Greek) was the author's grandson, who accomplished this task sometime after the thirty-eighth year of Euergetes (Ptolemy VII, whose thirty-eighth year was 132 B.C.). This means that the grandfather must have written down his teachings about 180 B.C.

The point of view pervading the whole book is that life in accordance with the Law is the highest wisdom (19:20). The author tells how Wisdom came to Israel. Wisdom came forth from the mouth of God and sought a dwelling place among the nations of men. In response to the commandment of the Creator she took her dwelling in Israel as "the book of the covenant of the Most High God," as "the law which Moses commanded us" (24:3-23). If one learns and keeps the commandments (both the written Law and the tradition of the fathers—8:9), he will be abundantly blessed by God with a prosperous and long life (1:12) and his memory will long endure (39:9, 41:13). For this author God's demands are both moral and ceremonial. He was the heir of both prophetic and priestly religion.

Like Proverbs, the book is loosely put together. There are small groups of sayings according to subjects, but there is no overall logical organization. It is possible that we have two volumes in our present book: Book I, chaps. 1–23; Book II, chaps. 24–50; with chap. 51 as an appendix. Divided thus, each book begins with the praise of Wisdom (chaps. 1 and 24).

The whole book is a treasure house of practical advice, set in the culture of second-century B.C. orthodox Judaism, concerning how young men, in particular, should deport themselves:

their table etiquette, their family relationships, their friendships, the care of their health, their self-discipline. There is a strong emphasis on the importance of prayer and good deeds. One of the best-known portions is the praise of famous men (Enoch to Nehemiah). Here the author yearns that there may be successors to them in his time (46:12; 49:10).

Joshua ben Sira's pupils were soon to be tested in the fires of the persecution instigated by Antiochus IV (Epiphanes) in 167-164 B.C. Undoubtedly, some of the wise who remained loyal to the covenant (Dan. 11:35; 12:3) drew their inspiration from this great teacher.

56. Baruch

Baruch was the disciple and secretary of Jeremiah, who, according to Jeremiah 36, wrote two scrolls at the prophet's dictation. The second of these is included in our present book of Jeremiah (see p. 156). It was to this trusted companion that Jeremiah gave the deed for property he bought at Anathoth as an act of faith in the future of the country (Jer. 32:12-16).

Because of Baruch's prominence in the book of Jeremiah in connection with writing and with Jeremiah's predictions concerning the future, his name was attached to various books in later periods, especially those dealing with Israel's future as the people of God. In this class belong the present book and the second-century A.D. Syriac Apocalypse of Baruch.

The book of Baruch in the Apocrypha claims to have been written by Baruch in Babylon after the destruction of Jerusalem by the Chaldeans, read to the captives there, and sent to Jerusalem for reading in the temple on feast days as a confession of sins (1:14).

The contents fall into two main parts, after a brief introduction explaining the book's origin (1:1-14).

Part I (1:15–3:8) is a confession of Israel's sins from the time of the Exodus from Egypt "to this day" (1: 20) and an appeal for forgiveness and return from exile. It is in the style of a national song of lamentation.

Part II (3:9–5:9) consists of two poems. The first praises Wisdom as God's gift to Israel in the Law, blames

Israel's misfortunes on the forsaking of Wisdom, and pleads for a return to Wisdom's ways. The second contains Jerusalem's lament over its pitiable condition and promises deliverance for its scattered children and its ultimate glorification.

The two parts are only loosely related and probably come from different writers.

The confession (Part I) shows heavy dependence on Daniel's prayer (Dan. 9), thus requiring a date for this portion later than the book of Daniel (167–164 B.C.). The poems (Part II) may be earlier or later in date. The book in its present form may come from sometime between 150 and 50 B.C.

Both parts seem to have been written in Hebrew. The identity of their authors is unknown.

57. The Letter of Jeremiah

The Latin Vulgate and the King James Version of the Apocrypha have the Letter of Jeremiah at the end of the book of Baruch.

Actually, this letter originally had nothing to do with the book of Baruch but was an independent composition. It stands in various places in ancient manuscripts and versions. The Septuagint (the Greek Old Testament), for example, places it in the sequence: Jeremiah, Baruch, Lamentations, the Letter of Jeremiah. The Revised Standard Version, therefore, prints the letter as a separate book, although it keeps the chapter and verse numbers of the King James Version.

The letter obviously was inspired by Jer. 29:1-23, where the prophet's letter to the Babylonian exiles is quoted, and by Jer. 10:1-16, where idols are ridiculed as man-made and powerless. The apocryphal letter contains a bitter and lengthy attack on idols. It expands Jeremiah 10 and echoes the language there.

It claims to have been written by Jeremiah for Jewish captives about to go into Babylonian exile (597 or 587 B.C.), in order to warn them of the length of their captivity and of the danger of idolatry in the land to which they were going. In fact, it is part of a fairly large body of Jewish literature in which exilic and postexilic writers ridiculed Gentile gods (Isa. 44:9-20; Pss. 115, 135; Wisd. of Sol. 13:1–15:17).

The original language was probably Hebrew or Aramaic, though Greek is possible. A tiny fragment in Greek on papyrus was found at Qumran by the Dead Sea, dating to about 100 B.C.

The letter may have been written at any time between the fourth and the second centuries B.C., the best time perhaps being near the beginning of the second century, when the Seleucids were enticing the Jews toward apostasy (see p. 165).

To Jews who were succumbing to false worship, the writer said eleven times (in various words), after scathing exposés of the idols' utter worthlessness, "We have no evidence whatever that they are gods; therefore do not fear them."

58. The Prayer of Azariah and the Song of the Three Young Men

The stories of the book of Daniel became so popular that they were soon embellished and expanded. Three additions to the book of Daniel appear in the Greek and Latin versions: the Prayer of Azariah and the Song of the Three Young Men, Susanna, and Bel and the Dragon.

Following the account of the throwing of Shadrach, Meshach, and Abednego into the fiery furnace (Dan. 3:19-23), the Greek and Latin versions insert the Prayer of Azariah (Abednego) and the Song of the Three Young Men.

Altogether the insertion consists of sixty-eight verses and falls into three parts.

1. The prayer of Azariah (vss. 3-22) contains a confession of national guilt and a plea for pardon of the nation, for its deliverance, and for vengeance on its oppressors. It is in the style of a national song of lamentation, not altogether suitable here.

It probably was adapted from an existing liturgical prayer.

2. Verses 23-27 offer information about the furnace: its intense heat; the burning of those who threw the three young men in; and the angel of the Lord who transformed the interior of the furnace to "a moist whistling wind" (vs. 27).

3. A song of praise to God by the three youths concludes the insert (vss. 28-68). This imitates Pss. 136 and 148. It seems to have been adapted from an earlier composition, as the closing reference to the three youths (vs. 66) and the stereotyped refrain—suggesting use in worship—indicate.

This addition to the text of Daniel makes the faith of the young men and the mighty deeds of the God of Israel yet more awesome.

When the addition was made is unknown, perhaps in the second or first century B.C. The original language was probably Hebrew.

59. Susanna

A second addition to Daniel (see the first, chap. 58) is the suspenseful tale about the beautiful and virtuous Susanna and her rescue from the lustful elders by the wise young Daniel. It

is a masterpiece of the storyteller's art.

In the Greek and Latin versions the story comes at the end of the book of Daniel as chap. 13. In other ancient texts and versions it appears as an introduction to the book of Daniel, perhaps because Daniel is described in Susanna as "a young lad" (vs. 45).

Daniel means "God has judged" or "God is my judge." In the Canaanite literature of the fourteenth century B.C., King Dan'el (Daniel) was a dispenser of justice to the widow and the orphan. In Ezek. 14:14 Daniel is associated with Noah and Job, and in Ezek. 28:3 his great wisdom is mentioned. Evidently there was a long tradition in Canaan-Israel about Daniel, the wise judge. The Susanna story, in which the young Daniel trips up the crafty and lecherous elders, is a further development of this tradition.

The story teaches that God supports the virtuous and punishes the wicked and that he who accuses his brother falsely shall have done to him what he intended against his brother (Deut. 19:18-21). In the book of Susanna the vicious elders, whose false testimony brought about the sentence of death for the innocent Susanna, were themselves put to death.

The book seems to have been written in Hebrew. The date is uncertain, but a good guess is the second or first century B.C.

60. Bel and the Dragon

This third addition to Daniel (see chaps. 58–59) consists of two fanciful tales in which Daniel demonstrates the unreality of foreign gods and the dishonesty of their priests. Judaism's contest with idolatry offered opportunity for sport as well as for serious theologizing.

The first tale shows how the wise Daniel exposed the trickery of the priests of Bel (Marduk), who made the statue of their god appear to consume large quantities of food and drink daily. Daniel proved that the statute was nothing but clay and brass and "never ate or drank anything" (vs. 7), and that the eating and drinking were done secretly by the priests and their families.

The second tale concerns Daniel's killing of a great dragon, which was worshiped as a god, by feeding it cakes made from pitch, fat, and hair. The worshipers, furious at Daniel, threw him into a lions' den for six days. While there Daniel was fed by the prophet Habakkuk, whom an angel transported from Judea to Babylon by the hair of his head and returned the same way to his home. The tale ends with the conversion of the king of Babylon and with Daniel's opponents thrown in the lions' den and devoured.

The theme of the stories is put on the lips of Daniel: "I do not revere man-made idols, but the living God, who created heaven and earth and has dominion over all flesh" (vs. 5; cf. vs. 25).

In Greek manuscripts Bel and the

Dragon appears at the end of the book of Daniel (after chap. 12). In the Latin Vulgate the story of Susanna forms chap. 13 of the book of Daniel,

and Bel and the Dragon is chap. 14.

The original language was probably Hebrew and the date the second or first century B.C.

61. The Prayer of Manasseh

This prayer of fifteen verses undoubtedly arose from the references in II Chron. 33:12-13, 18-19 to King Manasseh's prayer of repentance in exile through which God forgave him, restored him to his throne, and brought about the religious reformation of his kingdom.

II Chron. 33:18 states that Manasseh's prayer was available in a source known to the Chronicler. It is very clear that the prayer attributed to Manasseh in the Apocrypha cannot be the prayer referred to in II Chronicles.

First, the apocryphal prayer appears only in Greek form and has no firm anchorage in the Septuagint. In those Septuagint manuscripts where it does appear, it is introduced not in connection with Chronicles but in a

collection of hymns and odes attached to the Psalter.

Second, it is not present in the Old Latin translation, and Jerome seems not to have known it. The earliest surviving text of it is in the Syriac Didascalia, a church manual of the third century A.D.

Third, its form, contents, and language mark it as late in date, perhaps first century B.C. or A.D.

A late Jewish author, then, sought to supply the words of Manasseh's prayer. His composition, probably written first in Hebrew (though perhaps in Greek), is a noble one. It is infused with deep piety and mature theology. It stresses the mercy of God in forgiving even the blackest of sinners, as Manasseh was, according to Jewish tradition.

62. I Maccabees

I Maccabees is a book of high historical and literary worth. The religious faith which shines through it is of a quiet, strong type. In this respect it stands in contrast to II Maccabees, the pages of which are full of dramatic wonders and stupendous miracles (see chap. 63).

The book contains a detailed account of political and military affairs in Judea from the accession of Antiochus IV (Epiphanes) to the throne of Syria-Palestine (175 B.C.) to the death of Simon Maccabeus, ethnarch (ruler) and high priest, in 134 B.C. A brief reference to the reign of John Hyr-

Antiochus IV, called Antiochus Epiphanes;
from a silver tetradrachma

canus (134–104 B.C.) ends the book.

An introduction tells of the career of Alexander the Great and the division of his kingdom among his generals after his death (1:1-9). This leads to a discussion of the attempts of Antiochus IV, in cooperation with renegade Palestinian Jews, to impose Greek ideas and customs upon the Jewish nation. These attempts provoked loyal Jews, under the leadership of a family of priests, to organized resistance. Their remarkable military victories led not only to religious freedom but also eventually to complete political independence. The stories in the book center in the careers of Judas, Jonathan, and Simon of the family now known as the Maccabees (from a word probably meaning "the hammer," originally applied to Judas).

The book divides as follows:

Introduction: Alexander t h e Great and his successors (1:1-9)
I.　The causes and the beginning of the Maccabean revolt (1:10–2:70)
II.　Judas Maccabeus (3:1–9:22)
III.　Jonathan Maccabeus (9:23–12:53)
IV.　Simon Maccabeus (with brief reference to John Hyrcanus) (chaps. 13–16)

I Maccabees undoubtedly was written originally in Hebrew. What its Hebrew title was is unknown. "Maccabees" as a title for this and three other books (I-IV Maccabees) arose in the Christian church, probably with Clement of Alexandria in the second century.

The author, apparently living in Jerusalem, was almost certainly an eyewitness of some of the events he records. He used reliable sources—oral tradition, letters and official documents (probably from the Jerusalem archives), a Syrian (Seleucid) chronicle, a biography of Judas, chronicles of the high priests Jonathan and Simon, and the like. He must have written shortly after the end of the reign of John Hyrcanus (134–104 B.C.), probably about 100 B.C., although a date a few years earlier or later is possible.

His point of view is that if the Jews are faithful to God's Law and do their part in the struggle against God's enemies, an undergirding providence will guide and sustain them in their efforts. He does not claim that God intervenes in miraculous ways.

63.　II Maccabees

(See also the discussion above of I Maccabees.)

II Maccabees is an amusing and informative combination of history and legend.

The writer's goal was to please and

to profit the reader, while requiring little effort on his part (2:24-31; 15:38-39). The verdict of the centuries since has been that he succeeded notably.

The book, for the most part, is an abridgment of a five-volume history, no longer in existence, written by a certain Jason of Cyrene. The abridger tells his readers how diligently he worked to compress his source (2:23-32).

The abridgment, now II Maccabees, covers Jewish history from about 180 to 161 B.C.—from the time of Seleucus IV of Syria and of the high priest Onias III of Jerusalem to the defeat of the army of Nicanor, the Syrian governor of Judea, in the time of the Syrian king Demetrius I.

I Maccabees, as we have seen, spans the period 175–134 B.C. (apart from brief references to earlier and later events). By beginning at an earlier point, II Maccabees offers a much better understanding of what provoked the Maccabean rebellion and of the complex events associated with the recapture and rededication of the temple by Judas Maccabeus, with whose career the book ends.

II Maccabees divides as follows:

I. Introduction: Two letters from the Jews of Jerusalem and Judea to the Jews of Egypt, urging observance of the Feast of Dedication in Egypt (1:1–2:18)
II. Prologue: The abridger's explanation of the purpose and nature of his work (2:19-32)
III. The summary of Jewish history from Seleucus IV and Onias III to the defeat of Nicanor and the achieving of religious freedom (3:1–15:36)
  a. The miraculous punishment of Heliodorus, who attempted to rob the temple (chap. 3)
  b. The attempted conversion of Jerusalem to Greek ways by corrupt Jewish high priests and by the Syrian king Antiochus IV, including the murder of Onias III, the profanation of the temple by Antiochus, and the persecution of Jews who resisted (chaps. 4–7)
  c. The resistance of Judas Maccabeus and his followers, resulting in the recapture and rededication of the temple (8:1–10:9)
  d. Judas' victories during the reigns of Antiochus V and Demetrius I, especially his victory over Nicanor (10:10–15:36)
IV. Epilogue: A plea for the reader's indulgence (15:37-39)

On the religious side, the book is full of interesting emphases: God's miraculous interventions (through angelic warriors, for example) by which he revealed his mighty power; the sanctity of the temple; the justice of God as operating inflexibly in punishment and reward according to one's deeds; the suffering of the Jews as God's discipline; the atonement made by martyrs for the nation as a whole; the resurrection of the martyrs; prayers and sacrifices for the dead; emphasis on exact obedience to the Law. The general point of view is that of the Pharisees (see p. 407).

The book, like its five-volume source, was almost certainly composed in Greek. The source probably was written toward the end of the second century B.C. and the abridgment made in the first half of the first century B.C. Some scholars have argued that the letters at the beginning were added by an editor after the abridgment was made. Alexandria may have been the place where all the literary work was done.

The teaching about the suffering of the righteous martyrs as an atonement for the nation (7:38; 8:3) offers an important perspective for understanding the New Testament view of the meaning of Christ's sufferings (Mark 10:45, for example). The teaching concerning the resurrection (chap. 7) also offers valuable background material for understanding parts of the New Testament.

For Further Reading Concerning the Books of the Apocrypha

Brockington, L. H. *A Critical Introduction to the Apocrypha,* 1961.
Metzger, B. M. *An Introduction to the Apocrypha,* 1957.
Pfeiffer, R. H. *History of New Testament Times, with an Introduction to the Apocrypha,* 1949.

64. The Four Gospels

1. The Term "Gospel"

"Gospel" comes from "godspell," an Anglo-Saxon word meaning "good story" or "good news." It derives from the Latin *evangelium* and that word in turn from the Greek *euangelion.*

The Greek *euangelion* had several meanings: originally the reward given to one who brought good news; then the good news itself; then the good news proclaimed by Jesus; then the good news proclaimed about Jesus; then the books containing the church's memories of Jesus.

The last two meanings are seen in the opening verse and in the title of Mark's Gospel: "The beginning of the gospel of Jesus Christ," that is, the good news about Jesus Christ; and "The Gospel according to Mark," meaning the account of that good news about Jesus Christ written by Mark.

2. Importance

The four Gospels may well be the four most important books in human history. They present history's most influential man—Jesus of Nazareth. So influential was he that we divide all time by the date of his birth.

A coin of the Jewish King Alexander Janneus (103–76 B.C.), known in New Testament
times as the *lepton* (the "mite," Mark 12:42 KJV)

For Christians the Gospels are the apex of New Testament literature. If
the Christian faith that God became incarnate in the man Jesus is true,
then Christians must know what sort of man he was and what God was
purposing and saying in him. The Gospels offer us precisely this information: important facts about Jesus and what these facts mean or should
mean to us.

3. Literary Form

The Gospels constitute a new and distinctively Christian form of literature. Though they sketch Jesus' career and thus carry much biographical
information, they are not properly biographies. They show little interest
in subjects which are the stock in trade of the biographer, ancient or modern: the subject's family background and education, his physical and mental
qualities, his personal habits, the influences which shaped his attitudes and
outlook, the chronological sequence of the events of his life, and the like.

In some respects the Gospels are like sermons which proclaim and interpret facts and call for decision. The Gospels tell the story of Jesus' life in such a way as to convince readers of certain truths and move them to action. Peter's preaching in the house of Cornelius about God's saving activity in Jesus (Acts 10:34-43) is a Gospel in miniature. It is the peculiar combination of biographical material and proclamation that constitutes a "Gospel."

Now these elements—historical facts and interpretative proclamation— may be put together in differing proportions. Of the Gospels, Luke is the most historical and John the most theological and sermonic. Scholars once regarded Mark as the least theological and therefore as closer to the plain facts of Jesus' life. We now know Mark to be deeply shaped by theology, though more subtly than Matthew or John. All the Gospels, to some degree, share the purpose expressed by the author of the Gospel according to John when he said that he was writing "that you may believe that Jesus is the Christ, the Son of God, and that believing you may have life in his name" (20:31).

4. Why Four Gospels?

Irenaeus (c. A.D. 180) naïvely explained the fact of four Gospels by appealing to the pattern of fours in the universe and in Scripture: four principal regions of the world, four winds, four covenants, four living creatures around God's throne, etc.

The church's acceptance of four differing accounts of Jesus' career can be explained by assuming that each had become an official, authoritative document in a different area of primitive Christianity, before general acceptance by the church around the middle of the second century. Only thus can the inclusion of Mark be accounted for, since almost the whole of it is contained in Matthew and Luke and since it was widely ignored by the church in early Christian centuries.

5. Stages in the Creation of the Gospels

a. Jesus' Deeds and Teachings (A.D. 28–30)

As far as we know, Jesus committed none of his teachings or experiences to writing. He did, however, cast some of his sayings in a form that could be remembered easily. For example, various scholars have shown that Luke 12:24-28 is poetic in structure, as are many scattered sayings throughout the Synoptic Gospels.

It was customary for disciples of a revered teacher to preserve their master's instruction by memorization, by oral transmission, and eventually by collection in written form (as in the prophetic books of the Old Testament and the Mishnah of third-century Judaism). Fidelity to a rabbi's teaching was important to Jews.

b. The Oral Transmission of Jesus' Words and Deeds (c. A.D. 30–50)

For the following reasons the disciples were slow to record their memory of Jesus in writing:

(1) Like other Jews, they preferred oral, eyewitness testimony about happenings of importance, rather than written accounts of them. Written accounts were valuable to them when eyewitness testimony was no longer available.

(2) The first disciples were not well-educated, literary persons (Luke 10:21; I Cor. 1:26 ff.).

(3) Writing materials were expensive, and the reproduction of manuscripts was slow and costly.

(4) The first Christians believed that the end of the age was near (I Cor. 7:29-31; Rom. 13:11-13; I Pet. 4:7; James 5:8; Rev. 1:1-3; 22:6-7, 10, 12). Writing a record of the past and building up libraries of written material had less meaning for them than for those who expected an ongoing future in this world.

It was the spread of Christianity into the more literary Gentile world, the death of the eyewitnesses of Jesus' ministry, and the continuance of life in this age, with its accompanying problems within and without the church, that led to the creation of records of the church's past as an aid to its present and future.

Since 1919 New Testament scholars have probed the period of oral transmission (c. A.D. 30–50) in the attempt to determine how oral transmission affected the form and content of our surviving Gospel material. They have concluded that the church preserved those materials which were useful in preaching the good news, in instructing converts, in disciplining its members, in its services of worship, and in refuting its opponents.

They have found also that the material circulated in the church in small, independent units in fixed forms. These forms can now be identified in our Gospels. The two main groups of them are: sayings of Jesus (some introduced by a brief story, others without narrative setting, still others in the form of parables); and narratives about Jesus (his miracles, his

controversies, his individual experiences—baptism, temptation, transfiguration—the events of his passion).

Unknown persons assembled many of these units into small collections
of similar material (see next section). As far as we know, the author of
the Gospel of Mark was the first to join some of the collections together
according to a traditional recollection of the general outline of Jesus'
ministry.

The uses to which the traditional material was put in the church led
to some alterations—to contraction, to expansion, to loss or change of
original context, to redirection of meaning. The tradition was fairly flexible
during the oral period. This fact makes it difficult to reconstruct with
certainty the original teachings and happenings of Jesus' career. (See p.
439.)

The scholarly study of the oral period is known as *Formgeschichte*
(form history or form criticism).

c. Early Oral and Written Collections (*c.* 50–65)

Included in the Gospel of Mark are collections of material which presumably are older than that Gospel, such as conflict stories (2:1–3:6),
parables (4:1–32), miracles (4:35–5:43), prophecies concerning the end
(13:5–37), the Passion story (14:1–16:8). It is understandable that the
church needed to sort the material into categories that could be easily used.

About 250 verses containing sayings of Jesus appear in Matthew and
Luke in virtually identical wording but are not present at all in Mark.
These sayings seem to come from an early written collection which was
used independently by Matthew and Luke. Modern scholars call the supposed document "Q" (from the German *Quelle,* source). It apparently
had no Passion story and almost no narrative material. It probably was
a handbook of Jesus' sayings for the instruction of converts. The order of
its material has been reconstructed from the passages used by Luke, who
quoted material in blocks in the order in which they were in his sources.
Palestine or Antioch in Syria may be the place of its origin, and the date
about A.D. 50–60. Its author is unknown.

Contained only in Matthew are some 400 verses of material which
scholars call "Special Matthew." This consists mainly of about a dozen
quotations from the Old Testament (introduced by a formula noting fulfillment of prophecy), some twelve narratives (such as the nativity story,
Peter's walking on the water, the coin in the fish's mouth, and stories
connected with the Passion and Resurrection), and a large body of sayings

and parables in chaps. 5–25, notably about three fifths of the Sermon on the Mount.

This large body of sayings and parables may have come from a Jerusalem source, either written or oral. It is anti-Gentile in point of view, its scholarly symbol is "M," and its date is about A.D. 65. It is possible that Matthew drew on two or three sources besides "M" for his special material.

Similarly, more than one third of the Gospel of Luke has been labeled "Special Luke." "Special Luke" consists of both narratives and teaching matter and constitutes one of the most valuable parts of Luke's Gospel. Luke's nativity stories (chaps. 1–2) probably came from a different source than the rest of "Special Luke." We do not know whether most of "Special Luke" came from one written document ("L") or from several written records or from oral sources. There is a Palestinian flavor about "Special Luke," as well as a universal outlook. Caesarea may have been the place of the collection of this material, and the date about A.D. 60.

Some scholars have argued that "Q" and "L" were joined by the author of Luke before he came across Mark's Gospel, and that Luke then inserted sections of Mark into Q + L. These scholars give to Q + L the name "Proto-Luke." But there are weighty arguments against Proto-Luke, and most scholars deny that it ever existed.

It is evident that various collections of material, written and oral, lie behind our Synoptic Gospels as sources.

6. Our Four Gospels

a. The Gospel According to Mark

Mark was almost certainly the first of our four Gospels and the first book to be written in the literary form we now know as "Gospel."

Mark, probably John Mark of Jerusalem (see p. 230), joined together early traditional sayings and stories and supplied connecting links. He meant his book to explain the puzzling question, Why did the Messiah die at the hands of Jewish and Roman leaders? He aimed also to encourage Christians to bear their sufferings in imitation of Jesus.

He probably wrote in Rome about A.D. 65–70. (See p. 230.)

b. The Gospel According to Matthew

Matthew is an expanded version of Mark, supplemented by a collection of the sayings of Jesus (Q) and by material from a source or sources accessible only to its author (M).

This Gospel was shaped to meet the needs of the church in its struggle with Judaism (c. A.D. 85). It attempted to show that the church, not the synagogue, is the true people of God and the heir of the coming kingdom of Heaven. It urged the church to exhibit before the Jews and the world the moral standards expected of the people of God. It tried also to help the inner life of the church by reassuring it of the validity of its faith in Jesus; by guiding its discipline of members; by stimulating worship, evangelism, and brotherly service; and by encouraging patient endurance of suffering.

It seems to have been written in Syria, perhaps Antioch, by a learned Jewish Christian of a cosmopolitan turn of mind, who may have been heir to a tradition about Jesus associated with the Apostle Matthew. (See pp. 223, 225.)

c. The Gospel According to Luke

Luke is volume one of a two-volume work, called today "Luke-Acts." Luke-Acts constitutes more than one fourth of the total bulk of the New Testament.

As sources for his Gospel, Luke. used the Gospel of Mark, Q, and Special Luke (L), which he may have found at Caesarea.

He wished to defend and reinforce the church's position in the world of his time by showing that Christianity is true Judaism. It is a divinely initiated and guided movement, not a subversive political plot to overthrow either duly constituted Jewish institutions or Roman sovereignty. Therefore, neither Jews nor Romans have any valid grounds of complaint against the church. In fact, all who hear the true facts about Jesus and about the miraculous growth of the church, which issued from his ministry, should join the new faith. Christians, through knowledge of their venerable history, should take courage and fulfill their God-appointed evangelistic mission in the world until the eventual coming of the kingdom of God.

Its author probably was Luke, "the beloved physician" and missionary companion of Paul, who wrote somewhere in the Hellenistic world (Greece? Rome?) between A.D. 70 and 90. (See pp. 238-39.)

d. The Gospel According to John

This Gospel now appears to have been based on a tradition of Jesus' ministry, death, and resurrection which was independent of the tradition lying behind the Synoptic Gospels. This tradition may have stemmed from the Apostle John, who taught it to his disciples in Ephesus.

FROM JESUS TO THE FOUR GOSPELS

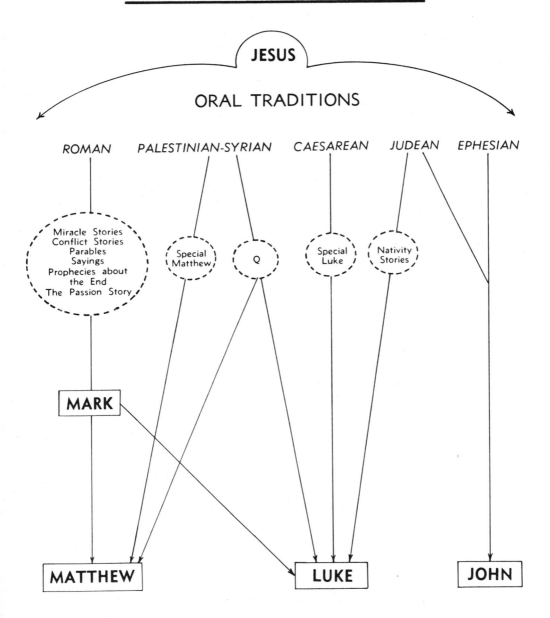

One of these disciples, a man of rare theological and literary gifts, shaped it into our present Gospel in the name and in the spirit of his teacher. He meant to strengthen Christians in the face of attacks by opponents outside and inside the church—by hostile Jews, possibly by the disciples of John the Baptist, and by false teachers within the church. By presenting Jesus as the incarnation of the Word and the Wisdom of God, whose glory was disclosed and attested by signs to the believing, he undoubtedly wished to make converts to the faith, as well as to strengthen believers.

The Gospel was written toward the end of the first century, probably in Ephesus. (See pp. 245-46.)

The careful study of the way the writers of the Gospels used the written sources and the oral traditions available to them is known today as redaction criticism (or composition criticism). From the contractions, expansions, omissions, substitutions, ways of connecting pieces of material, interjected comments, and alterations of fact or theological meaning, we can learn much about the writers' characteristics, historical situation, purpose, and theology—as the following discussion of the individual Gospels will show.

65. Matthew

The position of Matthew's Gospel at the head of the New Testament canon reflects the regard in which the early church held it. Research has shown that in the second century it was the most read, quoted, and valued book of our present New Testament. Especially prized, then as today, was the Sermon on the Mount. In the words of Jesus early Christians found guidance for the conduct of their lives and an explanation of the relationship between the new that came in Jesus and the old in Judaism.

1. Theme and Outline

Theme: Jesus, the divine-human Messiah, gathers together the people of the kingdom of heaven.

   I.   The lineage, birth, and childhood of Jesus, the divine-human Messiah (chaps. 1–2)

  II.   The preparation for his public work as the divine-human Messiah (3:1–4:11)

 III.   The gathering and teaching of his disciples (4:12–7:29) (First block of sayings—

"Concerning Discipleship"—
5:3–7:27)

IV. The redemptive deeds and
words of the Messiah and
his apostles (chaps. 8–10)
(Second block of sayings—
"Concerning Apostleship"—
10:5-42)

V. Reactions to the Messiah
(11:1–13:52)
(Third block of sayings—
"Concerning the Mystery of
the Kingdom of Heaven"—
13:3-52)

VI. The formation and organization of the Messiah's church
(13:53–18:35)
(Fourth block of sayings—
"Concerning Relationships
within the Church"—18:3-
35)

VII. The Messiah's preparation
for death and his prediction
concerning the establishment
of his kingdom (chaps. 19–
25)
(Fifth block of sayings—
"Concerning the Coming
Judgment"—chaps. 23–25)

VIII. The death of the Messiah
for the forgiveness of sins,
his resurrection, and his exaltation to universal authority
(chaps. 26–28)

Noteworthy are the five great blocks
of teaching (under points III, IV, V,
VI, VII) and the formula of transition
(in 7:28; 11:1; 13:53; 19:1; 26:1)
leading from one section to another.
The blocks of teaching concern discipleship: the nature of the goodness
expected by Jesus, the call to suffering
service involved in apostleship, the
character of the knowledge revealed
by Jesus to his followers, the relationship of brothers within the church, the
future to be expected by disciples in
the world and at the coming of the
kingdom.

2. View of Jesus

We may summarize Matthew's portrait of Jesus as follows: In the coming of Jesus of Nazareth God fulfilled
his announced purpose of sending a
Savior to mankind. This Savior (Messiah, Son of God, Son of man, Servant,
and second Moses) was recognized as
such by only some of the Jewish people, to whom the Father revealed his
true identity. Those who accepted the
revelation, believed in him, and became his disciples and apostles received forgiveness of sins, became his
righteous people (the "church"), and
were appointed heirs to the kingdom
of heaven, which he promised to inaugurate soon. As disciples they were
to trust implicitly in him, be inwardly
good rather than outwardly correct,
and imitate him in acts of loving
service. As apostles they were to
spread the good news to all men concerning the salvation available in him.
By being and doing what he asked,
they would be granted admission to
his kingdom.

A few comments on this summary
may make it more meaningful:

a. The Father's revelation to recep-
tive men of Jesus' true identity comes
to the fore in such passages as 3:17;
11:25-27; 13:11, 16-17, 51; 16:13-17;
17:5-6.

The multitudes, who did not understand who Jesus really was, regarded him as a "prophet" (21:10-11, 46), and the religious leaders saw him as a false "teacher" (9:11; 22:16, 24; 27:63). But the disciples, to whom God had revealed his true identity, knew that he was the unique Son of the Father, "God with us" for the salvation of men (1:21-23).

His supernatural birth (1:18-25), his miracles (14:28-33), and the Father's direct declaration (3:17; 17: 5-6) prove that Jesus belonged to the realm of deity, though he lived on earth as a human being. The many Old Testament prophecies he is said to have fulfilled (1:22-23; 2:15, 17-18, 23; 8:17; etc.) show that he is the Deliverer long promised to the Jews.

The Father raised him from the dead, exalted him to authority over the universe, and appointed him judge of all men and ruler of the coming kingdom of heaven (25:31-46; 28:18).

b. Jesus' work as redeemer from sin, not merely as teacher of the divine will, appears in 1:21; 18:18; 26:28 (only Matthew has "for the forgiveness of sins"). Jesus is the servant of the Lord, "an offering for sin" (Isa. 53:10; Matt. 12:18), and the second Moses (Matt. 2:15; 5:1 ff., where Jesus gives teaching [Torah] from a mountain). Both the first Moses and the second Moses were deliverers from bondage, as well as givers of Torah (teaching).

Jesus' work is to gather out from the world "the sons of the kingdom" (13:37-43), to call together the true Israel (16:18; 21:43), which he will admit to the kingdom at the last day (25:31-46). The terms of admission are: implicit faith in him (8:26; 14: 31; 16:8), inner goodness rather than external correctness (5:17-48; 6:1-18; 23:23), imitation of his acts of loving service (9:13; 10:42; 12:7; 25:31-46), and fidelity in the evangelistic mission (10:16-42; 28:19-20).

c. The Gospel of Matthew is deeply interested in the church as the true and truly righteous people of God. Among the Gospels, only Matthew uses the term "church" (*ekklesia*) as a designation for Jesus' followers (16: 18; 18:17).

3. Purpose

The Gospel of Matthew reflects the church's conflict with Judaism, which became acute in the last quarter of the first century.

The fall of Jerusalem (A.D. 70) led to the triumph of the Pharisees over all rival Jewish sects. The Pharisees insisted on obedience to the Law, as they interpreted it. They expelled Christians from the synagogues because they claimed to be the true Israel but did not obey the Law as the Pharisees understood it.

The writer of Matthew insists that the true people of God is the Christian church and the true interpretation of the Law is that offered by Jesus and practiced by his followers. The Law, says he, is properly observed when one becomes inwardly good (loving) and when one practices in his daily life what love requires of him (7:12; 22:37-40). The book is thus an apology for the church in its struggle with the synagogue.

But this Gospel was written also to

The synagogue at Masada, first built by Herod the Great and rebuilt by Zealots; the earliest synagogue yet discovered

build up the church within: to teach new converts the requirements of their adopted faith; to reassure Christians of the validity of their trust in Jesus as the world's Savior; to urge them to imitate him in personal goodness, in suffering service, and in spreading the gospel of the kingdom; to offer them materials from the church's memories of Jesus for the purposes of worship, evangelism, and inner discipline. Libertine, lawless teachers were threatening the moral life of the church (7:15-23; 13:36 ff.; 22:11-13) and compromising its witness to both Jews and Gentiles. The book warns the church that only those who are morally like Jesus

and do his work in the world will enter the kingdom of heaven.

This Gospel also interprets Jesus and the church in ways Gentiles, as well as Jews, could appreciate. The presentation of Jesus as the Son of God would be congenial to Gentiles of the author's time. They would be well disposed toward a divine-human being who had been born of a virgin, who had confirmed his supernatural origin by his miraculous powers, whose true identity and function God had revealed to men so that they might understand and be saved. They were accustomed to divine saviors (kings, emperors, roving prophets) who were revealed

The ruins of Herod the Great's palace at Masada

as such to the elect in many of the religions of their day.

4. Sources

Two views of the sources of Matthew's material have been dominant.

The first, the traditional Roman Catholic view, has held with Augustine that Matthew was the earliest of the Gospels, that it was written in Hebrew and subsequently translated into Greek, and that the Gospel of Mark is an abridgement of Matthew.

This view has present-day Roman Catholic and Protestant supporters. They argue that behind Matthew, Mark, and Luke lies a primitive Aramaic document, written by a Jewish Christian of Palestine (probably Matthew, the apostle) sometime before the destruction of Jerusalem in A.D. 70 and the scattering of Jerusalem Christians. The first apostles and missionaries may have used this document as an aid to memory in their preaching, teaching, and evangelizing. In Greek translation this document ("Proto-Matthew") became the basic source of our Synoptic Gospels. Materials from other sources were added to Proto-Matthew during the last quarter of the first century to form our present Gospel of Matthew.

The second view resulted from careful investigation of the literary similarities among the first three Gospels in the nineteenth century and the first quarter of the twentieth. The investigators concluded that Mark, rather than being an abridgment of Matthew, was one of Matthew's principal sources of information. The author of Matthew, who used over 90 percent of Mark, followed Mark's order of events, shortened many of Mark's narratives, improved Mark's style, and in places altered Mark's theology (compare Mark 6:5 with Matt. 13:58, and Mark 10:18 with Matt. 19:17).

This view holds also that the author of Matthew used, besides Mark, a sayings source (now called "Q," from the German word *Quelle*, meaning "source") for some 250 verses containing mostly words of Jesus. He had in addition a third source of information (Special Matthew) for many stories and sayings (such as the nativity narrative, Peter's walking on the water, the coin in the fish's mouth, Pilate's wife's dream, many sayings of the Sermon on the Mount, and many parables) not available to the other Gospel writers. The sayings and parables may have come from a written Jerusalem document (now called "M" by some), and the stories from a special line of oral tradition.

The second view is the dominant one today.

5. Date, Place of Origin, Authorship

The reasons for dating Matthew to the last quarter of the first century are: (1) the apparent reference to the fall of Jerusalem in Matt. 22:7; (2) Matthew's use of Mark (written A.D. 65–70); (3) the strong defense of the Christian church against the attacks of the synagogue, from which the church seems to have been completely separated by the author's time; (4) the nature of the teaching opposed in Matthew, known from the Pastoral Epistles, the letters of John, the book of Revelation, Jude, II Peter, and elsewhere as a strong threat in the late first and early second centuries; (5) the advanced theology contained in this Gospel (the church with a universal mission, the image of the apostles defended and enhanced, the rich and highly complex view of Christ).

We do not know the exact place of origin of this Gospel, but it probably came from the eastern end of the Mediterranean. Early church tradition places it "among the Hebrews in their own language," that is, Palestine (Irenaeus, c. A.D. 180); but the strong evidence that the Gospel of Matthew used the Gospel of Mark in Greek as a principal source and was probably written in Greek speaks against Palestine. The most likely place is Syria, and probably Antioch.

The early church ascribed this Gospel to the Apostle Matthew. Why it did so is not known. The title "According to Matthew" was added to manuscripts of the book in the second century.

Objections to Matthew's authorship of the book are weighty. Why would Matthew, an eyewitness, use over 90 percent of Mark, the work of someone not an eyewitness? Why do the changes of Mark made in Matthew look so little like the changes an eyewitness would have made?

It may be that the Apostle Mat-

THE HERODS

HEROD THE GREAT

(37–4 B.C.; Matt. 2:1; Luke 1:5)

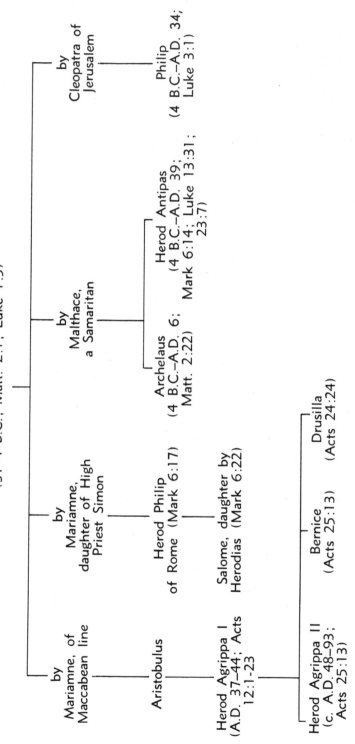

by
Mariamne, of
Maccabean line

Aristobulus

Herod Agrippa I
(A.D. 37–44; Acts
12:1-23

Herod Agrippa II
(c. A.D. 48–93;
Acts 25:13)

Bernice
(Acts 25:13)

Drusilla
(Acts 24:24)

by
Mariamne,
daughter of High
Priest Simon

Herod Philip
of Rome (Mark 6:17)

Salome, daughter by
Herodias (Mark 6:22)

by
Malthace,
a Samaritan

Archelaus
(4 B.C.–A.D. 6;
Matt. 2:22)

Herod Antipas
(4 B.C.–A.D. 39;
Mark 6:14; Luke 13:31;
23:7)

by
Cleopatra of
Jerusalem

Philip
(4 B.C.–A.D. 34;
Luke 3:1)

thew was the author or compiler of some source used in this Gospel (Q or M) and that his name thus passed over to the final book. It is also possible that the Apostle Matthew had gathered around himself followers who handed on his memories of Jesus. One of these toward the end of the first century may have put the present Gospel together in his name and, as it were, under his authority.

The final author was apparently a Jewish Christian who had been influenced by Greek culture, perhaps spiritually akin to Stephen's group at Jerusalem (Acts 6–7; 11:19-20). He wrote for Christians of this type in the emerging universal church of the late first century.

66. Mark

The Gospel of Mark is both a simple and a profound book. It contains a fast-moving story, told in plain language in dramatic episodes. These lead step by step to a bittersweet climax. When read at one sitting in a contemporary translation, it has the power to arouse the enthusiasm even of jaded teen-agers and adults, much as the rock opera *Jesus Christ, Superstar* has done.

It is at the same time a sophisticated book, full of profound theology. Scholars who are still probing its subtleties confess that its depths elude them. In some ways it is the most difficult of the four Gospels to comprehend.

Mark is regarded by most scholars of our time as the earliest of our Gospels and probably as the first "Gospel" ever written. With it a new literary form came into being—neither historical narrative nor preaching (proclamation), but preaching in the form of a story (see pp. 211-12).

1. Theme and Outline

Mark does not divide easily into sections, as the variety of outlines offered in commentaries and handbooks shows. It appears to be organized geographically, however.

Theme: Jesus, the mighty Son of God concealed in human form, accomplishes his redemptive work for all people through a ministry of sacrificial service and through vicarious death on a cross. (The key verse is 10:45.)

I.   Introduction: Jesus' preparation for his redemptive work through the ministry of John the Baptist and through his own baptism and temptation (1:1-13)

II. Jesus' redemptive work in Galilee and in adjacent areas (1: 14–9:50)

    A. In Galilee (1:14–7:23)

    B. In adjacent areas (Tyre, Sidon, Decapolis, Caesarea

PALESTINE
IN
JESUS' DAY

0   10   20
MILES

Tyre

PHOENICIA

GALILEE

Ceasarea Philippi

Capernaum

Bethsaida

Sea of Galilee

Cana

Tiberias

MT CARMEL

Nazareth

+ MT. TABOR

Nain

Mediterranean Sea

Caesarea

SAMARIA

Pella

DECAPOLIS

Samaria

Gerasa

MT GERIZIM

Jacob's Well

PERAEA

River Jordan

Joppa

Philadelphia

Lydda

Ephraim

Emmaus

Jericho

Jerusalem

Bethany

Bethlehem

Dead Sea

Machaerus

JUDAEA

Hebron

Gaza

DUMAEA

N

Philippi, with return journeys to Galilee) (7:24–9:50)

III. Jesus' redemptive work on the way to and in Jerusalem (10:1–16:8)
   A. On the way (10:1-52)
   B. In Jerusalem (11:1–16:8)
IV. A longer (16:9-20) and a shorter (two-sentence) ending

2. View of Jesus

Mark's Jesus is a divine being in human form, whose true identity and work are known to the demons (1:23-27, 34) but are hidden from men as a whole (4:11-12) and are only dimly and inaccurately perceived by his disciples (6:45-52; 8:14-21, 31-33; 9:10, 30-32).

This hidden Deity, the Son of God incarnate, has come to destroy the powers of evil and to inaugurate the kingdom of God. He is the Messiah (anointed King) of Jewish expectation and the heavenly Son of man (the coming judge of the world and inaugurator of the kingdom).

He achieves his redemptive work in a way surprising and mystifying to all: by unselfishly ministering to those bound by the demons' power, by suffering at the hands of his enemies, by dying on a cross, and by rising again. In his suffering and dying he pours out his life as a means of freeing "many" from their bondage, for they cannot free themselves (10:45). By his death he seals a covenant bond between God and men, offering them a new relationship based upon forgiveness and reconciliation (14:24).

As risen Lord, he will come soon in glory (13:24-31), perhaps appearing in Galilee to inaugurate his kingdom (14:28; 16:7).

3. Purposes

We must infer Mark's purposes in writing, since they are nowhere stated.

a. He tells the stories about Jesus' mighty deeds, about his work of teaching, and about his death and resurrection not as part of a history or biography of Jesus but as evidence that God has acted in Jesus for the redemption of all. He wants to promote faith in him. In short, Mark preaches "the gospel," the good news about Jesus, by means of episodes from the earthly life of Jesus.

b. Mark offers a defense of Christianity because of the official Jewish rejection of it and because of its offensiveness to many Gentiles. "Christ [Messiah] crucified" was "a stumbling block to Jews and folly to Gentiles" (I Cor. 1:23). Mark shows that God's way of salvation in the suffering, dying Jesus is indeed mysterious and mystifying—even the first disciples could not grasp it—but it is nonetheless the true and effective way of salvation for all people. The book thus grapples with the difficult problem of the scandal of the cross.

c. Mark's preoccupation with Jesus' ministry in Galilee (rather than in Jerusalem, as in the Gospel of John) and in the surrounding Gentile regions (Tyre, Sidon, Caesarea Philippi, the Decapolis, etc.) may suggest that he seeks to include the Gentile church in Jesus' intention. Mark sees the good

Reconstruction of the Synagogue at Capernaum

news as destined for the whole world (13:10; 14:9).

d. The emphasis in this Gospel on sacrificial suffering as the true mark of Christian discipleship (8:34-38; 10: 35-45), together with the picture of Jesus as the Messiah who had to suffer to fulfill his God-given mission (8:31; 9:12, 31; 10:33-34, 38, 45), may indicate that Mark wrote the Gospel for Christians everywhere who needed strengthening as they drank the bitter cup of suffering.

But he may have meant this emphasis especially for Christians in Rome. Early church tradition connects the writing of this Gospel with Rome during the last days of Peter there, or after the martyrdom of Peter and Paul

(see below). Nero's vicious slaughter of Roman Christians in A.D. 64 and the consequent hostility of the Roman populace would make an explanation such as Mark gives helpfully reassuring. This was: Christians have to suffer because Jesus had to suffer.

4. Sources

We know nothing certain about Mark's sources of information. Early church tradition (Papias, Irenaeus, Clement of Alexandria, and others) held that this Gospel was based on Mark's memory of the preaching of Peter, whose companion and interpreter Mark was.

Many scholars strongly challenge

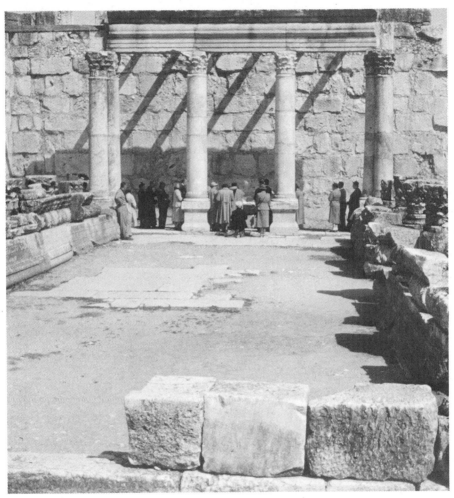

Remains of the 2nd and 3rd century synagogue at Capernaum, standing on the site of the synagogue of Jesus' time

this tradition today, since form criticism (see p. 214) has made it likely that Mark's Gospel was put together from many independent, or loosely associated, pieces of early Christian tradition. Furthermore, no details or points of view characteristic of Peter are clearly present in the Gospel.

The only closely knit piece of material in Mark is the Passion story (Mark 14:1–16:8). It is widely agreed today that the events leading immediately to the cross and the Resurrection were the first to be drawn together into a continuous narrative. These events explain why Jesus, the Messiah, died—a problem for faith, as we have seen. By drawing on individual stories and groups of stories circulating in the church, Mark extended the explanation backward from the final events to the beginning of Jesus' ministry in Galilee. Thus he offers a full story on the subject: Why did Jesus, the Messiah, die?

Mark seems to have found some collections of material at hand: conflict stories (2:1–3:6); parables (4:1-32); miracles (4:35–5:43); prophecies concerning the end (13:5-37); and the Passion story (14:1–16:8).

5. Authorship, Place, Date

The author of the Gospel of Mark was a collector and arranger of early church tradition concerning Jesus. No theory of authorship holds that he himself was an eyewitness of the ministry of Jesus.

Some have claimed, however, that he was the young man mentioned in 14:51-52, but there is no solid evidence to support this since the young man is not named or otherwise identified.

Early Christian writers (Papias, Irenaeus, Clement of Alexandria) tell us that the author's name was Mark. What Mark this was is debated today. Some scholars hold that he was an unknown Roman Marcus who gathered together Roman church tradition about Jesus. Others believe he was John Mark of Jerusalem, known to us from many New Testament passages (Acts 12:12, 25; 13:5, 13; 15:37-40; Philem. 24; Col. 4:10; II Tim. 4:11; I Pet. 5:13).

In spite of some problems relating to Mark's knowledge of the geography of Palestine and of certain Jewish legal practices, most experts today hold that the author was indeed John Mark of Jerusalem. His association with Peter in Rome (I Pet. 5:13, where "Babylon" is probably a symbolic name for Rome) undoubtedly was of help to him in his collecting and arranging of church traditions, even if his Gospel is not a transcript of Peter's preaching and was not produced until after the death of Peter (and Paul).

Arguments for Rome as the place of origin are stronger than for elsewhere (Antioch, Egypt, Galilee, Jerusalem). Supporting Rome are: the tradition (Papias, I Pet. 5:13, etc.) that Mark and Peter were associated in Rome; the apparent use of the Gospel of Mark in Roman Christian works (I Clement, the Shepherd of Hermas); the appropriateness for Roman Christians who had suffered under Nero of the strong emphasis in Mark on suffering as the normal expectation for Christians.

The explanation of Jewish customs and terms (7:3-4), as well as rather frequent Latin expressions (6:27; 12:14, 42; 15:16; etc.), while not arguing for Rome, makes Palestine unlikely.

The date of writing almost certainly falls between A.D. 65 and 70, as many considerations indicate. Early church tradition places the writing during Peter's ministry in Rome or after his death. Mark 13 anticipates the fall of Jerusalem (A.D. 70). This Gospel's interest in persecution and suffering fits the Roman situation after the persecution by Nero. The use of Mark by Matthew and Luke would fit this date.

6. Historical Reliability

Since Mark is a "Gospel" and not a biography or a chronicle of the events of Jesus' career, to what extent does it supply reliable information about Jesus of Nazareth?

Some scholars have said that Mark's outline of the ministry of Jesus is unreliable on the ground that it is his own construction, that it is a device to hold together the various bits of tradition that came to him, and that it serves his own theological interests.

However, the fact that Mark's story was adopted by Matthew and Luke as the backbone of their narratives and that this Gospel was accepted, cherished, and preserved in some important early Christian church (Rome? Antioch?) argues that it was recognized early as an essentially reliable portrait of Jesus.

While Mark's story of Jesus is far from complete, as the other Gospels show, the general sequence of events is historically probable. This sequence makes sense: Jesus began his ministry in Galilee after the imprisonment of John the Baptist; called disciples; carried out a healing and teaching ministry first in the synagogues; aroused opposition from straitlaced religious leaders; sent out the Twelve in an attempt speedily to reach the nation; withdrew from Galilee when Herod Antipas desired to arrest him as a dangerous troublemaker; faced, in a period of retreat, the question of the future course of his ministry; decided to go to Jerusalem for an appeal to the nation in its capital city; journeyed there with his disciples; attacked abuses in the temple and ran afoul of the religious and political leaders there; was consequently executed for treason. This outline is surely not something Mark created and imposed on traditional stories. It is true, of course, that there is no strict, detailed chronological order of events (3:1-6, for example, must come from relatively late in Jesus' career).

That Jesus, as Mark says, tried to stop people from proclaiming him openly as Messiah and that the disciples should have failed to grasp during his ministry what sort of a deliverer he regarded himself to be likewise make sense; it is not a theory imposed by Mark, as some have claimed. Messiahship to Jesus was a matter not of status but of redemptive action. The Messiah was suffering Servant—a concept hard to grasp, then as now!

7. The Ending of Mark's Gospel

Among ancient Greek manuscripts and versions there are differences in the way Mark's Gospel ends. Most of these documents contain what is now Mark 16:9-20, but in important early ones (e.g., Codex Sinaiticus and Codex Vaticanus—see pp. 362-63) vss. 9-20 are missing. Eusebius and Jerome (fourth century) indicate that the passage was absent from almost all manuscripts known to them.

Scholars agree today that 16:9-20

Inscription from Caesarea bearing the names of Tiberius and Pontius Pilate

and one important manuscript (Codex Washingtonensis—see p. 365) inserts between 16:14 and 16:15 a long passage containing a defense of the twelve apostles and an otherwise unrecorded saying of Jesus.

These various early endings suggest that for some reason the conclusion of Mark was thought unsatisfactory. Was the end accidentally or deliberately torn off at an early date? Or did Mark himself end the Gospel at 16:8, in a way that later seemed to others to be abrupt and deficient in the light of the other Gospels?

Scholars today increasingly believe that the Gospel of Mark as originally written ended at 16:8. Matthew and Luke seem to have known Mark as far as 16:8. And the fear (awe) on the part of the women confronted with the Resurrection is not an inappropriate way for Mark to have concluded his book.

differs considerably from Mark's vocabulary, style, and concepts and contains elements drawn from the other Gospels and the Acts. It is probably a second-century addition to the Gospel of Mark.

A brief (two-sentence) ending is found after 16:8 in a few manuscripts;

67. Luke

The French writer Ernest Renan called this Gospel "the most beautiful book in the world." Of the four Gospels, many Christians regard Luke as their favorite.

Its charm arises from many characteristics: its appealing picture of Jesus as the God-given, righteous humanitarian who sealed his redemptive love of outcasts, foreigners, the poor, and women with his death on the cross; its sheer literary artistry (in content, structure, phrasing); its

emotional heights (suspense, pathos); its comprehensiveness (much rich material, including parables, not found in the other Gospels); its cosmopolitan outlook; its devotional quality (emphasis on the importance of prayer and life in the Holy Spirit); its domestic scenes and tone; its charming birth and infancy stories; and much else.

We would be a great deal poorer in our knowledge of Jesus without this Gospel.

The Garden of Gethsemane, at the Church of All Nations, Jerusalem

1. Theme and Outline

The Gospel according to Luke is volume one of a two-volume work which we now call "Luke-Acts." The preface to the Acts of the Apostles (1:1-5) mentions and describes "the first book," clearly our Gospel of Luke, and mentions again the recipient of the two-book work, Theophilus (cf. Luke 1:3). The theme, contents, and style of the Acts show that the two volumes belong together. The following outline therefore will present the whole work.

The theme of Luke-Acts is: The Christian church is the true people of

God, called into being by God through the ministry, death, and resurrection of Jesus of Nazareth and empowered by God for a redemptive mission to all the earth; it is not a perversion of Judaism or a subversive society promoting rebellion against the Roman government.

Vol. I (The Gospel according to Luke): The Christian church originated in the ministry, death, and resurrection of Jesus of Nazareth, the Spirit-filled Savior, whom God sent to the Jewish people and to all nations.

    A. The preface—the author's sources of information and purpose in writing (1:1-4)

    B. The introduction—the birth and childhood of John the Baptist and Jesus (1:5–2:52)

    C. The preparation for Jesus' public ministry through the ministry of John the Baptist and through Jesus' baptism and temptation (3:1–4:13)

    D. Jesus' ministry in Galilee (4:14–9:50)

    E. Jesus' ministry on the way to Jerusalem (9:51–19:27)

    F. Jesus' ministry, death, and resurrection in Jerusalem (19:28–24:53)

Vol. II (The Acts of the Apostles): The universal Christian church came into being through the heroic, Spirit-filled witnessing of Jesus' disciples to Jews and Gentiles concerning the power of God which is redemptively active in the world through the crucified and resurrected Jesus. (For a detailed outline see p. 247.)

2. View of Jesus

This Gospel represents Jesus as a God-begotten, God-appointed, God-empowered, God-guided man, whose task was to free all people, without distinction as to race, sex, class, religion, from whatever bondage had victimized them. He would bring them to experience in this life in foretaste the blessings of the New Age over which he would reign as king.

According to the author of this Gospel, Jesus announced the purpose of his mission at the very beginning of his public activity by quoting Isa. 61:1-2:

The Spirit of the Lord is upon me,
because he has anointed me to
    preach good news to the poor.
He has sent me to proclaim release
    to the captives
and recovering of sight to the blind,
to set at liberty those who are
    oppressed,
to proclaim the acceptable year of
    the Lord. (Luke 4:18-19)

Luke shows that the Holy Spirit was not only the begetter of Jesus (1:35) but came upon him "in bodily form" at his baptism by John (3:22), guided him during his temptation in the wilderness (4:1-2), empowered him in his ministry in Galilee (4:14), and worked through him in healing diseases and casting out evil spirits (6:17-19). A life of constant prayer lay behind his possession of the Holy Spirit (3:21-22; 5:16-17; 6:12; 9:18; 10:21; 11:1).

Though he was a Jew sent to Jews ("the son of Abraham"—3:34), he was also sent to all people ("the son of Adam"—3:38). He was "a light for revelation to the Gentiles" (2:32). The hated Samaritans received his benefits (17:11-19). He ministered to women, even the harlots and the demon-possessed, and received them into his company of followers (7:36-50; 8:1-3; 10:38-42). He had special concern for the poor (4:18; 6:20; 7:22; 16:19-31), for tax collectors (5:27-32; 15:1-2; 19:1-10), and even for Pharisees (7:36 ff.; 11:37; 14:1).

Luke takes pains to show that Jesus, God's Spirit-filled Son (1:32, 35; 3:22; 4:41; etc.), the friend of all humanity, came to his death on the cross through no fault of his own. Pilate three times declared him innocent of any wrongdoing (23:4, 14-15, 22), as did Herod Antipas (23:6-12, 15) and the Roman centurion at the cross (23:47). The rejection of Jesus began among Jews in Galilee (4:16-30), was furthered by Jewish religious teachers (5:17–6:11; 11:53-54; 13:14-17; 15:2), and came to its climax among the Jewish religious authorities in Jerusalem (22:66–23:25; 24:20). He was a threat not to Roman authority but only to corrupt Jewish traditions and institutions.

Luke affirms that Jesus' death carried out the purpose of God for the redemption of all people (9:22, 30-31; 17:25; 24:25-27, 44-47). The long travel narrative, depicting Jesus on the way to Jerusalem (9:51–19:27),

Photo by H. T. Frank
Coin of Pontius Pilate, struck in A.D. 29

shows Jesus and the disciples treading the way of suffering marked out by the Father (13:33; 22:22, 37). Luke makes much of the concept of the *way* of Jesus and the *way* of the church as the *way* marked out by God. This way leads to "glory" (24:26), to the life of the kingdom of God.

The ascension, twice recorded (Luke 24:51; Acts 1:9), was for Luke the occasion of Jesus' divine enthronement. While as King he awaits the consummation of all things (Acts 3:21), he is active in the world through the Holy Spirit, which he has sent to the church (Acts 2:33) to enable it to proclaim the gospel to the nations (Acts 1:8).

Luke sees the purpose of God in the salvation of the world as embracing three historical stages: (1) the period of Israel (of the Law and the prophets, including John the Baptist); (2) the period of Jesus (his preaching of the coming kingdom and manifestation in his ministry of the power of that kingdom); (3) the period of the church (when the Spirit enables Jesus' disciples to carry the good news throughout the world and to draw together the universal people of God). (See Luke 16:16; 19:11; Acts 1:6-8; 3:21.)

The period of Jesus is thought of by Luke as "the center of history" (Hans Conzelmann). In Jesus, God has fulfilled the promises contained in the law and the prophets (Luke 4: 18-21; 24:25-27, 44-47). In Jesus, God has drawn together the people of the coming kingdom (the church). It is their task to continue in the work entrusted to them until the kingdom of God finally appears (19:11-27).

Luke's favorite titles for Jesus are Lord, Christ, and Son. In Luke-Acts these are applied to him both before and after his death and resurrection.

3. Sources

Luke says that he was not an eyewitness of the events of Jesus' ministry but that he had investigated carefully the information contained in the eyewitness traditions and the written accounts available to him (1:1-4).

Most scholars agree that Mark was one of Luke's principal sources. More than 60 percent of Mark appears in Luke, and Mark's sequence of events is largely followed. Luke abbreviated some of Mark's stories, often improved his language, and avoided expressions and stories that would be misleading or offensive to Gentile readers (e.g., Mark 7:24-30; 11:12-14, 20-25).

A second source appears to have been the document we call Q (see p. 214), which he employed as a source for the words of Jesus. He used materials from Mark and Q in blocks, following first one and then the other. He seems to have reproduced Q's order rather faithfully.

More than one third of Luke has no parallel in the other Gospels. Whether this material came from a written source or from miscellaneous oral traditions is not known. Its point of view is Palestinian. There is a strong interest in "the poor" and a close association of poverty with piety. Jesus' compassion toward women and the Samaritans is prominent in it. It may be that this material came into Luke's possession from his contact with the church at Caesarea when he was with Paul there (Acts 23:33–26:32).

It has been held that Q and Luke's special material had been joined into an earlier form of our Luke (Proto-Luke) before the sections from Mark were added. But this hypothesis is losing favor today.

Luke's birth and infancy stories (chaps. 1–2) seem to have come from yet another source (or sources), because of their peculiarities of style and language.

Luke welded his sources together skillfully.

4. Purposes

a. A Historical Purpose

The author realized that he lived a number of years after the events of

Jesus' life, that many traditions and records of that life existed, and that considerable controversy and uncertainty about Jesus prevailed in his time. He wished to set the facts straight by his record.

He makes a solid attempt to relate Jesus to world history by mentioning the census of Augustus under Quirinius (2:1-2), by the chronological context of the appearance of John the Baptist (3:1-2), and by naming Roman emperors and officials (Acts 11: 28; 18:2, 12).

He wishes also to explain how the church of his time arose. He regards it as important in the life of the empire and believes it will continue in the world for some time yet (19:11; 21: 7-9). Thus he connects Jesus not only with world history but with church history.

b. An Apologetic Purpose

He wishes by the historical facts to clear up misunderstandings about the Christian movement.

He refutes the charge that Jesus and the apostles and Christian missionaries were political revolutionists by showing that Pilate three times declared Jesus innocent (chap. 23), that Herod found no grounds for accusing him (23:6-12, 15), that the centurion at the cross attested his innocence (23: 47), that the Jewish authorities in Jerusalem (particularly Gamaliel) had reservations about the early Christians' guilt (Acts 5:33-40), and that Paul was repeatedly cleared or left uncharged by Roman authorities (Acts 18:12-17; chaps. 24–26). Ungodly Jews were the ones who instigated the opposition to Jesus and early Christian leaders. These leaders were true, God-pleasing Jews. Therefore, Christianity is entitled to the sufferance and protection that the Romans traditionally allowed Judaism.

He wishes also to show Jews and those Gentiles who were favorable to Judaism ("God-fearers"—see p. 238) that Christianity is not a perverted, but rather an authentic, Judaism. God (the Holy Spirit) was behind the Christian movement from the beginning. The apostles were loyal to the Old Testament rightly interpreted and to the temple (Luke 24:52; Acts 2:46). Paul received his call to Gentile missions in the temple (Acts 22:17-21). The church's true home was the holy city Jerusalem (Luke 24:52; Acts 1:4). The author was convinced that Old Testament hopes had found their fulfillment in the coming of Jesus, in the gift of the Holy Spirit to the church, and in the Christian world mission. Therefore the Jews have no real grounds of complaint against the Christian church.

c. An Evangelistic Purpose

It is evident that the author was a devout Christian, fully convinced of the truth of the Christian gospel, proud of the remarkable accomplishments of Jesus and the Christian church, and zealous to spread the new faith. Paul, the great missionary to the Gentiles, was obviously one of the author's heroes (Acts chaps. 13–28).

It may be that the author hoped to convert Theophilus and other readers to whom the book might come by clearing away objections commonly raised to Christianity.

5. Original Readers and Author

Theophilus, meaning "friend (or beloved) of God," was a proper name borne by both Greeks and Jews of the period. It is probably not to be understood here as meaning any reader beloved of God into whose hands the two-volume work might come.

The term "most excellent," used in Acts 23:26; 24:2; 26:25 in address to high government officials, seems to indicate that Theophilus was a man of importance. Whether he was a Christian or a "God-fearer" (a Gentile who had become a half-convert to Judaism—Acts 10:2; 13:16) or a high Gentile official suspicious of or opposed to Christianity has been much debated. Luke's eagerness to defend Christianity makes it unlikely that he was a Christian.

Apparently Luke, according to the custom of the time, expected Theophilus, as the addressee, to see to the distribution of the book. In this sense he was a patron of the author.

The author's identity is not beyond dispute. Early church tradition assigns the work to Luke, the physician and companion of Paul (Col. 4:14). An attempt has been made to prove from the language of Luke-Acts that its author was a physician, but this has been refuted by the fact that there is no more medical language in this work than in works known to be by nonmedical authors of the period. The "we" passages of Acts (16:10-17; 20:5-15; 21:1-18; 27:1–28:16) may indicate that the author was an eyewitness of the events narrated in these passages, but it is also possible that these sections are based on an itinerary or diary compiled by someone other than the author of Luke-Acts and do not, therefore, indicate our author's personal participation.

The strongest arguments against authorship by a companion of Paul have been raised on the ground of the author's apparent lack of accurate knowledge about Paul's career and his theology (see p. 252).

The strongest arguments in favor are: (1) since Luke was not an apostle, the church of the second century would hardly have assigned the authorship to him without sufficient reason; and (2) the author's cultural characteristics (excellent Greek style, historical interests, cosmopolitan outlook, etc.) imply a person such as Luke the physician must have been.

Whoever he was, he was the one great historian between Polybius, the last of the great Greek historians, and Eusebius, the first important church historian.

6. Date and Place of Composition

The use of the Gospel according to Mark (written A.D. 65–70) in Luke-Acts, the author's seeming knowledge of the destruction of Jerusalem by the Romans in A.D. 70 (Luke 19:41-44; 21:20-24), and the appropriateness of a learned defense of Christianity in the face of strong Jewish attacks and persistent Gentile suspicions suggest a date between A.D. 70 and 90. Some scholars have argued for a date before the end of Paul's trial in Rome,

Jerusalem in Jesus' Day

shortly after the last event described in the Acts; but this puts the writing of Mark too early.

Caesarea, Achaea (Greece), and Rome have been suggested as the place of writing, but these are only conjectures. A location outside Palestine is likely in view of the cultured, Greek-speaking readers for whom the work was intended.

68. John

Christian readers, ancient and modern, have reacted differently to the Gospel of John.

In the second century some Christians known as "Alogoi" judged its teaching, particularly about the Holy Spirit, unorthodox, denied its apostolic origin, and assigned its authorship to Cerinthus, a Gnostic heretic (see p. 335). Clement of Alexandria, on the other hand, thought this Gospel "inspired by the Spirit." He called it "a spiritual gospel."

In the nineteenth and twentieth centuries many scholars have denied its apostolic origin and its historical and religious value. Others, like William Temple, Archbishop of York, have confessed their deep love of the book.

Today, the pendulum is swinging strongly toward a positive appreciation of both its historical value and its religious significance.

1. Theme and Outline

Theme: Jesus is the heaven-sent Son of God and the giver of eternal life to all who believe in him.

Prologue: The Word of God became flesh (1:1-18).

I. Jesus' signs revealed his glory, as Son of God and giver of eternal life, to all who had eyes to see (1:19–12:50).

  A. Eyewitnesses at the beginning of his earthly ministry proclaimed his identity and glory (1:19–4:42).

  B. Many, especially the Jewish religious authorities, rejected his status and work as Son and life-giver, but others accepted him (4:43–12:50).

II. Jesus's parting instructions, his death, and his resurrection revealed his glory, as Son of God and giver of life, to his believing disciples (13:1–20:31).

  A. His parting instructions (chaps. 13–17)

  B. His death (chaps. 18–19)

  C. His resurrection (chap. 20)

Epilogue: The risen Jesus provides for the needs of his church until his (second) coming (chap. 21).

2. View of Jesus

The author's thought about Jesus revolves around three main centers.

a. Jesus Is the Son of God.

The phrases "Son of God" and "the Son" are found about twenty-eight times in this Gospel. Two emphases occur in them.

First, the Son has a unique intimacy with God, his Father. He is God's *only* Son (1:14; 3:16, 18), "only" meaning "unique" or "only one of its kind." This unique relationship involves essential identity with God, both in the Son's preexistent state (17:5, 24) and in his incarnate existence (5:17-18; 14:9). The Father's love for the Son is stressed (3:35; 5:20; 15:9; 17:23, 24, 26). Some scholars argue that the union between Father and Son claimed in this book is a love union, rather than a union of substance or essence (15:9; 17:23-26), since believers can share in it (14:20, 23; 17:21-23).

Second, the Son is subordinate to and dependent on the Father: "the Father is greater than I" (14:28); "I can do nothing on my own authority" (5:30). The Son is *sent* by the Father (8:42; 10:36; 11:42; 13:20; 17:3; etc.) to accomplish the Father's work in the world (5:30, 36; 14:10, 31).

Convent de Sion
Reconstruction of Herod's Antonia, the fortress that guarded the temple area
(Acts 21:31-36)

Here the Hebrew practice of appointing an official legal representative, who is invested with all the authority of the sender, is evident (13:20). The Son is completely obedient to the Father (4:34; 6:38; 15:10).

The work of the Son, like that of the Father, is to give life to men (5:21; 6:35, 48-51; 11:25) and to pass judgment on them (5:22, 27, 30; 9:39-41).

Jesus' sonship in this Gospel involves identity with and moral likeness to God.

Both Jews and Gentiles would find meaning in the characterization of Jesus as the Son of God. Jews referred to Israel, Israel's king, the righteous in Israel, the angels, and perhaps to the Messiah as the son or sons of God, while Gentiles used the term to suggest the divinity of their emperors and kings. In Judaism it signified close religious relationship with and obedient service to God, and in Greek usage it meant divine origin and essential divinity. In the Gospel of John both usages flow together.

b. Jesus Is the Son of Man.

Thirteen times Jesus is said to be "the Son of man." His true home is heaven (3:13; 6:62). He has come down to earth to be the Savior of men through exaltation on the cross (3:14-15; 8:28; 12:23). After gathering together the scattered children of God (11:52), he will ascend again into heaven (6:62). He is the judge of all men (5:27-29). This judgment is both a present and a future action (9:39-41; 5:27-29). As Son of man he is the point of contact between earth and heaven (1:51).

Jewish thought in the first century had been deeply influenced by Greek and oriental concepts. Widespread was the belief in a heavenly, ideal man, a glorious Adam, who was the pattern after which mankind was fashioned and who would descend at last to fallen earth and restore men to the blessedness they had lost. Paul speaks of Christ as "the last Adam," "the man of heaven," who will give believers spiritual bodies for the life of the age to come (I Cor. 15:45-49). Such a heavenly redeemer is described in Jewish apocalyptic books (I Enoch, II Esdras) and lies behind the theology of the Gospel of John.

c. Jesus Is the Word and the Wisdom of God.

The Prologue (1:1-18) interprets Jesus by use of the widespread concept of the Word (*Logos*) of God.

Greek philosophers spoke of inward thought and the outward expression of thought in speech as Word (*Logos*). They also spoke of God as *Logos,* as a fiery vapor capable of thinking, permeating all things, holding the universe together, and rationally governing all change. For them *Logos* was rational creative power and rational expression (revelation).

Judaism had a counterpart in the concept of Wisdom. Wisdom was with God before the creation (Prov. 8: 22 ff.) and served as an active agent in creation (Wisd. of Sol. 7:22). Wisdom is the binding force linking the world to its Creator (Wisd. of Sol. 1: 7). Wisdom came to earth and invited men to receive instruction (Prov. 8: 1-11), but foolish men refused (Prov. 1:24-25). Wisdom is the reflection of God's eternal light (Wisd. of Sol. 7: 26). It is God's truth, meant to lead men to life (Prov. 8:35) and immortality (Wisd. of Sol. 6:18-19). Wisdom seeks disciples (Prov. 1:20-23) and makes them friends of God (Wisd. of Sol. 7:14, 27). But Wisdom's coming divides men into receivers and rejecters, with the consequences of life or death.

The Gospel of John represents Jesus as having preexisted with God (1:1; 17:5). He served as agent in creation (1:3). He descended to earth to dwell among men (1:10-11, 14; 3: 13; 6:38). He revealed the mind and purposes of God (1:18; 7:16, 29). He sought out disciples, who were then united into one family of God (1:12-13; 11:52; 17:6-23). He experienced both acceptance and rejection (1:11-13; 3:20-21; 9:35-41). He brought light and life to believers (1:4; 8:12; 11:25-26) and death and judgment to unbelievers (3:18-20; 5:28-29; 12: 48).

Though much in this picture of Jesus comes from concepts current in the author's age, he is unique at one central point. He alone declares that the Word (or Wisdom) "became flesh" (1:14). To say that eternal creative

Photo by H. T. Frank
A Roman lamp of a type perhaps known
by Jesus (Matt. 5:15)

Reason appeared as a man among men
for the purpose of revelation and redemption was possible only by those
who had seen God's glory in the man
Jesus (1:14; 2:11; 17:22).

3. John and the Synoptic Gospels

Even the casual reader is aware of
the striking differences between the
Fourth Gospel and the first three. For
example:

The Fourth Gospel

Jesus' ministry is chiefly in Judea
and Jerusalem.
Jesus talks about himself and the
significance of his ministry.
Jesus teaches in long discourses,
often of a controversial nature.
Jesus' enemies are "the Jews."
The reason for the hostility to
Jesus is his claims regarding
himself.
Jesus' miracles are "signs" which
point to his true identity.

The Synoptics

Jesus' ministry is chiefly in Galilee.

Jesus preaches and teaches about
the kingdom of God.
Jesus teaches in short, pithy sayings, in parables, in conver-
sations in normal life situations as well as in controversy.
Jesus' enemies are the Pharisees.
The reason for the hostility is Jesus' revolutionary (liberal)
attitude toward the Law of
Moses.
Jesus' miracles are works of compassion for the needy.

The differences call for explanation.
Can both pictures of Jesus be correct?
Which better describes the historical
Jesus? Or are both needed for a true
understanding of him?

4. The Sources of the Gospel of John

In the first third of the twentieth
century many scholars believed that
the author of John had used the Synoptic Gospels (at least Mark and
Luke) in writing his Gospel, that he
was dissatisfied with their picture of
Jesus, and that he wished to replace
it with his own. They held that there
was little, if any, historical tradition
in his Gospel where he was not dependent on the Synoptics.

Today the pendulum is swinging toward the view that the author of John
did not use the Synoptics, that he drew
on a line of tradition unknown to the
Synoptic writers, and that this tradition contained considerable accurate
historical information about Jesus. It
appears that this tradition stemmed
from Palestine and was basically

Hebrew, not Greek, as proved by Aramaic words, Jewish grammatical constructions, Hebrew poetic forms, accurate geography and place names, and a Jewish-type theology, now known to us from the Dead Sea Scrolls.

Recent treatments of Jesus' career and teaching use some of the information peculiar to the Gospel of John, such as Jesus' enlistment of John the Baptist's disciples (1:19-51), the early Judean ministry of Jesus (3:22-24), several appearances at Jerusalem feasts (chaps. 5–10), and an earlier date for the Last Supper (18:28; 19:14).

5. Purposes

The Gospel itself suggests its purpose: "that you may believe that Jesus is the Christ, the Son of God, and that believing you may have life in his name" (20:31).

Unfortunately, all Greek manuscripts do not read the same in this verse. Some have a verbal form which must be translated "that you may continue to believe," and others have "that you may come to believe." The first would imply that the readers were Christians who needed support for their faith in Jesus, and the second that the readers had not yet come to faith in him. In 19:35 the same problem appears, but the best manuscripts have "continue to believe." This is probably the meaning in 20:31.

The author's purposes seem to have been:

a. To Strengthen the Faith of Christians in the Face of Attacks of Opponents

The Jews denied the messiahship of Jesus; John affirms it strongly (1:41; 4:25-26). The Jews insisted on the validity of their religious institutions and worship; John claims that in Jesus and the church these are superseded (2:13-22; 3:1-14; 4:20-24; 6:31-32). Since Christianity is the fulfillment of Judaism (5:39-47; 8:56; 12:41), Judaism has lost its preeminence. "The Jews" in the Gospel are evil men who, by rejecting Jesus, showed that they belonged to "the world," to darkness and the devil (8:44).

This Gospel may have been addressed to Christians still in Jewish synagogues of the Greco-Roman world who, in the last quarter of the first century, were being pressured to renounce faith in Jesus on pain of excommunication. The book would encourage them to persist in their trust in Jesus.

It is possible that it was meant also to counter the claims of the disciples of John the Baptist that their master, not Jesus, was the Messiah (1:6-8, 15, 19-36; 3:28-30).

Enemies of the faith were inside, as well as outside, the church. Some Christians claimed that Jesus was not really human, that God could not clothe himself in evil flesh. John's insistence on the real humanity of Jesus (1:14; 19:34) may be aimed to counteract this false teaching.

b. To Convert Non-Christians

Some scholars hold that this Gospel had as one of its aims the conversion of Jews and of intelligent pagans who were concerned about the true way of

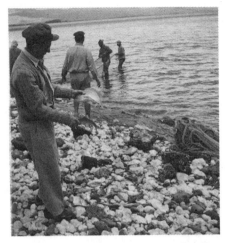

A modern-day fishing scene at the Sea of Galilee

salvation. Such a purpose would be in harmony with one way of reading 20: 31 (see above) and may have been included in the author's objective.

6. Author, Place of Writing, and Original Readers

Second-century church tradition ascribed this Gospel to "John, the disciple of the Lord, who also reclined on his bosom" (Irenaeus) and affirmed that John published it at Ephesus. Unfortunately, reliable evidence supporting John's residence in Ephesus is lacking in Christian literature before Irenaeus (end of second century). If John did live there, it must have been when he was very old.

Some think that certain facts about the Gospel of John (such as differences from the Synoptics and the speculative and sophisticated theology) make it impossible to accept the church's tradition of authorship by John the apostle. They point to a tradition in the church, dating to the fifth to ninth centuries, that said that both James and John were killed by Jews (as may be suggested in Mark 10: 39). They argue that Irenaeus was confused about the identity of the John who lived in Ephesus—that he was the Elder John, mentioned by Papias (c. A.D. 140), not John the son of Zebedee. Thus the author was not an eyewitness of the events he describes.

Today the discovery of the Semitic and Palestinian nature of the tradition lying behind this Gospel, of its independence of the Synoptic tradition, and of some marks of historical accuracy in its facts has brought a return to the view that the apostle John somehow stands behind it—as the source of the tradition, if not as the actual writer of the Gospel. Ancient teachers gathered around them disciples to whom they committed their teaching. One of the apostle John's disciples, whom we call the evangelist, may have been the actual writer, probably in the city of Ephesus. It would be natural for such a disciple to refer to his teacher as "the disciple whom Jesus loved" (13:23; 19:26; 20:2; 21:7, 20) and to issue the book in his name.

It is likely that chap. 21 and some passages in the rest of the Gospel were added to the book by an editor who belonged to the same group as the evangelist, as 21:24 suggests.

7. Date of Writing

The discovery of an early papyrus fragment of the Gospel of John (Papyrus Rylands Gk. 457 [known as Papyrus 52], containing John 18:31-33, 37-38, dating to about A.D. 135–50, and of Egyptian origin) seems to require a date around the end of the first century for this Gospel. If the papyrus was written in Ephesus, one would assume about a generation for its wide dissemination in Egypt.

If the author of the Gospel of John meant to encourage faith in Christians who were threatened with excommunication from synagogues in the Gentile world, the date may be as early as A.D. 80–90, or slightly later (90–100), a time when such pressure was acute. The Palestinian tradition contained in the Gospel probably took form before the fall of Jerusalem in A.D. 70.

69. The Acts of the Apostles

We pointed out in the discussion of the Gospel according to Luke that the Acts of the Apostles is volume 2 of a two-volume work, commonly known as Luke-Acts. The summary of the contents of volume 1 and the mention of Theophilus in Acts 1:1, plus the style, thought, and obvious purposes of the two volumes, make this clear.

In the second century, volume 2 was separated from volume 1 (the Gospel according to Luke). The latter was classed with the three other books of its type, and the four Gospels came

The great theater at Ephesus, seating 24,000, where Paul's enemies protested against his ministry (Acts 19:23-41)

as a group into early canonical lists. The Acts obviously belonged to a different category of literature and contained different subject matter. It was associated in early New Testament manuscripts with the Catholic (General) Epistles or with the Pauline Epistles.

Its present position is most fitting, for it shows how the work of Jesus continued after his death and resurrection in the spread of the church "to the end of the earth." And it makes understandable the letters of Paul and the other New Testament letters to the scattered churches.

1. Importance

The Acts has been called Christianity's "Hall of Fame." Here is the absorbing story of history-making events, centered in heroes of the faith who established the church in both the Jewish and Gentile worlds. Without this narrative we would have only scattered information, chiefly from the letters of Paul, about one of the most dynamic and creative movements of human history. It is the only bridge we possess between Jesus and Paul, between the gospel *of* Jesus and the gospel *about* Jesus, between the informal fellowship of disciples who gathered around Jesus and the sturdy organization called the church that sank deep roots in the soil of the first-century world.

2. Theme and Outline

Theme: The universal Christian church came into being through the heroic, Spirit-filled witnessing of Jesus' disciples to Jews and Gentiles concerning the power of God which is redemptively active in the world through the crucified and resurrected Jesus.

The Preface (1:1-2)
I. The establishment of the church in Jerusalem through the disciples' witnessing (1:3–8:3)
   A. The preparation for witnessing (1:3–2:13)
   B. The witnessing of Peter, John, and all the apostles and the establishment of the church through persecution (2:14–5:42)
   C. The witnessing and the persecution of the Hellenist (Greek-speaking) Christians (6:1–8:3)
II. The establishment of the church in Samaria and Judea through the disciples' witnessing (8:4–11:18)
   A. The witnessing of Philip in Samaria and the coastland (chap. 8)
   B. The preparation of Saul for Christian witnessing (9:1-31)
   C. The witnessing of Peter in Lydda, Joppa, and Caesarea and its sequel in Jerusalem (9:32–11:18)
III. The establishment of the church in Gentile lands through the witness of the Jerusalem Greek-speaking Christians and of Paul and his associates (11:19–28:31)
   A. The founding of the church in Antioch (11:19-30)

B. The persecution of the church in Jerusalem and the death of Herod, the persecutor (12:1-25)
C. The first witnessing mission of Paul (in Cyprus and southern Galatia) and its sequel at the Jerusalem Council (13:1–15:35)
D. The second witnessing mission of Paul (in lands around the Aegean Sea) (15:36–18:22)
E. The third witnessing mission of Paul (in Asia, Macedonia, Achaea) and his journey to Jerusalem (18:23–21:16)
F. Paul's arrest in Jerusalem, the hearings in Caesarea, and his journey to and activity in Rome (21:17–28:31)

This outline is one of several ways of analyzing the contents of the Acts. Some interpreters divide it into two parts: "The Acts of Peter" (chaps. 1–12) and "the Acts of Paul" (chaps. 13–28) or "From Jerusalem to Antioch" (chaps. 1–12) and "From Antioch to Rome" (chaps. 13–28). Others find five or more divisions and some none at all. The outline above takes as its clue Acts 1:8.

3. Theology

The word "witness," both as a noun and as a verb, is very prominent in this book. The theme of the Acts appears first in Luke 24:46-49, where it says that the disciples are witnesses of the fact and of the redemptive signifi-cance of the death and resurrection of Jesus. "Clothed with power from on high," they are to preach "repentance and forgiveness of sins . . . in his name to all nations."

According to Acts 5:29-32, this is precisely the role Peter and his associates fulfilled as "witnesses" to Israel. Throughout the Acts, testimony to the fact and the meaning of the Resurrection is (or is to be) offered by witnesses (1:22; 2:32, 40; 3:15; 4:33; 5:30-32; 10:39-42; etc.). Included also is witnessing to the God-anointed ministry of Jesus (10:38-39; cf. 1:21-22).

From these references we may conclude that a witness is one who has seen certain events. But he is also one who explains the meaning of the events he has seen. He speaks of both happenings and meanings. He is thus a kind of prophet (10:41-43).

In the Acts the term "witness" is used also for Paul, who had seen and heard the heavenly, not the earthly, Jesus (22:15; 26:16). Sometimes the prophets (10:43), God (14:3; 15:8), the Holy Spirit (20:23), the Council (the Sanhedrin—22:5), the Jews (26:5), and even the enemies of the faith (6:13; 7:58) are said to be witnesses. Basically the term is a legal one, meaning one who testifies (usually at a trial), on the basis of personal knowledge and experience, to the truth of something. In another usage in the church (Heb. 12:1; I Tim. 2:6) the term came to mean one who testified to the truth of the faith by sacrificing his life, that is, a martyr.

Many sermons in the Acts set forth the early testimony about Jesus, especially about his resurrection. These

Damascus: the street called Straight (Acts 9:11)

follow a somewhat common pattern, similar to Old Testament creedal recitals (such as Deut. 26:5-9; Josh. 24: 2-13) which recount God's acts in the redemption of his people. Early Christian preaching stressed God's redemptive activity and showed how it culminated in Jesus (Acts 13:16-41).

At least three major emphases occur in these sermons:

a. Jesus' death, resurrection, and exaltation are the deeds of God, who worked through the deeds of wicked men, in fulfillment of Old Testament prophecy concerning the redemption of Israel and the nations.

b. The resurrected, exalted Jesus is both Lord (Sovereign Master) and Christ (God's anointed King of the New Age and judge of all men).

c. In view of the rejection and crucifixion of Jesus, men should repent, accept Jesus as Savior in baptism, receive the gift of the Holy Spirit, and inherit God's promise of the New Age.

Sometimes, perhaps particularly for Gentile audiences, the witnesses included facts of Jesus' career (10:36-39).

The Acts tells us the witnessing was carried out in the power and under the direction of the Holy Spirit. The book's title might properly be "The Acts of the Holy Spirit Through the Apostles." The Holy Spirit was God's gift poured out on the disciples by the exalted Jesus (2:33), usually in an experience of prayer (Luke 3:21-22; Acts 1:14; 2:1 ff; 4:31; 8:15) but sometimes through baptism (2:38), often through the laying on of hands (8:12-17; 9:17-18; 19:2-6) or simply during the proclamation of the gospel (10:44-48). Receiving the Holy Spirit was an event which occurred more than once (2:1 ff.; 4:31). The Spirit was God's gift to every Christian.

The Holy Spirit's presence in believers resulted in miraculous achievements, such as speaking in tongues (2: 1 ff.; 10:46) and healings (5:12-16; cf. 10:38); courage and wisdom for witnessing (1:8; 4:8 ff., 31; 13:9); knowledge of future events (11:28; 20:23); guidance in decision-making (8:29; 10:19-20; 15:28; 16:6-8); moral and spiritual fruits in personal life (6:5; 9:31; 11:24; 13:52; 15:8-9); and brotherly sharing in the church (2:44-46; 4:32-35).

Prayer was the means by which God's guidance and power came to the church. The first Christians prayed in many circumstances: while awaiting the fulfillment of Jesus' promise concerning the coming of the Holy Spirit and of the New Age (1:14), when threatened by enemies or suffering at their hands (4:23-31; 12:12; 16:25), when confronted by the sickness and death of others (9:40; 28:8), when concerned about the spiritual needs of others (8:15), when parting from Christian brethren (20:36; 21:5), when selecting or commissioning persons for special service (1:24; 6:6; 13:3; 14:23), when facing martyrdom at the hands of persecutors (7:59-60). They prayed also at the set time and places of prayer (3:1; 6:4; 10:9). They prayed in homes (1:13-14; 12:12), in the temple (2:46; 3:1; 22:17-21), in jail (16:25), on the seashore (21:5), on shipboard (27:35). They prayed for the Holy Spirit for themselves and others, for guidance in choices, for courage in the face of opposition, for deliverance from danger, for the welfare of friends, for power to do the humanly impossible, for God's help for persons given special responsibility in the church, for forgiveness of enemies.

4. Purposes

On the historical, apologetic, and evangelistic purposes of Luke-Acts, see the discussion in chap. 67.

5. Sources

The question of the sources of the Acts is particularly difficult. Investigators have sought a solution in two directions:

a. Written Sources

Some have regarded Acts 1:1b–15: 35 as a translation into Greek of an Aramaic document, done by the author of 15:36–28:31. They hold that he wrote this latter part from personal knowledge. Others have thought that three or more written sources lie behind chaps. 1–15, these sources having come from Jerusalem, Antioch, and Caesarea.

The unexplained appearance of "we" in sections of the latter half of the Acts (16:10-17; 20:5-15; 21:1-18; 27:1–28:16) and the similarity of this material to a diary or itinerary have led some to conclude that a travel narrative, written by the author of Luke-Acts or by someone else, was the source of this portion of the book.

Photo by H. T. Frank

The Theodotus Inscription from a 1st-century A.D. synagogue in Jerusalem records the names of its donors and their purposes in building it.

b. Oral Sources

Form criticism (see p. 214) has led some scholars to conclude that underlying the Acts are no written sources but only pieces of oral tradition. The author of the Acts put these pieces together. He formed a framework of narrative for them and put his own stamp of thought and style on them. He may have used his own written notes for such events as he had personal knowledge of. But he had no lengthy, written documents.

It is likely that the many speeches of the Acts are summaries in the author's own language—not stenographic reports—of what he had been told or believed was said on the various occasions.

6. Authorship, Original Readers, Date, Place of Composition

See the discussion of the Gospel according to Luke, chap. 67.

7. Historical Accuracy

We shall forever be in debt to the author of Luke-Acts for gathering together information from many sources about the founding and spread of early Christianity. During those feverish and uncertain first days, few persons, if any, could have had much interest in, or even thoughts about, the preservation of exact records.

What we have in the Acts, particularly in chaps. 1–15, is more or less isolated, fragmentary, and disconnected pieces. But they are of great historical worth. The author's purposes and his language and style shaped their present form, to be sure, as they did the material he used in the writing of his Gospel.

It is plain that there are differences in fact and point of view between the material in the Acts and in the letters of Paul. For example, the Acts has Paul in Jerusalem twice before the Jerusalem Council (9:26-30; 11:27-30), whereas Paul himself states flatly he was there only once (Gal. 1:18–2:10). It is possible that Acts 11:27-30 and Acts 15 refer to the same journey and should not have been separated by the author of the Acts. And the picture of the nature of Paul's contacts with the Jerusalem Christian leaders on his first return to that city presents differences (in Gal. 1:18-24 private talks with Peter and James only; in Acts 9:26-30 contact with "the apostles" and a public ministry there). There are some important differences in the theology of Paul as represented in the Acts and in his letters.

But the Acts is certainly not "historical fiction rather than history," as some have claimed. The author is more than "a fascinating narrator" who wove together an entertaining story of Christian beginnings. His interest in dates, places, official terminology, customs, local color, and the like gives substance to his claim that he wished to write both accurately and in an orderly fashion and that he had a deep regard for the truth (Luke 1:3-4).

70. The Letters of Paul

Twenty-one books of the New Testament are in the form of letters. Of these, thirteen are expressly ascribed to Paul in their opening greeting:

Romans	Colossians
I and II Corinthians	I and II Thessalonians
Galatians	I and II Timothy
Ephesians	Titus
Philippians	Philemon

Almost all manuscripts of Paul's letters from the fourth century on include another biblical book—Hebrews. Its text does not claim authorship by Paul or by anyone else. Though in some respects it resembles Paul's letters, in others it differs widely from them and almost surely came from some other writer (see pp. 318-19).

The letters ascribed to Paul in most Greek manuscripts of the fourth century and later, as in our modern translations, are arranged according to

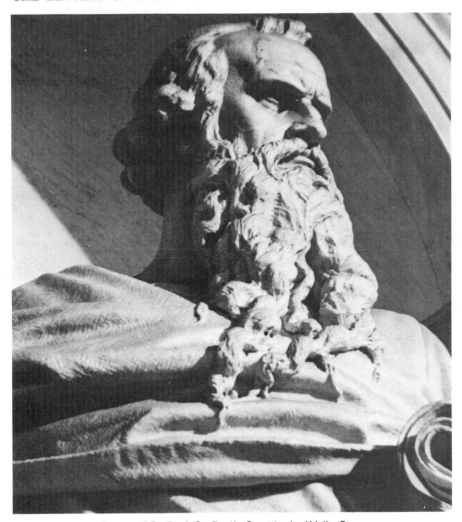

Statue of St. Paul, St. Paul's Outside the Walls, Rome

their recipients and their length. Letters to churches come first, from the longest (Romans) to the shortest (II Thessalonians). Next are the letters to individuals, again from the longest (I Timothy) to the shortest (Philemon). The anonymous Hebrews comes as an appendix.

Since the early nineteeth century many scholars have challenged Paul's authorship of the Pastoral Epistles (I and II Timothy and Titus) on the ground that the historical facts, the style, the language, and the theology in them make Paul's authorship impossible and point rather to a disciple of Paul. Some argue that genuine fragments by Paul may be included in them. The question about authorship and sources is still open (see pp. 307-9).

Some influential present-day scholars assign other letters to a disciple or disciples of Paul: Ephesians, Colossians, II Thessalonians. Here the variation from Paul's quite certainly authentic letters—I Thessalonians, I and II Corinthians, Galatians, Philippians, Philemon, and Romans—is considerably smaller than from the Pastoral Epistles. Consequently, other investigators staunchly defend Paul's authorship of Ephesians, Colossians, and II Thessalonians.

Computer research on the text of the letters traditionally assigned to Paul has led some to believe that even I Thessalonians, Philippians, and Philemon were not written by Paul. This would leave as authentic only Romans, Galatians, and I and II Corinthians. However, the computer method of studying the text has built-in limitations, and the results may not be accurate. So, at least, think most contemporary scholars.

We may say by way of summary that Paul quite certainly wrote the following: Romans, I and II Corinthians, Galatians, Philippians, I Thessalonians, Philemon. To these we may add, with less certainty, Ephesians, Colossians, II Thessalonians. More question exists about the Pastoral Epistles. They may contain authentic fragments from Paul. More probably, a disciple wrote all of them in the name of his admired teacher.

Paul's letters follow the form of the letters of his day, as known from thousands of papyrus letters found in Egypt since the end of the nineteenth century. This form consists of a greeting, a thanksgiving and a prayer for the readers, the message itself, and closing greetings and farewell. Paul added a benediction to his letters, often with the greetings and farewell, in his own handwriting (I Cor. 16:21-24; Gal. 6:11-18; Col. 4:18; II Thess. 3:17-18). This handwriting served to authenticate the letter.

Paul's letters are neither personal letters nor literary epistles. Even Philemon and the Pastorals (if regarded as Paul's) were meant to be read and used by the churches (Philem. 2; cf. the plurals in I Tim. 6:21; II Tim. 4:22; Titus 3:15). Literary epistles were addressed to the general public. Paul had specific readers in mind—individual churches or groups of churches—with specific problems and needs. He intended his letters to be read aloud in the public worship of the churches addressed, and sometimes they were to be exchanged with other churches (I Thess. 5:27; Col. 4:16).

His letters contain authoritative preaching, teaching, and exhortation. They come close to being sermons or addresses. Paul's purpose was to convey to the church the divine will for the edification of believers.

Several letters of Paul—Ephesians, Philippians, Colossians, and Philemon—form a group known as "The Prison (or Captivity) Epistles." This name arose because the letters themselves place their author in prison at the time of writing (Eph. 3:1; 4:1; 6:20; Phil. 1:7, 13; Col. 4:3, 10, 18; Philem. 1, 9, 23). If the Pastoral Epistles were written by Paul, II Timothy also belongs in this category (1:8, 17; 2:9).

From evidence in the letters many scholars have concluded that Ephesians, Colossians, and Philemon were written at the same time and sent with Tychicus (Eph. 6:21; Col. 4:7) and Onesimus (Col. 4:9; Philem. 10). Philippians was written at another time—and also II Timothy, if Paul's.

There is disagreement concerning the place of the writing of the Prison Epistles. Paul was in prison many times (II Cor. 6:5; 11:23; seven times, according to I Clement 5:6). The most likely places are Rome (Acts 28:16, 20), Caesarea (Acts 23:35; 24:23, 27), and Ephesus (I Cor. 15:30-32; II Cor. 1:8-10). Many arguments are possible in support of each place for all or some of the four (or five) letters, but no firm conclusion is possible now.

Fortunately, the exact place of writing of these letters is not particularly important for interpreting them.

71. Romans

Martin Luther wrote in his preface to Romans that this book is "rightly the chief part of the New Testament" and that it contains "the clearest gospel of all." He suggested that it would be well worth memorizing, so that it could be recited word for word.

The impact of Romans on the church through the centuries has been profound. Its effect on Augustine, Luther, Calvin, Wesley, and Karl Barth, and on the history-changing theological movements stemming from them, has led to its recognition as undoubtedly the most important theological book ever written.

1. Theme and Outline

Theme: The gospel—the power of God for salvation of everyone who has faith

I. Introduction (1:1-17)
   A. Greeting (a brief summary of the gospel) (1:1-7)
   B. Thanksgiving and explanations (1:8-15)
   C. Theme (1:16-17)

Roman road between Neapolis and Philippi in Macedonia

II. Body (1:18–15:13)
  A. The world's need of salvation (1:18–3:20)
    1. The need of the Gentiles (1:18-32)
    2. The need of the Jews (2:1–3:20)
  B. The way of salvation and its validity (3:21–4:25)
    1. Faith in Jesus Christ, whom God sent to take away human sin (3:21-31)
    2. Old Testament proof that salvation is by faith alone (4:1-25)
  C. The consequences of salvation through faith in Jesus Christ (5:1–8:39)
    1. From wrath and death to reconciliation and life (5:1-21)
    2. From the old life of sin and bondage to the new life of righteousness and service of God (6:1-23)
    3. From the Law and the sin it incites to freedom in Christ (7:1-25)
    4. From fleshly existence to life in the Spirit and final salvation (8:1-39)
  D. Jews and Gentiles in God's purpose of salvation (chaps. 9–11)
    1. Jewish rejection of the gospel in the light of

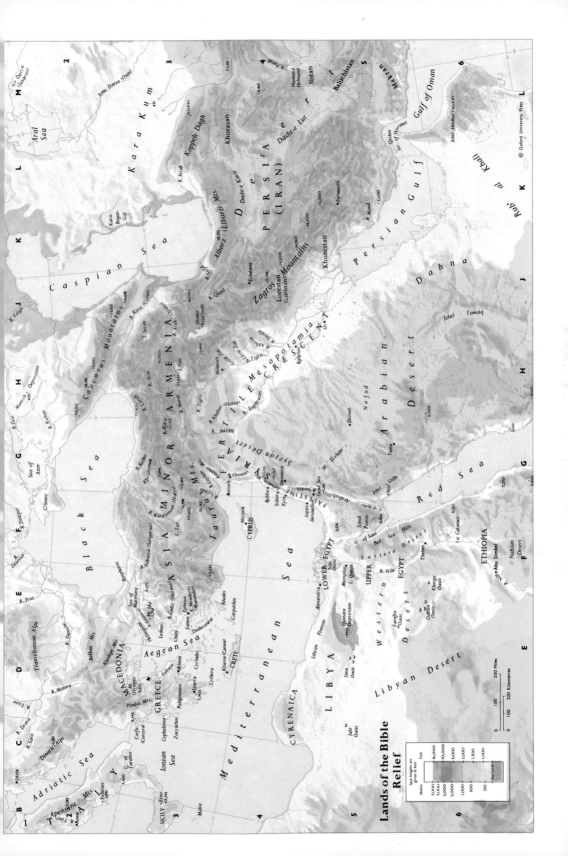

Lands of the Bible
Relief

feet
16,000
10,000
6,000
3,000
1,500
1,000
Metres   Sea Level
5,000
4,000
2,000
1,000
500
250
                                Sea level

Spot heights are
given in feet

0   100   200 Miles
0   100   200 Kilometres

© Oxford University Press

Seas and Bodies of Water:
Aral Sea
Caspian Sea
Black Sea
Sea of Azov
Aegean Sea
Ionian Sea
Adriatic Sea
Mediterranean Sea
Red Sea
Persian Gulf
Gulf of Oman
Dead Sea

Regions and Territories:
PERSIA (IRAN)
Khorasan
Baluchistan
Mekran
Khuzestan
Lorestan (Luristan)
ARMENIA
ASIA MINOR
MACEDONIA
GREECE
ITALY
SICILY
CYRENAICA
LIBYA
EGYPT
LOWER EGYPT
UPPER EGYPT
ETHIOPIA
SYRIA
PALESTINE
CYPRUS
Crimea
Sistan

Deserts and Physical Features:
Kara Kum
Dasht-e Lut
Dasht-e Kavir
Zagros Mountains
Caucasus Mountains
Taurus Mts.
Alborz (Elburz) Mts.
Koppeh Dagh
FERTILE CRESCENT
Mesopotamia
Syrian Desert
Arabian Desert
Nafud
Dahna
Rub' al Khali
Jebel Tuwaiq
Western Desert
Eastern Desert
Libyan Desert
Nubian Desert
Red Sea Hills
Sinai Penin.
Qattara Depression
Manych Depression
Transylvanian Alps
Dinaric Alps
Apennine Mts.
Pindus Mts.
Rhodope Mts.
Balkan Mts.
Antilebanon Mts.
Amanus Mts.

Rivers:
Syr Darya (Jaxartes)
Amu Darya (Oxus)
R. Volga
R. Don
R. Kuban
R. Dnieper
R. Prut
R. Danube
R. Morava
R. Drava
R. Sava
R. Tisza
R. Po
R. Tiber
R. Murat
R. Araks
R. Kura (Cyrus)
R. Çoruh
R. Seyhan
R. Ceyhan
R. Kizilirmak (Halys)
R. Sakarya (Sangarius)
R. Gediz
R. Menderes (Maeander)
R. Halys
R. Tigris
R. Euphrates
R. Balikh
R. Khabur (Habor)
Great Zab
Little Zab
R. Diyala
R. Adhaim
R. Orontes
R. Jordan
W. Sirhan
R. Nile
L. Tuz
L. Urmia (Rezai'yeh)
L. Van
Kara-Bogaz Gol

Cities and Places:
Persepolis
Ecbatana
Babylon
Nimrud
Nineveh
Dumah
Tema
Antioch
Damascus
Byblos
Sidon
Tyre
Joppa
Jerusalem
Nicosia
Memphis
Alexandria
Thebes
Abu Simbel
Siwa Oasis
Farafra Oasis
Bahria Oasis
Dakhla Oasis
Kharga Oasis
Jalo Oasis
Mt. Olympus
Corfu (Corcyra)
Cephalonia
Zacynthos
Cythera
Crete
CRETE
Rhodes
Cyclades
Dodecanese
Chios
Lesbos
Samos
Euboea
Peloponnese
Sparta
Ephesus
Smyrna
Sea of Marmara
Borysthenes
Khania (Canea)
Xanthus

G. of Suez
G. of Aqaba
Arabah
Str. of Hormuz
Qeshm
Jebel Akhdar
1st Cataract

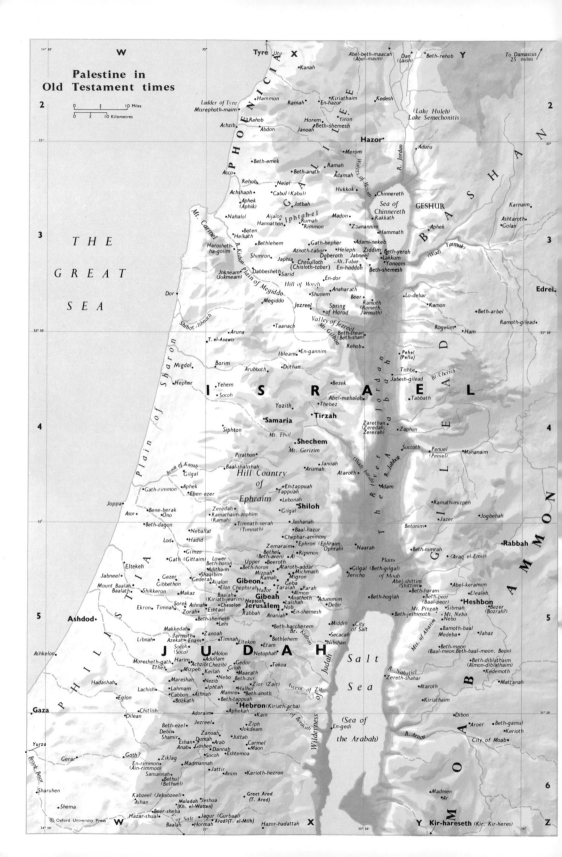

Palestine in
Old Testament times

0   5   10 Miles
0 5   10 Kilometres

W   35'   **W** Tyre Uzu **X**   Abel-beth-maacah (Abel-maim)   Dan (Laish)   Beth-rehob **Y**   To Damascus 25 miles

Kanah

PHOENICIA

Hammon Ramah• •Kiriathaim •Kedesh

Ladder of Tyre   •En-hazor
Misrephoth-maim•   Horem•

Achzib• •Rehob Yiron• (Lake Huleh)
Abdon• Beth-shemesh•   Lake Semechonitis

Janoah

Hazor•

GALILEE   •Merom   Aduru

•Beth-emek   Ramah•

Acco• •Beth-anath   Adamah•

•Rehob   Neiel•   Hukkok•   •Chinnereth

Achshaph•   •Cabul (Kabul)   Sea of   GESHUR   Karnaim•

Aphek (Aphik)•   •Jotbah   Chinnereth   Ashtaroth•

Nahalol•   Rumah• Madon• Rakkath   Golan•

Hannathon• Iphtah-el   •Rimmon   Zaanannim•   Aphek•   B A S H A N   Edrei•

•Beten   •Gath-hepher   Hammath•

Helkath•   •Bethlehem   Adami-nekeb•   (Wadi Yarmuk)

Harosheth- Shimron• Japhia• Aznoth-tabor• •Heleph Ziddim Beth-yerah•

ha-goiim Chesulloth •Deberath Jabneel• Lakkum•

Jokneam •Dabbesheth•Sarid (Chisloth-tabor) •Mt. Tabor Yanoam•

(Jokmeam)   En-haddah• Beth-shemesh•

Dor• Hill of Moreh   En-dor•

•Megiddo Jezreel• Shunem•   Anaharath•   Lo-debar•   Edrei•

Spring Beer• Ramoth (Remeth, Jarmuth)•   Kamon•

of Harod   •Beth-arbel

•Taanach   Mt. Gilboa   Beth-shean (Beth-shan)•   Rogelim• •Ham Ramoth-gilead•

Valley of Jezreel

T. el-Asawir•   Rehob•   GILEAD

Ibleam• •En-gannim   Pehel (Pella)•

Migdal•   Arubboth• •Dothan   Tishbe•   Br. Cherith

Borim•   •Bezek   Jabesh-gilead•

Hepher•   Yehem•   Abel-meholah•   Tabbath•

Yazith•   •Thebez

Socoh•   Zarethan (Zeredah, Zererah)• Zaphon•

Samaria   •**Tirzah**

Siphtan•   Succoth• Penuel (Peniel)• •Mahanaim

Mt. Ebal   •Shechem   (Wadi Jabbok)

Pirathon•   Mt. Gerizim   R. Jabbok

Baal-shalishah•   Janoah•   AMMON

•Gilgal   Arumah• Ataroth•   Ramath-mizpeh•

Brook of Kanah Hill Country   Adam• •Jogbehah

Aphek•   of   •En-tappuah

Eben-ezer•   Ephraim   Tappuah•   Betonim•   •Jazer

•Lebonah   Plains   ('Araq el-Emir)•

Joppa•   •**Shiloh**

Bene-berak•   Zeredah•   •Gilgal   •Jeshanah   •Beth-nimrah   •**Rabbah**

Asor• •Ono   •Ramathaim-zophim   •Baal-hazor

(Ramah)   Timnath-serah Gilgal (Beth-gilgal)•

•Beth-dagon   •Timnath (Timnath)   •Chephar-ammoni   •Naarah

Neballat•   Zemaraim• Ephron (Ephraim, Ophrah)•

Lod• •Hadid   Bethel (Beth-aven)• •Ai •Rimmon   •Beth-haram (Baal-peor)

Gimzo•   •Ai •Beeroth   Jericho•   Abel-shittim (Shittim)•

Gath (Gittaim)• Lower Upper Ataroth-adar•   •Beth-hoglah

Eltekeh•   Beth-horon •Michmash   Mt. Pisgah• •Beth-haram (Baal-peor)

Jabneel•   •Mithnah Beth-horon• Migron•   •Beth-jeshimoth Mt. Nebo•

Gezer•   Shaalbim• Mizpah• Ramah•   •Nebo

Mount Baalah Gibbethon• Gederah• Aijalon• Hazor• Geba•   **Heshbon**•

Baalath•   •Elon Chephirah• •**Gibeon** Taralah•   Bezer (Bozrah)•

Shikkeron• Makaz•   Baalah Almon•   City   Bamoth-baal•

Ekron• Timnah• Sorek• Ashnah• (Kiriath-jearim) •**Gibeah** Parah• of Salt•   Medeba•

Zorah• •Chesalon Neptoah• Anathoth•   •Middin   Mts. of Abarim

•Eshtaol **Jerusalem** Nob•   Jahaz•

Beth-shemesh•   Laishah•   Adummim•   Beth-meon (Baal-meon, Beth-baal-meon, Beon)•

Ashdod•   •Lehi   Ananiah• •En-shemesh   Debir•   •Nibshan   •Beth-diblathaim (Almon-diblathaim)

Makkedah•   Zanoah•   Secacah•   Kedemoth•

Libnah• Jarmuth• •Enam   •Beth-haccherem

Ashkelon•   Azekah•   Elteksn• •Etam   Salt   Zereth-shahar• Atarorh•   Mattanah•

Moresheth-gath• Socoh (Soco)• Bethlehem•   Sea

Ether•   Adullam• Netophah•   Kiriathaim•

Mizpeh• Keilah•   •Tekoa   R. Nahaliel•

Hadashah•   Achzib (Chezib)• Giloh•   Dibon• •Beth-gamul

Lachish•   Nezib• •Maarath   (Sea of

Lahmam• Cabbon• •Nebo Beth-zur•   En-gedi)

Gaza• Eglon• Mareshah• Iphtah• •Zior (Zair)   Aroer•   •Beth-gamul •Kerioth

Bozkath• Ashnah• •Beth-anoth   Ascent of Ziz   R. Arnon   City of Moab•

Dilean•   •Beth-tappuah   Atarorh•

Adoraim• Aphekah•   **Hebron** (Kiriath-arba)   the Arabah)   Kiriathaim•

Beth-ezel• Jezreel•   •Ziph   Wilderness

Debir• Shamir• Zanoah•   •Jokdeam   M O A B

Yurza•   Eshan• Arab• •Carmel   •Madmen •Ar

Gerar• **Gath?**•   Dumah• Goshen• •Maon   Kir-hareseth (Kir, Kir-heres)•

En-rimmon (Ain-rimmon)• Anab• Socoh• Eshtemoa•

Sansannah•   Madmannah•

Bethul (Bethuel)•   Jattir• Anim•   •Kerioth-hezron

Kabzeel (Jekabzeel)•   •Great Arad (T. Arad)

Ashan• Moladah Jeshua (Kh. el-Watten)•

Shema• Beer-sheba•   Jagur (Gurbaal)• •Arad? (T. el-Milh)

Hazar-shual•   •Gath of Salt   Baalah• •Hormah   Hazor-hadattah•

W   35'   **X**   35° 30'   **Y** Kir-hareseth (Kir, Kir-heres)•

THE
GREAT
SEA

PLAIN OF SHARON

PHILISTIA

I S R A E L

J U D A H

Mt. Carmel

R. Kishon Plain of Megiddo

Shihor-libnath

Brook Besor

Waters of Merom R. Jordan

The River Jordan

Salt Sea

© Oxford University Press

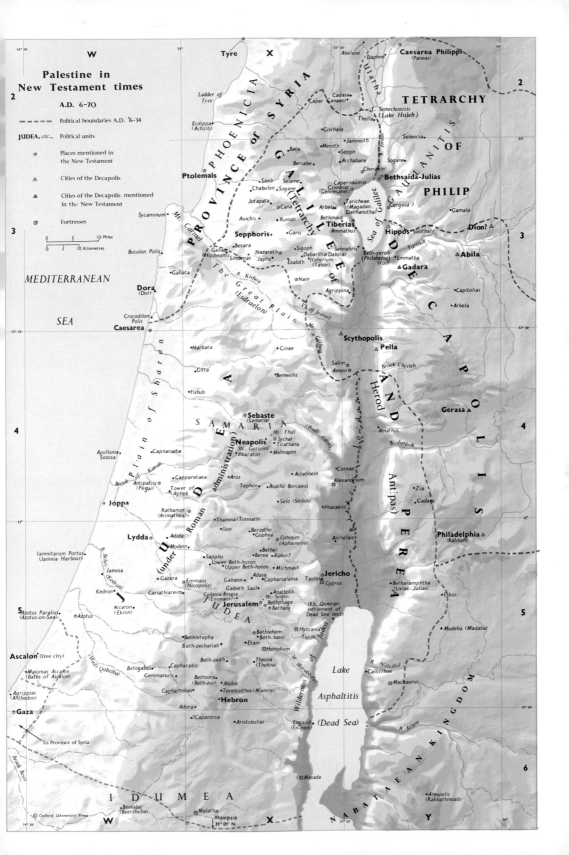

Palestine in New Testament times

A.D. 6-70

– – – – Political boundaries A.D. '6-34

JUDEA, etc., Political units

○ Places mentioned in the New Testament

△ Cities of the Decapolis

▲ Cities of the Decapolis mentioned in the New Testament

▣ Fortresses

0 ___ 5 ___ 10 Miles
0 _ 5 _ 10 Kilometres

MEDITERRANEAN

SEA

© Oxford University Press

W   **Tyre**   **X**

Abelane• •Daphne   •**Caesarea Philippi**
                  (Paneas)

TETRARCHY

Ladder of
Tyre•
     •Capar Canaeoi   •Cadasa
             L. Semechonitis
     Thella•   (Lake Huleh)

Ecdippa•
(Achzib)
   •Gischala
       •Jamneith   Seleucia•
  •Meroth •Sepph
Ptolemais   •Bersabe •Acchabare   Sogane•
      •Saab   Selame•   Chorazin•
     •Chabulon Sogane•   •Capernaum○ ○**Bethsaida-Julias**
Sycaminum•   Jotapata•   (Gennesaret?)
       •Cana   •Arbela   Taricheae○ ○Gergesa?
   Asochis•   •Rumah   (Magadan.
           Bethmaus   Dalmanutha)
         Sepphoris○ •Garis   Tiberias○ ○**Hippos** •Susithah?
    •Besara   Ammathus
Bucolon Polis•   Nazareth○ •Sigoph Sennabris•
      Gaba• Simonias• •Dabaritta(Dabira) Beth-yerah
    (Hippeum)   Japha• Exaloth •Itabyrium (Philoteria)
•Gabata   (Tabor)   •Emmatha
            •Nain   ▲**Gadara**

Dora
(Dor)
      •Agrippina   •Capitolias

Crocodilon
Polis•
Caesarea   •Arbela

               ▲**Scythopolis**   △**Pella**
    •Narbata   •Ginae
             Salim• Brook Cherith
•Gitta   Aenon•
     •Bemesilis
•Yishub   **Gerasa** △

    SAMARIA
   ●**Sebaste**
   (Samaria)   Mt Ebal
•Capnariaba   ●**Neapolis** ○Sychar
Apollonia•   Mt. Gerizim○ •Tirathana
Sozusa•   •Pharaton •Mahnayim
   Antipatris•   •Arus
   (Pegai)   Tephon• •Anathu Borcaeus
•**Joppa** Tower of   •Selo (Shiloh)   Alexandrium▣
   Aphek•   •Acrabbein   •Zia
   Rathamin•   •Coreae   •Gadara
   (Arimathea?)   •Phasaelis
   •Thamna (Timnath)   **Philadelphia** △
Lydda •Ilon •Berzetho   (Rabbah)
   •Adida •Gophna ○Ephraim
   •Modein   (Aphairema)   Archelais•
Iamnitarum Portus•   •Bethel
(Jamnia Harbour) •Sappho •Berea •Aialon?
         •Gabaon Lower Beth-horon•
•Jamnia   Upper Beth-horon• •Michmash
(Kedron)   •Gazara   •Adasa   •Betharamphtha
   •Kedron   Emmaus• •Capharsalama Taurus▣   (Livias-Julias)
     Cariathiarem• (Nicopolis) •Gabath Saul   **Jericho**
•Accaron   Colonia Amasa• •Anathoth ○ •Cyprus   •Erbus
(Ekron)   (Emmaus?)▣ •Mt. Scopus
         Jerusalem○ ○Bethphage
               ○Bethany
        •Bethletepha (Kh. Qumran:
            ○Bethlehem settlement of
       Beth-zechariah• Beth-bassi Dead Sea sect)
            •Etam ▣Hyrcania
Ascalon (Free city)   ▣Herodium
   •Maiumas Ascalon   Betogabri• •Capharabis   Thecoa•
   (Baths of Ascalon)   Gemmaruris• (Thekoa)
   •Agrippias   Bethsura• •Alulos
   (Anthedon)   Caphartobas• (Beth-zur) •Terebinthus (Mamre)
           •**Hebron**
○**Gaza**   •Adora
       ?Caparorsa   •Aristobulias
               •Engaddi (En-gedi)
→ To Province of Syria
              ▣Masada

Brook Besor

W   •Bersabe (Beersheba)   ▣Malatha
            ▣Mampsis   **X**
            31° 01' N

I D U M E A

NABATAEAN KINGDOM

•Areopolis (Rabbathmoab)   **Y**

PHOENICIA   *PROVINCE of SYRIA*   *GALILEE (Tetrarchy*   *GAULANITIS OF PHILIP*

Mt. Carmel   *The Great Plain (Esdraelon)*   *Sea of Galilee (Gennesaret)*   *V. of Jezreel*   *Mt. Gilboa*   *R. Kishon*

Plain of Sharon   *Brook of Kanah*   *R. Belus*   *R. (Kedron)*   *(Wadi Qubeiba)*

J U D E A (under Roman administration)   *Brook Cherith*   *R. Jabbok*   *D E C A P O L I S*

Yarmuk   *Wadi*   *Herod (and Antipas) P E R E A*   *R. Nahaliel*   *Callirrhoe*   *Machaerus*

Wilderness of Judea   *Lake Asphaltitis (Dead Sea)*   *R. Arnon*   *W. Murabbaat*   *Kidron*

Amathus   *Gamala*

Dion? △   *Abila* △

Photo by John C. Trever

Valley of Lebonah, in the hill country between Jerusalem and Shechem (Judg. 21:19)

Photo by John C. Trever

Pottery at Hebron. See Jer. 19:1-13

Cedars of Lebanon, like those Solomon used in building the Jerusalem temple (I Kings 5:6-10)

Photo by John C. Trever

The Jordan River near Jericho

A scroll of the Pentateuch (the Abisha Scroll), owned by Samaritans in Nablus, near Shechem

A threshing floor at Sebastiyeh, site of the ancient city of Samaria

Photo by John C. Trever

Cave I near Qumran, from which important Dead Sea Scrolls came

Photo by John C. Trever

Khirbet Qumran (Dead Sea in background), where writers of the Dead Sea Scrolls lived

Photo by John C. Trever

Fragments of a scroll of Daniel, from Qumran Cave I

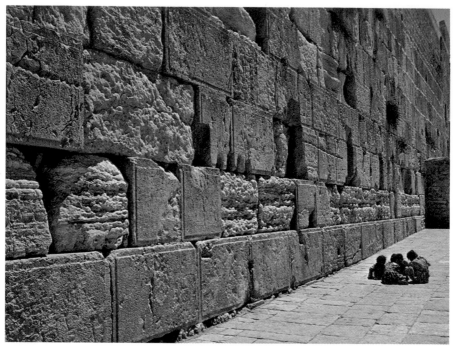

The "Wailing Wall," west side of the enclosure wall around Herod's temple in Jerusalem (Mark 13:1-2)

Sacred rock under the Dome of the Rock, in temple area, Jerusalem

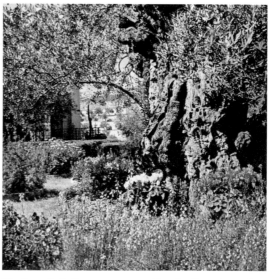

Garden of Gethsemane, according to Franciscan tradition, at the Church of All Nations

Photo by John C. Trever

Nazareth, Jesus' boyhood home, in the hills of southern Galilee, just north of the Plain of Esdraelon

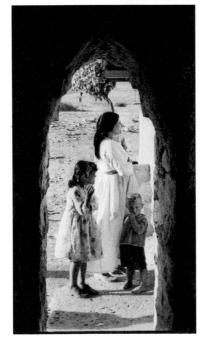

An Arab mother and children at the doorway of a village home

Star in the Grotto of the Nativity in Bethlehem, marking the traditional place of Jesus' birth

Mohammed edh-Dhib, the bedouin who discovered the Dead Sea Scrolls in Cave I near the Dead Sea

Girl of the village of Ramallah, north of Jerusalem

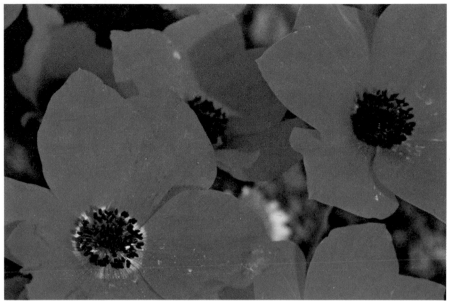

Photo by John C. Trever

Anemones, brilliant spring flow-
ers, which Jesus may have
referred to as "the lilies of the
field" (Matt. 6:28)

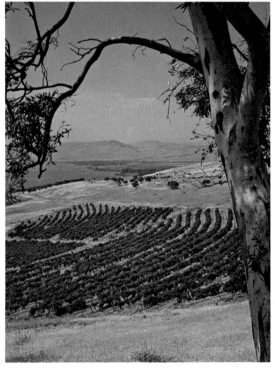

Fertile Plain of Gennesaret (on
NW side of the Sea of Galilee),
from whose lakeside town, Mag-
dala, Mary Magdalene probably
came

Photo by John C. Trever

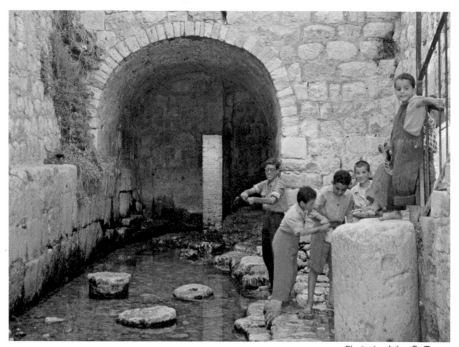

Pool of Siloam, at the southern end of Hezekiah's tunnel, Jerusalem (John 9:7; II Kings 20:20)

Garden tomb (in large opening) outside the north wall of Jerusalem, believed by some to be the place of Jesus' burial

North wall of Jerusalem, east of Herod's Gate

Marble street at Ephesus, once lined with temples and public buildings

Izmir, ancient Smyrna, in Turkey (Rev. 2:8-11)

Columns of the Temple of Apollo, Corinth, with Acrocorinth in background

Photo by John C. Trever

Acropolis in Athens, dominated by the Parthenon

Relief on the Arch of Titus, Rome, showing captured objects from the Jerusalem temple

Appian Way, approaching Rome from the south, over which Paul traveled (Acts 28:15)

Arch of Titus, erected A.D. 81 to honor the conqueror of Jerusalem in A.D. 70

Photo by John C. Trever

Harbor of the island of Patmos (Rev. 1:9), off the shore of Turkey

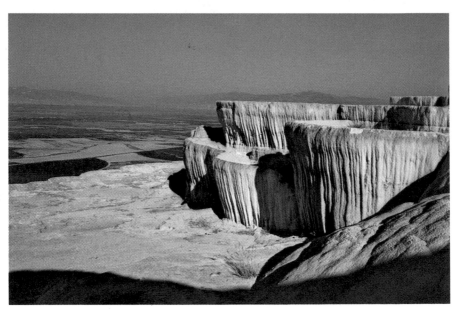

Lime terraces from hot springs at Hierapolis, Turkey, with the Lycus Valley in the background (Col. 4:13)

2. The Message

The letter to the Romans contains
a carefully formulated statement of
Paul's total message, a message that
appears in pieces, often illogically arranged, in his other letters.

The key to the contents of the letter
is Rom. 1:16-17. The subject of the
letter is "the gospel," the good news
concerning God's Son (1:3), which
has power to bring salvation to everyone (Jew and Gentile) who responds
in faith.

"Salvation" means man's becoming
righteous (that is, being put into right
relationship with God) through God's
righteousness (that is, his faithful, loving, redeeming activity in Jesus
Christ). The gospel reveals to people
this redemptive activity of God and
the salvation he offers them, if they
respond in faith (acceptance, trust,
obedience).

Paul's starting point is that people
are not in right relationship with God
(1:18–3:20). The gospel reveals, first
of all, the tragic plight of the human
race: man's guilt before God and his
present and future doom.

The Gentiles (1:18-32) cannot
plead ignorance of God, for they
have seen, in the wonders of creation,
God's everlasting power and his God-
ness (that is, that God is God and
not man). But they did not receive
this knowledge in gratitude and act on
it; they refused to recognize and worship God as God and worshiped what
was created rather than the Creator.
Their idolatry has led to a revolting
sensuality and to antisocial attitudes
and acts. At the lowest stage of depravity, they actually applaud the doing of evil. They stand under God's
wrath (his punishment, shown in the
progressive spiritual and moral degra-

dation of mankind) and under his sentence of death (present and future separation from God).

The Jews (2:1–3:20) also have knowledge of God. In addition to the revelation offered in nature, they have the Law of Moses and the Holy Scriptures ("the oracles of God"— 3:2). Of these they are justifiably proud, and on the basis of them they claim the right to be teachers of mankind. They condemn the Gentiles for their idolatry and immorality. But perversely and hypocritically, many Jews indulge in the very things they condemn in the Gentiles: stealing, adultery, sacrilege (or temple-robbing —2:22). Their hearts are proud and stubborn; they are self-centered and committed to wrongdoing. The covenant-mark on their bodies (circumcision) gives them no special standing before God, who requires inner dedication to himself and inner goodness, rather than outer correctness. They too stand under God's judgment, for he treats all men alike.

In short, all people are sinners. They have rebelled against the God who revealed himself to them in various ways: in the created order, in the inner light (2:15), and in the Scriptures. All live under the power of sin (3:9), and all are guilty before God.

But God has provided in Jesus Christ a way for guilty, alienated people to come into right relationship with himself (3:21-31). This way is not by earning acceptance through obedience to the Law, which no one can keep and which serves to reveal one's sin rather than to break its power (3:20). It is the way of faith (trust) in God's gracious, saving work in Jesus Christ. God does for people what they cannot do for themselves and asks only for their grateful response. Their freedom and new relationship flow from Christ Jesus' sacrificial death, which God made a means of taking away their sin and guilt. Since the new relationship comes from God's act, not man's, gratitude, not boasting in human achievement, is the appropriate attitude of the believer.

The consequences of trust in God's saving act in Jesus Christ are far-reaching (5:1–8:39). Believers have a new status before God. They enjoy the divine favor, have peace, are reconciled. They have a new spirit. They exult in their hope and in their sufferings. They have a new knowledge: that suffering has blessed results. They have a new self: the Holy Spirit and God's love within. They are participants in a new humanity. They are freed from the realm of sin and death, introduced by Adam, to a new order of right relations with God and new life, introduced by Jesus Christ.

They have a new kind of life under a new master. They no longer serve sin and the Law and earn wretchedness and death as their pay, but they experience a new quality of existence, serve God and righteousness, and receive the gift of eternal life. They at last escape the power of sin, which has the Law as its agent and the flesh as its host, and are introduced to life in the Spirit, a life pleasing to God, as befits the sons of God. As sons of God they are heirs of a glorious future, which no hostile power in the

THE CHURCH AT THE CLOSE OF PAUL'S MINISTRY

SCALE OF MILES

0   300   600

universe can prevent them from obtaining.

Who is going to participate in this this glorious future? Will it include both Jews and Gentiles (chaps. 9–11)? The hard fact is that most Jews have rejected the good news that right relation with God comes through faith in Jesus Christ. Does this mean that God is going to fail to bring about the salvation of his chosen people? Emphatically, no! The rejection by the majority of the Jews is to be seen in the light of the divine selectivity that has always been at work in Israel, by which God preserved a faithful remnant, a remnant useful for his purpose of salvation for all (9:1-29). But Jewish rejection can also be attributed to the Jews' free choice: having heard the gospel of salvation by faith in Jesus Christ, they preferred salvation by works (9:32; 10:3). Their zeal for God was misguided (10:2). They stand condemned before him (10:21).

Yet God brings good results out of man's evil decisions. Jewish rejection led to the preaching of the gospel to the Gentiles, and that in turn will lead to the ultimate salvation of the Jews. When the Jews see the Gentiles becoming heirs of the promises made to Abraham, they will desire to be included too and will turn to Christ in faith. Thus God's merciful plan for both Jews and Gentiles will be accomplished (11:11-32).

The new life in Christ determines the character of one's existence in the church and in the world (12:1–15:13). Right relations with God and man require total surrender of one's self to God and learning and doing his will.

God's will is that we love one another in the church (12:3-13), and even our enemies (12:14-21), and live as responsible citizens of the state (13:1-10). Love, furthermore, requires consideration of those whose convictions differ from our own (14:1–15:13). The Christian is not to please himself but to please God and his neighbor (14:3; 15:1-2). "Walking in love" (14:15) glorifies God and builds up the church. By such conduct children of the day await the coming of the day (13:11-14).

3. Original Contents

The precise contents of the original letter are in some doubt, because of the following facts:

a. Some ancient manuscripts omit the words "in Rome" in 1:7, 15.

b. In some manuscripts the Grace ("The grace of our Lord Jesus Christ be with you") occurs twice (16:20, 24), as in the King James Version; but in others it is found only once (either in 16:20 or 16:24), as in the Revised Standard Version (at 16:20).

c. The doxology (16:25-27) appears in different places in ancient manuscripts: at the end of chap. 16; after 14:23 (and sometimes also at the end of chap. 16); after 15:33; and once is omitted altogether.

d. The many personal greetings in 16:1-23, in a letter to a church (Rome) where Paul had never been, call for an explanation. Prisca and Aquila were in Ephesus shortly before the writing of this letter (I Cor. 16:19). Epaenetus' original home was Asia, probably Ephesus, not Rome (Rom. 16:5).

e. The doxology (16:25-27) seems to contain un-Pauline words and ideas.

It is difficult to account for these facts. Two major hypotheses have appeared, but neither has yet won general acceptance:

a. Paul's original letter to the Romans was 1:1–16:23.

Prisca and Aquila could have returned to Rome, where they formerly had lived (Acts 18:2); and Epaenetus and the other friends and acquaintances of Paul, mentioned in Rom. 16, may have moved to the capital city over a period of several years. Col. 4:10 ff., written to a church where Paul had never been, shows that he made use of personal contacts for his advantage.

The doxology in 16:25-27 is a second-century addition, composed to fit after 14:23. From Origen's writings, in the third century, it appears that the heretic Marcion (middle of the second century) abbreviated Romans at 14:23 for doctrinal reasons. A doxology was thus needed to conclude the letter. In some manuscripts this doxology became attached also to 16:23. Marcion's mutilation of the letter may have included the deleting of "in Rome" in 1:7, 15.

b. Paul's original letter to the Romans consisted of chaps. 1–15.

This, of course, contained the words "in Rome" in 1:7, 15.

Because of the suitability of this letter for other churches as well (see below), Paul sent a copy to the church at Ephesus without the words "in Rome." He added to this the material in 16:1-23. Phoebe of Cenchreae (near Corinth) may have carried this letter to Ephesus (16:1-2). The friends of Paul mentioned were thus residents of Ephesus, where Paul had spent nearly three years.

Marcion cut off chaps. 15 and 16. The doxology of 16:25-27 was first added to Marcion's shortened text (after 14:23) and later placed after 16:23.

The earliest manuscript of the letters of Paul now known (Papyrus 46, about A.D. 200), in placing the doxology after 15:33, lends support to this second view.

Other hypotheses exist, such as that chap. 16 came from (or comprises) an altogether separate letter of Paul's and was added to Rom. 1–15 by the first editor of Paul's letters. This is less likely than *a* and *b* above.

4. Occasion and Purpose

Paul apparently was at Corinth when he wrote Romans. He was about to leave for Jerusalem with the collection for the Jerusalem church (15:25-27). He was apprehensive about the trouble he might face there (15:31) and wished he could go west to Rome and Spain rather than east to Jerusalem (15:23-24, 28, 32). Acts 20:2-4 gives the general setting and lists his companions for the eastward journey.

Why he wanted to go to Rome is understandable. As God's priest for all the Gentile churches, he felt special responsibility for the Roman church (Rom. 15:16; 11:13), even though he did not found it. He wished to have fellowship with the members of this renowned church (1:8), which he had long wanted to visit (15:23), to contribute to their spiritual growth (1:11; 15:15 ff., 29), and to gain their moral and perhaps financial support for a missionary venture in Spain (15:24).

His reasons for writing this letter then become clear. He wanted to let the Romans know of his plans to come and arouse their enthusiasm for his project in the west. He also probably wished to counteract before his arrival any misunderstanding of his objectives and of the nature of his gospel, in view of the widespread slander directed at him by some fellow Christians and many Jews. Finally, he desired to make a contribution to the spiritual life of the Roman church by his letter.

The whole church, including the Romans, needed a clearer understanding of the theology of salvation: the relation of the new Christian movement to Judaism and the Old Testament; the proper terms of admission to the church; the status of Jew and Gentile outside and inside the church; God's future for Jew and Gentile; the moral and missionary demands of the new faith; Paul's own place in the purpose of God; and the like. Paul

and others had fiercely debated these matters in the years before the writing of Romans, and Paul wished the entire church to understand his hard-won positions. Thus he may have sent copies of this letter to both Rome and Ephesus.

5. Authorship and Date

Paul's authorship of Romans is undisputed. The date of writing falls somewhere between A.D. 55 and 59.

72. I Corinthians

The letter to the Romans and the first letter to the Corinthians, while they come from the same general period of Paul's life and contain the same mature, masterful theology, are very different in character.

Romans is theology-centered; I Corinthians is life-centered or problem-centered. Romans offers us little information about the situation of the Christians in Rome, but I Corinthians opens doors and windows through which we may view Corinthian Christians at home, in the marketplace, and in the church.

We find that the Corinthian Christians were living in a culture in many respects like our own, with many of the same temptations and problems. Nowhere else in the New Testament is the tension between the church and the world more apparent. I Corinthians is thus uniquely a book for our time.

1. Contents

I Corinthians is a string of varied gems, rather than one massive stone with several facets. Whether there is a string at all is uncertain.

Several unifying themes have been suggested: the Resurrection, the nature of Christian freedom, the place of love in building the church, and, negatively, the refutation of the Gnostic heresy (see below) that infected the Corinthian church. All are important in the letter, but none serves very well as a theme for the whole.

The parts of the letter are:
I. Introduction (1:1-9)
   A. Greeting (1:1-3)
   B. Thanksgiving (1:4-9)
II. Body (1:10–16:4)
   A. Paul's response to reports about the church at Corinth (1:10–6:20)

The Rostrum *(Bema)* at Corinth, where Paul was brought before Gallio (Acts 18:12-16)

2. Background of the Letter

The author of Luke-Acts places the evangelization of Corinth by Paul, Silvanus, and Timothy on Paul's second missionary journey. His stay in Corinth for about eighteen months (Acts 18:11) probably occurred in A.D. 50–51.

Paul first preached in the synagogue at Corinth, then in a house adjacent to the synagogue. The latter ministry, directed toward Gentile "God-fearers" (half-proselytes to Judaism), resulted in both conversions and fierce Jewish hostility. A court hearing before the proconsul Gallio, resulting from this hostility, led to a dismissal of the charges (Acts 18:12-17) and some protection for the infant church.

The Christians there were largely Gentiles (I Cor. 12:2) and mostly from the lower classes (1:26 ff.). A few were of higher status (Acts 18:8; I Cor. 11:21-22; Rom. 16:23), and some were Jews (Acts 18:4, 8; I Cor. 7:18).

Corinth, the capital city of the province of Achaea, strategically situated between two seas, was a bustling commercial city, notorious for sensuality. The temple of Aphrodite, according to the first-century Roman geographer and traveler Strabo, had one thousand prostitutes who sold themselves in service to the goddess. So wicked was the city that a verb was coined from the city's name—"to Corinthianize"—meaning to practice immorality. Paul was in Corinth when he wrote his startling description of the moral corruption of the pagan world (Rom. 1:18-32).

The inhabitants—Romans, Greeks, Orientals—brought with them almost every religion of the Mediterranean world. They worshiped such gods as Jupiter, Aphrodite, Isis, Osiris, Cybele, Attis, Atargatis, and Yahweh of the Jews. The biennial games brought thousands of visitors to Isthmia, an adjacent town. So fascinatingly seductive was the life of Corinth that a common saying of the time was, "Not every man should go to Corinth."

The church there was subject to the pressures of paganism: idolatry and idolatrous feasts, gluttony, lax sexual behavior, superstition, magic, demonism, religious frenzy, philosophical skepticism, materialism, and social strife.

After Paul left the city and before the composition of our I Corinthians, he wrote what is now called "The Previous Letter," mentioned in I Cor. 5:9. It dealt with the relations of moral and immoral church members at Corinth but was understood—or deliberately misunderstood—by them as having to do with Christians' relations to immoral people outside the church. The poison of paganism was at work in the life of the church. Some scholars have claimed that part of the Previous Letter is now present in II Cor. 6:14–7:1 (see below).

When Paul was at Ephesus (on the third missionary journey, according to the Acts), disturbing reports about the conditions at Corinth came to him, perhaps from Chloe's household (I Cor. 1:11). Paul sent Timothy to Corinth by way of Macedonia to deal with the problems there (I Cor. 4:17; 16:10; Acts 19:22). Whether he arrived, or when, we do not know.

Later the Corinthians Stephanus, Fortunatus, and Achaicus came to Paul (I Cor. 16:17) with a letter containing specific inquiries (I Cor. 7:1; 8:1; 12:1; 16:1). They described the situation at Corinth in detail and sought help from Paul. They apparently carried our I Corinthians home with them.

3. The Problems in the Church at Corinth

Apparently the most serious problem in Paul's eyes—for he treats it first and devotes most space to it—was the disunity of the church. Paul speaks of "divisions" and "quarrels" (1:10-11). The Corinthians claimed superiority over one another by virtue of their attachment to different Christian leaders—Paul, Apollos, Peter ("Cephas" is Aramaic for "rock"), and Christ (1:12). We do not know whether there were four distinct groups, each with a theology supposedly patterned after the views of its leader, or whether individuals were simply being loyal to the person who had baptized them into the faith.

If the groups were clearly defined, what may they have stood for?

Perhaps the Paul group stood for salvation by faith alone (*i.e.,* apart from merit through obedience to the Law). Its members believed that faith resulted from the preaching of Jesus, the Messiah, crucified for our sins and raised to put us right with God (Rom. 4:25; I Cor. 2:2-5).

The Apollos group may have gloried in that preacher's Greek intellectualism and rhetoric (Acts 18:24-28).

The Peter group may have stressed, to the disadvantage of Paul, Peter's superior rights as an apostle and valued Peter's approval of the observance of the Law by Jewish Christians.

The Christ group may have rejected the exaltation of human leaders and favored life under the direct control of Christ and of the Spirit (*cf.* II Cor. 10:7). This group probably wished to have no external controls on conduct.

Those scholars who believe that the squabble over leaders did not really divide the church into separate groups with differing theologies think there was one basic theological error underlying the individual preference for leaders. It consisted in a Gnostic (from a Greek word meaning "knowledge") interpretation of the gospel. The Gnostics, as we know them in the second century and later, stressed salvation by supernaturally revealed knowledge. This knowledge helped the soul, which had fallen from heaven into the evil world of matter, escape the prison of the flesh. The Gnostics believed that the resurrection, proclaimed as future in Judaism and Christianity, had already occurred in the liberation of man's spirit through faith in Jesus Christ and that they were already enjoying in its fullness the salvation of the kingdom of God (I Cor. 4:8). In their "freedom" many of them fell into immorality. (For further information about the Gnostics see pp. 304-7.)

It is true that most, if not all, of the problems treated in I Corinthians are more or less explainable in the light of Gnostic-type thinking.

Paul's downgrading of human wisdom (1:17-25; 2:1-5; 3:18-20) implies its glorification by some Corinthians. Their pride in their achievements (4:7-8) forces Paul to humble them (4:9-13, 18-20). Their arrogance over the case of incest in the church (5:1-8) illustrates their imagined freedom from all human regulations, as does their indifference to property rights, their consorting with harlots, and their general hell-raising (chap. 6).

When spirit and flesh are sharply distinguished and the latter is regarded as an impediment to the former, the problem of marriage becomes acute (chap. 7). Is marriage evil or good?

The "knowledge" that allowed Christians to eat meat sacrificed to idols and even to participate in feasts in heathen temples (chap. 8), regardless of the effect on less "enlightened" fellow Christians, fits the Gnostic perspective.

The "freedom" movement—exhibited by the women in flouting church regulation regarding the covering of their heads (11:2-16), by gluttony at the Lord's table (11:21), by unbridled Spirit-ecstasy in services of worship (chap. 14), and by disbelief in the future resurrection of the body (15:12)—points to this type of thinking.

If we assume that there were four theological groups, we may identify the Christ group as the Gnostic group. It was this group that offered the real danger to the church at Corinth.

4. Paul's Treatment of the Problems

a. Disunity (1:1–4:21)

Paul points out that excessive attachment to human leaders arises from a misunderstanding both of the basic nature of Christianity and of the proper function of Christian ministers (1:13–4:13).

The Christian's attachment is to Christ, not to human leaders. Baptism is in Christ's name. In Christianity salvation is obtained neither by ceremonies conducted by special mediators nor through the imparting, however eloquent, of human knowledge or wisdom. Salvation comes by hearing and responding in faith to the story

of God's deed for men in the cross of Jesus Christ, proclaimed in simple language (1:18–2:5). In this message, however, God discloses his true and secret purpose (wisdom) for the redemption and enrichment of man in the age to come (2:6-16).

Christian leaders are fellow laborers for God, not rivals (3:1-9). They are builders, accountable to God, whose materials and methods differ and whose work may not be of equal value (3:10-15). They are all cooperating in the plan of God for the good of those to whom they minister; they are not to be gloried in for what they may be individually (3:18-23). They are responsible to God, not to men, for their conduct (4:1-5). Their spirit of humility, suffering, and sacrifice is to be imitated by those whom they serve (4:6-13).

b. The Case of Incest (5:1-13)

A male member of the Corinthian church had married or was living with his stepmother, a relationship forbidden by both Jews and Gentiles. The church saw nothing wrong with this relationship and may even have gloated over it as an example of the new freedom over the flesh and over rules and regulations that their rebirth to the life of the New Age had brought (4:8).

Paul was horrified both by the relationship and by their attitude. They are to repent, not gloat, and officially remove the man from church membership as a means of his ultimate salvation. By being put outside the church into the world (the realm of

Satan), the offender would experience physical suffering and perhaps death at Satan's hands and through this refining experience find salvation at the day of judgment (*cf.* I Pet. 4:1).

All evil must be purged from the church because of its corrupting power. Christianity is a way of moral righteousness (right relations). Without morality church members are offensive to God (5:9-13).

c. Lawsuits Between Church Members (6:1-11)

The church should handle disputes among its members and not air them in Gentile courts. Members wise enough to judge disputes can be found. How inconsistent it is for Christians to be judged by pagans, when Christians are destined to participate with Christ in judging both the world (*cf.* Matt. 19:28; Rev. 20:4) and angels (*cf.* Jude 6; II Pet. 2:4)! It would be better to bear the wrong than to go to court about it. (Nonretaliation to evildoers is the Christian way of life—*cf.* Matt. 5:39 ff.; I Pet. 2:23.) But why should Christians be doing wrong at all? The Christian is called to a righteous life and to membership in the coming kingdom of God.

d. Union with Prostitutes (6:12-20)

Do not act on the principle "all things are lawful" in such a way that it leads you into immorality. You must consider the effects of what you do. Is what you do beneficial? Will doing it enslave you? And you must distinguish the areas in which the principle rightly applies. It properly applies to food but not to sexual relations. Sexual union with a harlot will separate you from union with Christ, to whom you properly belong and with whom you will be united in the resurrection life. What the Christian does with himself is important: he is the temple of the Holy Spirit; he is the property of God.

e. Marriage (chap. 7)

Paul's answer here was specifically requested in the Corinthians' letter (7:1). His counsel falls into two main categories.

(1) Counsel for the Unmarried

Celibacy is the best state (vss. 1, 7, 8, 26-27), because the celibate are free to serve the Lord without the distraction of marriage (vss. 34-35) and because of the closeness of the end of the age and its accompanying troubles (vss. 28-31).

But there is no evil in marriage. Marriage is advisable for most people. One should marry if it is necessary for the maintenance of virtue (vss. 2, 9, 36). This applies to the unmarried in general (vss. 1, 8), to widows (vs. 8), and to the engaged (vss. 36-38). Remarriage after the death of a spouse is legitimate if it is to a Christian (vs. 39). God has no set will for all men. Christian persons are free to decide for themselves what they should do (vs. 7).

(2) Counsel for the Married

The sexual needs of each partner should be fulfilled within the marriage relationship (vss. 3-5).

Divorce is forbidden on the authority of Christ (vss. 10-11). If the wife separates from her husband, she must remain single or be reconciled to her husband (vs. 11).

In mixed marriages (one partner Christian and the other not), the partners should remain together, if possible, in the hope that the non-Christian may be won to the Christian faith and life (vs. 16). The participation of a non-Christian partner does not make the marriage unclean; in fact, the Christian partner makes the marriage sacred and the children holy (vs. 14). In a mixed marriage, remaining together must be voluntary by both partners (vs. 15).

In the time remaining before the end of the age, let every person (the unmarried, the married, the uncircumcised, the circumcised, the slave, the free) remain in the status he had at the time of his conversion (vss. 17-24).

f. Food Offered to Idols (8:1–11:1)

Meat dedicated to gods in sacred rites at temples and then sold in the market for public consumption offered a serious problem for Jews and Christians.

It was offensive to Jews because it was associated with the worship of false gods. It had not been slaughtered in the proper way, and the tithe had not been paid on it.

Gentile Christians, though free from these considerations, were likewise bothered by its idolatrous associations. The bold—that is, the "enlightened" among them—such as the Corinthian

Gnostics, who professed knowledge that "an idol has no real existence" (8:4), ate the food with relish, unconcerned about the feelings of other Christians.

Paul treats the problem at length. Chap. 8 lays down the principle that knowledge, which leads to rights and freedoms, must be controlled by love for others. The unrestricted use of knowledge and the freedoms it offers will inflate the self-esteem of the enlightened, wreck the more conscientious, and ultimately destroy the church.

Chap. 9 illustrates the principle from Paul's own conduct. He has knowledge of his special relation to Christ as an apostle and the rights stemming from it, notably, the right to economic support from his converts for himself and a wife. This right is proved by the precedent of other apostles, by comparison to other fields of labor, by Scripture, and by command of Jesus. But love for others, shown in his desire to share with them the blessings of the gospel, has led him to forgo this right and thus to evangelize free of charge. All rights give way before the compelling power of love. Love requires any sacrifice for the sake of the salvation of others. Paul does not insist on exercising his rights, furthermore, because such exercise without discipline might harm his own prospect of final salvation.

Chap. 10 reinforces the principle by an appeal to history (vss. 1-13) and to logic (vss. 14-22). Knowledge, privilege, and the rights they bring may lead to spiritual disaster, as the experience of Israel after the Exodus shows. Though people of great privilege, they fell into immorality and did not inherit the promised land. Furthermore, common sense shows that the kind of boldness that leads to dabbling in idolatrous practices is inconsistent with one's unity with Christ. One cannot be united to Christ and to demons at the same time!

What is sold in the marketplace may be eaten, unless eating it will harm another. One should seek the good of his neighbor, not exercise his rights for his own selfish benefit (10: 23–11:1).

g. Disorders in Worship
(11:2–14:40)

Some Corinthian women were taking part in church worship (praying and speaking) with unveiled heads (11:2-16). In the culture of Paul's day women of good reputation did not appear in public without a head-covering. This rebellion against custom may have arisen partly out of Paul's teaching about the equality of men and women in Christ (Gal. 3:28) and partly out of Gnostic ways of thinking. Probably these women believed that their experience of the life of the New Age had lifted them above the limitations of the old "fleshly" order.

Paul uses several arguments to counter this overemphasis on "freedom," some of them rather curious to us: that there is a God-ordained order of relationships (in which women are subordinate to men) which must be honored; that the holy angels, present at the worship service as guardians of order, will be offended; that nature, by giving women long hair, favors head-covering; that veiling by women is the universal practice in Christian churches. Paul believed that as long as the present age lasts, the *status quo* in outward human relationships should be maintained (7:17-24), though he did hold that such relationships should be Christianized (see the discussion of the letter to Philemon).

The selfishness, gluttony, drunkenness, and divisiveness at the church's sacred meals (11:17-34) were shocking to Paul. Though the Supper was supposed to be in honor of the Lord Jesus, it did not honor him. It was an occasion for self-indulgence rather than an experience of sharing with others.

Paul deals with the situation by recalling the solemn meaning of Jesus' Last Supper with the disciples. At that Supper Jesus indicated that his death would accomplish for them a new relationship with God. He instructed them to observe the Supper in remembrance of his sacrificial act for others. His disciples should seriously examine their attitudes and their behavior in the knowledge that God's judgment falls on those who eat the Supper unworthily.

The Corinthians' confusion about the Holy Spirit's gifts and the use of them in the church is the subject of a long section (12:1–14:40). Paul had said that the Corinthians were well endowed with spiritual gifts (1: 5-7), and now we learn that there was bitter controversy over their relative value. Members who possessed the more dramatic gifts (especially speaking in tongues) received high honor, and those with less spectacular gifts were belittled. Exhibitionists in speech were creating bedlam in church meetings, so that outsiders were being repelled by the confusion.

The discussion on gifts runs through several phases:

(1) How to test whether a person is being moved by the Holy Spirit or some other spirit (12:2-3): does he exalt Jesus as Lord?

(2) The character and purpose of the Holy Spirit's gifts (12:4-11): they originated from one source; they are bestowed for the benefit of all; and they are of many types.

(3) The relation of members with different gifts to one another (12:12-31): church members, variously endowed, complement one another for the good of the whole body.

(4) The general gift underlying and directing the use of the gifts (chap. 13): love, God's gift to all Christians, makes all other gifts meaningful and useful.

(5) The comparative worth and proper use of the gifts (chap. 14): prophecy ("speaking God's message" —TEV) is of more value than tongues ("the language of ecstasy"—NEB). Since prophecy can be understood by everyone, it builds up the church and converts unbelievers. Christian worship should consist in an orderly use of the gifts for the good of all present.

h. Disbelief in the Resurrection (Chap. 15)

Disbelief in a final resurrection of the dead apparently had two roots: a high valuation of the spirit of man (a piece of divinity which had fallen from a higher realm), and a low valuation of the body (a prison from which the spirit would one day escape). The spirit-flesh dualism rendered the doctrine of the resurrection of the body unnecessary and ludicrous. Furthermore, the belief that in conversion the resurrection of the spirit had already occurred (cf. II Tim. 2:18) and that the life of the kingdom of God was already being experienced in fullness (I Cor. 4:8) left no place for a future resurrection.

Paul refutes the disbelief by showing that Jesus' resurrection is supported by Scripture, by the testimony of many witnesses to his post-resurrection appearances, and by the belief and preaching of the church. He affirms that Jesus' resurrection is the ground of the believers' coming resurrection. Jesus is "the firstfruits of the harvest of the dead" (NEB).

He clears away some wrong conceptions of resurrection by showing that the complete change of man from a physical to a nonphysical existence, not return to this earthly life, is meant.

i. The Collection (16:1-3)

The individual Corinthians are to set aside a sum each week to be paid into a central fund when Paul arrives. Delegates will carry the money to the church in Jerusalem.

5. Is the Letter a Unity?

Several scholars, because of supposed contradictions between certain sections of I Corinthians and seeming roughness in its subject and thought sequence, have supposed that two or more letters of Paul were joined by someone later on to form our I Corinthians. It has been thought, for example, that the Previous Letter of I Cor. 5:9 is not wholly lost but is to be found preserved in II Cor. 6:14–7:1; I Cor. 6:12-20; 9:24–10:22; 11:2-34; 15:1-58; 16:13-24. This would make the rest of our I Corinthians (1:1–6:11; 7:1–9:23; 10:23–11:1; 12:1–14:40; 16:1-12) the second letter.

Theories that dissect Corinthians into different letters have not convinced most scholars. Our I Corinthians is a long letter. Its roughness probably is due to its dictation over a considerable time and to changes in Paul's and the Corinthians' circumstances.

6. Place of Writing and Date

The letter was written in Ephesus (16:8). It was probably carried to Corinth by Stephanus, Fortunatus, and Achaicus (16:17). The date was the spring of A.D. 54 or 55.

73. II Corinthians

We have in II Corinthians the finest statement anywhere in the New Testament about the nature of the Christian ministry. Paul's enemies at Corinth and elsewhere forced him to defend his character and his ministry.

1. The Situation in the Corinthian Church

Our I Corinthians, for all its helpful content, did not cure the spiritual sickness at Corinth. Neither did Timothy's visit, if he actually arrived there (I Cor. 4:17; 16:10).

From references in II Corinthians we know that Paul journeyed to Corinth from Ephesus to deal with the situation himself, but he failed (2:1; 12:14, 21; 13:1-2). On that visit some member of the Corinthian church personally wronged Paul (7:12); how we are not told. Not only Paul but the whole church was injured by the act (2:5-8). We may guess that this member—possibly encouraged by some group within the church or by intruders from the outside (see below)—viciously attacked Paul's authority as an apostle.

Paul then returned to Ephesus, wrote a severe letter to the church in deep anguish of spirit (2:3-4; 7:8, 12), and sent it with Titus to Corinth. Whether this letter is wholly lost or is now preserved in part in II Corinthians is uncertain (see below).

Not long afterward, Paul went to Macedonia by way of Troas. He was greatly disappointed not to find Titus in Troas with a report about Corinth (2:12-13). In Macedonia, Titus finally relieved Paul's anxiety by reporting that the Corinthians had repented.

The remains of a town gate of Roman times, now called St. Paul's Gate, at Tarsus

Titus' mission and Paul's severe letter had achieved the desired result (7:5-16). The crisis was over. In great relief and thanksgiving Paul wrote our II Corinthians (in whole or in part—see below).

Paul then sent Titus back to Corinth with this letter and along with him two unnamed companions (8:16-24). He wished them to attend to the collection of the Corinthian contribution to the mother church in Jerusalem.

. Who Paul's enemies at Corinth were is far from clear. Their purpose, however, is unmistakable: they wanted to discredit Paul as an apostle of Jesus Christ and to advance their own "superior" claim to authority over the Corinthians. Among their charges against him were: insincerity and inconstancy (1:12 ff.); lack of credentials (3:1); misunderstanding of the gospel (4:3); emotional instability (5:13); self-seeking and possible dishonesty (7:2; 8:20-21; 12:16); feebleness when present (though bold when absent) (10:1, 10); unskilled speaking (11:6); false generosity (11:7-9; 12:13); false claims of being an apostle of Christ (12:12; 13:3); inferiority to other apostles in the church (11:5; 12:11).

Paul's criticism of them is no less sharp. They "trade on the word of God" (2:17 NAB) by accepting financial support (11:12, 20). They commend themselves (10:12, 18) and bolster their pretensions with letters of recommendation (3:1). They apparently boast of knowledge gained through visions and revelations (12:1, 11; 11:5-6) and of their special relationship to Christ (10:7; 11:23). They are proud of their Hebrew origin (11: 22). They preach a different Jesus and a different gospel from Paul's (11:4). They operate in missionary territory belonging to other people and take credit for work done by others (10: 15-16). They are immoral and do not repent (12:21; 13:2). They are false apostles and servants of Satan (11: 13-15).

These opponents have been variously identified: as the Gnostics known from I Corinthians; as Judaizers, like those in Galatia (see p. 281), who wanted to put the Corinthians under the Law; as wandering Jewish-Christian preachers; as Jewish Christians from Palestine who had contact with the original apostles and possibly personal knowledge of Jesus.

That they were Jewish Christians is certain (11:22). There is no evidence that they were Judaizers; Paul does not attack law observance as a way of salvation in II Corinthians. They were hostile to Paul and his Gentile mission. They joined forces with the Gnostic group at Corinth, which also was critical of Paul. A formidable opposition to Paul thus arose.

The situation at Corinth was more complex than at the time of the writing of I Corinthians.

2. Theme and Outline

The central subject of the letter is: Paul, a true minister of the New Covenant.

I. Introduction (1:1-11)
   A. Greeting (1:1-2)
   B. Thanksgiving for God's comfort in affliction (1:3-11)
II. Body (1:12–13:10)
   A. The recent crisis at Corinth (1:12–7:16)
      1. Explanation of his change of travel plans (1:12–2:13)
      2. His true ministry as an apostle (2:14–7:4)
      3. His joy over reconciliation with the Corinthians (7:5-16)
   B. The collection for the Jerusalem church (chaps. 8–9)
      1. The generosity of the Macedonian churches and the collectors (Titus and two others) he is sending (chap. 8)
      2. Reasons why the Corinthians should give generously to this project (chap. 9)
   C. The defense of his apostolic authority and ministry (10:1–13:10)
      1. The charge of face-to-face weakness, and boldness at a distance (10:1-11)
      2. The charge that he is overreaching the area of his authority (10:12-18)

3. His "boasting" versus the boasting of the "super" (but false) apostles (11: 1–12:13)
4. His paternal care for his Corinthian children and their proper preparation for his coming to Corinth (12:14–13: 10)

III.   Conclusion (13:11-14)

3. Paul's Authority and Ministry

II Corinthians is the most personal of all Paul's letters. Paul did not like to talk about himself, but his enemies forced him to defend his motives and his work. The charges made against him were vicious slander. In his defense he bared his soul in a most intimate way. We learn what it cost Paul to be a faithful minister of Jesus Christ and how he viewed Christian ministry in general.

Paul discusses the Christian ministry in this letter from several standpoints.

a. Its Authority

The basis of the Christian ministry is a call from God to live under the new covenant and to serve it. "It is God who establishes us with you in Christ, and has commissioned us" (1: 21). "The qualification we have comes from God; it is he who has qualified us to dispense his new covenant" (3: 5-6 NEB).

The new covenant differs sharply from the old. The old consisted of a written law which condemned men and brought them death (*cf.* Rom. 7: 7-11). The new covenant is God's law written in the heart through the life-giving activity of the Holy Spirit (II Cor. 3:6; *cf.* Rom. 2:28-29).

b. The Character of a Christian Minister

Sincerity (pure motives) is a necessary quality (1:12; 2:17). Unacceptable is the double-dealing involved in a hidden No when a Yes is uttered (1: 17-18). Shameful, cunning, underhanded ways on the part of those who proclaim the gospel (4:2) do not represent the ever trustworthy God, who faithfully fulfills his promises. As there is no duplicity in him or in his Son, Jesus Christ, there can be none in a true minister (1:18-20).

Humility, not boasting, should mark the spirit of the Christian minister. The false apostles boast of their knowledge (11:6), their heredity (11:22), their credentials (3:1), their special relation to Christ (10:7), their achievements (11:23). Self-commendation and boasting are incompatible with the spirit of the gospel (10:12, 17-18). Paul does not like to boast of "worldly things" but his enemies, by their bragging, have forced him to justify himself (12:11). But if he must, he will boast of his sufferings and weaknesses, for in these God's mighty power is seen (11:30–12:10).

Consideration for the welfare of others is characteristic of the true Christian minister. All of Paul's activities in relation to the Corinthians— his change of plans for his proposed visit to Corinth (1:23–2:3), his severe letter (2:3-4; 7:12), his self-support when evangelizing at Corinth (11:7-11), his bitter sufferings as an apostle (6:4-10; 11:23-29)—were meant to help them, not to enrich himself: "it is you I want, not your possessions" (12:14 JB).

Forgiveness is the hallmark of Christian ministry. Paul freely forgave the Corinthian man who had wronged him and urged the church there to do likewise (2:5-11).

Unflagging courage and indomitable hope in difficult circumstances reveal the true minister: "we never lose heart" (4:1 NEB); "we are often troubled, but not crushed; sometimes in doubt, but never in despair" (4:8 TEV). The servant of God, while suffering temporary afflictions and the daily wasting away of physical life and vitality, knows that his inner life is being renewed constantly (4:16). He knows that the resurrection life of the risen Jesus, at work in him now (4:7-12), points forward to the glory of the final life with God (4:14; 5:1-5). The Holy Spirit within is the guarantee of final victory (5:5).

c. The Christian Minister's Message

Paul summarizes it this way: "For what we preach is not ourselves, but Jesus Christ as Lord, with ourselves as your servants for Jesus' sake" (4:5). Jesus Christ (the Messiah), the risen Lord (Master), who is the likeness of God (4:4), brings to the believer at the new birth a wondrous inner light, dispelling the darkness of

unbelief and sin. It is God's light, as real as the light of creation, brought by Christ into the very center of the believer's being, that banishes the prince of darkness and with him the blindness he causes (4:4).

Jesus Christ, the God-given Redeemer, who died for all that he might reconcile them to God, has called his servants to a ministry of reconciliation (5:14-21). The minister's work is the abolition of hostility: man's hostility to God and to his fellow man. Thus the Corinthians and Paul, as God's reconciled children, must open their hearts to each other (6:11-13; 7:2), and the proclamation of God's reconciling activity must go on into unreached lands (10:15-16).

d. The Glory and Terror of the Christian Ministry

In spite of all opposition, God leads his apostles in a triumphal procession through the world, and knowledge of God is spread everywhere. The message of Christ's saving work, proclaimed by the apostles, has a double effect: those who reject it are sent farther on the way to death, but those who welcome it are sent progressively on the way to life. What a staggering responsibility it is to bring men to a decision with such far-reaching and irrevocable consequences! Who is adequate for such a task? Only a divine commission could make one assume this awesome role (2:14-17).

4. The Question of Unity

The letter has a certain disjointedness, which calls for explanation.

The three main parts (chaps. 1–7; 8–9; 10–13) are only loosely connected, and the first and second parts have sections that do not fit together well. In part 1, 2:13 is followed naturally by 7:5 (making 2:14–7:4 something of a digression). And within this digression, 6:14–7:1 seems to be a further digression (or an erratic block of material in the train of thought). Part 2 (chaps. 8–9) is not related closely to part 1 (chaps. 1–7). Furthermore, chap. 8 and chap. 9 present two accounts of the collection for the Jerusalem church, the second beginning in 9:1 as if chap. 8 did not exist.

But the most startling break in the flow of thought occurs between chaps. 9 and 10. At the end of chap. 9 Paul is serenely confident of the support of the Corinthians for the collection and full of gratitude for his restored, happy relationship with them. Then suddenly (in chaps. 10–13) he launches into a bitter attack on his enemies, as if no reconciliation had occurred. One wonders whether chaps. 10–13 would not have reopened the wound which Titus said had begun to heal.

Two major explanations of these facts have been offered.

a. Someone after Paul formed II Corinthians out of several letters written by Paul and possibly one fragment not from Paul.

In order of writing these might be:

(1) 6:14–7:1—a part of Paul's letter to the Corinthians mentioned in I Cor. 5:9 (or it might be a piece of non-Christian writing, possibly Essene [see p. 408], that had come into Christian hands);

(2) 2:14–6:13 and 7:2-4—a defense of Paul's ministry under the new covenant, written possibly from Ephesus after our I Corinthians and near the beginning of the trouble at Corinth;

(3) chaps. 10–13—from Paul's severe letter to the Corinthians, mentioned in II Cor. 2:3-4; 7:8, 12, written from Ephesus after his unsuccessful visit to Corinth;

(4) 1:1–2:13 and 7:5–16 — Paul's letter of thanksgiving for his reconciliation with the Corinthians, written from Macedonia;

(5) chaps. 8 and 9—two brief letters to Corinth about the collection, both from Macedonia, with only a short interval between them.

If we assume that II Corinthians contains parts or most of several letters of Paul, this would mean that someone after Paul joined these letters together into our II Corinthians, possibly at the beginning of the second century and perhaps at Corinth. Chaps. 10–13 (from the severe letter) may have been put last because it was the fashion in Christian writings of that period to warn readers at the end of documents concerning errors they would face in the time before the end of the age.

b. Though the letter is loosely constructed, Paul put it together himself in its present form.

Advocates of this position speak of Paul's tendency to digress and the probability of his having composed the letter at several sittings, thus accounting for the roughness of style and content. They argue that the difference between chaps. 1–9 and 10–13 is not as great as claimed: that Paul is defending himself in chaps. 1–9 (see, *e.g.*, 1:17 ff.; 2:17; 4:2-3; 5:12, 13), as well as in chaps. 10–13, for there was still a rebellious minority at Corinth (2:6). In this view chaps. 10–13 would be addressed to this rebellious minority, with the hope that their opposition might be overcome before his arrival there (12:14, 20; 13:1-2, 10). Or Paul may have received additional disturbing news that evoked the sharp tone of chaps. 10–13, or his "moods" may have caused him at a later dictating session to take a dimmer view of the Corinthian situation, or he may have followed the practice of reserving his strong words of warning for the end of his letters.

Scholars now are sharply divided on the problem of the letter's unity. If one claims unity, then he must hold that two letters of Paul to the Corinthians (referred to in I Cor. 5:9 and in II Cor. 2:3-4; 7:8, 12) are entirely lost.

5. Authorship, Place, Date

Only 6:14–7:1 has been assigned to some author other than Paul, and this on the basis of some variance in vocabulary and theology from Paul's normal usage. But the grounds are inconclusive.

If II Corinthians was put together from several letters, the different parts probably came from Ephesus and Macedonia and were joined by an editor, possibly at the beginning of the second century.

If we have II Corinthians in its original form, the place of writing was Macedonia and the date about A.D. 55 or 56.

74. Galatians

Martin Luther said, "The epistle to the Galatians is my epistle; I have betrothed myself to it: it is my wife." Someone has remarked that Luther put this epistle to his lips as a trumpet to blow the reveille of the Reformation. It is the Magna Carta of Christian freedom and the charter of evangelical faith. Through it and through the letter to the Romans, Paul has powerfully affected Christian theology.

1. Theme and Outline

Theme: My gospel of justification (*i.e.*, right relationship with God) by faith in Jesus Christ—and not by obedience to the requirements of the Law—is the one and only divine gospel.

   I. Introduction (1:1-10).
      A. Greeting and doxology (1: 1-5).
      B. Introductory censure (1: 6-10).
  II. Body (1:11–6:10).
      A. Facts of my personal life prove the divine origin of my gospel (1:11–2:21).
         1. My conversion from Judaism and its ac-

companying special re-
velation of the true
nature of the gospel
were an act of God
(1:11-16b).
2. My independent mis-
sionary activity and my
virtual lack of contact
with the apostles and
the churches of Judea
show that God, not
man, was directing my
activity,   as   those
churches openly con-
fessed (1:16c-24).
3. The endorsement of
my work by the lead-
ers of the Jerusalem
church shows that they
recognized the divine
origin of my gospel
(2:1-10).
4. My gospel won out in
Antioch in a struggle
with Cephas (Peter)
and with Jerusalem ad-
vocates of law observ-
ance by Gentiles (2:
11-21).
B. Experience, Scripture, and
reason support my gospel
(3:1–4:31).
1. You Galatians received
new life in the Spirit
and miraculous man-
ifestations of the Spir-
it's presence through
faith, not through obe-
dience to the Law's
demands,   and   you
should   continue   on
that course (3:1-5).
2. Abraham's right rela-

tionship with God was
the result of his faith
(trust) in God, and
God indicated to him
that   those   Gentiles
who later would have
a similar faith would
be his sons (3:6-9).
3. The Scripture testifies
that seeking a right re-
lationship with God by
obedience to the Law
leads to condemnation
by that Law; deliver-
ance from condemna-
tion   comes   only   by
faith in Jesus Christ
(3:10-14).
4. God's fundamental re-
lationship with his peo-
ple since Abraham has
been a promise-faith
relationship,   directed
toward the coming into
being of a universal
family of sons who
would   be   heirs   of
God's glorious future;
the Law, later in time,
communicated by an
inferior method, tem-
porary   in   purpose,
serves—but cannot re-
place—this   promise-
faith relationship (3:
15–4:7).
5. You Galatians, who be-
gan so well under
my ministry to fol-
low the path of justifi-
cation by faith, must
not turn away from
me and the true way

Bull's head with garlands at Antioch in Pisidia, where Paul preached (Acts 13:14 ff.)

to seek justification by obedience to the Law (4:8-20).

6. The Law itself teaches (in the story of Sarah and Hagar) that the true, free sons of God, who will inherit his promises, are those who have faith in Christ, not those who rely on the Law as a way of justification (4: 21-31).

C. My gospel leads to a life of controlled freedom in Christ (5:1–6:10).

1. Circumcision is the symbol of slavery; do not submit to it (5:1-12).

2. Love and the Spirit provide adequate controls for the life of Christian freedom; live by them (5:13–6:10).

II. Conclusion (6:11-18).

A. Beware of those who insist on circumcision (6:11-16).

B. Respect the authentic marks of my status and service as an apostle (6: 17).

C. Farewell in Christ (6:18).

2. The Basic Issue

Paul maintains in this letter that both Jews and Gentiles come into a right relationship with God and with one another through trust in Jesus Christ, God's incarnate Son (4:4), who by his death on the cross rescued believers from their bondage to sin and demonic powers and opened to them the life of the New Age (1:4).

He insists that men cannot win acceptance by God and a right relationship with him by conformity, however complete, to God's Law: "a man is not justified by works of the law but through faith in Jesus Christ . . . by works of the law shall no one be justified" (2:16).

Two ways of salvation are contrasted throughout this letter: salvation by divine rescue, provided in Jesus Christ and accepted gratefully and trustingly by men who know themselves to be sinners and in need of salvation; and salvation by human effort directed toward making oneself acceptable to God according to standards contained in what is regarded as a God-given moral code. Actually, all religions of the world today may be divided into religions of rescue and religions of achievement, though strains of both tend to appear in some of them.

Hebrew religion, as expressed by Israel's great prophets and psalmists, emphasized God's saving activity in behalf of rebellious, idolatrous Israel and mankind as a whole. It stressed the transformation by God's grace of man's inner life and the expression of his inner renewal in outward acts of justice and mercy. The priests, the wise men, and the rabbis tended rather to accent obedience to God's commands, as revealed in the Law of Moses, in order for the individual

and the nation to enjoy the approval of God and prove worthy of inheriting the promises he made to Israel. Many Jews came to think righteous and merciful acts were of so great merit that they could atone for sin (see Tobit 4:10-11; 12:9; Sirach 3:30). Some rabbis said that the patriarchs had laid up great stores of merit before God, and that others of lesser merit could draw on these stores.

This doctrine appeared in medieval Roman Catholicism as the merits of the saints, which could be transferred through prayer to those of lesser achievements. In modern Judaism the doctrine of merit continues. One Jewish scholar has written, "Rabbinic Jews and modern Jews believe that each person, through repentance and good deeds, works out his own personal atonement" (Samuel Sandmel, *A Jewish Understanding of the New Testament,* 1956, p. 38).

The doctrine appears also in those forms of contemporary Protestantism that stress salvation through education and becoming through doing. One theologian has written: "We know in the last analysis that our characters are the one thing we can and must create for ourselves. What is our character? It is our will to live by our ideals, 'sacrificing' whatever is needed to realize them ever more completely. And we know that our character is the fortress that we must build by our own efforts" (Peter Bertocci, *Religion as Creative Insecurity,* p. 61).

Paul held that man is gripped by forces too strong for him to conquer. Sin is an invading, corrupting power, making the will incapable of moral action and bringing the whole of mankind into bondage and ultimate death (Rom. 7:13-24; 5:12-14). Only God's identification with sinners through Jesus Christ and sinners' trusting identification with Jesus can bring deliverance for individual persons and for humanity as a whole. This faith-identification brings the gift of the Holy Spirit and inner renewal (Gal. 2:20; 4:6), and out of this renewal flow acts of Christian love and moral change (Gal. 5:13–6:10). (See the summary of the message of Romans, pp. 257-60).

Paul, therefore, resisted violently those who taught the Galatians that right relationship with God must be won by obedience to the Law, in addition to faith in Jesus Christ.

3. Location of the Galatian Churches

Two views are held today, with opinion about equally divided.

a. They were in upper central Asia Minor (modern Turkey), in the territory occupied by the Gauls (Celts) in the third century B.C., including the cities of Ancyra, Pessinus, and Tavium. Advocates of this view (commonly called the North Galatian theory) believe Paul founded these churches on his second missionary journey (Acts 16:6) and visited them on his third (Acts 18:23).

b. They were located in south central Asia Minor, in territory which had become part of the Roman province of Galatia in 25 B.C., including the cities of Antioch, Iconium, Lystra, and Derbe. Proponents of this view (the

South Galatian theory) hold that the churches were founded on Paul's first journey, as recorded in Acts 13:13–14:23, and visited by him on the second (16:6) and the third (18:23).

4. Opponents of Paul's Gospel

The facts concerning the exact identity of Paul's opponents are inconclusive. Some scholars have held that Paul may have had incomplete or inaccurate information about them. Several views are possible:

a. They were Jewish Christians from Jerusalem, who belonged to the legalistic wing of the church (Gal. 2:4; Acts 15:5). They insisted on conformity to the Law of Moses, as well as on faith in Jesus Christ, for the salvation of both Jews and Gentiles. They hotly opposed Paul's law-free gospel by journeying to his churches and attempting to set his converts right (II Cor. 11:4-5, 12-14, 22-23). Scholars have long called them "Judaizers."

b. They were Gentile Christians, living in Galatia, who had become Judaized (accepted circumcision and other requirements of the Law of Moses) and wished other Gentile Christians to do likewise.

c. They were Jewish-Christian Gnostics, somewhat like those at Corinth (see p. 265), who were leading the Galatian Christians into the worship of world powers and certain ritual observances (including circumcision and the keeping of sacred days and feasts—Gal. 4:9-10), as well as into immoral conduct. Those who hold this view believe Paul did not really understand these opponents and described them as if they were Jewish Christian legalists.

It is doubtful that we know more about these opponents than Paul did. Since he indicated clearly that they demanded acceptance of the Law as essential to salvation (4:21; 5:4; *cf.* 2:16; 3:21), it is perhaps best to identify them with the legalistic Jewish-Christian minority in the Jerusalem church (2:4; Acts 15:5), which seems to have strongly opposed Paul's law-free mission to the Gentiles.

5. Time and Place of Writing

Here again there is no agreement. The crucial questions are: (1) What does Paul mean in Gal. 4:13, where the Greek can mean either "at first" (or "originally") or "on the first of my two visits"? (2) Is Paul's journey to Jerusalem, described in Gal. 2:1-10, to be identified with that in Acts 15: 1-21 or with the one in Acts 11:27-30; 12:25?

If Paul had been in Galatia only once before the writing of this letter, and the Jerusalem council described in Acts 15:1-21 had not yet occurred but the famine relief visit of Paul had, the letter to the Galatians could have been the first of all Paul's letters (about A.D. 49, possibly from Antioch). If two visits to Galatia had taken place and Gal. 2:1-10 is Paul's account of the Jerusalem council, then the letter was written about A.D. 54 or 55, probably from Ephesus. The strong similarities in subject matter, language, and thought between Galatians and Romans make a date near the writing of Romans likely, though by no means certain. (See on Romans, p. 262.)

75. Ephesians

Samuel Taylor Coleridge called the epistle to the Ephesians "one of the divinest compositions of man." Theologians have long regarded it as the most profound of the writings ascribed to Paul, and some have held it to be the crown and climax of the entire New Testament.

The claim by one writer that it is "the most contemporary book in the Bible" is well founded. In an age like ours, characterized by rampant evil, widespread meaninglessness and despair, and deep social and religious divisions, Ephesians sings triumphantly about God's mighty activity in Christ and the church, through which all the hostile powers that tear life apart and seek to turn it back to chaos are defeated. Ephesians promises a new world of unity and harmony. The ecumenical movement of our time has found much inspiration in Ephesians.

1. Theme and Outline

Theme: It is God's purpose to unite the universe in Christ and the church.

    I. Greeting (1:1-2).

Statues along the main street, Ephesus

II. Body (1:3–6:20).
   A. The divine plan for the unification of all things in Christ and the church (1:3–3:21).
      1. Praise of "the Trinity" for projecting the plan (1:3-14).
      2. Prayer for the readers' understanding of the plan (1:15-23).
      3. The plan at work in the unification of Jews and Gentiles (2:1-22).
      4. Paul: God's instrument in the revelation of the plan (3:1-13).
      5. Prayer (resumed) for the readers' understanding of and full participation in the plan (3:14-19).
      6. Doxology (3:20-21).
   B. The Christians' role in the fulfillment of the plan (4:1–6:20).
      1. They must build the church up by mutual service and love (4:1-16).
      2. They must abandon completely the old pattern of life and espouse wholeheartedly the new (4:17–5:20).
      3. Family members must live together in mutual submission (5:21–6:9).
      4. Christians must be fully

equipped for the spiritual warfare in which they are engaged (6:10-20).

III. Conclusion (6:21-24).

2. Message

Ephesians begins with the purpose of God "before the foundation of the world" to bring into being a family of loving and morally blameless sons from all peoples of the earth. It shows that God realized this purpose through Jesus Christ and through the ministry of "holy apostles and prophets" and of Paul himself (3:1-13).

Ephesians describes the kind of life appropriate for God's "beloved children" who await the time when they will inherit the New Age (1:14, 21; 2:7; 4:30), that is, "the kingdom of Christ and of God" (5:5). And it sweeps on to brief and suggestive intimations of the character of that "fulness of time" when God will accomplish his purpose for the unification of all things—in heaven and on earth.

The opening thanksgiving hymn (1:3-14), marked by a refrain ("to the praise of his glory"—1:6, 12, 14), contemplates the God and Father who blessed, chose, and destined "us" (*i.e.,* the church) to be his family of morally blameless sons (vss. 3-6). The hymn considers "the Beloved" Jesus Christ, who through his sacrificial death brought forgiveness of sins and began the unification of the universe (vss. 7-12). It celebrates the gift of the Holy Spirit to the church as the guarantee of the promised heritage of the coming age (vss. 13-14).

Chap. 2 shows that God is uniting Jews and Gentiles. Both formerly were under the power of sin and the devil, hostile to one another, spiritually dead, and subject to God's judgment. Through God's great mercy, love, and graciousness they have shared together in the benefits of Christ's resurrection (victory over sin, death, and evil powers). This glorious result came about not through anything they themselves had done, but only through God's graciousness, met by their faith (trusting acceptance).

Jesus Christ is the bridge between Jews and Gentiles. A new humanity, a new international family of redeemed sons, at peace with God and with one another, has come into being. All members of the family have equal access to the Father through the Holy Spirit. Together they constitute the new temple in which God's Spirit dwells.

Paul's peculiar mission to preach to the Gentiles "the good news of the unfathomable riches of Christ" (3:8 NEB) and to make known to them the divine plan for the unification of all things leads on to what the members of the new family of God must be and do to further God's purpose.

They must have the qualities of spirit that promote unity (4:2-3); emphasize the things that unite them, not the things that divide them (4:4-6); use Christ's gifts for building up the church by mutual service and love (4:7-16); abandon completely the old pattern of life and wholeheartedly accept the new (4:17–5:20); "defer to one another" in family relationships "out of reverence for Christ" (5:21

NAB); become fully equipped for the spiritual warfare in which they are engaged (6:10-20).

The inheritance God will give the sons at "the day of redemption" (4:30), as this phrase implies, is freedom. It will be final freedom from sin, death, and evil powers—whose doom is already sealed (1:21-22; 3:10; 6:10-20)—and membership in "the kingdom of Christ and of God" (5:5). The New Age will be marked by God's immeasurable riches of grace (2:7). Universal harmony will come about (1:10), and God's sons will experience the wonder of all that God is and imparts to his children (3:19).

3. Authorship

Authorities divide about equally on the question of whether Paul wrote Ephesians.

Those who favor Paul's authorship cite:

a. The clear claim of the epistle itself (1:1; 3:1; 4:1; 6:20)
b. The second-century church's ascription of the epistle to Paul
c. Its Pauline literary structure (opening greeting, thanksgiving, doctrinal section, ethical section, conclusion and benediction)
d. Its Pauline language and theology (the language is 90 or 95 percent in accord with Paul's style; the thought in every important respect is Paul's)

Those who favor authorship by a disciple of Paul, who wrote from Paul's general point of view and in his name, cite:

a. The language of the epistle as being significantly different from the genuine Pauline letters (about 90 words in Ephesians not used elsewhere in Paul's letters; several non-Pauline expressions; long sentences and imposing liturgical style)
b. The literary relationships between Ephesians and other New Testament material (its curious overlapping with Colossians in such a way as to suggest an imitation and, to some degree, an alteration of ideas in Colossians; its similarity in vocabulary and thought to late New Testament literature such as I Peter, Luke-Acts, the books of John, and to the Apostolic Fathers of the second century)
c. The period and perspective of the writer as reflected in the letter (the Jewish-Gentile controversy is regarded as settled, a condition achieved only after Paul's time; the veneration of the apostles and prophets [2:20; 3:5] expresses a deference unlike Paul [Gal. 2])
d. The striking differences between the theology of Ephesians and that of the genuine letters of Paul (the high doctrine of the church in Ephesians, the different view of Christ's person and work, and the absence of the expectation of the return of Christ)
e. The known custom in New Testament times of ascribing a disciple's work to his master as a

means of honoring him and perpetuating his teaching and influence (see p. 308)

At present no final decision on authorship seems possible. Until the epistle's claim to authorship by Paul and the early church's acceptance of the letter as Paul's have been clearly disproved, it probably is wise to let its traditional authorship stand.

4. Original Readers and Purpose

The words "in Ephesus" are omitted in important early manuscripts (Vaticanus, Sinaiticus, Papyrus 46). Marcion, of the second century, regarded the letter as Paul's epistle to the Laodiceans (Col. 4:16); hence, "in Ephesus" could not have stood in Marcion's text.

The impersonal character of the epistle (no personal greetings, no practical problems) would be strange in a writing addressed to the church in Ephesus, where Paul had spent over two years (Acts 19:10). Furthermore, the writer has only "heard of your faith" (1:15) and assumes that the readers have heard of his special commission to a Gentile ministry (3:2).

If Paul was the author, and he was a prisoner at the time of writing (3:1; 6:20), we must assume that his long reflection on his mission to the Gentiles and on the church in many lands led to his writing a general statement to all the churches about the significance of the church in the universal purpose of God. He may have directed that several copies of the document be made and sent, perhaps by personal representatives, for reading in the churches (6:21). The copy we have may have come from the church in Ephesus, and hence the words "in Ephesus" were added by the collector of Paul's letters. Other copies, existing without those words, gave rise to uncertainty about the original destination.

If a disciple of Paul wrote the letter in Paul's name and spirit, we probably must assume that he was thoroughly familiar with Colossians and with Paul's letters as a whole. He wished to keep Gentile Christianity (by his time considerably influenced by Greek and Gnostic thought) aware of its roots in Jewish Christianity and in the eternal purpose of God as seen in the sending of Christ to the Jews (1:12; 2:12-13). If this hypothesis is correct, the author was a Jewish-Christian (1:12; 2:3, 11, 17) familiar with Greek and Gnostic thought. (On Gnosticism see pp. 304-7.)

One scholar has proposed that Ephesians was written by the collector of Paul's letters (Onesimus) to serve as an introduction to the whole collection.

5. Place and Date of Writing

If Paul was the author, the work must be assigned to one of several places where Paul was in prison: Rome, Ephesus, or Caesarea. The date would fall somewhere between A.D. 54 and 62. If a disciple was the writer, the date would seem to be about A.D. 80–95, the place indeterminable.

On the question of the place of origin of Paul's prison epistles, see p. 255.

76. Philippians

Philippians is Paul's most joyful letter.

It was not his circumstances that made him happy, for he was a prisoner (1:7, 13, 14, 17) facing the possibility of death (1:20-24; 2:23-24), misunderstood and opposed by fellow Christians (1:15-18), and threatened by the possible subversion of his converts by enemies outside and inside the church (3:2-21). From every human point of view life had fallen in on him.

The secret of his joy finds expression in his own words: "How great is the joy I have in my life in the Lord! . . . I have learned to be satisfied with what I have. . . . I have the strength to face all conditions by the power that Christ gives me" (4:10-13 TEV). He found that, by divine transformation, suffering becomes a source of strength.

1. Theme and Outline

Theme: The progress of the gospel
I. Introduction (1:1-11)
A. Greeting (1:1-2)
B. Thanksgiving for the Philippians' part in advancing the gospel and prayer for them (1:3-11)
II. Body (1:12–4:20)
A. The progress of the gospel through the events and circumstances of Paul's life (1:12-26)
1. His imprisonment (1:12-14)
2. His Christian opponents (1:15-18)
3. The coming verdict in his trial (1:19-26)
B. The advancing of the gospel within the church at Philippi (1:27–4:9)
1. By the achievement of unity through cooperative effort in behalf of the faith and through imitating the self-denying, brotherly spirit of Jesus Christ (1:27–2:11)
2. By cooperating with God in the effort to reach the goal of final salvation (2:12-18)
3. By accepting the help of deeply committed Christian leaders (2:19-30)
4. By rejecting false teaching and pressing on in the true way of salvation (3:1-21)
5. By mutual helpfulness, prayer, absolute trust in God, concentration on what is good, and imitation of Paul (4:1-9)
C. The Philippians' gift as evidence of their partnership in the advancing of the gospel (4:10-20)
III. Conclusion (4:21-23)

2. The Question of Unity

As the letter is now organized, there is considerable roughness in the sequence of materials. One would expect the personal matter concerning Timothy and Epaphroditus in 2:19-30 to come at the end of the letter, rather than in the middle. The sudden outburst in 3:2 ff. is surprising. The farewell and benediction of 4:4-9 seem appropriate for the end of the letter. However, the end does not come until after a long section on Epaphroditus and the Philippian gift (4:10-20). Furthermore, one would expect the thanks for the gift to appear at the beginning of the letter, rather than at the end. Paul's letters usually are more logical than this.

This roughness and a reference by Polycarp (a Christian martyr of the second century) to Paul's "letters" to the Philippians lead some scholars to conclude that our Philippians contains two or three letters joined together by someone after Paul, perhaps by the first collector of Paul's letters.

The hypothesis of two letters involves the following arrangement of material:

Letter 1 (3:2–4:23), written after the arrival of Epaphroditus with the Philippians' gift, to warn the Philippians against false teachers, whose activities Epaphroditus reported to Paul, and to express thanks for the gift. The one who joined the letters omitted the salutation.

Letter 2 (1:1–3:1), written about a year later to accompany Epaphroditus on his return to Philippi. Its purpose was to bring the Philippians up to date on Paul's situation, to inform them of the coming of Timothy, and to prevent any criticism of Epaphroditus. The ending of this letter was dropped (or may now be found in 4:21-23).

The hypothesis of three letters goes as follows:

Letter 1 (4:10-20), Paul's note of thanks after the arrival of Epaphroditus with the gift;

Letter 2 (1:1–2:30 [or 3:1] and 4:21-23; possibly also 4:2-9), written to accompany Epaphroditus on his return to Philippi;

Letter 3 (3:1 or 3:2 through 4:1 or 4:9), written just before Paul's death, as his last will and testament, warning against Jewish enemies, whom Paul blames for cutting short his life and ministry.

These hypotheses are interesting but unprovable. We do not know the precise circumstances and conditions under which Paul dictated the letter. Furthermore, it is an informal letter and may have been dictated over a period of some days. Abrupt changes of subject and style are not unknown in Paul (Rom. 16:17 ff.; II Cor. 2: 14 ff.). Those who hold that the letter is a unity find that the loss of the beginnings and endings of the supposed letters, as well as the curious way the hypothetical editor put them together, is as hard to explain as the roughness of thought and style.

3. Purpose

a. To thank the Philippians for their gift (1:5; 4:10-20)

b. To ensure a good reception for Epaphroditus, who was returning with the letter (2:25-30)

c. To inform the Philippians of Paul's present situation and his prospects for the future (1:12-26; 2:24)

d. To prepare the way for the coming of Timothy (2:19-23)

e. To assist in settling certain problems in the church of Philippi:

(1) Persecution by unknown opponents, possibly Gentiles stirred up by Jews (1:28-30; *cf.* Acts 16:11-40)

(2) False teaching by Jews or Jewish-Christian legalists or J e w i s h-Christian Gnostics (see pp. 265, 281) (3:2-19)

(3) Dissension among members (1:27; 2:2-3; 4:2-3)

4. Teaching

Philippians bubbles over with religious feeling sublimely expressed. It shows how one who is gripped by the power of God in Jesus Christ reacts to the hard realities of life and death. We are told that when the going is toughest, the footing is surest, the strength most abundant, and the joy most radiant.

a. Christian Joy

For the length of the letter, "joy" and "rejoice" occur a surprising num-

The river at Philippi, near which was a Jewish place of prayer where Paul met Lydia
(Acts 16:13-14)

ber of times (sixteen times in the various forms of the Greek word).

What occasioned Paul's joy? He found joy in prayer (1:4); in the proclamation of Christ, even by his enemies (1:18); in the knowledge that his prison experience and trial would honor Christ and aid in his ultimate salvation (1:19-20); in the thought that his death might have a sacrificial significance for the Philippians (2:17); in the hoped-for steadfastness and unity of his converts (4:1; 2:2); and in the Philippians' gift (4:10). And he wanted the Philippians to have joy in the progress of their faith (1:25); in the possibility of his sacrificial death for their sake (2:18); in their renewed fellowship with Epaphroditus (2:28-30); in the fact of their incorporation in Christ and the church ("rejoice *in the Lord*"—3:1; 4:4); and in the hope of Christ's coming (4:5).

Even if in some of these passages "rejoice" should be translated "farewell"—the other meaning of the word —as is possible in 3:1 and 4:4 (see NEB), the intensity of joy loses little; for "farewell" carried somewhat the meaning of "cheerio"—that is, "be happy," "be joyful."

The confident mood of the Christian life shines in the words, "I can do all things in him who strengthens me" (4:13).

b. Self-Denying Concern for Others

The greatest passage in the letter is undoubtedly 2:5-11, a hymn composed by Paul or possibly by some other Christian poet-theologian and used here by Paul. Its theme is Christ's self-denying concern for others and his exaltation by God. Paul introduced it here to counteract the selfish, grasping spirit of some of the Philippians who were bent on personal privilege and glory (2:3; 4:2-3) and were about to wreck the church.

Church members should have the attitude of Christ, says Paul. Christ, who bore the image (or the divine nature) of God, did not (like Adam) grasp greedily at equality with God, but, on the contrary, "made himself nothing" (NEB) by taking the nature of a slave. The heavenly Son of man became a man like us; and in obedience to God, whose slave he was, he accepted the most abject of humiliations: death on a cross. Because of his self-renunciation, God rewarded him with the sovereignty he did not grasp at: he made him King over the universe, to be worshiped by every creature, equal with God the Father in the exercise of divine sovereignty.

A disciple should imitate his Lord in radical self-renunciation. If he does so, divisions stemming from self-seeking will vanish from the church. God will set his seal on such self-renunciation.

c. The Path to the Glory of the Resurrection

False teachers were about to lure the Philippians from the path leading to the prize God had in store for them: life with Christ in the glory of the coming age.

Paul, therefore, marks out this path in the clearest terms. It involves the following:

(1) Renunciation of merit—all human assets from heredity, from personal choice, and from personal accomplishment (3:4-8)

(2) Identification with C h r i s t through faith—sharing in his sufferings, his death, and the power of his resurrection (3:9-11)

(3) Relentless concentration on reaching the goal of life eternal (or the resurrection from the dead), never being satisfied with one's degree of progress (3:12-16)

(4) Imitation of those Christian leaders who have set their minds on heavenly, rather than on earthly, realities and thus are destined for life in the New Age (3:17-21; *cf.* 4:9)

5. Place of Writing and Date

The probable location was Rome, Ephesus, or Caesarea, some time between about A.D. 54 and 62.

On the whole question of the place of writing of Paul's prison epistles, see p. 255.

77. Colossians

John Calvin called the epistle to the Colossians "an inestimable treasure." He based this judgment on its presentation of Christ: "What is of greater importance in the whole system of heavenly doctrine than to have Christ drawn to the life, so that we may clearly contemplate his excellence, his office, and all the fruits that accrue to us therefrom?"

Colossians' importance clearly lies in its view of Christ—in the way it relates Christ to God, to the church, and to the universe. The author drew his portrait of Christ against the backdrop of some heresy we do not fully understand. But our lack of knowledge here, while exasperating, is not particularly tragic. Whatever the heresy was, it stimulated the writer to a characterization of Christ which stretches the mind of the most competent theologian and mature Christian. The profundities of Colossians almost defy comprehension. Who indeed can grasp the full significance of the one "in whom are hid all the treasures of wisdom and knowledge" (2:3)?

1. Theme and Outline

Theme: The supremacy and all-sufficiency of Christ in the salvation of believers

I. Introduction (1:1-14)
   A. Greetings (1:1-2)
   B. Thanksgiving (1:3-8)
   C. Prayer (1:9-14)
II. Body (1:15–4:6)
   A. Christ versus the cosmic powers (1:15–2:23)
      1. The supremacy of Christ (1:15-23)
      2. Paul, the preacher of Christ's supremacy (1:24–2:5)
      3. The all-sufficiency of

Christ for salvation (2:6-15)

4. Freedom in Christ from the rules associated with the worship of cosmic powers (2:16-23)

B. The new, heavenly life in Christ versus the old, earthly life (3:1–4:6)

1. The readers' attitude toward the world in the light of their union with Christ and their heavenly destiny (3:1-4)

2. Their obligation to abandon their old way of living in view of their new life in Christ (3:5-11)

3. The attitudes and conduct appropriate to their new life in Christ (3:12-17)

4. How their new life should affect their domestic relations (3:18–4:1)

5. Counsels on prayer and witnessing (4:2-6)

III. Conclusion (4:7-18)

A. Introduction of Tychicus and Onesimus (4:7-9)

B. Greetings from Paul and his companions (4:10-15)

C. Instructions for an exchange of letters and for Archippus (4:16-17)

D. Benediction (4:18)

2. The Writer's Purposes

a. To counteract the Colossian heresy and to urge the Colossians to continue growing in the faith they had learned from Epaphras, Paul's convert and fellow worker (1:7).

It is clear from 1:4 and 2:1 that Paul did not know the Colossians personally. Epaphras, his fellow prisoner (Philem. 23), told him about the situation in Colossae. Because of his sense of responsibility for the Gentile church as a whole (1:23-29), Paul undertook to deal with the Colossians' problems. Epaphras, a native of Colossae (4:12), also had founded churches at the neighboring cities of Laodicea and Hierapolis (2:1; 4:13).

The Colossian church was mostly, if not completely, Gentile. The heresy, taught by unknown persons, involved the worship of angelic, cosmic powers (2:8, 18, 20) in addition to Christ. These were celestial spirits, who apparently were regarded as God's agents in governing the movements of the heavenly bodies. Thus these spirits in some respects controlled human destiny, as astrological thought holds. Their worshipers observed feast days, special seasons, and certain practices to honor and perhaps appease them (2:16-23).

Apparently all these powers, along with Christ, constituted God's "fullness," that is, the full range of his attributes and manifestations. Allegiance to Christ was not enough to guarantee salvation; the ruling powers also had to be recognized and pacified.

This "philosophy" (2:8) stressed special visions offering secret knowledge of ultimate reality and the way of salvation. The writer of Colossians thought such knowledge led to lofty pretensions and self-congratulation (2: 18).

The heresy was quite certainly an early form of Gnosticism, like that at Corinth (see p. 265). It is possible that some features of Judaism (circumcision, sabbath observance, dietary laws) were included in the Colossian "philosophy," though such practices also existed in Greek culture. The teaching debased Christ and introduced practices which were a threat to Christian freedom, according to this letter.

b. To introduce Tychicus, the carrier of the letter and envoy of the writer, who was to encourage the Colossians in the true way and inform them about Paul's circumstances (4: 7-8); and to ensure a good reception for Onesimus, the converted runaway slave, who was returning in company with Tychicus to his master at Colossae (4:9).

c. To enhance Epaphras' standing with the Colossians (4:12-13). The founder of the church in Colossae was apparently under attack by the heretics and needed Paul's support.

d. To prepare the way for the possible visit of Mark (4:10).

e. To urge Archippus to carry out faithfully some responsibility in the Lord's service entrusted to him (4:17).

What this responsibility was is unknown. Perhaps he was requested to carry on Epaphras' pastoral responsibilities, since the latter, like Paul, was a prisoner (Philem. 23); to continue the collection for the Jerusalem church which was so important to Paul (I Cor. 16:1-4; II Cor. 8–9); to receive Onesimus in a brotherly way and per-

haps free him for evangelistic service (an interpretation possible only if Archippus, not Philemon, was Onesimus' master [see p. 315]).

f. To establish Paul's authority and teaching firmly in the Gentile churches, both those founded directly by him and those raised up by his followers.

The instruction concerning the exchange of letters between churches (4: 16) is evidence of this purpose. (It has been suggested that "the letter from Laodicea" is our Ephesians or our Philemon; or the letter may be lost.) The strong emphasis on Paul's unique mission to the Gentiles (1: 23-29) and his authorization of Epaphras as a conveyor of the true faith also clearly support this purpose.

3. Teaching

a. The Supremacy and All-Sufficiency of Christ

The Colossian heretics taught that faith in Christ must be supplemented by recognition of the heavenly spirits which control human destiny. The author of Colossians did not deny the existence of these spirits, but he did deny that they have any power over believers in Christ and that worship and ceremonies of appeasement need be directed to them. Christ broke their hold over man by his triumph on the cross (2:15).

A great hymn of praise to Christ (1:15-20), which the writer may have created or adapted from an already existing composition, celebrates the absolute supremacy of Christ over all ruling spirits ("thrones," "dominions," "principalities," "authorities"—1:16).

It affirms Christ's all-sufficiency for the salvation of mankind and for the final unification of the universe.

The writer applies to Christ language and concepts usually applied to Wisdom and to the Word of God in the Old Testament and the Wisdom of Solomon (see chap. 54). Some characterisitc expressions are: "the image of the invisible God" ("the visible likeness of the invisible God"—TEV); "the first-born of all creation" ("the primacy over all created things"—NEB); the agent of God in creation; and the cohesive force which binds the whole universe together.

In Christ the divided and discordant universe is destined to be reunited. He himself, the resurrected one, is the beginning of the new creation, the head of the church (his Body). His death on the cross was the means of the final reconciliation of all powers in the universe.

In sum, God was in Christ, not partially but fully. Christ contains and represents all that God is, and he makes Christians participants in his magnificent completeness. Why, then, should any Christian pay deference to the discredited, defeated powers?

b. Christian Existence

The readers were at one time enemies of God (1:21), captives of the cosmic powers in the realm of darkness (1:13; 2:8, 20; cf. Eph. 6:12), and subject to the rules and regulations of these powers (2:16, 20-23). They lived as fleshly persons (2:11) and practiced evil deeds (1:21). They were spiritually dead by reason of their sins (2:13) and guilty before God's law (2:14). Their sins were "fornication, indecency, lust, foul cravings . . . ruthless greed . . . anger, passion, malice, cursing, filthy talk . . . lying" (3:5-9 NEB). Those who lived thus belonged to the world (2:20).

But God rescued them from the realm of darkness and bondage to its cosmic powers and made them members of the kingdom of his beloved Son (1:13). Their sins are forgiven (1:14). They are now alive together with Christ (2:13), "rooted and built up in him" (2:7). They have come to "full life in union with him" (2:10 TEV). They have been reconciled to God (1:22). They are now "saints", that is, set apart as God's people (1:2; 3:12). They have a new self, the old self having been destroyed (3:9-10). They are becoming like God in character (3:10). Love is the central quality of their life (3:14), thankfulness and singing its dominant mood (3:15-17), and faithful service of Christ in a life of good deeds its objective (1:10; 3:23-24). Since they have been raised with Christ, they live already in a new heavenly world, while they await the final victory of Christ in the establishment of his glorious kingdom (3:1-4). Union with God through Christ is not a wistful hope but a glorious accomplishment (3:3).

God's power at work in Christ's death on the cross and in his resurrection from the dead brought about their transformation. Preaching evoked trust in that power (1:23, 28), and baptism accomplished union with Christ in his death and resurrection (2:12). Baptism brought spiritual circumcision, that is, circumcision of the heart, and marked them as members of God's purified people (2:11-12).

4. Authorship

Two positions are widely held today:

a. Paul, as the letter clearly claims (1:1, 23; 4:18), was the author.

As was customary with him (I Cor. 16:21; Gal. 6:11; II Thess. 3:17), he added an authentication in his own handwriting (4:18). There is some variation in language, style, and theology from Paul's other letters, due to the special circumstances under which Colossians was written. But the similarity to these letters is greater than the dissimilarity.

No one in the early church, so far as we know, doubted Paul's authorship.

Moreover, strong ties to Philemon, undoubtedly written by Paul, argue for Paul's authorship of Colossians. One notes in both letters the same senders (Paul and Timothy); greetings from many of the same persons (Aristarchus, Mark, Epaphras, Luke, Demas), who were with Paul when the letters were written; the special mention of Archippus ("fellow soldier" with a special ministry to perform); and the reference to the return of the runaway slave Onesimus.

b. A disciple of Paul wrote the letter in Paul's name.

Many facts argue that Paul was not the author of the letter. A few are: the use of many words not found elsewhere in Paul's letters; the absence of Paul's characteristic ideas (righteousness, justification by faith alone, the purpose and function of the Law); the highly speculative view of Christ, especially in 1:15-20; and the strong emphasis on apostolic tradition as a way of counteracting heresy. It is possible that a disciple of Paul, who was thoroughly familiar with Paul's language and thoughts, used his master's authority as a way of meeting heresy sometime soon after Paul's death.

The defenders of Paul's authorship reply that most of the new and different features of Colossians are due to the peculiar nature of the heresy Paul opposed and to his subtle and flexible mind. We must not overlook the many similarities with letters that are definitely Paul's.

5. Place and Time of Writing

If the letter was written by Paul himself, the place probably was Rome, Ephesus, or Caesarea. (See on the prison letters, p. 255.) The date was about A.D. 54–62.

If a disciple wrote it, the time was about A.D. 70–90, the place unknown.

78. I Thessalonians

I Thessalonians is Paul's most solicitous, affectionate letter. Here the great apostle appears not as a warrior doing battle for the truth (as in Galatians), or as a lawyer arguing a case (as in Romans), or as a fireman rushing to extinguish a devastating blaze (as in I and II Corinthians). Here he is a tender shepherd of newborn lambs —a pastor—who lovingly feeds, protects, and encourages the young. To use the letter's own figures of speech, Paul is a nurse caring for children (2:7), a father gently encouraging his little ones (2:11).

The letter conveys a tender tone by the many times the readers are addressed as "brothers" (1:4; 2:1, 9, 14, 17; 3:7; 4:1, 9-10, 13; 5:1, 4, 12, 14). Paul expresses his delight in the Thessalonians in the words, "You are our pride and our joy" (2:20 TEV), and the depth of his emotional attachment to them in the exclamation, "Now we really live if you stand firm in your life in the Lord" (3:8 TEV).

1. Theme and Outline

Theme: Your new Christian faith and experience are valid; go on to maturity of life in Christ.

I. Introduction (1:1-3).
   A. Greeting (1:1).
   B. Thanksgiving (1:2-3).
      Note: Structurally the Thanksgiving concludes at 3:13. But from the standpoint of content, much of chaps. 2 and 3 is argument (defense of Paul's conduct) rather than thanksgiving.
II. Body (1:4–5:24).
   A. The remarkable conversion of the Thessalonians as evidence of the validity of their new faith and experience (1:4-10).

   B. Paul's and his associates' blameless conduct at Thessalonica and afterward as proof of the integrity of the missionaries and the validity of the Thessalonians' new faith and experience (2:1–3:13).
      1. At Thessalonica (2:1-16).
      2. After leaving (2:17–3:13).
   C. The Thessalonians' need for maturity of life in Christ (4:1–5:24).
      1. The call to maturity (4:1-2).
      2. Sexual purity (4:3-8).
      3. Brotherly love and personal industry (4:9-12).
      4. Growth in theological understanding (4:13–5:11).
         a. Concerning the fate of the Christian dead (4:13-18).
         b. Concerning the coming of the day of the Lord (5:1-11).
      5. General instructions concerning Christian life and experience (5:12-24).
III. Conclusion (5:25-28).

2. Occasion and Purpose

According to the Acts, Paul founded the church at Thessalonica on his second missionary journey (Acts 17:1-9). For three sabbaths he argued in the synagogue that the Old Testament predicts the coming of a suffering

Messiah and that Jesus of Nazareth fulfills this expectation.

His converts were mostly "godfearing Gentiles," "influential women" (Acts 17:4 NEB), and some Jews. The Gentiles were half-converts to Judaism (see p. 406).

Opposition by unbelieving Jews led to mob action against Paul's converts and to a charge of treason against the missionaries. A night journey to Beroea by Paul and his companions left the infant church alone, exposed to the fury of its enemies, and uncertain of its future.

Paul's ministry in Thessalonica was longer than a period of three sabbaths. This is apparent from the fact that the missionaries worked in the city to support themselves (I Thess. 2:9) and that they remained there long enough to receive two offerings from the church at Philippi (Phil. 4:16). A stay of two or three months is likely, including the three sabbaths at the synagogue.

When Paul arrived at Athens he sent Timothy back to Thessalonica to assist the infant congregation and to bring him word of its condition (I Thess. 3:1-5). Meanwhile, Paul crossed over to Corinth and began a mission there. Timothy brought a good report to Paul at Corinth (Acts 18:5; I Thess. 3:6). It is possible that he also brought a letter to him from the Thessalonians, inquiring about some matters to which Paul responded in I Thess. 4–5.

I Thessalonians is Paul's joyful reaction to the news of the fidelity of the Thessalonians in spite of their sufferings and also his attempt to guide them to a fuller Christian life through a solution to their problems.

Their problems were:

a. Persecution by fellow townsmen, probably spearheaded by the unbelieving Jews who had forced Paul from the city (Acts 17:5; I Thess. 2:14-16; 3:3-4)

b. Doubts about the integrity of the missionaries, spread probably by hostile Jews (I Thess. 2)

c. Confusion about the validity of their new faith and experience in the

The Areopagus (Mars Hill) in Athens, the meeting place of the court of the Areopagus, before which Paul may have appeared (Acts 17:19 ff.)

light of Jewish attacks (1:4-10); about
the Christian view of the future (the
fate of Christians who have died before the coming of Christ; the time
of Christ's coming and Christian activity meanwhile—4:13–5:11); and
about the place of suffering in the
life of Christians (3:3-4)

d. Sexual irregularities (4:3-8),
idleness and troublemaking (4:11-12),
carelessness (5:1-11), and quarreling
(5:13)

3. Message

The central message of I Thessalonians is: Stand fast in your newly
found faith in spite of opposition and
press on to Christian maturity!

The letter begins with a thanksgiving for the clear evidence Paul sees
that the Thessalonians have a secure
place in God's great redemptive purpose. This evidence consists of the
striking nature of their conversion experience and the character of its fruits.

Both the missionaries and the Thessalonians were moved by the Holy
Spirit, the former to mighty, persuasive
preaching of the gospel and the latter
to joyful reception of the message,
even though they were persecuted for
it.

The Thessalonians became imitators
of the missionaries and of Christ and
an example for Christians in other
places. Their faith showed itself in
action, their love resulted in labor,
and their hope produced great forti-
tude (see NEB 1:3). They turned
from idolatry to the worship of the
living and true God and to the hope

of the coming of Christ with final
salvation.

This dramatic conversion, with its
fruits of love and service, shows beyond a doubt, says Paul, that their
new faith and life are from God and
that the missionaries are his true and
faithful servants.

Paul next defends his conduct both
at Thessalonica and after leaving there
against the malicious charges of enemies. His ministry at Thessalonica was
courageous (2:2), sound doctrinally
(2:3-4), uncompromising (2:4-5),
selfless and self-giving (2:6-8), self-
supporting (2:9), blameless (2:10),
and patient (2:11).

To the charge that he cares little
about the Thessalonians, since he "ran
out" on them and has not returned
to help them with their problems, he
replies that it was impossible for him
to return because of factors beyond
his control (illness? hostile magistrates
or Jews at Thessalonica? problems at
Corinth?), interpreted by Paul as the
activity of Satan. His sending of Timothy to aid them and his joy over the
good news brought by him are evidence that he cares deeply about them.
Paul hopes yet to visit them; they are
very dear to him.

Meanwhile, they must face their
problems and come to spiritual maturity in Christ. Paul calls this maturity "holiness" or "sanctification"
(3:13; 4:3, 7; 5:23). These English
words come from Hebrew and Greek
terms which signify the condition of
persons or things which have been
separated from the common or profane by God and infused with his
power. By association with God they

bceome like God. Holiness (sanctification) is God's gift (5:23-24). For Paul holiness (sanctification) is both an accomplished fact (I Cor. 6:11) and something yet to be completed (II Cor. 7:1; I Thess. 4:3). Christians are to go on becoming, by God's gracious help, what they already are in principle. One does not progress *to* holiness but *in* holiness, according to Paul.

The life separated from the common and the unclean by God's activity in Christ (I Cor. 1:30; 6:11) and filled by God's Spirit (I Thess. 1:6; 4:8) has certain characteristics: sexual purity (4:3-8), brotherly love (4:9-10), attention to one's own business (4:11), industriousness (4:11-12), mature understanding of Christian truth and emotional stability (4:13-18), spiritual alertness (5:1-11), respect for leaders (5:12-13), patient helpfulness of others (5:14-15), thankfulness and prayerfulness (5:16-18), and moral discrimination (5:19-22).

Their lack of mature understanding of Christian truth and the harmful emotional and moral effects of this misunderstanding were associated with their wrong ideas about the future. Paul obviously had taught them about the second coming of Christ to judge the world and to gather believers into the final kingdom of God. He' had stressed the nearness of these events. He apparently left them with the impression either that Christians, with the divine life in them, would not die, or that the end of this age was so close that all who had believed at Thessalonica would be alive and participate in these glorious happenings. But the passage of time brought death to some Christians and with it the fear that the dead would not be included in Christ's triumphant inauguration of the New Age. Some may have begun to doubt Paul's teaching about the second coming of Christ because of the delay (5:3), and they began to live carelessly (5:4-8).

Paul's answer is, first, that death before Christ comes will not prevent Christians from fully participating in the blessings of the New Age. Through resurrection, based on the resurrection of Jesus to whom they are united, they will share with living Christians in perpetual life with their Lord. The coming Lord will summon both dead and living to himself at the time of his heavenly appearance. Therefore, there is no cause for grief over the fate of the departed brethren. Second, he reaffirms the reality and the suddenness of the second coming and warns that they must prepare for the strict judgment of that day.

4. Authorship and Date

A few scholars have argued that the letter comes from someone later than Paul, since certain Pauline notes are absent (*e.g.,* justification by faith alone) and some portions are unlike Paul (*e.g.,* the details about the coming of Christ in 4:13-18). But the vocabulary, style, and overall theology seem to be genuinely Paul's. Furthermore, it is unlikely that a later writer would have attributed to Paul the unfulfilled expectation that he would live until the second coming (4:15, 17).

I Thessalonians, dating to about A.D. 51, is probably the earliest of the preserved letters of Paul. This honor has been claimed for Galatians, but without adequate proof (see p. 282).

79. II Thessalonians

I Thessalonians is intensely personal, warmly affectionate, and gently persuasive. II Thessalonians is more formal, authoritarian, and theological.

In the first letter Paul encouraged the Thessalonians to continue in their faltering steps as little children in the faith. In the second he both encouraged them and scolded them for departures from Christian belief and practice. He mixed encouragement and discipline in differing proportions in his letters as the situation required.

II Thessalonians is noteworthy chiefly for its teaching about the second coming of Christ. Nowhere else in the letters of Paul is the teaching so explicit concerning the succession of events leading to it and its meaning for both sinners and saints.

1. Theme and Outline

Theme: The truth about the second coming of Christ.
I.   Introduction (1:1-4).
     A. Greeting (1:1-2).
     B. Thanksgiving (1:3-4).
        Note: Technically, thanksgiving and prayer continue to 2:17, but theological argument appears in 1:5-10 and 2:1-12. This makes structural and logical analysis difficult.

II. Body (1:5-3:15).
     A. The coming will bring the day of recompense for unbelieving persecutors and for faithful believers (1:5-10).
     B. The coming has not yet occurred; it will be preceded by events still to take place (2:1-12).
     C. To be prepared for the coming, Christians must obey the pattern of Christian doctrine and living taught by Paul and his associates (3:1-15).
III. Benediction and authentication (3:16-18).

2. Occasion and Purpose

The letter indicates that reports had come to Paul about problems in the church at Thessalonica (3:11).

The first problem concerned the persecution the church was experiencing, probably from both Jews and Gentiles (see p. 297).

The second problem centered in wrong ideas about the second coming of Christ. Someone claimed Paul as the authority for the false view that "the day of the Lord has come" (2:2). The practical result of this mistaken view was that some people quit their daily work; there was a great deal of idleness and meddling in other people's affairs (3:6, 11). Paul had faced the problem of lazy spongers when he was at Thessalonica (3:10), but his instructions went unheeded. Indeed, the situation had gotten much worse.

We can only guess who was teaching church members at Thessalonica that the day of the Lord had actually arrived. Gnostic Christians at Corinth (see p. 265) seem to have believed that they were enjoying the kingdom of God already (I Cor. 4:8), and a clear statement in II Tim. 2:18 attributes to two false teachers in the church the view that "the resurrection is past already." Such persons taught that Christians have been enlightened by secret knowledge; they have risen in spirit from the bondage of the flesh. Since redemption is already accomplished, nothing more is to be expected. The idle and disorderly way of life was the natural outgrowth of a view that claimed perfection of spirit and showed indifference and contempt for the flesh and the concerns of life in this "evil" world.

Paul denies that he is in any way responsible for this heresy. He has taught them nothing or written them nothing to this effect, whatever the false teachers claim (2:2). The sample of his handwriting Paul appended (3:17), possibly as a sign of genuineness, may suggest that a forged letter under his name was circulating at Thessalonica.

The purpose of II Thessalonians is thus to stop the false teaching and its devastating consequences for Christian living.

3. Teaching

The discussion of the coming of Christ begins from the situation of the Christians at Thessalonica. They were experiencing bitter persecution. Paul praises them for their steadfastness and continued growth in faith and love. He insists on doing so, in spite of their objection that they are unworthy of such praise (1:3).

He sees the patient endurance of persecution as proof of God's righteous (right, just) judgment. This judgment is seen now in God's support of the suffering Christians while he prepares them through their suffering for membership in the coming kingdom; it will be fully seen at the glorious coming of the Lord Jesus (1:5 ff.), when recompense will be meted out to the afflicted and their tormentors.

The reward for the persecuted Christians will be "rest" (relief from trouble and suffering) and eternal fellowship with the Lord in his kingdom, while the recompense of the wicked will be trouble and eternal ruin, that is, separation from the presence of the glorious and mighty Lord (1:7, 9).

Following the discussion of the coming of Christ at the day of recompense, Paul turns to the time of the coming (2:1-12). Here he deals with the error that the day of the Lord has already come by showing that the preliminary events on the divine timetable have not yet run their course.

Christ will not come until the self-deifying "man of lawlessness" appears. This one will come as the human incarnation of all evil. He will deceive men by Satanic power and induce them to false worship. Christ will appear to destroy this devil's messiah and to render judgment on his unrighteous worshipers. Now, Paul says, the mysterious force of lawlessness is at work in the world, but the coming of the "man of lawlessness" is being held back by something or someone—what or who the Thessalonians are said to know and are not told again here (2:5-6).

Who "the man of lawlessness" is and what or who the restrainer is elude us. Was some Gentile or Jewish leader, someone like Antiochus Epiphanes (see p. 165) or the mad emperor Caligula (A.D. 37-41), expected to appear as the embodiment of all evil and as the devil's instrument in the final great struggle between the forces of good and evil at the end of time? It is unlikely that Paul had some specific historical person in mind. Certainly he was not predicting the coming of a wicked pope, or of Mussolini, Hitler, Hirohito, Stalin, or Mao, as has been claimed! The passing of time has shown identifications of this sort to be illusions.

Some guesses about the identity of the restrainer are: the Roman empire (and the emperor), which held back the surge of lawlessness; an angel, perhaps Michael; the Holy Spirit; Paul and the proclamation of the gospel to the Gentiles. Speculation is useless. The main point is that God's calendar of historical events has not yet been fulfilled and, until it is, the end of the age and the coming of the kingdom of God—to be introduced by the return of Christ—cannot take place. The Gnostics, who claim that salvation has been *fully* realized in the resurrection and liberation of the self from the bondage of matter, are wrong. Salvation, whatever its present aspects (and these are not treated in this letter), is emphatically God's *future* gift (2: 10, 13-14).

While Christians await the second coming of Christ and the salvation to be bestowed in the gift of life in God's kingdom, they must be obedient to the pattern of doctrine and living taught them by Paul and his associates (2:15; 3:4, 6-12). This means a life of good works and words (2:17)— not idleness and gossip and troublemaking, but the Christian activity of prayer (3:1), personal industriousness (3:6-12), and tireless well-doing (3: 13).

4. Authorship, Date, Place of Writing

The two views on the problem of authorship are:

a. The letter was written by one of Paul's disciples in Paul's name.

The chief arguments for this conclusion are:

(1) The view of the future in II Thessalonians is not consistent with that in I Thessalonians. In the latter, the second coming of Christ is to occur soon and without warning signs; but in the former, the coming is not immediate and is to be preceded by specific signs. Both positions could hardly come from Paul. Furthermore, the "man of lawlessness" and the detailed preliminary signs have no parallel in the genuine letters of Paul.

(2) The many striking similarities in subject matter and wording between the two letters can be more easily explained as the result of a disciple's imitation of his master's thought and language than as the repetitiousness of the master himself, especially since there are theological differences as well.

(3) The historical situation behind II Thessalonians seems not to be a natural outgrowth of the situation we see in I Thessalonians. The church's concern about the delay in the second coming of Christ would hardly have turned so quickly into the belief that he had already come. If a disciple of Paul wrote II Thessalonians, there would have been adequate time for such a shift in perspective.

b. Paul is the author, as the letter claims (1:1; 3:17).

(1) Fluctuation between belief that the end was near and unpredictable and the view that certain events must occur first was common in visions concerning the future at the time of Jesus and Paul. Both emphases appear in the teaching of Jesus about the end (Matt. 24:36; Luke 21:34-36 and Matt. 24:32-33; Luke 21:29-30). They were therefore theologically possible for Paul.

(2) Similarities in thought and language between the two letters do not necessarily indicate imitation by a disciple. Two letters written to the same church within a few weeks would naturally involve some repetition, and desirably so, for the sake of emphasis. The letters are different as well as similar, the differences being due to new factors in the situation at Thessalonica.

(3) Gnostic teaching about redemption as a completely accomplished fact could arise quickly in a church in the Greek world, as indeed it did relatively soon at Corinth. We need not assume a long period of development and change.

Some scholars have suggested that the two letters were written in the reverse order or that II Thessalonians was addressed to a Jewish-Christian minority at Thessalonica and sent along with I Thessalonians, which was meant for the Gentile-Christian majority. Others have held that II Thessalonians was originally addressed to the church at Philippi or Beroea. None of these theories has convinced the majority of scholars.

That II Thessalonians was written by Paul within a few weeks of I Thessalonians (c. A.D. 51) remains the most satisfactory view.

The place of writing was probably Corinth.

80. I Timothy

I Timothy belongs to a subgroup of the letters ascribed to Paul which has been known since the eighteenth century as the Pastoral Epistles. The other letters in this group are II Timothy and Titus. These writings contain instructions and admonitions concerning the work of pastors in Christian churches.

In many respects these books are more like church manuals than personal letters. This is especially true of I Timothy, where personal information is almost entirely lacking. Since most of the material in these manuals would surely have been known already by Paul's long-time associates Timothy and Titus, it is likely that the books were written more for the benefit of church members than for the leaders mentioned—though the latter, of course, were included.

A hint that church members as well as the leaders were addressed appears in the benedictions of the three writings, where the "you" is plural in the Greek (in the best manuscripts). Furthermore, the center of interest in all three is the problems of faith and conduct of church members and how to meet these problems with the help of accredited leaders.

These books contain many crisp, salty sayings and instructions for the church. They do not probe the depths and scale the heights of life in Christ and the church as the other letters ascribed to Paul do, but their practical morality and wise counsel offer help to churches tempted to stray from the straight path of historic Christianity. Their keynote is: At all costs keep the faith delivered to you by the great apostle Paul!

1. Theme and Outline

Theme: Timothy's role in preserving the true faith and life of the church from the false instruction and way of life of heretical teachers

I. Greeting (1:1-2)
II. Body (1:3–6:19)
   A. Paul, the model of sound teaching and living, and Timothy, his true disciple, versus the false teachers and their message (1:3-20)
   B. Regulations concerning public worship and church leaders (2:1–3:13)
   C. Timothy's responsibility for teaching the Christian mystery (truth) and way of life (3:14–4:16)
   D. Timothy's role in preserving the family-like nature of the church (5:1–6:2)
   E. The false teachers' love for money; Timothy's and the true Christians' love for God and good deeds (6:3-19)
III. Concluding charge to Timothy and benediction (6:20-21)

2. False Teaching and Its Refutation

It is difficult to pin down the exact nature of the false teaching opposed in the Pastoral Epistles, so vague and general are the references to it. Several characteristics seem evident, however:

   a. An Emphasis on Myths and Genealogies (I Tim. 1:4; 4:7; II Tim. 4:4; Titus 1:14; 3:9)

According to Titus 1:14, these are "Jewish" and are propagated by those of "the circumcision party" (Titus 1:

10), meaning apparently Jewish Christians. "Quarrels over the law" (Titus 3:9), "speculations" (I Tim. 1:4), "vain discussion" (I Tim. 1:6), and "stupid controversies" (Titus 3:9) by those who desire to be "teachers of the law" (I Tim. 1:6-7) make it appear that fanciful Jewish interpretation of the Old Testament was being advocated in the church.

b. Salvation by Knowledge or Mystical Illumination

Christianity had stressed knowledge at the expense of faith (trust) and moral obedience, as the comments about "speculations," "vain discussions," "stupid controversies," and "what is falsely called knowledge" (I Tim. 6:20) show. The emphasis on traditional belief and good works in the Pastorals (see below) seems aimed to counterbalance this speculative emphasis.

It is likely that the knowledge these teachers offered included more than "proper" interpretation of the Old Testament. In the first and second centuries A.D. the philosophical-religious movement we call Gnosticism was spreading through the Mediterranean world. It offered people secret, saving knowledge of the universe: of the supreme, pure-spirit God, untouched by "evil" matter; of the many divine beings (aeons) thought to connect him with the evil world, which had been created by the lowest aeon; of man's nature as spirit enmeshed in an evil body; of the releasing of man's spirit from evil flesh for its ascent to its proper heavenly abode through enlightenment brought by a divine savior and through secret, sacramental rites

and mystical experiences; of practices permitted and forbidden those who have achieved freedom of spirit; of the coming liberation of the soul from the body at death, as the seal and consummation of a resurrection already achieved in mystical experience.

The following emphases in the Pastorals indicate that some such teaching was threatening the church: the oneness (not the plurality) of Deity; the single mediatorial position and role of "the man Christ Jesus" (I Tim. 2:5); the goodness of the created order and its free use by man (I Tim. 4:4); sin (disobedience to God's law) as the root of man's predicament, not his entanglement in evil matter (I Tim. 1:8-11; 4:7-8; 6:18; Titus 2:11-14; 3:3); a salvation involving true reverence for God ("godliness"), obedience to his will, faith in Christ as Savior, and the doing of good deeds (I Tim. 1:8-11; 4:7-8; 6:18; Titus 2:11-14); the certainty of the future coming of the Lord Jesus "to judge the living and the dead" (II Tim. 4:1; cf. I Tim. 6:14-15) and thus the certainty of a future resurrection.

c. The Practice of Magic Through Demonic Power

Like Pharaoh's legendary magicians Jannes and Jambres, these heretics sought to demonstrate their superior powers and capture allegiance to their heresy (II Tim. 3:6-9, 13). Behind them, we read, lay satanic, demonic power (I Tim. 4:1; II Tim. 2:26).

Gnosticism combined Jewish and Greek-oriental concepts into a system of impressive proportions. Its central error from the standpoint of Christian

The monument to St. Paul, Beroea, Greece, erected in 1952 to honor Paul's arrival 1900 years before truth was its cleavage between God and the world (matter), the latter being regarded as evil and the place of imprisonment of the unenlightened souls of men. Salvation as escape from evil matter was a perversion of the historic belief in salvation from sin. Perverted also was the view that God's good provisions for man (marriage, food, drink) were forbidden to him (I Tim. 4:3; 5:23). And to teach that the only resurrection the Christian would have was the resurrection experienced in his own rebirth was to empty the faith of its hope of the final resurrection of the whole person to communal life in the kingdom of God (I Cor. 15:35-57; Rev. 21:2-4).

The church resisted the heresy by insisting on the correctness of Paul's divinely given teaching. It claimed that Paul had delivered this teaching to his personal followers, and that they had passed it on to responsible teachers in the church (I Tim. 1:12-16; II Tim. 1:11-14; 2:2).

3. Authorship and Date of the Pastoral Epistles

No firm conclusion has been reached on these subjects. There are three main positions in regard to the authorship.

a. As the books themselves clearly claim, Paul was their author, either directly or indirectly.

From the late second century, at least, until the nineteenth, the church believed Paul wrote them.

Advocates of this view admit that the personal facts about Paul, Timothy, and Titus contained in the Pastorals do not fit into the outline of Paul's career as pictured in the Acts. The Acts has no mission by Paul and Titus on Crete (Titus 1:5), no evidence that Paul spent a winter at Nicopolis (Titus 3:12), or that shortly before his Roman imprisonment (II Tim. 1:16-17) he had been in Asia Minor, where he had left Trophimus ill at Miletus (II Tim. 4:20).

Defenders of Paul's authorship argue that Paul was released from the Roman captivity mentioned in Acts 28:16; that he evangelized on Crete and elsewhere in the Mediterranean area, even possibly in Spain; that the events and circumstances described in the Pastorals occurred during this period of release; and that he was arrested and imprisoned in Rome a second time. During the second imprisonment he wrote the Pastorals.

Supporters of this view explain that the many new words and ideas in the Pastorals are due to Paul's advancing age, his broadening contacts and experience, and the new situation addressed (the need for strengthening the church against rising heresy). They see the heresy Paul opposed in the Pastorals as somewhat like that attacked in Colossians and less formal and organized than the Gnostic systems of the second century A.D.

Some admit the possibility that Paul may have allowed a secretary (perhaps Tychicus or Luke) considerable freedom in the composition of the Pastorals. They suggest that this may account for some of the new features of these writings. In any case they were written at Paul's direction and under his authority.

b. The Pastorals were written by a disciple of Paul, considerably after Paul's death. He used Paul's name and influence to check the Gnostic heresy and to keep the church on the path marked out by the great apostle.

Scholars favoring this position point out that it was a recognized practice in antiquity for a disciple to write in the name of his teacher and to ascribe his insights to his honored master. This involved no dishonesty. Schools of learning gathered around great teachers and the traditions left by them. These traditions were handed down through successive generations.

Those holding this view offer four major objections to Paul's authorship (either direct or mediated through a secretary).

(1) The personal facts do not fit the career of Paul as we know it from the definitely genuine Pauline epistles and from the Acts. Since there is no solid evidence for a ministry between two Roman imprisonments, these facts can hardly be historical. In fact, some passages in the Acts (20:25, 38) rather clearly indicate that the author believed that Paul did not return again to his churches in the East.

(2) The situation in the church, reflected in the Pastorals, is not that of Paul's time but of a later period.

The organization of the church, as seen in the Pastorals, is too advanced for Paul's time. Timothy and Titus appear here as ruling bishops who appoint elders, discipline them, guard the church doctrinally and morally, and serve as a pattern for the church members to imitate. Such an episcopal role

did not come into being until the second century. Furthermore, the role of elders as ordained tradition-bearers (II Tim. 2:2) and the order of widows dedicated to continual prayer and sexual abstinence (I Tim. 5:3-16) seem to reflect a time considerably later than Paul.

(3) Some emphases in the theology of the Pastorals seem not to be Paul's. Many themes do accord with Paul's preaching and teaching, but others depart from his thought to some degree.

Paul's "faith" (trust) becomes in the Pastorals "the faith" (a body of truth handed down from an authoritative source). The Christian becomes one who has a "sound" or "healthy" faith to which he is loyal and which he passes on to others.

The Holy Spirit is not prominent in the Pastorals, as in the letters of Paul, and the Holy Spirit of the Pastorals is communicated not spontaneously and unpredictably but by the church rite of laying on of hands (I Tim. 4:14; II Tim. 1:6-7).

The emphasis in the Pastorals is on good works, on proper conduct, rather than on man's total response to God's grace as the way to a new relationship with God ("in Christ" or "in the Spirit").

(4) The vocabulary and the style of the Pastorals vary markedly from those in Paul's unquestionably genuine letters. About 175 words that appear in the Pastorals are found nowhere else in the New Testament. More than one third of the words used in the Pastorals are not found in Paul's certainly genuine letters, and many of Paul's words are used in a different

sense. Many terms and constructions peculiarly Greek occur in the Pastorals. The language and style as a whole are akin to those in late New Testament books and in writings of the second century.

On the assumption that the author was not Paul but a follower or admirer of Paul, the time of writing was either around the end of the first century or about the middle of the second century. Those who place the Pastorals at the later date believe their author meant them to counteract the teachings of the famous Gnostic heretic Marcion, whose views were refuted also by Irenaeus and other church leaders.

c. The third position mediates between the other two. It holds that both Paul and a disciple were involved in the making of the Pastorals. Paul wrote several short notes to his trusted helpers Timothy and Titus. A later admirer of Paul wove them into the present Pastorals in order to preserve them and to give his writings Pauline impact and authority.

Three such notes have been identified: (1) Titus 3:12-15; (2) II Tim. 4:9-15, 20, 21*a*, 22*b*; (3) II Tim. 1: 16-18; 3:10, 11; 4:1, 2*a*, 5*b*-8, 11-19, 21*b*-22*a*. It is possible to fit the information in them into Paul's known career. The first note may have been written to Titus from Macedonia just after Paul's severe letter to Corinth (see p. 271). The second may have gone to Timothy from Nicopolis a little later. The third, Paul's last letter, may have been written from Rome at the close of his imprisonment there (as mentioned in Acts 28:30, 31).

In conclusion we may say that the problem of the authorship of the Pastorals is one of the most vexing in the field of New Testament studies. The many striking differences in language, style, and theology between the Pastorals and Paul's certainly genuine letters make Paul's direct authorship of the Pastorals difficult to defend. It appears that either he gave a secretary large freedom in their composition or that a disciple put them together in his name and in his spirit (possibly using some of Paul's notes) to serve the needs of the church after the apostle's death. Who the disciple was and where he lived are quite unknown. Asia Minor has been suggested.

4. The Value of I Timothy

I Timothy, a handbook of church administration and discipline, is not filled with sublime and inspiring passages. The author did not blaze new trails in Christian thought, but rather sought to consolidate, conserve, and protect the conquests already made by the church. This is no small achievement, even if it is less dramatic than pioneering work.

Of lasting value are the following:

Loyalty to the truth and the preservation of a good conscience (1:5, 19; 3:9)—instead of succumbing to attractive, erroneous novelties which gratify the senses—belong to the essence of Christianity, as Christian martyrs later demonstrated.

The spiritual and moral requirements for church officials, set forth here, offer generally valid guidelines for every age (*e.g.*, "if a man does not know how to manage his own household, how can he care for God's church?"—3:5).

The Christian teacher, as an example to those whom he teaches (1: 16; 4:12-16), exhibits Christianity as truth incarnate.

The emphasis on the goodness of the created order and man's right to enjoy it (4:3-5) opposes recurring asceticism in Christian thought and life.

81. II Timothy

I Tim. and Titus are manuals of church administration. II Tim. is much more personal and is something of a last will and testament. Literary testaments (the instructions of a dying patriarch to his sons) were common in Judaism at that time. So here Paul, facing the hour of his death (4:6-8), instructs his beloved son Timothy (1: 2; 2:1) how to carry on after his departure. If Timothy follows these instructions, he will escape the dangers that threaten him and the people under his care.

1. Theme and Outline

Theme: Be loyal to me and my gospel, and you will be rewarded with eternal life.
   I.   Greeting (1:1-2)
   II. Body (1:3–4:21)
       A. An appeal for personal loyalty on the basis of past experience (1:3-18)
       B. An appeal for doctrinal loyalty on the basis of the gospel as preached, lived, and suffered for by Paul (2:1–4:8)

       C. Timothy's final ministrations to Paul (4:9-21)
   III. Benediction (4:22)

2. High Points in II Timothy

The intimate personal bond between Paul and Timothy is everywhere evident in the letter. Timothy is called "my beloved child" (1:2; *cf.* 2:1); Paul has knowledge about his family (1:5); Paul had participated in his ordination to the work of ministry (1:6; *cf.* I Tim. 4:14); Paul had been his teacher (1:13; 3:14); and Paul prays constantly for him (1:3). Paul wants to strengthen the bond of personal loyalty which his imprisonment might conceivably weaken (1:8). The close relationship between Paul and Timothy is evident also in Phil. 2:19-24.

The purpose of strengthening the bond is that Timothy may be fully loyal to Paul's gospel in the face of the destructive heresy that is threatening the church. (On the nature of this heresy see the discussion of I Timothy.) Timothy's opposition to the false teachers will cost him much suffering.

Excavated area at the harbor city of Miletus, where Paul addressed the elders from Ephesus (Acts 20:17 ff.)

He must be willing, as his teacher has been (1:8, 16; 2:9), to take his "share of suffering for the gospel in the power of God" (1:8; *cf.* 2:3).

The nature of Paul's gospel comes to clear focus in 2:8. It centers in Jesus as the fulfillment of Israel's history and hopes (the Messiah from the line of David, a real human person), who died and rose from the dead, as the mighty Son of God and inaugurator of the salvation of the New Age. (See also Rom. 1:3-4; 15:12.) His resurrection is the promise of the resurrection of all believers, contrary to the teaching of the heretics (II Tim. 2:17-18).

How Timothy is to deal with false teaching is treated in considerable detail:

a. He and his people should avoid senseless controversy and the false teachers who engage in it (2:14, 16, 23; 3:5). They should be kind, forbearing, and gentle (2:24-25).

b. He must be a good interpreter of Christian truth himself (an unashamed workman, "rightly handling the word of truth"—2:15).

c. He and his people must live righteously and associate with those who live in the same manner (2:22).

d. They must realize that God's church is basically unshakable, for God knows and cares for those who belong to him (2:19).

e. They must realize that the church is a mixed community, with good and bad members, and that individual and group discipline is constantly needed (2:20-21).

f. They must keep in mind what

hour it is on God's time clock—the time of great evil and suffering before the end, when God's people must defend the truth and persevere in righteousness, according to the teachings of the Holy Scriptures. On the day of judgment God will richly reward them (3:1–4:8).

3. Authorship, Date, Original Readers, Circumstances of Writing

See the discussion of I Timothy.

82. Titus

The letter to Titus is more similar in its contents to I Timothy than to II Timothy. The latter, as we have seen (chap. 81), contains the last will and testament of a father in the faith to his son in the gospel, while the others, on the whole, deal with church order and discipline. I Timothy offers fuller instructions on these matters than does the letter to Titus.

Titus, like Timothy, was a trusted companion of Paul and emissary to his churches. He was the spearhead of Paul's movement to free Christians from the Law of Moses. Paul made a test case before the mother church in Jerusalem and won acceptance of Titus as an uncircumcized Gentile Christian (Gal. 2:1-5). He was a gifted and skillful person, to judge from his successful reconciliation of the rebellious Corinthian church to Paul (II Cor. 7:6-16) and his effective service in collecting the offering for the church in Jerusalem (II Cor. 8:6, 16, 23).

The letter to Titus represents this Christian leader as head of the church in Crete by Paul's appointment (1:5). His task was to organize and discipline the church there—in an admittedly disorderly place (1:12). We hear of him last as on a mission to Dalmatia (II Tim. 4:10), a territory now in Yugoslavia.

Words in the greeting show that Titus was one of Paul's converts: "my true child in a common faith" (1:4).

1. Theme and Outline

Theme: Teach Christians in Crete to think straight and live right, for this is what God expects of those who have experienced his boundless generosity in Jesus Christ and are heirs of the eternal life he has promised.

I. Greeting (1:1-4).

II. Body (1:5–3:14).

    A. Appoint suitable elders (bishops) for leadership in the church (1:5-16).

        1. Their qualifications (1:5-9a).

        2. Their duties (1:9b-16).

    B. Teach and exemplify sound doctrine and right living in the church (2:1–3:11).

        1. Instruct the various church groups how to

think and act—and why
(2:2-15).

2. Teach all church members their responsibilities toward the state, their fellow citizens, and the life of good deeds—and why (3:1-8).

3. Avoid senseless controversy and those who promote it (3:9-11).

C. Perform acts of personal service and urge others to do the same (3:12-14).

1. Return to Paul after duty on Crete (3:12).

2. Assist two traveling fellow Christians (3:13).

3. Urge all Christians to do deeds of helpfulness (3:14).

III. Final Greetings and Benediction (3:15).

2. High Points

This brief letter is full of charm and help for effective Christian living.

Its setting is interesting. An old apostle is writing to a son in the gospel (1:4) to assist him in carrying out his mission in a tough spot (Crete). The son was living and working among people who were notorious as "liars, evil beasts, lazy gluttons" (1:12). The nature of the counsel offered him indicates that the church members there were undisciplined in personal habits, quarrelsome, insubordinate, and indolent in their Christian service. Their way of life was not markedly different from that of their heathen neighbors. And false teachers were destroying whatever

foundations of Christian understanding and living had been laid down when they had first been evangelized.

Titus' task is to improve the understanding of Christian truth and the level of Christian living and service in the Cretan church.

To do this, he must teach "sound" (*i.e.,* healthy) doctrine (1:9; 2:1), as opposed to the sick teachings of the heretics (see pp. 304-7). Sound doctrine teaches that:

a. God wills the salvation of all men from their "ungodly living and worldly passions" (2:12 TEV) and from their unloving attitudes (malice, envy, hatred—3:3).

b. This salvation is both present ("he saved us"—3:5) and future ("heirs in hope of eternal life"—3:7) and consists in rebirth and renewal in the Holy Spirit, effected in baptism, through Jesus Christ's act of redemption (2:14; 3:5-6).

c. One who has been saved and awaits final salvation lives a self-controlled, upright, and godly (*i.e.,* truly devout) life in this world (2:12). Specifically, this means these qualities: temperance, self-control, chastity, honesty, hospitality, kindness ("perfect courtesy toward all men"—3:2), submission to authority, brotherly helpfulness. Those who live thus "will add lustre to the doctrine of God our Saviour" (2:10 NEB).

d. Christians live in hope of the coming triumph of Christ (2:13) and of the life eternal (1:2; 3:7).

(On the problems of authorship, date, nature of the heresy opposed, and original readers see the discussion of I Timothy.)

83. Philemon

On the surface, this little letter looks like a private communication. Many readers have wondered why it was preserved among the church letters of Paul.

While it clearly is much like an ancient private letter, the fact that it is addressed not only to individuals but also to a house church (vss. 1, 2) shows that it was more than that.

From the Christian perspective the return of the runaway slave Onesimus, now a Christian brother (vs. 16), was as much a concern of the church as of his legal master. The church needed to understand what had happened to the returning slave, to be prepared to receive him warmly into its fellowship, and to use its influence with his master to ensure an appropriate reception.

The letter is important historically and theologically, because it shows how, in practical terms, the new Christian movement began to work and must work both personal and social change.

1. Circumstances of Writing

Paul was a prisoner when he led Onesimus to new life in Christ (vss. 9, 10). (On the location of Paul's imprisonment see p. 255.)

How Onesimus came to Paul is not known. Did one of Paul's helpers, perhaps Epaphras of Colossae (Onesimus' home town—Col. 4:9), come upon the slave accidentally and bring him to Paul? Did the runaway seek Paul out because of previous friendly contacts with him and because he was now homesick, lonely, out of money, and in need of a place of asylum? Or was Onesimus, by strange providence, housed in the same prison with Paul?

It is evident from the letter that Onesimus had fled with some of his master's money or property (vss. 18, 19). The stealing and the flight put the slave in a difficult legal position before his master, who had absolute power of life and death over him.

Paul wanted to keep Onesimus with him as an aide, for he found him useful (Onesimus means "useful"—vs. 11). But his service belonged to his master, and the Christian faith demanded repentance and restitution. Therefore, Onesimus had to return to his master, cast himself on his mercy, and seek forgiveness. With Onesimus went Tychicus (Col. 4:7-9) and this letter. Both were meant to intercede with the master for forgiveness and restoration.

Some students of the letter have contended that Paul indirectly asked for Onesimus' release from slavery and his return to Paul for subsequent service (vss. 13, 14, 21). But this is not stated, and vs. 15 ("that you might have him back for ever") argues against it.

Who was the slave owner, and where did he live? There are two views.

a. He was Philemon of Colossae, one of Paul's converts, perhaps in the city of Ephesus (since Paul had not been to Colossae—Col. 1:4; 2:1).

Philemon's house in Colossae was the meeting place of the church in that city. Apphia may have been his wife, and Archippus his son (vs. 2).

b. The owner was Archippus of Colossae, host of the house church there. Philemon was the overseer of the churches of the Lycus Valley, where Colossae, Laodicea, and Hierapolis were located. Philemon lived at Laodicea. Apphia was his wife. The letter was sent first to him so that he might add his influence to that of Paul when the letter was sent on to Archippus at Colossae. The ministry to be fulfilled by Archippus (Col. 4:17) was to free Onesimus for the work of evangelizing. Advocates of this view hold that the letter Paul sent to Laodicea (Col. 4:16) is our letter to Philemon.

The first view is to be preferred.

Philemon is first mentioned, not Archippus.

The ministry Archippus is to perform "in the Lord" was "received" (that is, "handed on," as by tradition) and must refer to some service in the church, not simply to the freeing of Onesimus.

The "letter from Laodicea," to be read by the Colossians, was more likely addressed primarily to that church, not primarily to an individual, as is the case with Philemon. The Laodicean letter seems to have perished. (An apocryphal epistle to the Laodiceans in Latin circulated widely in the early and medieval church. It consists of a number of passages by Paul, chiefly from Philippians, patched together to close this gap in the collected letters of Paul. It is obviously a forgery. Marcion in the second century, without adequate justification, regarded our Epistle to the Ephesians as the letter to the Laodiceans.)

2. Theme and Outline

Theme: Paul's appeal to Philemon for Christian forgiveness
I. Introduction (vss. 1-7)
   A. Greeting (vss. 1-3)
   B. Thanksgiving (vss. 4-7)
II. Body: The Entreaty Concerning Onesimus (vss. 8-21)
III. Conclusion (vss. 22-25)

3. The Nature of Paul's Appeal

The letter is a model of tactful persuasion. Paul's appeal to Philemon has many sides.

By addressing the letter to Philemon, his family, and the whole church Paul makes the problem of Onesimus' return more than a private matter between a master and a slave. The tactic practically ensures a Christian solution, not merely a legal consideration of the problem.

The mention of Philemon's reputation for loving attitudes and actions (vss. 4-7) would stimulate him to yet another act of generosity.

Paul's loving appeal, rather than an authoritative command based on status and rank, would tend to evoke a loving response (vss. 8, 9).

Paul's high regard for Onesimus (he is "useful to you and me," he is "my very heart," "my child") would motivate Philemon to a like regard (vss. 10-13).

Paul's consideration for Philemon's

rights as slave owner is deftly aimed at leaving the initiative toward generosity with Philemon (vs. 14).

Paul's suggestion that the hand of Providence is to be seen in the whole affair (vss. 15, 16) would move Philemon to gratitude to God, instead of personal vengeance.

The appeal to the common membership of Paul, Philemon, and Onesimus in the Christian brotherhood (vss. 16, 17) offers a theological ground for Paul's entreaty for mercy.

The reminder of what Philemon owes Paul, as well as Paul's willingness to assume financial responsibility for Onesimus' irresponsibility (vss. 18, 19), would have strong effect.

The request for a personal favor and the joyous anticipation that it would be abundantly granted (vss. 20, 21) would be hard to resist.

The suggestion that Philemon will soon meet Paul face to face in a proposed visit (vs. 22) would hasten speedy and favorable action.

By adding the names of his companions (vss. 23, 24) Paul suggests that they join him in the appeal for Onesimus.

4. Paul and Slavery

Neither Jesus, nor any of the first Christians, including Paul, had as a goal the abolition of slavery. Slavery was provided for in the Law of Moses and in contemporary Jewish and Greco-Roman law.

But the teachings of Jesus and the church ultimately undermined slavery. They set forth the infinite value of every person before God (Matt. 6:26; 10:29-31; Mark 10:13-16; Luke 15; etc.); the equality and essential oneness of all believers in Jesus Christ (Gal. 3:28: "there is neither slave nor free"; cf. Eph. 6:5-9; Col. 3:11). They emphasized love and deeds of mercy toward the unfortunate and the needy, as the central demand of Christian discipleship (Matt. 22:37-40; 25:31-46; John 13:35; I John 3:17; James 2:1-17). Since a Christian slave master was "a slave of Christ" and since a Christian slave was "a freedman of the Lord" (I Cor. 7:22), they occupied common ground in Christ.

Such a view and such a position could not but radically affect, and in time eliminate, the institution of slavery.

84. Hebrews

The Letter to the Hebrews contains the most eloquent writing in the New Testament. Its author was a brilliant early Christian thinker who scaled theological and literary heights equaled by few, if any, Christians of the first century.

Unfortunately, the text contains little information about its author, its original readers and their circumstances, its date, its purpose, and its theological background. Even its literary form is somewhat mysterious. It is like Melchizedek, "without father or mother or genealogy" (7:3), for we know so little about its antecedents and its family relationships.

1. Literary Character

Hebrews calls itself a "word of exhortation" (13:22). It is more like a sermon than a letter. It has no greeting at its opening, as letters almost always did (I John is like Hebrews here). However, its ending follows the normal pattern of letters, with personal matter, greetings, and benediction (13: 18-25).

The references to the author's *speaking* (2:5; 5:11; 6:9; 8:1; 9:5), while possible in a letter, fit better an oral address, especially the remark that "time would fail me to tell of" (11:32). The oratorical tone of the whole book would seem to indicate that it is a sermon.

If such was its original form, its author adapted it to serve as a message to be carried and read to some group of Christians. He may have at that time added 13:18-25 as an epistolary ending to his sermon.

The message requires about fifty minutes for reading aloud, not too long for an early Christian worship service.

The question of whether it is a sermon or a letter is not of much significance, however, since the New Testament letters were all addressed to churches and intended for reading at worship services (see p. 254).

2. Theme and Contents

Theme: Jesus, the eternal Son of God, by his completely effective high priestly work, offers all men perfect cleansing from their sins and admittance to the presence of the living God.

I. Jesus, God's Son (and, as such, superior in rank and function to angels and to Moses in God's redemptive purpose), is the God-appointed deliverer of men from sin, death, and the devil and the fulfiller of their destiny as sons of God (1:1–4:13).

II. Jesus, as a high priest in a superior priestly order (after the order of Melchizedek rather than of Aaron; see section 6 below) based upon a covenant superior to that given to Moses, by dying on the cross offered an effective sacrifice for the sins of all people, thus making possible their admittance to the very presence of God (4:14–10:18).

III. Jesus' completely effective redemptive work requires the response of faith, patience in suffering, reverent worship of God, obedience to his will and to church teaching, and loving activity in behalf of the brethren (10: 19–13:17).

IV. Epistolary ending: the fellowship of prayer, a final appeal, personal matters and greetings, benediction (13: 18-25).

3. Original Readers and Purpose

The title "To the Hebrews" represents the opinion of the church from the latter part of the second century concerning the first readers.

"Hebrews" apparently meant Jewish Christians, for the work plainly was intended for Christians, not Jews (3:1;

6:1-12; 12:22-24). The heavy use of the Old Testament, the constant reference to the ritual institutions and practices of Israel, the contrast of the old and the new covenants, and the like, might have led the early church to conclude that it was written to Hebrew (Jewish) Christians, quite apart from any tradition to that effect. Whether the title correctly defines the first readers is questionable.

The following major positions are possible:

a. The first readers were Jewish Christians.

The elaborate argument to show the superiority of Christianity over Judaism, together with the many indications that the readers were shrinking from full allegiance to Christ and the church (2:1-3*a*; 5:11-14; 6:1-12; 10; 23, 35-39), show that the recipients were about to give up Christianity and return to Judaism.

They may have lived in Jerusalem or in some other part of Palestine. Since the discovery of the Dead Sea Scrolls, some scholars have thought they were Essenes who had become Christians (see p. 408). It is possible also that they were a Jewish Christian minority group in some community like Rome, Corinth, Ephesus, the Lycus Valley, or Antioch.

b. They were Gentile Christians.

Gentile Christians used the Septuagint, were saturated in it, and regarded themselves as the true Israel (Gal. 6: 16; I Peter. 2:9-10).

Hebrews nowhere indicates that the readers were considering returning to Judaism. What threatened them was a general let-down due to the delay in the second coming of Christ (9:28; 10:23-25) and the bitter sufferings Christians were enduring at the hands of both Jews and Gentiles (12:3-13). The author wished to show these Gentile Christians that in Christ God had fulfilled his purpose for the redemption of *mankind*. To turn away from him was to turn away from God's future for *all* men.

On this second view, the readers could have been Gentiles living anywhere in the Gentile world.

c. They were both Jewish and Gentile Christians—simply Christians as Christians, irrespective of background. They had become discouraged (for the reasons suggested in *b*) and needed a ringing challenge to press on.

It is possible that the letter was intended for the mixed church at Rome or for some other church in Italy. Arguing for this is the acquaintance of Clement of Rome with Hebrews (*c.* A.D. 95; I Clement 17:1; 36: 2-5). In addition, the most natural interpretation of "those who come from Italy send you greetings" (13: 24) is that Italians present with the author outside Italy send greetings home to their fellow countrymen.

The third position seems the most likely.

4. Authorship

Many authors have been suggested.

a. Paul

The Eastern church, from the end of the second century, regarded Paul as the author and placed the book among the letters of Paul, after the

Letter to the Romans or after II Thessalonians. The Western church accepted Paul's authorship only from the second half of the fourth century, as a result of Eastern influence.

Almost all scholars agree today that the form, style, and theology are unlike Paul. Paul did not write anonymous letters. He did not alternate sections of argument and exhortation but usually reserved his major appeal for the end of his letters. The style is highly polished, whereas Paul's was frequently rough, marked by digression, and sometimes by unfinished sentences. Paul's distinctive themes are missing, or practically so: justification by faith, not by works of the Law; the equality of Jew and Gentile in God's purpose; the mystical union of the believer with Christ. The figure of Christ as high priest is absent from Paul's letters. Paul made little of the Law as a foundation for Israel's sin-removing sacrificial system, but rather stressed the Law as a sin-revealing and sin-stimulating instrument. Paul says nothing about the impossibility of a second repentance (6:4-8; 10:26-27; 12:17).

b. Apollos

Martin Luther's suggestion that Apollos of Alexandria was the author has won many advocates. Apollos was "an eloquent man, well versed in the scriptures" (Acts 18:24). His presumed training in Greek rhetoric and Greek philosophy would account for the style and thought of Hebrews (see below on "Formative Influences"). His contacts with Paul and Timothy (I Cor. 16:12) were close. This would explain both the Pauline characteristics of the book and his interest in Timothy (Heb. 13:23).

c. Luke

Clement of Alexandria (late second century) thought that Luke had translated Paul's original Hebrew text of this book into Greek. Some modern scholars have found similarities between Hebrews and the Acts of the Apostles, particularly in the speech of Stephen (Acts 7). However, the differences from Luke's theology as a whole are so striking that his authorship of Hebrews is extremely unlikely; and Hebrews shows no evidence of translation from a Hebrew text.

d. Barnabas

Tertullian (died c. A.D. 220) attributed Hebrews to Barnabas, a Levite from Cyprus (Acts 4:36). A Levite (a member of an ancient priestly group which attributed its origin to Levi, a son of Jacob) would have knowledge of temple ritual. Barnabas means "Son of encouragement" (cf. "word of encouragement," or "exhortation," mentioned in Heb. 13:22). He may have been an educated man capable of so profound a writing, but there is little to support the conjecture.

e. Others

Other suggestions are: Clement of Rome, Silvanus (Silas), Philip (one of the seven deacons), and Priscilla (wife of Aquila). Origen (third century) concluded, "Who wrote the epistle God alone knows certainly." Origen's judgment still stands, though the best candidates are Apollos and Barnabas.

5. Date of Writing

Clement of Rome's knowledge of Hebrews around A.D. 95 places it before that date, but how much before is uncertain.

There is no reference to the destruction of the temple in Jerusalem (A.D. 70). Timothy has been released (from some imprisonment?), but the time and circumstances are not given (13:23). The mention of "former days," when the readers were persecuted (10:32-34), could refer to the time (c. A.D. 49) when Claudius expelled the Jews from Rome (Acts 18:2) or to persecutions by Nero in A.D. 64. But the latter, which involved martyrdoms, seems unlikely from the statement in 12:4 that "you have not yet resisted to the point of shedding your blood." If the epistle was directed to the church at Rome, this statement would date it before A.D. 64—probably not long before, since the author and readers seem to be second-generation Christians (2:3).

If the epistle was not for the Roman church, where Nero's persecutions occurred, 12:4 would have no direct bearing on the date. It could then have been written as late as about A.D. 81–90, in the time of the erratic emperor Domitian, when the Christian's lot was becoming difficult.

The early 60s and the period 81–90 are the alternatives.

6. Theology

Hebrews is a Jesus-centered book. Its keynote is, "Let us keep our eyes fixed on Jesus, on whom our faith depends from beginning to end" (12:2 TEV; cf. 2:9).

The author's portrayal of Jesus and his meaning for the life of mankind is unique in the writings of the New Testament. Only Hebrews declares Jesus to be "a great high priest" and summarizes his achievement as the offering up of himself as a perfect sacrifice for the sins of all people. The daring of this concept is readily apparent. A high priest did not offer up himself but "the blood of goats and calves" (9:12). He was sacrificer but not also the one sacrificed.

In Hebrews Jesus is the perfect sacrifice for sins and the perfect sacrificer because he is the eternal Son of God. The highest language is used to characterize his relation to God: "he reflects the glory of God and bears the very stamp of his nature" (1:3). He was the agent of God in creation and is the upholder of the universe (1:2-3). This glorious Son became a true human being (2:14), "made like his brethren in every respect" (2:17). He suffered, prayed, and implored God's help (5:7). "He learned obedience through what he suffered; and being made perfect he became the source of eternal salvation to all who obey him" (5:8-9). The complete humanity of Jesus as incarnate Son of God is more prominent here than anywhere else in the New Testament. Because he became one of us (short of sinning), he was able to sympathize with us and our weaknesses (4:15) and thus to serve as our high priest before God.

His priestly ministry was perfectly effective. The ministry of the Jewish priesthood was not. The blood of animals could not take away sins (10:4,

11) and purge the conscience (9:9, 14). His ministry, while in some respects like that of the Jewish high priest, was in reality of a higher order. He belonged to the priestly order of Melchizedek, not to that of Aaron and Levi (5:10; 6:20–7:22).

Our author sees two priestly lines in the Old Testament. The superior one began with Melchizedek, the priest-king of Jerusalem at the time of Abraham. Abraham recognized his superiority by accepting his blessing and by paying him tithes (Gen. 14: 18-20). It was to this priestly line that King David belonged (Ps. 110:4). From this line the priest-king Messiah was to come.

The other line came from Levi, Jacob's son (Gen. 49:5-7; Exod. 32: 26-29). It included Aaron, Moses' brother, and Aaron's sons, who became Israel's priestly family (Lev. 8:5-30).

The author of Hebrews sees the priests descended from Levi and Aaron as inferior to the line of Melchizedek and to the Messiah and High Priest, Jesus, whom Melchizedek foreshadowed (Heb. 7).

Not only is Jesus' priestly line superior to the Levi-Aaron line, but his ministry is based on God's new covenant with his people, not the old, obsolete Mosaic covenant (8:8-13).

Jesus' place of ministry is also superior. He officiates not in an earthly sanctuary but in heaven (8:1-5). There he offered up before God the perfect sacrifice of his own life (9:11-12), and there he now intercedes before God in behalf of mankind (9:24; 7:25).

He accomplished what the Mosaic law and worship could not: the removal of the worshipers' sins, their sanctification, holiness, perfection (*i.e.,* their separation from all defilement and their becoming like God in character—10:10, 14; 12:14). Thus they became fit to stand in the very presence of God (10:19-22; 12:22-23).

He awaits the arrival of the Father's time for his return "to save those who are eagerly waiting for him" (9:28), to receive from God sovereignty over his enemies (10:13, 25, 37), and to enable men to enter with him into the promised sovereignty over all creation in the kingdom (or city) of God (2:5-13; 12:22-28; 13:14).

Those who have the Holy Spirit have already experienced the foretaste of life in that kingdom (6:4-5). Those who have had this high privilege must beware of becoming indifferent and unbelieving, of being carried away by "the deceitfulness of sin" (2:1; 3: 12-13) in their pilgrimage toward the final city. Else they may fall in the wilderness, as unbelieving Israel did (3:7-19). They must press on in faith, like the heroes of faith before them (chap. 11). They must devote themselves to righteous living and loving deeds (chap. 13), for the day of judgment and promise is drawing near (10:25).

7. Formative Influences

Jesus' high priesthood is echoed or assumed in other New Testament writings (*e.g.,* the high priestly prayer of John 17; the priestly garb worn by the Son of man of Rev. 1:13). The concept is based on the interpretation of Ps. 110 as referring to a future Messiah, and possibly on the belief within Judaism of the coming of both a priestly Messiah and a kingly Messiah. Its unique development in Hebrews arises from the profound reflection of a creative and subtle Christian mind at work on traditional materials.

The concept of the Law of Moses as "a shadow of the good things to come instead of the true form of these realities" (10:1) and the earthly tabernacle as "a copy of the true one" in heaven (9:23-24) probably reflects Greek views of the relation between the things of heaven and the things of earth and may point to the author's Hellenistic training.

Some scholars have seen at various points in Hebrews a marked similarity to the thought of the Greek-influenced Jewish philosopher Philo of Alexandria (c. 20 B.C. to A.D. 40). Others have identified Gnostic elements in the theology of Hebrews (on Gnosticism see pp. 304-7).

The extent of Paul's influence on the author is not clear. There are both similarities to and striking differences from Paul. On the whole, the approach in Hebrews to the Law and Israel's sacrificial system is fundamentally different from Paul's.

It is evident that Judaism, Greek culture, and primitive Christianity all contributed to the portrait of Jesus in Hebrews.

85. James

One of the most controversial books in the history of the church has been the Letter of James.

It first appeared in a time of hot controversy over the relative importance of faith and works in Christian belief and practice, and it entered the lists on the side of works.

The book was slow in gaining general acceptance in the church as a whole. The writings of important early church fathers such as Irenaeus, Tertullian, Cyprian, and Hippolytus do not quote from or mention it. Origen (third century) is the first church leader we know of to quote from it and to regard it as authoritative. Athanasius, in his Easter letter of A.D.

367, put it among the twenty-seven books (those now in our New Testament) which were to be regarded as canonical and "divine." Its place was finally made secure by Jerome's inclusion of it in the Latin Vulgate at the end of the fourth century. But some portions of the church, particularly in Syria, continued to contest its right to a place among the New Testament books.

Martin Luther called the book "an epistle of straw," in contrast to the pure gold of the gospel contained in Romans and Galatians. He felt that it did not properly teach Christ and the true way of salvation as set forth by Paul.

Today the Letter of James is looked on more sympathetically, as a valid protest against a form of heresy which exalted "faith" to the neglect of "deeds." Most interpreters now believe that Paul would have agreed with James that a faith which is not expressed in moral conduct is not *Christian* faith. The book argues powerfully and correctly that faith needs hands and feet—a point Paul also stressed.

1. Literary Character and Contents

At a first look, the book appears to be an epistle or letter. But, apart from the greeting of the first verse, it bears no marks of a letter. It has no conclusion and farewell; it offers no information about the readers to whom it might be addressed.

Its contents are like the book of Proverbs, Ecclesiasticus (the Wisdom of Jesus the Son of Sirach) of the Apocrypha, and various sections of New Testament books dealing with ethics. Some of its sayings echo the Sermon on the Mount. It presents crisp, salty wisdom about the true way of life after the manner of Israel's Wisdom teachers (including Jesus).

Like the Jewish Wisdom books, the Letter of James has no clear pattern of organization. The sections are somewhat loosely strung together.

The book deals with themes dear to the heart of Israel's wise men (true versus false wisdom, the power of the tongue, the lot and destiny of rich and poor, the meaning of suffering, the importance of God's law and obedience to it, the example of Old Testament figures). In form and content James is a book of wisdom, rather than an epistle or letter. It undoubtedly served in some portion of the early Christian church as a book of instruction in the meaning and way of Christian discipleship.

Its parts and subjects are as follows:

a. The Greeting: James to God's pilgrim people (the church) in many lands of the world (1:1)

b. The Teaching (1:2–5:20)
  (1) The joy of trials (1:2-4)
  (2) The double-minded man (1:5-8)
  (3) The perishing rich (1:9-11)
  (4) The enduring righteous (1:12-15)
  (5) God, the source of all good (1:16-18)
  (6) Hearing and doing (1:19-27)
  (7) Impartiality (2:1-13)
  (8) Faith and works (2:14-26)
  (9) Requirements for teachers in the church (3:1-18)
  (10) Submission to God (4:1-10)
  (11) The evil of evil-speaking (4:11-12)
  (12) The sin of presumption (4:13-17)
  (13) The doomed rich (5:1-6)
  (14) The coming of the Lord (5:7-11)
  (15) Absolute truthfulness (5:12)
  (16) Prayer and the power of God (5:13-18)
  (17) Restoration of the erring brother (5:19-20)

2. Purpose

The book seems to have both a specific and a general purpose.

The author attacks vigorously a

heresy which exalts faith and ignores works. He insists that "faith apart from works is dead" (2:26) and argues for the importance of works by an appeal to Old Testament examples (2:21-25). One might think he is attacking Paul directly (Rom. 3:28), even using Abraham to prove exactly the opposite conclusion from that drawn by Paul (Rom. 4).

Probably, he is attacking not Paul but a distortion of Paul's teaching by men who lacked Paul's balance. Paul believed that good works are the result of a trusting, loyal relationship to God. One's faith becomes active in deeds of love (Gal. 5:6). Paul and James emphasize different sides of the faith-works debate, but neither regards the other side as unimportant. Paul's teaching was seized on by men who turned it into an excuse for immorality (Rom. 6:1 ff.; I Cor. 5:1–6:20; Phil. 3:17-19). It is against men of this sort that the book of James argues.

More generally, the book speaks to Christians everywhere who find their cup of suffering full to overflowing. In addition to the sufferings that are the common lot of mankind, there are those which arise from Christian living in a pagan world. The writer wants the readers to see their sufferings as an opportunity for spiritual growth. He wants them to have confidence in God's good purpose for them and to remain loyal to him in every distressing circumstance. He holds out for the righteous the prospect of a blessed reward at the day of judgment, which he sees immediately ahead. Meanwhile they are to live in peace with one another, to avoid various dangers to their faith, to seek physical and spiritual health, and to act out their faith by deeds of love in daily life.

The Letter of James is a book of practical morality, a healthy corrective to a deviant form of Christianity. It contends that the kind of religion approved by God consists not simply in correct belief, inner feelings, and pious confessions but also in righteous conduct and deeds of mercy.

3. Authorship and Date

In the sixteenth century Erasmus, recognizing the excellent Greek in which the letter was written, denied that its author could have been James, the brother of Jesus.

In our time many scholars have argued that the book was written by some later James. Some have held that it was originally a Jewish work which was edited and reissued as a Christian book, chiefly by the insertion of the name "Jesus Christ" in two places (1:1; 2:1).

There are still many influential defenders of the traditional authorship. They claim that James, Jesus' brother, could indeed have come to a first-class knowledge of Greek and that the thought of the book agrees with what we know about this Jerusalem Christian leader from the Acts and Paul's letters. One recent commentator holds that Christian visitors to Jerusalem from the Gentile world, after hearing James's impressive teaching, wanted a written memo of it to carry back with them for use in their churches. James supplied this in an epistle-like message to the churches everywhere.

But doubts persist about the traditional authorship and purpose of the book. It is quite possible that it contains actual memories of the teaching of James, the brother of the Lord, put together by a disciple of James under his teacher's name. Such issuance of a famous teacher's material by a disciple under the teacher's name seems to have been common in that day.

If the letter was indeed written by James, the Lord's brother, the date falls before A.D. 62, when, according to Josephus, James was martyred. If a follower of James issued the book under his teacher's name, the date would be around the end of the first century.

4. Original Readers

The epistle is addressed to "the twelve tribes in the Dispersion" (1:1). Does this mean Jews of the Diaspora (Dispersion), thus Jews living outside Palestine? The contents of the book lead to a negative answer. The problems of Diaspora Jews are not discussed, and there is no missionary appeal.

Does it mean Jewish Christians, as distinguished from Gentile Christians, in various parts of the Greco-Roman world? Probably not, for Jewish and Gentile Christians were intermingled in the same churches in many places and would hardly be addressed separately. Furthermore, the teaching seems to apply to all Christians, not just to those of one ethnic background.

It is likely that "the twelve tribes" means to suggest that the whole Christian church is the true Israel, which lives on earth as a pilgrim or sojourner and whose home is heaven (Gal. 6:16; Phil. 3:20; I Pet. 2:11; Heb. 11:13-16).

Many Christian marks show that the book was not originally a Jewish work: for example, the name "Lord Jesus Christ" (1:1; 2:1); the reference to the readers as "first fruits" (1:18; cf. I Cor. 15:20; Rom. 8:29; Rev. 14:4); the characterization of God's law as "the perfect law, the law of liberty" (1:25), a phrase not used in Judaism; the many echoes of the teaching of Jesus (1:5, 17=Matt. 7:7 ff.; 1:22= Matt. 7:24 ff.; 4:12=Matt. 7:1; 5: 12=Matt. 5:34-37).

The author was a Christian, undoubtedly of Jewish background, who wrote for Christians everywhere.

86. I Peter

I Peter is undoubtedly one of the most attractive books in the New Testament.

It joins together several important strains in the Judeo-Christian religion: the priestly (e.g., 1:14-19; 2:5), the prophetic (e.g., 1:22-25; 2:9-12), the devotional (e.g., 1:6-8; 4:13-14), and the theological (e.g., the meaning of baptism and of undeserved suffering, and the Christian hope for the future).

The whole book glows with the warmth of personal and communal devotion to Jesus Christ. It looks forward in joyous anticipation to the great homecoming of all the children of God at the appearance of Jesus Christ and shows how one should spend his time in the pagan world meanwhile.

1. Theme and Outline

Theme: You are heirs of salvation through suffering

    I.   Greeting (1:1-2).

       The apostle Peter to God's scattered people, who lodge for awhile in Pontus, Galatia, Cappadocia, Asia, and Bithynia: Grace and peace.

    II.   Body (1:3–5:11).

       A.   God's purpose of salvation for you (1:3–2:10).

          1.   You are its appointed heirs (1:3-5).

          2.   You are its joyful, though disciplined, heirs (1:6-9).

          3.   You are its fortunate heirs (1:10-12).

          4.   You are to be its holy heirs (1:13-25).

          5.   You are to be its full-grown and fully-equipped heirs (2:1-10).

       B.   God's standard of conduct for you (2:11–4:11).

          1.   Maintain good conduct among the Gentiles, so that they may be con-

Statue of St. Peter, St. Paul's Outside the Walls, Rome

verted by your good behavior (2:11-12).

          2.   Be subject to God, to the emperor, to governors, and to every human authority so that you may silence ignorant and stupid criticism (2:13-17).

          3.   Let servants obey and respect their masters, both the considerate and the harsh ones, for in bearing patiently unjust suffering they are following the example of Christ (2:18-25).

          4.   Let wives be submissive to their husbands, reverent, chaste, and modest; and let husbands be

considerate of their wives—for they share together God's gracious gift of life (3:1-7).

5. Be zealous for what is right, caring nothing about any suffering that may result (3:8–4:6).

6. In the time before the end, pray, love one another, and use the gifts God gave you to serve one another (4:7-11).

C. God's discipline of suffering for you (4:12–5:11).

1. Suffering is for your benefit (4:12-19).

2. Suffering sheep must be tended by sympathetic shepherds (5:1-5).

3. Suffering is according to the will of God— to perfect, establish, and strengthen (5:6-11).

III. Conclusion (5:12-14).

2. First Readers and Purpose

The letter is addressed to "the exiles of the Dispersion in Pontus, Galatia, Cappadocia, Asia, and Bithynia" (1:1). These are places in Asia Minor, comprising most of the country we now know as Turkey.

The readers were Gentile Christians, some of them possibly former God-fearers (see Acts 10:2; 13:16, 26; 16:14; 17:17; 18:7). These uncircumcized Gentile members of the synagogues of the Greek world were prime prospects for conversion by the first Christian missionaries.

The pagan background of the readers is several times mentioned (1:14, 18; 2:9-10; 3:6; 4:3). The phrase "exiles of the Dispersion" in the address (1:1) indicates not that they were Jews living in the Gentile world but that they, as Christians, were children of God scattered abroad in the world, away from their true home in heaven (see Phil. 3:20; Heb. 13:14; James 1:1; I Pet. 2:11).

Grievous troubles had befallen these Christians. The exact nature of their situation is difficult to determine. Two views are possible.

First, the persecution may have consisted of vicious assaults by pagan neighbors who resented the Christians' new and exclusive manner of life (4:3-4; cf. 2:12, 15; 3:9, 14-16; 4:14) and possibly haled them before local police and magistrates. However, no references to imprisonments, confiscation of property, trials before judges, or bloody martyrdom appear in the book. And the counsel to be obedient to the emperor and to governors (2:13-14) seems to imply satisfactory relationships with the state.

Second, official governmental persecution is a possibility. "The fiery ordeal" (4:12) may refer to the drastic experience of trial by an imperial court for bearing the name of Christ (4:14, 16) and a subsequent death sentence. Such persecution took place in the time of the emperor Trajan and of Pliny, the imperial legate of Bithynia-Pontus (c. A.D. 110).

On the whole, the first view is preferable. The phrases "for the name of Christ" (4:14) and "as a Christian" (4:16) do not necessarily mean that being a Christian was an offense punishable by the government (as in the time of Trajan and Pliny). Since there was no organized, worldwide governmental persecution of the church until the third century, the suffering of the church mentioned in 5:9 cannot have been of this sort. It must rather have consisted of widespread local harassment, arising from the ill will of the pagan populace. The positive attitude toward the state in 2:13-14 supports this conclusion.

The purpose of the letter, then, was to encourage the Christians of the territories mentioned to bear patiently the undeserved suffering they were experiencing; they were to understand that such suffering is used by God to test, purify, and strengthen the sufferers and to prepare them for the day of judgment and the reward God will give to the faithful.

3. Composition

One theory is that the letter came into existence in two stages. Since 1:3–4:11 seems to be more of a sermon than a letter, since it appears to deal with suffering as possible rather than actual, and since it ends with a doxology (4:11), it may originally have been a baptismal sermon. Later, when there was an outbreak of severe persecution, this sermon was transformed into a letter by the addition of a greeting (1:1-2), specific comments about the readers' proper response to the present crisis (4:12–5:11), and a conclusion (5:12-14).

It is quite apparent that 1:3–4:11 has baptism and the new life into which it leads as a prominent theme

(1:3, 23; 2:2, 9-10, 25; 3:21). However, the argument that this section was originally a baptismal sermon falls short of proof.

That the suffering mentioned in 1:3–4:11 is possible rather than actual is contradicted by 1:6, where the Greek is best translated, "In this you exult, even though now you have been distressed for a short while (since it has to be) by various trials" (J. N. D. Kelly). In 4:4 the suffering is plainly indicated as present.

The doxology in 4:11 is probably not the sign of the conclusion of an earlier piece of writing but simply an outburst of awe and devotion in contemplation of the marvelous grace of God and the fulfillment of man's true end in the glorifying of God (cf. Rom. 11:33-36; Gal. 1:5; Phil. 4:20; Eph. 3:21).

It is best to hold that the author composed the whole of I Peter as a general letter to Christians spread over a wide area of Asia Minor. He meant it to be circulated among the churches for reading in services of worship. He called their baptismal experience to mind to bring into focus their status as children of God and to remind them of the implications of their new life in God's family for their existence in the world.

4. Authorship and Date

There are differing views on the authorship and date.

a. Peter the apostle was the author, either in a direct or an indirect sense. From at least the time of Irenaeus (end of second century) the church regarded Peter as the writer.

Certain facts in the letter may support Peter's authorship: references to the sufferings of Jesus (2:21-24; 3:18; 4:1; 5:1); echoes of Jesus' teaching, of a sort one would expect from Peter (*cf.* I Pet. 1:22 with John 13:34-35; I Pet. 2:12 with Matt. 5:16; I Pet. 2:13-17 with Matt. 17:24-27); and parallels with Peter's speeches in the Acts of the Apostles (*cf.* I Pet. 1:10-12 with Acts 2:14-36). However, these facts hardly prove Peter's authorship, since most of them would be known to any church teacher from the gospel tradition and from the church tradition in the Acts.

Some scholars have argued that Silvanus, a scribe or secretary (5:12), composed the letter at Peter's direction, perhaps using Peter's outline of contents and his basic ideas. Peter may have added personally the note about Silvanus and the rest of the text (5:12-14).

If Peter was the author, directly or indirectly, the date would fall during Peter's residence in Rome ("Babylon" —5:13), about A.D. 62–64.

b. The letter was written in Peter's name by an unknown author who lived at the time of Domitian's persecution of the church (*c.* A.D. 90–95) or in the time of Trajan and Pliny (*c.* A.D. 110). The Roman government carried out the persecution mentioned in the letter.

Some object to Peter's direct authorship on several grounds: that the Greek of I Peter is too flawless and sophisticated for a Galilean fisherman; that it is unlikely he would have quoted from the Greek (rather than the Hebrew) Old Testament; that his theology shows dependence on Paul's; and that the letter contains no special knowledge of Jesus of the sort an eyewitness would have possessed. And, as noted, they believe the persecution was the kind not experienced by the church until three decades after Peter's death.

Peter's direct authorship is unlikely. Silvanus or some other skilled writer seems to have played a major role in the creation of the letter, either in the sixties or around the end of the first century.

5. Teaching

The author regards the readers as newly begotten children of God who, according to the Father's will, are for a time scattered abroad in Asia Minor. They await the great homecoming in the Father's house, soon to be brought about by the return of Jesus Christ (1:5, 7, 13; 4:7, 17; 5:4).

As newborn babes, they are in need of spiritual food and spiritual growth (1:22–2:3). They must understand and value the high destiny their Father has in store for them and not be turned aside from the goal by unbelief (2:4-8), by "the passions of the flesh" (2:11; *cf.* 4:2-4), by love of earthly things (3:3-4; 5:2), by self-seeking and bickering (2:1; 3:8; 4:8; 5:5), and by the hostility they are experiencing from their fellow countrymen.

This hostility and the suffering it causes can be turned to good account. Christ's sufferings had blessed results, both for himself and for others. Through "being put to death in the flesh," he was "made alive in the spirit" (3:18—*i.e.,* through suffering he came from mortal life to resurrection life); and through his death he brought us to God. He achieved a complete triumph over the disobedient evil spirits (3:19, 22), which opposed him and afflict his followers.

Since Christ's sufferings had such blessed consequences, the readers ought to imitate him in patient endurance of suffering (2:21-25). They must realize that suffering "for the name of Christ" brings refinement of character (1:7), ethical fruit for one's own life (4:1), possession of the Holy Spirit (4:14), approval and reward at Christ's day of judgment (1:7; 4:13; 5:4), and ultimate participation in the glory of the coming age (1:7; 5:1, 4, 10).

"So even those whom God allows to suffer must trust themselves to the constancy of the creator and go on doing good" (4:19 JB).

87. II Peter

II Peter does not rise to the theological and literary heights of I Peter.

II Peter is more a tract for its own times than a writing for the ages. However, it presumably did its work in its own age, when the church was threatened by a subtle heresy; and that is no insignificant contribution to the ages.

There are, however, passages in the book significant for our times. These justify attention to the book by modern Christians.

1. Theme and Outline

Theme: The certainty of the second coming of Christ and the relation of that coming to Christian living.
 I. Greeting (1:1-2).
 II. Body (1:3–3:18*a*).
  A. The promise of the coming of Christ and his kingdom (1:3-21).
   1. Entrance to that kingdom depends on moral renewal and moral living (1:3-11).
   2. Fulfillment of the promise is assured by the experience on the Mount of Transfiguration and by divine revelation in Scripture (1:12-21).
  B. Those who deny the promise and their coming doom (2:1-22).
   1. In the past false prophets and disobedient angels were judged by God, and the righteous were preserved by him (2:1-10*a*).
   2. The present false proph-

ets will be destroyed (2:10*b*-22).

C. A refutation of the deniers and a reaffirmation of the promise and its moral requirements (3:1-18*a*).

1. The sure word of God, through the holy prophets and through the Lord Jesus and his apostles, announced both the appearance of these deniers and the certainty of the end of the world by fire (3:1-7).

2. The delay in Christ's coming and the end of the world must not be interpreted as a failure of the promise to be realized but as a brief opportunity for all to repent (3:8-10).

3. The hope for "the day of God" and the coming of the new age should stimulate believers to holy living (as Paul also urged) and to spiritual growth (3:11-18*a*).

III. Doxology (3:18*b*).

2. Purpose and Circumstances of Writing

This letter is "an apology for primitive Christian eschatology." This means a justification, in the face of attack, of the Christian hope of the second coming of Christ, the end of this world, and the establishment of the New Age.

Disbelievers ("scoffers") had arisen in the church. They questioned Christ's coming (3:3-4); they led self-indulgent lives; and they led others into disbelief and sensual living (2:1-3*a*, 10*b*-22), including those newly converted from paganism (2:18). They threatened to pervert the whole church by returning to the mire from which they had once been delivered and encouraging others to wallow there (1:9; 2:22).

The "scoffers" were a group within the church. They may have had their own dissolute love feasts (2:13 RSV margin). They stressed their freedom in Christ from all restraints (2:19). They seem to have resembled the Gnostics at Corinth who believed they were above temptation and any earthly controls because they already were living in the New Age (see p. 265). Since salvation for these Gnostics was fully present, the traditional teaching about the second coming of Christ and the arrival of the New Age thereafter made no sense. Furthermore, they pointed out scornfully that much time had elapsed since the promise was first made to "the fathers" (3:4, *i.e.*, the first Christians) and that the hope was therefore empty and meaningless.

II Peter was written to counteract this anti-apocalyptic and anti-moral teaching in the church at large (1:1). (On apocalyptic literature see pp. 242-43.)

3. Author, Date, and Place of Writing

The letter claims repeatedly that Peter the apostle was its author. Besides the direct mention of "Simon Peter" (1:1), facts about Peter are mentioned: a direct word from Jesus about Peter's imminent death (1:14); his presence at the transfiguration of Jesus (1:16-18); a reference to another letter written to the readers (3:1—probably our I Peter); and Peter's relation to Paul as that of a "beloved brother" (3:15).

Most scholars today believe that Peter could not have been the author but that the letter was written in his name by a disciple and admirer. The reasons for this belief are:

a. In the early church, up to the fourth century, some prominent leaders (Origen, Eusebius, and Jerome, for example) expressed or reported serious doubts that Peter the apostle wrote this letter. The letter was slow in gaining wide acceptance in the church.

b. The letter has a strong Greek character. Words and phrases like God's "excellence" (1:3), "virtue" (1:5), "partakers of the divine nature" (1:4), "eyewitnesses" (1:16 —a term designating those initiated into the highest grade of the mystery religions) seem unlikely from the mind of an uneducated Jew. The letter's wordy, pompous Greek style ill fits Peter.

c. The author of II Peter borrowed extensively from the letter of Jude (cf., for example, 2:1-18 with Jude 4-16, and 3:1-3 with Jude 17-18). This seems strange for the eminent Peter but not so strange for a lesser figure. And the late date of Jude (about the end of the first century) puts the later II Peter long after

Peter's death, which occurred between A.D. 64 and 67.

d. The nature of the heresy attacked, and particularly the heretics' scoffing at the church's unfulfilled hope for the future, points to a time considerably later than the death of Peter. We learn from I Clement (c. A.D. 95) that doubting and questioning of Christ's return was expressed in the church of that time.

e. The collection of Paul's letters, their acceptance as "scripture" (3:15b-16), and the implied authority of the church in the interpretation of scripture (1:20-21) point to a time later than Peter.

Though attempts have been made to disregard all these facts and to cling to Peter's direct authorship, most scholars consider them unsuccessful.

There grew up in the early church a considerable body of literature which claimed Peter as author but which clearly was not written by him (a Gospel of Peter, an Acts of Peter, and an Apocalypse of Peter). It was not uncommon for disciples of a great teacher to write works in his name.

Precisely who our author was is unknown. He probably was a Gentile Christian who wrote sometime between A.D. 100 and 150, probably nearer the later date. Many regard the letter as the latest writing in the New Testament.

The place of writing may have been Egypt, Rome, or Asia Minor.

4. Message

The church's historic faith is precious. The readers should value it and perpetuate it. Perverted men seek to undermine and destroy it.

Especially precious is the promise of the second coming of Christ and the inauguration of the "new heavens and a new earth in which righteousness dwells" (3:13). Contrary to the teaching of the heretics, we cannot fully obtain salvation in this life; we are called and elected to "entrance into the eternal kingdom of our Lord and Savior Jesus Christ" (1:11). Of the coming of this kingdom prophets and apostles—the latter at the command of Jesus—spoke (3:2).

The present world is a place where moral corruption dwells (1:4). The world will be destroyed (3:7). We have no stable, eternal order here, as the heretics maintain. (Here the author shares the early Christian view that Christians are pilgirms and strangers in the earth, who have here "no lasting city, but . . . seek the city which is to come" (Heb. 13:14;. cf.

Phil. 3:20; I Pet. 1:1; 2:11; Rev. 21:1)).

There are moral requirements for entrance to the coming kingdom. From the beginning of God's dealings with men, he has judged sinful men—and even sinful angels!—and has preserved the righteous. Thus the lewd, greedy, lawless heretics will be condemned to "the nether gloom of darkness" (2:17). The kingdom *now* or *then* is not theirs!

The delay in the coming of the kingdom is an expression of God's mercy. He wants all men to repent and enter it (3:9). While the righteous await that day, they should dedicate themselves to holy and godly living (1:5-11; 3:11, 14, 18).

Here are authentic teachings of early Christianity, warmheartedly urged on Christians of all ages. (On the second coming of Christ see chap. 102.)

88. I John

I John is one of the New Testament's most loved books. It shares this distinction with the Gospel of John, to which it is in many respects strikingly similar.

Its appeal is due to many features: its tender tone—an old man speaking to his "little children"; its clarity on what it means to be a disciple of Jesus; its balance between doctrine and behavior; its gems of wisdom; its simplicity and yet its profundity;

its personal nature—"that which *we* have seen and heard *we* proclaim . . . to *you*" (1:3); its joyful, victorious spirit; and much more. It stands near or at the height of New Testament literature.

1. Theme and Outline

While the book has an identifiable central emphasis, its contents are somewhat disorganized. Subjects do not follow one another in strict logical relationship but recur frequently in new combinations, like themes in a musical composition. A logical outline, therefore, can only approximately represent the contents.

    Theme: The message of the apostles is the standard of Christian truth and experience.

  I. Prologue: The apostolic testimony to the word of life (1:1-4).

 II. Body (1:5–5:12).

    A. The apostolic message concerning God's holiness, man's sin, and the way of salvation (1:5–2:17).

    B. The betrayers of the apostolic message and their deceptions (2:18-27).

    C. The apostolic message and life in the family of God (2:28–3:24).

    D. Tests of fidelity to the apostolic message and experience (4:1–5:12).

III. Epilogue: Summary of Christian certainties (5:13-21).

2. Literary Form and Destination

In form the document is more like a tract or a sermon than a letter. It has no opening and ending characteristic of a letter and no reference to individuals.

It is evident, however, that author and readers were well known to each other. The intimate forms of address show this: "my little children," "children," and "beloved." There is a pastoral tone to the book, such as would be normal if a trusted leader were giving counsel to followers who loved and respected him.

It is possible that the author or someone commissioned by him reproduced copies of this document and sent or carried them to churches in a certain geographic area, perhaps Asia Minor or Syria, to help them with a problem common to all.

Since the earliest evidence for the existence of I John comes from Polycarp and Papias (second quarter of second century), both of whom lived in Asia Minor, it is reasonable to conclude that the book originated there.

3. Circumstances of Writing

False teachers were unsettling the church by denying its long-standing faith in Jesus as the Messiah, the Son of God (2:22-23; 5:5), and as the Messiah–Son of God come in the flesh (4:2).

Apparently these teachers were not simply taking the Jewish position, which denied flatly that Jesus was the Messiah promised to God's people, for these heretics had been members of the church. Rather they denied that the heavenly Christ–Son of God was fully and inseparably to be identified with the man Jesus of Nazareth. This heavenly Christ–Son of God could not have become flesh, they reasoned, for flesh was essentially evil. The view of flesh as essentially evil was characteristic of the Gnostics (see below).

The false teachers boasted about

their superior knowledge and love of God (2:4; 4:20) and their fellowship with him (1:6; 2:9), but they did not follow Jesus' way of life (2:6). They lived in sin (2:4; 3:8, 10), even though they claimed to be above all sin (1:8, 10). They loved the world of sense and sensuality and apparently justified their indulging in its pleasures (2:15-17; 4:5).

They seem to have had little concern about preserving peaceful relations with their Christian brothers; in fact, they stirred up discord (2:9-11; 3:10-16). They were schismatics who withdrew from the brotherhood and formed a rival group (2:19). They sought to entice others into their circle (2:26; 3:7).

Our author calls them "antichrists" (2:18; 4:1-3). According to Jewish and early Christian belief, many antichrists were to come before the end of the age (Mark 13:6, 22; Matt. 24: 4-5; II Thess. 2:3-12). He sees these false teachers as agents of the devil to lead men astray. At his coming the Messiah (Christ) will destroy them and rescue the righteous for life in his kingdom. Their appearance is thus for our author a sign that it is "the last hour" (2:18). The appearance of Christ (2:28; 3:2) and the day of judgment (4:17) will expose the heretics for what they really are.

Their denial that the Savior came "in the flesh," their assertion that knowledge of God lifted people above all commandments and restraints, and their fleshly involvement with "the world" point clearly to the Gnostic heresy that arose in the church in the

second half of the first century and came to a head in the second century.

The heresy that I John seeks to counteract bears some resemblance to the teaching of a certain Cerinthus, who appeared in Asia Minor toward the end of the first century. He held that the world was made by a lower power, not the supreme God, that Jesus was conceived and born like all other men, that he became more righteous and wiser than others, and that after his baptism the Christ descended upon him in the form of a dove. Before his crucifixion the Christ withdrew from him, because the heavenly, spiritual Christ could not suffer.

The heretics' denial, described in I John, that the Christ–Son of God had come "in the flesh," fits this general outlook. Their claim that they were above sin accords with the Gnostic view that they had entered through baptism the life of the Resurrection and were therefore exempt from all earthly restraints (see p. 331). Their fleshly involvement with the world arose from their doctrine of creation, which held that the material world was created by a lower power and is essentially evil, while spirit is the creature of the Supreme Power. Since man is not a unity, what he does in the flesh cannot affect what he is in the spirit. To let worldly desire have free reign is to act in accordance with what one is by creation. Therefore, the flesh may legitimately be indulged.

Thus, the heresy struck at the very vitals of the Christian faith. Christians who clung to the traditional beliefs were being upset in doctrine, morals, and emotional certainty.

4. Message

The author says that he is writing to believers that they may know that they have eternal life (5:13). The message, then, is one of reassurance.

First, the author reassures them doctrinally. The faith handed down to the church from the beginning was based on the moral nature of God: "God is light and in him is no darkness at all" (1:5). Fellowship with God is possible only on the basis of man's moral renewal and obedience to God.

This renewal is gained through confession of one's sin and through divine forgiveness made effective for us through the death of Christ and his intercession for us (1:6–2:2). Moral obedience is the result of the imitation of Christ (2:3-6). So the church has always taught and must continue to teach!

The agent of man's moral redemption is Jesus Christ. He was the incarnate Son of God by whom the life of eternity was manifested in time. The church, through its first apostles, had indisputable experience of this God-in-flesh revelation. The humanity of Christ was real, not an appearance; it could be experienced by the senses (1:1-3).

Jesus' power to redeem rests not only on his receiving the Holy Spirit at his baptism (so that he could reveal divine mysteries to men) but also on his death as the incarnate Son of God (so that he might be "the remedy for the defilement of our sins"—2:2

NEB). Through the God-man, both in his baptism and death (5:6), our lives are enlightened and our sins are taken away. Furthermore, he is our present helper ("one to plead our cause with the Father"—2:1 NEB). So the church has always taught and must continue to teach!

Those who by faith in Christ find their sins canceled and their lives united to God are united also in the brotherhood of the family of God. The bond of union is love, "for God is love" (4:8). To live in love is to fulfill Christ's "new commandment" (2:8). To live in love means to serve the brothers in practical ways (3:16-18).

And life in union with God, Christ, and the brotherhood means a life of victory over sin. The believer is perpetually cleansed from his sins (1:8-10). "The man who lives 'in Christ' does not habitually sin" and "the man who is really God's son does not practice sin" (3:6, 9 Phillips). Thus, the heretics' fleshly indulgence is contrary to the gospel's demand as preached from the beginning.

How may one know for sure that he has eternal life and that the heretics are wrong? There are tests: (1) the test of love (do we love the brethren? —3:14; 4:7-8, 16); (2) the test of belief and confession (do we believe and confess Jesus as the Son of God incarnate?—4:2, 15; 5:1, 5); (3) the test of conduct (do we imitate Christ and do what is right?—2:5b-6, 29; 3:7, 10); (4) the test of conscience (does our heart condemn us?—3:21); (5) the test of the Spirit (does God's Spirit abide in us?—2:20, 27; 3:24;

4:13). Christians can know that they have eternal life (5:13).

5. Author and Date

The many striking agreements in vocabulary, style, and leading ideas between I John and the Gospel of John have led most scholars to believe that both books came from the same writer. Such differences as do exist may indicate that the books were written at different times without implying two authors.

Who the writer of the two books may have been is uncertain. II and III John identify their author as "the Elder" but offer no name. (On the meaning of "the Elder" see p. 339.)

The early church clearly attributed I John to the apostle John. We have seen the reason for believing that the apostle John stands in some way behind the Gospel of John—as the source of the tradition it contains, if not as its actual writer (see p. 245). Perhaps it was a disciple of the apostle John who put the tradition together in the present Gospel of John and who, probably somewhat later, wrote our I John.

The knowledge of I John by such early church writers as Polycarp and Papias (second quarter of second century) speaks for a date around the end of the first century, perhaps *c.* 90–115.

89. II-III John

These letters, probably each originally written on one sheet of papyrus, offer good examples of the informal letters of the Greco-Roman world.

They are not literary productions. They owe their survival to the fact that their author was an important person in the church. Their contents alone would hardly justify their inclusion in the New Testament.

In vocabulary, style, and general ideas they are strikingly similiar to I John and the Gospel of John. All must have come from the same author.

1. Themes and Outlines

II John

Theme: A warning against receiving and entertaining traveling false teachers

I. Greeting: The elder to "the elect lady" (some local church) (vss. 1-3)
II. Body (vss. 4-11)
    A. A commendation of some church members for fidelity to truth (vs. 4)
    B. A reminder of the commandment to love one another (vss. 5-6)
    C. A warning concerning traveling teachers of false doctrine about Jesus Christ and a command not to receive and entertain them (vss. 7-11)
III. Conclusion: The writer's plans and final greeting (vss. 12-13)

III John

Theme: Hospitality and financial

assistance for traveling missionaries who teach true Christian doctrine

I. Introduction (vss. 1-4)
   A. Greeting: The elder to Gaius (vs. 1)
   B. Prayer and thanksgiving: Prayer for Gaius' well-being and thanksgiving for his loyalty to the truth (vss. 2-4)
II. Body (vss. 5-12)
   A. Commendation of Gaius' past help for traveling missionaries and encouragement to continue it (vss. 5-8)
   B. Criticism of the arrogant Diotrephes for his opposition to the writer, his inhospitality to the traveling missionaries, and his excommunication of hospitable members (vss. 9-10); encouragement of Gaius to imitate good, rather than evil, persons (vs. 11)
   C. Commendation of Demetrius (vs. 12)
III. Conclusion: The writer's hope for a personal visit and his final greeting (vss. 13-15)

2. Situation and Purpose

All three letters of John reflect the same general situation: the spread of Gnostic teaching in the church, particularly the denial of the complete and indissoluble union of the eternal Son of God with the man Jesus (see pp. 334-36).

II John addresses a specific local church ("the elect lady"—1:1) to commend those in that church who have been faithful to the truth; to warn the members of the danger of the heresy for the life and future of the church; and to direct the readers to deny the heretics all hospitality and even friendly greeting. The heresy must be stopped through excommunication.

III John speaks to an individual, Gaius, apparently an important and somewhat affluent person. He was a beloved friend, and perhaps a convert, of the elder (vs. 4). He had been loyal to the true faith and had shown this by receiving and assisting financially certain traveling preachers of true doctrine. The author commends him for this and urges him to continue his good work.

Quite a contrary attitude characterized a certain Diotrephes, apparently in some local church known to Gaius but of which Gaius was not a member. (If Gaius and Diotrephes had lived in the same community and belonged to the same local church, the elder would hardly have needed to inform Gaius of Diotrephes' evil attitudes and deeds.) Diotrephes turned away the missionary representatives approved by the elder, forbade others to welcome them, and excommunicated—or attempted to excommunicate—those who had received them.

What authority for his actions Diotrephes claimed is not known. Was he a member of the board of elders of a local congregation? Had he assumed authority not rightfully his? Or was he (more probably) a bishop over a local church or possibly an area? Was he a Gnostic? He certainly stood opposed to the work the elder was trying to do, namely, to counteract Gnostic heresy. (See the discussion of I John.) The doctrinal clash had resulted in a clash of authority.

3. Author and Date

The writer calls himself "the elder." This can mean an old man or a member of the directing body of a local church. But more probably the title had a special meaning in Asia Minor. Irenaeus, from Smyrna in the second century, referred to "the Elders, disciples of the Apostles." The term thus designated one who, because of personal contact with the apostles, was honored as an authoritative teacher of the historic faith.

If this is the meaning of "the elder," he was a disciple of an apostle. This apostle may have been John, the Son of Zebedee (see p. 245), whose historical memories and interpretation of the faith the elder, as disciple, passed on.

The date was around the end of the first century, perhaps 90–115.

90. Jude

We know Jude best today for the doxology with which it concludes (vss. 24-25). Not many read the whole book, for its content is largely negative and its references to little-known persons and obscure apocryphal books give it a dated character.

It goes without saying that the book served a purpose in the life of the church at the time when it was written. Its urgent appeal to Christians to "contend for the faith which was once for all delivered to the saints" (vs. 3) was evidently a rallying cry in orthodox circles in its day.

This cry may well remind Christians that the backward look must be joined to the present and future look if authentic Christianity is to continue in the world. Tradition, while it must not hinder progress, must guide it and test it.

Jude's insistence that the face of God is set against evil doers—that is, that there is a moral demand deeply imbedded in the Christian faith—needs emphasis today quite as much as in the author's time.

1. Theme and Outline

Theme: God's judgment will fall on those in the church who undermine the faith and way of life once for all delivered to the saints.

I. Introduction (vss. 1-4)
   A. Greeting: Jude to called, beloved, and kept Christians (vss. 1-2)
   B. Occasion of writing: The appearance in the church of persons who are undermining the historic faith by perverting God's grace into

an opportunity for immorality and by rejecting Jesus Christ (vss. 3-4)

II. Body (vss. 5-23)

    A. Reminders from the past of God's judgment on the unbelieving, rebellious, and immoral (vss. 5-7)

    B. The sins of the godless people and others like them in the Old Testament (vss. 8-13)

    C. The prophecies of Enoch and the apostles concerning the coming of these evil persons and their judgment by God (vss. 14-19)

    D. What the faithful must do to protect themselves and counteract these godless ones (vss. 20-23)

III. Doxology (vss. 24-25)

2. Circumstances and Purpose

Here we again come face to face with a form of Gnosticism (see the discussions of I Corinthians, Colossians, I Timothy, II Peter, I John). Jude tells us little about its doctrine but a great deal about its moral consequences. Doctrine and practice are clearly tied together in the statement that these heretics "pervert the grace of our God into licentiousness and deny our only Master and Lord, Jesus Christ" (vs. 4).

Their evil practices evidently were based on the belief that God's grace allowed them freedom to indulge the flesh, in fact, commanded them to do so. Their reasoning seems to have been that by the resurrection experienced in baptism they became truly spiritual men, no longer subject to the laws of their pre-resurrection life. They were free sons of God. Furthermore, since by creation the flesh is essentially evil and the spirit good, and since only the spirit is eternal, what one does in the flesh cannot affect what one is in the spirit. They thus plunged into licentiousness and its associated evils with abandon and relish.

The statement that they "deny our only Master and Lord, Jesus Christ" may mean only that their immoral behavior denies the moral requirements laid down by Jesus (*e.g.,* Matt. 5:27-28). But it probably means more, as the author's interest in true doctrine indicates (vss. 3, 20-23, 25). In I John 2:22 the heretics deny "that Jesus is the Christ," that is, that the heavenly Christ, the Son of God, became flesh in the man Jesus. The suggestions that the immoral men attacked in Jude receive secret revelations (vs. 8) and regard themselves as Spirit-filled, but are not (vs. 19), point unmistakably to Gnostic views.

It appears that they did not withdraw from the church. They were present at the love feasts (vs. 12), that is, at church suppers in connection with which the Eucharist was often observed (I Cor. 11:17-34). They turned these into orgies.

Their disrespect for authority and the angels, appointed by God to enforce the natural and moral orders, was shocking to the author (vs. 8), as was their harsh, unloving spirit and their greed (vs. 11).

The author's purpose was to unmask these heretics and build up the faithful by encouraging them to continue in the traditional way. He exhorts them to pray in the Holy Spirit, to abide in God's love, to look forward in hope to eternal life, and to rescue as many fellow Christians as possible from the heretics' spell (vss. 22-23). They should avoid intimate contact with the heretics (vs. 23c).

3. Author and Date

Several possibilities exist.

a. He was Jude (Judas), the brother of Jesus. He is identified in 1:1 as a "brother of James," possibly the well-known James the brother of Jesus, who was head of the Jerusalem church (Gal. 1:19; 2:9; Acts 15:13 ff.; 21: 18). Jesus, James, and Jude are named together in Mark 6:3. Modesty may account for his identifying himself as "brother of James," rather than as "brother of Jesus."

b. He was an otherwise unknown Jude who had a brother named James, also otherwise unknown. Both names were common in those days. In this case we have no idea who Jude was.

c. He was a bishop Jude (Judas) of the Jerusalem church, early in the reign of the Emperor Trajan (A.D. 98–117).

d. The author wrote under the name of Jude, of whom he may have been a disciple or an admirer.

This book was widely accepted in the church of the second and third centuries, but in the fourth and fifth centuries it often was placed among the "disputed" writings, especially in the Eastern church. The author of II Peter, writing in perhaps the second quarter of the second century, reproduced in his work a large portion of the text of Jude (see p. 332). The early church thought the author was Jude, the brother of the Lord.

Possibility b leaves unexplained how the book gained acceptance in New Testament scripture, if the author was some nondescript Jude. Possibility c leaves unexplained the phrase "brother James," who obviously was some important, but now unknown, person. Some have assumed (without proof) that "brother" was inserted into the text after the book was written.

Arguments in favor of d are impressive to many scholars. Jude 17-18 seems to refer to the apostles as great men of the past. And the type of heresy the author was combatting in the book fits best the Gnosticism of the early second century—too late for Jude, the brother of Jesus.

However, it is possible that the book of Jude was written no later than A.D. 80–90. Gnostic trends had begun to appear at this time, and Jude, the Lord's brother, could have lived until A.D. 80 or a little later.

On balance, it seems best to hold that the brother of the Lord somehow stands behind the book, if not as its actual author, then as the teacher of the man who wrote it in his name.

4. The Use of Apocryphal Writings and the First Readers

There are two passages in Jude which directly depend on uncanonical books: vs. 9 and vss. 14-15. The first—the dispute of the archangel Michael with the devil over the body of Moses —according to early Christian writers comes from a first-century Jewish book, the Assumption of Moses. The second is a direct quotation from I Enoch 1:9. (See pp. 396-97.)

The high esteem in which the author obviously holds these Jewish apocalyptic books and the readers' presumed familiarity with them may imply a Jewish-Christian background for the author and possibly for his readers.

A good guess for the place of origin is some Greek-speaking community of Palestine or Syria, possibly Antioch, in view of some similarity between the heretical teachers and those opposed in the Gospel of Matthew.

91. The Revelation to John

"Revelation" (from a Greek word translated in English "apocalypse") means a disclosure of something hidden and unknown. In early Christianity it came to designate Jewish and Christian books which disclose the hidden future of the world.

The Revelation to John is the second great apocalypse in our Bible. The first is the book of Daniel (see chap. 35). Many other books of this sort existed among the Jews between about 165 B.C. and A.D. 135 (for example, I Enoch, the Assumption of Moses, the Apocalypse of Abraham, II Esdras, II Baruch, and several of the Dead Sea Scrolls; for a discussion of some of these, see pp. 396-403).

Christians also developed this kind of literature—for example, our Revelation to John, the Christian edition of the Jewish book the Testaments of the Twelve Patriarchs, the Ascension of Isaiah, and the Apocalypse of Peter.

1. Characteristics of Apocalyptic Literature

a. Characteristics of form: lengthy dialogue between the seer or prophet and an angelic interpreter; emphasis on the shock to the seer from what he sees; lengthy exhortations by the seer to the readers in view of what he has learned; the attributing of the visions and the book that reports them to some ancient man of God; the use of symbols drawn from nature (lions, bears, rams, locusts, trees, rushing water, etc.) to represent human and supernatural realities; and loose organization of materials.

b. Characteristics of thought: belief in the nearness of the end of the age and the destruction of this evil world; division of all history into time periods preordained by God; good versus evil (God, the angels, and the righteous locked in struggle with Satan, the demons, and the wicked); the coming of the kingdom of God by God's direct act or through the Messiah; and the new world as a return to the glories of paradise.

Apocalypses were meant to encourage the righteous to be faithful to God and their religious duties in times of persecution. The apocalypses said to the righteous: Trust in God, be loyal to his requirements, and soon the

The high altar of Zeus at Pergamum; possibly "Satan's throne" (Rev. 2:13)

dominion of evil authorities will come to an end; God will vindicate you and open to you a New Age of righteousness and glory. Apocalypses have been called "tracts for bad times."

2. Interpreting Apocalyptic Literature

We must make at least three approaches to this kind of literature:

a. An effort to understand communication which uses metaphors, symbols, and impressionistic drama

b. A consideration of the family characteristics of apocalyptic literature and the extent to which an individual apocalypse shares in these

c. An examination of the times in which the book was written and the circumstances of the original readers

Apocalypses do not yield their messages easily to us. We must study history to understand their references to ancient events and persons and the symbols and concepts of their cultures. We must first ask what the books had to say to their original readers. Then, and then only, can we ask what they have to say to people of our day and to us personally. Patient effort in this study will reward us, and God's truth will shine through the often strange symbols.

3. Theme and Outline of the Revelation to John

Theme: The triumph of Jesus Christ and his church

I. Introduction (1:1-11)

A. Superscription: The source, content, and importance of the revelation (1:1-3)

B. The greeting, doxology, and announcement of Christ's coming (1:4-8)
C. The occasion of the visions (1:9-11)
II. The visions (1:12–22:5)
   A. The heavenly Christ's message to the churches through his servant John (1:12–3:22)
     1. The description of the heavenly Christ (1:12-16)
     2. John's reaction and his commission to write (1:17-20)
     3. The letters to the seven churches (2:1–3:22)
   B. God's plan for the church's final triumph (4:1–22:5)
     1. The source of the church's triumph: God (chap. 4)
     2. The agent of the church's triumph: Christ, the Lion-Lamb (chap. 5)
     3. The grand strategy of the church's triumph (6:1–22:5)
       a. The seal judgments (6:1–8:1)
       b. The trumpet judgments (8:2–11:19)
       c. The anti-church "triple alliance": the certainty of its defeat and of the church's victory (12:1–15:4)
       d. The bowl judgments (15:5–16:21)
       e. The fall of Babylon (Rome) (17:1–19:5)
       f. God's final victory through Christ over all the powers of evil (19:6–20:15)
       g. The new heaven and the new earth (21:1–22:5)
III. The epilogue: Authentication of the message; warning not to alter the prophecy; the consequences of acceptance and rejection; benediction (22:6-21)

4. Literary Form

The book is both Jewish and Christian in form. It is both a letter and an apocalypse. It has a greeting like a letter (1:4-5a), messages of a practical and urgent nature to seven churches (chaps. 2–3), and the customary epistolary benediction (22:21). Most of the book consists of visions bearing the characteristics of an apocalypse (see above).

In theology the book is also Judeo-Christian. The author joins the Old and the New Covenants and shows that God's purpose involves Moses and Jesus, Israel and the church. We hear both the Song of Moses and the Song of the Lamb (15:3). The God of this book is the God of beginnings (Alpha) and endings (Omega) (1:8; 21:6).

One scholar has suggested that the book was patterned after Greek drama, and that it has seven acts, with seven scenes in each act. Though the number seven is indeed prominent in the book, a systematic arrangement by sevens seems not to have been the author's intention. And it is unlikely that a Christian writer who warned the church so urgently against paganism would have couched his message in theatrical form.

The book's form as a letter-apocalypse is unique.

5. Date and Circumstances

Irenaeus (c. A.D. 180) said that John "saw the revelation . . . at the close of Domitian's reign" (A.D. 81–96). Some scholars have argued for a date in the reigns of Vespasian (69–79) or Nero (54–68) for the writing of this book, but the evidence for its composition during the reign of Domitian is impressive.

Domitian, a moody, jealous, unpredictable tyrant, cut down all persons whom he regarded as a threat to his authority. He seems to have demanded worship of himself as Lord and God. He executed his niece's husband on a charge of atheism (perhaps the refusal to recognize his deity) and exiled the niece. Both may have been Christians. Many others were condemned for following a Jewish way of life— evidently for not supporting the religion of the state.

Domitian apparently was not an indiscriminate persecutor of the church, as Nero had been in Rome, but his selective terrorist tactics aroused fear in the church as well as in Roman society. The letter from Clement of Rome to the church at Corinth, known as I Clement (c. A.D. 95), refers to "the sudden and repeated misfortunes and calamities which have befallen us." The spread of emperor worship in the

provinces (for example, a new temple for the cult of the emperor in Ephesus in the time of Domitian) certainly put pressure on the Christians of Asia Minor, where the seven churches of the Apocalypse were located.

It is evident that some Christians there had suffered persecution. The author of Revelation had been exiled to Patmos, a penal island for political offenders, because of his loyalty to Christianity (1:9). A Christian named Antipas, a member of the church at Pergamum, had been put to death for his fidelity to Jesus (2:13). The phrase "where Satan's throne is" probably refers to Pergamum, which was the center of emperor worship. The author says that some Christians at Smyrna will face death (2:10). The souls under the altar are martyrs (6:9); others are to be killed as these have been (6:11). The harlot "drunk with the blood of the saints and the blood of the martyrs of Jesus" (17:6; cf. 18:24; 19:2) suggests that fierce persecution lies ahead for the church, if it has not already begun. An hour of trial is coming to the whole world (3:10), that is, the awful days before the end, known in Judaism as the Messianic Woes. Through the suffering of those days the righteous will be purged for membership in God's kingdom and the wicked warned and called to repentance.

The hostility of the Jews (2:9; 3:9) made the Christian plight more bitter. They undoubtedly slandered the church before governmental authorities, seeking thus to dissociate Christianity from Judaism. The charge made by the Jews may have been that Christians, by preaching "King Jesus," were traitors to the emperor and the state (*cf.* Acts 17:7).

The outer pressure on the church from emperor worship and the Jews was matched by inner dangers: false teaching, false living, and false attitudes. Nicolaitans, possibly named after Nicolaus of Antioch (Acts 6:5), seem to have advocated Gnostic teaching (see pp. 304-7). Ephesus had succeeded in silencing these heretics, Pergamum tolerated them, but at Thyatira they dominated the church. The controversy they evoked split the church (2:2-4). In some of the churches spiritual apathy and self-satisfaction, due in part to material prosperity, threatened their future.

Both external and internal conditions point to the period A.D. 90–95 as the time of the writing of the Revelation to John.

6. Author and Place of Writing

The author's name appears several times as John (1:1, 4, 9; 22:8). No title identifies him, such as "apostle." He wishes to be known as a "servant" of Christ, "brother" and fellow-sufferer of the readers (1:1, 9). He bases his right to be heard on a direct commission from Christ through a vision (1:10-11). He apparently was well known to the readers.

Which John was he? Possibilities are:

a. John, Son of Zebedee, the Apostle

Early church tradition (*e.g.,* Justin, Irenaeus, Clement of Alexandria, Origen) held to authorship by John the Apostle. Though there were some doubters in the second century, serious question about John the Apostle's authorship arose only in the third century, when Dionysius of Alexandria pointed out strong differences in style and thought between the Apocalypse and the Gospel of John. He credited the Apocalypse to some other John. From then on, the Eastern part of the church challenged the Apostle John's authorship.

Some scholars have cited evidence found in the book in support of authorship by the Apostle, such as the high sense of authority and inspiration the writer possessed, and the similarities in language and thought to the Gospel of John (Christ as "the Word," "the Lamb," the Shepherd; the references to water and manna; the strong contrast between truth and falsehood, light and darkness, God and the devil; the love of the number seven).

Against authorship by John the Apostle, one may argue as follows: there are some grounds for believing that John the Apostle may have died at the same time as his brother James (A.D. 44—Acts 12:2); there is no claim to apostolic authorship in the Apocalypse and no mention of facts about the life of Jesus such as an apostle would know; the references honoring the apostles in Rev. 18:20; 21:14 would hardly have come from an apostle; the differences from the Gospel of John are as strong as the similarities; and in no case could similarities prove John the Apostle wrote the Apocalypse, since his authorship of

THE
SEVEN CHURCHES of ASIA

0   50   100   150

Miles

PERGAMUM

THYATIRA   PROVINCE

SARDIS

SMYRNA   PHILADELPHIA

EPHESUS   OF

LAODICEA

PATMOS   ASIA

Aegean Sea

Mediterranean Sea

the Gospel has not been indisputably established.

b. John the Elder

Papias (c. A.D. 140) referred to an "Elder John," who passed on information about the Apostle John and the other apostles. "Elder" here probably has a special meaning: it designates a member of a group who formed a link between the apostles and the next generation. They were especially ven-erated for their contact with the original apostles (see p. 339).

It may be that this Elder John made use of apocalyptic material which originally came from the Apostle John or that he was later confused with the Apostle John.

c. An Otherwise Unknown Prophet John

Though he is unknown to us, it is obvious that the author was well known to the readers. Like the Old Testament prophets, he spoke with great authority. John was his real name, not an assumed name. The Semitic flavor of his Greek and his thorough acquaintance with the Hebrew Old Testament argue that he was a Jewish Christian.

The question of authorship cannot be settled yet, but possibilities b and c seem more likely than a.

The place of the visions was Patmos, but Patmos was not necessarily the place of writing. It is possible that after the author's release, he wrote in the city of Ephesus, where conditions were more favorable.

7. Interpretation of the Visions

Many ways of interpreting the visions have been proposed in the course of Christian history.

a. The Contemporary-Historical View

The supporters of this view regard the visions as wholly concerned with the circumstances of the author's time and with the future the author believed would soon issue out of those circumstances. They recognize as valid the author's picture of the struggle between good and evil and the certainty of God's and the church's ultimate triumph, but they do not believe any long-range predictions of future world events can be made from the visions.

b. The Continuous-Historical View

Some interpreters have seen the visions as containing predictions of events from the time of the author to the end of the world. They think that the letters to the seven churches predict successive periods in the life of the church—from the apostolic age to the second coming of Christ. A few have claimed to find references to the heresies of early Christian centuries, the spread of Islam, Charlemagne, the Crusades, the pope, etc. They have seen the book as a prophetic summary of the whole history of the church.

c. The Futurist View

According to this view, the visions refer entirely or principally to the final days before the end of the world. Futurists give little attention, if any, to the historical setting of the book and to how the book would have served the needs of the church in the latter part of the first century. In fact, they hold that only Christians in the time of fulfillment (i.e., at the end of time) could possibly understand the visions. According to this point of view, John wrote the book for the church at the end of history, not for the church of his own age.

d. The Mythic-Symbolic View

This approach holds that the author's purpose was to teach religious truths, not to predict the future. He accomplished this by the use of myths and symbols. To us they are at first grotesque and obscure, but behind them can be found meaningful theological concepts.

A symbolic interpretation appeared in the church of Alexandria around the end of the second century. According to this, the seven heads of the beast (chap. 13) are seven deadly sins; the ten horns of those heads are the serpent-like powers of sin; the stinging tails of the locusts (9:10) are the destructive power of immoral teachers in the church; the warrior on the white horse (19:11 ff.) is Christ, who opens heaven by giving the white light of truth to those who receive him; etc.

In our time some scholars have attempted to translate the myths and symbols into concepts of our time to show what they teach about man, his struggles in the world, his resources, and his future. They hold that the myths should not be taken literally and turned into predictions of future events but taken for what they really are: dramatic, poetic, mythic-symbolic representations of universal truth, whose meaning is not narrowly related to any set of historical circumstances.

Basic questions are before us today. Should we understand the book as primarily for ancient Christians and secondarily for us, or vice versa? And should we regard the book as a source of knowledge about world events of our time and of the future, or should we see it as a symbolic portrayal of religious truth about the ultimate triumph of God and the righteous? In short, is the book dramatized Christian theology, or is it predictive prophecy? Or is it both?

The basic rule of modern biblical study is that we must interpret all literature, including that in the Bible, in the light of the historical situation out of which it arose and to which

it was addressed. When we have determined as clearly as possible its meaning for its first readers, then and only then can we inquire about its meaning for us (see pp. 58-59). This fundamental principle eliminates *b* and *c* above and leaves a combination of *a* and *d* as the soundest approach.

8. Message to the First Readers

The author strikes several important notes:

a. The church will come to its final inheritance only if it remains absolutely faithful to God and to his Christ in the bitter persecutions which have begun and which will increase in fury.

There can be no doubt that the writer designed the book to meet the threat to the church caused by state-enforced emperor worship and by the hostility of the Jews. The author was exiled because of his fidelity to Jesus Christ (1:9); Antipas the faithful witness was killed (2:13); Christians were being slandered by Jews and some were about to be imprisoned (2:9-10); a group of martyrs under the heavenly altar awaits yet other martyrs (6:9-11); Rome will be "drunk with the blood of the saints and the blood of the martyrs of Jesus" (17:6; *cf.* 18:24). The book is "a call for the endurance of the saints, those who keep the commandments of God and the faith of Jesus" (14:12).

If Christians die "in the Lord," they are "blessed" (14:13). Christ and the author make extravagant promises to faithful Christians: the right "to eat of the tree of life, which is in the paradise of God" (2:7); "the crown of life" (2:10); "the hidden manna," miraculously preserved from the wilderness days for consumption at the banquet of the coming Messiah (2:17); "power over the nations" (2:26); and face-to-face fellowship with God in the glories of the new heaven and earth (21:1–22:5).

b. The church can meet its test only if it becomes strong and pure within.

Wrong teaching, wrong living, and wrong attitudes threaten the church from within. The church must deal with immoral Nicolaitans in a spirit of love, not in hostile criticism. Complacent, lukewarm Christians must repent and be revived. Involvement in pagan practices must cease. The church must be clothed in "fine linen, bright and pure," that is, in righteous deeds (19:8).

c. The time of trouble which is coming on the whole world is God's way of purging the righteous and calling the nations to repentance.

That the church must pass through "the hour of trial" (i.e., the period of distress preceding the coming of the Messiah with the New Age) and not be rescued miraculously by a "rapture" (I Thess. 4:17) is everywhere apparent in the book (7:14; 13:7, 10; 14:12; 17:6; 18:24).

But the hour of trial is a test for all the people on earth (3:10). The test shows both God's judgment on their sins and his desire that they should repent (9:20; 11:13; 16:11). The judgments of the seals, the trumpets, and the bowls are God's warnings to the wicked in the hope of their repentance. The God of the book of Revelation is a God who delights not in damning the wicked but in saving them.

d. Those who trust in God and are loyal to his Christ are eternally secure, but those who serve the devil and their own evil desires will perish.

Many members of the church will experience the first death (martyrdom) but will not be harmed by the second death (the lake of fire—2:11; 20:6, 14). True Christians will bear God's seal upon them so that the judgments that are coming on the earth will harm only the wicked (7:1-8). The entire faithful church (symbolized by the number 144,000), though martyred (7:14; 13:7; 17:6; 18:24), will dwell securely with the Lamb on Mount Zion (14:1-5). Though seemingly conquered by the two beasts (the Roman Empire with its self-deifying emperors, aided by the imperial priesthood), they are actually victors. They are the "first fruits for God and the Lamb" from all mankind (14:4). These faithful martyrs will enjoy special sovereignty with Christ (20:4-6).

God will destroy wicked idolaters, the mighty men of the earth, the free and the slave, the rich and the poor—all who have been deceived by false gods and false worship, inspired by the devil (6:15-17; 13:11-17)—together with the corrupt civilization they have built (chaps. 17–18).

e. The second coming of Christ and his final victory over the forces of evil is at hand.

It is clear that the author was talking about events of the near, rather than the distant, future. He stated flatly that "the time is near" (1:3), that the events "must soon take place" (22:6), and that Christ said he was coming soon (22:7, 12, 20). Therefore his book should not be sealed up, as the book of Daniel was sealed in prospect of long delay in fulfillment (Dan. 12:4). The Revelation to John should rather be left unsealed for urgent reading, since "the time is near" (22:10).

The whole early church believed that the second coming of Christ was near (Rom. 13:11-12; I Cor. 7:29-31; James 5:8; I Pet. 4:7; I John 2:18; and the above passages of the Revelation to John). The delay in the coming caused scoffers to doubt the validity of the hope; those who continued to believe had to defend their faith (II Pet. 3:3-10).

Even Jesus seems to have expected the coming of the final kingdom during his own generation (Mark 9:1; 13:30), though he insisted the time was known only to the Father and under his authority (Mark 13:32; Acts 1:7). The disciples were to hope and to work meanwhile (Luke 19:12-27; Acts 1:8), making the most of the remaining time by living righteously and speaking the Word boldly (Col. 4:2-6; Eph. 5:3-16).

Since the author was talking about events in the near future, largely connected with the fall of Rome, we can hardly suppose that he had in mind specific events of twenty centuries later, as some interpreters of today claim.

9. The Value of This Book for Us

If the book does not predict specific historical events of our time, what, if anything, does it say to us? It ministers to our spirits; it does not satisfy curiosity about the future. Among its great teachings are:

a. This world was created by a God of wisdom, power, righteousness, and mercy. As Creator he alone has the right to receive the worship of the creatures he has made. The rulers of earth have no real authority over the souls of men. Men should worship God.

b. God has a plan for the world, and he will carry it out to the end. The sorrows, the gains, the losses, the wars, the famines, the adventures and misadventures of the generations gone by and of our own somehow are used by God to contribute to a great pattern that he is weaving.

c. The goal toward which the universe is moving is intimate spiritual fellowship between God and man in an order free from sin and human limitation. In the new Jerusalem there will be no need to separate God from a defiled people by temple walls, for sin and sinners will have passed away, and he then can dwell freely among his people in intimate fellowship.

d. People are prepared for this holy fellowship by faith in the redemption accomplished by Jesus Christ. For John, Jesus is the Lamb of God who has "freed us from our sins by his blood" (1:5). In and through his death Jesus brought men to God.

e. If the church is to realize its high destiny, it must not allow itself to become contaminated by the immorality and paganism that surround it. It must remain faithful to righteousness in all of life's relationships.

For Further Reading Concerning the Books of the New Testament

Brown, R. E.; Fitzmyer, J. A.; and Murphy, R. E., eds. The Jerome Biblical Commentary, Vol. II, 1968.
Fuller, R. H. A Critical Introduction to the New Testament, 1966.
Guthrie, D. New Testament Introduction, 1965.
Harrison, E. F. Introduction to the New Testament, 1964.
Kee, H. C.; Young, F. W.; and Froelich, K. Understanding the New Testament, 3rd ed., 1973.

McArthur, Harvey K., "Computer Criticism," The Expository Times, 1965, pp. 367 ff.
Morton, A. Q., and McLeman, James. Christianity in the Computer Age, 1965.
———. Paul: The Man and the Myth, 1966.
Robert, A., and Feuillet, A. Introduction to the New Testament, 1965.
Spivey, R. A., and Smith, D. Moody. Anatomy of the New Testament, 1969.
Wikenhauser, A. New Testament Introduction, 1963.

BACKGROUND

Time Line of the Bible (by Periods)

B.C.	PERIOD	LITERATURE	CANONIZATION
1280	Wilderness Sojourn and Conquest of Canaan	Oral traditions Mosaic law	
1200	THE JUDGES	Early poetry G or T (earliest basic narrative)	
1020	THE UNITED KINGDOM	N (L, S, J1) Source J (Yahwist Epic) Court history of David (II Samuel 9–20; I Kings 1–2)	
922	THE	E (Elohist Epic) Deuteronomic laws Royal annals of Judah and Israel	
	DIVIDED	Amos (some later additions) Isaiah (most of chaps. 1–35)	
	KINGDOM	Hosea (later additions) Micah 1:2–3:12; 6:1–7:7 NJE joined Deuteronomy	

B.C.	PERIOD	LITERATURE	CANONIZATION
		Zephaniah (later additions) Nahum 2:1–3:19 Jeremiah 1–45 (later additions) Habakkuk	Deuteronomy—the basis of Josiah's reforms (622 B.C.)
587	THE BABYLONIAN EXILE	Ezekiel (later additions) Lamentations Obadiah Holiness Code (Lev. 17–26) Deuteronomic History (Deuteronomy–II Kings) P Source Isaiah 40–55	

539	THE
	PERSIAN
	PERIOD
		Haggai
		Zechariah 1–8
		Isaiah 56–66
		NJEDP joined to form our
		   Pentateuch
		Malachi
		Job (later additions)
		Ruth
		Chronicles-Ezra-Nehemiah
		Joel
		Zechariah 9–14
		Collection of Psalms and
		   Proverbs completed
		Jonah
		Song of Solomon
			Pentateuch canonized
			at time of Ezra
			(c. 400 B.C.)

332	THE GREEK PERIOD	Ecclesiastes Tobit; Letter of Jeremiah Esther Wisdom of Jesus, Son of Sirach Daniel Judith	Prophetic Books by 200 B.C.
143	INDEPENDENT HASMONEAN KINGDOM	I Maccabees I Esdras; Additions to Esther; Baruch; Additions to Daniel II Maccabees	

B.C.	PERIOD	LITERATURE	CANONIZATION
63	ROMAN	Wisdom of Solomon Prayer of Manasseh	
	PERIOD to end of New Testa- ment times	Letters of Paul Four Gospels Acts of the Apostles Hebrews I Peter Revelation to John; II Esdras Letters of John Pastoral Epistles (I-II Timothy, Titus) James, Jude II Peter	
c. A.D. 125			Paul's letters collected by c. A.D. 125 Our Four Gospels pre- eminent by A.D. 150–70 "The Writings" of the Jewish Scriptures closed by c. A.D. 200 Athanasius' Festal Letter (A.D. 367) listed our 27 New Testament books Councils of Hippo (393) and Carthage (397, 419) elevated our 27 New Testament books Council of Trent (1546) determined canon of Bible for Roman Catholics

92. The Manuscripts and the Search for the True Text

A "manuscript" is a document which was "written by hand." Until the invention of printing with movable type in the fifteenth century, all written materials were produced by hand. Making copies of books of considerable length was a laborious and expensive process. And the copies were likely to be full of errors, because of the limitations of eye, ear, and hand (see p. 366).

1. Biblical Languages and Writing

As far as we know, writing began in picture form in Mesopotamia about 3500–3300 B.C. Soon the pictures were modified into wedge-shaped ("cuneiform") impressions on clay.

In Egypt another form of picture-writing, called hieroglyphics, appeared shortly before 3000 B.C.

Sometime before 2000 B.C. the Canaanites created a script which was based on syllables. In the seventeenth century B.C. they invented an alphabet of some two dozen simple pictures, each representing one consonantal sound. The alphabet then passed from the Canaanites, or Phoenicians, to the Greeks and to modern languages.

We do not know how early the Hebrews began to write.

It is possible that Abraham could have written in some script or scripts, for writing had existed in Mesopotamia, from which he came, for more than a thousand years before his birth. A Canaanite script was in use when he came into Canaan, perhaps in the twentieth century B.C.

It is virtually certain that Moses could write, in view of his education at the court in Egypt and the availability of several scripts—Egyptian hieroglyphics, Akkadian cuneiform, and Canaanite scripts.

It is unlikely, however, that Abraham wrote any materials now contained in our book of Genesis, and nothing that can be attributed with certainty to Moses is now present in the Pentateuch (see pp. 82-83).

After the Exodus from Egypt, when the Israelites settled in Canaan in the thirteenth century B.C., they adopted the language of the Canaanites and their alphabetic writing.

After the Babylonian exile (sixth century B.C.) the Aramaic language and script came into common use among the Jews of Palestine. This language, closely related to Canaanite and Hebrew, originated in upper Mesopotamia in the late second millennium B.C. and spread widely as a language of international trade and diplomacy. It was used before the exile in Hebrew diplomatic circles (II Kings 18:26) and was perhaps spoken in Samaria by Assyrian colonists who settled there after the destruction of the Northern Kingdom in 721 B.C. (II Kings 17:24).

At the time of Jesus the popular language and script of the Jews was Aramaic. The Old Hebrew language continued in use in learned circles (*e.g.,* among the rabbis of Jerusalem and the priests of Qumran by the Dead Sea), and residents of Judea apparently still spoke it to some extent. Old Hebrew was emphasized in periods of religious and national revival, as during the Maccabean period of the second century B.C. and the Bar-

Photo by H. T. Frank

Codex Regius, a nearly complete manuscript of the four Gospels written in compressed uncials (8th century). Two endings to the Gospel of Mark are shown here.

Photo by H. T. Frank

An 11th century manuscript written in cursive Greek

Kochba revolt of A.D. 132–135. That Jesus knew Hebrew is evident from the fact that he read the lesson from the prophet Isaiah in the synagogue service at Nazareth (Luke 4:16-19), but the Galilean disciples probably did not know this language very well.

The language of the New Testament is Hellenistic Greek, which came mainly from the Attic dialect of the classical period (before c. 300 B.C.). The conquests of Alexander the Great (336–323 B.C.) and the resultant spread of the Greek language and culture through many lands brought about a simplification of the Attic dialect and produced a truly popular language for the empire. Though some literary men of the Hellenistic period imitated the Old Attic language, most of the Greek used was the "garden variety" sort—the language of the marketplace, the home, informal letters, and business documents.

Although some of the New Testament is written in a fairly cultivated Greek (such as parts of Luke-Acts, the Letter to the Hebrews, some sections in Paul's letters), most of the books use the common (*Koine*) Greek of everyday life.

Three styles of Greek handwriting were in use from intertestamental times to the invention of printing in the fifteenth century: (1) a cursive, informal hand for rapid writing of receipts, letters, deeds, and accounts; (2) a formal "book hand," consisting of separated letters somewhat like our capital letters, for literary works (the letters are called "uncials," meaning "a twelfth part" of a line of writing); (3) a flowing "book hand," with small connected letters, formal enough in style to be used for literary works (the letters are called "minuscules," meaning "rather small").

It is likely that Paul wrote to his churches in the cursive script. When his letters were later copied as literature, the scribes put them in the uncial script until about the ninth century, when minuscule writing came into use. No early cursive manuscripts of the New Testament have been found. Some nine tenths of all New Testament manuscripts known today are minuscules. Many of the most important New Testament manuscripts are in uncial letters (see pp. 362-65).

2. The Materials of Biblical Writings

In ancient times many materials were used for writing: clay (shaped into tablets), stone, skins of animals, bark, wood, bone, linen cloth, several metals, broken pieces of pottery (potsherds), and papyrus (a kind of paper made from the pith of the papyrus plant).

a. Skins (Leather)

In Egypt the use of skins for writing goes back to at least 2500 B.C.

How early skins were used for writing among the Hebrews is not known. Jeremiah's scroll, cut up with a scribe's knife and burned in 604 B.C. by Jehoiakim (Jer. 36:23), was of leather or papyrus. Either could have been cut with such a knife.

The wide use of leather scrolls by the Qumran community for their sacred books (see pp. 399-403) points to a tradition about the use of leather for such writings. The Talmud later required all copies of the Law used in public worship to be written on skins of clean animals and to be in roll form—no doubt a requirement of long standing.

The earliest leather scroll fragments from Qumran date to the third century B.C. Approximately one fourth of the manuscript finds at Qumran are copies on leather of the text of the Hebrew Scriptures. The manuscripts seem to have been prepared by scraping and rubbing, not by tanning. A superb example of a biblical scroll is the great Isaiah A manuscript, dating from about 100 B.C. It is 24½ feet long and 10½ inches wide, with 54 columns of text on 17 sheets (see photograph on p. 361).

Refinements in the preparation of skins yielded material now known as parchment and vellum. The skins were soaked in limewater and the hair scraped off; then they were rubbed with pumice, treated with chalk, and stretched on a frame. A fine writing surface resulted. Vellum, made from calfskin, provided the best surface of all.

Roman writers credited Eumenes II, king of Pergamum (197–159 B.C.), with the invention of parchment. Actually it is more likely that he was the principal developer of its manufacture and use.

In the fourth century A.D. the best copies of the Scriptures, such as our present Codex Sinaiticus and Codex Vaticanus (see pp. 362-63), were on vellum, and in book, rather then roll, form.

b. Papyrus

The home of papyrus was Egypt, where from early times, possibly as early as 3000 B.C., the tall plant from the marshes of the Nile delta furnished pith for the manufacture of a suitable writing material.

The triangular-shaped stalk, about the thickness of a man's wrist and from 6 to 15 feet in height, was cut into sections about a foot long. The pith was then cut into thin strips. These were laid vertically side by side, with another layer placed horizontally on top, and with some kind of glue bonding the two layers. Pressed until dry, cut to the size wanted, and smoothed with a piece of ivory or a shell, these layers became a sheet of relatively smooth and durable writing material.

Sheets normally varied in size from 6 by 9 inches to 12 by 15 inches. A roll of papyrus was made by overlapping the edges of individual sheets and gluing them together, until the desired length was achieved. The standard roll for literary works was about 30 to 35 feet long. Individual sheets were used for business accounts, brief letters, and the like. Writing was normally done on the side where the strips and fibers ran horizontally.

The original New Testament writers almost certainly used papyrus sheets and rolls. Such brief letters as Philemon and II and III John were written on single sheets. The Gospel of Matthew would fill a 30 to 35-foot roll.

When the New Testament writings were collected toward the end of the first century and during the second (see pp. 31-35), they were copied not on rolls but in papyrus codices (books).

For several centuries tablets of wood, waxed and held together at one edge by cords or clasps in a kind of book, had been in use among the Romans for memoranda, accounts, school exercises, etc. Parchment was sometimes substituted for wood and a parchment notebook created for special texts.

It was natural that papyrus sheets should be used in this same way. The individual sheets were folded down the middle and several of them laid atop one another with their folds adjacent. When several such folded groups of sheets were brought together and sewed at the folds, a book was created. The sheets were arranged so that vertical strips of papyrus would face one another on opposite pages and horizontal strips likewise.

Scrolls were bulky and awkward to unroll. This book form was convenient to use and economical through its use of both sides of the papyrus. It was thus suitable for the large collections of writings contained in the Christian Bible.

Strangely, the secular literature of the time continued to be written on rolls during early Christian centuries. And since the Jewish synagogues used rolls (scrolls) for their Scriptures, it is possible that Christians, particularly Gentile ones, wished to differentiate their Scriptures from those of Judaism, on the one hand, and from secular literature, on the other.

Writing on leather, parchment, vellum, and papyrus was done with a reed pen and ink. Some pens were split at the point to form a nib, and some were frayed like a small brush. One type of very black ink was made from lampblack (or smoke black) mixed with a solution of gum and water. The mixture was sometimes dried into small cakes and moistened when used. Another type came from nutgalls, green vitriol, and water. This ink turned in time into a rusty brown color.

3. The Manuscripts of the Bible

a. Old Testament Manuscripts

All original manuscripts of the Old and New Testament books have perished. When these books were first circulated, the original manuscripts were not thought particularly valuable. When they were later copied, the only concern of the copyists and their readers was for an accurate reproduction of their text.

The Jews retired their worn-out manuscripts to the Geniza—a chest or room in the synagogue for storage of holy, but no longer usable, books. Antiquity in a manuscript was no asset from their point of view. Fortunately for us, one such Geniza with its precious manuscripts, some dating as far back as the sixth century A.D., was found in Cairo, Egypt, at the end of the nineteenth century. From it came a flood of information about the text of Old Testament books.

Until the discovery of the Dead Sea Scrolls in 1947, the most ancient Old Testament manuscript known (the Cairo Prophets) came from the end of the ninth century A.D. The Dead Sea Scrolls have given us manuscripts that were made more than 1,000 years earlier; indeed, some fragments among the Dead Sea Scrolls go back to the third century B.C. (see below). It is possible now to trace the history of the transmission of the Old Testament text as never before.

Some important Old Testament manuscripts are:

(1) Fragments from Qumran cave 4
     Pieces of Exodus, I Samuel, Jeremiah (c. 250–175 B.C.).
(2) The Nash Papyrus (c. 150 B.C.)
     The Ten Commandments and the *Shema* (Deut. 6:4).
(3) Isaiah A Scroll (c. 100 B.C.)
     A complete copy of the text of Isaiah on seventeen sheets of leather.
(4) Isaiah B Scroll (first century A.D.)
     A fragmentary scroll of Isaiah, consisting mostly of chaps. 35–66 and some pieces of earlier chapters.
(5) The Dead Sea Psalms Scroll (first century A.D.)
     40 canonical psalms and some non-psalm material.

Photo by John C. Trever

The great Isaiah Scroll from Qumran

(6) The Targum [Translation] of Job (*c.* A.D. 50)

A fragmentary manuscript containing parts of Job 17:14–36:13 and 37:10–42:11 in Aramaic.

(7) The Cairo Prophets (A.D. 895)

The oldest dated Hebrew manuscript now known; contains both the former and the latter prophets of the Hebrew canon (see pp. 17-18).

(8) The Leningrad Codex (A.D. 1009)

A complete Old Testament text.

b. New Testament Manuscripts

Greek manuscripts of the New Testament fall into four classes: papyri, uncials, minuscules, lectionaries.

As of 1967 the following numbers of manuscripts had been catalogued in each group: papyri, 81; uncials, 266; minuscules, 2,754; lectionaries, 2,135—making a total of 5,236.

Students of the New Testament are exceedingly fortunate to have so many Greek manuscripts from which to reconstruct the original text of the

New Testament books. By contrast, students of the Greek classics are much more limited. We are told that Homer's Iliad is preserved in 457 papyri, 2 uncials, and 188 minuscules and that the writings of Euripides are preserved in 54 papyri and 276 parchment manuscripts (B. M. Metzger, *The Text of the New Testament,* 2nd ed., 1968, p. 34).

(1) The Papyrus Manuscripts

Almost all the papyri consist of, or clearly came from, manuscripts in book (codex) form. Only three or four are fragments from papyrus rolls. As noted above (p. 359), the church from the beginning of the second century found the papyrus codex cheaper and more convenient for its Scriptures.

The following are some of the important papyrus manuscripts and the symbols commonly used for them:

P⁴⁵—Chester Beatty Papyrus I

30 leaves (mostly of the text of Mark, Luke, and the Acts) out of some 220 leaves originally devoted to the four Gospels and the Acts, dating to the third century

P⁴⁶—Chester Beatty Papyrus II

86 leaves out of an original 104, containing Romans (some portions missing), Hebrews, I and II Corinthians, Ephesians, Galatians, Philippians, Colossians, I Thessalonians (portions missing), dating to about A.D. 200

P⁴⁷—Chester Beatty Papyrus III

10 leaves out of an original 32, containing Rev. 9:10–17:2, dating to the late third century

P⁵²—Papyrus Rylands Gk. 457

A tiny fragment (2½ by 3½ inches), containing John 18:31-33, 37-38 and dating to the first half of second century; the earliest of all manuscripts and fragments of any part of the New Testament

P⁶⁶—Bodmer Papyrus II

104 pages and fragments of 46 other pages of the Gospel of John (1:1–6:11; 6:35–14:26; parts of 14:29–21:9), dating to about A.D. 200

P⁷⁵—Bodmer Papyrus XIV–XV

102 pages out of an original 144 pages, containing most of the Gospels of Luke and John and dating to the early third century

(2) The Uncial Manuscripts

א—*Codex Sinaiticus* (the symbol is the Hebrew letter Aleph)

Discovered in the middle nineteenth century at the monastery of St. Catherine at Mt. Sinai by Constantin von Tischendorf.

Remaining today are 390 leaves out of about 730 leaves, 242 of the Old Testament and 148 of the New, including in the latter category the Epistle of Barnabas and the Shepherd of Hermas. Now in the British Museum.

Written in Egypt or Palestine about the middle of the fourth century and later corrected by several scribes. The only known complete copy of the Greek New Testament in uncial writing.

A—Codex Alexandrinus

Apparently brought from Egypt to Constantinople by Cyril Lucar, patriarch of that city, and presented by him in 1627 to Charles I of England.

Remaining today: 773 leaves out of about 820, 630 of the Old Testament and 143 of the New, with parts of Matthew, John, and II Corinthians missing. Now in the British Museum.

Written in the fifth century and corrected by later scribes.

B—Codex Vaticanus

For many centuries the property of the Vatican Library in Rome, though largely unknown to the outside world until 1889–90, when photographs of it appeared.

Remaining today: 759 leaves out of 820, 142 being of the New Testament.

Missing: portions of Genesis, Psalms, and Hebrews; the entire books of I and II Timothy, Titus, Philemon, Revelation, and the books of Maccabees.

Written in the fourth century, a tenth or eleventh century corrector having retraced the dim letters.

C—Codex Ephraemi Rescriptus

A palimpsest (re-scraped and reused) biblical manuscript of the fifth century, many of the pages rewritten in the twelfth century with a Greek translation of 38 discourses of St. Ephraem.

Remaining today: 209 leaves, 64 of the Old Testament and 145 of the New.

Missing: most of the Old Testament and the whole of II Thessalonians and II John.

Underlying biblical text deciphered by Constantin von Tischendorf in 1841–42 and improved on by later scholars with the help of ultraviolet rays.

D(05)—Codex Bezae Cantabrigiensis

Presented in 1581 by Theodore Beza of Geneva to the library at Cambridge University.

Contains most of the four Gospels and the Acts and a fragment of III John, all in both Greek and Latin, with the order of the Gospels being Matthew, John, Luke, Mark.

Written in the fifth or sixth century.

Photo by H. T. Frank

A page from the Lindisfarne Gospels, one of the most beautiful of the biblical manuscripts, showing the Latin text with an Anglo-Saxon paraphrase between the lines

W—Codex Washingtonensis

Brought from Egypt in 1906 by C. L. Freer and now in the Smithsonian Institution.

Contains the four Gospels in the order Matthew, John, Luke, Mark.

Dates from the late fourth or early fifth century.

Θ—*Codex Koridethianus* (the symbol is the Greek letter *theta*)

From Koridethi in the Caucasian Mountains and now at Tiflis, in the Soviet Socialist Republic of Georgia.

Contains the four Gospels.

Dates from the ninth century but reflects in part a third to fourth-century text type.

(3) The Minuscule Manuscripts

All are from the ninth century and later. They are more than ten times as numerous as the uncials (see p. 361). Some of them are ornate, one in gold letters on purple vellum.

Many are descended from early types of texts.

Of particular importance are the following: Families 1 and 13; and MSS. 33, 81, 565, 579, 1739, 2053. (For details see bibliography on p. 367.)

(4) The Lectionaries (Books of scripture readings for worship services)

The church adopted the synagogue practice of reading designated passages of Scripture in services of worship according to a set pattern throughout the year. In the church, beginning with Easter, the texts were assembled in proper sequence for reading on Sundays, Saturdays, and (in some manuscripts) on weekdays.

The lectionaries often preserve old forms of the New Testament texts.

It is not feasible to cite any individual lectionary manuscripts here, since they exceed 2,000 in number and scholars have not yet studied all of them in detail.

(5) Families of Manuscripts

As ever more manuscripts were discovered and their texts studied, it became apparent that they could be grouped into families on the basis of the errors and deliberate changes they contain.

The families or types now recognized are:

(a) The Alexandrian (including Codex Vaticanus, Codex Sinaiticus, P^{46}, P^{66}, P^{75}), probably the family preserving most nearly the original text of the New Testament

(b) The Western (including Codex Bezae and in part Codex Washingtonensis)

(c) The Caesarean (including Codex Koridethianus, minuscule families 1 and 13, and many lectionaries)

(d) The Byzantine (including Codex Alexandrinus in part and many late uncials and minuscules)

4. The Search for the Original Text

The Hebrew and Greek texts used by the translators of the King James Version rested on only a few—and often rather unreliable—manuscripts of the many now in the hands of biblical scholars. Today we know better than those translators did what the original wording of the biblical books was (see pp. 38-39).

Readers of the Bible in most contemporary versions can see from bracketed sections of the text and from footnotes that some words and passages they are accustomed to in the King James Version were contributed by persons other than the original authors of the books.

In Isaiah in the Revised Standard Version one finds a number of footnotes referring to "one ancient MS" which offers a different word or phrase from the one printed in the text. The reference is to the great Isaiah A scroll from Qumran, which presents some significant differences from the traditional Hebrew text. These footnotes point out also that the ancient versions offer other words, phrases, and meanings.

Mark 16:9-20, John 5:3-4, and John 7:53–8:11 contain material not present in the best manuscripts. These passages are bracketed or printed in a footnote in most recent English translations.

What led to the differences that appear in ancient manuscripts? And what kinds of differences are there?

Ancient copyists and editors are responsible for the differences. The changes they introduced were of two types: unintentional and deliberate.

Often copyists saw incorrectly; they confused look-alike letters, skipped lines of text, wrote words twice, transposed letters, etc. In commercial establishments, where several copyists wrote from one person's dictation, careless pronunciation, lack of attention, weariness, and distractions led to frequent mistakes. Errors arose also from writing passages from memory and from inaccurately judging whether marginal notes were to be included or omitted.

Sometimes copyists and editors deliberately altered language they regarded as rough, harmonized parallel passages where differences should have been preserved, removed discrepancies, left out or changed statements which were contrary to their theology, and filled out manuscripts that were damaged or thought incomplete.

In the search for the original text of the books of the Bible two general kinds of evidence from the manuscripts are important.

The first is *external* evidence. What manuscripts support a given reading (wording) and what is the date of those manuscripts or, more important, what is the type or family of text embodied in them? If a manuscript is of early date, its readings gain in importance. However, a relatively late manuscript may contain important readings, if it was copied from a significant early manuscript or manuscripts.

Important also is the geographical distribution of the manuscripts. A reading supported by manuscripts from a wide geographical area has a certain strength.

The second kind of evidence is *internal*. What is the original author most likely to have written in a passage where the manuscripts differ? Did a copyist smooth out a difficulty in the text? Is there an obvious blunder in copying? Was there a deliberate change in a passage for stylistic or doctrinal reasons? Which reading would most naturally explain the rise of the variants? In general, the more difficult reading is to be preferred, since a copyist would likely try to smooth out a difficulty. In view of the tendency of copyists to combine and preserve alternative readings of the manuscripts before them, the shorter reading is often to be chosen by us.

And which reading best fits the style, vocabulary, and theology of the original author? Which makes most sense in the immediate context?

By attending to such considerations manuscript variants can be evaluated and the true original text be approximated.

For all the differences among the manuscripts of the Bible, scholars generally agree that no central doctrines of the Judeo-Christian faith are undermined by these differences. As a whole, the copyists were remarkably faithful to the texts they reproduced.

For Further Reading

Greenlee, J. Harold. *Introduction to New Testament Textual Criticism,* 1964.
Kenyon, Frederic. *Our Bible and the Ancient Manuscripts,* 1958.
Metzger, Bruce M. *The Text of the New Testament,* 2nd ed., 1968.

93. Biblical Lands and Archaeology

1. The Lands

The bitter struggle between the Israelis and the Arabs during the last forty years or so and the recent clamor of Western powers for the oil of the Middle East have led to new interest in the lands at the eastern end of the Mediterranean Sea. Iran, Iraq, Syria, Lebanon, Israel, Jordan, and Egypt have become household words.

We may not fully understand the complex geography of this area and the reasons for the intense competition for its largely arid lands; but there is a general feeling that the future of mankind on this planet is somehow tied in with the destiny of this part of the world. All thinking people know that a major explosion in the Middle East would set fire to the whole world.

The importance of the Middle East is not simply a modern phenomenon. Here were the cradles of civilization: the Tigris-Euphrates river valley (modern Iraq); the long, green gash in the desert called Egypt; and the in-between "bridge" lands of Syria and Phoenicia (Canaan).

The land stretching from the Persian Gulf northwestward up the Tigris-Euphrates valley, through northern Syria, and down the Phoenician coast to the Sinai desert has been called "the Fertile Crescent." Here there was water enough—from the two great rivers in the east and the rainfall in the west—to sustain settled life and international trade and travel.

a. The Hebrews

The ancestors of the Hebrew people came from around the city of Haran in the territory of Paddan-aram of Upper Mesopotamia. One tradition in Genesis (11:28, 31; 15:7) connects the family of Abraham originally with Ur, near the Persian Gulf.

That the area around Haran was the family's homeland is evident from the identity of some place names of that region with personal names in Abraham's family; for example, Nahor, the name of both Abraham's grandfather and his brother, was also a place name (Nakhur) in the vicinity of Haran (cf. Gen. 24:10). From the fifteenth-century Nuzi tablets (found at Nuzi near the upper Tigris River) we learn that the laws and customs of Upper Mesopotamia in the first half of the second millennium B.C. agree in general with those referred to in the stories about the Patriarchs in Genesis (see p. 385). Abraham sought a wife for Isaac from Nahor, near Haran (Gen. 24:10), and Jacob fled to his relatives there (Gen.

THE FERTILE CRESCENT

SCALE OF MILES

0   100   200   300

29:4 ff.) The family was Aramean (Deut. 26:5) or at least from that stock that later became known as Aramean.

We do not know exactly why Abraham journeyed along the Fertile Crescent to its western end in Canaan. We read that he traveled there in response to a divine command (Gen. 12:1 ff.). One scholar has suggested that the Patriarchs were donkey caravaneers who followed the trade route to Canaan (and Egypt) and then turned to sheep- and cattle-raising in Canaan when opportunities in caravaning declined. However this may be, they did remain in Canaan and adopted the Canaanite language, of which Hebrew is a dialect.

The words "Canaan" and "Phoenicia" both mean "red-purple," apparently from the red-purple wool dye for which the country was famous. Several biblical references use "Canaanite" in the sense of "trader" or "merchant" (Zech. 14:21; Prov. 31:24), probably meaning traders in the dyeing industry.

b. The Geography of Palestine and the Surrounding Region

The structure of the lands along the eastern end of the Mediterranean is very complex. The mountains, valleys, gorges (rifts), and plateaus run mainly north-south, but also northeast to southwest, northwest to southeast, and in some cases east-west.

In southern Canaan ("Palestine," so named from the Philistines who lived there after about 1200 B.C.), starting from the Mediterranean shore, one travels eastward across (1) the coastal plain, (2) the rolling hills and the central mountains, (3) the Jordan Valley (Rift), and (4) the eastern plateau, which merges into the Arabian desert. The north-south lines, particularly of the coastal strip, have provided access to upper Canaan and Syria (and thus to Mesopotamia) and to Egypt on the southwest.

The great diversity in the surface of the area has always made political, economic, religious, and social unification difficult. With elevations ranging from about 9,100 feet above sea level at the crest of Mt. Hermon to about 1,290 feet below sea level at the Dead Sea, climates and flora and fauna varied widely. Houses of mud or sun-dried brick with straw roofs were adequate in the warm climate of the Jordan Valley, whereas stone houses roofed with beams of wood overlaid with branches and clay mixed with small stones, and furnished with braziers for heating in winter, were needed in the hill country. Because of its great diversity of land, climate, peoples, and natural life, Palestine is the world in miniature.

The lands occupied by the tribes of Israel east and west of the Jordan River covered some 10,000 square miles—about the size of Vermont. From Dan to Beersheba, the traditional north-south limits of Israel (*e.g.,* Judges 20:1), was about 145 air miles. In times of expansion, as under King David, Israelite territory took in southern and central Syria, including Damascus, and reached to the Red Sea on the south, a north-south distance of some 350 air miles.

In latitude Palestine falls in a line with southern Spain and Georgia in the U.S.A. In general its climate has two seasons: a rainy winter, with snow in the Lebanon mountains and occasionally in Jerusalem; and a long, dry summer.

The average temperature in Jerusalem (elevation *c.* 2500 feet) in August is about 74° F and in January about 48° F. During the same periods other places have temperatures as follows: Gaza 79° and 56°; Jericho (*c.* 825 feet below sea level) 88° and 59°; Acre 79° and 56°; Safad (elevation *c.* 2800 ft.) 75° and 45°.

The early (or "former") rains, which soften the ground for plowing, fall in October and November. The heavy rains come in December-February. And the late (or "latter") rains, which ripen the crops, descend in March and April.

The amount of rainfall varies widely according to elevation and location. The rain clouds come from the west. Where the mountains are highest (in Lebanon), annual rainfall reaches 60 inches. One high point in Galilee (Safad) has about 45 inches (New York City has some 40 inches), Jerusalem about 26 inches (London about 23 inches), the region south of Hebron to Beersheba about 10 to 15 inches, and Jericho about 5 inches. Northern Transjordan receives 20 to 30 inches because of the lower mountains of Samaria to the west, and southern Transjordan—opposite the higher Judean mountains—is dry (5 to 15 inches).

If the rains do not come at the right time in the right amounts, crops fail and famine may result. In Elijah's time a famine lasted more than two years (I Kings 17:1; 18:1-2). Other famines are reported in the Old Testament (*e.g.,* Gen. 12:10; 43:1; II Sam. 21:1; II Kings 6:25) and in the New (Acts 11:28). In recent times (1957–60) three very dry years caused considerable hardship in Israel and Jordan.

Prayers for rain (Zech. 10:1; *cf.* Joel 2:23) and rain-inducing ceremonies—such as occurred each day during the Feast of Tabernacles when water from the spring of Gihon was poured through a silver funnel into the ground below the altar of burnt offering of the temple in Jerusalem—were an important part of Israel's religious and economic life. The prophets of Israel strongly contended that Yahweh, not the Canaanite God Baal, controlled the rains and the crops the rains brought (Amos 4:7-8; Hos. 2.5, 8; Deut. 11:14; 28:12; Jer. 5:23-24; 14:22).

Palestine by our standards is a land poorly endowed, on the whole. The central portion of the country consists of limestone hills and mountains without much depth of soil. Once covered with considerable forests, the mountains have been denuded through the centuries and the sparse soil has eroded as a result of the heavy winter rains. Small valleys among the hills are suitable for agriculture, but thousands of square miles are of little use. The maritime plain, the plain of Esdraelon (Megiddo), parts of the Jordan Valley, and the valleys of Galilee are relatively good, especially when irrigated.

The cut-up, rocky, and generally arid country doomed its inhabitants to hard work for a minimal level of existence. Modern Israelis have produced remarkable results through fertilization, reforestation, irrigation, swamp drainage, industrialization, and the like.

The shoreline of the country, in contrast to Phoenicia (modern Lebanon) to the north, is largely unsuited for sea-going commerce. The only natural harbor is at Acre-Haifa. Herod the Great constructed an artificial harbor at Caesarea (22–10 B.C.) by building a huge seawall into the Mediterranean. Solomon built a port on the Gulf of Aqaba (at Ezion-geber). Today Eilat, near that site, serves the Israelis for that purpose.

The ancient Hebrews looked on their land as "a good land, a land of brooks of water, of fountains and springs, . . . a land of wheat and barley, of vines and fig trees and pomegranates, a land of olive trees and honey" (Deut. 8:7-8). As compared to the desert areas in which Israel wandered for a generation in the time of Moses, the description is justified. But it is the poorest part of the Fertile Crescent, and life on this international bridge was difficult and insecure economically and militarily. The Promised Land was no Garden of Eden; hence, seers and prophets looked forward to the coming of that Garden in the latter days.

2. Archaeology in the Lands of the Bible

a. Its Origin and History

Modern archaeology began at the time of Napoleon's invasion of Egypt in 1798. Along with his troops Napoleon took 175 scholars, artists, and scientists to study and draw the antiquities of Egypt. Their results were published in seven volumes between 1809 and 1822.

The most important discovery by the French in Egypt was the Rosetta Stone. While constructing a fort at Rosetta in the Nile delta in 1799, soldiers came across a large black stone inscribed in three scripts: hieroglyphic, Demotic (a form of Egyptian script), and Greek. Working from the Greek, which turned out to be a translation of the Demotic and hieroglyphic text, scholars by 1822 unlocked the secret of hieroglyphics and henceforth were able to read the thousands of inscriptions on the monuments of ancient Egypt.

Archaeological digging in Mesopotamia was undertaken by the French and British in the middle of the nineteenth century. Paul Botta of France discovered the palace of the Assyrian king Sargon II (721–705 B.C.) at Khorsabad. Henry Layard of England uncovered at Nimrud (ancient Calah) the palace of Asshur-nasir-pal II (884–860 B.C.) and at Kuyunjik (ancient Nineveh) the palaces of Sennacherib (704–681) and Asshurbanapal (668–627).

In the palace of Asshurbanapal the king's library of thousands of clay tablets was discovered by Rassam, Layard's associate. The tablets contained letters, contracts, dictionaries, grammars, receipts, tables of measures, lists of events, hymns, prayers, religious epics, medical reports, astronomical and astrological calculations, etc. They dealt with almost every field of learning known to scholars of that time. Among them were the Assyrian stories of the Creation and the Flood, which George Smith of the British Museum identified and interpreted (1872–76).

The deciphering of the wedge-shaped (cuneiform) writing was achieved mainly by an English army officer, Henry Rawlinson. At the risk of his life, between 1843 and 1847, he copied and finally interpreted Old Persian and Babylonian inscriptions placed by Darius I (522–486 B.C.) on a great rock cliff at Behistun, Persia.

Research in Palestine got under way near the beginning of the nineteenth century. The location of biblical towns was explored in 1838 by Americans Edward Robinson and Eli Smith. Their results were published in an important work entitled *Biblical Researches in Palestine, Mount Sinai, and Arabia Petraea* (1841).

French and British scholars carried on both surface and sub-surface explorations in the latter half of the nineteenth century. It was the British genius Flinders Petrie, who in 1890 at a mound in southwestern Palestine (Tell el-Hesi) set sub-surface exploration on a scientific basis. His careful methods of recording results, his recognition of mound stratification (see below), and, most of all, his discovery that levels of occupation in a mound can be dated from the type of pottery recovered from the different levels revolutionized archaeological method.

Photo by H. T. Frank

Excavators at work on top of Tell el-Hesi

Refinements of Petrie's methods and the introduction of still other techniques have gone on in the twentieth century under Reisner and Fisher, W. F. Albright, G. Ernest Wright, Kathleen Kenyon, and others. In the twentieth century, mounds all over Palestine, Transjordan, Syria, and Mesopotamia have been excavated with immensely significant results for our understanding of the Bible and the history of the Middle East.

b. Archaeological Method

(1) The first principle of modern, scientific archaeology is excavation by layers or strata.

It was in 1870 that Heinrich Schliemann learned at ancient Troy that ruined cities often had formed through the centuries into layered mounds, with the earliest layer at the bottom and successive cities atop each other, somewhat in layer-cake fashion. Flinders Petrie's expedition verified this at Tell el-Hesi in 1890, as has every scientifically conducted excavation of a mound since.

The Old Testament refers to a mound of this kind by the Hebrew word *tell,* a word whose meaning was not known when the King James Version was made in 1611. In that version Joshua 11:13 reads: "But as for the cities that stood still in their strength, Israel burned none of them, save Hazor only." The Revised Standard Version correctly renders the word *tell* by "mound" as follows: "But none of the cities that stood on mounds did Israel burn, except Hazor only."

Cities were destroyed in many ways: by earthquake, flood, volcanic eruption, fire, military conquest and pillaging, and abandonment due to the failure of the water supply. In many cases surviving inhabitants rebuilt the city, or a portion of it, on account of its many advantages: its strategic location (often on a prominent hill, at a good harbor, alongside a trade route, by a good source of water); its peculiar sanctity for some tribe or nation, often as a place of worship; its relative impregnability (its basically strong city walls, defensive towers, and water tunnel). It was easier and wiser to level off the destroyed buildings, patch up the walls, and rebuild inside the walls than start from scratch at a new location.

The layers, of course, are not well defined over a whole mound. Pits for storage and foundation trenches for buildings intrude into earlier levels. Stone from previous buildings appear in a later level. The top of the mound may be somewhat rounded, so that a stratum of occupation may not have the same elevation everywhere. A rebuilding in some period may have extended only over a portion of the mound. Confused layers are a headache for the archaeologist, but he must do his best to untangle them lest he confuse cultures of different historical periods.

Today archaeologists do not excavate a stratum over its whole extent. To do so would remove forever all evidence of that layer and thus leave nothing for future excavators, who will certainly have better methods than ours. But, more importantly, the removal of an entire stratum leaves the excavator and other archaeologists no on-the-spot evidence of the sequence of layers to serve as a check on interpretation of the history of the mound. Thus archaeologists today excavate only selected areas of mounds and leave "balks" (unexcavated strips with carefully cut vertical sides) running across the area being excavated. Here the layers of occupation can be observed in the vertical face of the balks.

The mounds vary in size from an acre or two to two hundred acres

(Hazor). In height the ruins vary from a few feet, representing one or two layers, to some eighty feet and eighteen layers (Bethshan).

(2) The second principle of scientific archaeology is the classification and study of objects according to their form and style—known technically as "typology."

Flinders Petrie in 1890 discovered that pottery from the different layers of a mound varied considerably in form, decoration, type of materials used, and methods of making. He finally proved, against considerable opposition, that the different types of pottery came from different cultural periods, that the types can be dated approximately (by comparison with types known from datable contexts in Egypt and elsewhere), and that pottery can establish the chronology of the layers of a mound.

The use of pottery as a clue to dating is now far advanced. Not only are pieces and intact pottery objects dated from knowledge of types, but their age can be determined by heating the pottery and measuring the radiation. Most buried mineral substances absorb the natural radiation given off by uranium, potassium, and thorium in the earth. Absorbed radiation is released when the substance is heated. Since the rate of absorption is known and the amount absorbed can be measured when heated, the time of burial in the earth can be determined. The technique is known as "thermoluminescence."

All objects discovered are helpful in dating a level: the types of tools made (from stone, copper, iron); the tombs and burial objects; the shapes and materials of houses and public buildings; the jewelry; etc.

When organic matter turns up in excavations, such as plants, wood, charcoal, shell, antler, burned bone, dung, and peat, the radiocarbon method of dating can fix its approximate age.

All living things absorb carbon 14 from the atmosphere. At the death of the organism no further carbon 14 is absorbed. Through the process of decay, the carbon 14 begins to disintegrate at a rate known to scientists. By measuring the amount of carbon 14 remaining in the specimen and by knowing the rate of atomic disintegration, the time when that specimen was alive can be calculated (with a 5 to 10 percent possibility of error). The method is valid back to about 20,000 years.

When dates have been established for a particular layer, all objects can be studied together and conclusions drawn about the kind of people who fashioned them and their relationship to one another and to their environment.

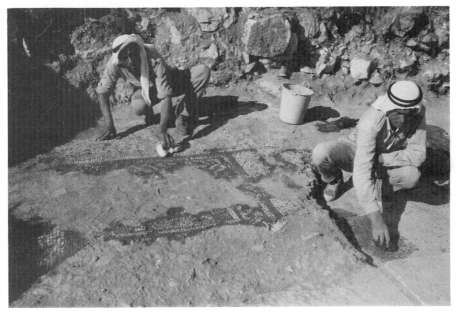

Arab workmen carefully uncover a Roman mosaic in the temple of Zeus on Mt. Gerizim

(3) The third principle in scientific archaeology is systematic and accurate recording of data.

When a layer has been picked apart and most of the objects removed from their context, the excavator must have the kind of records that will allow him completely to visualize that layer exactly as he found it.

Full and accurate recording calls for aerial photographs of the mound; a contour map of it; the division of the mound into numbered areas and strata so that objects can be labeled to indicate their exact place of discovery; photographs and sketches of important objects in their context; detailed, scale drawings (by a competent architect) of important areas of a stratum; cataloging of distinctive pieces of pottery and of isolated objects (jewelry, seals, statues, coins, inscriptions, etc.) with sketches, descriptions, and photographs; drawings and photographs of balks.

After the excavating is over, study of the artifacts may go on for long periods in laboratories and libraries. Geologists may analyze the stones to determine their type and place of origin. Botanists and zoologists may examine floral and faunal remains. Epigraphers and architects may pore over inscriptions and cornices. Historians of religion and culture may study the figurines and the statuary.

The aim of archaeology is not simply to recover ancient objects to fill museums but to understand as completely as possible the mentality, the manner of life, the achievements, the social relationships, and the relation to their physical environment of the people who made them. By understanding man's past, direction for his present and future may be gained.

3. Archaeology and the Bible

Archaeological research in Palestine and the rest of the Middle East has thrown light on man's life on this planet long before any parts of the Bible were written. So far as we can tell, the earliest parts of the Bible were composed after Israel settled in Canaan (thirteenth century B.C.), though the traditions on which they rest may go back far before that time (see pp. 95-96).

How long man has been on the earth is uncertain. Responsible estimates, based on discoveries at Olduvai Gorge in East Africa and elsewhere, are around 600,000 years or more. From the terraces of the Nile valley and northern Iraq have come crude stone tools estimated to be 200,000 or more years old. Caves in the side of Mt. Carmel have yielded skeletons and flint tools of 50,000 to 75,000 years ago.

Men moved out of caves, settled in villages, and began cultivating wild grains and domesticating animals around the ninth millennium B.C. Jericho, in the Jordan Valley, one of the oldest villages known, was in existence by about 8,000 B.C.

It is evident that Abraham, Isaac, Jacob, and Joseph—long thought to have lived near the dawn of history, which Archbishop Ussher in the seventeenth century put at 4004 B.C.—were latecomers on the human scene. These patriarchs are now dated between the twentieth and the seventeenth or early sixteenth centuries B.C. And the writing of the Bible began several centuries later still. Though the Bible and the characters with which it deals seem very old to us, on the time chart of human life on this planet the Hebrews and their literature came into being only yesterday.

A discussion of how the Bible and archaeology are related is almost impossible in brief compass. All we can do here is indicate types of relationship and offer a few examples of each. You may explore the vast and fascinating field of archaeology through the books suggested at the end of this section.

a. The Bible Guides the Work of Archaeologists.

In many parts of the world there are no literary sources to assist archaeologists in interpreting what they find or even to give them some idea what to look for. The archaeological task is much easier when ancient literary sources, such as the writings of Herodotus and Strabo (Greece), Manetho (Egypt), Josephus (Palestine), and the Bible in both its Testaments, give help in forming the questions and in putting together the jigsaw puzzle of ancient data.

Without the Bible archaeologists could make little out of the Lachish Letters, for example. In 1935 and 1938 twenty-one ostraca (inscribed pieces of pottery) were found in the ruins of Tell ed-Duweir (biblical Lachish), eighteen of them from the ashes of a guardroom at the city gate.

The letters are puzzling and fragmentary. Many of them were written by a Hoshaiah from an outpost near Lachish to a military commander named Yaosh at Lachish. They refer to situations apparently described in the book of Jeremiah. We read in them about signals—evidently fire or smoke—between two cities of southwestern Palestine, Lachish and Azekah. These towns were the last, apart from Jerusalem, to fall to the Babylonian army (Jer. 34:7). We hear of a journey of a commander named Coniah, the son of Elnathan, to Egypt, probably to enlist the help of Egypt against the Babylonians (cf. Jer. 37:5, 7-9). There is reference to a prophet who passed along a letter and said "Beware!"—possibly Jeremiah, who warned against resisting the Babylonians (Jer. 38:2-4). There is mention of princes who are "weakening the hands," apparently of the Judean army and of people in general in their resistance to the Babylonians—a charge laid against Jeremiah (38:4).

It is clear from the Letters, the burned level in which they were found, and the book of Jeremiah that they were written in 588 B.C. during the siege of the cities of Judah by Nebuchadnezzar. Without the biblical help in understanding them, they would be largely meaningless.

b. Archaeology Uncovers Places and Objects Mentioned in the Bible.

Robert Koldewey, at the turn of the twentieth century, uncovered magnificent Babylon, the creation of Nebuchadnezzar II (605–562 B.C.). Nebuchadnezzar designed and constructed a great system of fortifications. It included the double Ishtar Gate in a double city wall. Rows of bulls and dragons in enameled brick covered the gate. He built a processional way, lined with enameled lions, temples, and palaces. He rebuilt the Tower of

Babel, which was already a thousand years old in his time. This Tower is visible today only in its ground plan. We can see what it looked like in the much better preserved ziggurat at Ur.

Hezekiah's water system (II Kings 20:20; II Chron. 32:30), by which he ensured water for Jerusalem in case of siege by the Assyrians, is still visible in Jerusalem. His workmen dug a tunnel from the Spring of Gihon outside the city through about 1750 feet of limestone under the city to a reservoir inside the wall. An inscription in Hebrew on the tunnel wall described how the tunnel was cut through from both ends. This inscription is now in the Museum of the Ancient Orient in Istanbul.

We can stand today before the "wonderful stones" which the disciples referred to as they left Herod's temple (Mark 13:1). Recent excavation outside the huge retaining wall of the temple area has exposed many finely chiseled stones belonging to that wall. Some of them are more than thirty feet long and are set together without mortar. To maneuver them into place, to say nothing about cutting them out, is a feat greatly to be admired.

Archaeologists have uncovered many of the cities in which Paul preached. Notable is Corinth, where excavation has been going on since 1896. This fine city, the capital of Achaia and seat of the proconsul, was built on two terraces under the towering rock Acrocorinth (1886 feet high).

Photographing archaeological remains

At the city's center was the marketplace (agora) with its stately gate (propylaea), colonnades, shops, and basilicas (buildings for courts and public assembly). Towering over the marketplace on a hill just west was the Temple of Apollo. Seven of its original thirty-eight columns still stand.

At the center of the marketplace archaeologists found a large stone platform (bema) which served as a speakers' rostrum. Here the Roman proconsul and other officials heard petitions and addressed the public. The platform, originally covered with white and blue marble, had marble benches at the back and part way along the sides. Flanking the platform at ground level on either side were waiting rooms with marble benches, apparently for petitioners expecting audience with city officials. This platform is probably the very place where Paul was brought before the proconsul Gallio by his Jewish accusers (Acts 18:12-17).

We can now see and handle many of the coins mentioned in the New Testament. We can inspect the remains of synagogue buildings from near the time of Jesus. Scrolls like he read from (Luke 4:17) came from a cave at Qumran by the Dead Sea. Lamps like the wise and foolish maidens carried (Matt. 25:1-12) fill our museums.

Imagination has now given way to sight as a result of the work of archaeologists.

c. Archaeology Supplements and Explains Many Biblical Data.

The cherubim mentioned in the Old Testament as guarding the way to the tree of life (Gen. 3:24), as supporting the throne of God (Ps. 80:1), as overshadowing the ark of the covenant (Exod. 25:18-20), and as decorating the walls of the main room (the Holy Place) of the temple of Solomon (II Chron. 3:7) turn out to be winged lions with human heads, such as supported and decorated the thrones of ancient kings. They were not rosy-faced little angels as imagined by famous modern painters.

The ivory house built by Ahab (I Kings 22:39) was a house decorated with ivory ornaments (some inlaid in furniture and others hung on walls). The excavations of 1931–35 at Samaria uncovered many ivories of this type alongside the royal quarters in the debris of the Assyrian destruction of 721 B.C. For Ahab to have built a house entirely of ivory would have been a feat that even an Egyptian pharaoh's wealth could hardly have achieved!

Especially valuable information has come from excavations in territories occupied by Israel's neighbors. The peoples who throng the pages of the

Old Testament—the Amorites, the Horites, the Hittites, the Canaanites, the Arameans, the Philistines, the Egyptians, the Assyrians, the Moabites, the Ammonites, the Chaldeans, etc.—are now well known. Their cultures and their influence on Israel have come into clear view. Today we understand the stage on which Israel played out its life and destiny in a way undreamed of in the nineteenth century.

Biblical references to weights and measures (the cubit, the span, the omer, the ephah, the shekel, the talent, etc.), to utensils, to musical instruments, to weapons, to clothing, and the like are no longer mysterious, thanks to archaeology.

d. Archaeology Probes the Bible.

Archaeology raises important questions about information in the Bible and forces readers to look for adequate answers.

The book of Genesis tells of Abraham and Isaac having dealings with Abimelech, "king of the Philistines" (21:22-34; 26:1, 8, 14-15).

However, Abimelech is a Canaanite, not a Philistine, name. Furthermore, archaeological evidence from Egypt shows clearly that the Philistines and other sea peoples invaded Egypt and Canaan early in the twelfth century, that they were repulsed by Ramesses III in several battles, and that they then settled down as vassals of the Pharaoh on the coastal plain of southern Canaan. From the twelfth century on, this coastal plain became known as "the land of the Philistines." There were actually no Philistines in Canaan in the early second millenium B.C., the time of Abraham and Isaac.

The explanation of the biblical references to the Philistines in the time of Abraham and Isaac seems to be that the writer in Genesis used the later name of the country in referring to events of earlier history. Abimelech actually was king of Gerar in Canaan, a territory that later was known as "the land of the Philistines." Hence he was called anachronistically "king of the Philistines," much as we might in our time speak of "the first governor of New York" when we should more accurately speak of "the first governor of New Netherland" (the earlier name).

Archaeology also raises questions about the detailed biblical stories of the capture of Jericho and Ai (Josh. 6–8).

A generation ago a British archaeologist reported that he had found the walls of Jericho (double wall) at the time of Joshua and evidence of Jericho's destruction around 1400 B.C. by earthquake and fire. Recent excavations have shown that the double wall dates to a much earlier time (late third millennium B.C.) and cannot have been the one referred to in the biblical story. No walls certainly in use in the time of Joshua have come to light. In fact, only small traces of a town of the general period of Joshua (Late Bronze—c. 1550–1200) remain, and this town seems to have been destroyed and abandoned somewhere around 1325 B.C.—probably nearly a century before Joshua's time. Erosion of the mound has eliminated almost all trace of the fourteenth-century city. And there is no archaeological evidence for a city on this mound in the centuries following Joshua.

These archaeological conclusions raise serious questions for students of the Bible. Was Jericho a small city in the fourteenth century, and was it perhaps captured by people related to the Hebrews, who had never been in Egypt, rather than by Joshua and the children of those Hebrews who had come out of Egypt? And was the capture less dramatic than that described in Joshua 6? Is the story a folktale, recorded long after the Hebrew invasion, with a historical nucleus but considerable embellishment as well?

Ai, the next city conquered by Joshua—according to the book of Joshua —is as much a puzzle as Jericho. Extensive archaeological investigations at et-Tell near Bethel have shown that there was no city there in the thirteenth century—the assumed time of Joshua—and that there was a gap in the occupation of the site from about the middle of the third millennium B.C. until the twelfth century.

This archaeological evidence raises many questions. Is the true site of ancient Ai modern et-Tell? (Recent explorations in the area have answered in the affirmative.) Is the story of the capture of Ai in the book of Joshua legendary or etiological, *i.e.,* an attempt to explain the origin of a known ruin by a tale without substantial historical foundation? Is the story the record of the capture of nearby Bethel, which story somehow became wrongly attached to Ai? Or was the city of Ai, captured by the Hebrews, the small twelfth-century city found there—thus requiring the changing of the date of Ai's capture by a century and perhaps a different view of the nature of the Hebrew conquest?

Scholars are not yet in a position to offer conclusive answers to the puzzle of both Jericho and Ai, but the data from archaeology have forced them to examine the biblical material carefully for possible solutions.

e. Archaeology Confirms the Bible.

The conclusion that Israel's historical traditions were written down long after the events occurred (see chap. 9) led many scholars in the late nine-

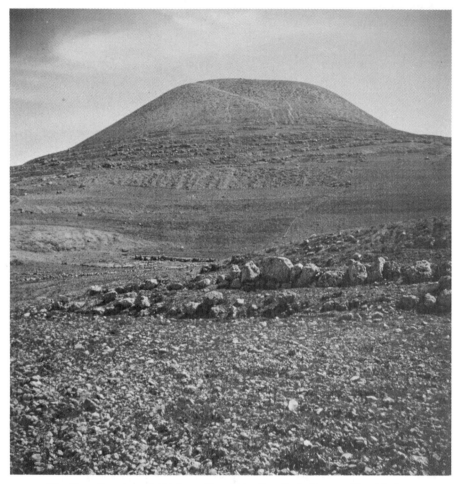

The Herodium near Bethlehem, Herod the Great's fortress and burial place

teenth and early twentieth centuries to say that the Pentateuch, and particularly the book of Genesis, contains little solid history but rather fanciful folktales about the forefathers of Israel. These scholars believed that any knowledge about Israel's past to be gained from these stories would concern the time when they were written down (ninth–fifth centuries B.C.), not the time with which they were supposed to deal (early second millennium B.C). They argued that the Patriarchs (Abraham, Isaac, Jacob, and the twelve sons of Jacob) probably were not historical individuals but personifications of clans, tribes, or ethnological groups or even originally deities.

Today we know that the cultural and sociological background of the patriarchal stories is generally accurate. We now have thousands of clay tablets contemporary or nearly contemporary with the patriarchal period. We have learned from them about the peoples, the names of places and persons, the laws, and the customs of those times. We see now that the stories about the Patriarchs fit remarkably well the times in which they are set.

The Mari tablets of the eighteenth century, from the upper Euphrates River region, show that some names in Abraham's family were used in Upper Mesopotamia in that time, sometimes as names of cities.

The Nuzi tablets of the fifteenth century, from the upper Tigris River area, throw light on several incidents in the patriarchal stories. We learn that it was the custom at Nuzi for childless couples to adopt a slave in order to have an heir and that, in the event of the birth of a true son, the adopted son would have to give way as principal heir (cf. Gen. 15:1-4). At Nuzi a childless wife was obliged to provide her husband with a concubine. The concubine and her offspring were protected legally against expulsion (cf. Gen. 16:1-4; 21:8-11). We can now understand Rachel's theft of Laban's household gods (Gen. 31:30-35) in light of the information in the Nuzi texts that the position of head of the family and, accordingly, inheritance rights were associated with possession of the household gods.

Israel's relationships with surrounding peoples during its long national history, as presented in the Old Testament, receives support from archaeology: the conquest of Canaan by both an intensive initial campaign and later tribal assimilation; the struggle with the Philistines by Saul and David; Solomon's extensive building operations and his cultural and commercial relationships with the people of Tyre; the encroachments of, accommodation to, and conflicts with the Assyrians and Babylonians; the Babylonian exile and subsequent restoration. In thousands of ways archaeology has shown that the biblical picture of the history of Israel is essentially accurate.

The same is true for the background of the life of Jesus and Paul. The kings, the governors, the places, the social, economic, and religious conditions of the times, and many of the major events—all receive general, and often specific, confirmation from archaeology.

Archaeology has shown that the historical memory of Israel and the New Israel (the church), preserved in their long transmitted traditions, was surprisingly accurate.

   f. Archaeology Reveals the Uniqueness of the Judeo-Christian Religion and Literature.

Since the latter decades of the nineteenth century archaeological discoveries have let us see striking similarities and differences between the life,
thought, and literature of the Hebrews and other Near Eastern peoples,
particularly the Canaanites and the inhabitants of Mesopotamia.

The stories of Genesis 1–11 are parallel at many points to tablets found
in the library of Asshurbanapal (see p. 373) and elsewhere in Mesopotamia. Three examples are:

   (1) The Creation Epic (*Enuma Elish*)
This is written on seven clay tablets of about one thousand lines. It
concerns the origin of the gods from the union of the powers of chaos
(Apsu and Tiamat) and the subsequent war between the gods and Tiamat
in which Marduk destroys Tiamat and from her body forms heaven and
earth. Marduk establishes the sun, moon, and stars and creates man from
the blood of a god (Kingu, Tiamat's general) in order that he may be the
servant of the gods. The gods acclaim Marduk as their chief and exalt
Babylon as his place of worship.

Both the Hebrew story (Gen. 1:1–2:3) and this Assyrian-Akkadian creation epic refer to a watery chaos at or near the beginning of all things
(Tiamat equals *Tehom*, Hebrew for "deep" in Gen. 1:2). The division of
Tiamat into heaven and earth equals the dividing of the waters from the
waters (Gen. 1:6-7). The order of creative acts is the same. The seven days
of creation equal the seven tablets. And so on.

The differences, however, are far-reaching. In the Hebrew story God is
the transcendent creator of matter. In the Assyrian-Akkadian myth god is
male and female matter, and the many gods originate from sexual union.
In the Hebrew story man is a creature, not essentially divine, who is made
in God's likeness to be lord of the created order. In the other story man is
essentially divine, since he was made from the blood of a god. He is to be
the servant of the gods in order that the gods may be at ease. The Hebrew
story is properly a creation story, whereas the other is a glorification of
Marduk and his place of worship.

   (2) Enki and Ninhursag: A Paradise Myth
This myth comes from Nippur, in lower Mesopotamia. The six-column
tablet on which it is written dates to the first half of the second millennium
B.C.

It describes the land of Dilmun, the Sumerian "Abode of the Blessed," as a pure, clean, and bright land where there is no sickness, sorrow, old age, or death, and where fresh water from the earth rises to nourish plant and human life.

The god Enki successively impregnates the Sumerian mother goddess Ninhursag and their female offspring to the fourth generation. The last (the great granddaughter) yields to him only after a gift of cucumbers, apples (?), and grapes. Enki's semen is used to produce eight different plants, which, when eaten by Enki in order to know their nature, cause him to become sick in eight organs of his body, one being a rib. Ninhursag then curses Enki and subsequently heals him through the birth of eight deities, who in some way cure the sick members of his body.

Similarities to the Garden of Eden story in Genesis 2–3 are: the perfection of Dilmun; the fresh water from the earth (Gen. 2:6); the birth of the successive goddesses seemingly without pain or travail to the mother (cf. Gen. 3:16); the eating of the plants which resulted in a curse (Gen. 3:17-19); the reference to the rib (in Sumerian the word for rib means "to make live"), thus perhaps explaining why Eve ("the mother of all living"—Gen. 3:20) was taken from Adam's rib.

The differences, of course, are immense—notably, the crude, sexually-oriented polytheism and the lack of any ethical content in the story from Nippur.

(3) The Gilgamesh Epic

Several versions of this epic from various periods and places of the Middle East have come to light. The best preserved came from the library of Asshurbanapal (668–627 B.C.) at Nineveh. George Smith of the British Museum in 1872 identified a portion of this epic as a flood story, calling it "The Chaldean Account of the Deluge." The epic was written on twelve tablets, the eleventh being the account of the flood, and was probably composed originally around 2000 B.C.

The epic deals with the exploits of Gilgamesh, the youthful, half-god and half-man ruler of Uruk, who, after many civic accomplishments and heroic acts, often in company with his close friend Enkidu, is brought to grief by Enkidu's death.

Haunted by the thought of his own coming death, he seeks out his ancestor Utnapishtim, who has escaped death and become immortal. After a long and arduous journey to the west, through the mountains and over the Sea, he arrives at the land of the blessed, where Utnapishtim tells him how he has escaped the great flood and has been given immortal life by the gods. He advises Gilgamesh to secure a plant from the bottom of the sea and to eat it to gain immortality. Gilgamesh gets the plant, but a serpent snatches and devours it. In disappointment he returns to Uruk, seeking to be content with his mortality, finding such joy in life as he can.

Tablet 11, Utnapishtim's account of the flood, parallels the biblical story in many details. The god Ea warns Utnapishtim in a dream about a coming deluge planned by the gods and advises him to build a ship in which he and "the seed of all living things" might survive. According to Ea's instructions Utnapishtim builds the ship in the form of a cube, with six decks (*i.e.,* seven stories) and sixty-three compartments. He smears it with bitumen, provisions it, and loads it with gold and silver, family members, kin, boatmen, craftsmen, and beasts and wild creatures of the field—then battens down the ship's door and waits for the storm. For six days and nights the storm rages. On the seventh day it ceases. The ship comes to rest on Mt. Nizir, where it remains motionless for six days. On the seventh day Utnapishtim sends forth a dove, a swallow, and a raven. The first two return, but the raven does not. Utnapishtim and his companions disembark and offer sacrifices. The gods smell the sweet savor and "crowd like flies about the sacrificer." Ea reproaches Enlil for attempting the wholesale destruction of people. "On the sinner impose his sin" he says, and then he offers suggestions of better ways than a flood to diminish mankind (by a lion, a wolf, a famine, a pestilence). Enlil thereupon blesses Utnapishtim and his wife and elevates them to a place among the gods in the land of the blessed.

So close are the parallels to the biblical story that we must suppose that some kind of relationship exists.

Archaeology has not proved that a worldwide flood actually occurred, but it has produced evidence of serious local floods. Thick layers of river mud have been found at several ancient sites in Mesopotamia (Ur, Kish, Fara, Nineveh). The dates of the layers do not coincide, and sometimes the layers did not even cover the whole site or nearby places. We probably must assume that the Hebrew and Babylonian flood stories go back to the memory of some destructive local flood in Mesopotamia.

Claims from time to time that explorers have found the ark on Mt. Ararat or Mt. Judi have no scientific support.

The religious outlook of the Genesis story sets it apart from the Assyrian-Akkadian myth. Genesis declares that a purposeful and moral God, not capricious and feuding gods, caused the flood as a responsible judgment on evil men. The flood story thus became for Israelite writers the opportunity for illustrating the righteous mercy of God.

Parallels exist also between Hittite and Israelite covenants; Egyptian and Israelite proverbs; Canaanite and Israelite psalms, prophecy, and sacrifices; Persian (Zoroastrian) and Jewish views of the future; and Greek and Jewish concepts of the way God is related to the world (as Logos, Spirit, Wisdom).

The Hebrews did not live in a vacuum. They shared world views and traditions with the peoples among whom they lived. They used the thought forms and language of their day.

The way to explain the similarities between the stories of Gen. 1–11 and Mesopotamian literature is probably to assume that Abraham and his family brought Mesopotamian traditions with them when they migrated to Canaan. Israel's growing faith and experience transformed these traditions and made them the vehicle of its witness to God's activity in history and the world.

It is clear that the best minds and spirits of Israel adopted and adapted those elements of their cultural heritage and environment—myths, customs, laws, institutions, literary forms, and vocabulary—that were useful in expressing their view and experience of God. The great souls, like Amos, Isaiah, and Jeremiah, whose lives had been shaped by a righteous God, took the common clay in their hands and molded it into exquisite vessels for God's service. The clay was not unique; but the design, the workmanship, and the service to be rendered were.

For Further Reading

Baly, Denis. *Geographical Companion to the Bible,* 1963.

Finegan, Jack. *Light from the Ancient Past,* 2nd ed., 1959.

————. *The Archaeology of the New Testament,* 1969.

Frank, Harry Thomas. *Bible, Archaeology, and Faith,* 1971.

Kenyon, Kathleen. *Beginning in Archaeology,* 1952.

————. *Archaeology in the Holy Land,* 3rd ed., 1970.

Pritchard, James B., ed. *The Ancient Near East in Pictures Relating to the Old Testament,* 1954.

————. *Ancient Near Eastern Texts Relating to the Old Testament,* 2nd ed., 1955.

Thompson, J. A. *The Bible and Archaeology,* 1962.

Wright, G. Ernest, *Biblical Archaeology,* 1961.

————, et al. (the editors of the *Reader's Digest*). *Great People of the Bible and How They Lived,* 1974.

94. Between the Testaments

By the period between the Testaments we mean, strictly speaking, the time between the latest Old Testament book and the earliest New Testament book. There is no exact agreement about which books are to be thus identified; therefore we cannot define the exact limits of the period.

Scholars of a liberal outlook regard Daniel as the latest Old Testament

Photo by H. T. Frank

Steps of Herod the Great's temple at Samaria, dedicated to Caesar Augustus

book (*c*. 165 B.C.). Conservative scholars hold that no Old Testament book is later than the fifth/fourth centuries B.C., when such works as I-II Chronicles, Ezra-Nehemiah, Malachi, and Esther appeared.

We are also not certain about the earliest New Testament book. Some conservative scholars believe that the Gospel of Matthew was written around A.D. 50, and some liberals and conservatives assign Paul's letter to the Galatians to about A.D. 48 or 49. Others, both conservatives and liberals, think I Thessalonians (*c*. A.D. 51) is the earliest.

The time then *on outside dates* runs from around 400 B.C. to around A.D. 50.

1. Historical Events

The time between the Testaments divides into several periods:

a. The Jews under the Persians (539–332 B.C.)

Cyrus, the conqueror of Babylon (539 B.C.), and his successors (the most important being Darius I [522–486], Xerxes [486–465], Artaxerxes I [465–424], and Artaxerxes II [404–358]) allowed the Jews a large degree of self-determination. Restored to their homeland under Cyrus, Darius I, and others, they lived under the rule of a Persian governor and a Jewish high priest.

Economic conditions in the restored land were bleak, and religious life, centering in the renewed temple in Jerusalem, was perfunctory. Religious leaders made a strong effort to segregate the Jews from surrounding "unclean" peoples, including the Samaritans.

Toward the end of the period, Persia's struggles with Egypt and Greece and internal conflicts weakened its authority and power. Alexander the Great (336–323 B.C.) brought about the fall of Persia at the battles of Issus (333 B.C.) and Gaugamela (331 B.C.).

b. The Jews under Alexander the Great and the Ptolemies (332–198 B.C.)

The brief time of Alexander's conquests (334–323) was followed by a period in which Alexander's generals shared authority over the conquered regions.

Ptolemy gained control first of Egypt (323) and then of Palestine (301). Under Ptolemy and his successors the Jews apparently continued to have a large degree of freedom, limited largely by the payment of taxes to Egypt.

A large Jewish community, with possibly a million persons, flourished in Egypt. The translation of the Old Testament into Greek for these and other Greek-language readers began in the third century, according to tradition under Ptolemy II Philadelphus (285–246 B.C.).

c. The Jews under the Seleucids (198–143 B.C.)

Seleucus, one of Alexander the Great's generals, made himself master of Babylonia in 312 B.C. and of parts of Syria in 301. In 198 the Seleucid king Antiochus III defeated the Egyptian army at Panium near Mt. Hermon and thereafter annexed Palestine.

The Jews were glad to be rid of Egyptian control but soon found the rule

Coin showing the profile of
Alexander the Great

Photo by H. T. Frank

of the Seleucids far worse. Though Antiochus III accorded his Jewish subjects many freedoms and privileges, Antiochus IV (Epiphanes, *i.e.,* "the
God manifest"—175–163 B.C.) tried to force his diverse territories and
subjects into a cultural and religious unity.

He promoted the worship of Greek gods, whom he identified with local
deities, and demanded the veneration of himself as Zeus manifest in flesh.
He confiscated money and valuables from various temples, including the
temple of Yahweh in Jerusalem in 169 B.C. (I Macc. 1:20-24; II Mac. 5:
15-21). He rewarded Jews who cooperated in his program of Hellenization
(*i.e.,* of promoting the acceptance of Greek culture and religion by Jews)
and at last demanded that the Jews cease the practice of circumcision,
Sabbath observance, and the food laws. He appointed the highest bidders
to the post of high priest (II Macc. 4:7-9, 23-27). One such appointee
stole precious vessels from the temple and sold them to pay his obligation
to Antiochus (II Macc. 4:32).

Antiochus' troops put down in blood Jewish resistance to the Hellaniza-
tion of Judaism. They looted Jerusalem, butchered innocent people, and
carried others into slavery. Antiochus built a citadel called the Acra near

the temple and garrisoned it with foreign troops. It became the center for the Hellenizing activities of renegade Jews and their Gentile allies.

Copies of the Jewish Law were burned. Pagan altars were erected throughout the land. Jews were forced to eat the flesh of pigs. The worst offense of all to Jews was the erecting of an altar to Zeus in the temple itself and the offering of swine on it.

Jewish resistance was both literary and military. A writer loyal to the Law and the traditions of Judaism penned our book of Daniel at the height of the crisis (chap. 35) to encourage the faithful to resist Antiochus' demands. He showed how God brought the faithful through their ordeal in a similar crisis of the past and how he would soon destroy the oppressing tyrant and give the long-promised kingdom (world sovereignty) to Israel.

A rural priest named Mattathias and his five sons began military resistance. This priest stoutly refused to offer sacrifice to a pagan god, slew the king's officer who demanded it, fled to the hills, and conducted guerrilla warfare from there. Those loyal to the Law (the *Hasidim,* "pious ones") joined him. They destroyed pagan altars and forcibly circumcized Jewish children. Mattathias' son Judas Maccabeus (*i.e.,* "the hammer") carried on the struggle. He achieved smashing victories over the king's forces. He gained possession of the temple, tore down its pagan altar, erected a new one, installed faithful priests, and held a great ceremony of rededication (Hanukkah, *i.e.,* "Dedication") in December, 164 B.C.

Under Judas' brothers Jonathan and Simon the resistance continued until political, as well as religious, independence was gained. Jonathan (160–143 B.C.) became the first Maccabean high priest, and Simon (143–134) became both high priest and ethnarch (*i.e.,* "ruler of the people").

d. The Independent Hasmonean Kingdom (143–63 B.C.)

According to the Jewish historian Josephus, the great-grandfather of Mattathias was Asamonaios (Hashmon). Hence the family was called Hasmonean.

These priests, turned political leaders as well, became more and more secular. They lost the support of the *Hasidim* ("pious ones"), formed alliances with the Romans, undertook foreign wars, and eventually adopted the title "king." Under John Hyrcanus (134–104 B.C.), Aristobulus I

(104–103), and especially Alexander Janneus (103–76) zeal for conquest increased. Conquest was sometimes followed by the forcible conversion of conquered enemies to Judaism. Alexander Janneus oppressed the Pharisees, an opposition party within Judaism. Queen Alexandra (76–67), however, made friends of the Pharisees and brought peace and a degree of prosperity to the land.

A struggle between Hyrcanus II and Aristobulus II for the throne and the high priesthood (between *c.* 66 and 63) brought in the Romans to settle the dispute and ended the period of Jewish independence.

e. The Jews under the Romans (63 B.C.–A.D. 135 and later)

The Romans appointed Hyrcanus II as high priest and ethnarch but put him under the control of Syrian and Idumean governors.

Before long Herod the Great (37–4 B.C.) was made king by Rome. His reign was marked by family conspiracies and murders. He carried out immense building operations, including a new temple in Jerusalem. On Herod's death a Jewish embassy to Rome asked for the abolition of kingly rule in Palestine.

Herod's territories were divided among his sons. Archelaus became ethnarch of Judea, Samaria, and Idumea (4 B.C.–A.D. 6). Herod Antipas became tetrarch ("ruler of a fourth of a kingdom") of Galilee and Perea (4 B.C.–A.D. 39). Herod Philip became tetrarch of Gaulanitis, Trachonitis, Batanea, and Auranitis (4 B.C.–A.D. 34).

Jesus spent his youth and public ministry in Galilee under "that fox" Herod Antipas (Luke 13:32); and Jesus appeared before Herod after his arrest in Jerusalem (Luke 23:6-12).

Herod Agrippa I (A.D. 37–44), the grandson of Herod the Great, was appointed "king" by the Romans, first over Herod Philip's territories, then also over those of Herod Antipas, and finally over Judea, Samaria, and Idumea. From A.D. 6 to 41 Judea, Samaria, and Idumea had been under Roman governors. Thus finally Herod Agrippa I ruled over all the territories held by his grandfather.

After Herod Agrippa I's death (A.D. 44), Rome placed all his realm under Roman procurators (governors).

Herod Agrippa II (A.D. 48–*c.* 93), the son of Herod Agrippa I, before whom Paul appeared in Caesarea (Acts 25:13–26:32), was a puppet king for Rome in largely Gentile territories in the north and northeast of Palestine (Chalcis, Iturea).

Photo by H. T. Frank

Caesarea: The Roman aqueduct, built by Herod the Great and enlarged by Hadrian, which ran some 20 miles to the heights of Mt. Carmel to bring water to the city

The Jews rebelled several times against the Romans: A.D. 6 under Judas of Gamala ("Judas the Galilean," Acts 5:37); around 44 under Theudas (Acts 5:36); 66–73 under Eleazar, Menahem, and the Zealots; 132–135 under Simon ben Kosibah (Bar Kochba) and Rabbi Aqiba.

In every revolt the Romans were victorious. Titus destroyed Jerusalem and the temple in A.D. 70, and Hadrian put down the rebellion of 132–135. He subsequently rebuilt Jerusalem as a pagan city, peopled it with Gentiles exclusively, and named it Aelia Capitolina.

2. The Literature

We can mention only Jewish literature here. (For Greek, Roman, and other literature of significance for an understanding of the New Testament, see the bibliography on p. 409.)

a. The Apocrypha

The books of the Apocrypha (called deuterocanonical books by Roman Catholics) are intertestamental writings. There are fifteen of these books;

three, however, are not considered deuterocanonical by Roman Catholics (I and II Esdras and the Prayer of Manasseh).

The books of the Apocrypha are listed and described in chaps. 48–63.

b. The Pseudepigrapha (called Apocrypha by Roman Catholics) are numerous and important.

The *Book of Jubilees* divides history, from creation to the covenant at Sinai, into forty-nine periods of forty-nine years each (in this book forty-nine years is a "jubilee" period). It rewrites Gen. 1–Exod. 14 to glorify the Jewish Law of the author's time by showing that it originated in heaven, was practiced by the patriarchs and other ancients, and has eternal validity. It urges loyalty to the Law and separation from Gentiles. It probably was written by a Pharisee or an Essene between 175 and 125 B.C., when the Jews were resisting Gentile culture.

Aristeas to Philocrates claims to be a letter written by a Gentile courtier of the Egyptian ruler Ptolemy II Philadelphus (285–246 B.C.) to his brother about his personal knowledge of events connected with the Greek translation of the Jewish Torah. Actually it is a second- or first-century Jewish propaganda piece to show the miraculous origin of the Septuagint (the Greek Old Testament) and to glorify Jewish wisdom as superior to Gentile thought. It probably was written in Alexandria, Egypt.

Ethiopic Enoch (*I Enoch*) was preserved in the Ethiopian church and came to the West in 1773. It is a great collection (108 chaps. in 5 sections) of Jewish apocalyptic materials (see pp. 342-43) from the last two pre-Christian centuries, with some early Christian additions and editing. It concerns the visions of Enoch after he was taken to heaven (Gen. 5:24; *cf.* Jubilees 4:17-25). These visions pertain to the secrets of the heavenly world and the hidden purposes of God for the life of man, especially the coming of the Messiah–Son of Man and the final judgment of the world. The book contains much Jewish speculation about angels, demons, astrology (astronomy), and the proper calendar (solar rather than lunar). It probably was written originally in Aramaic. Aramaic fragments of some parts of the book have been found at Qumran by the Dead Sea (see pp. 399-403). Scholars consider I Enoch to be the most influential book of the Pseudepigrapha on the New Testament. Jude 14-15 cites I Enoch 1:9.

The Testaments of the Twelve Patriarchs employs the last-will-and-testament literary form, found in Gen. 49 and in many Jewish and Christian writings of the New Testament period. It presents the words of dying

leaders (here each of Jacob's twelve sons), who review crucial events of
their lives for their children, offer the children ethical instruction on the
basis of their own experiences, and reveal the direction of the children's
future lives and destinies. In its earliest form it probably was an Essene
writing of the second century B.C. Hebrew and Aramaic fragments of some
of the Testaments have been found at Qumran by the Dead Sea. Early
Christian writers edited the book. It offers a striking combination of Jewish
haggadah (edifying expansions of Old Testament material), high ethical
teaching, and speculation about the future (including the doctrine of the
coming of two Messiahs, one a high priest and the other a Davidic king).
In ethical content it is nearer the New Testament than any other intertestamental writing.

The Psalms of Solomon is a collection of eighteen psalms, originally
written in Hebrew, much like the psalms of the Old Testament. Essenes
probably composed these psalms (*c.* 63–30 B.C.) to show their opposition
to the secularized religious leadership of the Sadducees. They were written
also to encourage members of the Essene community to obey the Law of
Moses as taught within the community, so that God might reward them
with the gift of the Messiah and his glorious kingdom. The book was
called "The Psalms of Solomon" to gain for it importance and acceptance,
since the Psalter of David (our book of Psalms) was a closed collection
by this time and Solomon was the next in fame as a songwriter (I Kings
4:32).

The Assumption of Moses was once a longer book which contained,
first, a last will and testament of Moses and, second, a story of Michael's
dispute with the devil over Moses' body (referred to in Jude 9) and of
Moses' subsequent assumption into heaven. The book now contains only
the first part. This deals with Moses' disclosure to Joshua of the future
experiences of Israel from the conquest of Canaan to the coming of God's
kingdom. Its author may have been an Essene who wrote between 4 B.C.
and A.D. 30 (*i.e.,* during the lifetime of Jesus). He wished to point out the
sins of the godless Hasmonean priest-kings and their Roman successors,
God's certain judgment of them, and the importance of absolute loyalty to
the Law, even unto martyrdom.

III Maccabees (*the Ptolemaica*) contains three legendary stories about
the Egyptian king Ptolemy IV's (221–203 B.C.) oppression of Jews, from
which they were miraculously delivered. It warns would-be persecutors of
the invincibility of the Jewish people, and it urges the Jews to continued

loyalty to God's laws. An Alexandrian Jew composed it in Greek in the first century B.C.

IV Maccabees (On the Supremacy of Reason) is a philosophical treatise on the supremacy of reason over the passions and sufferings of the body and soul. It illustrates this supremacy by examples from the Old Testament (Joseph over sexual desire, Moses over anger, etc.) and from recent Jewish history (the triumph of Maccabean martyrs over their sufferings). It aims to show that the Law of Moses contains philosophy of the truest sort and that obedience to that Law leads to the highest virtue. It was written in Greek by a Jew of the Diaspora (Dispersion), perhaps of Alexandria or Antioch, probably in the first half of the first century A.D.

The Sibylline Oracles are books III–V from a twelve-book collection (originally there were fifteen books) of wise sayings and prophecies attributed to sibyls, that is, old women who were believed to have spoken under the influence of a deity. Prized by pagans, Jews, and Christians alike, such oracles were written, collected, and edited by all three groups between about 200 B.C. and A.D. 500. Books III–V are Jewish propaganda pieces (written second century B.C. to second century A.D.) in which the sibyl predicts the course of world history, the coming of the Messiah, and the triumph of the Jews over all idolatrous opponents, and also glorifies Moses and the Jewish Law.

II Baruch (The Syriac Apocalypse of Baruch) is preserved only in a Syriac translation, though it was written originally in Hebrew or Aramaic. It consists of a series of visions Baruch (Jeremiah's secretary) supposedly had after the fall of Jerusalem in 587 B.C. These visions explain that fall as God's judgment on sinful Israel in order to purge it, and they promise the resurrection of the dead and the vindication of Israel under the Messiah in the coming glorious age. The book makes participation in the final age dependent on faithful obedience to the Law. It probably was written after the fall of Jerusalem in A.D. 70 to throw light on the meaning of that tragedy. It contains many similarities to the Revelation to John in the New Testament.

c. The Writings of Philo Judeus

Philo (*c.* 20 B.C.–*c.* A.D. 45), a distinguished Alexandrian Jew, learned in both Judaism and Hellenism (especially Greek philosophy), left a large body of writings. Their purpose was to show that Judaism and Hellenism occupy common ground—that the best thought of the Greek world is also found in the Jewish Scriptures and Jewish theology. He was thus a defender of Judaism in an often hostile pagan environment.

Some of his important works are: Life of Moses; Exposition of the Law; Allegory of the Jewish Law; Questions and Answers in Genesis and Exodus.

d. The Works of Flavius Josephus (c. A.D. 37–c. 100)

Though not strictly a writer of the intertestamental period, Josephus is listed here because of his importance.

He was a priestly descendant of the Hasmoneans, a student of the various religious sects of Judaism, a commanding officer of Galilean Jewish forces in the war against Rome (A.D. 66–70), a captive of the Romans, and then a sympathetic interpreter and mediator for them. He at length settled in Rome on an imperial pension and gave himself to a literary career. He tried to make Judaism understandable and acceptable to Romans. As a Roman sympathizer, he was often criticized by Jews.

His works are: The Jewish War; The Antiquities of the Jews; The Life (of Josephus); Against Apion.

e. The Dead Sea Scrolls (The Qumran Texts)

From caves in the cliffs along the northwest side of the Dead Sea have come the greatest manuscript discoveries of modern times.

The manuscripts belonged to a monastic Jewish community which settled by the Dead Sea, at a place now called by Arabs Qumran, around the middle of the second century B.C. The Romans destroyed the community in A.D. 68. It seems that the members deposited their manuscripts in caves to protect them from possible destruction at the hands of the Romans.

The founder or principal organizer of the community, "The Righteous Teacher," whose name is unknown, may have been a member of the *Hasidim* ("the pious ones"), who opposed the efforts of Antiochus Epiphanes and his Jewish accomplices to introduce Greek culture and resisted Jonathan and Simon Maccabeus' assuming the high priesthood (see p. 393). The *Hasidim* felt that the legitimate priestly line, the house of Zadok, had been unjustifiably ousted and worship in the temple at Jerusalem was being carried on by priests without divine authorization. Perhaps fearing for their lives and wishing to continue proper worship, a group of these *Hasidim* withdrew to the wilderness and established a community of their own. They probably were "the Essenes," referred to by several ancient writers as having lived by the Dead Sea.

About a dozen complete or fairly complete compositions have sur-
vived, most of them having come from Caves I and XI. Fragments run
into the tens of thousands, varying from a column or two of text to tiny
pieces containing a single letter of the alphabet. Some 600 manuscripts
have been identified thus far.

They fall into various classes:

(1) Biblical Texts

About one fourth of the manuscript finds are copies of the text of the
Hebrew Scriptures. A scroll of Isaiah is in an excellent state of preservation
(see p. 361). Every Old Testament book except Esther is represented among

Photo by H. T. Frank

Qumran: steps to one of the cisterns. The cracks show the effects of the earthquake
of 31 B.C.

the manuscript discoveries, some in a number of copies. The books most frequently represented are the Psalms, Isaiah, and Deuteronomy. Some fragments of the books of the Apocrypha appear also.

(2) Commentaries, Anthologies, and Paraphrases

Members of the community composed commentaries on biblical books (*e.g.,* on Habakkuk, Nahum, Isaiah, Micah, Zephaniah, and several psalms). The community believed that the commentator's interpretation was divinely given in order that the members might understand how the mysteries of God's purpose, as announced by the Old Testament writers, were being fulfilled in the community and in the events of the author's own day.

Collections of Old Testament passages (anthologies) and paraphrases of Old Testament materials were made to teach readers the community's theology, pattern of life, and way of worship.

(3) Apocalyptic Works

Books that unveiled the future were very popular, as indicated by the presence of a considerable number of fragments of the book of Daniel and of several nonbiblical apocalypses (on apocalyptic literature see pp. 342-43).

Noteworthy is the War Scroll (also called "The War of the Sons of Light and the Sons of Darkness"), which describes the forty-year war the Essene community ("the sons of light") will wage with the wicked nations round about ("the sons of darkness"). The war will be cosmic, with God, the angels, and the righteous fighting against Belial (the devil), the evil spirits, and the wicked nations. The final victory, the community believed, will end the period of great tribulation and the dominion of evil and introduce the eternal rule of light and goodness.

(4) Psalms and Hymns

An important scroll contains hymns of thanksgiving, originally about forty of them. Some twenty-five are preserved. A number have an autobiographical flavor, reflecting the sufferings of a leader of the community (perhaps "the Righteous Teacher" or "Right Teacher") who so greatly shaped the community. The hymns thank God for salvation from pollution and transgression, for revealing his secrets to unworthy men, and for helping his creatures of clay toward perfection of way.

One scroll contains forty-four psalms, of which thirty-six are in our book of Psalms. The extra eight glorify David, wisdom, and Zion, and praise the Creator of all.

(5) Liturgical Works

These works include collections of prayers for the days of the week and for festival occasions; angelic blessings of the righteous; blessing of the community and its groups and individuals by the overseer of the community; and other liturgical materials. These compositions show the nature of the piety and worship of the Essenes.

The Temple Scroll, the longest scroll yet discovered (over twenty-eight feet), is largely concerned with proper worship. It offers detailed rules concerning the celebration of the various festivals (Tabernacles, Passover, Day of Atonement, New Wine, New Oil), with their sacrifices, meal-offerings, and ritual practices.

Centrally important in this scroll is a description of the temple in Jerusalem as it ought to be according to God's intention. The scroll specifies three courts, each an exact square, inside one another, the arrangements for sacrifices, and the procedures to be followed at the various festivals. The middle and outer courts are to have twelve gates each, named for the twelve tribes of Israel (*cf.* Rev. 21:12-13).

It is obvious that the Essenes who possessed this scroll would be dissatisfied with Herod's temple (begun *c.* 20 B.C.), since it did not meet the scroll's specifications and thus the divine intention for the temple.

(6) Writings About the Community

The most important document found in the caves is unquestionably the Manual of Discipline (or Order of the Community). The Manual covers initiation into the community, including the vows to be taken, the ritual of initiation, and the standards of admission; a brief summary of Essene beliefs; the rules of the community; and a hymn on the community's doctrines and practices.

The community's rules are presented also in a second document called the Damascus Document, known from fragments found in the caves and from medieval copies of the entire work. Life in the community was strictly controlled and austere. The rules were more strict than those practiced by the Pharisees and other parties of Judaism.

This sect regarded itself as the true people of God, which alone offered him proper worship according to the right calendar (solar rather than lunar) and in proper ceremonies under properly accredited priests, and which alone gave him true obedience according to the Law of Moses as interpreted by their "Right Teacher." They expected God to reward their obedience soon with the gifts of an end-time Prophet, two Messiahs (one a priest and the other a Davidic King), and the blessings of the New Age about to dawn.

3. Religion

Some of the major characteristics of Jewish religion between the Testaments were:

a. A Firm Ethical Monotheism

This is the belief that there is *one* God, who is good and who requires goodness of men.

After the return from Exile the Jews never again officially recognized foreign gods, as was done by certain preexilic Jewish kings (*e.g.,* Ahaz and Manasseh). There were periods when paganism pressed heavily on the Jews, especially under the Seleucid king Antiochus IV (see pp. 392-93). Some Jews yielded to the pressures, as we have seen, but strong resistance destroyed the threat and led to a reaffirmation of ethical monotheism as the national faith.

The Jews had learned the lesson taught by the great prophets: Yahweh holds the nations in his hands; their gods are vanity; their idols are nothing (Isa. 41:21-24; 44:9-20). The postexilic Jews fully accepted the prophetic teaching that the disaster of the Exile was Yahweh's judgment for their idolatry (*e.g.,* Ezek. 8–9). Individuals did indeed fall away, but never again the nation!

In fact, Judaism so honored and exalted Yahweh that his name became too sacred to utter, except in the ritual of the temple. People referred to him as God, Lord, God of heaven, King of heaven, Heaven, the Lord of Spirits, the Great Glory, the Head of Days, and the Most High God. They thought of him as living in the highest heaven, with archangels and myriads of angels at his command as his ministers in the world. Representing him in the world were also his Wisdom, his Word, his Spirit, his Presence. The elevation of God and the multiplication of intermediary beings in Judaism was both a strength and a weakness: it made God absolutely supreme but it tended to remove him from intimate relation to men and the world.

b. The Supremacy of the Law

It was Ezra (458 or 428 or 398 B.C.) who established the Law of Moses, apparently as found in the Pentateuch, squarely at the heart of

Judaism (see p. 89). He reformed the nation on the basis of the demands of that Law. From this time on, God's will for the total life of man was thought to be found in the Law. All that was needed was to read, interpret, and apply it to every situation in life.

There soon grew up a body of interpretation of the Law that became as binding as the Law itself. Since the prescriptions of the ancient written Law did not apply directly to constantly changing cultural situations, it was necessary for experts, called scribes, to draw out the Law's general intent and apply it to those situations (as the Supreme Court of the United States must do with respect to another ancient document, the Constitution). The scribes claimed that their interpretations had come from Moses also, through a long chain of oral tradition.

The scribes worked sometimes as a body but often individually. Disciples of individual scribes passed along their teacher's interpretations. Thus "schools" of interpretation arose which developed into parties or sects. The tradition of the Pharisees, for example, differed from that of the Essenes.

Since the Jews came to believe that the whole will of God for all time was written down in the Law of Moses, they saw no further need for prophets. Prophetic spirits, in order to be heard, had to write books under an ancient name (see the Pseudepigrapha, pp. 396-98). What the nation needed, rather than prophets, was scribes—to reconcile conflicting laws, to show what individual laws meant, and to indicate how to apply the Law in particular cases.

Synagogues—local places of worship—came into being in the postexilic period as places of instruction in the Law and the other scriptures.

The Law was elevated, praised, and glorified; it was regarded as eternally existing. Jewish teachers said that it existed on heavenly tablets before the creation of the world; that angels practiced it in heaven; and that it would be practiced in the Age to Come.

Wisdom and the Law were practically equated. Wisdom writers claimed that Wisdom had descended from heaven and embodied itself in the Law. People were to meditate on the Law day and night, love it, and obey it in every detail. By obeying it they would find perfection before God and become worthy of God's rewards.

Such elevation of the Law inevitably introduced a strong element of legalism into Judaism. The individual did not always clearly see that strict obedience to the Law was his response to God's gracious forgiveness and help; often obedience to the Law became the means by which he sought to obtain grace. Thus one writer of the time remarks, "Almsgiving delivers from death, and it will purge away every sin" (Tobit 12:9).

This exaltation of the Law did not lead solely to a burdensome legalistic system. Many Jews loved the Law and sought to live by it as their response to God's merciful deeds in Israel's behalf. But in Judaism heart religion did tend to retreat behind a religion of outward conformity; this is clearly seen in Jesus' words about the legalism of the Pharisees and other contemporaries. Indeed, this has been a problem in Christianity through the centuries also!

c. Israel as a Holy People in Mission

The Jews never forgot that God had called them to a special relationship with himself that involved both separation from the world and service to the world. The prophets had taught that Israel's election was not only to special privilege but also to special responsibility.

Since God was "holy" (*i.e.,* separated from all that is common, profane, and unclean and within himself morally pure), Israel was to share God's holiness (Lev. 19:2: "You shall be holy; for I the Lord your God am holy"). The separation of Israel from the uncleanness of pagan peoples, though advocated by religious teachers before the Exile, was seriously undertaken first by Nehemiah and Ezra.

The most drastic accomplishment in Ezra's reform of the life of the nation under the Law brought from Babylonia was the divorce of foreign wives (Ezra 9–10). Ezra emphasized those demands of the Law which marked Jews as Jews (circumcision, rigid Sabbath observance, tithes for the support of the temple, etc.). Samaritans were especially to be avoided as unclean. Because of Jewish ostracism, the Samaritans founded a temple of their own on Mt. Gerizim in Samaria (John 4:20). The Jews, now sworn to uphold the Law in every respect (Neh. 9:38; 10:29), became an exclusive, separatist community, wholly committed to life in accordance with the Law and "holiness" by the standards of that Law.

The *Hasidim* ("the pious ones") reaffirmed the separatist standard in the struggle against Greek defilement under Antiochus IV (175–163 B.C.). From the *Hasidim* appear to have come the separatist parties known as the Pharisees and the Essenes, which were so influential in Jesus' time.

Though it seems fundamentally contradictory to all that has been said, Israel's service to the nations was not entirely lost sight of in this period.

The Second Isaiah and his disciples drew out the implications of Israel's monotheism for its understanding of its role under God. If there was no other God than Yahweh, he was implicitly Lord of all nations; and all peoples were someday to recognize his Lordship. Israel by her God-likeness was to draw all nations to Zion (Isa. 56:3-8; 66:18-21; Zech. 8:22-23; Mal. 1:11). The author of the book of Jonah was fully aware of Israel's mission under God to the nations (see chap. 40).

Some of the books of the Apocrypha and Pseudepigrapha emphasize the inclusion of Gentiles as part of God's purpose for the end-time (Tobit 13:11; 14:6-7; I Enoch 10:21-22; Test. of Levi 4:4; 14:3-4; Test. of Naphtali 8:3).

In the period between the Testaments some Gentiles became converts to Judaism (Judith 14:10; Acts 6:5; 13:43; Matt. 23:15). Paul encountered half-converts, known as "God fearers," in the Jewish synagogues almost everywhere (Acts 13:16, 26; 17:4, 17; 18:7).

d. A Glowing Hope for the Future

Israel's conviction that it was God's special possession among all peoples (Exod. 19:5) carried with it another conviction: God had planned a wonderful future for his chosen people (Gen. 12:2-3). A part of early covenant ceremonies between God and Israel was the utterance of blessings and curses. The blessings set forth God's rich rewards for obedience to the covenant (Deut. 27–28; Josh. 8:30-35).

The exact details of the future were differently conceived by various writers. At the heart of it was Yahweh's coming to an acknowledged supremacy over the whole earth, with Israel's temple as the place of contact between God and all people.

At the Day of Yahweh he will defeat all his enemies in a mighty display of power and exalt Israel to prosperity, full righteousness, and perpetual security. God's temple in Jerusalem will be the center of worship and learning for all people and the seat of judgment for all disputes (Isa. 2:2-4).

The Old Testament prophets thought of God's kingdom as a glorified earthly order. Some of them saw this order as ruled by a descendant of David, who will be fully righteous, Spirit-endowed, God-fearing, and wise. Absolute justice in an order of peace, embracing even the animal kingdom, will prevail (Isa. 11:1-9).

Some writers held that two Messiahs would come: a political leader from the tribe of Judah and a priestly head from Levi or Aaron (Zech. 6:9-14 [see p. 192]; Test. of Simeon 7:2; Manual of Discipline 9:10-11). Others saw no Messiah at all—only God as King.

The writers of apocalypses (see pp. 342-43) sometimes saw the coming of a new world after God's judgment of the earth, not a continuance, even in glorified form, of this earthly existence. One says that God's kingdom "will appear throughout all his creation" (Assumption of Moses 10:1). Israel will be exalted "to the heaven of the stars" and will see her foes in Gehenna (10:9-10).

And still other writers saw first a temporary earthly kingdom to be followed by an eternal heavenly kingdom (I Enoch 91-104; II Baruch; II Esdras), the pattern adopted in the Revelation to John (chaps. 20–22) in the New Testament.

Underneath all the forms of the hope was the conviction that "things beyond our seeing, things beyond our hearing, things beyond our imagining (are) all prepared by God for those who love him" (I Cor. 2:9 NEB).

Between the Testaments the faithful looked not only back to Moses and the Law for guidance but forward to the New Age for strength and courage to walk in the path Moses had marked out.

4. Religious Groups in Judaism

How many religious parties or sects there were in the period between the Testaments we do not know. Josephus (see p. 399) identified four groups, which he called "philosophies":

a. The Pharisees

The name probably means "the separated (or separate) ones." From what they were separated we do not know—probably from defilement and from those defiled (Gentiles and Jews who did not carefully obey the Law).

This group emerged around 140 B.C. from the *Hasidim* (see p. 393). Chiefly a lay group, it taught, developed, and passed on the oral interpretation of the Law. The aim of this interpretation was to bring the whole of life under the control of the Law. This oral tradition, now in the Mishnah (see bibliography at the end of this chapter), was often opposed by Jesus (*e.g.,* Mark 7:1-23).

The Pharisees believed in human freedom under the divine sovereignty, in angels and demons, in the resurrection of the body, and in the coming of the Messiah and the kingdom of God. They held that the kingdom of God will come through God's power, not by force of human arms.

Their numbers were not great (Josephus says some six thousand), but their influence with the people was weighty.

b. The Sadducees

Their name seems to derive from Zadok, the head of the old priestly family which long officiated in the temple in Jerusalem (I Kings 1:26).

As a definite party within Judaism, the Sadducees seem to have arisen in Maccabean times, probably in the time of Jonathan (160–143 B.C.) or Simon (143–134 B.C.). They appear to have been supporters of the Hasmonean high priests, who eventually also became kings; and they remained allied with these priest-kings most of the time until the coming of the Romans in 63 B.C.

They continued in power under the Romans, whom they probably reluctantly served. They undoubtedly wished for the return of theocratic government in which they, as high priests, would head the state.

They were an aristocratic, priestly party (possibly containing some wealthy lay Jerusalemites) concerned with Israel as a nation as well as with religion. They challenged the lay Pharisees' right to interpret the Law for the nation—their own priestly prerogative—and thus disputed the authority of Pharisaic oral tradition. They denied the Pharisees' doctrines of the resurrection of the body, rewards and punishment after death, and the existence of angels and spirits—probably since these teachings were not present in the Law.

With the fall of the temple in A.D. 70 they no longer played a significant role in Jewish life.

c. The Essenes

The name seems to come from the Aramaic equivalent of the Hebrew word *Hasidim,* meaning "the pious ones."

As we noted above (p. 399), this group seems to have formed out of the *Hasidim* about 150 B.C. in protest to Jonathan Maccabeus' becoming high priest. They built their community center by the Dead Sea. They believed their "Right Teacher" had given the true interpretation of the Law and the Prophets. According to this, the Essenes were the true and righteous Remnant to whom God would give the joys of the Coming Age. They were a rigidly ascetic and legalistic community, contemptuous of all Jews outside. They awaited the coming of a Prophet and two Messiahs and the transformation of the barren desert around the Dead Sea into a new Garden of Eden. Some two hundred lived at Qumran and others in groups elsewhere in Palestine and the Near East. According to Josephus and Philo, their total number was about four thousand.

d. The Zealots

The Zealots were not a single party but many groups of a revolutionary nature that developed in the Roman period. In Acts 5:36-37 we hear of Judas the Galilean and Theudas. Josephus tells us of Eleazar and the "dagger-men" who brought on the war with Rome (66–73). The name comes from a Hebrew word meaning "to be jealous or zealous."

These groups took their inspiration from Old Testament characters (Simeon, Levi, Phinehas, Elijah) who, in zeal for God's Law, slew those enemies of Israel—whether within or without—who attempted to subvert Israel's loyalty to God and his laws. Their heroes were also the Maccabees, who slew Antiochus IV's officers and soldiers, together with apostate Jews (see p. 393). To them, rebellion against Rome was a religious act, in the tradition of the fathers.

They thought that such zeal, and particularly the martyrdom which resulted from it, would atone for the nation's sin (Num. 25:10-13; Sirach 45:23-24; II Macc. 7:30-38).

Simon the Zealot was a member of the Twelve (Luke 6:15; Acts 1:13), and other disciples (possibly Peter, James and John, and Judas Iscariot) seem to have been affected by this point of view.

For Further Reading

> Barrett, C. K. *The New Testament Background: Selected Documents,* 1957.
> Charles, R. H., ed. *The Apocrypha and Pseudepigrapha of the Old Testament,* 2 vols., 1913.
> Danby, H. E. *The Mishnah,* 1933.
> Mansoor, Menahem. *The Dead Sea Scrolls,* 1964.
> Russell, D. S. *Between the Testaments,* 1960.
> _____. *The Method and Message of Jewish Apocalyptic,* 1964.
> Tenney, Merrill C. *New Testament Times,* 1965.
> Vermes, Geza. *The Dead Sea Scrolls in English,* 1962.

95. Historical Outline and Chronology*

I. Before the Hebrew Patriarchs (Abraham, Isaac, Jacob)
(before the twentieth century B.C.)
Old Stone (Paleolithic) Age — 200,000(?)–10,000 B.C.
Life in caves; food collecting stage

* Dates are derived largely from John Bright, *A History of Israel,* 2nd ed. 1972, pp. 476-87. Many dates are approximate, although *"c."* ("about") does not appear.

Photo by H. T. Frank

The pre-historic Tabun Cave at Wadi el-Mughara. Human occupation dates back at least 50,000 years.

Middle Stone (Mesolithic) Age — 10,000–7000
   Cave-dwellers emerged from caves; food-producing stage
   Jericho settled — 8000
New Stone (Neolithic) Age — 7000–4000
   Pottery invented — 5500
Copper-Stone (Chalcolithic) Age — 4000–3200
   Writing invented by Sumerians in Mesopotamia—3500–3300
Early Bronze Age—3200–2100
   Egyptians and Mesopotamians (Sumerians, Akkadians) developed advanced civilizations, with tools and weapons of bronze

II. **The Patriarchs (twentieth–seventeenth centuries)**
Middle Bronze Age — 2100–1550
   Abraham, Isaac, Jacob — somewhere between the twentieth–
   seventeenth centuries
   Invention of the alphabet in Canaan — seventeenth century
   Hyksos ("rulers of foreign lands") in control of Canaan and
   Egypt — eightenth–sixteenth centuries
   Descent of Hebrew groups into Egypt — end of eighteenth or
   first half of seventeenth century

III. **Israel in Egypt (eighteenth or seventeenth–early thirteenth century)**
   Joseph — seventeenth century
Late Bronze Age — 1550–1200
   Expulsion of Hyksos from Egypt — 1540
   Building of Egypt's empire under eighteenth and nineteenth
   dynasties — 1552–1200
   Egyptian solar monotheism under Amenophis IV (Akhenaten)
   — 1364–1347; the Amarna Letters
   Oppression of the Hebrews under Sethos I (1305–1290) and
   Ramesses II (1290–1224)
   Moses and the Exodus from Egypt — 1280

IV. **The Wilderness Sojourn and the Conquest of Canaan (1280–1200)**
   Ramesses II's treaty of peace with the Hittites — 1275
   Israel's covenant with Yahweh at Mt. Sinai and life at Kadesh-
   barnea for about a generation
   The conquest of Canaan under Joshua — 1250–1200
   Merneptah's campaign in Canaan and his victory stele mention-
   ing Israel — 1220
   Destruction of Hittite empire by sea peoples—1240–1200;
   their invasion of Egypt repelled by Merneptah — 1220

V. **The Judges (1200–1020)**
Early Iron Age — 1200–900
   Sea peoples (including the Philistines) settled in Canaan —
   1175
   Deborah, Barak, Gideon — 1125

Destruction of Shiloh by the Philistines — 1050
Samuel — latter two thirds of the eleventh century

VI. The United Kingdom (1020–922)
Saul — 1020–1000
David — 1000–961
Solomon — 961–922
Temple built — 958–952

Photo by H. T. Frank

Reconstruction of Megiddo, a major Canaanite and Israelite city

VII. The Divided Kingdom (922–587) (more important kings and prophets only)

Israel	Judah	Assyria and Babylonia
Jeroboam I — 922–901	Rehoboam — 922–915	Adad-nirari II — 912–892
Omri — 876–869	Jehoshaphat — 873–849	Asshur-nasir-pal II — 884–860
Ahab — 869–850; ELIJAH		Shalmaneser III—859–825
Jehu — 842–815; ELISHA		Adad-nirari III — 811–784

Photo by H. T. Frank

The ruins of the stables of Megiddo, probably dating to the time of Ahab

Israel	*Judah*			*Assyria and Babylonia*
Jeroboam II — 786–746; AMOS, HOSEA	Uzziah (Azariah) — 783–742			
	Jotham — 742–735	I S	M I	Tiglath-pileser III — 745–727
Fall of Samaria and deportation of 27,290 to Assyria — 721	Ahaz — 735–715	A I	C A	Shalmaneser V — 726–722
	Hezekiah — 715–686	A H	H	Sargon II — 721–705
	Manasseh — 686–642			Sennacherib — 704–681
				Esarhaddon — 680–669
	Josiah — 640–609			Asshurbanapal — 668–627

Israel	Judah		Assyria and Babylonia
		J	Fall of Nineveh—612
	Jehoiakim — 609–	E	Nebuchadnezzar —
	598	R	605–562
	Jehoiachin —	E	
	598/97	M	
	1st deportation	I	
	Zedekiah — 597–	A	
	587	H	
	Fall of Jeru-		
	salem — 587,		
	2nd deportation;		
	582, 3rd depor-		
	tation		

VIII.   Babylonian Exile (597 or 587–539)
Nebuchadnezzar — 605–562; EZEKIEL
Nabonidus (556–539) and Belshazzar; II ISAIAH
Cyrus (550–530) captured Babylon — 539

IX.   The Jews Under the Persians (539–332)

	Persian Kings
Edict of Cyrus — 538	Cyrus — 550–530
Rebuilding of temple in Jerusalem — 520–515	Cambyses — 530–522
Zerubbabel, Joshua, HAGGAI,	Darius I — 522–486
ZECHARIAH	Xerxes — 486–465
MALACHI — 460	Artaxerxes I — 465–424
Ezra's reforms — 458 or 428 or 398	Artaxerxes II — 404–358
Nehemiah as governor — 445–425	Darius III — 336–331

X.   The Jews Under Alexander the Great and the Ptolemies (332–198)
Alexander the Great (336–323) defeated Persians — 333 and 331; took Palestine and Egypt — 332
Death of Alexander (323) and struggle for control of his empire by his generals — 323–301
  Babylonia under Seleucus I — 312; parts of Syria added — 301
  Egypt under Ptolemy I — 323; Palestine and parts of Syria added — 301
Greek translation of the Old Testament (the Septuagint) begun under Ptolemy II Philadelphus (285–246)

XI. **The Jews Under the Seleucids (198–143)**
Antiochus III's (223–187) defeat of the Egyptians at Panium and
   his annexation of Palestine — 198
Antiochus IV Epiphanes' (175–163) desecration of the temple in
   Jerusalem — 167
Writing of the book of Daniel — 166 or 165
Judas Maccabeus (166–160); the rededication of temple — 164
Jonathan Maccabeus (160–143), the first Maccabean high priest
Rise of the Essenes and founding of Qumran — 150

XII. **The Independent Hasmonean Kingdom (143–63)**
Simon Maccabeus, ethnarch and high priest — 143–134
Rise of Sadducees and Pharisees
John Hyrcanus, ethnarch and high priest — 134–104
Aristobulus I, king and high priest — 104–103
Alexander Janneus, cruel warrior king and high priest — 103–76
Salome Alexandra as ruler; Hyrcanus II as high priest — 76–67
Aristobulus II, king and high priest — 67–63
Pompey's capture of Jerusalem — 63

XIII. **The Jews and Christians Under the Romans (63 B.C.–A.D. 135
and following)**

The Jews	*The Christians*	*Roman Generals, Emperors, Governors*
Hyrcanus II, high priest (63–41) and eth- narch (47–41) under Roman governors		Pompey over Palestine — 63–48
Antipater II (father of Herod the Great) appointed prefect of Judea by Julius Caesar — 47		Julius Caesar over Palestine — 48–44
Herod the Great, ap- pointed king by the Romans — 40; ruled over Palestine — 37– 4 B.C. began to build the temple in Jerusalem — 20–19		Octavian (Augustus) —31 B.C.–A.D. 14

The Jews	*The Christians*	*Roman Generals, Emperors, Governors*
	Birth of JESUS — between 7 and 4 B.C.*	
Archelaus, ethnarch of Judea, Samaria, Idumea — 4 B.C.–A.D. 6		
Herod Antipas, tetrarch of Galilee and Perea — 4 B.C.–A.D. 39	JOHN THE BAPTIST'S ministry — 27–28	Tiberius — 14–37 Pontius Pilate — 26–36
Herod Philip, tetrarch of Auranitis, Batanea, etc. — 4 B.C.–A.D. 34	Crucifixion of JESUS — 30 Conversion of Saul (Paul) — 34	
Herod Agrippa I, king by stages over all the territories of Herod the Great — 37–44	Mission of Paul and Barnabas in Cyprus and Asia Minor — 47–48	Gaius Caligula — 37–41 Claudius — 41–54 Roman governors over Palestine — 44 on
Herod Agrippa II, king of Gentile territories north of Palestine (Chalcis, Iturea) — 48–93	Jerusalem Council — 49 Paul's mission in Asia Minor, Macedonia, Achaia — 49 (50)–52	Gallio, governor of Achaia — 51–52
	Paul's mission in Asia Minor, Macedonia, Achaia — 53–58 Paul in prison at Caesarea — 58–60; in prison at Rome — 61–63 Martyrdom of James, Jesus' brother, in Jerusalem — 62 Martyrdom of Paul and Peter in Rome — 64–67	Felix, governor of Palestine — 52–60 (?) Nero — 54–68 Festus, governor of Palestine — 60 (?)–62

The Jews	The Christians	Roman Generals, Emperors, Governors
First Jewish revolt against the Romans — 66–73; fall of Jerusalem — 70		Vespasian — 69–79 Titus — 79–81 Domitian — 81–96 Nerva — 96–98 Trajan — 98–117 Hadrian — 117–138
Second Jewish revolt — 132–135; destruction of Jerusalem — 135 Jerusalem rebuilt by Hadrian as Aelia Capitolina, a non-Jewish city — 135 and following		

* The date of Jesus' birth was put at least 4 years too late by Dionysius Exiguus, the head of a Roman monastery, in the early sixth century. He placed it 754 years after the founding of Rome. We know from data in Josephus' works that Herod the Great died 750 years after the founding of that city. That Jesus was born before Herod's death is clear from the Gospels (Luke 1:5; Matt. 2:1), but how much before is not known.

96. Measures, Weights and Money, Calendar, Festivals

1. Measures

a. Of Length

finger	0.7	inches
handbreadth (four fingers)	2.9	inches
span (three handbreadths)	8.7	inches
cubit		
common (from elbow to tip of middle finger)	17.5	inches
long (as above, plus a handbreadth)	20.4	inches
fathom	6	feet
stadion (furlong)	606	feet
mile (Roman)	1,618	yards
Sabbath day's journey	0.6	mile

b. Of Volume

kab	1.1	quarts
omer	2	quarts
seah	0.67	peck
ephah	0.5	bushel
lethech	2.5	bushel
homer, cor	5.1	bushel
log	0.6	pint
hin	1	gallon
bath	5.5	gallon
homer, cor (liquid)	55	gallon
sextarius	1	pint
metretes	9	gallon
modios	1	peck

Comments on Measures:
1. The equivalents in the table above are approximate.
2. There was no standard system of measures throughout Hebrew history. The Hebrews were influenced by Babylonian, Egyptian, Canaanite, and Greco-Roman systems, and within any one historical period there was no exact standardization. Thus there were frequent complaints about unjust measures and weights (Amos 8:5; Deut. 25:13-14).
3. Early people used the human body as a standard of measurement: the fingerbreadth, the handbreadth, the length of the forearm, the distance of the horizontal arm reach, the stride. In time they devised more sophisticated measures.

2. Weights and Money

gerah	8.7	grains
bekah	0.2	ounces
pim	0.26	ounces
shekel	0.4	ounces
litra	12	ounces
mina	1.2	pound
talent	75.6	pounds
lepton	0.25	cent
quadrans	0.5	cent
denarius, drachma (a day laborer's wage)	25	cents
half shekel	50	cents

shekel (silver), stater	1	dollar
mina (silver)	25	dollars
talent (silver)	1,500	dollars

Comments on Weights and Money:

1. The money equivalents above in today's U.S. currency are approximate.

2. Weights were usually of stone and sometimes inscribed. Often in Egypt and Babylonia they were in the shape of animals or fowl.

3. Before the minting of coins began, in the seventh century B.C., precious metals, usually in the form of ingots, were weighed and used as a medium of exchange. The names of the weights were sometimes carried over as the names of the coins.

4. In New Testament times the rapid political changes in Judah and in the Greco-Roman world left in their wake a confusing number of monetary systems. Jews brought coins to Jerusalem of many kinds from all over the Middle East. Money changers therefore flourished in that city, especially since only silver coins of Tyre could be used in the temple.

3. The Calendar

Comments on the Calendar:

1. The beginning of the Hebrew year shown here falls at our March 21, the spring equinox. The Hebrews took this point of beginning from the Babylonians, probably after 605 B.C., when the Babylonians gained control of Judah and the West. After the conquest of Canaan (late thirteenth century B.C.) and through the periods of the united and divided monarchies (roughly eleventh through the seventh centuries B.C.), the Hebrews followed the Canaanite calendar, which began the year at the fall equinox (September 21).

2. The names of the Hebrew months shown on page 420 are of Babylonian origin. The earlier names given for some are Canaanite.

3. The Hebrew calendar was solar-lunar. The year ran from one equinox to another. Months were calculated from new moon to new moon. Thus months were of about 30 days' length (one lunation actually lasts about 29½ days, and twelve lunations about 354¼ days). To make up the loss of 11 days per year (the solar year is 365¼ days) an extra month was inserted every two or three years. Usually Adar, the twelfth month, was duplicated.

4. The Essenes of Qumran by the Dead Sea (see p. 408) seem to

have followed a purely solar calendar of 364 days, divided into four seasons of 13 weeks each (91 days), each season having two months of 30
days and one of 31. This scheme caused festivals to fall always on the
same day of the week. We do not know when this calendar first arose.

5. The Hebrew day began at sundown.

4. Special Days and Festivals in Israel

a. The Sabbath

From a root meaning "to rest" or "to cease"; the seventh day of the
Hebrew week; origin of the Hebrew Sabbath unknown, though possibly
from Moses; a day of rest for Israelites, animals, and slaves (Exod. 20:8-10;
Amos 8:5; Neh. 13:15-22); in the postexilic period a day of religious
assembly (Lev. 23:1-3); considered, along with circumcision, to be a dis-
tinguishing mark of Judaism; thirty-nine types of work on the Sabbath pro-
hibited by Jewish rabbis.

b. Feast of Trumpets (New Year?)

A one-day celebration (first day of Tishri [September-October]) consisting of cessation from work, blast of trumpets, solemn assembly, special

offerings in the temple, and singing (Lev. 23:24-25; Num. 29:1-6); perhaps the preexilic New Year, celebrated at that time in the fall (see p. 420).

c. Day of Atonement

Tenth of Tishri (September-October); a day of national fasting and repentance; sacrifices offered to cleanse the temple, the priests, and the people; the sins of Israel borne into the desert by a goat (Lev. 16:8-10, 20-22); only day of the year when the high priest entered the Holy of Holies in the temple.

d. Passover and the Feast of Unleavened Bread

Passover—probably originally a nomadic fertility (or lambing) festival, older than the Exodus from Egypt (Exod. 5:1; 10:9), which gained special meaning from the events of the Exodus (Exod. 12:1-28); became a family dinner around the eating of a roasted yearling lamb, with ceremonies that helped participants relive the Exodus from Egypt; a one-day celebration on the fourteenth of Nisan (March-April).

Unleavened Bread—originally an agricultural festival of thanksgiving at the beginning of barley harvest; featured the consecration of the first-born of man and beast to God and the redemption of first-born human males (Exod. 13:1-16); required abstinence from the use of leaven for seven days; Passover and Unleaven Bread observed together, Passover becoming the first day of an eight-day commemoration of the deliverance from Egypt (Exod. 12:1-20), Nisan 14–21.

e. Feast of Weeks (Pentecost)

A one-day, end-of-harvest, thanksgiving festival centering in the offering to God of a portion of the wheat harvest; occurred on the fiftieth day after the offering of the barley sheaf to God during the ceremonies of the Feast of Unleavened Bread (usually on sixth of Sivan [May-June]), roughly fifty days after Passover (Lev. 23:15-21); became in the postexilic period also a festival commemorating the gift of the Law (the Covenant) to Israel.

f. Feast of Tabernacles (Booths)

An eight-day (originally seven-day) autumnal festival of thanksgiving for all the harvests (grain, fruits, grapes, olives); also called "the feast of ingathering" (Exod. 34:22) or "the feast of the Lord" (Lev. 23:39); involved pilgrimage to the temple, elaborate animal sacrifices and cereal offerings (Num. 29:12-38), dwelling in leafy huts or booths (Neh.8:14-18), and foliage (palm-branch) processions (II Macc. 10:6-7); huts—originally booths for shelter in harvest time—reinterpreted later as symbols of Israel's wilderness wandering (Lev. 23:43); held Tishri 15–22 (September-October).

g. Feast of Dedication (Hanukkah)

Commemorated the rededication of the temple by Judas Maccabeus Kislev 25 [November-December], 164 B.C.), after its defiling three years earlier by Antiochus Epiphanes (see pp. 392-93); an eight-day feast, with temple sacrifices, foliage processions, daily lighting of lamps and torches in front of houses and in the temple, and much singing and rejoicing.

h. Feast of Purim

A two-day festival (Adar 14–15 [February-March]), celebrating the victory of Persian Jews over their persecutors (Esther 9:17-22); public reading of the Book of Esther, cursing of Israel's enemies and blessing of Israel, exchanging gifts and giving alms, and much drinking and hilarity.

PART III
THE BIBLE
AND FAITH AND LIFE

97. God and Satan

1. God

The Bible is a book about God. It begins with a story about the creation of the heavens and the earth and ends with an account of a new creation in which God's purpose in the original creation is fulfilled. In the Bible God is said to be the Alpha and the Omega, the first and the last (Rev. 1:8; 22:13); and, to judge from the Bible's story as a whole, he is also all the letters in between.

Biblical writers did not hesitate to think and talk about God. Though biblical men were impressed with the mystery of God—Isaiah saw the Lord as "high and lifted up" (Isa. 6:1) and Paul puzzled over God's mysterious ways (Rom. 11:33)—they also were powerfully aware that God to some degree had disclosed himself to them and declared his purpose for their life and for all people.

What has God revealed to men, according to the Bible?

a. He Is to Be Known and Worshiped as "Yahweh."

In the ancient Near East a person's name was of great importance, for it represented the person's character and experiences (Gen. 17:5; 32:28; I Sam. 25:25). Similarly, a god's real person and character were concentrated in his name and that name was therefore powerful (Exod. 23:20-21; Jer. 10:6; Ps. 20:7).

God was worshiped by the patriarchs before Moses as "El" (a general name meaning "God" or "deity"). Often characterizing words were added, as in the name El Shaddai (Exod. 6:3, where "Shaddai" probably means "the Mountain One," though it is usually translated "Almighty").

It was Moses who introduced the name "Yahweh" to the Hebrew people (Exod. 6:2-3; here the RSV renders the Hebrew YHWH as "the Lord").

The meaning of "Yahweh" is not certain. Probably it means "he causes to be" in the sense that he is the Creator. In Exod. 3:14 the translation "I am who I am" probably should be rendered, "I cause to be what comes into existence."

"Jehovah" is not a Hebrew word but an artificial combination (perhaps made in the sixteenth century A.D.) of YHWH and the vowels of the Hebrew word "Adonai," meaning "my Lord." These vowels were placed beneath the consonants YHWH in the sixth–seventh centuries A.D. by Jewish editors of the Hebrew Scriptures (the Masoretes) to indicate that the sacred name Yahweh out of reverence should not be pronounced but that "Adonai" should be spoken instead. It was never intended by the Masoretes that the vowels should be combined with the consonants to create the word Jehovah. This word has thus been dropped in most of the recent English translations in favor of the term of long use among the Jews: "the Lord."

b. God Is Spirit.

(1) He Is Both Far Away and Near at Hand.

Jesus declared, according to John 4:24, that, since God is Spirit, worship of him is not to be confined to any particular place. He is not a local deity.

Israel had long believed that God was invisible, universal Spirit, whose tabernacle and temple in Israel were places of his earthly manifestation. Other nations around believed also that their deities were universal gods whose temples were places where they could be encountered by men.

While non-Israelite temples contained a statue of the god which was thought to house the god's person or essence, Israel forbade the making of statues or images of Yahweh and thought of him as invisibly enthroned above the two olive-wood cherubim (winged sphinxes) contained in the Holy of Holies of the temple.

(2) God Is One Spirit.

Unlike the peoples around, Israel believed that God was One, not many: "The Lord our God is one Lord" (Deut. 6:4).

In the religions of other nations the forces of nature were personified, conceived of as male and female deities, organized into a structured relationship (a pantheon), and duly worshiped so that their benefits could be obtained. The worshiper's aim was to conform to the rhythms of nature so that the powers of nature would be good to them.

The Hebrews saw their God as Lord of nature. For them nature was the handiwork of God, but nature was not God (Ps. 8:3). Nature was the arena in which men encountered God as the Lord of their lives and their destiny. In the world of nature men are called to fellowship with God and to obedience to his will. It is a quality of life that God wants, not simply indulgence in the bounties of nature.

(3) Spirit Is Power.

The basic meaning of the Hebrew word for "spirit" is "air," which early man saw as "wind" in nature and "breath" in living beings. The concept of "power" or "energy" is fundamental to the word.

God's Spirit is thus his active power: *creating* the physical universe (Gen. 1:2; Ps. 33:6); *enabling* people to accomplish heroic deeds (Judges 14:6; Acts 10:38) and to utter God's Word (Mic. 3:8; Luke 4:18); *transforming* the inner life of persons (Acts 15:9; Gal. 5:22-23); and *guaranteeing* the believers' participation in the life of the Age to Come (II Cor. 1:22; Eph. 1:14).

c. God Is Light.

I John 1:5 says, "God is light and in him is no darkness at all." The context here shows clearly that by "light" the writer means holiness, goodness, or righteousness, not natural light.

Natural light is indeed said in the Bible to come from God (Gen. 1:3; Isa. 45:7). But it results from his creative activity; it does not define what he is.

The symbolic use of "light" is strong in the Bible. In the New Testament Jesus Christ, God's Son, is "the light of the world," who, if followed, will deliver from the darkness of sin (John 8:12-24). Christians are "sons of God" and thus "sons of light" (Luke 16:8; John 12:36; I Thess. 5:5). They, too, are "the light of the world." Men are to see their good deeds and praise the Father in heaven (Matt. 5:14-16).

When biblical writers said that God is "holy" and that his people must be "holy" (Lev. 19:2; I Pet. 1:15-16), they meant that he and they belong together in a realm of mysterious power and moral purity altogether different from the weak, profane, and sinful order in which the sons of darkness dwell. "Holiness" (I Thess. 3:11–4:8; Heb. 12:14) is separation from the common and the unclean and is moral likeness to God (see pp. 455-56).

The understanding of light as a symbol of truth or knowledge (Ps. 43:3; 119:104-105) is in harmony with the understanding of light as moral goodness, for the truth God gives, according to the Bible, is knowledge of the true way of life, not of abstract truths.

d. God Is Love.

This famous statement in I John 4:8 needs to be joined with the declaration that God has loved us (John 3:16; I John 4:10).

To say only that "God is love" might imply that God is impersonal, an abstract principle. To say only that God loved or loves might imply that loving is one of several activities, such as creating or judging. But to affirm both is to hold that he is fully personal and that "all that he does is an expression of his nature, which is—to love" (C. H. Dodd).

We often hear that the God of the Old Testament is a God of wrath and that the God of the New Testament is a God of love. The contrast is not true to either Testament. Both emphasize both God's love and his justice or wrath (see pp. 453-54).

The writers of the Old Testament repeatedly declared God's love for Israel (Deut. 7:7-8; Hos. 11:1; Jer. 31:3; Ps. 103:17).

The concept of God as Father appears in the Old Testament as well as the New (Isa. 63:16; Ps. 103:13; Jer. 3:19; Mal. 2:10). The term Father implies authority and justice as well as tender affection. A father lays requirements on his children, if he truly loves them.

It is indeed true that the range and depth of God's love is more fully shown in the New Testament. Although the Old Testament occasionally declares God's concern for the salvation of the nations, which is to be accomplished through the life and witness of Israel (Gen. 12:3; Isa. 2:2-4; 45:22; 49:6; Zech. 8:23; the book of Jonah), the New Testament almost everywhere assumes the universality of salvation. In the church there are no distinctions of race, class, or sex (Gal. 3:28; Col. 3:11) and the final salvation of the kingdom of God embraces people of every nation and tongue (Rev. 7:9).

And the depth of God's love is greater in the New Testament. There is little evidence in the Old Testament that deliberate, individual sinners within Israel were to be offered mercy, forgiveness, and restoration. They were to be cut off from the people of God (Num. 15:22-36; Deut. 22:13-27). The God of infinite compassion, who loves his enemies and bids his sons do likewise (Matt. 5:43-48; Rom. 5:6-8), is the God Jesus exalted in his teaching and actions and thereby set the standard for the belief and activity of the Christian church (see p. 454).

e. God Is King.

The figure of the king in the ancient Near East offered an apt way of thinking and speaking about God. The king was sovereign, and his subjects were servants. As king he was provider, shepherd, and judge of his people.

We now know that the covenant sealed between God and Israel at Mt. Sinai (Exod. 20–24) and reaffirmed at Shechem by Joshua (Josh. 8:30-35;

chap. 24) followed the pattern of covenants made between ancient kings and vassal states to insure unswerving loyalty of the vassals and proper reward for loyal support. The covenants included a preamble in which the author of the covenant was named, with his titles, attributes, and genealogy; a prologue describing the previous acts of benevolence of the king in relation to his vassal; a statement of the obligations to be accepted by the vassal; blessings and curses as sanctions of the covenant; and some other elements (see pp. 81-82).

The kingship of God was taken so seriously that the establishment of a monarchy in Israel was resisted by Gideon (Judges 8:23) and Samuel (I Sam. 8) as an affront to the kingship of Yahweh.

Israel's worship extolled the kingship of God (Ps. 24:7-10; 95:3; 97:1; 146:10).

The prophets believed that someday God would extend his kingship over all the earth. At that day, either directly or through a chosen human representative, he would judge the nations and inaugurate a new order of peace, prosperity, and felicity (Isa. 9:2-7; 11:1-9; Hag. 2:6-9; Zech. 14:1-9). The New Testament makes much of the coming reign of God (the kingdom of God) and indicates clearly that early Christians believed it to be close at hand (Rom. 13:11-14; I Cor. 7:25-31; I Thess. 4:15-17; I Pet. 4:7; James 5:8). See chap. 102 on "the second coming of Christ."

2. Satan

Before the Babylonian Exile (sixth century B.C.) the Hebrews seem to have thought of God as the source of both good and evil. They viewed natural disasters as his punishment of wrongdoing (Deut. chap. 28; 31:17; I Kings 14:9-10). Because they believed God used the evil acts of men to advance his purposes (e.g., Isa. 10:5-11, where the Assyrians are said to be sent by God to punish Israel), the Old Testament sometimes represents God as the author of evil (Job 2:10; Isa. 45:7; Amos 3:6).

Even moral evil was sometimes attributed to him, as when the Lord sent a lying spirit into the mouth of false prophets to deceive Ahab (I Kings 22:19-23) and an evil spirit "from the Lord" came to torment Saul (I Sam. 16:14-15).

In the late Old Testament period and in the intertestamental period the increasing sense of God's holiness made his responsibility for evil, both moral and natural, seem difficult to accept. The problem is dealt with in part in the book of Job (see chap. 25). The influence of Zoroastrianism on Judaism during the Persian period (539–332 B.C.), with its strong emphasis on an evil being (Angra Mainyu) as the source of evil and the enemy of God, undoubtedly affected Jewish theology and helped to give rise to the concept of Satan developed in this period and contained in the New Testament.

The word Satan means "adversary" or "opposer."

It is used in the Bible principally in two senses:

a. As an angelic agent of God who opposes or tests men

(1) An angelic being, who acted under the authority of God, put Job to the test (Job 1:6-12; 2:1-7); see also I Kings 22:19-23, where a heavenly spirit (here not called Satan) deceives Ahab through false prophets.

(2) The adversary accused the high priest Joshua before the heavenly court because he was guilty of sin along with his people (Zech. 3:1-5).

(3) The adversary told David to count the men of Israel (I Chron. 21:1). The adversary here apparently acted as God's agent (see II Sam. 24:1).

b. As a being hostile to God and the originator and embodiment of all evil

(1) He was referred to by names other than Satan in intertestamental writings and in the New Testament: Belial or Beliar, meaning "the worthless one" (II Cor. 6:15); Mastema, meaning "hostility" (the Book of Jubilees); Beelzebul, meaning perhaps "lord of dung" (Mark 3:22); the devil, meaning "the slanderer" (John 8:44).

(2) Some of his activities according to the New Testament are: ruling over this age (John 12:31; II Cor. 4:4); blinding the minds of unbelievers (II Cor. 4:4); tempting believers to sin (I Cor. 7:5); causing physical affliction (Luke 13:16); frustrating the activities of God's servants (I Thess. 2:18); accusing believers before God (Rev. 12:10); causing persecution of Christians (I Pet. 5:8); empowering the Antichrist for the final war against Christ and the righteous (II Thess. 2:7-12).

(3) His origin is not indicated in the Bible, though some Bible students have claimed that Isa. 14:12 ff. and Ezek. 28:12-19 suggest that Satan was an ambitious angel who was cast out of heaven. But in both passages the reference is clearly to arrogant human kings—of Babylon and Tyre—and not to any ambitious angel.

(4) What Satan is we shall never know, even as we cannot know what God is! Whether Satan is a personal antagonist of God who stands outside people as the inspirer of their evil thoughts and deeds, and who would exist whether people did or not, or whether Satan is man's personifi-

cation of all the evil in individual persons and in society has long been debated.

The Bible is content to stress the reality of evil, whatever its source and exact nature, and to declare that God has acted in Jesus Christ to destroy its power.

98. Man and Miracles

1. Mankind

We have seen that the Bible is a book about God and other supernatural powers (chap. 97). It is also a book about mankind. In fact, its interest in people is so strong that recently some scholars have said that its central concern is persons—their place in the world, their problems as human beings, their resources, and their prospects for the future. From this point of view the Bible contains more "anthropology" (statements about man) than "theology" (statements about God).

Actually, both are in the center of the stage. The biblical drama involves three levels of existence: the supernatural (God, the angels, and the powers of evil); human beings; and animals and the world of nature.

The Bible's description of mankind is complex and varied. We cannot do justice to it in a few summary statements. But we can indicate some general emphases.

a. Human Beings Are God's Creatures.

In Hebrew-Christian thought mankind did not spring from the loins or from the blood of a god—as some ancient religions taught—but was *created* by God (Gen. 1). God formed man from the dust of the earth and gave him life by his own breath (Gen. 2).

There is thus a fundamental distinction between God and mankind. God is above the world and mankind. The world and people are not a part of God but are the result of his creative activity. Man is not divine and self-sufficient. He is dependent on God.

b. Human Beings Are Closely Related to Animals and Nature and, by the Creator's Will, Are Custodians of Both.

The dust from the ground, out of which the Creator formed man (Gen. 2:7), suggests the bond that unites man and nature. People are at home in the world of nature, derive their nourishment from it, and to some extent make the animals their friends and companions (Gen. 2:19-20).

But mankind is superior to the animals and maintains some distance from nature. He names the animals and uses many of them for food. He is not absolute master of the animals and nature, however. Animals and the land have rights too (Deut. 22:10; 27:21; Exod. 23:10-12).

c. Mankind Was Created in Two Sexes; and Persons Are Social in Nature.

Sex is a gift of God, and children are its fruit (Gen. 1:28). Woman was created to be man's companion and helper. God formed her from man's rib. She is from him and part of him and thus his equal—bone of his bone and flesh of his flesh (Gen. 2:23). The animals did not satisfy man's social needs, but the woman (and children) did. In union man and woman become "one flesh" (Gen. 2:24; Mark 10:7-8).

d. A Person Is a Living Being, an Animated Body, an Indivisible Unity of Flesh and Spirit.

When God breathed into man's nostrils the breath of life, he became "a living being" (Gen. 2:7). The Hebrews thought of man not as an incarnated soul, but as a living body.

This body had many characteristics. The physical side was called "flesh." Then there was the "aliveness," the vitality they called *nephesh* (translated "soul" in the King James Version).

They termed the divinely given energies of the individual person his "spirit." "Heart" was the seat of feeling, will, and thought.

In summary, we may say that the Hebrew-Christian view of a human being is that he is *one* self in many aspects or functions—not a self composed of separate parts—body, soul, and spirit.

e. Human Beings Were Created to Live in Fellowship with God and in Obedience to His Will.

They were created in the "image" of God (Gen. 1:26-27; 9:6; Wisd. of Sol. 2:23; I Cor. 11:7; Col. 3:10). This means that people have a relationship to God not shared by animals. As persons standing before a Person, they are not simply a part of nature. They reflect in their persons the qualities of God who created them. They are thus capable of a degree of sovereignty over nature.

Each person is of value to God (Gen. 3:9; Luke 12:6-7; II Pet. 3:9) and is individually responsible to him. Israel's early law codes made the individual offender responsible for his own actions (*e.g.,* Exod. chaps. 21–23). The prophets called for individual repentance and for personal obedience to God (Mic. 6:8), just as Jesus and New Testament writers did (Matt. 21:28-32; Rom. 12:1-3; Heb. 2:1-3). People are also collectively responsible to God (Num. chap. 16; Josh. chap. 7; Deut. 21:1-9).

f. Human Beings Are Frail and Sinful and, in Their Rebellion Against God, Often Become Utterly Corrupt in Their Thinking and Behavior.

Since they came from dust and return to dust, they are weak and mortal. "All flesh is grass . . . the grass withers, the flower fades" (Isa. 40:6-8; I Pet. 1:24). Imperfection, ignorance, and suffering are their lot (Ps. 51:5; Eccles. 8:17; Job 5:7).

By rebelling against God and following their own desires, they become corrupt—at odds with God and with one another.

Gen. 6:5 pictures man's sinfulness before the flood in dark terms: "The Lord saw that the wickedness of man was great in the earth, and that every imagination of the thoughts of his heart was only evil continually."

Paul links the moral depravity of the world to men's refusal to give thanks for God's self-revelation in the created order. Their failure to honor and obey the God thus revealed led to idolatry, "a base mind," and frightful conduct (Rom. 1:18-32). Sin, a diabolical power, laid hold of their lives and brought them into slavery (Rom. 7:13-23). "Death [*i.e.,* spiritual death, final death] spread to all men because all men sinned" (Rom. 5:12).

Paul did not say that all men sin and die because they are physically descended from Adam (*i.e.,* that sin is inherited by every descendant of Adam). He does say that Adam opened the door to sin and sinning and that sin is a monstrous reality in the world. But death comes by man's "yes" to sin. His personal responsibility remains.

g. Sinful Human Beings Have the Potential for God-likeness.

The Bible tells the story of God's long pursuit of sinful mankind: through the righteous line from Seth and Enosh (Gen. 4:25-26) through Enoch (5:22-24), Noah (6:9), Shem (11:10 ff.), and Abram (Abraham); through the work of Moses and the giving of the covenant at Mt. Sinai; through the activity of the prophets; and through the mission of Jesus and the church.

The Bible promises that the tree of life, which God placed in the Garden at the beginning, will at last become fruit and medicine for the nations (Rev. 22:2). It is God's will that sin, death, ignorance, and suffering be vanquished forever (I Cor. 15:54-55; 13:9-12, Rev. 21:4).

The God-likeness intended for mankind at the beginning (Gen. 1:26-27) becomes possible and actual through Jesus Christ, who is the likeness of God (Rom. 8:29; Col. 1:15-20; 3:9-10).

2. Miracles

The Bible holds that God, on the one hand, and the powers of evil, on the other, are active in the world and in the life of mankind and that both are capable of amazing deeds.

These supernatural powers often operate through persons. Pharaoh's magicians, agents of the Egyptian gods, were able to match some of the miracles of Moses and Aaron (Exod. 7:11, 22). We are told that false prophets and false messiahs will deceive many by signs and wonders, even endangering the elect (Matt. 24:24; II Thess. 2:9-12; Rev. 13:11-15).

a. Definition of Miracle

Most of the miracles in the Bible are deeds of Yahweh. The Bible sees a miracle of Yahweh as an act that shows his presence and purpose in the world—usually in an unexpected and intense way, and only to those who have eyes of faith.

Biblical writers did not conceive of nature as an ironclad system of law, in which every effect had a natural cause. They did not think of miracle as an act of God contrary to nature's laws. Since God created the world, it was absolutely dependent on him and he was continually active in it—in sustaining its ordained patterns and intervening from time to time in special ways to carry out his purposes.

b. Purposes of Miracles

(1) To Reveal God and Evoke Faith

Miracles are often called "signs" in both Testaments. A sign is something which points beyond itself to an ultimate reality. It is a signpost or a finger pointing toward God.

The miracles ("signs") Moses did—*e.g.,* the rod turned into a serpent, and the leprous hand—were to point to the fact that God had appeared to Moses and that he was God's agent for the liberation of Israel (Exod. 4:1-8). Israel was to learn through the signs and wonders of the Exodus that Yahweh was God alone (Deut. 4:34-35). Jesus' miracle at Cana was a "sign" pointing toward his "glory" (i.e., God's presence in him—John 2:11).

Biblical writers knew that miracles or signs do not automatically convince people. Pharaoh was not convinced (Exod. 7:8-13) and neither were Jesus' enemies: "Though he had done so many signs before them, yet they did not believe in him" (John 12:37). Signs should call forth faith, but they do not compel it.

Miracles were meant to evoke faith not only in Israel but also among the nations (Ps. 86:8-10; 105:1-6; Isa. 40:3-5; 52:10; John 20:30-31).

(2) The Pledge of Future Fulfillment

God's marvelous deeds in the past are the pledge and guarantee of his help in the future.

The God who defeated the Egyptians by signs, wonders, mighty hand, and outstretched arm will drive out Israel's enemies from the Promised Land (Deut. 7:17-24). The God who fed Israel with manna in the wilderness will see that it eats to the full in that land (8:3-10).

Correspondingly, the miracles of the New Testament are the manifestation in the present of the power of the coming kingdom of God. Jesus claimed that his deeds were signs that the kingdom of God was present and active in his ministry (Luke 11:20; Matt. 12:28). By his deeds he was rescuing lives broken by the devil's power and destroying the power of the devil himself (Mark 3:22-27; Luke 10:18). The early church believed it had tasted of "the powers of the age to come" (Heb. 6:5). It saw in the resurrection of Jesus "the first fruits" of the resurrection of all Christians (I Cor. 15:23).

c. Types of Miracles

(1) Nature miracles: e.g., the strong wind and the parting of the Red Sea at the Exodus (Exod. 14:21-22); the shadow that moved backward on the sundial (II Kings 20:8-11); the floating axe head (II Kings 6:5-7); Jesus' calming the tempest (Mark 4:35-41); the turning of water into wine (John 2:1-11).

(2) Miracles of conception: e.g., Sarah, Rachel, Hannah, and Elizabeth (Gen. 17:15-21; 30:22; I Sam. 1:19-20; Luke 1:8-25); the virgin Mary by the power of the Holy Spirit alone (Luke 1:26-38).

(3) Miracles of national conquest and preservation: e.g., the conquest of Jericho (Josh. 6), the victory by hailstones (Josh. 10:11), the

destruction of the Assyrians and the preservation of Jerusalem in the time of Isaiah (II Kings 19:35).

(4) Miracles of personal preservation and healing: *e.g.,* Elijah fed by the ravens (I Kings 17:4-6); the Hebrews in the fiery furnace and Daniel in the lions' den (Dan. 3:19-27; 6:16-23); Jonah and the great fish (Jon. 1:17); Paul unharmed by the sting of a viper (Acts 28:3-6); Miriam and Naaman saved from leprosy (Num. 12:9-15; II Kings 5:1-14); various sick people by Jesus (*e.g.,* Mark 2:3-12; 5:25-34; Luke 13:11-13), by Peter and the apostles (Acts 3:1-10; 5:12-16), by Paul (Acts 20:7-12; 28:8-9).

(5) Miracles of resurrection: Elisha and the Shunammite woman's son (II Kings 4:32-37), Jesus and the widow's son at Nain (Luke 7:11-15), Jesus and Lazarus (John 11:17-44), Jewish saints at the time of Jesus' crucifixion (Matt. 27:52-53), the resurrection of Jesus (the four Gospels; I Cor. 15:4-8).

d. Workers of Miracles

The miracles recorded in the Bible occurred chiefly in four periods: (1) at the time of Moses, the Exodus, and the establishing of the nation in the Promised Land; (2) at the beginning of the age of the prophets (with Elijah and Elisha), a time of great pressure from Baal religion; (3) at the height of the Assyrian threat against the independence of Judah in the days of Isaiah; (4) in the period of the fulfillment of Old Testament prophesies concerning the end-time begun by Jesus and continued by the early church.

Miracles were part of the work of God's prophets. (Moses and Jesus [Luke 13:33-34] are to be included among the prophets.) The prophet acted for God and released the power of God in the crises of the nation's life.

The early church believed that Jesus did his mighty works by the power of the Holy Spirit (Matt. 12:28; Luke 4:14, 18; 5:17; Acts 10:38). It declared that this power was available to Christians to do the same works, and even greater works (John 14:12). Some Christians, under the power of the Holy Spirit, became workers of miracles and healers (I Cor. 12:9-10, 28).

e. Evaluation of Miracles

The importance of a miracle depends on the extent to which it reveals God and his purpose. The resurrection of Jesus obviously tells us more about God's purpose and activity than does a floating axe head (II Kings 6:5-7) or a fish with a coin in its mouth for payment of the temple tax (Matt. 17:24-27).

We must look at miracles in their literary contexts.

The "miracle" of the sun's standing still (Josh. 10:13-14) resulted from the author's taking literally the poetic imagery in a source he used (vss. 12-13). The story cannot therefore be taken as a true miracle.

The book of Jonah is a short story which aims to teach a religious truth: God loves the Assyrians and desires their repentance and salvation. We are hardly justified in pressing the story about the fish into the category of genuine miracle.

If the book of Daniel was written between 167 and 164 B.C., as seems certain, then the stories of chaps. 1-6 are probably *haggadah,* popular stories designed to set forth religious and moral truths, not sober history (see p. 164).

As far as possible, we must look at miracle stories in the light of their oral and literary history.

Scholars have found that many of the miracle stories of the Gospels have a stereotyped form like miracle stories in other literature (chiefly non-Jewish) of the period (*e.g.,* Mark 7:32-37; 8:22-26). In cases of healing such stories often run through several steps: the seriousness of the sickness and the attempted cures; the method used in the present healing; a demonstration of the reality of the cure; and the impression made on onlookers. Stories not told in this pattern (*e.g.,* Mark 10:46-52; Luke 14:1-6) seem to be older and nearer the original facts.

Parallel stories in the Gospels must be checked in order to find the more original version. For example, Mark 1:34 says, "He [Jesus] healed many who were sick with various diseases," whereas in the parallel passage in Matthew 8:16 we read, "he . . . healed all who were sick." (See also Mark 6:5 and Matt. 13:58.) Matthew tended to heighten the miraculous element in Mark's account.

Such sifting of the miracle stories yields a solid residue of mighty deeds.

The heart of Israel's faith was that Yahweh is the living God, that nothing is too hard (wonderful) for him (Gen. 18:14), and that with him all things are possible (Mark 10:27). If the universe is not a closed, inflexible system—and many scientists today agree that it is not—and if God is the reality the Hebrews claimed him to be, his activity in the world in unexpected and intense ways, as well as in familiar and undramatic ones, will not seem strange to people of faith.

That God should work in the world chiefly through Spirit-empowered people is in line with his purpose to save the world by incarnating himself in the man Jesus.

99. Jesus Christ and the Way of Salvation

1. Jesus Christ

The flood of books in recent years about Jesus and, even more, his impact today on playwrights, athletes, and unchurched youth testify once again that Jesus is a man for all times.

What sort of person *was* he?

Some theologians of a generation ago thought it unnecessary and unrewarding to ask. They said that what is important is not Jesus as he actually was, but only what the apostles believed him to be. It is the Christ of the apostles' faith and preaching who is the proper object of faith, not the historical Jesus. And, furthermore, they said, we can no longer recover the historical Jesus.

Today we think that it is both necessary and rewarding to inquire. We now see what ought to have been obvious all along: that Christianity's real roots are in Jesus himself; it was he who brought about the church's faith and message. If faith in him is to arise in our time, it will come about by *his* impact on us, not simply by the church's proclaimed and recorded faith.

If Jesus is God's example of what people ought to be, and if we are to grow into his likeness, as the New Testament holds (Rom. 8:29), then we must know what sort of man he was.

In spite of the limited and sometimes conflicting information about the life of Jesus in the Gospels (see chap. 64), we now believe that we can recover a reasonably clear portrait of him. This portrait puts us in the crisis of decision—for Jesus or against him.

And what sort of person *is* he?

If he is "alive for evermore" (Rev. 1:18), if he can be with us "to the close of the age" (Matt. 28:20), and if he has "the keys of Death and Hades" (Rev. 1:18), it is imperative that we know him for what he is—for our destiny is in his hands and depends on our relation to him.

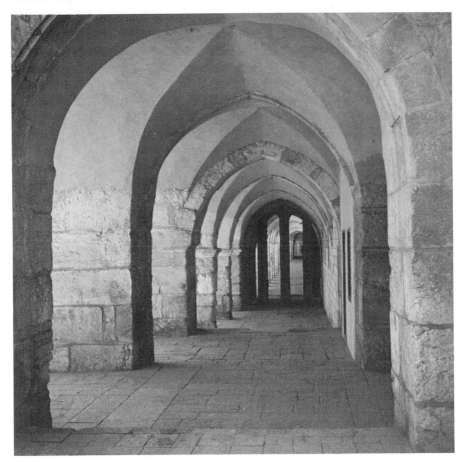

The western colonnaded portico of the present Jerusalem temple area

a. The Career of Jesus

Today scholars agree that it is not possible to write a life of Jesus (see p. 214). We cannot arrange the events of his career chronologically or identify with certainty its major turning points. Neither can we trace his psychological development and changes of strategy. Only the passion narrative offers anything like a connected account of his words and experiences.

Nevertheless, we do have considerable information about him.

He was born in Bethlehem (some have argued for Galilee as his birth place) before the death of Herod the Great in 4 B.C. (see p. 417). A date between 7 and 4 B.C. is probable.

He attended the synagogue as a youth (Luke 4:16). As a boy he showed aptitude for learning and religious discussion (Luke 2:41-51). He worked as a carpenter before he began his ministry (Mark 6:3). He had no formal training for public teaching (John 7:15). He seems to have remained unmarried, though claims to the contrary have been made in recent years. Joseph may have died during Jesus' youth, and Jesus may have become the chief support of the family.

In A.D. 26 or 28 (Luke 3:1-2) he responded to John the Baptist's appeal for repentance, an appeal based on John's conviction that the end of the age and the Messiah's fiery judgment were at hand (Luke 3:7-17). Along with multitudes of Jews, he was baptized by John in the Jordan river (Mark 1:4-11). At that baptism he was filled with the Holy Spirit, with the consciousness of a unique relationship with God, and with a sense of special mission (Mark 1:11).

He began to gather disciples, some of them from among the followers of John the Baptist (John 1:35 ff.; Mark 1:16-20). He taught and baptized for a time in Judea (John 3:22) and then, after the arrest of John the Baptist by Herod Antipas (Mark 1:14), he launched a preaching and teaching mission in the synagogues of Galilee (Luke 4:14-15). He taught also by the lakeside and in the open fields.

His Galilean mission, implemented by a mission carried out by twelve disciples (Mark 6:7-13), was acclaimed by multitudes who heard his teaching and witnessed his amazing deeds (Mark 3:7-10).

But he soon aroused the hostility of influential Pharisees and the suspicions of Herod Antipas, the ruler of Galilee.

The Pharisees objected to his liberal teaching and practice of the Law as they understood and observed it. They were offended most of all, apparently, by his claim of authority to declare what was binding in the Law and what was not (Mark 7:1-23; 10:2-9).

Herod Antipas feared the political consequences of Jesus' popularity with the multitudes and decided to take measures against him (Mark 6:14-16; Luke 13:31). Jesus withdrew for a time into territory to the north of Galilee. While there he seems to have decided on an appeal to the nation in its capital city.

He journeyed to Jerusalem with his disciples. It seems that he had been in Jerusalem at national festivals several times during his ministry. The Gospel of John refers to three Passovers there (2:13; 6:4; 11:55), thus implying at least a two-year ministry. Or the Synoptic Gospels may be accurate in assuming a ministry of a few months more than a year. His final visit to Jerusalem may have occurred at Passover time, A.D. 30.

His act of cleansing the temple caused the priestly authorities to arrest him—by stealth because of his popularity (Mark 14:1-2). Following a grand-jury type hearing before a priestly body, he was turned over to the Roman procurator Pontius Pilate with the recommendation that he be sentenced to death. After hearings before Pilate and Herod Antipas (Luke 23:6-12), he was executed by crucifixion.

His disciples subsequently claimed that God raised him from death and that he had appeared to them individually and collectively.

b. Jesus' Activities

Jesus' activity during his career assumed many forms:

(1) Preaching and Teaching

He announced the coming of the kingdom of God (Mark 1:14-15; Luke 8:1) and instructed the disciples, in particular, concerning its nature and conditions for admission (Matt. 5:1 ff.). He had much to say about God and the will of God for those who believed in him and his message about the kingdom.

(2) Exorcisms and Healing

The Gospels are full of accounts about Jesus' freeing people from demonic control and from afflictions of many kinds. He refused, however, to devote himself principally to a ministry of physical healing (Mark 1:35-39) and to authenticate his mission by miraculous acts (Mark 8:11-12).

(3) Mission to Religious and Social Outcasts

Much of his time and energy was spent in the attempt to reach those outside the synagogue—the "unchurched" people who made little or no attempt to observe traditional Jewish law.

Many of them were engaged in occupations which were thought to be immoral or dishonest, such as money-changing, money-lending, gambling, prostitution, thieving, and, above all, tax-collecting for Rome. These people are the "sinners" or "tax collectors and sinners" so often mentioned in the Gospels (Mark 2:15-17; Matt. 11:19; 21:32; Luke 7:37, 39; 15:1-2, 19:7).

Jesus repeatedly ate their "unclean" and untithed food, and allowed them to touch him (Luke 7:39). He offered them forgiveness, membership in God's family, and a share in the blessings of the coming age (Mark 2:13-14; Luke 19:1-10; 7:36-50; 8:2). His meals with them were symbolic of their coming banquet together in the kingdom of God. In his culture eating with others was a sign of acceptance, reconciliation, mutual trust, and a sharing of life.

Jesus was attacked bitterly for his free association with such people (Mark 2:15-17; Matt. 11:16-19). He defended himself by comparing his mission to that of a physician (Mark 2:17). Much of his teaching was a defense of his conduct in calling "sinners" to God's table (Luke 15; 18:9-14; Matt. 20:1-15; 21:28-32).

(4) Controversies with Religious Leaders

These controversies centered not only on his "scandalous" association with "sinners" but on his attitude toward the Jewish Law and his claim to authority.

He challenged the validity of the food laws (Mark 7:14-23), broke Sabbath laws (2:23–3:5), set Genesis against Deuteronomy on the matter of divorce (Mark 10:2-9), and claimed the right to declare the true meaning of the Law (Matt. 5:21-48). He claimed authority to forgive sins (Mark 2:5) and to have God's power over Satan and the demons (Mark 3:22-27; Luke 11:20). He claimed the right to cleanse the temple of abuses (Mark 11:15-18). His controversy with religious leaders is recorded in both the Synoptic Gospels and the Gospel of John.

(5) Personal Counseling

He dealt often with individuals: the rich man (Mark 10:17-22), Nicodemus (John 3:1 ff.), Zacchaeus (Luke 19:2-9), Mary (Luke 10:38-42), Simon the Pharisee (Luke 7:36 ff.). He made clear the cost of discipleship and brought about personal repentance and rebirth (Luke 19:2-10).

(6) Formation of a Fellowship of Prayer, Obedience, and Suffering Service

He led his disciples in the practice of prayer (Luke 5:16; 6:12; 9:18; 11:1-4). He taught them by example and word the meaning of radical obedience to God, whatever the personal cost (Luke 9:57-62; 13:31-33; Mark 8:31-35). He sent his disciples on a missionary journey (Mark 6:7-13) and led such journeys himself (Luke 4:14-15; 8:1; 9:51 ff.). He regarded his disciples as God's "little flock" to which God would give the coming kingdom (Luke 12:32).

c. His Statements About His Mission

Mark summarized the essence of Jesus' proclamation thus: "The time is fulfilled, and the kingdom of God is at hand; repent, and believe in the gospel" (1:15).

John the Baptist announced the imminent judgment of God on the Jews and the nations. Jesus focused on the kingdom of God, or the rule of God, which would follow that judgment.

Jesus seems to have expected the coming of God's kingdom during his generation (Mark 9:1; 13:30; Matt. 10:23), though he disclaimed knowledge of the exact date (Mark 13:32; *cf.* Acts 1:7).

He did not describe the kingdom but spoke of it in terms of a banquet (Mark 14:25; Matt. 8:11), "life" (Mark 9:43; Matt. 7:14), and "joy" (Matt. 25:21, 23).

He clearly repudiated the political understanding of the kingdom advocated by the Zealots (see p. 409) and refused to join their movement to establish it by force of arms (Mark 12:17; Luke 6:35; Matt. 5:41).

While the kingdom of God was for him principally future, he clearly believed that its power was at work in his deeds and his preaching and that the Scriptures concerning the last days (Isa. 35:5-6; 61:1) were being fulfilled in his ministry (Matt. 11:4-6).

Crucially important is Luke 11:20 (Matt. 12:28): "If it is by the finger of God [Matthew has "the Spirit of God"] that I cast out demons, then the kingdom of God has come upon you." One writer has paraphrased this to read: "If I by God's power take men and women, set them on their feet, and enable them to live a life worth living, that is a clear indication that the kingdom of God is a present active reality among you" (T. W. Manson, *Jesus and the Non-Jews,* p. 17).

Jesus believed he was destroying Satan's hold over people (Mark 3:22-27); God's promised salvation was dawning for those who accepted his announcement of the kingdom and experienced its power through him. (See also chap. 101.)

Did Jesus think that he was or was to be "the Messiah," the anointed king of the coming kingdom of God? There is strong evidence that he disliked the term and the role as his contemporaries conceived it. For them the Messiah was to be a descendant of David, who would destroy all the enemies of the Jews and rule in splendor over the reassembled, holy people of God (Psalms of Solomon, chap. 17). Or he would be the high priest of the New Age ("the Messiah of Aaron" mentioned in the Dead Sea Scrolls), who would serve in the Holy of Holies of the temple in the New Jerusalem, have fellowship with angels, be a light for the world, and have "a branch of David" ("the Messiah of Israel") at his side. Jesus seems to have recognized that he was or would be neither of these.

The Gospel of Mark depicts Jesus as silencing those who accorded him

Photo by H. T. Frank

Modern Tiberias, on the west side of the Sea of Galilee

exalted status (1:24-25, 34; 3:11-12; 8:29-30). Before the high priest he admitted that he regarded himself as the Messiah, but quickly shifted to the term "the Son of man" as more descriptive of his role (14:61-62). One scholar has said, "Jesus imposed silence because of the nature of Messiah- ship as He conceived it to be. To Him it was not primarily a matter of status but of action" (Vincent Taylor, *The Gospel According to St. Mark*, p. 123). He was Messiah only in the breaking of Satan's power, in healing the sick, in forgiving sins, and in preparing a holy people for the coming kingdom of God.

Jesus was more concerned about his work than he was about titles. The only title he made much use of was "the Son of man." What he meant by this is not clear. The term could mean simply a human being (Ps. 8:4) or a Spirit-filled prophet (some 90 times in Ezekiel) or the righteous people of God (Dan. 7:13-18, 27) or the heavenly Judge of all men at the day of judgment and the Savior of the righteous (I Enoch 62:1-14; II Esdras, chap. 13).

Probably he used it in the last sense. If he believed that the power of God's coming kingdom was at work in him—in his preaching and in his deeds—it is not inconceivable that he should have believed God would make him King, Judge, and Savior at the end of the age. He said that if men respond in faith to the earthly Jesus the exalted Jesus (the Son of man) will acknowledge them before the angels of God (Luke 12:8). The question was, Would people believe that the future Son of man was present in their midst? If Jesus understood and used the term in this sense, he claimed that he was God's end-time representative.

There is much evidence that Jesus regarded himself as God's representative, as speaking and acting for God. He was "sent" as the Father's official delegate (Matt. 10:40; John 6:29; 13:20). He offered forgiveness, as if he stood in God's place (Mark 2:10). He interpreted the Law, even setting one part of it against another (Mark 10:2-9), as if he had sovereign authority. His "I say to you," over against the Law and human tradition, had the ring of divine right (Matt. 5:21-48). He offered salvation to tax collectors, harlots, and to the multitudes who did not observe traditional law, as if he had the right to give it. He identified his finger with God's (Luke 11:20).

Did he anticipate his death and speak of it as having redemptive significance? This is a difficult and much discussed question. Though it has often been denied that Jesus foresaw his death, the evidence supports the conclusion that he did. The course he pursued in his ministry was deliberately radical, and many of the charges laid against him had as their punishment death (practicing magic, blaspheming God, being a false prophet, deliberately breaking the Sabbath). He knew of the tradition of the martyrdom of the prophets and saw himself in the succession of the prophets (Luke 13:33-34). And almost before his eyes he had seen John the Baptist put to death.

Some scholars admit that he foresaw his death but deny that he gave it redemptive significance. He saw his death only as his personal "transition to the divine glory" as coming King.

Some facts point to the opposite conclusion. Judaism at Jesus' time contained ideas about the atoning power of death, particularly the death of righteous martyrs (*e.g.,* II Macc. 7:37-38; IV Macc. 6:29). Mark 10:45 ("For the Son of man also came not to be served but to serve, and to give his life as a ransom for many") echoes Isa. 53:10. Here "ransom" corresponds to "offering for sin." Whether the statement came from Jesus or arose in the early church as the church's interpretation of the meaning of his death has long been debated. The words spoken over the bread and wine at the Last Supper (Mark 14:22-24; I Cor. 11:24-25) suggest that Jesus may have regarded himself as a Passover sacrifice for "many" (Mark 14:24; Isa. 53:12), *i.e.,* "the many," everybody.

It would be strange indeed if Jesus entertained no thoughts about the meaning of his death in relation to God's purpose for the salvation of mankind.

If he thought that God had ordained triumph for him and a future as the Judge of all men and the inaugurator of the kingdom of God, we may infer that he also believed in his coming resurrection, vindication, and exaltation to authority (Mark 8:31; 9:31; 10:34; 14:28).

d. The Source of His Power

The New Testament takes both the deity and the humanity of Jesus seriously.

Mark represents Jesus as a divine being in human form, whose true identity and work are known to the demons but are hidden from men as a whole and even, for the most part, from the disciples (see p. 227). Paul and John held that the eternal Word (Son) became flesh (Phil. 2:5-11; II Cor. 8:9; John 1:1-18).

Most readers of the New Testament do not realize how strongly its writers conceived the humanity of Jesus. Heretics in the early church denied that the Son of God, the heavenly Christ, had really come in the flesh (I John 4:1-2; see pp. 334-35). Many passages show that Jesus was indeed authentically human.

Though Jesus had great perception and insight (John 2:25), he was limited in knowledge. He did not know when the Son of man would come (Mark 13:32). He asked questions for information, as ordinary men do (Mark 6:38). The disciples did not assume that he had all knowledge (Matt. 15:12). Luke says that he grew in wisdom (2:52).

Spiritual growth marked his relationship with God and man: he "increased . . . in favor with God and man" (Luke 2:52); "he learned obedience through what he suffered; and being made perfect he became the source of eternal salvation" (Heb. 5:8-9).

He prayed much during his ministry (Luke 3:21; 5:16; 6:12; 9:18; 11:1), and the power of the Holy Spirit came upon him (3:21-22; 4:14; 5:16-17; 6:19). He did his works by the power of the Spirit (Matt. 12:28; Luke 11:20; Acts 10:38). He promised the disciples that they would do the works he did, and greater works, because the Spirit would be given to them (John 7:39; 14:12; 20:22).

He pondered the Scriptures and found meaning in them for his life and ministry (Luke 4:16-20; Mark 2:25-27).

The eternal Son became like us in every respect except our sinning (Heb. 2:14-17; 4:15). Therefore, he is our brother (2:11-13, 17).

The New Testament view is that in the days of Jesus' earthly life he did not draw on any hidden reservoir of deity, but found strength and did his work in the way open to all men.

We may conclude that he was uniquely endowed with intellectual and spiritual capacities, but his endowments fell within the boundaries of what we call human. His resurrection and exaltation removed him from the realm of the human (Matt. 28:18; Phil. 2:9-11). He is now universal Lord (Phil. 2:11; Rev. 1:5; 17:14).

Finally, we may note two general views of Jesus in the New Testament:

(1) He is God's official end-time delegate to mankind. He is the point where God's graciousness and power contact people in their sin and bondage and give them a foretaste of the coming kingdom of God. And he will be God's agent in the inauguration of that coming kingdom.

(2) He is mankind's representative before God. Jesus was fully human. He was tempted by Satan; he prayed; he read the Scriptures; he worked in the power of the Holy Spirit; and he suffered hostility, rejection, and death. Yet he overcame Satan and his enemies and called others to follow him. He seems to have believed—certainly the church after him did—that his life, death, and resurrection would be redemptive for all mankind.

He is thus the one in whom deity and humanity meet. He is both God's eternal Son and mankind's High Priest before God, as the author of the Letter to the Hebrews saw.

2. The Way of Salvation

When the early church called people to faith in Jesus as the promised Redeemer (Acts 2:22-40; 13:23-39; Rom. 1:1-4; I Cor. 15:3-4) and as the point of contact between heaven and earth (John 1:1-18; Phil. 2:6-11; Heb. 1:2-4; 2:9-18), it followed Jesus' own view of his God-appointed position and role.

What did the church mean when it promised "salvation" through Jesus?

Salvation is God's deliverance from all that threatens persons, individually and collectively: sickness, poverty, personal and national enemies, Satan and the demons, sin, death, judgment, the lake of fire. Those whom God saves he restores to wholeness, health, well-being, and right relations with himself and their fellows. Salvation, deliverance, restoration begins in this life and is completed in the coming kingdom of God.

What is the way of salvation, as presented in the New Testament?

a. Seeing or Hearing

Jesus believed that his deeds were signs of the kingdom's presence in his ministry (Luke 11:20), which, when seen, ought to lead to faith (Matt. 11:4-6). He congratulated the disciples for their opportunity to see and hear what prophets and kings had desired to witness (Luke 10:23-24). Sight should lead to insight (John 9). But he knew it did not always do so—for the disciples (Mark 8:18) or the multitudes (Matt. 11:20-24). He marveled that the people of Nazareth, who had seen or heard of his mighty works, still did not believe (Mark 6:2, 6).

Early Christian preaching often, if not always, told the story of Jesus' doings and bore witness to his resurrection (Acts 10:34-43; 13:23-31). Paul said that "faith comes from what is heard, and what is heard comes by the preaching of Christ" (Rom. 10:17). Faith came to the Galatians by Paul's preaching of Christ crucified and by their hearing the message (Gal. 3:1-5). And, like Jesus, the church experienced the agony of seeing its message rejected (Acts 13:44-46; Rom. 10:18-21).

b. Faith (Trust)

Jesus called for faith in God (Mark 11:22) and faith in himself as the one in whom God's power was working and as God's spokesman (Matt. 11:2-6; Mark 1:15; Matt. 8:5-10). He declared, "Everything is possible to one who has faith" (Mark 9:23 NEB).

Faith for Jesus was trust in God's grace and power and in Jesus' own ability to help when human resources had failed (Mark 5:25-34; 9:17-29). Faith was absolute trust in a person and trust in that person's willingness and ability to supply what was needed.

Faith for Paul was complete reliance on Jesus Christ, God's Son, the one sent by God to deliver mankind from the power of sin and death (Rom. 7:21-25; 8:3-4; Gal. 1:4). Faith was openness to and acceptance of the power of God at work in the death and resurrection of Christ (Col. 2:12; Rom. 4:24-25).

In the New Testament, faith is man's response to God's act in Jesus Christ when that act is declared (Rom. 10:17; I Cor. 1:21; 2:1-5). Faith is not an attitude one manages to stir up by his own effort; it is the response to the Father's initiative in Jesus Christ (John 6:37, 44).

c. Repentance (Conversion)

Repentance was preached by John the Baptist (Luke 3:3, 7-14), Jesus (Mark 1:15; Luke 13:3; 15:7, 10), Peter (Acts 2:38; 3:19), Paul (II Cor. 7:10; I Thess. 1:9), and other New Testament writers.

John the Baptist, by a 15th-century Florentine artist

Repentance in the New Testament is not remorse, or even "a change of mind." It is a radical turning around in one's total life (Luke 3:8-14). It is absolute renunciation of false gods and a false way of life and the embracing of the true God and true life (Matt. 11:20-24). It is glad acceptance of the salvation God offers in Jesus (Matt. 12:41-42; 13:44-46; Luke 9:57-62).

Repentance is not the precondition of God's grace; it is a person's response to it. It both accompanies and follows the moment of faith, or trust. It is putting one's house in order as the domicile for God.

Baptism is associated with repentance. It was so in the teaching and practice of John the Baptist (Mark 1:4-11). What baptism meant to John is not altogether clear. It probably was a rite of cleansing away of sins to prepare one who had "turned around" to pass the test of the final judgment.

Jesus and his disciples baptized (John 3:22). It is likely that it was for them a sacrament of preparation for entrance into the coming kingdom of God.

The early church baptized (Acts 2:41; 8:36-38), and Paul assumed that all Christians had been baptized (Rom. 6:3). For Christians, besides an act of preparation for the judgment and entering the coming kingdom, it was the act of incorporation into the death and resurrection of Jesus, the Messiah, and his resurrection-body, the church (Rom. 6:3-4; I Cor. 12:13). It was the occasion of the bestowal of the Holy Spirit (Acts 2:38; I Cor. 12:13), when one experienced in foretaste the power of the Age to Come (II Cor. 1:22; Eph. 1:13-14; Heb. 6:4-5).

d. Obedience

For Jesus and the church, faith involved faithfulness, or obedience.

Jesus warned the disciples against those who called him "Lord" but did not do the will of God (Matt. 7:21). Praise of Jesus' mother—and indirectly of Jesus himself—has little meaning, he said, if one does not "hear the word of God and keep it" (Luke 11:27-28). He who *does* the words of Jesus is the wise man who builds on rock (Matt. 7:24-27).

So, for Paul, faith involves obedience to Jesus as Lord (Master). As Christ was obedient to God (Rom. 5:19; Phil. 2:8), so the Christian is to be obedient to God (Rom. 6:22) and to the Lord Jesus Christ, even in every thought (II Cor. 10:5). He is to be obedient to the gospel (Rom. 10:16) and to the truth (Rom. 2:8). Paul can even speak of "the obedience of faith" (Rom. 1:5).

What this means in practical terms is elaborately treated in the New Testament. It is having the mind of Christ, which means loving God and one's neighbor, and doing the works of love (Phil. 2:5 ff.; Rom. 12:3-21; 13:8-10; I Pet. 2:20-24; Heb. 13:1-6).

Obedience to Christ involves observing the Lord's Supper as the memorial of his sacrifice in our behalf and the pledge of future triumph and fellowship in the kingdom of God (I Cor. 11:23-26; Mark 14:25).

And obedience means making disciples of people of all nations in the time before the coming of the kingdom (Matt. 28:19-20; Mark 14:9; Acts 1:8; Rom. 1:5).

100. The Old Community and the New

Someone has said, "One man is *no* man."

The Bible expresses this truth in such statements as: "It is not good that man should be alone; I will make him a helper fit for him" (Gen. 2:18); "My dwelling place shall be with them; and I will be their God, and they shall be my people" (Ezek. 37:27); and "I bow my knees before the Father, from whom every family in heaven and on earth is named" (Eph. 3:14). Even God is represented as surrounded by heavenly councilors (Ps. 82:1; 89:5-7; Rev. 4:4). According to the Bible, God and men are social beings.

It was at Mt. Sinai under Moses that the slaves from Egypt became an organized religious community. It was the second Moses, Jesus, who by his life, death, and resurrection brought into being the new community, the true Israel (Gal. 6:16; Mark 12:9; John 15:5; Phil. 3:3).

The new community, the Christian church, saw itself as fulfilling God's purpose when he formed the old community: the creation of a holy people, the members of which would live in loyal love with himself and one another, testify to his glory before the nations, and inherit, along with the converted nations, the wonderful future he was planning.

Several characteristics of both communities stand out in the Bible.

1. A Strong Self-Awareness as the People of God

We do not know how early the belief arose that Israel was God's called and chosen people. The early J writer (see pp. 84-86) attributed this belief to Abraham (Gen. 12:1-3). It certainly flowered out in the times of Moses, when the covenant was sealed at Mt. Sinai between Yahweh and the liberated slaves. The J writer's whole history revolves around this belief. The great prophets Amos, Hosea, Isaiah, and Jeremiah repeatedly emphasized God's choice of Israel and Israel's obligations in view of that choice. The author of Deuteronomy discusses the reality and the mystery of Israel's election (7:6-11; 9:4 ff.). The Second Isaiah, during the Exile, undertook to restore the nation's shattered confidence in its place in God's love and concern and to help it fulfill its proper role as God's Servant.

The prophets pointed out that election was not simply to special privilege but to special responsibility and special service. The responsibility and service consisted in receiving God's self-revelation, becoming like him in character, doing his will, and sharing the revelation with all people.

The prophets knew that Israel had failed to be loyal to the terms of its covenant with God and predicted the destruction of the nation. They said that God would preserve a remnant, to which he would give a victorious and righteous king, the Messiah. This remnant would carry out his purpose in the world (e.g., Mic. 4:6-8; 5:2-9; Isa. 4:2-6; 10:20-22; Zeph. 2:7; Jer. 23:3-6; Joel 2:32).

Some scholars have argued that Jesus believed he was the Messiah of the remnant, that he symbolized this claim by appointing *twelve* disciples as "the nuclear Israel," and that he deliberately sought through these disciples to call out the remnant as his followers.

The argument founders on the fact that the Messiah of the remnant was a political-military figure who was to destroy the enemies of Israel (Mic. 5:2-9), a role Jesus clearly repudiated for himself (see p. 443).

Jesus regarded his little company of followers as God's flock, which was to inherit the coming kingdom of God (Luke 12:32). But he does not seem to have used the idea of the remnant in connection with his disciples.

Paul made some use of that idea in stating his understanding of the church (Rom. 11:5). But he preferred to think of the church as the true sons of Abraham (Gal. 3:6-9, 14, 16, 29; Rom. 4:11-12, 16-18), as those who were circumcised in heart not in the flesh (Rom. 2:28-29; Phil. 3:3). By this he meant people whose relationship with God rested on their faith, not on their meritorious works.

It was a constant source of wonder to Christians that they were privileged to be the people of God. This was especially true of Gentiles, who once had been "separated from Christ, alienated from the commonwealth of Israel, and strangers to the covenants of promise" (Eph. 2:12). They were now "a chosen race, a royal priesthood, a holy nation, God's own people," whose purpose was to declare God's wonderful deeds (I Pet. 2:9). They rhapsodized about God's choice of the church, which was made "before the foundation of the world" (Eph. 1:4). "We are God's children now," they said (I John 3:2). As children they knew they were heirs of the glories of the coming kingdom (Rom. 8:14-25; Gal. 4:1-7; Eph. 1:14).

The early Christians believed that the old Israel's relationship with God, based on Moses and the Mosaic covenant, had been superseded by a new relationship, based on the Messiah Jesus and a New Covenant (II Cor. 3:5-18; Heb. 8:6-13). God's law, they said, is now written in the hearts of his true sons, not on tables of stone, and his sons are his true witnesses to the nations.

The conviction that they were God's chosen people, destined for entrance to the kingdom of God in the near future, and now experiencing a foretaste of that future (see chap. 101) gave zest to their life and zeal to their witness.

2. Remembrance of the Past and Anticipation of the Future

The life of the old community was designed to call the past to remembrance. The feasts, the memorial objects (like the ark of the covenant), the literature, and the ceremonies of worship all pointed to God's gracious deeds in the past.

Israel's early creedal statements contained a review of God's redeeming acts (Deut. 6:20-25; 26:5-10; Josh. 24:2-13). The book of Psalms, the hymnbook of temple worship, celebrated his wonders of old. The sermons of Moses in Deuteronomy review in great detail God's marvelous works in Israel's history. The Passover ceremony made Israelite families participants forever in that holy occurrence when God rescued his chosen people from Egypt.

By remembering the marvelous deeds of God in ceremony and worship, the Israelites kept alive their national and religious consciousness. They were thus obligated to obey the terms of the covenant their God had given them at the founding of the nation.

The remembrance of the past also provided ground for their hope for the future. The God who had led them hitherto would lead them henceforth. By their fidelity to his covenant demands, he would fulfill his covenant promises. The Lord would make Israel "the head, and not the tail" (Deut. 28:13). The wealth of the nations would come to the temple (Hag. 2:7); the branch of David would rule in justice over Israel and the nations (Isa. 11:1-9; Jer. 23:5-6); and the earth would be full of the knowledge of the Lord (Isa. 11:9).

The call to remembrance was strong in early Christianity. The preaching dealt with God's gracious deeds in the history of Israel, culminating in the gift of the Savior Jesus Christ (Acts 13:16-41). In II Timothy readers are exhorted to "remember Jesus Christ, risen from the dead, descended from David" (2:8). Paul asked the Ephesian elders to remember the words of the Lord Jesus (Acts 20:35). We owe the existence of the four Gospels to the church's remembering in its worship, teaching, preaching, disciplining of members, and controversy with opponents what Jesus had said and done (see p. 213).

The supreme act of remembrance, of course, was the Lord's Supper, at which Jesus' passion was recalled. Through the taking of the bread and wine the participants entered personally into the meaning of the original event.

Again, the remembering of the past offered ground for hope in the future. The Jesus who ate with them in the homes of Galilee (Mark 2:15; Matt. 11:18-19), on the green grass near the sea (Mark 6:30-44), and in an upper room in Jerusalem (Mark 14:15 ff.) would dine with them at the banquet in the kingdom of God (Mark 14:25). In fact, these meals were a foretaste of life in the kingdom (see chap. 101).

3. Loving Loyalty in Attitude and Deeds

Many people today believe that the New Testament is a book about God's love and the Old Testament is a book about God's wrath. Actually, in both Testaments God's love forms the basis of his actions and his requirements; and both have a place for God's wrath, or judgment.

The old community saw God's love in his choice of Israel to be his people and in his gift of the covenant at Mt. Sinai. We can illustrate this from the book of Deuteronomy.

We read in this remarkable book that the God of the fathers brought the nation into being. He revealed his holy will to it. He guided, protected, and disciplined it. He planned for it peace and prosperity in a good land. He showered unmerited love on it (Deut. 7:6-11). In view of his gracious attitudes and acts, his love should be reciprocated with love. This love should express itself in exclusive worship of him and in loving, just relationships with all members of the covenant community.

Deuteronomy defines in great detail the loving loyalty which members of the community were to express toward one another (see p. 106). God provides the motive for such attitudes and acts. God loved and showed mercy on a weak, afflicted people (5:15). His love for Israel can be explained by no characteristics or qualities of Israel itself (7:7; 9:4-5). Therefore, members of the community should show mercy to one another, even to foreigners in their midst (10:19).

In the church God's love was also the basis for Christians' loving attitudes and deeds. "We love, because he first loved us" (I John 4:19). He manifested his love above all in the gift of his Son, "that we might live through him" (I John 4:9; John 3:16).

Jesus built firmly on the Old Testament teaching about God. He enriched it, of course, by showing its depth and breadth. He addressed God in a way and with a meaning the Old Testament and Judaism had never known: *Abba,* that is, "Dear Father" or something close to "Papa" or "Daddy" in English (Mark 14:36; *cf.* Rom. 8:15). He taught his disciples to address God thus (Luke 11:2). He pictured God's love and concern as including the sparrows and the hairs of our head (Luke 12:6-7). He dramatized God's love for outcasts and thereby scandalized the Pharisees (see pp. 441-42). He showed God's love as embracing the hated Samaritans (Luke 10:30-37) and even national enemies (Matt. 5:41, 44)—at a time when some Jews were advocating bitter hatred of outsiders.

Paul and other Christian writers followed Jesus in requiring love of enemies (Rom. 12:14, 20; I Pet. 2:20-23).

What love requires in practical terms was not spelled out in a code of law for the church as it was in Judaism. In principle, Christians were adult sons, capable of determining what love demands (Gal. 3:23-29). However, there were guidelines for conduct.

Sometimes commands of the Old Testament were appealed to (Rom. 12:19-20; Gal. 5:14; Eph. 6:1-3).

Church traditions and customs offered directions for behavior (I Cor. 11:16).

Codes of household responsibilities, based on Jewish and pagan codes, appeared in the church to guide the relationships between husbands and wives, parents and children, masters and slaves (Col. 3:18–4:1; Eph. 5:22–6:9; I Pet. 2:18–3:7).

Lists of vices and virtues, more or less patterned after Jewish and Greek models, gave guidance (Rom. 1:29-31; Gal. 5:19-23; Phil. 4:8).

Christian wisdom teachers, like the author of the book of James, worked out norms of conduct which expressed the essential character of Christianity.

Intimate concern for one another led to mutual prayers (Rom. 15:30; Col. 4:2-4; James 5:14), confession of sins to one another (James 5:16), the admonishing of fellow Christians (I Thess. 5:14), and financial support of the needy (Acts 11:29-30; II Cor. 8–9).

Christians addressed fellow church members as "brothers." Paul used the term eighteen times in the short letter I Thessalonians, apparently to convey to the Thessalonians his deep concern for them. The term was also used in Judaism in addressing fellow Jews (II Macc. 1:1).

God's loving loyalty to his people set the standard for social attitudes and acts in both the old and the new community.

4. A Holy People in Mission

The purpose of God's choice of Israel, according to both Testaments, was that Israel should be a holy people in mission to all the world.

This purpose finds expression in many passages of the Old Testament: "You shall be holy to me; for I the Lord am holy, and have separated you from the peoples, that you should be mine" (Lev. 20:26; cf. 19:2; Deut. 7:6; 14:2); "you shall be to me a kingdom of priests and a holy nation" (Exod. 19:6; cf. Isa. 4:3; 6:1-8).

In the New Testament the concept of a holy people is strong also: "as he who called you is holy, be holy yourselves in all your conduct; since it is written, 'You shall be holy, for I am holy'" (I Pet. 1:15-16); "God's temple is holy, and that temple you [the church at Corinth] are" (I Cor. 3:17; cf. Eph. 1:4; 2:21; Heb. 3:1); "you are a chosen race, a royal priesthood, a holy nation, God's own people" (I Pet. 2:9; cf. Rev. 1:5-6).

What did it mean to be a holy people?

When a Hebrew said that God was "holy," he meant that he was above and beyond the universe (transcendent), different from man and all his works, separated from the common and profane, and powerful, brilliant, and glorious beyond imagining. Under the influence of the teaching of the great prophets God's separation from man's sin came to the fore (e.g., Isa. 6:1-8), and his holiness came to mean also his goodness or rightness. The basic ideas in God's "holiness," then, are separation, glorious power, and rightness or goodness.

A holy people, accordingly, is a community set apart from the common and profane for God's possession and use. By virtue of its association with him, it shares in his glorious power, and acts in accordance with his rightness or goodness by keeping his law.

From the standpoint of the great prophets Israel failed to become a holy people and to serve as his light to the nations. Why did this happen? Historical circumstances played their part.

Israelites felt both the appeal and the pressure of the idolatrous religions in and around their land.

Agricultural life in Canaan had long been tied to fertility deities, whose worship in sexual rites was thought important in bringing about fertility of lands, animals, and people. These practices were seductively attractive and economically important, it seemed, especially since Yahweh was a God of the desert!

The road to military security in that day (and today!) was alliance with a strong, friendly, outside power. The cost was the payment of tribute and recognition of the gods of that power (II Kings 16:6-16). A fearful corruption of Israel's life and religion resulted from paying this price.

The religious establishments of the great powers around were impressive: ornate temples, many priests and priestesses, dramatic ceremonies, and elaborate sacrifices. Kings like Solomon and Ahab aped the architecture and worship practices of surrounding peoples. Hebrew religion turned in a ceremonial, rather than an ethical, direction—to the horror of the prophets (Amos 5:21-24; Mic. 6:6-8; Jer. 7:21-23).

The preoccupation with the Law, after the fall of Jerusalem and the destruction of the temple, and its exaltation over the life of the people led in the direction of legalism and salvation by works (see pp. 404-5).

There were great souls, of course, who kept alive the covenant faith and way of life and sought to fulfill Israel's responsibility to the nations (the Old Testament prophets and the writers of the books of Jonah and Ruth), but the nation's record as a whole was dismal.

John the Baptist, Jesus, and the church called the nation to turn away from ceremonial and legalistic religion to a religion of heart and life.

Jesus reaffirmed the emphases of the great prophets: exclusive loyalty to God and the rejection of all false gods ("You cannot serve God and

Money"—Matt. 6:24 NEB); and the subordination of sacrifice to mercy (Matt. 9:13; 12:7; 23:3).

The church viewed all animal sacrifice as ineffective. Jesus' effective sacrifice of himself had replaced it (I Cor. 5:7; Heb. 9:12-14). The church saw proper sacrifice as the offering of oneself to God in spiritual worship (Rom. 12:1; I Pet. 2:5).

Jesus and the church placed strong emphasis on personal, inner cleansing. God requires inner goodness and purity, not outward correctness (Mark 7:14-23; Matt. 5:21 ff.; Rom. 2:28-29; Col. 3:5-17).

Holiness—that is, separation from all moral defilement—Spirit-empowerment, and godly character, were the hallmarks of early Christianity: "Strive for peace with all men, and for the holiness without which no one will see the Lord" (Heb. 12:14); "May God himself, the God of peace, make you holy in every part, and keep you sound in spirit, soul, and body, without fault when our Lord Jesus Christ comes" (I Thess. 5:23 NEB).

Holiness of life was God's gift ("He who calls you is to be trusted; he will do it"—I Thess. 5:24 NEB) and resulted from the presence of the Holy Spirit, or Christ, or God in the Christian (Rom. 8:9-11).

The author of I Peter wrote that the Christians' task, as the holy people of God, was to "declare the wonderful deeds of him who called you out of darkness into his marvelous light" (2:9). Under Paul and other Christian preachers the new community reached out to the Gentile world to fulfill Israel's mission to the nations. Paul regarded himself as God's apostle (special envoy) to the whole Gentile world (Rom. 11:13; 15:16). With incredible zeal he sought to complete his God-given mission in the brief period—as he viewed God's time clock—before the end of the age (Rom. 13:11-14; I Cor. 7:29-31). (See chap. 102.)

The church became God's "holy temple in the Lord" (Eph. 2:21) in which a new humanity, without distinctions of race, class, or sex (Gal. 3:28; Col. 3:11), worshiped God in spirit and truth (John 4:24) and pressed on toward perfection of life (Phil. 3:12-15).

While the old and the new communities had much in common, there were strong differences as well.

As we noted above, the two communities shared in remembrance and anticipation. A third word must be added to characterize the church properly: realization.

The church believed that it was the community for which righteous men long had hoped (I Cor. 10:11; I Pet. 1:10-12). God had sent his Messiah in the person of Jesus of Nazareth (Acts 2:36). Through his ministry, death, and resurrection God had broken the power of Satan (Col. 2:15;

Heb. 2:14-15). God had made the resurrected Christ reigning Lord. Christ awaited only the Father's time for introducing the final kingdom of God (Phil. 2:9-11; Acts 3:19-21).

Through Jesus' coming and work, the Holy Spirit, long expected as God's gift for the Messianic Age (Joel 2:28-32), had been poured out on the church (John 20:22; Acts 2:1 ff.). The church, because of the Spirit's presence in it, was the outpost of the coming kingdom of God, the kingdom in foretaste (see chap. 101).

In view of all this, radiant joy marked the church's life, and miraculous powers attended its ministry (see p. 436). There was a keener sense of the reality of personal and corporate redemption in the church and a brighter hope for the immediate future than in Judaism.

Finally, Judaism was less missionary in spirit than early Christianity. Though there were attempts to reach Gentiles through the synagogues of the Dispersion, the Old Testament expectation that Yahweh's temple and obedient, glorified Israel would draw the nations to Jerusalem in the Messianic Age (see pp. 405-6) did not provide a strong motive for active evangelization of the nations.

Christians, in the belief that the Messiah had come, that the life of the kingdom of God could be tasted in anticipation in the church, and that the establishment of the kingdom was very near, sought converts among the Gentiles with an enthusiasm never before witnessed by Jews.

101. The Christian in the World

What precisely is the Christian's relation to the kingdom of God, on the one hand, and to the world in which he lives, on the other? Answering this question will require careful attention to the meaning of the kingdom of God, the characteristics that mark the life of a Christian, and the nature of the world.

1. The Kingdom of God

In general, four views of what Jesus meant by the kingdom of God have been advanced in the last hundred years or so.

a. A new order of society here on the earth in which humanity will be organized through action inspired by love. It will come as men obey the will of God as taught by Jesus. We might call this *a religious-sociological conception.*

b. A new community (the church) raised up by Jesus and given authority over the lives of men—*an ecclesiastical conception.*

c. The rule of God in the individual human heart, that is, the inner acceptance of God's authority over one's life—*a spiritual conception.*

d. An order to be introduced by God at the end of history—*an eschatological* (having to do with "last things") *conception.*

The last view is the one most New Testament scholars today believe Jesus held. He may have held it in one of four forms. There have been scholarly advocates for each form.

(1) *The kingdom future.* Jesus expected the end of the world very soon, to be followed by the final judgment and the inauguration of a new heavenly order. He called people to repent so that they might enter this New Age. The kingdom was, for him, in no real sense present. He regarded it as near—in fact, there were signs of its coming—but it was still future. Its nearness placed people in an intense crisis and made extraordinary ethical demands on them. It forced them to a crucial decision for or against him and his announcement.

(2) *The kingdom present.* Jesus believed the eschatological kingdom had actually arrived in his appearance, his works of power, his defeat of the forces of evil in personal and corporate life, and his formation of the church. The kingdom of God is really the rule of God over a redeemed people, and *that* is possible within history. Though he talked about the coming of the kingdom in symbolic language (which makes it sound other-worldly), in actuality he expected life to continue on this earth and the gospel to spread to the ends of it. Christians are, then, in the kingdom as members of God's community, the church. This view has strong points of contact with *a, b,* and *c* above.

(3) *The kingdom both present and future.* For Jesus the kingdom was chiefly future, but he believed it was so near it had driven a wedge into history in such a way that it could be said to have begun. In his works he saw the power of evil being broken, a new community being formed which would soon enter the coming kingdom, and life in this community anticipating life in the coming age. He taught that in response to God's gracious redemption, members were expected to live now by the standards of the New Age. Failure to do so would bring exclusion from the final kingdom soon to arrive.

(4) *The kingdom interpreted existentially.* Jesus, using the dramatic language and thought forms of his age, announced the coming end of all

things and urged people to repent and believe in him as the bringer of God's good news of final salvation. He was not really concerned with the end of the world and the inauguration of an objective new world order in its place. He was rather concerned with the end of history for the person in either life or death. He was offering people God's authentic existence (life) and calling them to be open to God's future, whatever that might involve. He also warned them of the tragic consequences of refusal (death or inadequate existence). People are called to do God's will with all their might while they continue in authentic living.

The third form above is probably faithful to more of the evidence concerning Jesus' view of the kingdom of God than any other. We may represent it as follows:

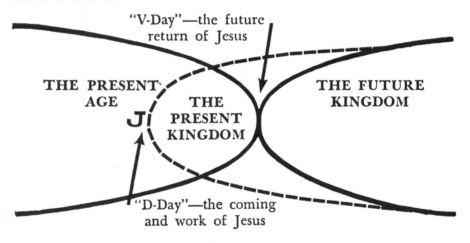

The solid arc at the left indicates the limits of the present age. Jesus, who is represented here by J, felt he was living in the last days of the present age. He saw the future kingdom of God (solid arc at right), which was to end the present age, as near. Its powers had overlapped the present age (broken arc) and were at work in his preaching, teaching, healings, and expulsion of demons. His redeemed followers were already living in the manner of the future kingdom of God while they awaited the final kingdom. To use one scholar's terms, Jesus believed that "D-Day" had occurred in his appearance and ministry (for Satan's kingdom had been breached); "V-Day" would occur soon, at his return as the Son of man from heaven with the future kingdom, when Satan would be finally and absolutely defeated.

If such was Jesus' view of the kingdom of God, the church after him was faithful to it, on the whole. The Christian community in Jerusalem believed that the Holy Spirit, the power of the age to come (Joel 2:28-32; Heb. 6:4-5), had been given to it (Acts 2:16 ff.). It seems to have patterned its worship after its idea of the nature of worship in the kingdom of God. Its communal dinners (Acts 2:42, 46), like those enjoyed with Jesus (Mark 2:15; Matt. 11:19; Mark 6:35-44; Luke 22:14 ff.), were anticipations of the great banquet in the coming kingdom of God (Mark 14:25; Matt. 8:11). Its spirit of brotherhood, in which economic and social distinctions had largely disappeared (Acts 2:44-45; 4:32-35; 6:1 ff.), anticipated the brotherhood of the coming kingdom.

Paul emphasized the present aspect of the kingdom when he wrote to the Romans: "the kingdom of God is not eating and drinking, but justice, peace, and joy, inspired by the Holy Spirit" (14:17 NEB). He said to the Colossians, "He [God] has delivered us from the dominion of darkness and transferred us to the kingdom of his beloved Son, in whom we have redemption, the forgiveness of sins" (1:13-14; cf. II Cor. 5:17).

This sense of present membership in the kingdom of God must have been very strong in the church at Corinth. False teachers there persuaded many in the church to give up entirely belief in resurrection to life in a future kingdom and to concentrate on *present* redemption (see p. 270). Paul had to call that church back to the view that present experience was an anticipation, not a complete fulfillment, of the hope of Jesus and the church concerning the coming of the kingdom of God. The day of the Lord had not already come, as some had claimed (II Thess. 2:2 ff.).

The church's view of itself seems to have been that it was "a colony of heaven" (Phil. 3:20 Moffatt), an outpost of the final kingdom of God. It enjoyed in advance the powers and privileges of that kingdom, and it lived by its standards now. It expected the glorious coming of the kingdom of God in the near future (Rom. 13:11-12; I Cor. 7:29-31; James 5:8).

2. The Marks of a Christian

Nowhere in the New Testament are the marks of a Christian so completely presented as in the Sermon on the Mount (Matt. chaps. 5-7). The church preserved Jesus' teaching about the nature of Christian discipleship, and the author of the Gospel of Matthew gathered it together in a great sermon.

The sermon was put together for church members—for those who already had made the decision of faith in Jesus. It was not intended to be a pattern of discipline to qualify those who followed it for admission to the kingdom of heaven. According to the New Testament, we do not act our way into salvation; we act *in* salvation. This means increasingly acting out our response to the gracious deed of God in the gift of Jesus Christ and coming to maturity in him (Eph. 4:13). The Sermon on the Mount offers us a guide to this kind of growth.

Characteristics of a Disciple of Jesus in the Sermon on the Mount

Inner Life	Relation to God	Relation to Fellow Men	Relation to Things
Feels spiritual need (5:3)			
Repentant (5:4)		Merciful (5:7)	
Humble (5:5)		Reconciled (5:21-26)	
Desires right's triumph (or to do God's will) (5:6)		Chaste (5:27-30)	
		Faithful in marriage (5:31-32)	
Single-minded (5:8)		Truthful (5:33-37)	
Peace-making (5:9)		Actively benevolent (5:38-42)	
Joyful in persecution (5:10-12)		Loves enemies (5:43-48)	
Inner sincerity (6:1-18)	Seeks God's favor (6:1-18)	Unostentatious in giving (6:2-4)	
	Prays privately and simply (6:5-8)		
	Submits to God's will (6:10)		
	Depends on God for bread, forgiveness, and deliverance from evil (6:11-13)	Forgives trespassers (6:12, 14)	
	Penitent before God (6:16-18)		
Serenity (6:25-33)	Worships God alone and trusts completely in him (6:19-34)		Needs them but is not mastered by them (6:24-34)
	Eager in prayer (7:7-11)	Generous in judgment (7:1-5)	
	Radical in commitment (7:13-14)	Discriminating in approach (7:6)	
	Obedient to God's will as spoken through Christ (7:21-27)	Large-hearted (7:12) Devoted to good works (7:15-20)	
Summary: Inner goodness and integrity	Summary: An obedient son of the Father	Summary: Actively all-loving	Summary: Needs them but is not mastered by them

Such character, relationship to God, and actions toward one's fellowmen make the disciple salt and light in the world (5:13-16).

From the Sermon on the Mount and the Gospel of Matthew as a whole, we may draw up Matthew's portrait of a Christian.

A Christian has accepted the Father's revelation of Jesus as the end-time Deliverer (Messiah, Son of God, Son of man, "God with us"). He has trusted implicitly in him, received forgiveness of sins, and become inwardly good (sincere, humble, loving) rather than outwardly correct. He has dedicated himself to imitating Jesus in acts of loving service in behalf of all people. He has faithfully carried out his mission of spreading the good news to all men concerning the salvation available in Jesus. He is like the Father in character and activity (a son of the Father—Matt. 5:45). (See the discussion of the Gospel of Matthew, chap. 65.)

By faithfully obeying and imitating Jesus he will be light and salt in the world and will be admitted to the kingdom of God (kingdom of heaven) at its coming.

Paul also saw the Christian as a son of God (Gal. 3:26; Rom. 8:15-16), who has trusted completely in Jesus as the end-time Deliverer sent from God (Rom. 3:22-25).

The Christian has been freed from sin (Rom. 6:6-7) and bondage to evil powers (Gal. 4:8-9). He has received the Holy Spirit as God's gift and pledge of final salvation (Rom. 5:5; II Cor. 1:22).

He has the mind of Christ (I Cor. 2:16) and thus seeks to benefit others rather than himself (Phil. 2:3 ff.). He lives and serves in the church in the spirit of love, using his gifts for the benefit of all (Rom. 12:3-21; I Cor. 12:27–13:13). He fulfills the law of God by loving his neighbor as himself (Rom. 13:8-10). Though he is free in Christ, he restricts his liberty if he finds that his conduct is injuring his brother in the church (I Cor. 8:7-13).

He is a loyal citizen in the state, honoring established authority and paying his taxes (Rom. 13:1-7).

He presses on toward moral perfection through imitating Christ and Christian leaders (I Cor. 11:1; I Thess. 1:6; Phil. 3:12-17). He is spiritually and morally alert while he awaits the coming of Christ and the kingdom of God (Rom. 13:11-14; I Thess. 5:1-11).

He actively preaches the gospel or supports those who do (II Cor. 5:11-20; I Cor. 16:10-11; Gal. 6:6; Eph. 6:18-20).

3. The World

It is in the Gospel and epistles of John that we hear most about "the world."

The term is used in these writings in several senses: the physical universe (John 1:10; 11:9; 17:5); the earth, as distinct from heaven (John 8:23;

18:36); mankind (John 3:16; 12:19); and evil people and their way of thinking and living (John 7:7; 17:14; I John 2:15-16). The last meaning is the dominant one in these books.

Characteristics of these evil people are: ignorance (John 12:35); unbelief (John 5:38); hatred of fellows (I John 2:11); falsehood (I John 2:22); and bondage to sin (John 8:34), death (I John 3:14), and the devil (John 8:44).

For this author the world in the sense of the physical universe is good. It was created through the Word (John 1:3, 10). Human existence is not in itself evil, for the Word "became flesh" (John 1:14). Although life on the earth is a lower form of existence than life in heaven—from which Jesus came, to which he returns, and in which he prepares a place for us (John 14:2)—it is a suitable meeting place for God incarnate and mankind and for human decision.

Both God and the devil are operating on the earth, and people must decide between them. Those who decide for Christ have life here and now (John 5:24). Those who decide against him remain under the devil's power (I John 5:19)—in sin and in death (John 8:24).

The earth, then, is a battleground where human destiny is decided. Evil people, who love the world and the things of the world (I John 2:15-16)— that is, who find their satisfactions in the earthly and the created—attract people to their way of thinking and living. But other people are drawn by the Father to Jesus Christ and a higher life here and hereafter (John 6:37, 44).

The writer of the Gospel and the epistles of John was not an ascetic who renounced the created order as evil (see p. 305); rather he affirmed it as God's and as suited for God's purpose. He saw that the devil ("the ruler of this world"—12:31) gets people in his power and makes their way of living appealing, even to those who have chosen Christ (I John 2:15-16). But Christ's power is greater than the devil's (I John 3:8; 4:4), and Christians need not fall victim to him.

Christians must live in the evil world (John 17:11, 15). They have a mission to the world, as Jesus had a mission to the world. They are to represent Jesus, even as Jesus represented God (John 17:18; 13:20). Like Jesus, they are to gather out of the world those whom the Father draws to Jesus (John 17:6, 9, 20).

But while they are "in the world," they are not to be "of the world" (John 17:14-16). They are not to love the world but to love the Father (I John 2:15). Sensuality, covetousness, and empty boasting, characteristic of people of the world, are not to capture them (I John 2:16). They are to be set apart from the world's spirit and protected from the devil by God's powerful name (John 17:11; cf. Prov. 18:10) and by his Spirit (John 14:16-17; I John 4:4). They are separated from the world (John 17:16, 19) in order that they may have a mission to it (vs. 18).

Paul also stressed the Christian's separation from the world ("holiness"— see pp. 298-99), but he also had something to say about his involvement with the world. As long as Christians are in the present age in an outpost of the coming kingdom of God, they have obligations toward this age as well as toward the coming kingdom. Christians are to honor the governing authorities and to pay their taxes (Rom. 13:1-7; cf. I Pet. 2:13-17).

Paul may have known that Jesus said, "Render to Caesar the things that are Caesar's, and to God the things that are God's" (Mark 12:17).

When the emperor and the state usurped the place belonging to God, then Christian teachers counseled moral and spiritual resistance (see on the Revelation to John, pp. 349-51).

The writer of the second- or third-century Letter to Diognetus stressed the dual obligation of Christians:

> Christians cannot be distinguished from the rest of the human race by country or language or customs. They do not live in cities of their own; they do not use a peculiar form of speech; they do not follow an eccentric manner of life. . . . Yet, although they live in Greek and barbarian cities alike, as each man's lot has been cast, and follow the customs of the country in clothing and food and other matters of daily living, at the same time they give proof of the remarkable and admittedly extraordinary constitution of their own commonwealth. They live in their own countries, but only as aliens. They have a share in everything as citizens, and endure everything as foreigners. Every foreign land is their fatherland, and yet for them every fatherland is a foreign land. They marry, like everyone else, and they beget children, but they do not cast out their offspring. They share their board with each other, but not their marriage bed. It is true that they are "in the flesh," but they do not live "according to the flesh." They busy themselves on earth, but their citizenship is in heaven. They obey the established laws, but in their own lives they go far beyond what the laws require. They love all men, and by all men are persecuted. . . . They are reviled, and yet they bless. . . . What the soul is in the body, that Christians are in the world. (*Letter to Diognetus* 5:1–6:1, Eugene R. Fairweather translation)

Because Christians live only in the outpost of the kingdom of God they pray, "Thy kingdom come"; and because they live in the present, evil age, they cry out, "Lead us not into temptation, but deliver us from evil [the evil one]" (Matt. 6:13).

102. The Second Coming of Christ

The whole New Testament looks forward to the final triumph of Jesus Christ and his establishment of the glorious kingdom of God.

New Testament writers believed that Jesus, who appeared among men in humility and suffering, unheralded and unrecognized, would soon be revealed for what he really was: the mighty, long-promised Messiah, the God-appointed inaugurator of the end-time kingdom of God.

The tiny mustard seed he had planted during his earthly career (the present kingdom), valued in faith by his disciples but ignored or despised by "the wise" (Matt. 11:25), would become a great tree (the future kingdom) for the nesting of the birds of the earth (the nations) (Matt. 13:31-34). At that time, they said, every knee would bow and every tongue confess his sovereign authority (Phil. 2:10-11).

The material in the New Testament concerning the future triumph of Christ is so abundant, so complex, and so difficult to interpret that it almost defies brief discussion. But we may take note of a few major points.

1. Terms Characterizing Christ's Triumph

Some passages speak of "the revealing" of Jesus Christ (I Cor. 1:7; I Pet. 1:7). Others refer to his "appearing" (II Thess. 2:8; I Tim. 6:14) or his "coming" (Mark 13:26; Matt. 25:31) or to "the day" of the Lord Jesus or Christ or Son of man (I Cor. 1:8; Phil. 2:16; Luke 17:22).

Most striking of all the terms is the Greek word *parousia* (translated "coming" in RSV) (Matt. 24:3; I Cor. 15:23; James 5:7). In a secular, everyday sense this word meant "arrival" or "presence" (I Cor. 16:17; II Cor. 10:10). It was used in New Testament times as a special term to refer to the presence of a hidden deity or the visit to a province of a king, an emperor, or some other official. People were asked to get ready for the "presence" of the king. The word therefore was especially appropriate for Jesus' future manifestation as King.

The New Testament does not speak of Jesus' "second coming," though Heb. 9:28 comes close to it. "Second coming" goes back at least to the second century (to Justin Martyr).

2. The Purposes of Christ's "Coming" or "Presence"

a. Judgment of sinners (Matt. 24:48-51; 25:31-46; II Thess. 1:6-10)

b. The reward of the righteous by the gift of the kingdom (II Thess. 1:5-10; II Cor. 5:10; Matt. 25:31-46)

c. The destruction of evil powers (I Cor. 15:24-26; II Thess. 2:8; Rev. 19:11-21), thus the preparation for Christ's thousand-year reign (Rev. 20:4-6) and/or the absolute reign of God (I Cor. 15:28; Rev. 21:5)

3. The Time of Christ's Coming

The whole New Testament represents it as near.

Jesus apparently expected it during the generation of those living when he was speaking (Mark 9:1; 13:28-30; Matt. 10:23). Paul was convinced that it was near (Rom. 13:11-12; I Cor. 7:29-31; I Thess. 4:15-17; 5:1-10; Phil. 4:5). Other New Testament writers expected it soon (I Pet. 4:7; James 5:8; I John 2:18; Rev. 1:1; 22:6-7, 10, 12).

How soon they thought of it as coming is uncertain.

Jesus seems to have expected an interim between his death and the end during which the gospel would be preached inside and outside Israel by his disciples (Mark 13:10; 14:9). In that endeavor they would suffer persecution and sorrow (Mark 2:19-20; Luke 6:22; Matt. 10:28; Mark 8:34-35). Jesus' open attitude toward Gentiles during his ministry (Matt. 8:5-13; Mark 7:24-30) offers ground for believing that he intended the disciples to carry out a mission to them, which he himself could not do.

Paul clearly thought God had raised him up to preach to the Gentiles in the time before the end (I Cor. 1:1, 7; Rom. 1:5; 11:13; 15:15-16; II Thess. 2:14). Some scholars have suggested that Paul believed the end would not come until his ministry was completed. But the evidence is inconclusive.

Luke expected some time yet before the end (19:11-27). He saw spreading the gospel to the nations as the church's ordained task in this period (Acts 1:6-8).

Neither Jesus nor the church set dates. Jesus denied knowledge of the time of the end (Mark 13:32) and counseled the disciples not to speculate. He told them to leave the time to God and to concentrate on their mission (Acts 1:7-8).

Jesus predicted the destruction of Jerusalem by the Romans (Mark 13:1-2; Luke 13:3-5, 34-35; 21:20-24). But how it was related in his mind to the end of the age is not clear.

There are no real clues in either Testament for setting the time of the second coming of Christ. (On the "signs of the times" see the remarks under point 5 below.) We are told to leave the date to God, to be about

our Master's work in the meantime, and to be ready for the coming when-
ever it occurs (Mark 13:33-37; Luke 12:35-37).

4. The Manner of Christ's Coming

The coming of Christ is set forth in the New Testament in symbolic or
picture language. Christ (the Son of man) will come veiled in clouds,
surrounded by angels, in supernatural glory (Mark 13:26). There will be
an archangel's call, a blast of a trumpet, a cry of command, and Christ's
fiery descent from heaven (I Thess. 4:16; II Thess. 1:7). Or he will come
on a white horse at the head of the armies of heaven (Rev. 19:11-16). His
coming will be sudden and unpredictable (Mark 13:33-37; Luke 17:20-37;
I Thess. 5:2-4).

Usually the coming is represented as a descent from heaven to earth
(I Thess. 4:16; Acts 1:11; Rev. 1:7). But in some passages the manifestation of Christ's triumph seems to consist in his elevation from earth—that
is, a movement from below upward (Luke 22:69, in contrast to Mark
14:62; Acts 7:56; Luke 24:26; John 12:23). Some scholars therefore
think that Jesus' concept of his coming was a coming upward into his
sovereignty—an exaltation—and that the church understood it as a coming
back to earth. Whatever Jesus' concept, the church clearly believed in
both Jesus' exaltation and his return (Acts 1:11).

5. The Interpretation of Christ's Coming

a. The Literalist View
Some interpreters attempt to fit together all passages in the Bible concerning Christ's (or God's) coming at the end of time and to construct
from them a total picture of its nature and the exact sequence of events
related to it.

No consistent understanding results from such an attempt, as the many
contradictory systems of the past and present show. Such interpreters simply
tear passages from their historical and literary contexts and deny to biblical
writers their individuality (see p. 60).

How does one fit Paul's view of the rapture of living Christians at the
time of Christ's coming (I Thess. 4:16-17) with the scheme in the Revelation to John where no such rapture is mentioned? Will Christians go
through the awful times that are coming on the earth, as predicted in Rev.
6:11; 13:7, 10, 15; or will they be rescued before these times come, as
Paul possibly suggests in I Thess. 4:16-17?

How can one fit together the many "signs" of the end suggested in the Old and New Testaments? They simply defy logical or chronological arrangement. And many of them are frequently occurring natural phenomena with no significant value as definite signs of the end (Matt. 24:6-8). Their purpose seems to be to call the believer to preparedness, watchfulness, and steadfastness—to keep him examining his own life and situation in the light of trends in the world in which he lives—not to tell him when the end will arrive.

How does one reconcile Christ's coming "in the same way as you saw him go into heaven" (Acts 1:11) with his coming on a white horse at the head of the armies of heaven (Rev. 19:11-16)? Are there two different comings, one to rescue living Christians and the other to destroy the forces of evil, or is there to be only one? Does the coming (or do the comings) precede the millennium (Rev. 20:4-6)—thus "premillennialism" —or does it follow the millennium ("postmillennialism")?

And what is the religious significance of this speculation anyhow, especially when Jesus forbade such preoccupation (Acts 1:6-7)? If it is God's business, he will see to it, and we should see to ours (Acts 1:8)!

The problems are legion in this literalist approach.

b. The Conservative View

Other interpreters seek to take the coming of Christ seriously without taking it literally.

They admit the pictorial and often inconsistent character of the New Testament descriptions of Christ's coming. They do not hunt out unmistakable signs of the end and arrange them in a sequence designed to determine its time. They do not seek to identify the Antichrist with some contemporary person or group. They do not place the millennium before or after the *parousia* (presence).

But they do insist on a real return of Christ to be with his people and to complete what he began. Though he is present with us now as the living Christ, his presence is veiled. We do not fully know him as he is and will be to us in the kingdom of God. Though his power is at work in us and in the world now, his mighty arm is restrained. At his coming his sovereignty will be manifested in all the earth. The kingdom he began in weakness, suffering, and death will be consummated in power. He will bring an end to the forces of chaos, sin, and death, and transform the created order into the Garden of Eden it was meant to be.

As one such scholar puts it, "the importance of the *parousia* hope is not its representation of Jesus as moving from one point to another in the firmament, but its insistence that then he performs his awaited work of fulfilment" (G. R. Beasley-Murray).

Supporters of this view believe with biblical writers that human existence and the world itself are impermanent—"here we have no lasting city, but we seek the city which is to come" (Heb. 13:14; *cf.* I Cor. 7:29-31; II Pet. 3:10)—and that God will complete in another order of existence what he began in this.

In short, they hold to the heart of the New Testament hope, while allowing for the inconsistent and ancient forms in which it is expressed.

c. The Liberal Position

There are those who think that the New Testament teaching about the second coming of Christ does not rest on Jesus' belief about his future role. Jesus spoke not about a return in glory to the earth (a visitation) but only about a future vindication. He had nothing to say about the end of the world. He looked forward to the spread of the kingdom of God through the world and to the universal acceptance of his teaching and work. That would be his vindication. He did, however, predict the fall of Jerusalem.

The early church took Jesus' words about his vindication and reshaped them in the light of Old Testament views concerning the day of the Lord and of apocalyptic materials from such books as I Enoch (see p. 396).

We should recognize the church's apocalyptic reinterpretation of Jesus for what it is and free Jesus from it. There will be no second coming as the New Testament pictures it.

d. The Existentialist View

This position assumes that the whole New Testament view of the second coming of Christ is shaped by Jewish apocalyptic myths and by myths that circulated in the Greek world. Its advocates say that modern people cannot accept the myth of the descent of Christ with his angels to destroy the powers of evil and rescue the saints, whom he takes to heaven with him or into a transformed earthly order. The world view in this myth is an ancient one: heaven above; the earth below, under the power of the devil and demons; war between supernatural powers; etc. Though we cannot accept this myth, we can ask what the myth is trying to say to us.

It does not tell us anything about the course of events in the future. Such knowledge is not given to mankind. We live in faith. We can only be open to God's future, whatever the future may be. However, mythology of this kind can tell us what meaning Jesus has for our existence *in this world*.

It says to us that by our faith Jesus can be master of our inner life, that his spirit can dwell within us. The second coming of Christ and the coming of the Spirit to the believer are the same. There will be no future coming as an external event. As the Gospel of John tells us, both eternal life and judgment are present experiences. Jesus' victory is a victory inside the believer, not outside him.

The world will run its course. If there is an end, it will come about by natural causes, not by the mythical event the New Testament expects.

These positions cannot be evaluated properly here. Probably the second stands nearest to the faith of the writers of the New Testament. It holds that "God will bring to perfect completion the work begun through Christ, and that the same Christ who stands at the center of Christian faith will also stand at the final boundary of human experience in time, in space, and in eternity" (Harvey K. McArthur).

103. The Bible's Inspiration and Authority

We come, finally, to the most difficult questions about the Bible. What, if anything, did God have to do with its origin? In what sense may we speak of the Bible as the Word of God? And how do we determine what in the Bible is binding on us as Christians?

It is true that many intellectuals of our time regard the Bible not as the Word of God but as a noble collection of ancient books which contain valuable teachings concerning human relationships and many human interest stories. Since it is part of our cultural heritage, they agree that an educated person probably ought to know something about it. But the church's claim that it came from God is mysterious to them and difficult to swallow. And that this ancient book has any right to dictate the shape of contemporary life—and particularly their own lives—is a questionable, if not an offensive, concept.

Even committed Christians are troubled by many things in the Bible that appear inconsistent with its alleged divine origin. The Bible seems too human and fallible to be the Word of God for mankind. To some Christians the ancient book is an embarrassment. They are quite content to leave it on the shelf to gather dust. Others feel that they ought to appreciate it and read it more, but its dated character turns them off. If anyone could speak up for the book, they would be glad to listen. Can anyone say for sure just what kind of book this is?

Frankly, the answer is no. But students of the Bible through the centuries have made a valiant attempt at an answer—and they are still trying. What the church means when it says that the Bible is a God-inspired book is a central question in contemporary theological discussion.

1. The Meaning and Purpose of "Inspiration"

Behind this noun is the Latin verb *inspirare,* meaning "to breathe into." When we describe the Scriptures as God-inspired writings, we mean that God has somehow breathed into them.

This claim is made in an important passage in II Timothy: "from childhood you have been acquainted with the sacred writings which are able to instruct you for salvation through faith in Christ Jesus. All scripture is inspired by God and [or, Every scripture inspired by God is also] profitable for teaching, for reproof, for correction, and for training in righteousness, that the man of God may be complete, equipped for every good work" (3:15-17).

In the Greek text "inspired by God" is one word: *theopneustos,* meaning "God-breathed." Thus one recent translation (NIV) has: "All Scripture is God-breathed . . ."

The Old Testament concept of God's breath-spirit, particularly as the breath of life which he breathed into man's nostrils (Gen. 2:7), comes to mind at once. God's breath is the divine vitality which makes man and the animals (Ps. 104:29-30) "live." The statement in II Timothy thus means that God's vitality, his life, is in the Scriptures so that they are able to achieve his purposes.

What these purposes are is stated in II Timothy: to lead to salvation through faith in Christ Jesus, and to educate the Christian (the Christian leader especially) intellectually and morally so that he will be equipped for his service for God.

The passage claims that the Scriptures are the instrument through which God works, that they are functionally powerful, that they can achieve in people who are instructed by them the life and service God desires.

The purpose of inspiration, according to the Bible as a whole, is not to satisfy people's curiosity about God, the world, or the inner life of persons. Neither is it to instruct them in magic, in the arts, or in science so that they may control evil spirits and wrest from nature its benefits. It is not primarily the communication of knowledge. The purpose of inspiration is rather the establishing of a relationship with God in which people become like him in character, share in his strength, and do his will in daily life. While inspiration involves the communication of knowledge, this knowledge is always the basis for becoming and doing.

Some theologians have distinguished between inspiration and revelation. They have said that revelation is that process by which God showed chosen people what otherwise they could not have known, and that inspiration was the way he kept them from error when they communicated to others, verbally or in writing, what he had shown them.

It is doubtful that the distinction is valid. It supports the position that the Bible is inerrant—a view very difficult to defend, as the following discussion will show. The terms refer to the same reality, namely, God's self-disclosure to and conversation with chosen and responsive people and the continuing effects of this disclosure.

2. The Nature of Inspiration

How did God's vitality get into the Scriptures? Obviously he did not write the Scriptures with his finger, as we are told he did the tables of stone he gave to Moses (Exod. 31:18).

In the church there have been those who have believed that God dictated to human writers both the ideas and the words they were to write down. Others have conjectured that the human authors were free to write what they wished and that the Holy Spirit and the church subsequently approved what was written. Some have held that the Holy Spirit only guarded the human authors from making any errors. Still others have said that God inspired the thoughts of the human writers but left them free to choose their own words, style, and literary forms.

In our time it has become increasingly clear that the inspiration of the Scriptures is the result or by-product of God's inspiration of people whom he called to receive his self-revelation. These people were transformed and commissioned for service by God's self-disclosure. They then bore witness to the mighty deeds and words they had seen and heard—first in oral testimony and then directly or indirectly (*i.e.,* through their disciples) in writing. God's revelation came *through* people into the Scriptures. Ordinarily he did not suspend their personalities (see pp. 474-75) but worked in and through them in their individuality. He was limited by their abilities, eccentricities, and faltering response. Accordingly, certain biblical writers' understanding of God's character and purposes was partial and distorted.

Recently, some scholars (particularly Roman Catholics) have been stressing the social character of inspiration. They see inspiration as God's gift to the community of Israel and to the Christian church, rather than to individual persons only.

These scholars contend that the Holy Spirit inspired the whole Judeo-Christian movement out of which the Scriptures came—its leaders and doers, as well as its writers. "Men [were] chosen by God to act and to live the biblical 'deed' before it was recounted or written" (P. Benoit). They say that only thus can literature such as the Pentateuch or the Gospels, to which many people contributed over a long period of time (see chaps. 9 and 64), be regarded as inspired. Surely God directed the work of the J writer and the compiler of the document we call Q as well as the work of the person or persons who combined the sources into our present documents. Those who wrote were representatives of the community, and the community is therefore the real author of the literature.

Probably the truth lies in a combination of the last two positions. Israel and the church lived their literature before individuals wrote it down, but certainly those individuals had special gifts as writers and editors and have left on the literature marks of their own personalities.

Exactly how inspiration came to the old and the new communities and to their leaders and writers is a difficult question. God's self-disclosure and its accompanying message came to people in many ways, according to the Bible: in personal appearances, such as God made to Moses (Exod. 33:12-23); through an angel (Gen. 16:7-14; Luke 1:11 ff., 26 ff.); dreams (Gen. 28:10-17; Matt. 2:22); visions (Isa. chap. 6; Acts 10:3, 9-16); a direct voice (I Kings 19:9-18; Mark 9:7); observation of nature (Jer. 1:11-14); and personal domestic experience (Hosea).

The exact nature of the divine appearances, visions, and auditory experiences escapes us. In late Old Testament and intertestamental times visions became the standard means of revelation and in some of the literature the use of visions is to be regarded as a literary device (as in Dan. chaps. 7–12). Ecstatic inspiration, highly esteemed in Greek life and culture, was valued in the church at Corinth (I Cor. chap. 14).

Today we think that inspiration came to biblical people principally as the heightening of the total personality through personal relationship with God, even in many of the cases where the biblical record attributes it to visions and ecstatic states. God came to people through the events of their lives and times and through the interpretation of those events by sensitive, insightful people. Without interpretation the events would have been meaningless. The great prophets saw themselves as God's interpreters (Amos 3:7).

Jeremiah, for example, was a keen observer of national and international affairs. Through the events of his time he saw that in the game of power politics Israel's attempt to gain security by foreign alliances would lead to its destruction. The conclusion troubled him deeply. If Israel was to be destroyed, how then could God fulfill his purpose for the world through the mission of Israel? He came one day into the house of a potter, and there, through observing the potter's treatment of the clay, he received his answer: God could rework the clay into another vessel (Jer. 18:1-6).

Hosea's tragic marriage was God's means of leading him to a profound understanding of God's love for Israel.

Jesus saw the tragic situation of his time and became convinced that Roman armies would destroy Jerusalem (Mark 13:1-2; Luke 21:20-24).

Although Paul did not rule out inspiration by way of ecstatic experience, he rated it low on his list of the gifts of the Spirit (I Cor. 12:10, 28-30) and glorified the place of the mind in religious expression (I Cor. 14:6-19).

The conclusion is justified that "inspiration came, not by the suspension of personality, but through the organ of personality" (H. H. Rowley) and through all its facets—mind, will, and emotions.

3. The Scope of Inspiration

We have seen that God breathed life and with it understanding of his purposes into both individuals and the community of which they were a part. To what extent did inspiration affect the Scriptures in their various aspects?

Some Jews of the interestamental period believed that the Septuagint (the Greek Old Testament) was verbally inspired. God guaranteed the accuracy of the translation by causing all the translators, working independently, to agree word for word in their renditions.

The rabbis of the New Testament period held that every syllable, every letter, and even peculiarities of spelling were the work of God's Spirit.

Verbal inspiration, and thus verbal inerrancy, was long a dogma in Judaism and Christianity. It has present-day advocates. "What Scripture says, God says" and "God so inspired the biblical writers that their word is also His Word" (J. I. Packer) are slogans of contemporary verbalists.

Such absolute equating of God's Word with the words of Scripture certainly was not done by Jesus and the New Testament writers. Though they spoke of the Scriptures in the highest terms (John 10:35; II Pet. 1:20-21), they clearly did not equate God's will with the exact words of Scripture.

Jesus quoted Genesis with the intent of setting aside Moses' provision concerning divorce (Mark 10:2-9), and he nullified the Mosaic commandments concerning unclean foods (Mark 7:14-23).

The church regarded the whole sacrificial system of Israel as ended by Christ's sacrifice of himself and by the "living sacrifice" of oneself to God (Heb. 10:1-10; Rom. 12:1). Christians regarded themselves as God's true sons and therefore free from the letter of Jewish law and under the control of God's Spirit and the power of love within them (Gal. 5:13-18). Their assumed freedom with respect to the Law was scandalous in Jewish eyes. Christians saw the Old Testament as pointing toward and authenticating what had come to pass in Jesus and the church.

Both Old and New Testament writers used previous literary material with a freedom that argues against verbal literalism on their part. Early sources of the Pentateuch were interpreted and edited by later writers to suit new purposes (see chap. 9). The author of I and II Chronicles freely adapted material from I and II Samuel and I and II Kings (see chap. 21). Matthew abbreviated Mark's narratives, improved Mark's style, and in places altered his theology (see p. 223). It is evident from the fact that the church approved *four* Gospels, often differing widely from one another, that it did not regard verbal and factual agreement as of any particular importance. All presented Jesus Christ as Savior and Lord and called for faith in and obedience to him—and that was sufficient.

Furthermore, the Bible's historical statements are not always accurate and consistent. A few examples must suffice.

Was Jesus' last supper before his crucifixion the Passover supper (Mark 14:12-16), or was it held on the evening prior to the Passover (John 18:28; 19:14)? Did Jesus cleanse the temple at the beginning of his ministry (John 2:13-22) or at the end (Mark 11:15-18)? Did Jesus say to the rich man, "Why do you call me good?" (Mark 10:18) or "Why do you ask me about what is good?" (Matt. 19:17)—a considerable difference in meaning. Did the Lord tell David to number Israel and Judah (II Sam. 24:1), or was Satan responsible for this (I Chron. 21:1)? Did Abraham leave Haran after his father Terah's death (Acts 7:4) or sixty years before he died (Gen. 11:26, 32; 12:4)? Such problems and inconsistencies are abundant in the Scriptures.

For early Christians the fountain of life, revelation, and inspiration was not the Scriptures but Jesus Christ, the one to whom the Scriptures bore witness. In John 5:39-40 we read, "You [the Jews] search the scriptures, because you think that in them you have eternal life; and it is they that bear witness to me; yet you refuse to come to me that you may have life." The church read the Scriptures for signs pointing toward Jesus and wrote books, like the Gospel of Matthew, to show how Jesus had fulfilled the hopes expressed in the sacred writings. The church sought life not in the Scriptures but in him to whom the Scriptures pointed.

For guidance in everyday life, Christians turned chiefly to the deeds and words of Jesus (I Cor. 7:10), to Spirit-filled teachers and prophets in the church (I Cor. 7:25), to church tradition (I Cor. 11:16), to the guidance of the Spirit within themselves (Gal. 5:18), and to the Scriptures. Paul held that the records of the past were written down for the church's instruction. They were a mirror in which the church should be able to recognize itself and be warned and helped on its way to the promised future by what it saw there (I Cor. 10:11). Anything in the Scriptures that did not point to Jesus and the church, shed light on the significance of Jesus' redemptive work—past, present, or future—or give direction to the church's life and mission in the world was largely bypassed.

Whether the Scriptures in all parts contained an infallible record of Israel's history or presented a sound world view or even a proper picture of God apparently was of little concern to them. Luke, for example, was impressed chiefly, and perhaps only, with the way Jesus was mirrored in Moses, the prophets, and all the Scriptures (24:27, 44-47) and how he fulfilled in his birth, personal life, ministry, death, and resurrection the deepest hopes of the Scriptures for the full redemption of mankind.

The New Testament church's approach to the Holy Scriptures was a Christ-centered approach. The Christians measured everything they found there by the revelation that had come in and through their Lord.

4. The Authority of the Bible

It has been said that there were two incarnations of the Word of God: one in human flesh (in Jesus of Nazareth) and one in human language (in the Bible).

While the comparison is attractive and partially true, it is to some extent misleading, for only the first was an "enfleshment" of the Word of God. The second is the written record of that enfleshment—the testimony to its reality, the explanation of its necessity, the description of the form of its manifestation, and the disclosure of its consequences for human life.

The belief that the Bible is an incarnation of the Word of God parallel to and on the same level as the incarnation in Jesus has misled many in the church. For them the Bible has been an object of worship, a fetish, an idol, which has wrongly received the reverence that belongs to God alone.

The Bible points to the absolute authority that stands over human beings: God himself. From the moment of Creation both people and animals have been subject to his commandments. He revealed his will for mankind in covenants given to the Patriarchs and especially in the Mosaic covenant. He punished disobedience to the terms of the latter covenant in the disaster of the Exile. He established a new covenant through the sending of Jesus, whose covenant law was the law of love. Through Jesus and by that law he will judge mankind at the last day (Matt. 25:31-46). God is Creator and Ruler and as such has absolute authority over his creatures.

The Bible is indispensable for us in that it tells us about the activity of God in the life of mankind and how people whom he called experienced and interpreted that activity. We can learn about God's activity and purpose nowhere but in the Bible.

We cannot prove that God was active in the experience of Israel and the Christian church. There are no unmistakable marks of divinity on the literature that arose in those communities. Even as it was not obvious to Jesus' contemporaries that God had sent his Son into the world as the end-time Deliverer, so it is not obvious that the Bible is a God-inspired book. In both cases certainty comes only through the venture of faith. But there are signs or signposts pointing toward God's activity.

First, there is a remarkable unity in Israel's historical experience. A sense of election, mission, and destiny dominated the whole of Israel's history. Moses, the nation's founder, structured Israel's position and function before God in a covenant. The prophets strove to hold the nation to its God-ordained course and predicted the fulfillment of the nation's service and destiny in the future. The church declared that this service and destiny were being accomplished through the appearance of Jesus and the establishment of a new community based on a new covenant, as predicted in Old Testament prophecy. There is a unity, a coherence, in all this historical experience that is amazing, to say the least.

Second, even as Jesus' mighty works were signposts pointing to his identity and mission (see p. 448), so there were signs of God's activity in Israel: in the wonderful events connected with the Exodus from Egypt, in the remarkable experience in the wilderness, and in the establishment of the nation in the Promised Land, for example. The Christian church saw evidences of God's activity in its works of power (Gal. 3:5; Rom. 15:18-19).

Third, the character of the people and the kind of society created under

INCIPITLIBER
ISAIAE·PRO
PHETAE ▾

cap. i.

ISIOISA
IAEFILII
AMOS·
quamui
DITSUP
IUDAM·
ETHIERU
SALEMIN
DIEBUS·O
ZIAEIOATHA

achaz ezechiae regum iuda· Audite caeli
et auribuf percipite terra· qnm dnf locutuf
eft· filiof enutriui et exaltaui· Ipfi autem
fpreuerunt me· Cognouit bof poffefforē
fuum et afinuf praefepe domini fui· Ifrahel
non cognouit me· populuf meuf non intelle
xit· Uae genti peccatrici populograui· Ini
quitate· femini nequam filiif fceleratif·

Photo by H. T. Frank

A page from a copy of the Vulgate dated about 800 A.D., showing Isa. 1:1-4 the old and the new covenants point to God's working. Majestic spirits like Moses, Amos, Jeremiah, the Second Isaiah, Jesus, and Paul, and their impact for good in human society, evidence a divine purpose at work in Israel's history.

Fourth, the Bible's explanation of man's nature, situation in the world, and final destiny gives meaning and direction to his life and agrees with knowledge about man derived from other sources.

Since *people* wrote about their experiences with God, we ought not to expect inerrant fact and perfect understanding from their writings. When light shines through a glass, there is inevitably some distortion of the light. God took the risk of human distortion in order to communicate with us in our language and forms of thought. The clearest revelation, of course, came through those persons in whom there was the least opaqueness and imperfection. Only through the one perfect human personality, Jesus Christ, did the light shine without distortion.

We should therefore expect different levels of truth and some error in the Bible. The standard which we apply to all parts is the truth that came through Jesus Christ. We do not take vengeance on people who wrong us by hacking them to pieces in holy war, as Samuel ordered Saul to do in the name of the Lord and finally did himself (I Sam. 15). We instead follow Jesus, who told us to love our enemies and who practiced what he counseled others to do.

We recognize that biblical standards were conditioned by the times and the situations in which they were set. In one situation readers were exhorted to obey governmental authorities (Rom. 13:1-7) and in another to resist them (see the discussion of the books of Daniel and Revelation).

There is no rule of thumb by which one can decide what biblical counsels are binding on us. There are, however, aids to decision-making.

First, we should examine any biblical command in the light of its literary and historical context. Only thus can its precise meaning be discovered. It may have been shaped for a particular situation and be valid in no other set of circumstances.

Second, we must judge it by the mind of Christ. If it does not agree with his spirit and deeds, it cannot be binding on us.

Third, we should pray for the guidance of the Holy Spirit. Christians are promised the help of the Spirit in knowing and doing the truth (John 14:26; 16:13).

Fourth, we ought to interpret the Scriptures and scriptural demands through studying with other Christians in groups. Christian comrades who struggle together with the Scriptures will often see the truth or error in a passage more clearly than individuals reading alone. And they will throw light on one another's problems by their individual perceptions and experiences.

Fifth, if possible, we should check our interpretation against the conclusions of the great minds of the church, past and present, and evaluate it against truth from other fields of learning (psychology, sociology, etc.).

Sixth, when truth commends itself to us after we have taken these steps, we must act on it in faith. Deep certainty and further truth come only by obeying the truth we have found, not by praising it or toying with it.

It has been the experience of multitudes through the centuries that when they approached the Scriptures thoughtfully and prayerfully a wonderful thing happened to them. The veil of doubt, unbelief, and cynicism fell from their eyes. They began to see the glory of the Lord Jesus and to be changed into his likeness (II Cor. 3:12-18). Then they recognized the "limitations" of the Bible for what they really are—the marks of God's condescension to reach us in our humanness and fallibility.

For Further Reading on the Subjects in Part III

Anderson, B. W., ed. *The Old Testament and Christian Faith*, 1964.
Beegle, Dewey M. *Scripture, Tradition, and Infallibility*, 1973.
Blenkinsopp, Joseph. *A Sketchbook of Biblical Theology*, 1968.
Burrows, Millar. *An Outline of Biblical Theology*, 1946.
Hunter, Archibald, *Introducing New Testament Theology*, 1957.
Jacob, Edmond. *Theology of the Old Testament*, 1958.
Kümmel, W. G. *The Theology of the New Testament*, 1973.
Macquarrie, John. *The Faith of the People of God*, 1972.
Miller, Donald G. *The Authority of the Bible*, 1972.
Richardson, Alan. *An Introduction to the Theology of the New Testament*, 1958.
Rowley, H. H. *The Relevance of the Bible*, 1944.
_____. *The Unity of the Bible*, 1953.
Schnackenburg, Rudolf. *The Church in the New Testament*, 1965.
Vriezen, Th. C. *An Outline of Old Testament Theology*, 1960.

One-Volume Commentaries on the Bible

Black, M., and Rowley, H. H., eds. *Peake's Commentary on the Bible*, 1962.
Brown, R. E.; Fitzmyer, J. A.; and Murphy, R. E., eds. *The Jerome Biblical Commentary*, 1968.
Laymon, Charles M., ed. *The Interpreter's One-Volume Commentary on the Bible*, 1971.

INDEX

483

488   ABINGDON BIBLE HANDBOOK

Damascus, 174, 249
Damascus Document, 402
Dan, 110, 119, 121, 174
Dangerous Bride, 199
Daniel, book of, 146, 204, 342, 351,
    390, 393, 437
  additions to (apocryphal), 205-7
  as apocalyptic literature, 162-63
  author and date of, 164-65, 166-
    67
  contemporary significance of, 166,
    167
  contents of, 163-64
  historical situation and message
    of, 165-66
Daniel (Dan'el), King, 165, 206
Darius, 127, 166, 197, 373, 391
David, 115, 116, 119, 123, 321, 371,
    385, 430
  psalms of, 136, 137
Day of Atonement, 421
Day of the Lord (day of Yahweh;
    day of judgment), 176, 177,
    187, 191, 194, 301, 331, 324,
    406. *See also* Kingdom of God
Dead Sea scrolls, 30, 134, 186, 244,
    318, 342, 360, 366, 399-403,
    443
Debir, 110
Deborah, 111
Dedication, Feast of, 422
Demas, 295
Demetrius I, 209
Demotic script, 373
Derbe, 281
Deuterocanonical books, 29, 196,
    197, 199, 395-96. *See also*
    Apocrypha
Deutero-Isaiah. *See* Second Isaiah
Deuteronomy, 29, 81, 87-88, 451,
    452, 454
  circumstances of writing of, 105
  contents of, 104-5
  continuing significance of, 106

  controversy on position of, in
    Bible, 107-8
  and I-II Kings, 121
  theological emphases of, 105-6,
    109
  title and importance of, 104
DeVaux, Roland, 52
Dialogue of the Redeemer, 34
Diatessaron, 33
Didactic poetry, 130
Didascalia, 207
Dilmun, 387
Diognetus, Letter to, 465
Dionysius Exiguus, 417
Dionysius of Alexandria, 346
Diotrephes, 338-39
Dirges, 148, 158
Disciples, 213, 218, 219, 220, 247,
    248, 440, 448, 451-52
Discipleship, 219, 323, 461, 462
Divino Afflante Spiritus (Pius XII),
    56
Divorce, 268, 405
Dodd, C. H., 50, 428
Domitian, 320, 329, 345
Douay-Rheims-Challoner Version, 44
Doxologies, 260, 261, 328, 339
Driver, G. R., 50

E ("Elohistic") source, 86, 87, 92,
    102, 107, 109, 112, 116, 120
Ea, 388
Easter letter of Athanasius, 35, 322
Ecclesiastes, 140, 146
  author and date of, 142, 143
  philosophical and religious out-
    look of, 141-42
  significance of, 142-43
  title and arrangement of material
    of, 141
Ecclesiasticus, 165, 202-3, 323
Ecumenical movement, 282
Edom, Edomites, 139, 174, 176-77

Green, Jay P., 40
Guilt, 257, 258

Habakkuk, 149, 184, 206
Habakkuk, book of, 167
contents and literary form of, 184-85
date and historical situation of, 185
message of, 185-86
significance of, 186
title of, and name of the prophet, 184
Hadassah (Esther), 128
Hadrian, 395
Haggadah, 164, 397, 437
Haggai, 127, 149, 190, 193, 194
Haggai, book of, 167
contents and compilation of, 189
message and abiding value of, 189-90
name, date, and historical situation of, 188-89
Haifa, 372
Hanukkah, 422
Haran, 95, 368
Hasidim, 393, 399, 405, 407, 408
Hasmonean kingdom, 393-94, 415
Hazor, 110, 376
Healing
by Jesus, 441
miracles of, 436
Hebrew Bible, 17-18, 29-31
Chronicles and Ezra-Nehemiah in, 122, 125-26, 193
Esther in, 128
Isaiah in, 149
Joel in, 172
Judges in, 111
Lamentations in, 158
prophetic books in, 107, 146, 167
Ruth in, 113
Samuel and Kings in, 114, 118
Hebrew language, 355-57, 370

Hebrew people, 368-70. *See also* Jews
Hebrew poetry, 59, 73, 130-31, 158-59
Hebrews, letter to, 252, 253, 316, 357, 447
authorship of, 318-19
date of writing of, 320
formative influences in, 321-22
literary character, theme, and contents of, 317
original readers and purpose of, 317-18
theology of, 320-21
Heliodorus, 209
Hellenization, 201, 357, 392, 393, 398-99. *See also* Greek influence
Heresy, 292-93, 301, 305-7, 308, 323, 324, 332. *See also* Gnosticism
Herod Agrippa, 394
Herod Antipas, 231, 235, 237, 394, 440, 441
Herodotus, 128, 129, 187, 379
Herod Philip, 394
Herod the Great, 372, 394, 417
"Hexateuch," 107
Hezekiah, 119, 120, 138 150, 151, 180, 186, 380
Hierapolis, 292, 315
Hieroglyphics, 355, 373
Hilkiah, 87
Hippo, Council of, 30, 35
Hippolytus, 322
Historical New Testament (Moffatt), 42
History
interpreted and apologetic, 124
of Israel, unity in, 478
writing of, 116-18
Holiness (sanctification), 298, 299, 321, 427, 455-58
Holiness code, 101